1996

THE RISE AND FALL OF THE

French Revolution

Studies in European History from the
Journal of Modern History

John W. Boyer and Julius Kirshner
Series Editors

THE RISE AND FALL OF THE

French Revolution

Edited by

T. C. W. BLANNING

The University of Chicago Press

Chicago and London

The essays in this volume originally appeared in the *Journal of Modern History.* Acknowledgment of the original publication date may be found on the first page of each essay.

"The Monarchy and Procedures for the Elections of 1789" by François Furet, "The Crowd and Politics between *Ancien Régime* and Revolution in France" by Colin Lucas, and " 'Public Opinion' at the End of the Old Regime" by Mona Ozouf are reprinted with kind permission from Elsevier Science, Ltd., Oxford, England.

The University of Chicago Press, Chicago, 60637
The University of Chicago Press, Ltd., London
© 1996 by the University of Chicago
All rights reserved. Published 1996
Printed in the United States of America
ISBN (cl)   0-226-05691-0
ISBN (pa)   0-226-05692-9

00 99 98 97 96   5 4 3 2 1

Library of Congress Cataloging in Publication Data

The rise and fall of the French Revolution / edited by Timothy C.
  Blanning.
        p.   cm. -- (Studies in European history from the Journal of
  modern history)
    Includes bibliographical references and index.
    ISBN 0-226-05691-0 (cl). -- ISBN 0-226-05692-9 (pa)
    1. France--History--Revolution, 1789–1799.   I. Blanning, T. C. W.
II. Series.
DC148.R56 1996
944.04--dc20   95-43310
                                                                         CIP

The paper used in the publication meets the minimum requirements of American National Standard for Information Sciences - Permanence of Paper for Printed Library Materials, ANSI Z39.48. 1984.

Contents

Introduction: The Rise and Fall of the French Revolution

T. C. W. Blanning

Confronted with the never-ending flow of literature on the French Revolution, even the most voracious speed-reader can only despair. It is a problem as old as the Revolution itself: during the first four months of 1789, as the elections for the Estates General got under way, at least 2,639 pamphlets appeared.[1] Every important anniversary since then has brought a renewed surge of activity, none proving more productive than the bicentenary of the fall of the Bastille, which was commemorated by about 170 conferences worldwide. Just one of them—the great jamboree held at the Sorbonne in July 1989—led to the publication of four fat volumes, containing nearly three hundred papers and 2,709 pages.[2]

If this print inflation has not driven out all the good money, it has certainly brought into circulation much clipped and debased coinage. The undiscriminating investor is all too likely to find a heavy investment of intellectual effort repaid by meager dividends or even negative equity. What is needed is a quality control that will separate the occasional louis d'or from a heap of assignats. To the fore in this vital assaying exercise have been the editors of the *Journal of Modern History,* who have allowed only the genuine article to pass their scrutiny. Even a cursory glance at the table of contents of this volume will reveal that they have attracted contributions from most of the market leaders in French Revolutionary historiography. Indeed, only limitation of space has prevented the addition of many more articles of equal distinction. From this *embarras de richesses* I have chosen those that offer original and illuminating approaches to three crucial topics: the decline and fall of the Old Regime, the creation of a new political culture, and the emergence of a vigorous counterrevolution.

The Decline and Fall of the Old Regime

Long gone are the days when Marxist historians led by the redoubtable Albert Soboul could advance as commonplace the "truth" that the French Revolution

---

[1] Jeremy D. Popkin, *Revolutionary News: The Press in France, 1789–99* (Durham, N.C., 1990), p. 26.

[2] Michel Vovelle, ed., *L'Image de la Révolution française: Communications présentées lors du Congrès Mondial pour le Bicentenaire de la Révolution Sorbonne Paris 6–12 juillet 1989,* 4 vols. (Paris, 1990).

represented "the culmination of a long economic and social evolution that made the bourgeoisie the mistress of the world" and that therefore "the essential cause of the Revolution was the power of a bourgeoisie arrived at its maturity and confronted by a decadent aristocracy holding tenaciously to its privileges."[3] Those words were published in the year that Stalin died, when the transition from feudalism to capitalism to socialism could still seem inevitable. At one of the bicentennial lectures a generation later, just as the Soviet empire was collapsing, the audience was told that any attempt to place the bourgeoisie at the center of attention now appeared "gloriously *dépassé*."[4] In the meantime, the conceptual world of revolutionary causation had been turned upside down. What had once been parts of the superstructure—culture and politics—had been liberated from subjection to the forces of production and given their own autonomous status, indeed had been promoted to primacy.

Just a year after the publication of Soboul's confident dictum quoted above, the opening salvo in this methodological war of independence was fired by Alfred Cobban, in his inaugural lecture at the University of London provocatively titled "The Myth of the French Revolution."[5] Once a breach had been opened in "notre bonne orthodoxie" (as Soboul liked to call it) and the defenders had proved to be much less formidable than their martial rhetoric had suggested, a growing number of scholars donned revisionist armor and joined the fray. That they fired from different directions, used weapons of varying caliber, and often shot each other did not matter. Their collective firepower proved explosive. Significantly, they were almost all British or American and—also significantly—their work was rarely translated into French.[6] Yet after the citadel had been razed, it was not at all clear what the victors might erect in its place. As the vanquished and their numerous fellow

[3] Albert Soboul, "Classes and Class Struggles during the French Revolution," *Science and Society* 17 (1953): 238, 245.

[4] Colin Jones, "Bourgeois Revolution Revivified: 1789 and Social Change," in *Rewriting the French Revolution,* ed. Colin Lucas (Oxford, 1991), p. 71. This is a stimulating and ingenious but not entirely convincing attempt to breathe fresh life into the old concept of a bourgeois revolution.

[5] Reprinted in his collected essays, *Aspects of the French Revolution* (London, 1968).

[6] It is a constant source of annoyance to non-Francophone historians (and perhaps a salutary lesson in humility) that French publishers greatly prefer to publish a translation of yet another gushing and superficial biography of Madame du Barry or Marie Antoinette rather than works of original scholarship. I have discussed the struggle for and against the "bourgeois revolution" in a short study titled *The French Revolution: Aristocrats versus Bourgeois?* (London, 1987). There is an excellent and fuller discussion in William Doyle, *Origins of the French Revolution,* 2d ed. (Oxford, 1988).

travelers enjoyed pointing out, it was much easier to say what had not caused the French Revolution than what had.

The most influential of the alternative constructions has been that offered by François Furet, the first important French scholar to join the revisionist forces. With all the zeal of the convert, this former communist set about the Marxist interpretation with a will. Especially in a coruscating attack on Claude Mazauric and Albert Soboul, published in *Annales* in 1971, he showed that he could be as destructive as any of his Anglophone allies.[7] Yet over the years he has also put together his own overarching interpretation of the rise and fall of the Revolution. There is no space to follow each stage of his development here.[8] It should be noted, however, that a wide gulf separates his first general account, written in collaboration with Denis Richet and published in 1965, from his most recent, a history of France from 1770 until 1880, published in 1988.[9] In this latter definitive statement of his position, economic forces are replaced by politics, which no longer occupy a marginalized part of the superstructure but form an autonomous determinant.

Furet sees as the chief contradiction of the Old Regime the fact that at the very time the monarchy was seeking to impose standardization on France, it was also multiplying the obstacles.[10] It was a contradiction that derived from the monarchy's inability to generate sufficient regular income to finance its state building. Driven to sell offices to its privileged elites, it also alienated a significant part of public power in the process. So the administrative monarchy created in the seventeenth century was "an unstable compromise between the construction of a modern state and an aristocratic society remodelled by the state."[11] When the old king died in 1715, the crucial relationship between crown and nobility had been forced into a cul-de-sac. The Polish exit to nostalgic aristocratic anarchy had been bricked up forever by Louis XIV; for nobles as bloated with wealth as the French, the gate was too strait and the way was too narrow that led to a Prussian solution of state

[7] François Furet, "Sur le catéchisme de la Révolution française," *Annales: Économies, Sociétés, Civilisations,* vol. 26, no. 2 (1971). This was translated as "The Revolutionary Catechism," with the addition of a section on the Old Regime state, in his *Interpreting the French Revolution* (Cambridge, 1981).

[8] Readers wishing to follow his odyssey can begin with Donald Sutherland, "An Assessment of the Writings of François Furet," *French Historical Studies,* vol. 16 (1990).

[9] François Furet and Denis Richet, *La Révolution* (Paris, 1965), published in English as *The French Revolution* (London, 1970); and François Furet, *La Révolution de Turgot à Jules Ferry, 1770–1880* (Paris, 1988), published in English as *Revolutionary France, 1770–1880* (Oxford and Cambridge, Mass., 1992).

[10] Furet, *Revolutionary France,* p. 7.

[11] Ibid., pp. 8–9.

service; while the price of admission to the more attractive English model of a plutocratic parliamentary aristocracy was just too high, requiring as it did at least the abolition of tax exemptions. It was in this impasse, Furet argues, that there lay "the origins of the social and political crisis of eighteenth century France, giving rise to a part of the French Revolution and its prolongation into the nineteenth century. Neither the French king nor the nobility put forward a policy which might unite state and ruling society around a minimum consensus: because of that, royal action oscillated between despotism and capitulation."[12]

So when the terminal crisis erupted at the end of the 1780s, Louis XVI had nothing on which to fall back: "A victim of its own practices, the absolute monarchy possessed no heritage, no tradition that would have enabled it to consult opinion according to incontestable forms; it was responsible for having destroyed that heritage and that tradition."[13]

This fatal propensity for having the worst of all worlds also prompted the monarchy to foster the democratic forces that would move in to pick up the pieces left by the collapse of the Old Regime. Centralization of decision making at Versailles, together with the denial of representation to the provinces, ensured that Paris would become the center of opposition. During the course of the eighteenth century there developed in the capital an alternative sovereign, nonetheless potent for being abstract. This was public opinion:

It constituted a public tribunal, in contrast with the secrecy of the king; it was universal, in contrast with the particularism of "feudal" laws; and objective, in contrast with monarchic arbitrariness: in short, a court of appeal of reason, judging all matters of state, in the name of public interest alone. It was a means of getting away from a society of orders and guilds without falling into the disarray of private interests and factions. Well before the Revolution, this idea transferred the feature of royal sovereignty to a new authority, also unique, which was an exact copy of the monarchic idea: on the ruins of feudal monarchy, it had only to build a monarchy of reason. It was in this transfer that a revolution took place.[14]

In short, the history of the decline and fall of the absolute monarchy in France was the history of the rise and triumph of public opinion. In the succinct formulation of Mona Ozouf in her article reprinted herein: "There was no public opinion under Louis XIV, for the brilliance of the monarch outshone it. Similarly, when public opinion had become king, it left no place

---

[12] Ibid., p. 13.

[13] François Furet, "The Monarchy and Procedures for the Elections of 1789" (in this volume), p. 183.

[14] Furet, *Revolutionary France,* pp. 16–17.

for royal authority."[15] This new sovereign developed in a new kind of cultural space—"the public sphere"—to which historians of eighteenth-century Europe have devoted a great deal of attention recently. They have drawn much of their inspiration from what at first sight seems a most unlikely source—a dissertation by a German philosopher and sociologist, Jürgen Habermas, with the uninviting title *The Structural Transformation of the Public Sphere: An Inquiry into a Category of Bourgeois Society*. First published in Germany in 1965, its impact on students of eighteenth-century France was delayed until its translation into French in 1978.[16]

Habermas's main concern in *The Structural Transformation of the Public Sphere* is not historical. His primary purpose is to identify, analyze, and rectify what he regards as the current cultural malaise. He does this by illustrating and explaining the change in the function of culture from the middle ages to the present day, thus providing an explanation for the rise of what he and his fellow members of the Frankfurt school like to call "the culture industry," a phrase that was first coined by Theodor Adorno and Max Horkheimer in 1944.[17] At the center of his analysis is the relationship between what is regarded as public and what is regarded as private. In the middle ages, he argues, there was no clear distinction between public and private because there was no clear concept of private property.[18] Those who exercised power— monarch, nobles, prelates—expressed their status in public in a concrete nonabstract way, through insignia, clothing, gesture, or rhetoric. Power was both exercised and represented directly: "as long as the prince and the estates of the realm still were the country and not just its representatives, they could represent it in a specific sense; they represented their lordship not for but 'before' the people."[19]

This is what he calls "repräsentative Öffentlichkeit," which can best be translated as "the representational public sphere."[20] Confined to those who

[15] Mona Ozouf, "Public Opinion at the End of the Old Regime" (in this volume), p. 99.

[16] The original German edition was *Strukturwandel der Öffentlichkeit: Untersuchungen zu einer Kategorie der bürgerlichen Gesellschaft* (Neuwied, 1962). The French translation was titled *L'Espace public: Archéologie de la publicité comme dimension constitutive de la société bourgeoise* (Paris, 1978). An English translation was published in 1989.

[17] Peter Uwe Hohendahl, "Critical Theory, Public Sphere and Culture: Jürgen Habermas and His Critics," *New German Critique* 16 (1979): 90.

[18] Habermas, p. 5.

[19] Ibid., p. 8.

[20] Ibid., p. 7. "The representational public sphere" seems to me to be a better translation of "repräsentative Öffentlichkeit" than the "publicness (or publicity) of representation" offered in this translation.

exercise power, it assumes an entirely passive attitude on the part of the rest of the population. It reached its apogee in the courtly-chivalric court culture of France and Burgundy in the fifteenth century, but it lived on through the early modern period, transforming itself into the baroque. By now, however, representation had become more confined, moving from the streets of the city to the parks and state apartments of the château. In a bourgeois house even the ceremonial rooms are designed to be lived in; in a baroque château, even the living rooms have a ceremonial purpose. Indeed, the most intimate—the bedroom—is also the most important, the scene of the grand ceremonial *levée*. The sumptuous display of the representational public sphere was not supposed to be recreational; its purpose was to represent the power of the sovereign before the people. So the sovereign had to be on parade even when he was eating—the people were still allowed to watch. It was only bourgeois banquets that became entirely private.[21]

Two interconnected developments eroded the representational public sphere: the exchange of goods and the exchange of information. Together they created a fundamentally different kind of public sphere—the bourgeois. While the feudal public sphere had been founded on authority, received passively, the essence of the bourgeois public sphere is rational argument. The bourgeois public sphere can be defined as the medium through which private persons can reason in public. In doing so, they perform the vital function of mediating relations between the essentially separate realms of civil society and the state.[22] Habermas argues not that there was a public mind but that there was a public sphere. What matters most about it is not what it contains in terms of ideas or feelings or even its social composition, but the fact that those contents are actively communicated. It is the effort of communication which creates the "public" and gives it qualities of cohesion and authority quite different from mere aggregates of individuals. In other words, what is so special about this process is the historically unique medium in which political debate now took place: public argument.[23]

Habermas does not suppose that this was a sudden process. Those who established the public sphere were private citizens, not immediately involved in the exercise of power. They did not bid directly for a share of power; rather, they undermined the very principle of the existing regime's rule by advocating publicity (*Publizität*) as a principle of control.[24] With the forces of production on their side, it could only be a matter of time before their concept of the

---

[21] Ibid., p. 10.

[22] Thomas McCarthy, *The Critical Theory of Jürgen Habermas* (London, 1978), p. 381.

[23] Habermas, p. 27.

[24] Ibid., p. 28.

public sphere triumphed completely. Long before political victory was achieved, however, the bourgeois succeeded in establishing nonpolitical forms of their new public concept. This they did through cultural media that now became accessible to the public—lecture halls, theaters, museums, and concerts.[25] This in turn was made possible by the same economic forces that began the erosion of the feudal public sphere. Culture was transformed from something that is representational into a commodity that could be desired for its own sake and purchased. Cultural commercialization had begun. The more that cultural artifacts were produced for the market, the more they escaped from the control of the old patrons—the court, the church, and the nobles. The more they became accessible to anyone who could pay for them, the more they lost their aura, their sacramental character.

This excursus seems to have taken us straight back to a Marxist scenario dominated by the inexorable forces of production. The revisionists demonstrated, however, that it was possible to take from Habermas his concept of the public sphere and of the progression from cultural to political criticism while rejecting his Marxist terminology and assumptions. In the words of the most acute historian of the development of the public sphere in Old Regime France, Keith Michael Baker, "it seems difficult to characterise the new public space as a specifically bourgeois phenomenon or to see 'public opinion' as the device by which a specifically bourgeois civil society sought to defend its needs and interests against the absolute state."[26] The public sphere developed not as part of a transition from feudalism to capitalism but as "a political invention appearing in the context of a crisis of political authority."[27] In his contribution to this present volume, Baker justifies and illustrates this insight with specific reference to the early stages of Louis XVI's reign, beginning with a fascinating analysis of the coronation at Rheims on June 11, 1775.[28]

By that time the political crisis of the Old Regime had long been under way. Its roots were more than a century old, sinking back into the rich black soil of the Jansenist dispute, which had begun with the posthumous publication of Bishop Cornelius Jansen's *Augustinus* in 1640. By enlisting papal support to

[25] Ibid., p. 29.

[26] Keith Michael Baker, "Defining the Public Sphere in Eighteenth Century France: Variations on a Theme by Habermas," in *Habermas and the Public Sphere,* ed. Craig Calhoun (Cambridge, Mass., and London, 1992), pp. 191–92.

[27] Ibid. See also Baker's article, "Public Opinion as Political Invention," reprinted in his *Inventing the French Revolution* (Cambridge, 1990), pp. 167–99.

[28] See Keith Michael Baker, "French Political Thought at the Accession of Louis XVI" (in this volume), p. 65. Also illuminating on the same subject is Hermann Weber, "Das Sacre Ludwigs XVI. vom 11. Juni 1775 und die Krise des Ancien Régime," in *Vom Ancien Régime zur Französischen Revolution: Forschungen und Ergebnisse,* ed. Ernst Hinrichs, Eberhard Schmitt, and Rudolf Vierhaus (Göttingen, 1978).

extirpate Jansenism, Louis XIV had identified the monarchy with ultramontanism, thus allowing the Parlements to seize the Gallican card and play it for all it was worth. The importance of the Jansenist issue in prizing apart state and society in eighteenth-century France has long been recognized. It is almost forty years since J. S. Bromley wrote, "national sovereignty was the most dynamic concept that was crystallised out of the parliamentary struggle. . . . Parliamentary Jansenism, and with it what d'Argenson called Jansenist nationalism, did more to shake the fabric of French absolutism, in its theory and its practice, than the philosophers. . . . Perhaps they [the Parlements] were the real educators of the *sans-culottes.*"[29] Much work has been done meanwhile to substantiate these observations, especially by Dale Van Kley, who is well represented in this volume by a penetrating analysis of the role played by the Jansenist issue in the origins of the Revolution. As he concludes, "The coming of the bull *Unigenitus* in 1713, the 'miracles' of Saint-Medard in the early 1730s, the refusal of sacraments to Jansenists in the 1750s, the expulsion of the Jesuits in the 1760s—these were the major landmarks on a polemical road which gradually bifurcated toward both Revolution and counter-Revolution."[30]

The religious controversies forced both contestants to enter the public sphere and to appeal to public opinion as the ultimate arbiter, the crucial difference being that the Parlements did it gladly and deftly, the Crown reluctantly and clumsily. In taking their dispute out of the secrecy of the court and the courts, they both helped to educate the force that would ultimately destroy them both. It is important to note that this sort of account of the destabilization of the Old Regime downgrades the importance of the philosophes. As Van Kley points out, adherents of the Enlightenment were to be found on both sides and none: "Not a single participant in this controversy fully qualifies as a member of Peter Gay's 'little flock' of the truly enlightened, whose distinguished bleating constitutes in fact no more than the most distant echo in any of these disputes."[31] In other words, it was not so much the ideas that proved corrosive as the forum in which they were propagated. Once established, an axiom such as that advanced by Raynal in 1770—"In a nation that thinks and talks, public opinion is the rule of government, and govern-

[29] J. S. Bromley, "The Decline of Absolute Monarchy," in *France: Government and Society,* 2d ed., ed. J. Wallace-Hadrill and J. McManners (London, 1970), pp. 144–45. The first edition of this excellent collection was published in 1957.

[30] See Dale Van Kley, "Church, State, and the Ideological Origins of the French Revolution" (in this volume), p. 60.

[31] Ibid., p. 61. The "little flock of philosophes" refers to the heading Peter Gay gave to his introduction to his *The Enlightenment: An Interpretation,* vol. 1, *The Rise of Modern Paganism* (London, 1967).

ment must never act against it without giving public reasons nor thwart it without disabusing it"—required the monarchy to adapt or perish.[32]

The hapless Louis XVI was as ill-suited to organize the modernization of his kingship as it is possible to imagine. Timid, taciturn, indecisive, signally deficient in charisma, and hardly ever seen outside the gilded world of Versailles or the other royal châteaus, he was like a fish out of water when it came to operating in the public sphere. Yet many of his fellow sovereigns did succeed in adapting their image, discovering in the process that when it came to public relations, the monarchy still held most of the best cards. In their very different ways, both George III and Frederick the Great, for example, made themselves respected by contemporaries and venerated by posterity. In 1782–83 George III faced a political crisis so severe that he contemplated abdication and departure for Hanover. In the event, by a combination of resolution and skill he emerged the victor and was rewarded with seventeen years of political stability. Faced with his own crisis in the summer of 1788, Louis XVI in effect abdicated, allowing the political opposition to seize an initiative they never lost: "The bankruptcy of the monarchy was not only financial, but political and intellectual too. It had collapsed in every sense, leaving an enormous vacuum of power."[33]

Although Louis XVI's personal shortcomings were as manifest as they were fatal, it is undeniable that he came to the throne handicapped by an "image problem" none of his own making. In particular, the Austrian alliance secured by the "diplomatic revolution" of 1756 had been a disastrous failure. To public opinion, it seemed responsible for the multiple defeats of the Seven Years' War at the hands of the British and the Prussians, costing France much of her overseas empire and most of her influence in Europe. Further humiliations such as the first partition of Poland, the Russian annexation of the Crimea, or Frederick the Great's formation of the League of Princes suggested that France had become "the auxiliary of Austria" (Soulavie) and had "ceased to be a first-rank power" (Ségur).[34] Louis inherited this problem from his predecessor. Any attempt to deal with it was virtually ruled out from the start by another poisoned chalice passed on by Louis XV in the bittersweet shape of the Austrian Archduchess Marie Antoinette, sister of Joseph II and married

---

[32] Quoted in Baker, "Public Opinion as Political Invention," p. 187.

[33] William Doyle, *The Oxford History of the French Revolution* (Oxford, 1989), p. 85.

[34] Jean-Louis Soulavie, *Mémoires historiques et politiques du règne de Louis XVI, depuis son mariage jusqu'à son mort, ouvrage composé sur des pièces authentiques fourniés à l'auteur avant la Révolution, par plusieurs ministres* (Paris, 1801), 1:8; Louis-Philippe comte de Ségur, *Mémoires ou souvenirs et anecdotes*, vols. 1–3 of *Oeuvres complètes* (Paris, 1824–26), 1:22.

to the Dauphin (as Louis XVI then was) in 1770. Everyone knew that she was much stronger-willed than her feeble consort, and most chose to believe that she was an Austrian agent determined to run French policy in her brother's interests. That in fact Louis did not allow her to dictate French foreign policy does not matter. His intensely unpopular wife always vitiated any chance of remodeling the monarchy's image in a national mold.

The last chance was thrown away in the summer of 1787, when the king supported the decision taken by his first minister, Brienne, not to intervene to prevent the Prussian invasion of the United Provinces. So the French had to stand idly by, as their supporters were arrested, the Prince of Orange was restored to power, and the country was obliged to abandon France in favor of an alliance with Prussia and Great Britain. If Louis XVI could not afford the expense of a military action, still less could he afford to remain inactive. More than any other episode, this fiasco demonstrated how low once-mighty France had fallen in the world. Unable to defend its vital interests even in its own backyard, the Old Regime had virtually abdicated.[35] Yet the defense and assertion of the country's interests lay at the very heart of monarchy's legitimation. This is an aspect of the Revolution's prehistory that will repay closer examination. Although out of fashion for most the twentieth century, the "primacy of foreign policy" is long overdue for a comeback in French Revolutionary historiography.

The rapidly intensifying political crisis at the end of the 1780s coincided with a sharply deteriorating socioeconomic situation, culminating in the subsistence crisis of 1788–89. Now the great mass of the urban and rural population could be mobilized. Their fears, resentments, and ambitions may have pointed in many different and often contradictory directions, but they combined for long enough in the spring and summer of 1789 to destroy the Old Regime. No group has suffered more from the concentration of current historiography on politics and culture than the peasantry, by far the most numerous sector of society, comprising around 67 percent of the population.[36] Their demotion can be illustrated by their relative treatment by François Furet in his two general accounts. In 1965 he devoted several pages to them in his chapter titled "The France of Louis XVI." In 1988 his chapter on "The *Ancien Régime*" did not mention them at all, finding room only for sections on "The Monarchy" (seven pages), "The Nobility" (four pages), "The Enlightenment" (four pages), "Projects for Reform" (nine pages), "Louis

---

[35] I have discussed this episode and its ramifications in greater detail in *The French Revolutionary Wars, 1787–1802* (London, 1996), chap. 1.

[36] Peter Jones, *The Peasantry in the French Revolution* (Cambridge, 1988), p. 4. This is by far the best account of the subject available in any language and is strongly recommended.

XVI" (four pages), "Marie Antoinette" (three pages), and "The Financial Crisis" (eight pages).[37]

The presence of John Markoff's article in this collection therefore has a symbolic as well as a substantive value. Not only does he provide the reader with an invaluable introduction to the current historiography, he also provides a rigorous quantitative analysis of the *cahiers de doléances* to reveal patterns of rural grievances in 1789. His meticulous, carefully qualified, and modest conclusions highlight by contrast both the attractions and the limitations of the broad-brush, grand-canvas approach to revolutionary politics and culture favored by Furet and his followers. It must be conceded that the revisionists' neglect of rural France in general and the peasantry in particular forms the Achilles' heel of their account. As one of their most effective critics, Gwynne Lewis, has pointed out, "Revisionist historians, anxious to improve the image of the *ancien régime* at the cost of the Revolution, too often ignore the social fact that the vast majority of country-dwellers laboured within an increasingly despised and archaic feudal and theocratic system which exacted from those who worked the soil a multiplicity of dues and personal services."[38] Whatever else it may have done or not done, the Revolution at least put an end to that situation, although whether the majority of peasants reaped any appreciable material benefit is a different matter.

REVOLUTIONARY POLITICAL CULTURE

The primacy of politics is even more pronounced in revisionist accounts of the creation of a new France. Once again, it was Furet who set the pace. In an essay with the gnomic title "The French Revolution Is Over," he argued that the fierce struggle that marked the first five years of the Revolution was not between classes or even interest groups. Rather, it was a contest for power through the appropriation of the symbols of revolutionary legitimacy. At its core was the axiom, taken from Rousseau, that the power of the people cannot be alienated through representation. As direct democracy is impracticable in a country the size of France or even in a city the size of Paris, the essential task of the politician is to present himself and his cause in such a way as to personify popular sovereignty. This is the crucial passage that underpins Furet's account of revolutionary politics: "Legitimacy (and victory) therefore belonged to those who symbolically embodied the people's will and were able to monopolise the appeal to it. It is the inevitable paradox of direct democracy

---

[37] Furet and Richet (n. 9 above), pp. 7–44; Furet, *Revolutionary France* (n. 9 above), pp. 3–40.

[38] Gwynne Lewis, *The French Revolution: Rethinking the Debate* (London, 1993), pp. 73–74.

that it replaces electoral representation with a system of abstract equivalences in which the people's will always coincides with power and in which political action is exactly identical with its legitimacy."[39] In other words, the language and ritual of political struggle were not just the external symptoms of some deeper social reality, they themselves were real:

> The Revolution . . . ushered in a world where mental representations of power governed all actions, and where a network of signs completely dominated political life. Politics was a matter of establishing just who represented the people, or equality, or the nation: victory was in the hands of those who were capable of occupying and keeping that symbolic position. The history of the Revolution between 1789 and 1794, in its period of development, can therefore be seen as the rapid drift from a compromise with the principle of representation toward the unconditional triumph of rule by opinion. It was a logical evolution, considering that the Revolution had from the outset made power out of opinion.[40]

For this reason, recent historiography has concentrated on the development of revolutionary political culture. This phrase—"political culture"—recurs so often that it is essential to nail down a clear definition. The best is that offered by Keith Michael Baker: "It sees politics as about making claims; as the activity through which individuals and groups in any society articulate, negotiate, implement, and enforce the competing claims they make upon one another and upon the whole. Political culture is, in this sense, the set of discourses or symbolic practices by which these claims are made."[41]

This approach has had the advantage of taking scholars out of the important but overfrequented debating chambers of the National Assembly or Jacobin Clubs into the streets, to look at the press, pamphlets, prints, songs, and ceremonies that made up this new culture.[42] It has also led them to bring back to the center of attention aspects of revolutionary activity previously neglected. The Old Regime collapsed so quickly and completely in the summer of 1789 that the opportunity arose to remodel society from top to bottom in accordance with the dictates of reason and nature. In his contribution to this volume, William Sewell calls it "the ideological restructuring of social life," citing as an example the metric system in which the meter was set as exactly

---

[39] François Furet, "The French Revolution Is Over," in *Interpreting the French Revolution,* p. 48.

[40] Ibid., pp. 48–49.

[41] Baker, *Inventing the French Revolution* (n. 27 above), p. 4.

[42] The literature is already vast. A good sample can be found in Colin Lucas, ed., *The Political Culture of the French Revolution* (Oxford, 1988). Especially interesting are Lynn Hunt, *Politics, Culture and Class in the French Revolution* (London, 1986); and Mona Ozouf, *Festivals and the French Revolution* (Cambridge, Mass., 1988). The latter is equipped with a helpful preface by Lynn Hunt, which conveniently summarizes the book's argument.

one ten-millionth of the distance from the North Pole to the equator: "the new system measured out the world in terms at once uniform, rational, easily manipulable, and based on immutable facts of nature."[43]

The metric system has proved the most durable, universal, and arguably the most benign of all the consequences of the French Revolution. It should not be seen as a peripheral by-product of a more fundamental social process. As Lynn Hunt has written, "The concern with words, festivals, seals, and measures of time, space and distance was not a diversion from some more real or important political issue; it was essential to the definition of the revolutionary process and to the identity of the new political class."[44] Parts of this revolutionary culture did not stand the test of time—in particular, we should all be grateful that the ten-day week perished—but in general it represented "the chief accomplishment of the French Revolution."[45] This verdict also advertises the primacy of politics. As Hunt argues, the social and economic changes brought about by the Revolution were not revolutionary. If anything, they retarded French industrialization, while it has become something of a cliché to observe that socially the France of Louis Philippe resembled nothing more than the France of Louis XVI. But, she goes on, "in the realm of politics, in contrast, almost everything changed. Thousands of men and even many women gained firsthand experience in the political arena: they talked, read, and listened in new ways; they voted; they joined new organisations; and they marched for their political goals. Revolution became a tradition, and republicanism an enduring option. Afterward, kings could not rule without assemblies, and noble domination of public affairs only provoked more revolution. As a result, France in the nineteenth century had the most bourgeois polity in Europe, even though France was never the leading industrial power."[46]

There was a less appealing side to this new democratic culture, demonstrated by periodic eruptions of popular violence. Atrocities such as the lynching of Foulon and Berthier in July 1789 or the September Massacres of 1792 shocked not only conservatives. Both at home and abroad they saddled the Revolution with a criminal image as destabilizing as it was long-lived. Well might Colin Lucas point out in his contribution herein that "the Revolution hastened the process of separation of the elites from the popular community, from its claims and its values. The crowd's actions in the Revolution may be seen as instrumental in accelerating the alienation of the

---

[43] See William H. Sewell Jr., "Ideologies and Social Revolutions: Reflections on the French Case" (in this volume), p. 305.

[44] Hunt, p. 215.

[45] Ibid., p. 15.

[46] Ibid., p. 221.

propertied classes from the popular community."[47] Yet he is also at pains to find meaning beneath the blood-lust. The crowd, he suggests, was the means by which ordinary people expressed their collective identity and values, regulated their relationship with authority, defended their place in society, and imposed their collective values on deviant members. It was also a judicial instrument. Even the stomach-churning butchery of Foulon and Berthier was presented as an act of justice, the former being subjected to a "trial" before being dragged to the Place de Grève, just like a regular criminal, before being decapitated.

It may be doubted, however, whether most readers will feel able to endorse Lucas's reassuring conclusion that "the crowd action in July was essentially reactive. It was engendered by panic and its motive was fundamentally self-defense."[48] It is at this point that one feels that a natural inclination to regard as legitimate anything perpetrated by the common people may be obscuring understanding. It is a sad but well-documented fact that any revolution allows what can only be called psychopaths to emerge from their dark private world and turn their fantasies into reality. Not only is the risk of apprehension reduced by the collapse of the rule of law, violence is now condoned, even encouraged, if it is directed against the revolution's enemies. Almost all the murderers who slaughtered aristocrats, priests, and "traitors" of every class with such relish between 1789 and 1794 escaped unpunished. The politicians who exploited the violence for their own fell purposes were not always so fortunate. When asked whether the murders of Foulon and Berthier really served the cause of liberty, Barnave replied with a sneer: "What, then, is their blood so pure?" One can only hope that those words came back to haunt him when he mounted the steps to the guillotine on November 29, 1793.

As the fate of Barnave indicated, a man regarded as a radical revolutionary in 1789 could be executed as a "traitor to the people" only four years later. What William Sewell calls the "ideological dynamic" of the Revolution brought a rapid process of radicalization.[49] No group was affected more drastically than the liberal nobles who had played such a destructive role in the collapse of the Old Regime and such a constructive role in remaking France in the Constituent Assembly in 1789–91. As the Revolution whirled leftward, former supporters—even former leaders—were left gasping in its wake. As Alison Patrick argues in her chapter herein, "For most of the outstanding contributors, the considerable noble share in the great reforms of the

---

[47] See Colin Lucas, "The Crowd and Politics between *Ancien Régime* and Revolution in France" (in this volume), p. 210.

[48] Ibid., p. 221.

[49] Sewell, p. 300.

revolution came to a jarring halt when a final choice between monarchy and revolution had to be made. To accept revolution in 1789, or even 1791, was not necessarily to accept the 1792 Republic."[50] As those who abandoned ship included Lafayette, who had been the first commander of the Paris National Guard and was commander of the Army of the Centre when he defected to the Austrians on August 19, 1792, and the equally prominent liberal noble Alexandre de Lameth, it is not surprising that so many nobles' sterling services to the Revolution should have made way for a collective image of counterrevolutionary treason.

This brings us to the Terror of Year II (1793–94) and the heart of current historiography.[51] It is particularly instructive to compare the two versions given by François Furet of this episode. In *The French Revolution* of 1965 he repeated the conventional version, which saw the Terror as a response to an emergency. With the military situation deteriorating rapidly, on February 23, 1793, the National Convention decreed the conscription of 300,000 men. The result was the counterrevolutionary rising in the Vendée. On March 16 the Austrians scored a great victory at Neerwinden, reconquered Belgium, and prepared to march on Paris. The violent overthrow of the Girondin government at the beginning of June provoked widespread "federalist" revolts against the new regime in Paris. The nadir of revolutionary fortunes was reached on August 27 when Toulon, the main naval base in the Mediterranean, surrendered to the British. It seemed only a question of whether the Revolution would succumb first to foreign or civil war, so it also seems only common sense to conclude with Furet that "far from being an inevitable part of the revolutionary process, the dictatorship of Year II bears all the marks of contingency, of a nation that had found itself in dire straits."[52]

By the time he came to write "The French Revolution Is Over," he had changed his mind. He now saw the Terror as "an integral part of revolutionary ideology."[53] In the definitive version, published in the bicentennial year, he went further, describing the Terror as "a demand based on political convictions or beliefs, a characteristic feature of the mentality of revolutionary activism. As such, it predated the dictatorship of Year II, the Republic, and the war with Europe. It had existed since the early summer of 1789, along with

---

[50] See Alison Patrick, "The Second Estate in the Constituent Assembly, 1789–1791" (in this volume), p. 262.

[51] The new revolutionary calendar was adopted on October 5, 1793. The first day of the first revolutionary year was deemed to be September 22, 1792, the day of the inauguration of the French Republic following the abolition of the monarchy by the National Convention on the previous day.

[52] Furet and Richet (n. 9 above), p. 184.

[53] Furet, "The French Revolution Is Over" (n. 39 above), p. 62.

the related idea that the Revolution was threatened by an aristocratic plot that only prompt measures could thwart."[54] Two kinds of arguments are advanced to support this position. First, Furet goes back to the essence of revolutionary ideology, stressing its Rousseauist demand for unanimity. This insistence on the unity of the general will was matched by an equally firm belief in the existence of an aristocratic plot. Honest disagreement about policy or procedures could not be entertained in this fundamentally nonpluralist political culture. When discord reared its ugly head, it could only be explained by the treachery or delusion plotted by the Revolution's enemies. As dissent was illegitimate, it had to be rooted out by any means that seemed appropriate. In other words, the Terror was part of revolutionary ideology from the start, generated by the dialectic between the general will and the belief in the aristocratic plot.[55]

A second and less abstract argument draws attention to the timing of the Terror. Made "the order of the day" on September 5, 1793, it took many weeks—months indeed—to be fully realized. Yet the military situation improved rapidly during the autumn and winter of 1793–94 for reasons unconnected with events in Paris. On September 6 a French victory over the British expeditionary force at Hondschoote relieved Dunkirk; on October 6 victory over the Austrians at Wattignies secured the northern frontier; at the end of December Hoche defeated the Austrians at Froeschwiller and Geisberg, forcing them to evacuate Alsace; at the same time, the Prussians evacuated the Palatinate. By the time the "great terror" began in June 1794, the war was well and truly won.[56] Indeed, in her article on "War and Terror" in this volume, Mona Ozouf shows that there was a triumphalist mood abroad as the Terror was pushed to its climax.[57]

So was the Terror, in Simon Schama's characteristically pithy phrase, "merely 1789 with a higher body count"?[58] This is surely going too far. While the revisionists have made the point well that all echelons of the Revolution were bloodstained from the start, the Terror of Year II was so much more intense and so much more deliberate as to be different in kind. Monsters such as Fouquier-Tinville, Collot-d'Herbois, Saint-Just, or Turreau could not have flourished four years earlier. A recent examination of the judicial procedures

[54] François Furet, "Terror," in *A Critical Dictionary of the French Revolution,* ed. François Furet and Mona Ozouf (Cambridge, Mass., 1989), p. 137.

[55] See Sewell, p. 301. This article contains a particularly clear exegesis of Furet's argument.

[56] Furet, "The French Revolution Is Over," p. 62.

[57] See Mona Ozouf, "War and Terror in the French Revolution" (in this volume), p. 266.

[58] Simon Schama, *Citizens: A Chronicle of the French Revolution* (New York, 1989), p. 447.

of 1789–90 has concluded that the new regime treated its opponents on both right and left with a restraint and indulgence that confirms that the Revolution did enjoy a liberal, pluralist phase. Only one counterrevolutionary conspirator was executed before the fall of the monarchy (the Marquis de Favras).[59] Certainly there was much uncompromising rhetoric that pointed in the direction of the guillotine, but there was just as much to suggest that France was moving toward a stable if lively polity of the kind recently established in the United States of America.

The best explanation for the rapid radicalization and descent into state terrorism that the Revolution then experienced remains the war. Of course there were many domestic forces working in the same direction, notably material deprivation; the political education of the *menu peuple;* the capture and removal from Versailles to Paris of both the royal family and the National Assembly; and—yes, too—the nature and development of revolutionary political culture. Yet what turned a crisis into a second revolution was the threat of intervention from outside. It is important to remember that the "revolutionary wars" did not begin on April 20, 1792. The war declared on that day by the National Assembly was only part of a much wider conflict that had begun almost five years earlier. The revolutionaries did not make the mistake of so many subsequent historians and confine their attention to the situation inside France, for they had seen the Prussians invading and conquering the Dutch Republic in September 1787 and the Austrians invading and conquering Belgium in November 1790.[60] So when the Prussians and the Austrians prepared to invade France in the summer of 1792, there was a reaction of corresponding magnitude—especially when the allied commander-in-chief, the Duke of Brunswick, published a manifesto threatening to put Paris to the torch and the sword if the safety of the royal family was impaired. That brought the overthrow of the monarchy on August 10.

Yet the radicalizing effect of the war had begun long before its formal declaration. It was during the Brissotin campaign for war, launched in the Legislative Assembly as soon as it convened on October 1, 1791, that the last liberal elements of revolutionary political culture were submerged by great waves of bellicose rhetoric. On December 26, 1791, for example, Gensonné proclaimed the end of pluralism. In the old days, he stated, when the operations of the émigrés seemed harmless and the "great foreign conspiracy

---

[59] Barry M. Shapiro, *Revolutionary Justice in Paris, 1789–1790* (Cambridge, 1993), pp. xii–xiii, 124.

[60] I have argued this case in "The French Revolution and Europe," in Lucas, ed. (n. 4 above), pp. 183–206, and at greater length in *The French Revolutionary Wars, 1787–1802* (London, 1996), esp. chaps. 2–4. Very welcome support has recently been added by Paul W. Schroeder, *The Transformation of European Politics, 1763–1848* (Oxford, 1994), p. 53.

against French liberty" was not yet apparent, it had been possible for men of good will to belong to all political groupings. But no longer. Now there could be only two parties—for the Revolution and against it, good and evil. This Manichaean pronouncement was then given an even more sinister twist: " 'The common enemy is at the gates of the city; a general assault threatens us; so now there can be no more beating about the bush; let us rush to the breach, we must defend our ramparts or bury ourselves beneath their ruins' (*Stormy applause*)."[61] As the Brissotin orators were quick to discover, what brought the deputies and the public galleries to their feet cheering were speeches calling for total victory or total destruction, liberty or death, coupled with demands for the punishment of the enemy within. On January 14, 1792, after orchestrating the great demonstration when the deputies took the oath, "We shall live in freedom or we shall die, the constitution or death!" Guadet concluded with the following threat: "In a word, let us mark out in advance a place for traitors, and that place will be on the scaffold (*Bravo! Bravo! Stormy applause*)."[62] Unfortunately for both men, the definition of treason in the Revolution proved to be mobile: Gensonné was guillotined on October 31, 1793, Guadet on June 15, 1794.

COUNTERREVOLUTION

If the war took the Revolution to the left, it also took the counterrevolution to the right. Without the war there would have been no conscription, and without conscription there would have been no rising in the Vendée. Or would there? So combustible was the heap of resentments by 1793 that any spark might have ignited the conflagration that then swept across the west. No episode of the Revolution proved more fiercely controversial in France during the bicentennial celebrations, the flavor of the debate being well captured by the title of one of the more intemperate contributions: *Le génocide franco-français, la Vendée-Vengé.*[63] Two centuries on, the old battles between the "whites" and the "blues" are still being fought with relish.

The combatants now have a great deal more information at their disposal. Soboul's "bonne orthodoxie" did not care for heretics, paying them as little attention as possible and marginalizing them as the deluded puppets of the

---

[61] *Archives Parlementaires de 1787 à 1860: Recueil complet des débats législatifs et politiques des chambres françaises,* 127 vols. (Paris, 1879–1913), 36:406.

[62] Ibid., 37:413–14. It might be thought that Mona Ozouf does not take sufficient account of the debates of 1791–92 in her discussion of the relationship between war and terror in the chapter herein.

[63] By Reynald Sécher (Paris, 1986). For a judicious discussion of the controversy, see Hugh Gough, "Genocide and the Bicentenary: The French Revolution and the Revenge of the Vendée," *Historical Journal,* vol. 30, no. 4 (1987).

privileged orders: "stirred up by their priests, the peasants were neither royalists nor supporters of the old regime, they just refused to go to war a long way away from their villages."[64] In the 1960s, however, two trailblazing studies appeared that lifted counterrevolutionary studies to quite a new plane: Paul Bois's *Paysans de l'Ouest,* which began life in 1960 as a dissertation of the École Pratique des Hautes Études (Furet's stronghold) and Charles Tilly's *The Vendée,* first published in 1964. In their different ways they both applied the tools provided by the non-Marxist social sciences to explain why some parts of the west were counterrevolutionary and some parts were not, Bois dealing with the department of the Sarthe and Tilly with southern Anjou. There is no room here even to summarize their conclusions. What is important for our present purpose is to point out that both insisted that the behavior of their subjects was determined by socioeconomic structures. The composition of the substructure was no longer defined in Marxist terms, but its relationship with the superstructure remained the same. As Harvey Mitchell pointed out in a critique of both men's work, their concentration on social structure meant that "their models cannot deal adequately with the problem of social and psychological processes. As a result, although we now have a much clearer conception of why parts of the west became ripe for turmoil and rebellion, we remain unenlightened on how the chiefs of the rebellion exploited the sources of discontent and how they identified their goals with the goals of those whom the Revolution had alienated."[65]

It was the liberation of politics and culture discussed earlier that pointed the way to a better understanding of what motivated the counterrevolutionaries. A sine qua non, however, was the abandoning of any ideologically motivated aversion to the Counterrevolution. As Colin Lucas points out in his contribution to this volume, George Rudé's classic study of *The Crowd in the French Revolution* was limited by his denial of validity to any form of mass action

[64] Albert Soboul, *Histoire de la Révolution française,* 2 vols. (Paris, 1962), 1:353–54. Soboul's account of the Vendée repeats the earlier version of Lefebvre almost word-for-word. Compare, for example, "Les paysans vendéens cependant n'avaient pas soutenu la révolte nobiliaire d'août 1791; ils n'avaient pas bougé en 1792 pour sauver leurs *bons* prêtres de la déportation" (ibid., p. 353), and "In August, 1791, the peasants had not supported the revolt of the nobles; nor had they risen in 1792 to protect the 'good' priests from deportation" (Georges Lefebvre, *The French Revolution from 1793 to 1799* [London, 1964], p. 46; this is the translation of the 2d ed. of *La Révolution française* published in 1957).

[65] Harvey Mitchell, "The Vendée and Counter-Revolution: A Review Essay," *French Historical Studies* 5 (1967–68): 426–27. For further cogent criticism of the application of modernization theory in the style of Tilly, see also T. J. A. Le Goff and D. M. G. Sutherland, "Religion and Rural Revolt in the French Revolution: An Overview," in *Religion and Rural Revolt,* ed. Janos M. Bak and Gerhard Benecke (Manchester, 1984).

that might be deemed right-wing.[66] Far from being the deluded puppets of evil clerics and nobles, the counterrevolutionaries had a clear conception of where their interests lay and set about defending them as best they could. In his exceptionally illuminating and important study of the role played by religious loyalties in the west of France printed herein, Timothy Tackett asserts the autonomy of culture:

In the final analysis, there can be no denying the importance of economic relations, of patterns of land tenure, of the issue of military conscription as factors in the outbreak of the *Vendée* and the *Chouannerie*. Yet it seems clear that the socioeconomic clashes between town and country were paralleled and greatly reinforced by an independent cultural clash; and that the peculiar constellation of religious structures and attitudes rendered this clash as sharp and pronounced as in any other region of France. And we must seriously entertain the possibility that it was this very religious confrontation which served as a key catalyst in the relative cohesion and unity of so much of the rural west, galvanizing and energizing the diverse and sometimes contradictory patterns of social and economic conflict at the local level.[67]

Not only has the tide now turned in favor of the previously despised and marginalized "whites," it is running so fast in their favor that they are being swept to hegemony as the most powerful popular movement of the period. That at least is the view of Donald Sutherland: "The history of the entire period can be understood as the struggle against a counter-revolution that was not so much aristocratic as massive, extensive, durable and popular."[68] And fueling that counterrevolution was religion. Although there may have been more enthusiasm for the King than Lefebvre and Soboul liked to think, few of his subjects were prepared to die in a ditch for his brother—the Comte d'Artois—or any of the other émigrés seeking to foment counterrevolution. The emigratio.., which began immediately after the fall of the Bastille, was important for politics at the center because it provided a basis of reality for that belief in an aristocratic plot Furet deems so important. Indeed, it was Albert Sorel's opinion that "no event was more disastrous for the monarchy or more pernicious for the course of the Revolution than the emigration."[69] But a mass basis for counterrevolution could only be created by an issue that could galvanize ordinary people.

That was the role of religion. Almost from the start it demonstrated its disruptive potential by forcing natural supporters of the Revolution to move into the opposition camp. Especially in the southeast of France, where there

[66] See Lucas (n. 47 above), p. 201.

[67] See Timothy Tackett, "The West in France in 1789: The Religious Factor in the Origins of the Counterrevolution" (in this volume), p. 357.

[68] D. M. G. Sutherland, *France, 1789–1815* (London, 1985), p. 14.

[69] Albert Sorel, *L'Europe et la Révolution jiançaise,* 8 vols. (Paris, 1885–1905), 2:5.

was a heavy concentration of Protestants, the abolition of religious disabilities allowed heretics for the first time to compete on equal terms. Like many minorities before and since, they seized their opportunity with gusto, taking control of municipal government and other instruments of local control such as the National Guard. Catholics who had greeted the Revolution with enthusiasm soon began to have second thoughts as they were elbowed aside. Tension grew during the winter and spring of 1790, as armed camps began to form. On June 13–14 there was an eruption of violence at Nîmes when some three hundred Catholics were butchered by a mob of Protestant peasants and artisans, ushering in a decade of sectarian violence in the Rhône valley.[70] Although it was aversion to Protestantism as heresy that supplied the common thread running through all the various manifestations of counterrevolution in the southeast,[71] there were undeniably socioeconomic forces at work too, as James Hood makes amply clear in his contribution to this volume.

Here as elsewhere in France, the politics of the 1790s cannot be reduced to a simple confrontation between revolution and counterrevolution, pitting radical republicans against clerical royalists. However confusing the overall picture may become, integrity requires the variations and hybrids to be charted. There are two good examples in this volume. In a model exercise in local history, Suzanne Desan demonstrates that many devout Catholics were equally ardent supporters of the Revolution, praying for the success of the Republic's armies and borrowing revolutionary arguments to support their call for toleration. It is certainly arresting to discover that early in the Revolution a group of villagers in Périgord made their *curé* put a tricolor cockade on the Host and leave the doors open "so that the good God might be free."[72] Bill Edmonds also finds revolutionary arguments being used by dissident groups, in this case by the "federalists" who revolted against the new regime in Paris following the fall of the Girondins. Looking again at the pattern of resistance, he finds that the popular generalization that "two-thirds" of the departments were federalist is a gross exaggeration—even verbal support for the cause could be found in only forty-three (of eighty-three) departments and of these only fourteen took their protest to the point of military action. Federalism was not a general war waged by the provincial bourgeoisie against Paris, he concludes, but a limited defensive reaction to Montagnard centralism.[73]

[70] The best account is to be found in Gwynne Lewis, *The Second Vendée: The Continuity of Counter-Revolution in the Department of the Gard, 1789–1815* (Oxford, 1978).

[71] Ibid., p. 27.

[72] See Suzanne Desan, "Redefining Revolutionary Liberty: The Rhetoric of Religious Revival during the French Revolution" (in this volume), p. 384.

[73] See Bill Edmonds, "Federalism and Urban Revolt in France in 1793" (in this volume).

Whatever the source of its various forms, opposition to the regime was powerful and continuous throughout the revolutionary decade. Never was there a time when the Rousseauist dream of a united general will looked feasible. Yet its baleful influence never waned. Even the veteran politicians of the Directory were still in its thrall, refusing to make the compromises with disordered reality that might have allowed the construction of a viable polity. This is the conclusion of Lynn Hunt, David Lansky and Paul Hanson, who in their joint article reprinted herein argue that the Directors' fatal aversion to political parties stemmed from their rejection of anything suggesting division within "the community of citizens": "The Brumaire coup—its possibility and its success—grew out of a fundamental contradiction in the way the Revolutionary notables thought about and acted out their politics. The legislators of 1795 instituted a representative government based on electoral politics, but they were unwilling to accept the consequences of their handiwork, the growth of organized political parties.... In essence, the republicans of 1795 wanted to establish a liberal republic without accepting the imperatives of liberal politics."[74] So eventually their resistance to the notion that any opposition could be legitimate drove them to endorse "the technocratic, authoritarian and antiparty vision of government that Napoleon put into practice."[75]

This is a subtle and persuasive analysis but perhaps does not explain adequately why it was General Bonaparte who took power in 1799. It is at least arguable that it was the defeats of 1799 and the first real invasion-scare since 1793 that inflicted the terminal delegitimation of the Directorial regime. In sorting out conceptually what happened on 18 brumaire, the tools offered by Max Weber are particularly helpful. Weber identified three forms of political legitimacy: traditional, legal, and charismatic. The French Revolution had deliberately revoked the first of those when it sought to create "a new national community based on reason and nature without reference to the customs of the past."[76] What little legality still attached to the Revolution after the Terror, counterrevolution, and the repeated coups d'état from above under the Directory was finally eliminated by the patent illegality of General Bonaparte's coup of 18 brumaire. That left only charismatic authority, famously defined by Weber as "the domination, as exercised by the prophet or—in the field of politics—by the elected war lord, the plebiscitarian ruler, the great demagogue, or the political party leader. Devotion to the charisma of the prophet, or the leader in war, or to the great demagogue in the church or

[74] See Lynn Hunt, David Lansky, and Paul Hanson, "The Failure of the Liberal Republic in France, 1795–1799: The Road to Brumaire" (in this volume), p. 470.

[75] Ibid., p. 490.

[76] Hunt (n. 42 above), p. 213.

in parliament, means that the leader is personally recognised as the innerly 'called' leader of men. Men do not obey him by virtue of tradition or statute but because they believe in him."[77] In revolutionary France—a secular state whose political culture was essentially at odds with party politics—that could only mean the warlord. To paraphrase François Furet, now the Revolution really was over.

* * *

No single volume can encompass all possible approaches to the French Revolution. Presented here are seventeen contributions that allow the major trends in current historiography to be experienced in all their exciting variety. It is an indication of the subject's seminal importance in the history of modern Europe that it has attracted the attention of so many powerful minds. Moreover, its undimmed topicality naturally lends to even the more specialized studies an invigorating polemical edge. By approaching the rise and fall of the French Revolution in this company, the reader will be stimulated as well as informed.

---

[77] H. H. Gerth and C. Wright Mills, eds., *From Max Weber: Essays in Sociology*, new edition (London, 1991), pp. 78–79.

THE DECLINE AND FALL
OF THE OLD REGIME

Church, State, and the Ideological Origins of the French Revolution: The Debate over the General Assembly of the Gallican Clergy in 1765*

Dale Van Kley

I. Introduction

The lot of the provincial parish priest has no doubt always been a hard one, but it seemed even harder than usual to Hubert Chalumeau, curé of Saint Pierre in Vézelay, in the spring of 1766. It was bad enough that numbers of "pernicious books" had penetrated this remote Burgundian town, most notably some by Jean-Jacques Rousseau, and that the curé's parishioners had been "devouring" them. At least for this evil a powerful antidote was at hand—or so the curé thought. For as it providentially happened, the general assembly of the Gallican Clergy had just anathematized some of these books, specifically Rousseau's *Emile, Social Contract,* and *Letters Written from the Mountain,* and had moreover published their condemnation as part of its *Actes,* which some bishops had sent to their parish priests.[1] So when the vigilant Chalumeau received his copy toward the beginning of 1766, he could think of no better means of countering the "extreme peril" threatening his parishioners' souls than to read to them the section condemning the "books against Religion" as an introduction to his sermon. But who should have thought that for this gesture of edification the local

* Painstaking stylistic criticism by my colleagues David Diephouse and Edwin J. Van Kley as well as by John La Grand and Carroll Joynes of Carleton University and the University of Chicago, respectively, has greatly improved this article. It has also benefited from the counsels of professors Keith Baker, David Bien, Robert Palmer, Alexander Sedgwick, and Timothy Tackett, all of whom read the manuscript in its entirety. A John Simon Guggenheim Fellowship and a supplementary stipend from the Calvin Foundation enabled me to undertake the necessary research in Paris. To all of these I express my profoundest gratitude. Michel Peronnet's *Les Eveques de l'ancienne France,* 2 vols. (Lille, 1977), came to my attention too late to influence the writing of this paper, the focus of which is very different from the one adopted in the few pages (2:790–821) Peronnet devotes to the general assembly of 1765.

[1] *Actes de l'assemblée générale du clergé de France sur la religion, extraits du procès-verbal de ladite assemblée, tenue à Paris, par permission du Roi, au couvent des Grands-Augustins, en mil sept cent soixante-cinq* (Paris, 1765), "Condamnation de plusieurs livres contre la religion," pp. 3–9, esp. p. 9 (hereafter cited as *Actes*).

This essay originally appeared in the *Journal of Modern History* 51 (December 1979).

procureur fiscal, who had not even attended the sermon, would denounce the good curé to the attorney general of the parlement of Paris as a rebellious subject and a disturber of the public peace? Yet that is in fact what happened. "Ah, monsigneur," he sighed, in a letter to the attorney general on April 29, "how unhappy is the lot of the curé these days." It is hard to disagree.[2]

What had this curé done wrong? How could his modest stand against provincial apostasy have merited the martyrdom of a scrape with the law, which for its part had "lacerated and burned" Rousseau's *Emile* as recently as 1762? On one level, the answer is quite simple. Only the first and smaller portion of the *Actes,* published by the general assembly of 1765 dealt with the "criminal productions" of the French Enlightenment; the second and far larger portion defined the rights of the Church in relation to the State.[3] Now this second part of *Actes* had provoked the ire of the parlement of Paris, which therefore condemned the entire document and tried to prevent its dissemination. So when Vézelay's *procureur fiscal* obtained word that the curé of Saint Pierre had publicly read these *Actes,* he wrongly concluded that the curé had read the whole document, rather than only the part against the irreligious books. It was all a pathetic mistake—avoidable, no doubt, had the *procureur fiscal* only gone to mass.

But on another level the incident is rather more complicated than that, and invites a closer look at the whole range of issues dividing the clergy from the parlement which had culminated in the publication of the *Actes.* Important no doubt in their own right, the issues separating the two major *corps* of the realm seem all the more so in the light of the pamphlet literature the controversy provoked, For a careful examination of this literature reveals a "liberal" France in confrontation with a "conservative" France long before the nineteenth century or even the Revolution to which these divisions are generally credited. The controversy moreover reveals a ubiquitous Enlightenment cutting across these divisions, seemingly without specific political direction of its own. So let us leave this poor curé to his provincial misery, and proceed directly to the episcopal *Actes* which occasioned it, and the controversies of the capital which caused it.

It was most unusual for a general assembly of the Gallican Clergy

---

[2] Bibliothèque Nationale (hereafter BN), Collection Joly de Fleury, fol. 1480, MS 345, Billon, procureur fiscal, to attorney general, Vézelay, February 13, 1766, and MSS 348–49, Chalumeau to attorney general, Vézelay, April 29, 1766.

[3] *Actes,* "Exposition sur les droits de la puissance spirituelle," pp. 11–46, and "Déclaration sur la constitution *Unigenitus,*" pp. 47–51.

to promulgate a doctrinal statement such as these *Actes* contained. For the general assembly was not strictly speaking a Church council, but rather a delegation of the clergy in its temporal capacity as first order of the realm. Its origin was fairly recent, as Old Regime institutions go: the monarchy virtually created it at the Colloquy of Poissy in 1561 when it guaranteed the clergy's corporate autonomy and fiscal immunities in return for a large financial contribution. Since then the first estate's assembly had ordinarily met every five years in order to renegotiate this contract, verify its financial accounts, and present remonstrances to the king.[4] All the same, the assembly had occasionally made doctrinal judgments, most notably in 1682 when, cajoled by Louis XIV and guided by Bishop Bossuet, it defined the four famous "liberties" of the Gallican Church uniting adherence to the Council of Constance's assertion of the ecumenical council's supremacy in matters of faith to a declaration of the monarchy's complete independence of any ecclesiastical authority in temporal affairs.[5] But on this and other occasions the assembly had acted at the behest or at least with the blessings of the monarchy. In contrast, what the assembly first did timidly in 1760 and 1762, then with great fanfare in 1765, was quite without precedent: it published a doctrinal statement against the "temporal power" in spite of the unexpressed but sufficiently known displeasure of its crowned head. It was indeed, as one historian has called it, an act of "almost revolutionary audacity."[6]

The circumstances accounting for the clergy's belligerence in 1765 are not obscure. In the course of the previous decade, the macabre campaign by a group of episcopal zealots to deny the Eucharist and extreme unction to penitents suspected of Jansenism had broken against the inflexible resistance of the parlements which, led by that of Paris, defended the right of all Catholics to public participation in the sacraments. At first the king had seemed to side with the episcopacy against his Parisian magistrates, who sustained the unmistakable marks of royal displeasure in 1753 and again in 1757. But

[4] Louis Greenbaum, "The General Assembly of the Clergy of France and Its Situation at the End of the Ancien Régime," *Catholic Historical Review* 53 (July 1967): 156–59.

[5] On Gallicanism, Bossuet, and the assembly of 1682, see Victor Martin, *Le Gallicanisme politique et le clergé de France* (Paris, 1929); and Aimé-Georges Martimort, *Le Gallicanisme de Bossuet* (Paris, 1953). Both point out that the 1682 declaration's first article asserting the monarchy's complete independence of any ecclesiastical authority was a latecomer to the Gallican tradition, and that prior to the wars of religion Gallicanism had held the king responsible, if not to the papacy in particular, at least to the Church in general. Martimort's thesis minimizes Bossuet's role in the assembly of 1682.

[6] Bourlon, *Les Assemblées du clergé et le jansénisme* (Paris, 1909), p. 274.

in September of that year the parlement returned triumphant and, under cover of the king's Law of Silence, thereafter ordered priests to administer the sacraments to appellants of *Unigenitus* and harried them out of the land if they refused. In sum, not only had the parlement "Thrust its hand into the censer" and seized ultimate jurisdictional authority over the Church's most "august" sacraments, but it had seriously undermined the episcopacy's control over its parish priests. Then came the parlement's suppression of the Jesuit Order, entailing two additional profane tramplings upon the holy ground of ecclesiastical jurisdiction. First, the parlement annulled the Jesuits' vows as abusive and pronounced the whole order to be "perverse." Then, not content with having arrogated to itself a purely spiritual authority by condemning a collection of extracts from Jesuits' theological treatises—the infamous *Assertions dangereuses*—the parlement added the effrontery of sending this collection to all the realm's bishops, not for their judgment, but for their instruction and edification.[7] Decidedly, by 1765 the bishops had had enough. For them the time had again come, as it had for Saint Flavian in the fifth century, "to raise our voices and proclaim our doctrine."[8]

So proclaim they did. The resultant "Exposition of the Rights of the Spiritual Power" began innocuously enough with a proclamation of Gallican banalities. Two powers had been established to govern man: "the sacred authority of priests and that of kings"; both came from God, from whom emanated all "well-ordered power on the earth." The goal of the second of these powers was man's well-being in the present life; the object of the first was to prepare him for eternity. In establishing these two powers, God had intended not their strife but their cooperation, so that they might lend mutual aid and support. But neither power was to be subordinate to the other, for each was "sovereign, independent and absolute" in its own domain. For that reason "the Clergy of France" had always taught that the Church's power was confined to "spiritual things," and that kings were "not subordinate to any ecclesiastical power . . . in temporal things," because they held their power from God himself.

---

[7] On these developments, see Dale Van Kley, *The Jansenists and the Expulsion of the Jesuits from France* (New Haven, Conn., 1975), pp. 108–36; and D. Van Kley, "The Refusal of Sacraments Controversy in France and the Political Crisis of 1756–7" (paper presented at the meeting of the American Society for Eighteenth-Century Studies, Chicago, April 1978). To be precise, the parlement of Paris, in its August 6, 1761 *arrêts* provisionally suppressing the order, condemned the *"formules de voeux"* rather than the vows as such, typically trying to distinguish between the vows themselves and the exterior form in which they were embodied.

[8] *Actes*, accompanying circular letter dated August 27, 1765, p. 91.

But if kings commanded in temporal affairs, "the universal Church" had always taught that they were "obliged to obey priests in the order of Religion," to whom "alone the government of the Church belongs."[9]

But it was not so much the glittering teeth of its principles as the tailend whiplash of their applications that constituted the *Actes'* chief force. " . . . Silence," the *Actes* for example proclaimed, "can never be imposed upon those whom God had instituted as His mouthpiece." This was a not very covert condemnation of Louis XV's Law of Silence of September 2, 1754, which had forbidden mention of the bull *Unigenitus* and polemical terms such as Jansenist and Molinist. Again, " . . . The Civil Power . . . cannot . . . be permitted to contradict the Doctrine received by the Church, to suspend the execution of her judgments, or to elude their effects . . . . " Instead read: the parlement of Paris flagrantly exceeded its authority on April 18, 1752, when it declared that no one could be refused the sacraments by virtue of opposition to *Unigenitus*. Moreover, "the Laws of the Church can receive no qualifications except from the authority which pronounced them." In other words, even Louis XV exceeded his authority in his Declaration of December 10, 1756, by saying that *Unigenitus* was not a "rule of faith," thereby implying that the bull's opponents were not really heretics. Further, "The Keys of the Kingdom of Heaven would have been remitted to [the Church] in vain, were she able to authorize a corrupt ethic . . . , and the judgment she pronounces on moral truths, is just as independent of Princes and their Ministers, as that which she makes concerning the objects of belief." That is to say that the parlement's condemnation of lax casuistical propositions taken from Jesuit authors was both unnecessary and jurisdictionally illicit. And finally, " . . . The refusal of the most august of our sacraments can never be the object of the competence of the civil authority." This passage speaks clearly enough for itself.[10]

The general assembly's *Actes* were no sooner printed than the parlement of Paris declared them "null" and condemned an accompanying circular letter as "fanatical and seditious" in judgments on September 4 and 5. These judgments in turn initiated a spectacle of jurisdictional and corporate anarchy—a three-cornered slugfest between the parlement, the episcopacy, and the royal council—to which the realm had grown strangely accustomed since 1750.[11] Not

[9] Ibid., pp. 15–27.
[10] Ibid., pp. 31–39.
[11] The parlement's *parti janséniste* typically engineered the courts' condemnation of

wholly devoid, for its part, of means of "temporal" persuasion—the
clergy had been dragging its feet on the 12 million *don gratuit*
requested by the government—the general assembly promptly solicited and on September 15 obtained a royal order in council annul-
ling the parlementary judgments. The royal action predictably en-
raged the parlement of Paris, which set to work on remonstrances,
but also left the clergy imperfectly avenged by reserving for the king
the cognizance of the contested matters. The provincial parlements
now entered the fray: in the parlement of Aix-en-Provence, the
solicitor general Le Blanc de Castillon delivered a *réquisitoire* so
virulent against the *Actes* that the general assembly felt obliged to
ask the king to disavow it. A conciliar order obligingly did so on
May 24, 1766, but not strongly enough to suit the clergy: the same
day, another conciliar order articulated the royal position on the
proper boundaries between Sacerdoce and Empire, which predictably satisfied neither side. A parlementary judgment on July 8, which
outlawed episcopal attempts to solicit adhesions to the *Actes*, provoked yet another conciliar order of annullment on November 25,
which nonetheless displeased the clergy by adding its own prohibition of soliciting signatures.[12] The controversy slowly melted away
during the spring and early summer of 1767, then disappeared
altogether beneath the avalanche of the La Chalotais-d'Aiguillon
affair in the following years.

the *Actes*. On the composition of the *parti janséniste*, see Van Kley, *The Jansenists*,
pp. 37–61. Guillaume Lambert, counselor in the second chamber of *enquêtes*, saw to
the actual condemnation by the assembled chambers on September 4 while his good
friend Adrien Le Paige, the party's unofficial head and one of the parlement's chief
oracles in ecclesiastical matters, laid the groundwork for what later became the
remonstrances of August 30–31, 1766, in response to a request for his advice on
September 12. He found the *Actes* to consist of "principles which no one has ever
contested" plus "very inconsequent consequences which have been drawn from
them." See Bibliothèque de Port Royal (hereafter BPR), Collection Le Paige 562, MS
29, note by Le Paige "pour la cour après la lecture rapide des actes qu'on m'avoit fait
passer ad hoc," and MS 19, memoir by Lambert. Also see *Nouvelles écclésiastiques*,
henceforth NNEE, November 6, 1765, pp. 183–84; June 30, 1766, p. 21; December 9,
1767, p. 197; and *Extraits des registres du parlement: Des 4 et 5 septembre 1765*
(Paris, 1765).

  [12] NNEE, March 27, 1766, pp. 53–65 (December 9, 16, and 24, 1767), pp. 197–207;
*Procès-verbal de l'assemblée générale du clergé tenue à Paris, au couvent des
Grands-Augustins, en l'année 1765, et continuée en l'année 1766* (Paris, 1773); on *don
gratuit*, pp. 55, 122; on assembly's immediate reaction to the parlement's *arrêts* of
September 4–5, pp. 309–11, 320; on king's response, pp. 836–37; and clergy's
complaint that royal condemnation of Le Blanc de Castillon's *Réquisitoire* of October
30 was not strong enough, pp. 788–89. For parlement's *arrêts*, see Jules Flammermont, ed., *Remontrances du parlement de Paris au XVIIIe siècle* (1888–98; reprint
ed., Geneva, 1978), 2:596.

II. JANSENISM, GALLICANISM, AND PARLEMENTARY
     CONSTITUTIONALISM

Before disappearing altogether, however, the controversy over the
general assembly of 1765 set off a minor avalanche of its own in the
form of anonymous polemical pamphlets and a few full-scale
treatises, the great majority of which took the side of the parlements. Among these were some *Observations on the Acts of the
Assembly of the Clergy of 1765* by the canon lawyer and Jansenist
polemicist Adrien LePaige, who could generally be counted on to
contribute one or two pamphlets per *affaire*. But the *Actes* were also
the object of *Reflections, Diverse Remarks, Anathemas, Legitimate
Complaints*, a *Preservative Against*, and even a *Request on the Part
of a Great Number of the Faithful*, to say nothing of numbers of
Letter[s], including one by a *Military Philosophe*.[13]

The point of view, or "mentality," common to most of these
pamphlets might be described as a peculiar mix of Gallicanism,
Jansenism, and parlementary constitutionalism—or perhaps distor-
tions of all three.[14] The mentality's Gallicanism, first of all, was not
in principle antiepiscopal and professed great reverence for the
authority of Bishop Bossuet. But its taste for antiquity carried it
beyond the episcopal conciliarism of 1682 to the more radical lay
conciliarism of the fourteenth and fifteenth centuries, which invested
the bibical "keys" with the entire "assembly of the faithful," not
the episcopacy alone.[15] The consequent pouring of the new wine of

[13] Of these titles, only *Plaintes légitimes, ou Réclamation contre les Actes de
l'assemblée du clergé de France* (n.p., n.d.), is not cited on the following pages.
Adrien Le Paige's authorship of *Observations sur les Actes de l'assemblée du clergé
de 1765* (n.p., n.d.) can be ascertained by a note in Le Paige's handwriting in his
personal copy of this work, in BPR, Le Paige 785, MS 12, p. 127. This note contains
(1) a paragraph written by Le Paige in 1765 but not published with his *Observations*,
warning that if the French bishops persisted in their "maximes révoltantes ils
s'exposent aux plus grands perils" including a reaction such as the Protestant
Reformation which "embrasserent avec empressement une nouvelle hérésie, pour se
délivrer du fardeau de ces évêques, en abolissant l'Episcopat," and (2) Le Paige's
reflections on the omitted passage as an octogenarian in 1790: "L'auteur ne voulut pas
laisser imprimer ce morceau, pour ne pas être un prophète de malheur. Mais il l'a
conservée; et l'on voit aujourd'hui comment 25 ans après, en évitant cependant les 2
crimes [l'hérésie et l'abolition de l'Episcopat] tout le reste s'est realisé quant à la
personne des Eveques." Le Paige accepted the Civil Constitution of the Clergy.
[14] For another attempt to describe this mentality with the emphasis, however, on
Jansenism, see Van Kley, *The Jansenists*, pp. 6–36.
[15] Most immediately, this brand of Gallicanism harks back to such seventeenth- and
early eighteenth-century figures as Edmond Richer, Vivien de la Borde, and Nicolas
Le Gros. On these, see Edmond Préclin, *Les Jansénistes du XVIIIe siècle et la
constitution civile du clergé: Le développement du richerisme, sa propagation dans le
bas clergé, 1713–1791* (Paris, 1929), pp. 1–12, 41–51, 60–65. But both Carroll Joynes

eighteenth-century religious and ecclesiastical controversy into the
old wine skins of late medieval conciliarism produced a Gallicanism
prejudicial not only to the papacy but to the Gallican bishops
themselves, making them "simple dispensers of the holy mysteries"
accountable to the equally "holy canons" and—ultimately—to their
lay congregations.[16] All gestures of independence of judgment on
their part were so many displays of "despotism" and the "spirit of
domination."

To curb the bishops' "despotism" and confine them to the "holy
canons," this mentality looked immediately to the crown, although
its democratic conciliarism and frequent appeals to the "nation"
raise the suspicion that it was here, if only half consciously, that it
tended to locate sovereignty. In any case the appeal to the king was
authorized by the royal and parlementary strains in its Gallicanism,
enshrined in the first article of the Gallican Declaration of 1682
guaranteeing the temporal power's independence of any ecclesiastical—specifically papal—supervision. But it hammered this
axiom into a formidable engine of war against the Gallican bishops
themselves and what little remained of their independent jurisdiction—called their "system of independence"—and against even
the king to the degree he tried to maintain this jurisdiction.

The oppositional outlook's use of royal Gallicanism against the
king is warning enough that its strident royalism in the matter of
Church-State relations is somewhat deceptive and not without constitutional limitations. To be sure, this constitutionalism was not
self-consciously antimonarchical and owed something to theorists as
royalist as Jean Bodin (although considerably more to the constitutionalism of the Fronde and even the scholastic political analyses of the late medieval Sorbonnists).[17] But it so venerated the

and Keith Baker have called my attention to its direct and major dependence upon
such late medieval conciliarists as Pierre d'Ailly, Jean Gerson, Jacques Almain, and
John Mair. On these figures, see Martimort, pp. 17–70; Victor Martin, *Les Origines
du gallicanisme*, 2 vols. (Paris, 1939), 2:31–54, 131–47; Quentin Skinner, *The
Foundations of Modern Political Thought*, vol. 2, *The Reformation* (Cambridge,
1978), pp. 34–50; and Brian Tierney, *Foundations of the Conciliar Theory: The
Contribution of the Medieval Canonists from Gratian to the Great Schism* (Cambridge, 1955).

[16] *Lettre de M. l'évêque de xxx à monseigneur l'archévêque de Rheims, sur les
Actes de l'assemblée de 1765, envoyés à tous les évêques du Royaume* (n.p., n.d.),
p. 6.

[17] On parlementary constitutionalism during the eighteenth century, see Roger
Bickart, *Les Parlements et la notion de souveraineté nationale au XVIIIe siècle* (Paris,
1932); Jean Egret, *Louis XV et l'opposition parlementaire, 1715–1774* (Paris, 1970);
and Elie Carcassonne, *Montesquieu et le problème de la constitution française au
XVIIIe siècle* (Paris, 1926). On the constitutionalism of the Fronde, see Paul Rice
Doolin, *The Fronde* (Cambridge, Mass., 1935); and on the political thought of the late

immutability of "fundamental" law and the parlements' immemorial role in the matter that it tended to view every irregularity in monarchical behavior as another example of "despotism," and it so impersonally conceived of the monarchical state—not always sharply distinguished from the "nation"—as to leave little room for flesh and blood monarchs who were "nothing but its administrators."[18] As in the case of its Gallicanism, then, the mentality was fearfully preoccupied with "despotism" and "domination," although in this stage of its development the opposite of these spectres was not so much the Whiggish "liberty" described by Bernard Bailyn in England and the American colonies as it was the majesty of impartial "justice" and "law."[19]

The element of Jansenism is the most elusive and difficult to isolate because it seldom took the theologically explicit form of adherence to the Augustinian doctrines of predestination and efficacious grace. Yet like Le Paige, most of the pamphleteers in this instance were probably Jansenists in even this rigorous sense, and in any case numbers of originally Jansenist themes had become so thoroughly a part of the mentality that they functioned within it quite independently of the theological convictions of those who shared it. The Jansenist component most clearly surfaced in the convictions that the bull *Unigenitus* had endangered Catholic dogmas, that Jansenism itself was an imaginary heresy, that the eighteenth-century Catholic Church was corrupt doctrinally, morally, and structurally, and finally, in an omnipresent tone of righteous indignation. Specifically, the mentality so accentuated Jansenism's long-standing theological quarrel with the Jesuit Order that, in explosive combination with Gallicanism's antipapalism, it became a xenophobic hatred of the "court of Rome," everything Italian or "over the mountains," plus a conspiratorial-mindedness capable of believing that the Jesuit Order lurked behind everything which had run amok in Christendom since the mid-sixteenth century.[20]

It was moreover the various papal condemnations of Jansenism, culminating in the bull *Unigenitus,* which had fused the originally

---

medieval Sorbonnists, especially Jacques Almain and John Maier, see Skinner, pp. 113–23. Again, I owe to Carroll Joynes and to Keith Baker my awareness of the mentality's dependence on these sources.

[18] [Gabriel-Nicolas Maultrot and Claude Mey], *Apologie de tous les jugements rendue par les tribunaux séculiers en France contre le schisme . . .* , 2 vols. (France, 1752), 2:357.

[19] Bernard Bailyn, *The Ideological Origins of the American Revolution* (Cambridge, Mass., 1971), pp. 55–93.

[20] Van Kley, *The Jansenists,* pp. 6–36, 233–37. See also René Taveneaux, *Jansénisme et politique* (Paris, 1965).

ct elements of Jansenism, the several strains of Gallicanism, nd parlementary constitutionalism in the first place. Promulgated in 1713, this bull offended both Augustinian and Gallican suscep- tibilities, and the monarchy's persistent attempts to enforce it suc- ceeded only in swelling the ranks of the opponents and in adding the crown as a target of their arrows.[21] As early as the 1730s the resultant coherent (if not altogether internally consistent) mentality of opposition was at once denouncing the Jesuits' "Molinism" in the name of all good Catholics, the "court of Rome's" alien influence in the name of "all good Frenchmen," the Gallican bishops' "spirit of domination" in the name of the king's loyal subjects, and the monarchy's "despotism" in the name of the "fundamental laws of the realm." Conceived, in a word, by Jansenism, born of the bull *Unigenitus*, this mentality suffered greatly but waxed in obscurity under the archbishop of Paris and his infernal *billets de confession*, only to rise full-blown and triumphant over the Jesuits in the 1760s. It was more than ready for the general assembly's *Actes* in 1765.

This pamphlet literature fell upon the *Actes* with a violence which made the parlement's official reaction seem polite by comparison. Le Paige, for example, more melodramatic as pamphleteer than as parlementary *éminence grise*, proclaimed that the *Actes* "tend to- wards nothing less than to make a universal revolution in the Church of France and to engulf everything in the State," to constitute a regular "war declared by the Sacerdoce against the Empire."[22] The "enflamed style" of the circular letter which accompanied the *Actes*, the publication of these documents in various dioceses, the quest for adhesions and signatures—were not these together the "signal of reunion" of an "episcopal League," similar to the one in the sixteenth century?[23] If not all were as certain as Le Paige that they witnessed the renaissance of the Catholic League, most detected the hand of the sinister and omnipresent Jesuit Order, the same yester- day, today, and tomorrow despite its definitive dissolution in France a year earlier. "This imperious and vindictive society," warned one polemicist in the name of a *Great Number of the Faithful*, "in the days of our father the heart of such a terrible confederation [the League], is today perhaps more than ever animated by the same spirit . . . ; and the Public is persuaded that it is she who by her

---

[21] Jacques-François Thomas, *La Querelle de l'Unigenitus* (Paris, 1949).
[22] [Le Paige], *Observations*, pp. 1, 68.
[23] Ibid., p. 126.

members spread out in every direction is the secret motor of all the operations of Your Assembly."[24]

If any part of the general assembly's *Actes* could have won the approval of these polemicists, it would surely have been the condemnation of unbelief. And indeed, acknowledged the anonymous fulminator of *The Anathemas*, "one cannot sufficiently praise the attention of our prelates to stop its rapid torrent. But our Bishops will in vain raise their voices against irreligion," he hastened to add, "as long as they do not add the luminous principles and holy maxims of the Faith."[25] Too little, too late: such, in sum, was the general verdict. "The Assembly of 1765," intoned the Jansenist weekly *Nouvelles écclésiastiques,* "points out in its *Actes* a part of the evil; but it applies to it only a powerless remedy: so long as [ecclesiastical] censures, especially censures as vague as these, preempt the place of instruction, religion will be badly defended."[26]

If such was their reaction to the *Actes'* first section, what were they to think of the next section concerning the "rights of the Spiritual power?" Here, predictably, they discovered yawning cavities beneath the pearly white of the principles themselves. To what mischievous end, for example, did the author of the *Actes* place the comma in Rom. 13:1 after *Deo* rather than *sunt,* where the Vulgate put it *(Non est enim potestas nisi a Deo; quae autem sunt *a Deo* ordinatae sunt).* Whereas the Vulgate's punctuation conveyed the message that every power on earth was ordained by God, the *Actes* clearly cajoled the verse into saying that only "well-ordered" powers had God's blessing. Who, in the latter case, was to decide whether a given polity was "well-ordered" or not? The bishops? The Pope? And if not "well-ordered," was obedience suspended?[27] The fact that Boniface VIII had punctuated the verse

[24] *Requête d'un grand nombre de fidèles adressée à Monseigneur l'archévêque de Reims, président de l'assemblée générale du clergé, qui se tient actuellement à Paris, pour être par lui communiquée à tous les prélats de ladite assemblée, au sujet des Acts qu'elle a fait imprimer* (n.p., 1765), pp. 94–95.

[25] *Les Anathèmes, ou Lettre à monseigneur l'évêque d'xxx sur la publication qu'il a faite dans son diocèse des nouveaux Actes du clergé* (n.p., 1766), pp. 6–7.

[26] NNEE, January 2, 1767, p. 2.

[27] *Actes*, p. 15. The French translation in the text reads: "Deux puissances sout établies pour gouverner les hommes: l'autorité sacrée des Pontifes et celle des Rois; l'une et l'autre viennent de Dieu, de qui émane tout pouvoir bien ordonné sur la terre." Nearly all the pamphlets published on the occasion objected to this punctuation, as did the parlement of Paris and its moderate attorney general, Guillaume-François Joly de Fleury. See Flammermont, *Remontrances*, 2:621; and J.-F. Joly de Fleury's manuscript "Réflexions sur les Actes de 1765" in BN, Collection Joly de Fleury, fol. 1479, MS 85.

this eccentric fashion in *Unam Sanctam* (1302), or that the archbishop of Paris, Christophe de Beaumont, had done likewise in a *mandement* published in the wake of Damiens's attempt to assassinate Louis XV in 1757, could scarcely be expected to allay suspicions.[28] These were instead reinforced by the *Actes'* failure to imitate the Assembly of 1682 in explicitly condemning Cardinal Bellarmin's theory of indirect ecclesiastical authority, which allowed for papal intervention in temporal affairs in cases where sin was clearly involved.[29]

To be sure, the *Actes* in principle concurred with the "divine right" theory of the Gallican Declaration of 1682 in teaching that kings were not accountable to any ecclesiastical authority in temporal matters, and that they received their power from God directly. But this high-principled dust thrown into the eyes of the inattentive citizen was not sufficiently dense to prevent the perspicacious editor of the *Nouvelles écclésiastiques* from noting that "even the independence of the Crown is only presented in the *Actes* as the sentiment of the *Clergy of France;* whereas all the pretensions of the Spiritual Power . . . are presented as the teaching of the *Universal Church.*"[30] Other pamphleteers were quick to concur. The Declaration of the Assembly of 1682, explained the canon lawyer G.-N. Maultrot in *The Rights of the Temporal Power Defended,* had proclaimed the independence of the temporal authority "as a truth conformed to the word of God, the tradition of the Fathers, and to the examples of the Saints. In 1765 this doctrine is no more than the teaching of the Clergy of France. The reader is therefore entitled to conclude that it is a national opinion concerning which doubts are legitimate. . . . "[31] And if the *Actes'* pronouncements on the subject of the first Gallican article lacked constancy, the consistency of its commitment to the others was that of the purest sponge rubber. Its

---

[28] *Lettre d'un solitaire sur le mandement de M l'archévêque de Paris, du 1 mars 1757* (n.p., 1757), pp. 9–10.

[29] Jean-François-André Le Blanc de Castillon, *Réquisitoire du 30 octobre 1765* in BPR, Le Paige 562, MS 562, pp. 22–23.

[30] NNEE, March 27, 1766, p. 54.

[31] [Gabriel-Nicolas Maultrot], *Les Droits de la puissance temporelle, défendue contre la seconde partie des Actes de l'assemblée du clergé de 1765 concernant la religion* (Amsterdam, 1777), pp. 7–8. This belated contribution to the controversy was provoked by the reprinting of the *Actes,* along with the *Procès-verbaux* of the general assemblies, by Guillaume Desprez during the 1770s. For stylistic and organizational reasons, this pamphlet is treated as if it had appeared along with the others around 1765. If, as Barbier assures us, the author is the Jansenist canon lawyer Maultrot, it represents no advance over what he with the Abbé Mey and Le Paige were saying in the 1750s and 1760s. So if the pamphlet was not actually written in 1765, it clearly should have been. A few paragraphs from this work are reproduced in Taveneaux, *Jansénisme et politique,* pp. 190–95.

description of the bull *Unigenitus* as an "irreformable judgment," its
publication of Pope Benedict's encyclical letter of 1756 without
protestation against this document's presumption of papal infallibility—all this and more, complained Le Blanc de Castillon of
the parlement of Aix, breathed an "ultramontanist spirit" in blatant
disharmony with the conciliarist tradition of the Gallican Church.[32]
Taken together, concluded the *Nouvelles écclésiastiques*, these traits
entitled one "to regard the *Actes* of the Assembly of 1765 as a
revocation of the Declaration of 1682."[33]

Yet the polemicizing so far gives only an insufficient notion of the
extent of the chasm dividing the rival conceptions of the Church and
its relation to the State. On the episcopal side, a rigidly authoritarian
and hierarchical structure dominated by the episcopacy in cooperation with the pope stood proudly on an equal footing with the State.
On the Gallicano-Jansenist side, a more malleable and egalitarian
structure allowing parish priests and laymen a role of active participation maneuvered exclusively within the confines of the State.

Among these elements it was undoubtedly the latter, the degree to
which Gallicano-Jansenist polemicists were willing to subordinate
even the most "spiritual" of the Church's functions to the supervision of the State, that emerges most strikingly in the controversy.
The authorities they most frequently cited in doing so were treatises
on canon law written around the turn of the last century, especially
those by Van Espen and Pierre de Marca, and the example of the
early Church, especially under the emperors Constantine and
Theodosius, as presented in the ecclesiastical histories of Noel
Alexandre and Claude Fleury. Perhaps the chief principle they
invoked and claimed to have found in these sources was that the
Church was within the "Empire," and not the "Empire" within the
Church, which in turn they took to mean that the State or "prince"
alone possessed coercive power on earth, that the Church's ministry
was in contrast exclusively spiritual, and that such authority as it did
possess could be regulated by the "prince" in the interests of the
temporal welfare of his subjects.[34] Even pagan or heretical princes

[32] Le Blanc de Castillon, *Réquisitoire*, pp. 29–31, 97–98.

[33] NNEE, March 27, 1766, pp. 54–55. The parlement of Paris, in its remonstrances
of August 30–31, 1766, made the same comparison between 1682 and 1765. See
Flammermont, *Remontrances*, 2:599–600.

[34] Pierre de Marca's *De concordia sacerdotii et imperii, seu de libertatibus
ecclesiae gallicanae* was first published in Paris in 1663; a third Paris edition appeared
in 1703. Zeghert Bernhard Van Espen's *Opera canonica in quatuor partes distributa*
first appeared in two volumes in Louvain in 1700; another Louvain edition followed in
1721. A Paris edition in seven volumes of Noel Alexandre's *Historia ecclesiastica
veteris Novique Testamenti, ab orbe condito ad annum post Christum natum mil-*

were entitled to do this by virtue of their God-conferred capacity as
"political magistrate," but since the regular establishment of Christianity after the conversion of the Roman emperors and the Ger-
manic kings, the "Christian Prince" was further authorized by his
role as "outside bishop" and "protector of the canons," enabling
him to enforce and uphold the Church's own laws and
constitutions—even against churchmen themselves, they stressed,
should this become necessary. The very active role of a Constantine, Theodosius, or Charlemagne in decisions of ecclesiastical discipline and even doctrine were the historical examples they had in
mind; they seemed imperfectly aware that the cultural context was
no longer the same.[35]

Yet these principles could not have produced the radical consequences they did except in alliance with the corrosive and closely
related distinctions between externality and spiritual internality, fact
and principle. The latter represents one of the more authentically
Jansenist contributions to the Gallican, Jansenist, and parlementary
mix, and goes back to "the great" Antoine Arnauld's division
between the questions of whether the five famous propositions
supposedly extracted from Jansenius's *Augustinus* were *in fact* to be
found in this treatise, and whether these proportions should *in
principle* be regarded as heretical. Arnauld argued that the papacy
was indeed infallible in matters of principle *(droit)* and hence entitled
to declare the propositions heretical, but that it was quite fallible in
matters of contingent fact *(fait)* and therefore incompetent to say
that Jansenius's treatise contained these propositions.[36] Arnauld
himself was only partially Gallican, as his concessions to papal
infallibility demonstrate, but after the merging of Gallicanism and
Jansenism in the wake of the bull *Unigenitus* his distinction was
extended to ecumenical councils, indeed the Church universal,

---

lesimum sexcentesimum appeared in 1699; the thirty-six volumes of Claude Fleury's
Histoire écclésiastique were published in Paris from 1691 to 1738. The maxim that the
Church was in the State, not the State within the Church, was most specifically taken
from Saint Optatus, the fourth-century bishop of Mileve. See Carolus Ziwsa, ed., *S.
Optati milevitani libri VII* (Prague, 1893), p. 74, line 3: ". . . non respublica in
ecclesia, sed ecclesia in respublica." For some examples of appeals to this principle
in the controversy over the *Actes*, see Le Paige, *Observations*, pp. 38 and 102, where
Optatus of Mileve is specifically mentioned. See also Le Blanc de Castillon, *Réquisitoire*, p. 87.

[35] The best examples of these principles at work are [Maultrot and Mey], *Apologie;*
and Adrien Le Paige, *Lettres adressés à MM. les commissaires nommés par le roi
pour délibérer sur l'affaire présente du parlement au sujet du refus des sacrements ou
Lettres pacifiques au suject des contestations présentes* (n.p., 1752).

[36] Alexander Sedgwick, *Jansenism in Seventeenth-Century France; Voices from the
Wilderness* (Charlottesville, Va., 1977), pp. 107–38. See also Louis Cognet, *Le
Jansénisme*, no. 960, of "Que sais-je?" series (Paris, 1964), pp. 62–75.

which was similarly held to be infallible in matters of doctrine but not of fact. Now all the territory annexed by the realm of *fait* and externality at the expense of the realm of *droit* and internality was territory opened up to the intervention of the "prince" and "reason," which could as competently judge matters of fact as any prelate, pope, or ecumenical council. As it turned out, moreover, there were few if any matters so vaporously spiritual that they could not be condensed into matters of temporal fact and thereby rendered accessible to profane inspection.

Not only were councils quite fallible in matters of fact, according to these pamphleteers, but whether they were ecumenical or not was itself a matter of fact which the "prince" was competent to judge. "Once the universal Church has pronounced, the laity has no choice except that of submission," conceded the self-annointed defender of *The Rights of the Temporal Power*. "But the Prince, the Magistrates, even the simple Faithful," he added, "have the right to examine the exterior character of the judgment which is attributed to the Church in order to see if she has really spoken, if it is not just a small number of Bishops who have usurped her name." They moreover "have the right to examine if the judgment has been reached freely and unanimously," that is, canonically, "and whether it has been formulated clearly, in such a manner as to abate the controversy."[37] And should any of these criteria remain unfulfilled, the prince, as "protector of the canons" was obliged to reject the judgment; or even if it met them all, as did the Council of Trent, the prince as "Political magistrate" had the right to see if under the name of doctrine nothing had "slipped by which is contrary to the rights of the Prince, to the interests of his Crown, to the tranquility of his Realm" and to accept or reject it "according to the utility or the danger of which it is susceptible in his States."[38]

If such were the rights of princes with regard to decisions by ecumenical councils, how much more amply entitled was Louis XV in imposing silence on the subject of the bull *Unigenitus*—that mere product of Jesuitical intrigue—and in declaring that it was not a "rule of faith." By imposing silence, this prince was not, as the *Actes* implied, infringing upon the bishops' sacred right to teach, but merely forbidding them to make reference to the "exterior charac-

---

[37] [Maultrot], *Les Droits de la puissance temporelle*, pp. 26–27.

[38] [Maultrot and Mey], *Apologie*, 1:348; and *Lettre d'un philosophe militaire à monsieur l'archévêque de Rheims, en qualité de président de l'assemblée générale du clergé de France en 1765; sur les affaires du temps, et sur les Actes du clergé* (n.p., n.d.), p. 8.

ter'' in which certain teachings were embodied.[39] In rendering the bull this dubious ''honor . . . , one can in truth no longer speak about it,'' elucidated Le Paige, speaking about it, ''yet one can continue to teach the great and beautiful verities it has reputedly decided.'' In declaring the *Unigenitus* was not a ''rule of faith,'' on the other hand, the king as both political magistrate and protector of the canons had only decided whether it taught ''without ambiguity what should be believed and what should be rejected,'' and whether it was ''more apt to augment the disputes than to terminate them.[40] ''Such an examination,'' assured the *Request by a Great Number of the Faithful,* ''has no article of doctrine as its object, but rather pure and palpable exterior facts of which the eyes are natural judges, and of which princes and magistrates can rightfully take cognizance.''[41]

The same held for the *Actes'* other particular claims to independent ecclesiastical jurisdiction. The sole and infallible right to make moral judgments? ''Who doubts that in certain doctrinal matters the prince cannot go much further'' than what is purely factual and exterior, argued the defender of *The Rights of the Temporal Power,* with an eye toward justifying the parlement's recent condemnation of the Jesuitical *Assertions.* ''There are certain points of doctrine''— namely, moral ones—''which have an intimate connection with the State. Is all cognizance of them to be denied to the Prince, because they fall into the category of a spiritual matter?''[42] The sole right to judge religious vows? One must distinguish—Le Paige again— between *''le droit et le fait.''* If it is a case of a simple vow validly contracted with God, ''it is for the Ecclesiastical Power alone . . . to decide concerning its substance, to commute it, even to dispense someone from it. . . . '' But whether the vow was validly contracted at all was a matter of fact, which the prince could judge ''by the light of reason'' alone.[43] The exclusive jurisdiction, finally, over the Eucharist and extreme unction, the Church's most ''august'' sacraments? One must again distinguish, with Le Paige, between the ''interior dispositions required to approach the sacraments worthily''—altogether spiritual, this, and the business of the confessor—and the ''conditions required to refuse them publicly,'' another matter altogether.[44] In the latter case canon law was the

---

[39] In the authors' words, ''la formule dans laquelle elle est proposée'' or ''la forme sous laquelle il est conçue.'' [Maultrot and Mey], *Apologie,* 1:176.
[40] [Le Paige], *Observations,* p. 40.
[41] *Requête d'un grand nombre de fidèles,* p. 64.
[42] [Maultrot], *Les Droits de la puissance temporelle,* p. 27.
[43] [Le Paige], *Observations,* pp. 71, 79–80.
[44] Ibid., p. 91.

guide, and the prince—read: the parlement—as protector of the canons, could "bend a Bishop to the Laws of the Church when he has violated these overtly." As political magistrate, moreover, to believe the relentless defender of *The Temporal Power*, he had the right "to maintain a citizen in the possession of the exterior advantages assured to all Christians, because the legal possession [*possessoire*] of even spiritual things is a purely profane matter."[45]

Despite these and other audacities, all these pamphleteers stopped short before what they condemned as the heresy of "Anglican supremacy"; all, too, would have anathematized the "civil religion" of Rousseau's *Social Contract*.[46] Self-consciously Catholic, they sincerely believed that by granting the Church jurisdiction over matters "purely spiritual" they were safeguarding what was essential to ecclesiastical authority; the "capital error of the *Actes*," complained Le Blanc de Castillon, was "to have excluded the authority and even the Prince's right of inspection over everything which is not entirely profane, instead of restricting the innate power of the Church to what is purely spiritual," thereby opening the door, in his opinion, to the dreaded ultramontanist theory of indirect power.[47] Yet by restricting the Church to what was ethereally and internally spiritual and in fastening upon the temporal dimension of all that remained, these polemicists ran close to the opposite extreme of temporalizing the spiritual all the better to control it. The bishop of Le Puy, Lefranc de Pompignan, was not altogether sacreligious in calling their "purely interior and invisible belief" a matter of "no consequence"; not wholly unjust in describing their theory of indirect princely power as different from ultramontanism only in the goal it proposed, but not in the means it employed. Neither the "Anglican supremacy" nor Rousseau's civil religion, he thought, had really pushed the subordination of religion to the State "any further."[48] Such, without doubt, was later his sentiment concerning the Civil Constitution of the Clergy, despite his tergiversations in the matter as Louis XVI's minister in 1790.[49]

---

[45] [Maultrot], *Les Droits de la puissance temporelle*, p. 82.

[46] Jean-Jacques Rousseau, *Oeuvres complètes*, ed. Bernard Gagnebin and Marcel Raymond, vol. 3, *Du contrat social* (Paris, 1964), pp. 460–69.

[47] Le Blanc de Castillon, *Réquisitoire*, pp. 57–58.

[48] Lefranc de Pompignan, *Défénse des Actes du clergé de France, publiée en l'assemblée de 1765, par M. l'évêque du Puy* (Louvain, 1769), pp. 285, 290, 304, 390.

[49] On Lefranc de Pompignan's policy with regard to the Civil Constitution, see Pierre de la Gorce, *Histoire religieuse de la Révolution française*, 6 vols. (1912–13; reprint ed., New York, 1969), 1:285–89; and W. Henley Jervis, *The Gallican Church and the Revolution* (London, 1882), pp. 72–78.

III. REASON, CONTRACT, AND THE PURSUIT OF HAPPINESS

Lefranc de Pompignan however seemed less upset by the mass of pamphlets discussed thus far than by a few treatise-like productions which appeared later than the others, and which to his mind displayed an affinity to the principles of the "so-called *esprits forts* of our days," in particular Rousseau.[50] Nor were the worthy bishop's fears in this matter uniquely the figment of a paranoid episcopal imagination. The productions in question indeed differ from the others in their more frequent appeals to "reason," in their employment of the concept of political and social contract, in their easier acceptance of human nature and the pursuit of terrestrial happiness—intellectual traits one associates automatically with the Enlightenment in France. This "enlightened" conceptual apparatus perhaps enabled these pamphleteers to go somewhat further than the others in subordinating religious (or at least ecclesiastical) to purely political and social considerations.

Lefranc de Pompignan directed the bulk of his fire against a two-volume treatise entitled *On the Authority of the Clergy and the Power of the Political Magistrate in the Exercise of the Functions of the Ecclesiastical Ministry*, written by the lawyer François Richer and published in 1766.[51] Like the Rousseau of the *Social Contract*, Richer began with the question of why, given his natural liberty, man had everywhere accepted the restraints of society. Richer found the answer not so much in man's technological prowess as in the long period of helplessness preceding his maturity, rendering stable and authoritarian families indispensable. Large and extended families had therefore been the first sorts of societies. But after these had broken up due to the death of patriarchal chiefs, the "passions and the inherent vices of humanity" had created a state of perpetual war, whence the need to appoint a "conventional chief" in place of the "natural chief," thereby creating society. In the resulting social contract, the chief or "sovereign" agreed to promulgate "the most suitable rules" for the general welfare, in return for which the "nation" promised "the most prompt and blind obedience." The Hobbesian rigor of the contract's terms was nonetheless softened by their apparent compatibility with the sovereign's divine right—he

---

[50] Ibid., p. 207.

[51] [Francois Richer], *De l'autorité du clergé, et du pouvoir du magistrat politique sur l'exercise des fonctions du ministere écclesiastique. Par M xxx, avocat au parlement*, 2 vols. (Amsterdam, 1766). On the authorship, see Préclin, *Les Jansénistes du XVIIIe siècle*, p. 416. On the circulation of this book under Jansenist auspices in Maria Theresa's Austria, see ibid., p. 432.

accounted to God alone—and with his quality as a "representative" and even "mandatory" of the "nation."[52]

This somewhat precarious balance of constitutional authorities was revealed to the author by a combination of "reason," "nature," and the "essence of things," although it was also confirmed by biblical authority. These sources of inspiration again collaborated to produce another principle, that the "conservation and the agreements of terrestrial life" had been the "unique motive" behind the formation of civil societies. . . ." Religion had had no hand in it. For "the cult inspired by enlightened nature and guided by reason" (the only one which the Supreme Being had demanded before revealing "a more particular one") was not dependent upon society for its celebration. "Each man," in Emile-like fashion, had fulfilled all he owed to his Creator "within the most profound solitude and without any sort of communication with his fellows." Classical history here came to his aid by revealing that the "first legislators" had been almost solely occupied with temporal concerns; to the small extent that the "religious cult" had distracted them, it was "only as a subordinate dimension of politics. . . . " They were "almost always observed to accommodate the exterior ceremonies to the civil order they established."[53]

The intended effect of all this was obviously to give priority to the interests of civil society over those of religion, at least so far as temporal arrangements were concerned. Nor had the advent of Christianity much altered this primitive state of affairs. For Christianity had established an altogether different sort of society—the Church—consisting of a "corps of travelers on earth" en route to their "other country" or "the bosom of God himself." In contrast to the State, which employed physical force to rule corporeal bodies, the Church employed the gentler arms of grace and reason to persuade "our souls, or pure spirits" to accept its authority. The Church could proceed in no other fashion because our souls were "essentially free"; it was a "formal heresy" to suppose that even God coerced them.[54] Such spiritual authority as the Church rightfully possessed was moreover the property of the whole Church, or the assembly of all the faithful; the ecclesiastical hierarchy only administered the power of the keys. Though it was true that priests received their ministry directly from Christ, it was "no less true," Richer insisted, that they exercised it "only in the name of the

[52] Ibid., 1:1–27.
[53] Ibid.
[54] Ibid., pp. 27–32, 39–40.

Church" and could undertake nothing "without its presumed consent." The ministers were "only representatives" and could only do "what the represented would do if he were acting upon his own."[55]

Despite the un-Jansenist emphasis upon the freedom of will, much of this seems vaguely familiar. It is as if Richer had imperceptibly strayed from the stark, austere heights of simple contracts and states of nature into a thickening forest of scriptural and early Church precedents below. Before descending any further, however, the ascent of another contract intervened, this one between the Church and the prince become Christian. For when the band of travelers which was the Church had first asked the prince for the "liberty of passage" through his lands, the prince's duty to maintain "good order" had obliged him to undertake a detailed examination of "all the views and intentions of these foreigners," including their doctrine, morals, liturgy, and government. None of this meant, to believe the author, that the prince had actually judged dogma; he had only ascertained that the "good order of the State" was in no way compromised. Now if as a result of this examination the travelers had obtained a safe conduct, they for their part had agreed to abide strictly by the Scriptures and the tradition of the early Church, while the Sovereign for his part had sworn "to maintain them in the free exercise of the dogmas, moral code and discipline" which formed "the basis of the contract" and its essential "clauses."[56]

With the conclusion of this second contract, however, the truth finally emerges. Like the Church he defines, our author has all along been a stranger in a foreign land, that of philosophical states of nature and natural religions. Yet far from impeding his homeward course, the last contract rather plummets him headlong toward the promised land of Gallicano-Jansenist conclusions. For this contract, not as two-sided as it might appear, has already put the "Sovereign" as "political magistrate" in control of everything affecting "good order," therefore everything external about the Church. The prince's promise to protect the Church's doctrine and discipline—read; his rights as "outside bishop" and "protector of the canons"—further entitles him to protect these rules against the ministers themselves. Hence, for example, the prince's obligation to oppose any novel doctrine—the bull *Unigenitus?*—that an ecclesiastical cabal might attempt to foist upon the Church. Hence, too, his obligation to examine all the exterior circumstances of the Church council to

[55] Ibid., pp. 75–77, 107.
[56] Ibid., pp. 125–29.

ascertain its ecumenicity, as well as his right to impose silence on religious disputes, invalidate unjust excommunications, prevent public refusals of sacraments—all this and more, without ever infringing upon the spiritual. But whether holy or not, most of this is familiar ground.[57]

Not so entirely, however. For the treatise's enlightened social contracts and states of nature do not simply serve as neutral containers of Jansenist and Gallican contents. They display, rather, a cocoon-like effect, in some cases making more explicit what was implicit before; in others, metamorphosing the contents altogether. More explicit are the author's transformation of the Catholic priest into moral henchman for the State—"the organ of those charged with announcing the divine word ought always to be at the orders of the government"—as well as his starker statement of Gallicano-Jansenism's criteria for infallibility on the part of Church councils—"only when human passions are silent" and "the necessary liberty to receive the Holy Spirit" obtains.[58] Some examples of metamorphosis are his advocacy of the marriage of priests—the "good order" of the State included the propagation of the human species—and his willingness to legalize divorce, which he justified by distinguishing between the civil contract, or "matter," and the inessential sacrament or its "benediction."[59] Under the same heading falls his attack upon ecclesiastical property as a contradiction in terms. The "improperly called property of the Church," he maintained, belonged not to the Church but to some clerics, and to these in turn not as clerics, but only as a privileged order of citizens. Having desacralized the property, he then subjected it to the "fundamental law" that all property was taxable. The "general will" of the "Sovereign" therefore demanded that the "particular interest" of these citizens cede, and that their property be, if not confiscated for the benefit of the State, at least taxed like "secular" property.[60]

It was this particular distillation of Richer's unique blend of Gallicano-Jansenism and "enlightened" concepts that several anonymously published pamphlets seized upon in their turn. The most spectacular of these, entitled *The Right of the Sovereign over the Property of the Clergy and Monks, and the Usage to Which He Can*

[57] Ibid., pp. 393–96, 414–21; 2:8–9, 38–43, 95–99. For an idea of how far he strays from the Enlightenment, consider the following utterance: " . . . or il suffit en matière de religion, qu'une doctrine soit nouvelle et inconnue aux premiers tems, pour être fausse" (ibid., 1:133).

[58] Ibid., 1:211–14, 238, 247–48, 418. Note the similarity of these criteria to those which Rousseau lays down for an assembly's articulation of the general will.

[59] Ibid., 2:146–59, 190–93.

[60] Ibid., 1:149–94, esp. 151–53, 163–65, 174–75, 189–92.

Put This Property for the Happiness of the Citizens, appeared in 1770.[61] Unlike Richer, this pamphleteer began his pilgrimage in the forest of Gallicano-Jansenist appeals to the authority of the New Testament, especially the gospels and Saint Paul, and to the example of "the first centuries of the Church." Thoroughly within this tradition, too, are his subordination of the clergy to the Church defined as the assembly of all the faithful and his insistence that the Church was purely spiritual and "not of this world"—all this, of course, to the familiar purpose of establishing the State's control over everything external, temporal, and factual.[62] Christ's precept to "sell everything you have, give it to the poor, and come follow me" was a formal condemnation in advance, he thought, of "every kind of [temporal] pretension on the part of members of the Sacerdoce," most especially including the possession of property. Anyway, he argued, since the Church could not by definition possess property, all donations of property to priests "under the borrowed name of God or the Church" were legally invalid because they involved "an error of persons."[63]

Yet one might well enquire why he restricted the application of Christ's precept to the clergy alone. If the Church is the assembly of all the faithful, and if the faithful are the followers of Christ, then should not laymen and clergy alike sell all they have and give to the poor—or at least to the Church which succors the poor? Sensing this difficulty all the more acutely because ecclesiastical property constituted the grail-like object of his unholy quest, he retreated the better to advance. Having all but obscured the distinction between clergy

[61] [Cervol], *Du droit du souverain sur les biens fonds du clergé et des moines, et de l'usage qu'il peut faire de ces biens pour le bonheur des citoyens* (Naples, 1770). This pamphlet, however, is not the only one elicited by this controversy which directly assaulted ecclesiastical property. Another, entitled *Discussion interessante, sur la prétention du clergé d'être le premier order d'un état* (La Haye, 1767) by the marquis de Puységur, according to Barbier, likewise insisted upon the incompatibility between the clergy's possession of landed property and their essential quality as "strangers" in the world divested of "all terrestrial attachments" (pp. 19–20). This definition of the clergy, plus its definition of the Church as the "assemblée des fidèles," constitutes this pamphlet's most recognizable connection to Gallicano-Jansenism. The pamphlet's most interesting feature, however, is perhaps its aristocratic grouping of the "nation's" population into the three "orders" of the "sovereign power" and its officers, the "corps of Patricians" consisting of landowners, and the mass of "pure wage-earners" or "*gagistes*" (pp. 20–24, 31). This last category, in which he included the clergy, were "unattached to the soil," possessed "no interest in the general welfare of the Nation" and were hence "nothing less than true Cosmopolites" (pp. 13–14). As a whole, the pamphlet seems a somewhat aristocratic anticipation of national liberalism. Lefranc de Pompignan took the bother to refer to it, in his *Defense,* as "l'idée bizarre d'un écrivain anonyme et moderne," p. 373.

[62] [Cervol], *Du droit du souverain,* pp. 11–14, 55–56.

[63] Ibid., pp. 38–39, 87.

and laity with the one hand, he then stealthily reintroduced it with the other, for we learn with surprise that "sell all you have" is not a precept after all, but rather a "counsel" applicable to the Church's "Holy Ministers" alone.[64] Yet his left hand knew very well what his right hand was up to—Christ's injunction to the contrary was undoubtedly just another counsel—for he was also aware that his task was now to justify the acquisition of property in particular and the pursuit of physical well-being in general.

His strategic retreat completed, he now jumps—indeed fairly catapults himself—onto the high ground of Enlightenment rhetoric. Like Rousseau's, his remaining "letters" are written from the mountain; the air grows abruptly chilly with appeals to "reason" and its "imprescriptible rights." Jolted, first of all, with the most un-Jansenist comment that it is not really necessary for a Christian to relate all his actions to God, that some actions are "indifferent in themselves," we are next astonished to hear that *"le bonheur physique"* is a gift of heaven, "that happiness and unhappiness are the results of our conduct," and that "the springs, producers of one as well as the other of these two states, are purely physical." Nor is that all. The proposition that society's "inspection extends even to the precepts of Religion, not to contradict them, but in order to turn then to the profit of the State" may sound familiar enough, but not so the lengths to which it is taken. For not only is the Church's "exterior cult" purely "ceremonial and commemorative," but the State could eliminate it altogether and "restrict the Christian's cult to an interior act and the recitation of Dominical prayer, without forcing him to violate his religious obligations."[65] Now if the State may do all that, can the Church legitimately resist the "Supreme Legislator" should he cast covetous eyes upon ecclesiastical property, especially when "armed with the equitable and transcendent motive of the public good . . . ?"[66]

The answer is clearly no. The author then proceeded to imagine precisely the situation in which the monarchy and the National Assembly successively found themselves in 1789. The State owed 3 billion livres, and the payment of the interest on this debt, which consumed nearly half of the annual revenues, did not leave enough to meet the State's ordinary expenses. Taxes could not be augmented because of the *"cherté* of nearly all sorts of goods. . . . " What was then to be done? After considering and dismissing sundry

[64] Ibid., pp. 13–14.
[65] Ibid., pp. 89–97.
[66] Ibid., p. 120.

alternatives, such as bankruptcy, economy measures, and additional loans, he opted for the "surgical, decisive," and "simple" solution also adopted in 1789, namely, the confiscation of all ecclesiastical property and its sale to private citizens, together with the transformation of ecclesiastics into paid "pensionaries of the State."[67] Nowhere, not even in the literature immediately preceding the Revolution, was the revolutionary solution to the State's financial problems more clearly anticipated than here.[68]

IV.   TOWARD THRONE AND ALTAR

Quantitatively, at least, the episcopal cause mustered no more than a Noah's ark–like response to the deluge of writings submerging its *Actes:* the anonymous *Respective Rights of the State and the Church Reminded of Their Principles* (1766), the bishop of Grenoble's uninteresting *Dissertation* (1767), and the bishop of Le Puy's monumental *Defense of the Acts of the Clergy of France concerning Religion* (1769).[69] Taken together, however, these responses are not without some interesting features, one of which is a marked preference for explicitly engaging the more "enlightened" of their opponents. In doing so, moreover, they proved themselves as adept at

---

[67] Ibid., p. 138 and in general, pp. 121–146.

[68] Some indication of the relationship between the likes of Richer and Cervol on the one hand, and indisputably Jansenist pamphleteers such as Le Paige on the other, is furnished by the latter's reaction to the *Discours de rentrée* which Le Blanc de Castillon delivered before the parlement of Aix on October 1, 1765. Very much like Richer's treatise, this discourse began with a flurry of "enlightened" appeals to reason and natural law and condemnations of prejudice and religious superstition. Most notably, it attributed the formation of civil society to natural law alone understood as enlightened self-interest. These "enlightened" remarks, however, served only as an introduction to a much lengthier and thoroughly Gallicano-Jansenist diatribe against ultramontanism in particular, ecclesiastical "despotism" and "independence" in general. When local "devout" reaction plunged Castillon into the predictable bath of hot water, he turned for advice, not to Jean d'Alembert (with whom he was apparently on cordial terms), but to Le Paige himself. Le Paige in turn objected, not to the unique agency attributed to natural law in the formation of civil society or to anything in the body of the discourse generally (all of which he found "very accurate, very well stated"), but to the few places in the introduction which hinted at skepticism concerning the authenticity of divine revelation and the miraculous. See BPR, Le Paige 588, Le Blanc de Castillon's manuscript *discours,* MS 13, esp. pp. 1–9; and Le Paige to Castillon, January 17, 1766, MS 15. Castillon's letter to Le Paige of October 14, 1768 (MS 26) indicates that the abbés Mey and Gourlin, good Jansenists both, functioned as his theological and canonical advisers. On Castillon's relations to d'Alembert, see Ronald Grimsley, *Jean d'Alembert, 1717–1783* (Oxford, 1963), p. 215.

[69] *Les Droits respectifs de l'état et l'église rappellés à leurs principes* (Avignon, 1766), and [Jean de Caulet, bishop of Grenoble], *Dissertation à l'occasion des Actes de l'assemblée générale du clergé de France de 1765 sur la religion* (n.p., 1767).

manipulating "enlightened" vocabulary and concepts in defense of their own cause as some of their enemies had been in attacking it.

Take, for example, the anonymous reminder of *The Respective Rights,* apparently an aristocratic defender of the first order rather than a member of it himself. His system, like that of the episcopacy's more "enlightened" opponents, made "civil" or "social" laws both chronologically and anthropologically prior to "religious" and "ecclesiastical" laws because of the more imperious character of physical needs. Further, these civil laws originated in "first conventions" based on natural law, more readily perceived, he thought, by "the vivacity of sentiments" than by some "method of reasoning." The resultant State, at first enlightened by means of natural religion alone, had accepted Christianity and the Church only subsequently, and on condition—a second contract, this—that its "ecclesiastical laws" did not run counter to its own. The State therefore reserved the right to inspect, approve, or reject ecclesiastical legislation, since it exercised an influence over "exterior morals" which in turn formed part of the State's *"haute police."* The Church, although not expressly the ecumenical council, the author defined as the assembly of all the faithful, and he insisted that the clergy's functions had been "originally entirely spiritual."[70]

So far the author seemed headed down the path carved out by François Richer in *On the Authority of the Clergy and the Power of the Civil Magistrate,* which was published the same year. But at precisely this juncture his path diverged sharply. This was perhaps due in part to his accent on "sentiment" as opposed to reason, but mainly to his Montesquieuian, empirical, yet unimpeachably "enlightened" emphasis on the "strange circumstantial vicissitudes" and "conjunctural whimsicalities" encountered by different peoples. The main effect of these, in his view, had been to refract the application of natural law into the bewildering variety of particular laws we observe. Though natural law had inspired the formation of all constitutions, each "legislator" had had to adjust it according to the nation's physical and climactic circumstances, "factitious inclinations," and even errors, but infallibly with a view toward the "best possible condition." Even the most apparently bizarre laws were therefore "nonetheless respectable" because the "idea of the best possible" had dictated their formation; to understand them a detailed empirical examination of the circumstances which produced them was necessary. And the science of politics was therefore not

[70] *Les Droits respectifs,* pp. 19, 28–30, 36–37, 57–59, 71–72.

reducible to a "system of geometrical order," but was rather a "calculus of proximities and simple approximations."[71]

The author's more empirical cast of mind thus led him to a proto-Burkean veneration for the delicately complex and infinitely variegated texture of all positive law, seen as the embodiment of the wisdom of the past. Consistent with himself, he did not exclude the clergy's privileged constitutional position from his all-embracing ken. The existence of a separate and even coercive ecclesiastical juris-diction, the clergy's "titles of honor" and "exterior prerogatives," the Church's extensive property holdings—all these represented "universal reason's" infallible application of "natural law" to achieve the "best possible," which included the respect due to the ministers of a religion serving as spiritual foundation to the State. For "if in order to assure the repose of society, it was necessary to fortify the observation of human laws by means of a principle of religion and a motive of conscience," was it not "equally advan-tageous," he rhetorically asked, "to imprint on the people's soul a particular sentiment of respect for the censors of their conscience and the ministers of their religion . . . ?"[72]

Whereas the anonymous author of *The Respective Rights* thus anticipated counter-Revolutionary conservatism's veneration for traditional law and historic wisdom, Lefranc de Pompignan, in his monumental *Defense,* pointed no less clearly toward its theocratic and ultramonarchical tendencies. Yet he too, by pitting himself specifically against Richer's *On the Authority of the Clergy,* chose to do battle on unmistakably "enlightened" terrain. Though complain-ing throughout his treatise about "the false and modern philosophy" of "our day" and its addiction to states of nature and reciprocal contracts, he nonetheless accepted these concepts for practical pur-poses, and contrived to maneuver within their constraints.[73]

This maneuvering is not unimpressive, in a purely forensic way. Tactically postulating society's emergence from a state of nature, the future bishop of Vienne first argued the "enlightened" utility of religion

---

[71] Ibid., pp. 19 24.

[72] Ibid., pp. 64–66, 71–73, 102–104. I fully accept the corollary that Edmund Burke himself is to be regarded as a legitimate child of Enlightenment thought. On this, see Frederick Drayer, "The Genesis of Burke's *Reflections,*" *Journal of Modern History* 50 (September 1978): 462–79.

[73] "On aime," he complained, "dans ce siècle ces prétendus contrat, dont la date remonte à l'origine des choses, dont les stipulations soient réciproques, dont les obligations et les effets soient imprescriptibles, malgré la plus longue possession. Ces chimères éblouissent des esprits superficiels que se flattent de penser profondément, quoiqu'ils pensent peu et n'approfondissent rien" (Lefranc de Pompignan, *Défense des Actes du clergé de France,* p. 346).

by contesting the principle that mundane considerations alone could have effected such a transition. It was to "outrage providence," he protested, "to suppose that civil societies were formed without her, or that her principal purpose in presiding over their formation was not to unite men so that they could render the sovereign arbiter of their destinies the common duties required of them." Although he conceded that terrestrial considerations might have been the occasion for the formation of civil societies, the deeper cause, he clearly implied, was religious. From Adam through Noah, the "first men" had indeed been recipients of a "particular revelation" which, however distorted with the passage of time in all but God's chosen race, made the father of every family at once a sacrificer and priest, rights inherited by the eldest son. Just as each family, then, had been basically a "religious association," so also the body politic, after men's "unchained passions" had led them to unite in civil society. Religion therefore entered into the very "constitution of every body politic, and it would have been impossible to associate men under a civil government if Religion, anterior to these human establishments, had not been the foundation and the tie." The redoubtable bishop thought it "easy to prove that, far from accommodating the exterior ceremonies of the religious cult to the civil order they established," the first legislators had more often "accommodated their political laws to the religious ideas established before them."[74]

Having sufficiently loosened Richer's social contract to incorporate religion at its core, the bishop of Le Puy proceeded to bind by his anathemas a principle he viewed as basic to the opposition's case, namely, that "by natural law and imprescriptible right" every society possessed the "power of government" and only delegated the usage to its chiefs. In ecclesiastical form, this principle gave the possession of the "keys" to the assembly of all the faithful, leaving the clergy with only their use; in political form, it located sovereignty within the nation which delegated its exercise by means of a contract. Now it goes without saying that the bishop vigorously combated the ecclesiastical manifestation of this principle, that he insisted that the episcopal hierarchy alone possessed the power of the keys and together with the pope formed a "very singular type" of "monarchy essentially tempered by an aristocracy." But in choosing Richer's book as his chief foil, de Pompignan cleverly linked lay conciliarism to national sovereignty and then concentrated his fire on the latter. It was a bit unfair, of course, for the bishop to insinuate thereby that the political form of this principle was

[74] Ibid., pp. 132–34.

explicitly attributable to *all* opponents of the *Actes,* or even that it was unambiguously held by Richer himself. But he was shrewd enough to see that it represented the profound current of their thought, and to aim his depth charges at the least avowable of their half-conscious assumptions.[75]

Accepting, again, the notion of a passage from a state of nature to one of civil government accompanied by a contract, de Pompignan contested the principle that it was sovereignty itself—the power of life and death over other humans—which the community had ever delegated to any government by virtue of natural law. Proceeding from the Rousseauean principle of men's "natural equality" in the "primitive state," the bishop cogently argued that nature gave to no man or group of men the right to human life. Sheer numbers or express conventions did not legitimize a power which no man rightfully possessed over either his own life or anyone else's, even if exercised in the act of self defense. Rendered powerless by this very equality to mitigate the fall's disorderly effects, men had received from the hand of their creator the gift of sovereignty necessary to create governments. "It is He who has come to their aid. His absolute power has enabled their impotence." With a stridency and accent which look forward to the early Lamennais or De Maistre, the bishop of Le Puy concluded that the "Supreme Arbiter of their life" was "also the unique and necessary principle of all sovereign authority."[76]

That religion was fundamental to the formation of civil societies, that God alone was the source of political sovereignty—neither of these principles led necessarily in a monarchical direction. The bishop acknowledged as much, and allowed that "all the nations of the earth [had] originally possessed the liberty to choose the form of government which suited them best." To the nations which had opted for monarchy he further allowed the choice of their first monarch, as well as between elective and hereditary monarchy. But could a nation so constituted subsequently rescind its original choice? Or could it ever dethrone a particular monarch by virtue of the nonfulfillment of some reciprocal contract? De Pompignan could hardly deny that some monarchical nations possessed such contracts, but he emphatically denied that these derived from natural

---

[75] Ibid., pp. 206–07, 233.

[76] Ibid., pp. 207–10. The corollary is again intended and accepted that Lamennais and De Maistre are just as legitimately the Enlightenment's progeny as, say, Benjamin Constant or Madame de Staël. For the connections between Maistre's thought and the Enlightenment, see Jack Lively's excellent introduction to his translation and edition of *The Works of Joseph de Maistre* (New York and London, 1965), pp. 1–45.

law. He further failed to see how they could derive from the original liberty by which God had allowed men to choose their governments if this same liberty, "a gift of God's providence," could become the "germ of inexhaustible discords and intestine factions, of revolutions and castastrophes." Obviously, the bishop wanted to say no; the whole discussion put him out of sorts. What he clearly wished to affirm, on the contrary, was that the founders of hereditary monarchies could have very well tied the hands of their descendants and that, for the governance of their kingdoms, monarchs answered "to God alone."[77]

In thus defending "divine right" monarchy against the threat of national sovereignty, the bishop was opposing the parlementary constitutionalism of the great majority of his opponents as much as the *"école de nos prétendus esprits forts,"* Le Paige as much as Rousseau. That this was the case he made clear by an off-handed and less than reverent reference to the "fundamental laws" of the Realm, a key phrase in the parlementary constitutional rhetoric of the time.[78] Not, of course, that in 1765 either the parlement of Paris or the Gallicano-Jansenist press was publicly espousing a theory of national sovereignty or reciprocal political contract. But de Pompignan was not ignorant of the fact that the parlement, in its remonstrances, was then styling itself as "born with the monarchy" and the temple of its fundamental laws; or defining its duty as the defense of the "national constitution" against the "absolute power" of misguided monarchs, for which it was accountable to the "nation."[79] In view of this rhetoric, it was a calculated provocation on the bishop's part to define the French monarch as "absolute" and to add that his magistrates were "his first subjects, and nothing more" who "received his orders and gave none except in his name."[80]

Evidence suggests that the bishop of Le Puy spoke for a growing body of episcopal thinking on this score which, in predictable reaction to the constitutionalism of their Gallican and Jansenist foes, was redefining its conception of the monarchy in ever more absolutistic, anticonstitutional, or "despotic" terms.[81] But if so, had

---

[77] Ibid., pp. 213–19.

[78] Ibid., p. 217.

[79] For some random examples, see Flammermont, *Remontrances,* 2:523–24, 534, 543, 546, 549.

[80] Lefranc de Pompignan, *Défense,* pp. 232–33.

[81] The evidence is not as satisfactory as it might be, partly because bishops had too few occasions to pronounce themselves on this subject. Nonetheless the evidence in Van Kley, *The Jansenists,* pp. 150–58, is applicable if the French Jesuits' thinking about the monarchy and its "constitution" can be taken as representative of at least zealously "constitutionary" (e.g., pro-*Unigenitus*) and ultramontanist bishops such as

Lefranc de Pompignan and the episcopal thinking he represented progressed no further than Bossuet and the assembly of 1682? Were they still, albeit with naturalistic argumentation, defending the marriage of ecclesiastical conciliarism and royal absolutism which this celebrated assembly had solemnized? Hardly. Recall the *Actes'* dubious punctuation and translation of Romans 13:1; its spirited defense of the spiritual power as "sovereign, independent and absolute;" its insistence that kings themselves should obey priests; its ominous admonition, finally, that priests were to obey "God rather than men."[82] For if the episcopacy was extending the monarchy's power over the laity with the one hand, it was tending severely to curtail it in relation to the Church with the other. Unlike the assembly of 1682, after all, which had defended the temporal power against the Church, the assembly of 1765 rather defended the Church against the temporal power.

Now the demands of this new task, added to those of defending episcopal prerogatives against Jansenist laicism, put unaccustomed strains on the Gallican clergy, segments of which developed the symptoms of an identity crisis. Among these symptoms was a guarded disavowal of the whole Gallican Declaration of 1682—thus confirming episcopal enemies' darkest suspicions. In response, for example, to the accusation that the general assembly had avoided the expressions consecrated by the celebrated assembly of 1682, the bishop of Le Puy confessed to the opinion that "whatever the respect" which subsequent assemblies of the clergy had paid to the

---

Christophe de Beaumont of Paris, Orléans de la Motte of Amiens, Montmorency de Laval of Condom (formerly Orléans), Caritat de Condorcet of Auxerre, or Rosset de Ceiles of Tours. This is almost certainly the case in view of the general assembly's spirited defense of the absolute power of the Jesuits' general within that order as "le chef d'oeuvre de la sagesse du fondateur de cet institut" (Archives Nationales: K 1361, dr. 1^A, "procès verbal de l'assemblée extraordinaire des évêques en 1761," pp. 18–19). For in the context of that debate, to defend the absolute power of the general within the Jesuit Order was tantamount to defending the absolute power of the king within his realm. All the same, it is not my intention to associate too closely the development of ideological or "integral" absolutism and the episcopacy *as an order*, particularly in view of the eleventh-hour rapprochement between the parlements and the clergy and the growing capacity of the latter to sound like Montesquieu in proportion as the threat to its immunities came from the monarchy itself. On this, see Michel Peronnet, "Les assemblées du clergé de France sous le règne de Louis XVI, 1775–1788," *Annales historiques de la Révolution française* 34 (1962): 8–35; and Jean Egret, "La Derniere Assemblée du clergé de France," *Revue historique* 219 (1958): 1–15. It is reassuring to note, however, that even in 1788 Lefranc de Pompignan, then bishop of Vienne, was demanding absolute obedience to the crown—even at the cost of 8 million lives in *don gratuit*.

[82] *Actes*, p. 43. Norman Ravitch first called attention to Lefranc de Pompignan's "hedging" in this matter in *Sword and Mitre: Government and Episcopate in France and England in the Age of Aristocracy* (The Hague, 1966), p. 23.

one held in 1682, they had "never considered its authority as equal to that of the Universal Church or an Ecumenical Council." They had learned from this assembly itself "not to regard its Declaration as a symbol of faith."[83] A compromising admission, this, nonetheless outdone by Henri-Jacques de Montesquiou, bishop of Sarlat, who a few years earlier had informed his diocesan clergy in a *Pastoral Instruction* that God's word was "not the foundation of our [Gallican] liberties; for the word being unchangeable and uniform, all the Churches which do not possess such liberties would then be governed against the word of God."[84] At about the same time, the bishop of Langres, Montmorin de Saint-Herem, gave it out as his opinion that the Declaration of 1682 was more than just an opinion. But in the same breath he told his diocesan clergy that the "particular certitude" attributable to the article concerning the independence of the temporal power was "much superior to that of the other articles," leaving his clergy to wonder what precisely he thought of these.[85]

Not enough, in any event, to suit the Gallicano-Jansenist press, which snarled its condemnation in the pages of the *Nouvelles écclésiastiques*, going so far as to accuse Montmorin of "treason."[86] For within the nationalized Catholicism of the *parti janséniste*, the four Gallican articles of 1682 had become, in the words of the bishop of Soissons, "holy truths which belong to revelation, which form part of the sacred *dépôt* which Jesus Christ confided to his Disciples, which has come down to us by the tradition of all the centuries. . . ."[87] If the universal Church in an ecumenical council had not enshrined these truths in a "formula of faith," it was only because for too many Catholics, especially Spanish and Italian ones, the eighteenth century remained a time of "obscurity" and "combat"—in short, they gnashed their teeth in outer darkness.[88]

As a concurrent controversy swirling around Fitz-James of Sois-

---

[83] Lefranc de Pompignan, *Défense*, p. 472.

[84] Henri-Jacques de Montesquieu, *Instruction pastorale de monseigneur l'évêque de Sarlat au clergé séculier et régulier et à tous les fidèles de son diocèse. 28 nov 1764* (n.p. n.d.), pp. 11, 16.

[85] Montmorin de Saint-Herem, *Lettre pastorale de Mgr. l'évêque de Langres au clergé de son diocèse. 1 aout 1763* (n.p. n.d.), p. 9.

[86] NNEE, January 23, 1764, p. 14. For the review of the bishop of Sarlat's pastoral instruction, see ibid., September 11, 1765, pp. 149–51.

[87] François de Fitz-James, *Oeuvres posthumes de monseigneur le duc de Fitz-James évesque de Soissons. . . ,* vol. 1, *Ordonnance et instruction pastorale de monseigneur l'évêque de Soissons, au sujet des assertions extraites par le parlement des livres, thèses, cahiers composés, publiés et dictés par les jésuites* (Avignon, 1769), pp. 289–90.

[88] Ibid., vol. 2, *Projet de réponse de m. l'évêque de Saint Pons*, pp. 374–75.

sons's 1763 pastoral instruction made clear, not many of his episcopal peers shared this renegade Jansenist bishop's high view of the
Gallican articles of 1682. At least the four bishops on the commission appointed by Louis XV to examine his instruction seemed more
inclined to agree with Montmorin and Montesquiou that the Declaration represented a venerable but debatable "opinion" or "sentiment" which, however compatible with revelation, did not really
belong to the realm of faith or dogma.[89] And it is not easy to see
how they could have felt much differently in 1765. For to say that
the Declaration enunciated articles of faith had become tantamount
to endorsing nearly everything which Gallicano-Jansenism had construed it to mean: that is, the nearly total subordination of Church to
State under the hammer of the Declaration's first article; the democratization and laicization of the Church itself under the cover of the
remaining three. In the face of the former, the bishops felt bound to
resist what Lefranc de Pompignan called the "shameful slavery" of
the "ecclesiastical ministry to the secular Power."[90] Concerning the
latter, the bishop of Le Puy again probably spoke for most of his
peers when he said that given the choice between being "vicars of
the Pope," on the one side, and "mandatories of the people"
accountable to "laymen" and even "women," on the other, he
would choose the former. For all practical purposes, at least, the
"ultramontanist theologians" maintained the Church as a "mixture
of aristocracy with monarchy" instead of reducing it to the
"tumults" and "discords" of "popular Tribunals."[91] The bishop of
Le Puy could protest all he wished his loyalty to the classically
Gallican "*juste milieu* between these two extremities," but in spirit,
at least—and decades before the French Revolution hurled them into
the arms of the papacy—he and his peers were ultramontane.

Ultramontanism and absolutism or the Civil Constitution of the
Clergy—that was how matters stood by 1765. Whatever the original
intentions of the celebrated assembly of 1682, they were irrelevant
now; whatever bridge classical Gallicanism yet maintained across

[89] Ibid., *Mémoire au sujet de l'instruction pastorale*, pp. 197–200, 212–13, 224–25.
The royal *commissaires* were Roche-Aimon, Montazet, Dillon and Jarente, archbishops of Narbonne, Lyon, and Toulouse, and bishop of Orléans, respectively.
Ibid., vol. 1, *Vie*, pp. lxix–lxx. The general assembly's inclination to convene a
provincial council to examine the bishop of Anger's 1763 pastoral instruction, which
had similarly expressed a high view of the Declaration of 1682, perhaps also indicates
something of the majority of bishops' thinking on this subject. See *Procès-verbal*,
September 27, 1765, pp. 440–41; and Jacques de Grasse, *Ordonnance et instruction
pastorale de monseigneur l'évêque d'Angers, portant condamnation de la doctrine
contenue dans les Extraits des assertions* (n.p., n.d.), pp. 14, 16–17.
[90] Lefranc de Pompignan, *Défense*, p. 348.
[91] Ibid., pp. 203, 205.

the widening chasm was rapidly collapsing. Symptomatically, the royal council's judgment of May 24, 1765, which attempted to articulate and reinforce this bridge, was beset by both sides, as increasingly these sides had beset most everything the king had done affecting their relations since 1750.[92] The Gallican Declaration of 1682, that great legislative tapestry from the age of Louis XIV weaving conciliar Church and divine right monarchy together, was now in shreds.

New patterns and combinations were therefore in order, and they were not long in coming. For the emerging clerical party in France, it remained ahistorically to unite its new ultramontanism to its solicitude for the monarchy against the perceived threat to both. Lefranc de Pompignan implicitly did this by identifying the same subversive principle of national sovereignty undermining both Church and State, maintaining that if it were really true, as critics of the *Actes* tended to say, that the bishops "in their chairs" were only "mandatories" and "representatives" of the people, then "the most absolute monarchs should be and are as much on their thrones."[93] But others were more explicit. *The Impartial Reflexions of a Papist and Royalist Frenchman*, the title of a pro-Jesuit pamphlet published in 1764 as part of the controversy over the suppression of that order, by itself speaks volumes, as does a *Letter from a Cosmopolite*, published the same year, which announced the formation and growth of a conspiracy against throne and altar.[94] Yet another clerical pamphleteer challenged Gallicano-Jansenism's hitherto quasi monopoly of what one Jesuit had already dubbed "the jargon of patriotism," and in his "double title" of "Catholic" and "Frenchman," raised a "cry of indignation" in reaction to Le Blanc de Castillon's *Réquisitoire*, especially its disrespectful attitude toward the papacy.[95] Well before it described a political reality of the counter-Revolution or became a watchword of the Bourbon and Catholic Restoration, Bourbon "throne" and papal "altar" began

[92] For the text of the royal council's *arrêt* of May 24, 1765, as well as a good indication of both parties' response to it, see NNEE, December 9 and 16, 1767, pp. 197–204.

[93] Lefranc de Pompignan, *Défense*, p. 223.

[94] *Réflexions impartiales d'un françois papiste et roialiste sur le réquisitoire de maitre Omer Joly de Fleury et l'arrêt du parlement de Paris du 1 juin 1764 qui suprime les brefs de n.s.p. le pape Clement XIII au roi de Pologne, duc de Lorraine et de Bar et à m. l'archévêque de Paris* (à Alais, chés Narcisse Buisson imprimeur à l'enseigne du probabalisme, ce 12 juin 1764). For the *Lettre d'un cosmopolite*, see *NNEE* (August 28, 1765), p. 142.

[95] *Cri d'un françois catholique après la lecture du Réquisitoire de m. Le Blanc de Castillon sur les Actes du clergé* (Soleure, 1766), p. 12. The Jesuit is Joseph-Antoine-J. Cerutti, *Apologie de l'institut des jésuites* 2 vols. (n.p., 1763), 1:10.

huddling together—if not in fact, at least in the minds of the emerging clerical party in France.

V.   CONCLUSION

The controversy over the general assembly of the Gallican clergy in 1765 was really the last in a series of mixed religious, ecclesiastical, and political disputes which had dominated the eighteenth-century French domestic scene until then. The coming of the bull *Unigenitus* in 1713, the "miracles" of Saint-Médard in the early 1730s, the refusal of sacraments to Jansenists in the 1750s, the expulsion of the Jesuits in the 1760s—these were the major landmarks on a polemical road which gradually bifurcated toward both Revolution and counter-Revolution. By 1765 these directions were well established and clear enough. Not only had the Jansenist, Gallican, and parlementary syndrome conceived of the Civil Constitution of the Clergy and contemplated the confiscation of ecclesiastical property, but is it wholly fanciful to recognize the lineaments of future "liberalism" in its constitutionalism, protonationalism, and the thoroughgoing laicism of its ecclesiastical conceptions? And does it, again, stretch the imagination unduly to discern the basic contours of counter-Revolution—indeed, of early nineteenth-century "conservatism" generally—within the episcopal defenders' veneration for the past, theocratic social conceptions, and synthesis of anticonstitutional royalism and ultramontanism? Most conspicuously missing, at this stage, is aristocracy as such as a bone of contention.[96] But the anti-aristocratic egalitarianism which played so important a role in the revolutionary mentality of the 1790s was a latecomer to the eighteenth-century scene; it was nowhere to be found in concentrated form during its middle decades.

If there is anything to this, then the marquis d'Argenson was not far wrong—in fact, much righter than he knew—when he observed of these midcentury ecclesiastical and religious controversies that they no longer so much pitted Jansenists against Molinists as "na-

[96] The lines of division over aristocracy and privilege as such, when these became important towards the end of the century, tended to cut across and therefore confuse the issues outlined in this paper. It is this which in no small measure accounts for the gradual rapprochement between episcopacy and parlement after 1774. For examples of how at mid-century *both* parties to the controversy described in this paper could be "aristocratic," see n. 62 and the discussion of *Les Droits respectifs* in Section IV, above. For an example in a neighboring Catholic country of how controversy between "ultramontanists" and "Jansenists" lay at the origins of modern conservatism and liberalism, see Richard Herr, *The Eighteenth-Century Revolution in Spain* (Princeton, N.J., 1958). To a greater extent than in France, the Enlightenment was not very divisive; it was shared by both parties to the Jansenist-ultramontanist controversy.

tionals" (*nationaux*) against "sacerdotals" (*sacerdotaux*).[97] It also follows that, at least prior to the Maupeou "revolution" of the 1770s, these mixed religious, ecclesiastical, and political controversies were central, not peripheral, to the unraveling of the Old Regime and the coming of the French Revolution. For they appear to have engendered the ideological and political divisions which later burst forth with greater clarity during the Revolution itself, which was hence as much a product of these divisions as it was a progenitor of them in its turn.

If the 1765 meeting of the general assembly touched off the last major *Unigenitus*-related controversy in France, it also occasioned the Gallican clergy's first explicit condemnation of Enlightenment works. This contrast raises the difficult question of the relationship between the Enlightenment and the emerging ideological and political divisions in France, which seem to have arisen quite independently of the celebrated "movement of lights." The question becomes the more difficult in proportion as one associates "Enlightenment" with "unbelief" because, as the study of this particular affair has indicated, these mixed religious, ecclesiastical, and political controversies tended to divide Catholic from Catholic much more than Catholic from unbeliever. Lefranc de Pompignan undoubtedly had doubts about the Catholicity of some of his opponents whom he called "enemies of the clergy," but he still distinguished between these and "unbelievers," and professed to respect the sincerity of the former who, he acknowledged, "call themselves Christians."[98] Not a single participant in this controversy fully qualifies as a member of Peter Gay's "little flock" of the truly enlightened, whose distinguished bleating constitutes in fact no more than the most distant echo in any of these disputes.[99] In the debate over the general assembly of 1765 there is moreover across-the-board agreement among all participants that Catholicism should

[97] René-Louis d'Argenson, *Journal et mémoires*, ed. E.-J.-B. Rathery, 9 vols. (Paris, 1859–67), 8:313.

[98] Lefranc de Pompignan, *Défense*, pp. 132, 399.

[99] Perhaps "enlightened" is not the right adjective to describe the "little flock," because Peter Gay distinguishes between "philosophes" and "other enlightened men of their age" who were presumably not part of the "little flock." The *philosophes*, unlike this broader category of the more or less enlightened, "used their classical learning to free themselves from their Christian heritage, and then, having done with the ancients, turned their face toward a modern world view. The Enlightenment was a volatile mixture of classicism, impiety, and science; the philosophes, in a phrase, were modern pagans" (Peter Gay, *The Enlightenment: An Interpretation*, vol. 1, *The Rise of Modern Paganism* [New York, 1967] p. 8, and, in general, "The Little Flock of Philosophes," pp. 3–20).

function as the moral and spiritual foundation of the State.[100] This much seems to suggest that even the very immediate origins of the ideological divisions of the Revolution and nineteenth-century France lie primarily in the century-long disputes between Catholic and Catholic, at best secondarily in the more loudly sung conflict between Catholic and unbeliever.

The privileged place which historians have traditionally accorded the Enlightenment *understood as unbelief* among the ideological origins of the French Revolution is surely in part the result of viewing the eighteenth century through the distorting lens of the Revolution itself, which in its frenzied pursuit of the refractory priest-*cum*-aristocrat had recourse to the most virulent form of anticlericalism available. But partly, too, it is a result of naively taking at face value a forensic device frequently employed by Old Regime defenders of the ecclesiastical establishment, that of concentrating all their polemical energies in corralling the most conspicuously "enlightened" of their opponents the better to brand them all with the stigma of unbelief. That is what Lefranc de Pompignan was really up to, of course, in choosing Richer's *On the Authority of the Clergy* as his chief foil; in a way, it was also the strategy of the general assembly's *Actes* in juxtaposing its condemnation of "impious works" to its defense of the rights of the "spiritual power." The Jesuits had earlier shown the way by lavishing all their attention, in the debate accompanying their expulsion, on the relatively "enlightened" *Compte rendu* of the attorney general of the parlement of Brittany while feigning ignorance of the hundred or more pamphlets of purely Gallicano-Jansenist inspiration which were delivering them the most damaging blows.[101] But what was perhaps justifiable or at least clever as a forensic device in the eighteenth century seems precarious as a foundation of historical interpretation in the twentieth.

If, however, the Enlightenment is understood more broadly as a set of appeals, whether to reason, nature, or sensate experience, which replaced older ones such as to revelation and traditional precedents, then the problem of its relationship to the emerging ideological and political divisions of France is possibly susceptible of

---

[100] The abbé Bernard Plongeron has convincingly insisted upon the persistence of the idea of "Christendom" among the constitutional clergy during the Revolution in *Théologie et politique au siècle des lumières, 1770–1820* (Geneva, 1973), pp. 149–82, but more specifically in "Permanence d'une idéologie de 'civilisation chrétienne' dans le clergé constitutionnel" in *Studies in Eighteenth-Century Culture,* ed. Roseann Runt (Madison, Wis., 1978), 7:263–87. It is moreover to Plongeron that I owe the phrase "Gallicano-Jansenism."

[101] Van Kley, *The Jansenists,* pp. 137–62.

solution. And what this small study suggests is that "enlightened" concepts and vocabulary were sufficiently elastic to accommodate themselves to either side of the controversy, not just one, with perhaps a slight tendency for the Enlightenment's empirical side to run in a conservative direction, its natural rights inheritance in a revolutionary one. (This much, incidentally, might serve as a word of caution to those who wish to define the Enlightenment in exclusively empirical terms on the one hand, and persist in seeing it as the sole ancestor of modern liberalism on the other.) Can it be said, then, that the mixed religious, ecclesiastical, and political controversies generated the fundamental political and ideological directions of eighteenth-century France; whereas the Enlightenment, a broad cultural movement affecting the thought patterns of all literate groups, provided the conceptual apparatus and vocabulary in which either direction progressively expressed itself?

This is not to say that the choice of concepts and vocabulary was completely neutral or inconsequential. During the controversy in question, the recourse to contracts and states of nature obviously carried the Gallicano-Jansenist argument further than appeals to the early Church and distinctions between *fait* and *droit* by themselves could have done; something analogous could perhaps be observed on the other side. Nor is this to say that the Enlightenment did not develop affiliations of a more particular kind with either side. On the one side, both Bernhard Groethuysen and Robert Palmer have successfully called attention to the close similarity between "enlightened" conceptions of human nature and reason and those of certain segments of the French "devout" party, especially the Jesuits.[102] On the other side, this small study has attempted to underscore the very close proximity of Gallicano-Jansenism's subjection of Church to State to the ideas of the *philosophes* on this matter, particularly the "civil religion" of Rousseau's *Social Contract*.

This takes us back, at long last, to the old pilgrimage town of Vézelay, and to Hubert Chalumeau, curé of the parish of Saint Pierre. The good curé could not have been more than dimly aware, as he resolved upon his diminutive stand against Rousseau and local apostasy, of the immense and somewhat irrelevant cross fire into which he was about to stumble. He wished only to sermonize against Rousseau, innocent of the fact that in using the assembly's

---

[102] Bernhard Groethuysen, *Die Entstehung der Bürgerlichen Welt-und Lebensanschaung in Frankreich* (Halle/Salle, 1927); and Robert R. Palmer, *Catholics and Unbelievers in Eighteenth-Century France* (Princeton, N.J., 1939), esp. pp. 23–52.

Actes to do so, he was publicizing a document which the parlement of Paris had condemned for quite different reasons. On this superficial level, then, his affair was an accident, a mere and irrelevant anecdote, although illuminating rather poignantly the difficulties one could encounter in combating unbelief in eighteenth-century France. Yet Gallican and Jansenist thinking about Church and State, so close in some ways to the *Social Contract,* were also pretty much those of the parlement of Paris. In fact, the parlement's remonstrances of August 31, 1766, rather nicely sum up decades of Gallicano-Jansenist theorizing on relations between Church and State; it is as succinct a statement of these conceptions as exists anywhere. What is more, the authors of these remonstrances were malign enough to cite Chalumeau's case as an example of the "publication" of the *Actes*—in a footnote, to be fair—even though they almost certainly knew better by that time.[103] In view of these supplementary considerations, it is perhaps permissible to wonder whether, on some profounder level, the parlement's prosecution of the curé of Saint Pierre was so accidental, after all. What is in any event certain is that the lot of the curé was indeed an unhappy one in those days.

---

[103] "Dans d'autres diocèses, la publication en a été faite aux prônes des paroisses.
. . . " (Flammermont, *Remontrances,* 2:638). Footnote 4 cites the dioceses of Chartres and Autun as examples; Vézelay was located in the diocese of Autun. The case referred to in the diocese of Chartres was however just as phony. See the letter of March 27, 1766, from the unhappy curé of Mévoisin to the attorney general in BN, Collection Joly de Fleury, fol. 1480, MSS 254–55.

French Political Thought at the Accession of Louis XVI*

Keith Michael Baker

The last coronation of the Old Regime, which took place at Rheims on June 11, 1775, was by all accounts a lavish, costly, and touching affair. The magnificence of the coronation regalia, which drew crowds when exhibited in Paris in the weeks preceding the ceremony, was matched by the ostentatiousness of the festivities in the city of Rheims itself and by the emotional exuberance of the moment when, at the culmination of the coronation service, the great doors of the cathedral were opened and the populace was admitted to hail its king. "At that moment, spontaneous tears of joy ran down every cheek," the duc de Croÿ recorded in his diary.

I am sure that I have never experienced such enthusiasm; I was completely astonished to find myself in tears and to see everyone else in the same condition. The Queen was so seized with pleasure that her eyes streamed in torrents; she was obliged to draw her handkerchief, and this increased the general emotion. The King appeared really touched by this beautiful moment; and we saw, finally, something that can only be seen here: our King, clothed in all the radiance of royalty, on the true throne, a vision so powerful that it cannot be expressed. The emotional rapture was really general.[1]

Whatever the strength of this emotional tidal wave, however, it did not entirely erase other currents of concern. Well informed of Turgot's efforts as Controller-General to reduce the expenses of the coronation service by transferring it to Paris, conscious of the contrast between the general euphoria at Rheims and the intensity of the bread riots that had swept through the countryside into the

* Research for this article was completed with the help of a grant-in-aid from the Penrose Fund of the American Philosophical Society (summer 1976), for which I am happy to express my thanks. Support was also gratefully received from the Social Sciences Divisional Research Fund of the University of Chicago. Aspects of this research were presented in papers to the 1976 annual meetings of the Society for French Historical Studies and of the Conference for the Study of Political Thought. A slightly different version of this article was also delivered to the Association for Eighteenth-Century Studies of McMaster University (March 1977). Help and criticism were generously given by John Bosher, Roger Hahn, David Higgs, Emile Karafiol, and William Smeaton.

[1] *Journal inédit du duc de Croÿ* (1718–84), ed. vicomte E. H. de Grouchy and Paul Cottin, 4 vols. (Paris, 1906–7), 3:186; see also [Pidansat de Mairobert], *Mémoires secrets pour servir à l'histoire de la republique des lettres en France, depuis MDCCLXII jusqu'à nos jours*, 36 vols. (London [Amsterdam], 1784–89), 8:84 (June 16, 1775) (hereafter cited as *Mémoires secrets*).

This essay originally appeared in the *Journal of Modern History* 50 (June 1978).

capital scarcely a month before, the abbé de Véri expressed a more sober view. "The popular acclamations which touched the King and especially the Queen, whose tears of tenderness were shared by everyone, always accompany ceremonies that are extraordinary and full of pomp. But unfortunately they are inebriating and they can give a false notion of the common opinion. Flatterers make great use of them. It is nonetheless true that the generality of the people of Paris and the provinces are distressed to see the expenses that the coronation has occasioned and those which are not yet pruned, or even marked out for pruning."[2] More radical in his criticism, Pidansat de Mairobert used his clandestine newsletters to emphasize the extent to which the public works occasioned by "this coronation, so ostentatious and so useless" depended on the forced labor of the *corvée*, levied at a time of the year particularly valuable to the peasantry. "The unfortunate peasants employed on these works during the most precious time of the year, as soon as they saw a traveler in the distance, fell upon their knees before him (so I have been told), raising their hands to the sky and then directing them towards their mouth, as in a gesture demanding bread. And it is to this people that Louis XVI was going to take a vow promising security and protection."[3]

Nor were reservations concerning the coronation limited to the expenses thereby incurred. Tensions and ambiguities in the service itself revealed ideological strains within the contemporary conception of the monarchy and reflected the institutional conflicts of the last years of the reign of Louis XV. A proposal by Turgot to modernize and secularize the coronation oaths, most particularly in a way that would respect the claims of protestants for civil rights, was rejected by Louis XVI. But when the service reached the stage of the royal oath to exterminate all heretics within the realm, the king apparently found it less embarrassing to mumble an unintelligible phrase.[4] The same ambiguity occurred at the point in the ceremony at which the bishops of Laon and Beauvais were to present Louis

[2] *Journal de l'abbé de Véri*, ed. baron Jehan de Witte, 2 vols. (Paris, 1928–30), 1:304. On Turgot's efforts to reduce the expenses of the coronation service, see G. Schelle, ed., *Oeuvres de Turgot*, 5 vols. (Paris, 1913–23), 4:119–20.

[3] [Pidansat de Mairobert], *L'Observateur anglais, ou Correspondance secrète entre Milord All-eye et Milord All'ear*, 4 vols. (London [Amsterdam], 1777–78), 1:327, 328; see also *Mémoires secrets*, 8:38–39 (May 19, 1775). On the clandestine circulation and publishing history of the *Mémoires secrets*, see Robert S. Tate, Jr., "Petit de Bachaumont: His Circle and the *Mémoires secrets*," *Studies on Voltaire and the Eighteenth Century*, vol. 65 (1968).

[4] Schelle, 4:551–54. For a discussion of the ridiculousness of the coronation oath, see [Pidansat de Mairobert], *L'Observateur anglais*, 1:346–47.

XVI to the assembled peers and people, demanding whether they would accept him as king. This latter formality seems to have been omitted by the two bishops. "What caused indignation among the patriots," reported the *Mémoires secrets* on June 20, 1775, "was the suppression of that part of the ceremony in which one seemed to demand the consent of the people for the election of the king. However vain this formula, and derisory today, there is great disapproval of the fact that the clergy, for whom this pious spectacle seems especially designed, should have ventured on its own initiative to cut out the other part and preserve only that which especially concerned it."[5]

Some of the "patriots" to whom the *Mémoires secrets* referred were doubtless confirmed in their indignation at this omission by the appearance, shortly after the coronation of Louis XVI, of an exhaustive tract entitled *Le Sacre royal, ou Les droits de la nation française, reconnus et confirmés par cette cérémonie,* which combed the traditional coronation ceremony (together with much of biblical and French constitutional history) for evidence demonstrating the principle of the social contract.[6] As propaganda for the rights of the nation, however, *Le Sacre royal* was perhaps too dry in its prose and too congested in its scholarly apparatus to be really effective. Such at least was the view of that connoisseur of the art of political pamphleteering, Pidansat de Mairobert.[7] But there were other writings, the author of the *Mémoires secrets* was happy to report, that could more appropriately "combat the formulas of adulation"[8] adopted at the coronation of Louis XVI. Two of these works, *L'Ami des lois* attributed to the Parisian *avocat,* Jacques-Claude Martin de Mariveaux, and *Le Catéchisme du citoyen,* attributed to the Bor-

---

[5] *Mémoires secrets,* 8:87 (June 20, 1775). The omission was also reported by the duc de Croÿ, who later asked the two bishops about it: "ils me dirent que cela n'était pas dans leur instruction, et que ce soulèvement qu'ils font du Roi est ce qui reste de cet ancien usage. Ainsi voila le vrai: cette fameuse demande ne se fait plus" (*Journal inédit du duc de Croÿ,* 3:183). For the traditional form of the demand, see Nicolas Ménin, *Traité historique et chronologique du sacre et couronnement des rois et des reines de France . . .* (Paris, 1723), p. 255. The semiofficial account of the coronation by the abbé Pichon followed the traditional form: see *Sacre et couronnement de Louis XVI, Roi de France et de Navarre, à Rheims, le 11 juin 1775; précédé de recherches sur le sacre des Rois de France, depuis Clovis jusqu'à Louis XV; et suivi d'un Journal historique de ce qui s'est passé à cette auguste cérémonie* (Paris, 1775), p. 41 (*Journal historique*).

[6] [Martin Morizot], *Le Sacre royal, ou Les droits de la nation française, reconnus et confirmés par cette cérémonie,* 2 vols. (Amsterdam, 1776). Although dated 1776, *Le Sacre royal* was already circulating in July 1775 (see *Mémoires secrets,* 8:117–18, 125–26). The demand omitted is discussed at 2:99.

[7] *Mémoires secrets,* 8:117–18, 125–26 (July 15 and 22, 1775).

[8] Ibid., 8:83 (June 17, 1775).

deaux *avocat,* Guillaume-Joseph Saige, were condemned by the Parlement of Paris on June 30, 1775.[9] Ordered burned as "seditious, subversive of royal sovereignty, and contrary to the fundamental laws of the realm," both these pamphlets developed the argument for national sovereignty in brief, unambiguous terms. "Since very long demonstrations are unnecessary to maintain propositions as true as these in the matter of right," Pidansat de Mairobert reported of *L'Ami des lois* on June 17, 1775, "the author is content to appeal in this regard to elementary truths."[10] Mairobert was no less enthusiastic about the appeal of the *Catéchisme du citoyen,* some copies of which continued to escape the vigilance of the police. "Once one has read it, one is not surprised that the partisans of despotism have made such efforts to annihilate it," he wrote a year later, on June 15, 1776. "Moreover, it marvelously fulfills its title, which is to say that it puts within the grasp of the most simple and inept a doctrine that *L'Esprit des lois* and *Le Contrat social* have clouded in a metaphysics very difficult to understand."[11]

Le Sacre royal, L'Ami des lois, and *Le Catéchisme du citoyen* had one thing in common. Although published in 1775, each of these works was a response to the "revolution" that had occurred in France in 1771, when Chancellor Maupeou had abolished venality of parlementary offices, reorganized parlementary jurisdictions, limited the judicial right of remonstrance, and staffed his remodeled "parlements" with men willing to exercise their functions on condition of removability subject to the royal will.[12] Each of these works be-

---

[9] *Arrêt de la cour de parlement, qui condamne deux libelles intitulés, le premier: "Catéchisme du citoyen, ou Eléments du droit public français, par demandes et par réponses"; le second: "L'Ami des lois, etc.",* à être lacérés et brulés au pied du grand escalier du Palais, par l'exécuteur de la Haute-Justice (Paris, 1775); *Mémoires secrets,* 8:103 (July 3, 1775); *Nouvelles extraordinaires de divers endroits (Gazette de Leyde)* (July 18, 1775), suppl. The *Catéchisme* was also condemned in similar terms by the parlement of Bordeaux, its probable place of publication, on June 28, 1775: see "Arrêt du Parlement de Bordeaux condamnant au feu un livre intitulé *Catéchisme du citoyen ou Eléments du droit public,*" *Archives historiques du département de la Gironde* 23 (1883): 297–98.

[10] *Mémoires secrets,* 8:83 (June 17, 1775).

[11] Ibid., 9:134 (June 15, 1776).

[12] Morizot, the author of *Le Sacre royal,* had published an earlier (and briefer) pamphlet on the same theme shortly after the Maupeou coup (see *Inauguration de Pharamond, ou Exposition des lois fondamentales de la monarchie française avec les preuves de leur exécution* [n.p., 1772]). *L'Ami des lois* explicitly sets out to refute a claim to legislative sovereignty made on the king's behalf by Maupeou in the *lit de justice* of December 7, 1770. The response of the *Catéchisme du citoyen* to the Maupeou coup is discussed in the course of this article. On the Maupeou reforms, the standard work remains Jules Flammermont, *Le Chancelier Maupeou et les parlements* (Paris, 1885). Jean Egret (*Louis XV et l'opposition parlementaire, 1715–1774* [Paris, 1970]) provides an excellent general discussion of the parlementary struggles which

longed to the large body of anti-Maupeou pamphlet literature that Pidansat de Mairobert attributed collectively to those *"Patriots, who going back to the source of the Laws and of the Constitution of Governments, demonstrated the reciprocal obligations of Subjects and Sovereigns, developed the study of history and its movements, and fixed the great principles of Administration."*[13] Maupeou's reforms did not, of course, long survive his fall. When Louis XVI succeeded to the throne in 1774, the old parlementaires were quickly restored to their offices, and the chancellor's most radical measures were abrogated. But if Maupeou's reforms could be reversed at the beginning of the new reign, their essential effect could not. For by demonstrating unambiguously and dramatically the danger of despotism in a no longer well-tempered monarchy, Maupeou had cast the tensions in the political order into a new and more compelling light. His "revolution" had underlined the need for a restatement of the principles of the political order, a reconstitution of the body politic, and a reconsideration of the traditional theory of representation. Even as the coronation of Louis XVI seemed to affirm the traditional relationship between king and people, that process of redefinition was well under way.

In the present article, I shall discuss three particular expressions of this process which appeared at the beginning of Louis XVI's reign. The first such expression is the *Remontrances* presented to their new sovereign on May 6, 1775, by the magistrates of the

---

culminated in 1771, while Lucien Laugier (*Un Ministère réformateur sous Louis XV: le Triumvirat (1770–1774)* [Paris, 1775]) offers a fresh analysis of the final years of the reign. William Doyle ("The Parlements of France and the Breakdown of the Old Regime, 1771–1788," *French Historical Studies* 6 [1970]: 415–58) presents a provocative reconsideration of the implications of the Maupeou coup and its reversal in 1774. David Hudson ("In Defense of Reform: French Government Propaganda during the Maupeou Crisis," *French Historical Studies* 8 [1973]: 51–76) and André Cocatre-Zilgien ("Les Doctrines politiques des milieux parlementaires dans la seconde moitié du XVIIIe siècle, ou les avocats dans la bataille idéologique revolutionnaire," in *Annales de la Faculté de droit et des sciences économiques de Lille, année 1963* [Lille, 1963], pp. 29–154) discuss the propaganda of the period.

[13] *Mémoires secrets*, 1:4 (*Avertissement*). Mairobert devoted considerable editorial energies to popularizing the writings of the "patriots." In addition to the collection of anti-Maupeou propoganda published under the title, *Maupeouana, ou Recueil complet des écrits patriotiques publiés pendant le règne du chancelier Maupeou, pour démontrer l'absurdité du despotisme qu'il voulait établir, et pour maintenir dans toute sa splendeur la monarchie française*, 5 vols. (Paris, 1775), he also edited the multivolume *Journal historique du rétablissement de la magistrature pour servir de suite à celui de la révolution operée dans la constitution de la monarchie française, par M. de Maupeou, chancelier de France*, 7 vols. (London [Amsterdam], 1775). Moreover, he clearly regarded the *Mémoires secrets* as a vehicle by which to keep the spirit of the opposition to Maupeou alive, by informing his audience of the existence and arguments of these works. See Tate (n. 3 above).

restored court of appeals for fiscal affairs, the Paris Cour des Aides. This lengthy analysis of administrative abuses was written on behalf of his colleagues by the *premier président* of the court, Malesherbes, soon to be named minister for the Maison du Roi. It was formally received by Louis XVI with the assurance that the reform of the abuses it described, if not the work of a moment, would nevertheless be the work of his entire reign. Significantly enough, however, the court's minutes of these remonstrances were confiscated on the king's orders to ensure against their publication, which was thereby delayed until 1778.[14]

After discussing the *Remontrances* of the Cour des Aides, I shall turn in comparison to the reforming vision of Malesherbes's close associate, Turgot, who served as Controller-General from 1774 to 1776. Turgot's comprehensive project for the reform of French government and society was drafted during this period by his confidant, the economist Dupont de Nemours, in the form of a memorandum intended for Louis XVI. That memorandum was apparently never delivered. Not made public until 1787, the *Mémoire sur les municipalités* nevertheless exercised a clear influence on the proposals of reforming ministers in the period of the pre-revolution.[15]

---

[14] *Très-humbles et très respectueuses remontrances, que présentent au Roi notre très honoré Souverain et Seigneur, les gens tenants sa Cour des Aides à Paris* (Paris, 1778) (hereafter cited as *Remontrances*). The *Remontrances*, as initially published in pamphlet form in 1778, has been reprinted by James Harvey Robinson (with an English translation by Grace Reade Robinson) in Translations and Reprints from the Original Sources of European History, vol. 5, no. 2 (Philadelphia, 1912). That edition will be cited here. However, Robinson errs in giving the date of presentation as April 10, 1775 (the date of another important remonstrance) rather than May 6, 1775. The work appeared again in 1779 in [Dionis de Séjour], *Mémoires pour servir à l'histoire du droit public de la France en matières d'impôts, ou Recueil de ce qui s'est passé de plus intéressant à la Cour des Aides, depuis 1756 jusqu'au mois de juin 1775* (Brussels, 1779), pp. 628–93; for the reception afforded the *Remontrances* by the king and the response of the Cour des Aides, see pp. 694–96. On Malesherbes's long and complicated career, see Pierre Grosclaude, *Malesherbes. Témoin et interprète de son temps* (Paris, 1961).

[15] Three versions of the *Mémoire sur les municipalités* exist. The first, communicated to the Margrave of Baden by Dupont in 1778 (see Carl Knies, ed., *Carl Friedrichs von Baden Brieflicher Verkehr mit Mirabeau und DuPont*, 2 vols. [Heidelberg, 1892], 1:236–84), is reprinted in Schelle, 4:568–628 (n. 2 above). This version will be cited here. The *Mémoire* was first made public in France (with minor changes) by the comte de Mirabeau under the title *Oeuvres posthumes de M. Turgot, ou Mémoire de M. Turgot sur les administrations provinciales* (Lausanne, 1787). Finally, Dupont himself published a revised version of the *Mémoire* in his own edition of the *Oeuvres de Turgot*, 9 vols. (Paris, 1808–11). The range of interpretation to which the *Mémoire sur les municipalités* has been subject is sobering. The principal issues are well stated in Gerald J. Cavanaugh, "Turgot: The Rejection of Enlightened Despotism," *French Historical Studies* 6 (1969): 31–58. The best introductions to Tur-

To that work, in turn, I shall compare a writing that also reappeared in the immediate prerevolutionary period, the *Catéchisme du citoyen* of the Bordeaux *avocat,* Guillaume-Joseph Saige.[16] First published in 1775, the *Catéchisme* circulated again in 1787 and (more widely) in 1788, when royal ministers again took measures against the parlements similar to those of Maupeou.[17] If this work was radical in the context of 1788, it was (as we shall see) even more radical in the context of 1775. The fact that it has been largely neglected by historians suggests that we still know far less than we might about the nature of the political ideas and arguments that circulated in France in the mid-1770s and the way in which they

got's career are Douglas Dakin, *Turgot and the Ancien Régime in France* (London, 1939); and Edgar Faure, *La Disgrâce de Turgot* (Paris, 1961). For a provocative analysis of the relationship between Turgot's views and those expressed in the *Remontrances* of the Cour des Aides, see M. Marion, "Turgot et les grandes remontrances de la Cour des Aides (1775)," *Vierteljahrschrift für Social-und Wirtschaftsgeschichte* 1 (1903): 303–13.

[16] [Guillaume-Joseph Saige], *Catéchisme du citoyen, ou Eléments du droit public français, par demandes et par réponses. A Genève [Bordeaux], aux depens de la Compagnie* (1775) (hereafter cited as *Catéchisme du citoyen*). Copies of this work are rare: they exist in the Bibliothèque de l'Arsénal (Paris) and the Bibliothèque municipale de Bordeaux. Concerning Guillaume-Joseph Saige himself, relatively little is known. Member of a prominent merchant family in Bordeaux, he was born in 1746 and became an *avocat* in the parlement of Bordeaux in 1768. He was also one of the earliest and most energetic members of the literary and philosophical society known as the Musée de Bordeaux (see Marie-Thérèse Bouyssy, *Le Musée de Bordeaux (1783–1789), élude psycho-sociologique d'une société de lumières,* diplôme d'études supérieures, Paris-Sorbonne, 1967 [Paris, Microfiche, 1973]). He played an active part in the prerevolutionary movement in that city (see Michel L'Héritier, *La Révolution à Bordeaux dans l'histoire de la Révolution française. I. La fin de l'ancien régime et la préparation des Etats-généraux (1787–1789)* [Paris, 1942]), but his career during the Revolution remains obscure. He died in 1804. In addition to the *Catéchisme du citoyen,* Saige was also the author of several other political tracts, most notably, *Manuel de l'homme libre, ou Exposition raisonnée des points fondamentaux du droit politique* (Amsterdam [Bordeaux?], 1787), which appeared in English translation as *The Manual of a Free Man, or Reasonable Exposition of the Fundamental Points of Universal Political Right . . . Translated from the French by a Citizen of Virginia* (Richmond, 1799); and *L'Ami des trois ordres, ou Réflexions sur les dissensions actuelles, par l'auteur du "Catéchisme du citoyen"* (n.p., 1789). For a brief discussion of Saige's career (and the most reliable to date), see Clarke W. Garrett, "The Moniteur of 1788," *French Historical Studies* 5 (1968): 263–73. I hope shortly to offer a fuller account of the life and writings of this forgotten publicist.

[17] [Guillaume-Joseph Saige], *Catéchisme du citoyen, ou Eléments du droit public français, par demandes et par réponses; suivi de fragments politiques par le même auteur. 2e édition. A Genève [Bordeaux] 1787.* Three further printings of this pamphlet (published "en France, 1788") exist in the Bibliothèque nationale. The work is discussed briefly in André Lemaire, *Les Lois fondamentales de la monarchie française d'après les théoriciens de l'ancien régime* (Paris, 1907), pp. 238–39, and (more intelligently) in Elie Carcassonne, *Montesquieu et le problème de la constitution française au XVIIIe siècle* (Paris, 1927), pp. 473–78. See also Durand Echeverria, "The Pre-Revolutionary Influence of Rousseau's *Contrat Social,*" *Journal of the History of Ideas* 33 (1972): 555–56.

were mobilized a decade or so later in the constitutional struggle that eventually brought about the French Revolution.

None of these three documents can properly be regarded as a classic work of political theory as we tend to define that genre, though at many points they may bear the imprint of such works. Taken together, however, they clearly suggest the problems which French political thinkers faced on the accession of Louis XVI, the range of language in which such thinkers attempted to resolve those problems, and the tensions that language often displayed. They also suggest how close French Political thought was in the early 1770s to the formulations that became so compelling in 1789.

I

The general framework within which these works took form can perhaps best be suggested by resorting to a quotation from Bossuet, whose famous *Politique tirée des propres paroles de l'Ecriture sainte* so effectively set forth the language of politics in the age of absolutism. "The end of government is the good and the preservation of the State. To preserve it, first one must maintain therein a good constitution," Bossuet wrote in a section of that work outlining his discussion of the general duties and responsibilities of the prince. "The good constitution of the body of the State consists in two things, namely religion and justice: these are the internal and constitutive principles of States. By the former, God is given his due, and by the latter, men are given that which is fitting and proper to them. The resources essential to royalty and necessary for government are arms, counsel, wealth or finances. . . ."[18] According to this definition, what Bossuet calls the "state" is a passive rather than an active subject. It is that which is to be preserved; it is that state of things, that social order, which is constituted by two fundamental principles, religion and justice. The social order, then, is ultimately grounded on a religious order, which is to say that it is ultimately dependent upon divine providence. For this reason, monarchy is a spiritual function providentially conferred through the mechanism of dynastic inheritance, and the person of the king is accordingly sacred.

Within this religious framework, however, the state is constituted by justice, that justice "by which men are given what is fitting and proper to them." For Bossuet it went literally without saying that all things are not fit and proper for all men. In 1776, faced with a

---

[18] Jacques-Bénigne Bossuet, *Politique tirée des propres paroles de l'Ecriture sainte*, ed. Jacques Le Brun (Geneva, 1967), p. 212.

reform of Turgot's that threatened to introduce the principle of equality into the social order, the Parlement of Paris was obliged to be more explicit. "Justice, Sire, is the first duty of kings," the magistrates reminded their sovereign on that occasion. "The first rule of justice is to preserve for every man what belongs to him . . . a rule that consists not only in maintaining the rights of property, but also in preserving rights attached to the person and those which derive from the prerogatives of birth and estate."[19] Within the social state of things that is to be maintained, there are all states and conditions of men; within the body of the state, there is a diversity, a multiplicity, of corporate bodies, orders and Estates, whose rights and responsibilities, whose *privilèges,* in effect constitute and are constituted by the traditional order of things. Given this traditional order, justice must be the fundamental mode of governmental activity. And justice, in this sense, means giving each his due in a particularistic society of orders and Estates.

It follows from this definition of absolutism that the king, and the king alone, is a public person. The king, alone among his subjects, sees the whole and can take counsel for the whole; his alone is a truly public will. Frenchmen as a body—or, more precisely, as a congeries of corporate bodies—are related to each other only indirectly as subjects of the crown. They participate in government only to the extent that they are officers of the crown (and hence share in its judicial function) or retain a traditionally constituted right to make representations of their partial interests. There can be no useful public discussion of political questions since there is no public apart from the person of the king. It was for this reason that in the famous *séance de la flagellation* in 1766 Louis XV quite appropriately prohibited the various parlements from making public their judicial remonstrances, or even circulating them from one parlement to another.[20]

That is was necessary for the king so to prohibit his parlements in 1766 suggests the obvious fact that this model of politics was not exactly working, that there was indeed a profound structural crisis in the French monarchy during this period. To understand some of the most general aspects of this crisis, it is necessary to recall the way in which the monarchy had itself been transformed in the course of

---

[19] Jules Flammermont, ed., *Rémontrances du parlement de Paris au XVIIIe siècle,* 3 vols. (Paris, 1888–98), 3:278.

[20] Ibid., 2:559. In this and the following paragraph, I have drawn on the discussion in my book, *Condorcet: From Natural Philosophy to Social Mathematics* (Chicago, 1975), pp. 203–5.

the seventeenth and eighteenth centuries.[21] In a society of orders and Estates, the king served as arbiter of the common good, guarantor of public order, defender of the realm. To the extent that his responsibilities to the common weal required, he could (as Bossuet maintains) command his subjects according to their rank and Estate to aid him spiritually with their counsel and materially by their financial contributions. So it was that in seventeenth-century conditions of war, religious and political division, economic decline, and social unrest, the French monarchy had exercised its traditional role by increasing its power to mobilize the resources of society and coordinate the activities of communities and corporations for the common good. So it was that new taxes (at first extraordinary but gradually regularized) began eating into ancient privileges, that counsel traditionally expressed in representative corporate bodies gradually gave way to command, that local government of *officiers* and Estates gradually gave way to the more centralized control represented by the intendants, that justice as the mode of royal government gradually gave way to administration.

As a result of these developments, the institutional order of the old regime was by the 1750s and 1760s displaying a series of tensions, which (in Parsonian terms) can be regarded as aspects of the differentiation of the policy from the societal community. These tensions can be very schematically listed as follows:

1. A tension between the traditional foundations of royal absolutism in a particularistic social order and the universalistic implications of the growth of more centralized government. This tension expressed itself in conflicts over taxation and local privileges, in the confusion of aims of much royal policy, and in the differentiation within the administrative elite between those officials who tended to emphasize the more particularistic and those who tended to emphasize the more universalistic aspects of their role.

---

[21] The following discussion is necessarily schematic. Some of these themes are treated in the following general works: Roland Mousnier, *Les Institutions de la France sous la monarchie absolue, 1598–1789* (Paris, 1974), and *La Plume, la faucille et le marteau; institutions et société en France du moyen âge à la Révolution* (Paris, 1970); François Olivier-Martin, *Histoire du droit français des origines à la Révolution* (Paris, 1948), and *L'Organisation corporative de la France d'ancien régime* (Paris, 1938); Emile Lousse, *La Société d'ancien régime. Organisation et représentation corporatives* (Louvain, 1943); Michel Antoine, *Le Conseil du Roi sous le règne de Louis XV* (Geneva, 1970); Furio Diaz, *Filosofia e politica nel Settecento francese* (Turin, 1962); Eberhard Schmitt, *Repräsentation und Revolution. Eine Untersuchung zur Genesis der kontinentalen Theorie und Praxis parlamentarischer Repräsentation aus der Herrschaftspraxis des Ancien régime in Frankreich (1760–1789)* (Munich, 1969). In general terms, the approach I am taking owes much to Tocqueville (see Alexis de Tocqueville, *The Ancien Regime and the French Revolution*, trans. Stuart Gilbert [Garden City, N.Y., 1955]).

2. A tension between justice, as the mode of government action in preserving each his due, and administration, as mobilizing social resources to maximize the public welfare. This tension expressed itself in the conflict between the older judicial *officiers* and the newer administrative elite which Auget de Montyon (an astute analyst of the administration of his day) described as "a fairly continuous and often too intense war between two powers, the *jurisdictional* and the *ministerial*."[22] It revealed itself also in diverging views of justice as a mode of royal activity, on the one hand, or as an agency limiting royal activity, on the other.

3. A tension between the need for monocratic authority in an institutional order ultimately grounded in the person of the king and the lack of such authority in a system of government now too complex and chaotic to allow for it. This tension expressed itself in the inconsistencies and vacillations of government policy; in the inefficiencies, contradictions, and arbitrariness of much of the administrative system; and in the weakening of personal respect for the monarch as a symbol of unity.

4. A tension between the increased public demand for and expectation of the social benefits that came from the integration of public authority and the growing criticism of the irresponsible power by which these benefits were achieved. This tension revealed itself in discussion of such issues as the *corvée*, for example, as in the demands for administrative decentralization that became frequent in the last years of the old regime.

All these tensions found their expression, too, in a more general phenomenon: the increasing importance of public opinion, as institutional actors appealed beyond the traditional political arena to an educated audience denied active participation but by no means indifferent to the issues involved, and the growing demand for publicity in all aspects of government. The case for such publicity was well presented at the beginning of Louis XVI's reign by the

[22] Antoine-Jean-Baptiste Auget de Montyon, "Des Agents de l'administration" (Archives de l'Assistance publique de Paris, Fonds Montyon, carton 8), section entitled "Des intendants de province" (emphasis added). Montyon's notes and drafts for this uncompleted treatise on the science of administration form an invaluable source for the development of the administrative role in eighteenth-century France. His comments on the differences between the administrative and the judicial mentality are of particular interest in this context. On Montyon, see Louis Guimbaud, *Un Grand bourgeois au XVIIIᵉ siècle: Auget de Montyon (1733–1820) d'après des documents inédits* (Paris, 1909). His treatise on administration is thoughtfully discussed by John Bosher (*French Finances, 1770–1795: From Business to Bureaucracy* [Cambridge, 1970], pp. 130–33). See also Claude Hohl, "Le Fonds Montyon aux Archives de l'Assistance publique à Paris," *Annales historiques de la Révolution française* 42 (1970): 506–18.

abbé Morellet, whose *Réflexions sur les avantages de la liberté d'écrire et d'imprimer sur les matières de l'administration* presented a vigorous defense of the right of the public to read about—and of publicists to write about—the conduct of public affairs.[23] For who was to lay down the terms of a public discussion which raised fundamental questions concerning the nature of man in society, if not the men of letters whose professional function it was (in the words of d'Alembert) to "fix the use of language" and to "legislate for the rest of the nation in matters of philosophy and taste"?[24] "Nowadays everything is put into dictionaries, almanacs, journals," commented Pidansat de Mairobert in 1776. "The men of letters continue to concern themselves with matters that were formerly foreign to them; they have so thoroughly analyzed the field of politics that there scarcely remains anything new in this genre."[25] The history of the term "publicist" is, in this respect, itself very suggestive. Appearing in French about the middle of the eighteenth century, it seems first to have been invoked in reference to established authorities on public law. By the time of the French Revolution, its usage had broadened to include journalists and political writers more generally.[26] In 1776, interestingly enough, Mairobert was already prepared to apply it to a pamphleteer such as the author of the anonymous *Catéchisme du citoyen*.[27] For if, on the accession of Louis XVI, the monarchical ideal still seemed to some to imply the notion that the art of politics remained "le secret du roi," political affairs were nevertheless being discussed in an unprecedented manner; publicists were defining and extending their intellectual role; a public was being brought into being. It was not without reason that, in his denunciation of *Le Catéchisme du citoyen* and *L'Ami des lois* before the Parlement of Paris on June 30, 1775, the *avocat-général* Séguier lamented the loss of "the veil with which

[23] [André Morellet], *Réflexions sur les avantages de la liberté d'écrire et d'imprimer sur les matières de l'administration . . . Par M. l'A.M.* (London and Paris, 1775). These reflections were first written in 1764, but they were not published until Turgot's ministry seemed to offer a more favorable political climate. Morellet himself was the author of an elaborate project for a dictionary of political economy, in which the obscurities of that subject would be dispelled by the precise definition of terms (see *Prospectus d'un nouveau Dictionnaire de commerce. Par M. l'abbé Morellet. En cinq volumes in-folio. Proposés par souscription* [Paris, 1769]).

[24] Jean le Rond d'Alembert, *Essai sur la société des gens de lettres et des grands, Mélanges de littérature, d'histoire et de philosophie. Nouvelle edition,* 5 vols. (Amsterdam, 1759–68), 1:385, 410.

[25] *Mémoires secrets,* 9:243 (October 24, 1776); 9:270–71 (November 24, 1776).

[26] See Ferdinand Brunot, *Histoire de la langue française des origines à 1900,* new ed., 13 vols. (Paris, 1966–72), 6, pt. 1:36; Walther von Wartburg, *Französisches etymologisches Wörterbuch,* 21 vols. (Bonn, Basel, 1928–65), 9:508.

[27] *Mémoires secrets* 9:134 (June 15, 1776).

the prudence of our Fathers had enveloped all that which pertains to Government and Administration."[28] The demand for publicity in all aspects of political life had become the order of the day. Even the conservative University of Paris felt moved in 1776, in proposing the subject of its prize for Latin eloquence for the following year, to question the appropriateness of preventing men of letters from discussing public affairs.[29]

II

With the claims of men of letters to exercise their public ministry, Malesherbes was very well acquainted. As *directeur de la librairie* from 1750 to 1763, he had found ample opportunity to exercise his power to protect the philosophes' enterprise and sufficient grounds to confirm his belief in freedom of the press. Not surprisingly, then, the importance of printing and publicity is a central theme of the *Remontrances* he drafted on behalf of the magistrates of the Cour des Aides in 1775. Passing quickly from criticism of taxes introduced under Maupeou to an indictment of the system of taxation in general, the *Remontrances* proceeded more deliberately from that indictment to a sweeping condemnation of the system of "oriental despotism" that was threatening to destroy the very principles of absolute monarchy in France. This system, the magistrates charged, had three principal characteristics. First, it involved an attempt to do away with the real representatives of the nation. The Estates-General no longer met, *pays d'états* had seen their provincial assemblies reduced to insignificance, and *pays d'élections* had long since been deprived of the elected representatives participating in the allocation of taxes from which they originally took their name.

---

[28] *Arrêt de la cour de parlement* (n. 9 above); *Gazette de Leyde* (July 18, 1775), suppl. (n. 9 above).

[29] *Mémoires secrets*, 9:280–81 (December 5, 1776). "Since it represents an indirect censure of several prohibitions, reiterated in varying circumstances, against writing on matters of administration," commented Mairobert, "it is surprising that the government has let this subject pass, and it would not be astonishing if an order to change it appeared." Public interest in this issue had been aroused in 1776 by the case of the physiocratic journalist, abbé Baudeau, editor of the *Nouvelles éphémérides du citoyen*. After the fall of Turgot, Baudeau was sued by the financiers of the so-called *Caisse de Poissy* (which Turgot had proposed to abolish) for his exposure of their profits. His speeches in his defense, which mixed vigorous denunciation of the financiers with passionate defense of Turgot, made the government so nervous that printers were prohibited from publishing anything on his behalf and the case was abruptly brought to an end (*Mémoires secrets*, 9:110–12, 114–15, 165, 168–69, 170, 171–72). Even while the trial was continuing, Baudeau compounded his difficulties by printing an article critical of government finance during the Seven Years' War. His journal was suppressed for "thus publicly revealing the secrets of the ministry," and he was ordered into exile in Auvergne (ibid., 9:176–77, 180–81, 188).

Even the right of communities and corporate bodies to administer their own affairs—"a right which we shall not say forms part of the primitive constitution of the realm, for it has a more fundamental basis than that, in natural right and the law of reason"[30]—had been invaded and destroyed. In short, "the whole Nation has, so to speak, been declared incapable of managing its own affairs and placed in the charge of guardians."[31]

Not only had the exercise of the traditional rights of representation been suppressed. In addition, argued the *Remontrances,* the protests of those bodies who in the absence of such assemblies had been obliged to represent the interests of the nation had also been rendered illusory. The parlements and other superior courts had been forbidden to discuss matters of administration, their members had been punished for bringing justice to the foot of the throne, and their remonstrances had been suppressed as dangerous measures from which the government should protect itself. "Under this pretext, a government has been introduced into France far more fatal than despotism and worthy of oriental barbarism: the clandestine administration by which, under the eyes of a just sovereign and in the midst of an enlightened nation, injustice can show itself and, moreover, be flagrantly committed."[32]

This clandestine administrative system, divorced from judicial restraint and sanctioned by the name of the king, was the third and most fundamental aspect of the despotism denounced in the *Remontrances.* It was the product of a separation of justice from administration that Malesherbes placed in the context of a novel analysis of French judicial history. In the earliest times, the age of the spoken word, he argued, justice and administration were inseparable: both were exercised by the king himself, who gave his justice to the nation in the assembly of the Champ de Mars. Publicity was accordingly the hallmark of justice, and publicity was necessary because contracts and agreements among men were oral and laws were ill-formulated and not written down. As the king gave justice in person to the nation assembled, so did the nobles render justice to the people, each in his own domain.

---

[30] *Remontrances* (n. 14 above), p. 27.

[31] Ibid., p. 28.

[32] Ibid., p. 26. On the concept of "oriental despotism" here invoked, see Franco Venturi, "Oriental Despotism," *Journal of the History of Ideas* 24 (1963): 133–42; Sven Stelling-Michaud, "Le Mythe du despotisme oriental," *Schweizer Beiträge zur Allgemeinen Geschichte* 18/19 (1960–61): 328–46. More generally, see R. Koebner, "Despot and Despotism: Vicissitudes of a Political Term," *Journal of the Warburg and Courtauld Institutes* 14 (1951): 275–302; Melvin Richter, "Despotism," in *Dictionary of the History of Ideas,* ed. Philip P. Wiener, 4 vols. (New York, 1973), 2:1–18.

All this changed in the next period, the age of writing. A code of written laws came into existence, upon which the rights of citizens could be more securely based. As this code became more complicated, however, a "new order of citizens" emerged as specialists in the law, and the administration of justice accordingly became less public. Jurisprudence became so profound a science that it was no longer possible for the king and the nobles to give justice in person. "The kings therefore confided this function to the magistrates, jurisconsults and graduates in the law, but reserved to themselves the administration; and since this latter was exercised by royal letters, instead of the public proclamations of earlier times, everything was done in the secrecy of the king's cabinet."[33]

Under this veil of secrecy, the *Remontrances* charged, a new system of administration had developed and elaborated itself. Ministers and their clerks, intendants and their subdelegates, tax farmers and their police agents acted in the name of the king and claimed the sanctity of the "secret du Roi." Freeing themselves from the restraints imposed by representative assemblies, benefiting from the lack of clearly defined responsibility within the administrative system, these men were able to insulate themselves effectively from all criticism. Lacking direct constitutional basis in the state, formally responsible to no one but the king whose views they were powerful enough to misrepresent, they were arbitrary and repressive in their actions and clandestine in their operations. They exercised a tyranny that threatened the structure of the monarchy itself, a tyranny that could only be destroyed by attacking the entire system of administration and reestablishing a direct relationship between the king and the nation.

The attack which the *Remontrances* proposed comprised two principal measures. The first entailed the restoration of the traditional right of representation at all levels: in the *élections,* in the provincial estates, and, above all, in the Estates-General. For how could a direct link between king and nation be reestablished? The simplest and most natural means, the magistrates informed their monarch, was also that most conformable to the constitution of the realm: "to listen to the Nation itself assembled, or at least to permit assemblies in each Province. No one must have the cowardice to tell you otherwise; no one must leave you in ignorance that the unanimous wish of the Nation is to obtain either the Estates-General, or at least the provincial Estates."[34]

---

[33] *Remontrances,* pp. 71–72.
[34] Ibid., p. 66.

The second measure proposed by the Cour des Aides, which the *Remontrances* allowed might be an intermediate step toward the first, was to introduce publicity into every aspect of the government. For if the age of writing had brought about the separation of justice and administration, with its consequent abuses, the age of printing now offered the means to reform these abuses and transcend that separation. The benefits of printing had not quickly been realized. It had taken several centuries before the nation had developed the habit of instructing itself by reading and before there appeared "enough men skillful in the art of writing to extend their ministry to the whole public and take the place of those who, endowed with natural eloquence, made themselves heard by our forefathers on the Champ de Mars or in public trials."[35] But the moment had arrived in which the conduct of justice and administration could once again be given the same publicity they had enjoyed in that early age, this time on the basis of the printed page. The moment had arrived in which, enlightened as to its public role through the ministry of men of letters, the nation could resume the conduct of its own affairs. The moment had arrived, in short, when the King of France—following the example of those ancestors who did not feel endangered by the liberty of their subjects to speak in the presence of an assembled nation—could once again "reign at the head of a Nation that will be in its entirety your council; and from which you will derive far greater resources, because you live in a far more enlightened century."[36]

Written on behalf of the Cour des Aides by one of the most enlightened and liberal magistrates of the Old Regime, the man who was to defend his sovereign before the Convention in 1793, the *Remontrances* represented a vision of the traditional constitution restored and revivified in the light of new conditions. Publicity was to be the hallmark of government in an enlightened age; simplicity and order were to characterize the laws. The creation of an enlightened public, through the saving grace of the printed word, would reconstitute the wholeness of the body politic and recreate the link between king and people. The revival of the traditional representative assemblies would restore to the nation its right to participate in the management of its own affairs. And that right in its turn would be exercised and defended not simply in terms of an ancient

---

[35] Ibid., p. 72. For a modern view of this process, see Elizabeth Eisenstein, "Some Conjectures about the Impact of Printing on Western Society and Thought: A Preliminary Report," *Journal of Modern History* 40 (1968): 1–56.

[36] *Remontrances,* p. 74.

constitution now restored but on the more fundamental basis of "natural right and the law of reason."[37]

Malesherbes's vision was probably the most attractive ever endorsed by the parlementary magistrates. Like most moderate statements, however, it was a compromise. It appealed to the traditional rights of the nation in a language that came close to invoking the rights of man; it claimed, in defense of a particularistic order, the publicity more appropriate to a universalistic one; it appealed for the reintegration of the body politic to a king whose defined role as a public person implied and assumed the very lack of such a polity. The tensions inherent in the *Remontrances* can perhaps best be illustrated by comparison, first with the *Mémoire sur les municipalités* of the reforming minister Turgot, and then with the *Catéchisme du citoyen* of the radical *avocat*, Saige.

The *Mémoire sur les municipalités* opened its discussion with an analysis of the administrative confusion, arbitrariness, and inefficiency of French government that parallels Malesherbes's analysis in many respects. If the symptoms described are often similar, however, the diagnosis of the fundamental problem is very different. "The cause of the evil, Sire," Turgot would have told his sovereign, "goes back to the fact that your nation has no constitution."

It is a society composed of different orders badly united, and of a people in which there are but very few social ties between the members. . . . It follows that there exists a perpetual war of claims and counter-claims which reason and mutual understanding have never regulated, in which Your Majesty is obliged to decide everything personally or through your agents. . . . You are forced to decree on everything, in most cases by particular acts of will, while you could govern like God by general laws if the various parts composing your realm had a regular organization and a clear understanding of their relations.[38]

In Turgot's view as an informed and enlightened adminstrator, experienced as former intendant of the Limousin in the problems of local government, the tensions that were coming to paralyze French government and disrupt French society could not be relieved by resorting to claims for a traditional constitution which no longer existed. On the contrary, it was necessary to recognize that the French monarchy quite simply lacked a constitution—lacked, that is, a regular and orderly structure—and had to be reconstituted in such a way as to make government simpler, more responsive to the needs of the people, and more effective in tapping the resources of society at large for the public welfare.

[37] Ibid., p. 27.

[38] Schelle, 4:576. In the following discussion of Turgot, I have drawn on the arguments of my *Condorcet*, pp. 202–14.

This reconstitution of the monarchy was to be based on simple and indubitable principles: "The rights of men united in society [which] are founded not on their history, but on their nature."[39] For Turgot, therefore, the doctrine of the rights of man gave theoretical form and justification to the universalistic implications of the development of the monarchy. Ultimately, it implied the reconstitution of the monarchy on the basis of civic equality, the elaboration of a system of taxation in which all property owners were taxed on an equal basis, and the creation of a legal system in which individual subjects were equally protected under the law.

The conditions under which such reforms might eventually be implemented were to be achieved by two measures. The first was the creation of a national educational system that would inculcate the public spirit Turgot (like Malesherbes) found so clearly lacking in France. The second was the institution of a hierarchy of representative assemblies from the village to the national level, charged with the details of tax assessment and the direction of public works. At the primary level, participation in these assemblies would be open to property owners in proportion to their property. Participation being thus based on property, the claim to participate would ultimately imply a public statement of taxability. The desire of an individual to minimize his tax obligations would be counterbalanced by his desire to maximize his participation in the local assembly, while the accuracy of individual claims would also be guaranteed by their very publicity. As a result, "the proportions of fortunes being known, the allocation of taxes will be carried out with the allocation of votes, by the inhabitants themselves without any difficulty."[40] The details of tax assessment accurately and automatically carried out, the primary assemblies would then be free to concern themselves with discussion of the public works necessary in the community, together with the provision of additional funds for their execution. All particular questions would therefore be handled by those most directly concerned. And the government, no longer overburdened with details, would be free to devote itself to "the general considerations of a wise legislation."[41]

In showing how this same pattern of automatic taxation and self-administration would be repeated at each level of the hierarchy of assemblies, the *Mémoire sur les municipalités* was careful to emphasize that these assemblies were to be instituted not on the

[39] Schelle, 4:575.

[40] Ibid., p. 589. This was Turgot's solution to the problem of assessment, also discussed at some length in the *Remontrances*, pp. 52–57.

[41] Schelle, 4:620.

antiquated basis of corporate membership in a society of orders and Estates but in terms of the natural and objective criterion of the landed wealth of *citoyens propriétaires,* those whose rational interest was ensured by a stake in the country. They would not be assemblies of Estates, the appropriate constitutional image of the monarchy in a corporate society. But "grouping citizens in relation to their utility to the State and the indelible place they occupy on the soil as property-owners, they would tend to make of the nation but a single body perpetually animated by one sole objective, the public good and the preservation of the rights of each individual."[42] Such assemblies, Turgot insisted, would have the right to enlighten the administration in the formulation of general policy. But unlike the traditional assemblies of Estates, they would not claim the power to prevent the implementation of rational reforms.

Nor was this latter argument simply a device to secure Louis XVI's acceptance of Turgot's proposed assemblies. These assemblies were not intended to give direct expression to the political will of the nation. True to their administrative inspiration, they were to be instituted, on the contrary, in order to provide accurate social information and public enlightenment through the exercise of the common reason. Throughout the *Mémoire sur les municipalités,* there is a marked concern to ensure the rationality of decision making by institutional mechanisms that would transform particular wills into the expression of public reason. For if Turgot admitted the theoretical sovereignty of the people—which he regarded as demonstrated by Rousseau[43]—the whole thrust of his political thinking was to minimize the importance of its direct and immediate exercise. The right of sovereignty is not anterior to society but owes its existence to it, Condorcet argued in his biography of Turgot, explaining the Controller-General's views. It should not therefore be confused with those essential rights of man for the preservation of which individuals entered into society. Nor should the direct exercise of sovereignty be allowed to a people who might use its power to abuse the natural rights of its members. Indeed, given the preservation of these rights in society, the direct exercise of popular sovereignty is of relatively little significance. This is all the more true, Condorcet insisted in his *Vie de M. Turgot,* once the laws are regarded not as the expression of the arbitrary will of the greatest number but as truths rationally derived from the principles of natural right.[44]

---

[42] Ibid., p. 619.
[43] Ibid., 2:660.
[44] F. Arago and A. Condorcet O'Connor, eds., *Oeuvres de Condorcet,* 12 vols. (Paris, 1847–49), 5:182, 211.

In Turgot's political thinking, then, the rationality of legislation is more important than the locus of legislative power. His schemes for a hierarchy of representative assemblies were not intended to effect the transfer of power from one arbitrary will to another. On the contrary, he aimed at the transformation of power through enlightenment. In a reconstituted France, where the king ruled "like God, by general laws," the personal will of the ruler would give way to the legal-rational authority of the reformed administrative system. Such a system would find its ultimate justification in service to the nation. But it would serve not the popular will but the common reason, as defined in consultation with assemblies that were at once agencies of local self-administration and vehicles for the rational expression of public interest.

Not surprisingly, then, given the close association between their authors, there are important similarities between the *Remontrances* of the Cour des Aides and the *Mémoire sur les municipalités*. Both aimed at the creation of a public spirit through enlightenment, the participation of the ruled in the conduct of public affairs, and the establishment (or reestablishment) of local assemblies. Both aimed to replace the arbitrary action of despotic will with the exercise of a rational politics made possible through the printed word. Both aimed at the simplification of the laws and administration. Yet if there are important similarities between these two works, there are also powerful differences. Malesherbes, speaking on behalf of the magistrates of the Cour des Aides, offered a vision of a restored traditional constitution that would maintain the rights of the nation by safeguarding the ability of traditional judicial institutions and representative assemblies to check the arbitrary exercise of administrative power. Turgot, as a reforming minister, offered the vision of a transformed administrative system that would implement the rights of man and bring about the rule of reason. Representative assemblies were to have a fundamental part in his reconstituted political order, not as repositories of the popular will but as vehicles for the articulation of public reason. For Turgot, the rights of man were ultimately more important than the rights of the nation.

In terms of this distinction, the doctrine of the *Catéchisme du citoyen* becomes most interesting. The aim of this pamphlet, displayed by its question-and-answer form as in its announced purpose, was to educate citizens in the principles of the national political existence: *le droit public français*. The basic right and obligation of every citizen, the *Catéchisme* argued, instruction in this subject is above all necessary when there is a direct contestation of "the principles of all legitimate politics and particularly the fundamental laws of our constitution."[45] Like the *Remontrances* of the Cour des Aides and the *Mémoire sur les municipalités,* then, the *Catéchisme du citoyen* emphasized the need for a citizen body fully conscious of its rights and obligations. Like the *Mémoire sur les municipalités,* it also made an explicit appeal to the principle of the rights of man. Political society, the author announced at the very outset, is an assemblage of men freely united, by a primitive contract, for their common advantage. Such a contract, whether express or tacit, "is absolutely necessary to the formation of societies, to preserve the imprescriptible rights of the individuals uniting, and to determine the cause and the goal of the association."[46] But if the *Mémoire sur les municipalités* invoked the principle of the rights of man to support an argument for a rational politics founded on civic equality, the *Catéchisme du citoyen* used it to draw radically different conclusions. It rapidly becomes clear, as the *Catéchisme* proceeds, that its author was less immediately interested in the rights of man than in the rights of the nation, and particularly in that "most incontestable right of the nation to legislative power."[47] The purpose of the *Catéchisme* was to invoke one arbitrary will in restraint of another.

The inalienable right of the nation to exercise sovereign power, Saige argued, is necessarily implied by the very nature of the social contract. For since the nature of that contract is to secure the general good, it follows that the sovereign power it creates must reside in a will that has a permanent tendency toward that good. Such a tendency exists only in the general will, which is to say "the common will of all the members of society, clearly manifested, and relative to an object of public interest."[48] The principle of national sovereignty thereby demonstrated in the manner suggested by Rousseau, the author of the *Catéchisme du citoyen* drew the conclusion that all existing political and social arrangements depend ultimately and directly upon the will of the nation. No magistracy, no form of political organization, is independent of that will or indestructible by it. The political realm is an entirely contingent one: "for there is nothing essential in the political body but the social contract and the exercise of the general will; apart from that, everything is absolutely contingent, and depends, for its form as for its existence, on the supreme will of the nation, of which every civil power is an emanation. . . . Thus the nation can create, destroy and change all the

---

[45] *Catéchisme du citoyen* (n. 16 above), p. 15.
[46] Ibid., p. 4.
[47] Ibid., p. 17.
[48] Ibid., p. 7.

Magistracies of the state, modify the constitution or annihilate it totally in order to form a new one.''[49]

It is difficult to imagine a less ambiguous formulation of the principle of national sovereignty than that voiced in this pamphlet. I know of no more radical statement in the pamphlet literature of 1788 and early 1789. It becomes all the more startling if we remember that it had already been penned in 1775. But if the author of the *Catéchisme du citoyen* enunciated the principle of inalienable and illimitable national sovereignty, however, he found no contradiction in mobilizing this principle in defense of the traditional constitution. Since the constitution of the state at any given time depends ultimately upon the will of the nation, it follows that any attack upon that constitution is a challenge to the popular will, to be met by the formal expression of that will in the Estates-General. Attempts of generations of royal administrators to diminish the practical importance of this body, and other representative assemblies in the monarchy, could not affect the right of the nation to meet in this way, nor was such a body dependent upon the royal will to convoke it.[50] If a monarch refused to call the Estates-General when the public good so required, it could (and should) be convoked by the Cour des Pairs, a "senate as old as the monarchy," sharing with the monarchy in the exercise of executive power.[51] According to the *Catéchisme du citoyen,* this Cour des Pairs was comprised, first and foremost, of the peers of the realm. It had also come to include the magistrates of the Parlement of Paris, together with those of the provincial parlements. Although these judicial magistrates did not hold their place by the same hereditary political right as the peerage, they could not be removed from office (as they had been by Maupeou) except by the nation or with its express consent. No minister, not even the king himself, could destroy this senate or deprive one of its members of his place without open violation of the constitutive laws of the monarchy.[52]

This body, forming an integral part of the constitution, can only be annihilated by the power which has formed the constitution; that is to say, by the nation itself; such an attempt, on the part of any other authority whatsoever, would be an act of the most violent despotism and an open attack upon the

[49] Ibid., p. 12.

[50] Ibid., pp. 22–23. This same argument was also forcibly developed in the 2d ed. of perhaps the most influential "patriotic" work [Claude Mey et al.], *Maximes du droit public français,* 2 vols. (Amsterdam, 1775). This edition contained a powerful "Dissertation sur le droit de convoquer les Etats-généraux" not included in the original edition of 1772.

[51] *Catéchisme du citoyen,* pp. 23, 25, 32.

[52] Ibid., p. 35.

rights of the society. . . . However elevated his dignity, the Magistrate who deprived one of these Senators of his place, or prohibited him to exercise his functions, would render himself guilty of a very great abuse of authority, and would consequently deserve to be punished by the supreme authority of the Body of the nation.[53]

On the rights of the nation, and particularly its right to exercise supreme power, the *Catéchisme du citoyen* is therefore emphatic and unambiguous. On the rights of man which that power is intended to sanction, it displays a rather interesting ambiguity. According to Saige, the rights common to individuals in French society are two-fold: liberty and property. They do not explicitly include equality. For in addition to the common rights of all Frenchmen, there are privileges particular to each of the three orders of which French society is composed. These privileges the *Catéchisme* discusses in a series of chapters devoted to the Clergy, the Nobility, and the Third Estate. The latter, the *Catéchisme* insists in a voice we inevitably associate with the abbé Sieyès, is not only "the most numerous part of the Nation, and consequently the most important."[54] More fundamentally than that, "the Third Estate, finding itself composed of the greatest part of the Members of the society, forms, properly speaking, the society itself; and the two other orders must only be considered as particular associations, whose interests are, by the very constitution of the civil State, really subordinate to that of this numerous Order. . . ."[55]

There was indeed a time, the author of the *Catéchisme* allowed, when this order of things had been turned upside down: when the nobility had arrogated the legislative authority and laid hold of all the property of the state. Crushed beneath the burdens of feudal bar-barism, reduced to the most humiliating slavery, the Third Estate had then "lived without a home in the midst of the *patrie,* and without influence in the social body, of which it constituted the principal force."[56] But if the people had not always sat in the Estates-General, it had always possessed an imprescriptible right to do so. And only with the rise of the communes did the legislative assemblies of the monarchy again become "true assemblies of the nation, since they comprised the universality of the Citizens."[57]

The implications of this passage seem clear. Claims to civic equality are indeed inherent in the *Catéchisme du citoyen*. Yet they make their appearance not as a direct consequence of the rights of man, but as an

[53] Ibid., p. 74.
[54] Ibid., p. 54.
[55] Ibid., p. 55.
[56] Ibid.
[57] Ibid.

indirect implication of the rights of the citizen—or, more precisely, of the sovereignty and universality of the nation. For if the Third Estate properly forms the nation, and the first two orders are consequently only "particular associations whose interests are . . . really subordinate" to it, equality becomes a necessary attribute of citizenship. Moreover, it needs only an expression of the sovereign will of the nation to give this argument legal effect. The conclusion of *Qu'est-ce que le Tiers Etat?* in 1789 is already implied in the *Catéchisme du citoyen* in 1775.

III

The different documents just discussed present three different views of a public political order, of an open and enlightened politics, of a reconstitution of the body politic through recognition of the claims of the national community. They do not exhaust the range of ways in which, on the accession of Louis XVI, Frenchmen were reaching out for a redefinition of their social order. But they do suggest the existence of three broad strands of thinking, from the interaction of which the revolutionary ideology was eventually born.

Taken together, these three strands of thinking would seem to represent a disaggregation of the attributes traditionally bound together in the concept of royal authority into competing definitions of the nature of political order. Taken singly, each may be seen as emphasizing in the language of the Enlightenment the priority of one aspect of the royal authority as traditionally conceived: justice, reason, or will. The *Remontrances* of the Cour des Aides represents, in its most enlightened form, what I shall call a judicial vision. It remains closest to the essentially judicial conceptions underlying the traditional constitution, which it seeks to reformulate in a manner appropriate to an enlightened age, and it represents a powerful statement of the institutional claims of the judicial magistrates on whose behalf it was written. In Malesherbes's conception, then, the particularistic rights and liberties of the nation are to be restored and respected, administrative power is to be subject to judicial restraint, and reason and counsel are to prevent the exercise of an arbitrary and despotic will. All of this is to be achieved by an appeal to the principles of justice according to which the state is constituted and by recognition of the central institutional role of the magistrates who are, and must remain, the guardians of that justice.

The *Mémoire sur les municipalités* represents what I shall call, perhaps at the risk of paradox, an administrative vision. Relatively few of Turgot's administrative colleagues would have expressed themselves as radically as he did; it would be misleading to regard his ideas as entirely typical. Nevertheless, the *Mémoire sur les municipalités* seems to draw to their logical and most radical conclusion the implications of the development of bureaucratic absolutism in France. In Turgot's conception, the nation is to be reconstituted on the basis of universalistic norms, as embodied in the doctrine of the rights of man; and legal-rational authority is to be exercised with the support of an enlightened public opinion as expressed in representative assemblies. Reason, not will, is to be the hallmark of public authority.

The *Catéchisme du citoyen,* in contrast, represents what I shall call a political vision. It appeals to the conception of an ultimate political will inherent in the nation, a will that knows neither judicial restraint nor constitutional limitation. In Saige's view, all political and social arrangements are contingent upon that will. The nation has the power and the right to punish all infractions against the traditional constitution. It has, by implication, the power and the right to transform not only the political arrangements inherent in that constitution but the social arrangements upon which it depends. National sovereignty is for Saige the ultimate principle, and implied in that principle is the demand for political equality for the most numerous part of the nation, the Third Estate.

In 1789 that demand was realized in precisely the manner suggested by Saige: by an act of sovereign national will. The rights of man were achieved by direct expression of the rights of the citizen as a member of the body sovereign, and the two sets of rights were identified as one in the celebrated *Declaration of the Rights of Man and of the Citizen.* This welding of the principles of the rights of man and of the rights of the nation concealed a tension which had existed in much Enlightenment thinking and was to have a continuing influence on the development of French Revolutionary thought.[58] For the Revolution came about as the result of a conflict between the efforts of reforming administrators to advance the principle of civic equality, along lines similar to those suggested by Turgot, and the resistance of those who defended the rights of the nation, first along lines suggested by Malesherbes and other parlementary theorists and then along the more radical lines suggested by Saige. Only when the rights of the nation had been secured did the revolutionaries claim the rights of man.

[58] On this point, see Alfred Cobban, *In Search of Humanity: The Role of the Enlightenment in Modern History* (London, 1960), pp. 208–210.

"Public Opinion" at the End of the Old Regime

Mona Ozouf

> To speak to us of the public spirit [*l'esprit public*] is to persist
> in giving a common name to the most heterogeneous opin-
> ions. Those who construct it out of the thought of their own
> coterie pretend to be unaware that they are surrounded by
> other coteries that feed on quite different illusions and that
> [even] within the same circle, people change system, party,
> and principles every month, every decade, and often over-
> night. The dictionary of the Revolution already contains some
> words that have become obsolete.

This anonymous revolutionary text, taken from the *Abréviateur Universel,* 18 germinal III, attempts to assess the results of the French
Revolution's passion for statistics and the success of its attempts to
poll opinion. In this, too, the Revolution was innovative, for it was
constantly preoccupied with evaluating the state of public opinion or
the "public mind" and set its administrators to that task.[1] The anonymous author of this article concludes in disappointment that both the
enterprise and the concept were swept away by the torrent of revolutionary innovations. A much better known passage from Louis-
Sébastien Mercier reflects an identical sense of feverish but ephemeral
vitality.[2]

The idea that had disappeared was a recent one. A glance at the
dictionaries shows that we have to wait for the 1798 edition of the
Dictionnaire de l'Académie française to find a definition of *opinion
publique.* Until that date, the dictionaries treat *opinion* as doubtful or
probable knowledge, following the Platonic opposition of sure knowledge and opinion. If opinion was defined at the time in a collection of
confused and disparate maxims, it was because all dictionaries—including those of Trévoux, Furetière, and the *Encyclopédie*—linked it

---

[1] The terms *opinion publique* and *esprit public* competed for favor during
the entire second half of the eighteenth century. The Revolution tended to opt
for *esprit public,* and even for *conscience publique.*

[2] Louis-Sébastien Mercier, *Paris pendant la Révolution, ou le Nouveau Paris*
(Paris, 1862), pp. 50–52.

This essay originally appeared in the *Journal of Modern History* 60, suppl. (September 1988).

with individual sentiment, which would be a paradox if applied to "public." *Public,* in the dictionaries, was not yet opposed to *privé* (private)—and would not be until the 1835 edition of the dictionary of the French Academy—but, rather, to *particulier* (particular, individual). This is why the word *public,* which could qualify a place, a records office, a road, or a woman, could not be used as a modifier for "opinions," which were seemingly mired forever in particularity.

Here and there the dictionaries hinted at the later coupling of the two terms, however. First, the notion of the uncertain flow of opinions contained the feeling (even when the connotations were pejorative) that opinions constituted an inexorable torrent of irresistible force. Furthermore, the notion of the power of opinion echoed that of the power of the public: "no matter how much the public is disparaged, there is no more incorruptible judge, and sooner or later it will sit in judgment."[3] The firm belief that opinion would always find a way—an accepted offshoot of the maxim that opinion was the queen of the world—and that sooner or later the judgment of the public would triumph coupled the noun and the adjective surreptitiously. Other themes that were crystallizing in the dictionaries under definitions of *publier, publicité,* or *publication* were the conspicuousness of public opinion and, even more, the operation of the will that consisted in bringing secrets out into the open. It made no sense to speak of "publishing" what everyone sees, which was why the *Dictionnaire de Trévoux* took Racine to task for saying that he was "publishing the beauties of Bérénice." The term *publiciste* (journalist, political writer) was still unknown at this time, except, in the *Dictionnaire de Trévoux,* as "one who writes and lectures on public law," but the theme of public expression, a decisive political stake in the thought of the century, was already being prepared.

Dictionaries record innovations only after due deliberation. In reality, the concept of public opinion had appeared in France as early as the middle of the century, with Rousseau generally granted the honors of precedence (but it is well known that first attribution is a risky affair). The works of the second half of the century offer a rich harvest of definitions, as a recent article by Keith Baker amply demonstrates.[4]

[3] Nicolas Boileau-Despréaux, cited in the *Dictionnaire de Trévoux,* ed. Abbé Brillant (Nanay, 1734), s.v. "Opinion."

[4] Keith Michael Baker, "Politics and Public Opinion under the Old Regime: Some Reflections," in *Press and Politics in Pre-Revolutionary France,* ed. Jack Censer and Jeremy Popkin (Berkeley and Los Angeles, 1987), pp. 204–46, and "Politique et opinion publique sous l'Ancien Régime," *Annales ESC* (January–February 1987): 41–71.

Some scholars—A. W. Gunn, for example—argue that unlike England, where the terms "public opinion" and the "opinion of the public" had a clear status as early as 1730, French usage remained uncertain.[5] On the one hand, the old kinship between opinion and prejudice continued to influence thought as late as 1789, when Jean-Pierre Papon was still likening opinion to "a metaphysical being" impossible to grasp rationally.[6] This was even true among the inventors of the term *opinion public*. Rousseau put it most brutally: "Remove the word opinions and put in its place the word prejudices, and the correction will be made."[7] On the other hand, "public opinion," even among those fondest of the expression, such as Necker, was used within a constellation of terms that included *esprit public* (public mind or spirit), *bien public* (common weal, the common good), *cri public* (public demand), *murmure public* (generalized protest), *voie publique* (free-access road), *conscience publique* (public conscience), and *amour public* (public admiration)—notions related by their use in contexts of the contestation of absolutism.[8] It is clear that these concepts drew their polemic efficacy from the adjective "public" and, what is more, from the use of the term in the singular since Rousseau's public opinions in the plural were short-lived and returned immediately to the realm of personal prejudices. The change to "public opinion" in the singular reflects a true conversion. This is illustrated in physiocratic literature and defined in a letter in which Condorcet pointed out to Turgot, to console him, the abyss that separated *la voix du public,* which was logically plural, since it was made up of "a hundred yelpings excited by the edicts" and *la voix publique,* which was one.[9] It is true, however, that even authors admired for having placed the unity of public opinion above the motley

[5] J. A. W. Gunn, "Public Opinion and l'Opinion Publique: Some Contrasts" (paper presented at a joint session of the Canadian Historical Association and the Canadian Political Science Association, Vancouver, 1983).

[6] Jean-Pierre Papon, *De l'action de l'opinion sur les gouvernements* (n.p., 1789), p. 1.

[7] Cited in Colette Ganochaud, *L'opinion publique chez Jean-Jacques Rousseau* (Lille, 1980), p. 18.

[8] See, e.g., Henri Griffet, *Mémoires pour servir à l'histoire de Louis, dauphin de France . . . avec un traité de la connaissance des hommes de France. Fait par ses ordres en 1758* (Paris, 1777): "A taste for republic and for popular government has seized all minds, and it makes itself felt even in the language. People abuse the words of public good, of public repose and public tranquillity. All one hears is praise for the qualities of citizen and patriot" (p. 100).

[9] Charles Henry, ed., *Correspondance inédite de Condorcet et de Turgot (1770–1779)* (Paris, 1883), p. 265.

realm of opinions showed a degree of intellectual inertia that often led back to the old theme of contrary opinions.[10]

With its late appearance, uncertain usage, and early demise, the short and dubious career of public opinion in prerevolutionary France presents us with a problem: why did it appear so late and with such confusion, when contemporary German thought credited France with having invented both the word and the thing?[11] Gunn's answer to this question runs counter to the present essay. According to Gunn, France—in spite of the brilliance of the philosophes—was a land in which public opinion could only stammer for lack of institutional channels of expression and by virtue of the extremely limited opportunities for public political life in eighteenth-century France. This means that French authors never had reason to see public opinion as positive. The concept, Gunn continues, fulfilled a purely polemic function. It conveyed no significant information and referred to no actual practice, political or cultural. A first direction for my research was thus to reread the texts to see whether they are indeed as indifferent to reality as Gunn thought them to be. I will accompany him a little farther as I seek to define the function of the concept. I will part company with him to ask whether the brevity of the career of the notion of "public opinion" came from problems inherent in the concept itself: how to construct public opinion on the basis of a collection of individual opinions; how to imagine its workings.

I. THE POSITIVITY OF PUBLIC OPINION

First, let us follow Gunn to the heart of his argument: the choice of England, not France, as the favored terrain for public opinion. A good many French writers would have accepted the notion that England was the native land of public opinion, either because they connected public opinion with the circulation and the diffusion of public papers (as with d'Argenson) or because they saw it as a reflection of parliamentary debates that passed from person to person to echo throughout the nation (as with Voltaire). Others, like Mably, saw this as the fruit of an obsession with the common weal; still others, like those ingenuous,

[10] This theme is treated throughout the collection of Gilbert-Charles Legendre, Marquis of Saint-Aubin, *Traité de l'opinion, ou mémoires pour servir à l'histoire de l'esprit humain,* 6 vols. (Paris, 1733).

[11] See Jürgen Habermas, *L'espace public: Archéologie de la publicité comme dimension constitutive de la société bourgeoise,* trans. Marc B. de Launay (Paris, 1978). Habermas sees the concept of public opinion as defined precisely for the first time by the physiocrats.

wonder-struck tourists who found their prototype in the Abbé Coyer, credited all English innovations from sidewalks to taxes on carriages to an all-powerful *esprit public* ("When one walks through London, public spirit shows itself at every step").[12] We could even range a certain Rousseau among England's partisans, the Rousseau of the *Lettres écrites de la Montagne,* writing, to be sure, within the constraints of the polemic that he was offering to the Council of Geneva.[13] Nevertheless, the praise of the British Parliament that so neatly fit his argument rested on the periodic convocation of that body, guarantor of public opinion.

Certainly, as in all French debate concerning England during the eighteenth century, these quotations could be counterbalanced by an equal number of statements of vehement anglophobia that strove to show that freedom of the press and parliamentary debate offered opportunities for "multiplied commotions" and "menacing tempests"[14] and were a sign, not of liberty but of instability, thus the very opposite of a concordant public opinion. All physiocratic criticism made use of such descriptions of stormy political weather in England. Public opinion could "take" only in a country devoted to unity, which meant that France, not England, must be the true homeland of public opinion.

What is important in this geographic quarrel is not so much what divided the two sides as what united them, for it was with the same argument that one side accepted and the other rejected the localization of public opinion in England. Both sides were arguing from universal principles and agreed that the moment one consulted one's own individual sentiments (Mably was speaking of the French, Linguet of the English), public opinion is no longer possible. In this unspoken agreement we can sense the growing reconciliation of the two political cultures, which Hume had theorized and which was exemplified every day by the spread of public papers in France, by parlementary demands and by the inefficacy of measures against the publication of parlementary *remontrances.* It is also clear—and I shall return to this point—that to a great extent public opinion was debated in France within a religion of unity.

Such debate shows that French writers were a good deal more interested in finding concrete referents for public opinion than Gunn

[12] Abbé Gabriel-François Coyer, *Nouvelles observations sur l'Angleterre, par un voyageur* (Paris, 1779), p. 15.

[13] Jean-Jacques Rousseau, *Lettres écrites sur la montagne,* in *Oeuvres complètes,* ed. B. Gagnebin and M. Raymond, 4 vols. (Paris, 1959–64), vol. 3.

[14] Abbé Henri Dubois de Launay, *Coup d'oeil sur le gouvernement anglais* (n.p., 1786), p. 191.

believed. They not only attempted to ascertain a place for public opinion but assigned a precise time to it as well. All writers were struck by the sudden upsurge—in a veritable and datable birth—of public opinion. Rousseau was the first: "Among the singularities that distinguish the century in which we live from all others is the spirit of method and consistency that has guided public opinions for the last twenty years. Until now, these opinions have strayed, with no aftermath and no rule, at the whim of men's passions, and these ceaselessly clashing passions made the public drift from one [opinion] to the other with no constant direction."[15] Let us leave aside for the moment the problem of the principle by which these drifting opinions could be brought together to note the precise moment: Rousseau, writing in 1776, says "for the last twenty years." Rulhière is even more precise.[16] For him, public opinion was born in the few years between the peace of 1748 and the Seven Years War and even, if a date were absolutely necessary, in 1749. Why? This was when Montesquieu published *L'esprit des Lois* and when Rousseau launched his career. It is interesting to note the importance of literary events here (and in other texts), further proof that the connection between public opinion and a certain sociocultural milieu was considered self-evident.[17]

What groups were the bearers of public opinion? The most frequent response to this question (asked by contemporaries as well) attaches public opinion to the opinion of men of letters, to changes in their objectives (when a desire to instruct replaced their desire to please), and to their now recognized role as arbiters. Such men of letters were, to be sure, designated by other men of letters, in clearly apparent narcissism. We see them in an entire literature of academic discourses and eulogies, seemingly enchanted to envision this special role for their little troupe, detached from the feverish necessities of action and totally absorbed in the dream of constituting an enlightened public opinion.

[15] Jean-Jacques Rousseau, *Rousseau juge de Jean-Jacques*, troisième dialogue, in *Oeuvres complètes*, 1:1964.

[16] See Claude-Carloman de Rulhière, *Discours prononcés dans l'Académie française* (Paris, 1787): "However, the capital, so long a prompt and docile imitator of the sentiments, the tastes, and the opinions of the court, ceased at the same time to have this ancient deference for it. It was then that there arose among us what we have called the empire of public opinion" (p. 18). See also Claude-Carloman de Rulhière, "De l'action de l'opinion sur les gouvernements," in *Oeuvres* (Paris, 1819).

[17] See Chrétien-Guillaume de Lamoignon de Malesherbes, *Discours prononcé dans l'Académie française le jeudi 16 février [1775]* (Paris, 1775), p. 5. Malesherbes sees the birth of public opinion as earlier and contemporary to the institution of the Académie française.

To their eyes, this claim was founded on the practice of equality imposed by the rules of parity within the utopian space of the academies and the other literary bodies: "The man who had only power lost it as he crossed the threshold of the Temple of the Arts; he sought to exist by enlightenment or he was nothing."[18] Their claim to speak for public opinion was also founded on the permanence of the written word, the guarantor, as Diderot wrote to Falconet, of the public message.

The second sociologically qualifiable group of bearers of opinion (and the second contemporary answer to the question as well) was the milieux of the *parlements*. Although political speech did not yet carry theoretical legitimacy, the *parlements* had become, thanks to the various "affairs" that shook the century, to the exilings, collective resignations, and dissolutions, "communities of scholars" (as d'Argenson said) buzzing with discussions on public law and capable of raising "public enthusiasm" in their favor. (This time, the term is Moreau's, and he could hardly be suspected of complaisance).[19] Not that the discourses of the *parlementaires* (Malesherbes excepted) were particularly fertile ground for evocations of "public spirit" or public opinion.[20] Still, all the episodes in the parlementary drama followed the same scenario: the king manifested his irritation at "the license with which the remonstrances of his Parlements are spread among the public";[21] the *parlements* then protested that this was an attempt "to stifle the public voice." Were the *parlements,* then, truly the environment in which public opinion took root, or simply the milieu so designated by an adroit but arbitrary propaganda? The question, which still divides French historiography, divided contemporaries as well. It is more to the point to note in their divergent views that "publicity," which meant making the *remontrances* public knowledge and was the chief weapon of the *parlements,* met with a unanimous response. Partisans of the monarchy dreamed of having an equivalent weapon—by no means secrecy or silence, which the monarchy had so long and so ineffectively sought to use, but a counterpublicity. The monarchy's campaign, with Moreau as its standard-bearer, tells us better than anything else that public opinion was a concrete reality. Censorship, police surveillance,

---

[18] Jean Delisle de Sales, *Mémoire pour les Académies* (Paris, 1800), p. 93.

[19] Jacob-Nicolas Moreau, *Mes souvenirs*, ed. Camille Hermelin, 2 vols. (Paris, 1898–1901), 1:110.

[20] First mentioned, to my knowledge, in the protests of the Parlement of Paris in 1788.

[21] Letter of chancellor Maupeou to the lieutenant of police Sartine, cited in Pierre Grosclaude, *Malesherbes témoin et interprète de son temps* (Paris, 1961), p. 239.

and police spies (the *mouches*) had also long borne witness to its existence.

It would be inaccurate to present the practice of public opinion as operating only in a context of the criticism of absolutism. The monarchy itself turned its attention to the phenomenon and went as far as to invent ingenious means of measuring it. Nothing demonstrates this better than the investigation launched in 1745 by the *contrôleur général,* Orry, who attempted to evaluate, in quite traditional terms, "the situation of the peoples of France."[22] But the investigation included an experimental innovation: at a time when the state was seeking to increase its financial resources and was concerned about the potential effect of a rise in taxes, Orry asked the royal *intendants* to "spread the word" of a rise in the *droit des entrées* (entry taxes and duties) related to a forthcoming militia levy. Then, once these rumors had been "sown," the *intendants* were to gather information on the emotional reactions and comments the rumors had inspired and report back. The observations gathered by the *subdélégués* and collated by the *intendants* are quite persuasive of the reality of public opinion. Not only is its preferred environment defined (cafés and public places), but its forms are also recognized (grumblings, oaths, and even insults directed toward the minister). Even more, the government had anticipated its reactions and had attempted to elicit them experimentally. In short, public opinion was seen, at this early date, in terms of a situation in which a plurality of the individuals concerned expresses approval or support of an action within a group regular enough to serve as a reference for a specific political project. This has an oddly modern ring to it.

Literary and parlementary practices that involved alerting the public and monarchical practices that involved surveillance and containment of the public are positive acts that postulate a much more lively political life than Gunn would have us believe. It is true, however, that public opinion was not yet clearly defined. Its only unanimously recognized characteristic was negative: it was not the opinion of the multitude, which Necker saw as *toute sauvage.*[23] The public was not the people, who were so quick to err, so undefinable, and so easily inflamed.[24] A

[22] See Bernard Lécuyer, "Une quasi-expérimentation sur les rumeurs au dix-huitième siècle: L'enquête proto-scientifique du contrôleur général Orry," in his *Science et théorie de l'opinion publique* (Paris, 1981), pp. 170–85.

[23] Jacques Necker, *Éloge de Jean-Baptiste Colbert* (Paris, 1773), p. 60.

[24] A great many texts could illustrate this distinction between public opinion and the opinion of the multitude. We could cite Condorcet: "As these gentlemen [the *parlementaires*] are unaware of opinion or scorn it, the only thing they

positive portrayal, however, is quite rarely found, the connection that our own age makes almost mechanically between opinion and freedom of the press is quite loose, and any reference to numbers (circulation figures for journals, press runs of books) is lacking. Why do the texts give so few particulars? Because they are less concerned with providing information than with utilizing the concept of public opinion for polemic ends. Description gives way before the normative.

II. AN IMAGINARY AUTHORITY

The key word in contemporary evocations of public opinion was "tribunal." As with the divine tribunal, all must appear before this infallible judge. Malesherbes defined this notion most eloquently: "A tribunal has been raised independent of all powers and respected by all powers, which evaluates all talents, and pronounces on all people of merit. And in an enlightened century, in a century in which each citizen can speak to the entire nation by means of print, those who have the talent for instructing men and the gift of moving them—men of letters, in a word—are, among the dispersed public, what the orators of Rome and Athens were in the midst of the public assembly."[25] All these terms bear meaning: the independence that discredits traditional authorities, the capacity to pass judgment on everything—that is, the demand for the recognition of sweeping powers—the comparison of the people of the classical city physically assembled to hear the spoken word to the modern public, dispersed but ideally united by the written word, and, finally, the brusque appearance of this tribunal.

The appearance of this tribunal was tied, in a functional sense, to a disappearance. In order for public opinion to appear as a supreme authority, the world had to be swept clean of other, inherited authorities. This was already almost true in the maxim that public opinion

---

will ever strive for is to have the favors of the population" (Henry, ed. [n. 9 above], p. 202). See also Jean Le Rond d'Alembert, *Éloges lus dans les séances publiques de l'Académie française* (Paris, 1779): "[The historian] often tends to distinguish the truly enlightened public, which must guide his pen, from that blind and noisy multitude that believes it fixes ranks because it busies itself with assigning them" (p. ix). Or, once again, Condorcet, *Réflexions sur le commerce des blés* (London, 1776): "When one speaks of opinion, one must distinguish three species: the opinion of enlightened people, which precedes public opinion and ultimately dictates to it; the opinion whose authority sweeps along the opinion of the people; popular opinion, finally, which remains that of the most stupid and most misery-stricken part of the people" (p. 140).

[25] Malesherbes, p. 5.

was "the queen of the world": how could such a queen be under the sway of kings? Quite the contrary, it was she who sat in judgment of them, reserving the right to pass sentence, as Rousseau put it, on "princes who were merely princes." When men of this century sought a visual equivalent for public opinion, they portrayed it perched on a throne engaged in distributing laurels. This was how Necker pictured it, and he perceived better than anyone the substitutive nature of public opinion.[26] As long as a material embodiment of authority occupied the forefront of the scene, there was no room for another authority, even an immaterial one. There was no public opinion under Louis XIV, for the brilliance of the monarch outshone it. Similarly, when public opinion had become king, it left no place for royal authority. This is why the duc d'Aiguillon, when he attempted to best the Parlement of Rennes in his zeal for the *esprit du roi*, only managed to bring on his own disgrace through the *esprit du public*. According to La Chalotais, who confided his thoughts to Monsieur de Caradeuc, he had picked the wrong epoch and the wrong tribunal.[27]

The divine word was still quite audible in this new tribunal—or so we might be led to think by the way public opinion imposed its decrees like mysterious revelations. It is even more striking, however, to see humanity's tribunal do without divine authority. This can be sensed in the large body of academic literature in which public opinion righted wrongs and avenged the great man for the scorn he had encountered in this world, substituting for heaven an enlightened posterity. The substitution of public opinion for divinity is even more striking when its spokesman was an adversary of the new ideas. Jacob-Nicolas Moreau, like Bossuet, held that the only possible counterweight to the injustice of sovereigns—an old and ceaselessly debated problem—was the voice "of the sole sovereign whose scepter [mankind] cannot refuse to acknowledge."[28] But the novelty in Moreau, which Bossuet would never have imagined, was his connection of this sovereign voice to the *conscience publique*—that is, to the reactions of "those who, having by themselves no coactive power, seize the strongest of all powers" and offer to interpret the voice of God. The "public voice" is nearly

[26] Jacques Necker, *De l'administration des finances de la France* (Paris, 1784), p. 58.

[27] Letter of de la Chalotais to M. de Caradeuc, cited in A. de Moy, *Le Parlement de Bretagne et le pouvoir royal au XVIIIᵉ siècle* (Angers, 1909), p. 303.

[28] Jacob-Nicolas Moreau, *Principes de morale, de politique et de droit public* (Paris, 1777–89), 1:59. Moreau defines public conscience as "the general cry of reason, justice, [and] humanity."

identical here to the divine voice. That Moreau felt the need to call *la conscience publique* to his aid testifies better than anything else to the extent to which the concept of public opinion had a polemic function at the time. (Indeed, it lay at the heart of all polemic, as seen in the use that Palissot made of the concept against the philosophes.)[29] Public opinion was a "counterforce." It was even, in physiocratic thought, the only imaginable counterforce. It was trotted out whenever thought turned to opposition. The next problem is to ascertain the source of the new tribunal's authority.

First of all, its authority came from the conditions under which it functioned. Public opinion was an impersonal and anonymous tribunal. In its verdicts every individual could hear the voice of all, thus the voice of no one, and could, in the last analysis, believe he was hearing his own voice—an irresistible argument for all schools of thought, from Rousseau to the physiocrats, that held mediation in horror. Furthermore, these unsigned verdicts were published—that is, they were set before everyone's eyes—an operation that at the time was accorded much intellectual, aesthetic, and moral merit. To make visible was to instruct, in the direct line of a sensationalism that held it sufficient to show in order to educate and convince. This was demonstrated by the growing demand, as the century progressed, for opening archives, museums, and gardens to the public. To make visible was also to cure the ills of a state mined by clandestinity and the practice of secrecy. Compared with this openness, the royal position quite evidently was working against the trend when it tirelessly reminded the *parlements* that the king would receive their *remontrances* "when secrecy conserves their decency and utility." It was also ineffective. To think for even a moment that the law of silence would suffice, Prost de Royer remarked, was to misunderstand the foreign press, "avid to publish everything and to disfigure everything."[30] Furthermore, it was to misunderstand men, who, according to Morellet, one must never lead "blindly."[31] Finally, it was to misunderstand the interests of the ministry. Malesherbes's writings are exemplary of the disadvantages to a minister in surrounding administrative acts with a "legal and impenetrable" mystery. From the *Mémoire sur la librairie* to the *remontrances* of the Cour

[29] Charles Palissot, *Petites lettres sur de grands philosophes* (Paris, 1757).

[30] Antoine Prost de Royer, *Dictionnaire de jurisprudence* (Lyon, 1781–88), 2:837–38. He adds, "What? Have we so long permitted a mysterious and impenetrable mystery to envelop the two things most important to public well-being, criminal procedure and the administration?"

[31] Abbé André Morellet, *Réflexions sur les avantages de la liberté d'écrire et d'imprimer* (London, 1775), p. 39.

des Aides, his writings owe their unity to this obsession for visibility. They opposed to absolutist policy, which was never public, a monarchic policy of total openness, in which the written word would guarantee constancy and regularity and the chief advantage of which would be a greater morality in comportment.[32] This was, in fact, the solution discovered by the government of Poland: "to have all citizens feel themselves incessantly before the eyes of the public."[33] This was a way of tearing people away from the pursuit of their personal interests and of bringing about a veritable conversion, also described by Necker.[34] On the one hand, the individual gave up the approbation of a supportive circle of friends; on the other, he earned "the love of the public" (*l'amour public*).

An anonymous tribunal visible to all. There was general agreement on the conditions of its judgment, but its criteria of judgment had changed in equal measure. The literature of eulogy clearly demonstrates this. Merit was contrasted here to birth, the city to the court, liberty to deference. This meant that the new tribunal acted as a court of appeals, that it offered a second chance to victims of injustice and arbitrary fortune. It was presented as a great dream of reparation and compensation bolstered by highly symbolic victories such as the rehabilitation of Calas. Public opinion had become a concept of recourse just as ductile and elastic as the opposing concept of abuse, the polemic function of which seemed boundless.

Countertribunal or not, public opinion was still a tribunal. Far from breaking with the older ways of thinking, this new court took over from its model—with a revealing inertia—components of infallibility, externality, and unity. If not infallible, at least its efficacy flowed like an unstoppable torrent. All writers from Rousseau to Beaumarchais held that one could never contest the *cri public* with impunity, for "if at times judges pronounce [sentence] on every citizen, at all times the

---

[32] In Malesherbes's mind, "publicity" establishes a direct communication between the people and the king; there was a pact sealed between administrators, whose task it was to hide and to dissimulate.

[33] Jean-Jacques Rousseau, *Considérations sur le Gouvernement de Pologne,* in *Oeuvres complètes* (n. 13 above), 3:1019.

[34] Necker, *De l'administration des finances de la France* (Paris, 1784), p. 21. Necker presents a portrait of the sensitive administrator: "The favors [and] the acts of courtesy of the Great trouble the imagination of the private man, but they are an object of indifference for the true public man. . . . He will thus renounce particular recognition. . . . To praise, he will prefer those secret blessings of the people which he will not hear, and that public opinion that is slow to form and whose judgments one must await with patience."

mass of the citizens pronounce on each judge."[35] As the century progressed, this efficacy tended increasingly to be confused with the movement of history itself. Historical change was to be credited to the universal force of what Condillac called "the law of opinion," in particular to changes "advantageous to the people," as Sieyès said of the Third Estate.[36]

The second borrowed trait was externality. As a prime mover of history, public opinion constrained individual opinion to recognize it as a superior external force. It seemed just as vain to quarrel with it as with the self-evidence of the geometrical truths that the physiocrats, in their contempt for diversity, celebrated as the one authority. It is here that the substitutive function of public opinion was best revealed. It had, in theory, replaced the powers of heaven and earth in returning men to possession of their decisions, but it had not eliminated appeal to a transcendent authority, the unifying and coercive characteristics of which it had taken over. By the same token, just as authorities in classical antiquity were faced with the insubordination of individual liberty, public opinion was faced with the caprice of individual opinion, with which it had to come to terms.

III. Public Opinion and Individual Opinion

Compromise was imperative since public opinion could not exist without individual opinion—that is, without independent beings capable of opining. I might even suggest that public opinion had this force of appeal only because the social bond was no longer felt as primary and its weakening permitted the discovery of logically anterior, logically independent, and logically coequal individual opinions. The moment one admitted the absolute priority and self-sufficiency of individual opinion, the existence and the authority of public opinion became problematic. How to escape the "vexations" of opinion?[37] How, out of the teeming mass of individual opinions that had already been delivered, could one draw anything but arbitrary decisions? Two formidable questions needed to be resolved: the nature of individual obligation toward public opinion, since authority must be founded so as to assure that the individual

---

[35] Pierre-Augustin Caron de Beaumarchais, "Addition au supplément du mémoire à consulter servant de réponse à Madame Goezman," in *Oeuvres complètes* (Paris, 1876), p. 261.

[36] Emmanuel Sieyès, *Qu'est-ce que le Tiers-Etat?* ed. Roberto Zapperi (Geneva, 1970), p. 215.

[37] This was a topic that reappeared constantly throughout the century. See Legendre de Saint-Aubin (n. 10 above).

ceding to it ceded to himself, and the formation of public opinion, since it was clear that once formed, it swept individual consent along with it. But what exactly was it composed of?

The solution that the century invented (and that moved Habermas to give it credit for having invented the concept of public opinion) came from the physiocrats.[38] In order for public opinion to have the infallibility that engaged unquestioned and unanimous assent, it was necessary and sufficient that it be another name for the self-evident. To cede to the self-evident was not to cede. It was to imitate geometers in the face of mathematical verities: they "cede" only to their own inherent reason, which was, as Euclid insisted,[39] the true despot. All writers held that "no public denies an obvious truth."[40] These Cartesians found an eminently anti-Cartesian solution to their problem. The insubordination of the will to the intelligence seemed to them so improbable that, unlike Descartes, they could not imagine that man confronted with the truth could fail to adhere to it. Physiocratic thought, even when forced to admit the inconstancy of opinion (as in Le Mercier de la Rivière), held that opinion always ended up ceding to the evident. Intellectual evidence in fact did not reside in the individual: it was a relation between objects that remained rigorous and fixed no matter what being contemplated it. Understandably, public opinion as viewed by the physiocrats (along with the public instruction that they held desirable) was totally free of psychopedagogy. When an individual listened to public opinion, he did not need to effect a conversion involving his dispositions and his particular inclinations. He was subjecting himself to a searching light all the more unavoidable because it emanated from his own reason. Even the sovereign of the physiocrats, the despot "imbued with his obligations," was none other than reason moved by the evident, incapable of erecting any government but a rational one.

Should individuals wait to be illuminated by an encounter with public opinion in a self-evident form, or is it their task to bring it to light? Choice of the first made individual opinion a consequence; choice of the second made it an antecedent. The question was often resolved in a circular fashion. With one choice, individual opinion was indeed the fruit of the new sociability tried and tested in a century of enlightenment. With the other, individual initiative effectively took charge of bringing public

[38] Habermas (n. 11 above).

[39] Pierre-Paul Le Mercier de la Rivière, *L'ordre naturel et essentiel des sociétés politiques* (London, 1767), p. 142.

[40] Said by Malesherbes concerning the cadastral survey, cited in Elisabeth Badinter, *Les "Remontrances" de Malesherbes, 1771–1775* (Paris, 1985), p. 247.

opinion to maturity. "The effect of a clever administration," Necker wrote, "is to fortify moral ideas, to bind together opinions and sentiments by the bond of trust."[41] This supposed a current state in which a unified opinion of this sort did not yet exist and in which, as Le Mercier de la Rivière said, "men are not truly men," and a future time in which it would reign uncontested.[42] Consequently, there were two moments at which opinion matured, and even the enlightened prince must submit to "the unanimous opinion of an enlightened nation, of a vast public opinion."[43] A master architect of the self-evident was needed in order to reach this epoch of philosophic plenitude. Here was where the enlightened man entered the picture, and this was what explained his prestige. He had already met and recognized evidence in the books he had read and the circles he had frequented. He must now occupy himself with presenting it to the less enlightened. He was not a mediator but a conductor of the evident. This was how Condorcet viewed him.

When they chose the enlightened man as their means for conveying evidence, the physiocrats took an easy way out. To accept that public opinion be made simply imitation (supposing, like Hume, that the unavoidable overlapping of individuals in society irresistibly brought nations and cultures closer together) would be tantamount to allowing the mediation of influences. But the enlightened man was not a mediator but a spokesman for and a carrier of evidence. His role was totally provisory and ended when he had managed to transmit what was evident to him. His very dullness made clear that his role was not that of a manipulator but a revealer of opinion.

This was an elegant solution, but it shows all the more clearly the strange mixture of archaism and modernity that went into the concept of public opinion during this period. The "spirit of the times" had at least three reasons to hesitate before the concept of public opinion as a pure aggregate of individual wills, a compromise of varying origins and results struck between dissidences and divergences. These three reasons show proof, each in its way, of the difficulty of giving up the archaic dream of integration within the collective. They also show how

[41] Necker, *De l'administration des finances* (n. 26 above), p. 12.

[42] Le Mercier de la Rivière. But this "inconstant" and "stormy" state did not last long. It ceded to "the evidence which subjects it while enlightening it and denaturing it" (pp. 357–58).

[43] Guillaume-François le Trosne, *De l'ordre social, ouvrage suivi d'un traité élémentaire sur la valeur, l'argent, la circulation, l'industrie et le commerce intéreur et extérieur* (Paris, 1777), p. 259. At a first stage, the enlightened prince must accept the advice and counsel of a senate of landed proprietors; at a later stage, he can refer to public opinion.

strongly divergence of opinion was still connected to the idea of misfortune in people's minds.

The first difficulty consisted in admitting that enlightened men could think differently and that individual opinion could maintain its right to refuse the yoke of collectivity. Oddly enough, the only writer to have a clear awareness of the problem was Mably, in whom we are more accustomed to finding the naive and didactic voluntarism of the enlightened legislator, but who nonetheless maintained that individual opinions have a vocation to resist obliteration in a public opinion that imposed fusion and rationality. This is, on the one hand, because he was not ready to accept that opinion, which, he admitted, governed men, could be equated with evidence, which, failed to govern them. On the other hand, it is because Mably, imbued with the Cartesian psychology of the passions, had reflected on the conditions of belief: "We are not so difficult as to believe only the truth of evidence. We would like to believe, we need to believe; a passably reasonable opinion suffices us. For lack of a likely opinion, we will adopt a ridiculous one."[44]

Mably's disagreement with the physiocrats arose out of a reflection that started from an identical base but led to opposite results on what unites men. The belief that men are the same is obviously essential to the concept of public opinion. But what exactly was meant by "the same men"? "Same," for the physiocrats, meant that men were absolutely interchangeable because their intelligence was identical. Thus they felt no conflict and showed no resistance to what was evident. This, in turn, meant that public opinion was by necessity united. For Mably, men were subjected in equal measure to passions and special interests, thus they were in conflict with one another, which allowed only ephemeral coalescences of opinions. But Mably was alone in accepting without difficulty the conflictual nature of social life, which a modern view of public opinion takes as axiomatic.

The legitimacy of numbers offered a second drawback. If one chose to believe that the isolated opinions that formed public opinion bore equal weight and if one wanted to compare aggregates of individual opinions, one had to count. How was this possible? Garat objected to Suard that numerical equality was chimerical. Out of thirty million opinions, at least twenty million would be "voiceless." How could one

---

[44] Gabriel Bonnot de Mably, *Doutes proposés aux philosophes économistes sur l'ordre naturel et essentiel des sociétés politiques* (The Hague, 1768), pp. 48–49.

prevent having "phrases"[45]—that is, once again, the discourses of men gifted with a particular quality, of enlightened men—come between those voiceless opinions and the opinion counters? In short, this would not really be counting, which was a manner of saying that it was impossible to accept the omnipotence of the majority. The only author to consider the question squarely was perhaps Beaumarchais, and he did so only in the quite special domain of judgment on taste. Beaumarchais held the public to be a fiction that did not hold up under examination and a collective being permanently threatened with dissolution and dispersion, constrained to give way to "the judgment of the smaller number"—to intrigue and to influence. But what was true in the intellectual domain was no longer true in the realm of the "objects of taste and of sentiment."[46] Where feeling was concerned, one man's judgment was as good as another's. In aesthetic matters, judgments could be counted and the choice of the majority trusted: numbers decided. This is a strange statement, but its very singularity has the merit of showing how much the century hesitated at the idea of the legitimacy of the majority. Even the man who had treated the logical problem of the procedure by which individual preferences joined to become a collective decision imposable as law on the collectivity— even Condorcet—hesitated to recognize validity in the law of majority rule unless at the same time the rationality of that law could be demonstrated. The sole social obligation was "to obey, in the actions that must follow a common rule, not one's own reason, but the collective reason of the greatest number. I say its reason, and not its will. For the power of the majority over the minority . . . does not extend to obliging submission when it evidently contradicts reason."[47]

This hesitation obviously implied a similar retreat before the idea of representation, which would have had the effect of putting numbers to divisions of opinion. In the same book in which Garat reported a clash of opinions between Suard and Wilkes (in reality, a discussion "between two Englishmen, so much was M. Suard one by enlightenment"—though of the Tory variety, to be sure), he has Suard deliver the principal argument against representation. As representatives would be capable only of representing public opinion, and as this was single,

---

[45] Dominique-Joseph Garat, *Mémoires historiques sur la vie de M. Suard, sur ses écrits et sur le XVIIIᵉ siècle*, 2 vols. (Paris, 1820), 2:92–98.

[46] Beaumarchais, *Essai sur le genre dramatique sérieux*, published in introduction to the first edition of *Eugénie* (Paris, 1767), p. 7.

[47] Condorcet, "De la nature des pouvoirs politiques dans une nation libre," in *Oeuvres complètes*, ed. D. J. Garat and P. J. G. Cabanis (Paris, 1804), 15:113.

representatives could not divide into parties. To be sure, there were debates. But they arose and developed "before the gallery of the nation, which listens with meditative attention but does not divide." Since the resolution of a political problem was no different from the solution to a mathematical problem or a problem in chess, "everyone deposes and gives witness according to his conscience and goes in peace." The consciences of those who listened could not be affected differently, and parties had no need to form. We are close here to Saige's *Catéchisme du citoyen*.[48] For Saige, representation constantly threatened to plunge all of society back into the dangers of the state of nature. And of course we are also close to Rousseau.

Definitions of public opinion in Rousseau varied considerably. One could garner a good many passages from his writings in which *l'estime public* or *le murmure public* served as barriers to despotism or in which public opinion had a valuable supervisory and regulatory function during those moments at which sovereignty was dispersed without being, as Rousseau put it, annihilated or dead. But there are also a good many texts in which the tendency of public opinion to crystallize in cliques or in special interest associations rendered it irremediably suspect: "The French have no personal existence; they think and act only in masses, each of them by himself alone is nothing. However, there is never in a collective body any disinterested love of justice."[49] The logic of public opinion was to express itself in a number of fragmented meetings that diluted the political bond by fixing the citizen's gaze on those meetings. This public opinion, furthermore, was manipulable, as the Rousseau of the *Considérations sur le gouvernement de Pologne* well knew. This meant that there would always be the threat of there being deceivers and the deceived and of sectarian interests making themselves masters of public opinion. Rousseau, more perspicacious than the dreamers who envisioned a unified public opinion, foresaw that its underlying nature was to shatter into differing representations. Thus it had not the least infallibility and needed constant rectification. In short, it was not a rule of justice, and it portrayed the general will only by usurpation.

This brief recapitulation of thought concerning public opinion in the eighteenth century shows both profound agreement and great perplexity. There was agreement that public opinion played a major role in the dynamism of history. This conviction, as we have seen, was prepared by the old image of an unsinkable opinion impossible to stifle on a long-

---

[48] Joseph Saige, *Catéchisme du citoyen; ou, Elémens du droit public français par demandes et réponses* ("In France," 1788).

[49] Rousseau, *Rousseau juge de Jean-Jacques* (n. 15 above), 1:965.

term basis. Henceforth, everyone saw public opinion as the primary cause of historical vicissitudes, which followed its deepest currents. It was, Constant was to say, "the life of states."[50] When public opinion faltered, states wasted away; when it rebounded, they revived. This subterranean pulse, what little one could gather of it, was what kept history from madness.

Since these movements, even when they were contravened in the short term, ultimately presented an unambiguous trajectory, since they furnished a progressive revelation of reason and a concordance of events with values and of minds with the truth, it is quite understandable that this early version of historicism presented a far from somber picture. The triumph of public opinion could be delayed, collective assent could even be coerced or constrained by doubtful means and pass for public opinion (and, an important point, success might not be the criterion of truth). Reason could temporarily lack enlightenment. The fact remained that sooner or later true public opinion would triumph. The history of the world led up to the arrival of a government of reason and of the progressive assimilation by the common consciousness of truth, which the philosophes had discovered.

This necessary forward march, I might note, was not the march of necessity. Even if by rights historical reality could be rationalized, it was not rational from beginning to end. Individual opinion remained the interpreter of public opinion, and subjectivity the point of departure for the temporal process. This was a tempered historicism, in which historical dynamism was the work of human action.

There were two quite different ways to represent public opinion on the basis of this agreement, however. One was modern, and carried the individualistic and egalitarian premises of public opinion to their logical consequences. This view refused to see public opinion as more than the spontaneous result of combined dissidences and divergences, which thrust up from the bottom, starting with opinions, those teeming, eternally preexistent volitional atoms. In this perspective, public opinion, which arose from the social, was not in the hands of political authority. The idea that governments could direct the opinions of men was absurd: authority could not "lull peoples to sleep or awaken them in accordance with its pleasures or momentary fancies."[51]

---

[50] Benjamin Constant, *Principes de politique* (Geneva, 1980), p. 137.

[51] Ibid., p. 128. According to Constant, the relation between the government and public opinion was even to be completely reversed: "The lethargy of a nation in which there is no public opinion is communicated to its government, no matter what it does; not being able to keep [the nation] awake, it finishes by dozing off with it" (p. 149).

What were the rules of suitable conduct for the philosopher, the moralist, the educator, or the politician who adopted this idea of public opinion? They were all negative since one needed only to wait, to know how to set limits, and to forbid oneself to forbid. Knowing how to wait was important, for impatience was useless, and it was enough to let national judgment form without interference. Setting limits was necessary, for there was in mankind's existence a space that escaped public opinion and fell under a purely individual jurisdiction. Avoidance of constraint was needed, for the only way one could claim to direct opinion was by disguising one's own voice as an impersonal pronouncement. Political writers, Constant was to say, believed that they were saying something substantive when they said "one must direct the opinions of men. One must not abandon men to their own divagations. But these words, 'one must, one should,' do they not refer to men? One might believe that they apply to a different species."[52] The logic of a belief in the preeminence of the social over the political and a public opinion rooted in the liberty of subjects dictated a renunciation of political voluntarism. One could not make public opinion come to pass; it was enough to receive its message.

This tranquil acceptance of a spontaneous movement of the social, most strikingly seen in Constant, was not, however, the most widely held belief at the end of the century. Almost all writers recalled Hobbes's divided opinion, which was even a source of unhappiness. It was this sort of opinion, as Rousseau wrote, that by "obliging us always to ask others what we are," makes all mankind sworn enemies.[53] But who among his contemporaries did not share Rousseau's horror of partial communities such as these? Who accepted without difficulty the permanent reconciling of divergences? Who was not concerned with conjuring away the threat of dissolution of political and social bonds? All these fears joined together to bring back the archaic dream of full integration in the collectivity and unified public opinion.

In this backward-looking view of public opinion, the rules of conduct for the legislator and the educator are obviously reversed: do not wait, do not limit, but intervene. Do not wait, for individual opinions need energetic rectification, the constant presence of a materialized social bond, and ongoing practice in citizenship. Do not limit, for the separating out of a private sphere proffers a threat of dissolution that authorizes an omnipotent power to keep even the most intimate manifestations of indi-

[52] Ibid., p. 74.
[53] Jean-Jacques Rousseau, *Discours sur l'origine et les fondements de l'inégalité parmi les hommes,* in *Oeuvres complètes* (n. 13 above), 3:193.

vidual opinion under surveillance. Intervene, since public opinion is imposed on corrupt and depraved opinions from above; thus the primacy of the political over the social.

One might interpret this cohesive and coercive depiction of public opinion as anachronistic. The archaic and the modern do not represent two moments, however, but two faces of a genuinely contradictory concept that supposed that one could simultaneously conceive of divergences and unity. In this sense, we must not be surprised to see public opinion recoil before modern innovations as the century waned, even though it took the place of conventional authorities. It is precisely because it replaced them that it borrowed archaic traits from them and that its most fervent partisans, imprisoned in an earlier mental framework, continued to assign it a master[54] and to see it as stable.

It is in no way forcing the picture to see the French Revolution as an illustration of the two aspects of this concept. The Revolution was indeed, as its partisans described it, the moment at which obedience to external necessity stopped and obedience to the presence of reason in itself and to the realization of the universal ideal by means of the opinion of reasonable men—public opinion—began. But it was also the moment of an unexpected return to an adoration of necessity under the pretext of a horror of factions and in the interests of a dream of perfect unity between the community and its guides and the complete absorption of individuals in citizenship. This explains why the Jacobin texts so quickly dropped the term "public opinion"—still too marked by liberty and subjectivity—in favor of the more unifying and coercive concept of *esprit public* or the more virtuous *conscience publique,* as Saint-Just preferred.[55] Reduced emphasis on public opinion during the revolutionary decade is a perfect illustration of the paradox that Constant noted: uniformity never met with more favor than during a revolution carried out in the name of the rights and the liberty of man.

---

[54] On this question, see Paul-Henri-Dietrich, baron d'Holbach, *Ethocratie, ou le gouvernement fondé sur la morale* (Amsterdam, 1776), in particular the last chapter, "Des moyens que le gouvernement peut employer pour réformer les moeurs et pour exciter les hommes à la vertu."

[55] Antoine-Louis-Léon de Saint-Just, *Rapport à la Convention sur la police générale,* 26 germinal II (Paris, 1794): "The word is not *esprit,* but *conscience.* The public spirit is in [people's] heads; and as everyone cannot have an equal influence of understanding and enlightenment, public spirit is an impetus from without. Have a public conscience, then, for all hearts are equal by their sense of evil and good, and it is composed of the penchant of the people for the common good" (p. 9).

A Mutation in Elite Political Culture: The French Notables and the Defense of Property and Participation, 1787*

Vivian R. Gruder

> . . . It is as advantageous to the maintenance of royal authority as it is in conformity with the fundamental principles of monarchy that there should exist a national interest which ties subjects to their sovereign. Nothing is better to revive this interest and through it to give a new resilience to the entire body politic than to have the taxpayers' representatives deliberate on the allotment of taxes . . . [which] excites a sort of patriotic effervescence that, if managed wisely, can do much good. [Mid-November 1786]

> Authority is never stronger than when it . . . is supported by reason and the national interest. . . . To create this interest, or to permit it to develop, will reinforce rather than weaken monarchical power . . . and will silence particular interests by enabling the general interest to express itself. [Late November 1786][1]

With these words the controller general Calonne tried to convince Louis XVI to accept his program of reforms. Though the menace of impending bankruptcy had driven the minister to draft his reforms, he was attempting to give to his plan a meaning larger than a desperate effort to salvage

* This article first took form as a paper entitled " 'No Taxation without Representation': The Assembly of Notables of 1787 and the 'Pre-Revolution' in France," presented in March 1981 at the Conference on the History of Parliaments at Emory University, Atlanta, Georgia, and was among the conference papers that appeared in a special issue of *Legislative Studies Quarterly* (7, no. 2 [May 1982]: 263–79). This paper was also presented in May 1981 at the first annual History Conference of the City University of New York. My thanks to Peter Manicas and Carlo Poni for reading earlier versions, and to Keith Baker for his valuable advice.

[1] Archives nationales (AN), K 164, no. 4^{2A} fols. 18–19, 23–26, and K 677, no. 138 (both published in Hans Glagau, *Reformversuche und Sturz des absolutismus in Frankreich [1774–1788]* [Munich, 1908], pp. 352–75).

This essay originally appeared in the *Journal of Modern History* 56 (December 1984).

the royal treasury through higher taxes. He had in mind a political design founded on three premises: royal authority would be fortified; public opinion would support the kinds of changes he intended to introduce; and all the reforms, in particular the establishment of provincial assemblies, would revive a political consciousness in the nation, would attach the public to the pursuit of "national interests." Those engaging in public activities in the new institutions he proposed would become better aware of the problems of government and of the interests shared by the Crown and the public. They would more willingly obey laws which in part they would help to make by advising the king. If, nonetheless, opposition arose, Calonne had an explanation ready. Opposition would come only from the "privileged, who do not fear opposing their particular interest to the general interest, and would dare complain about paying general taxes in proportion to their property. But . . . their voice would be drowned out by the voice of the public, which would necessarily be stronger; especially would the establishment of assemblies . . . in districts and provinces give to authority the aid of that national interest which presently is nothing, and which if well-directed can smooth away all difficulties."[2] Here were introduced the two themes which, in contrapuntal fashion, became the leitmotiv in the flurry of events and crises of the two succeeding years, in particular in the history of that Assembly of Notables which Calonne would soon call into being: "privilege" versus "national interest."

The controller general perceived that change was at work among Frenchmen, that for some time they desired reforms — a unified national market, freer trade, more equitable taxes, and a role in public affairs. Yet his insights remained partial, limited by the habits and attitudes formed through years of service as a royal official and perhaps also by the needs of a minister to defer to the wishes of the king.[3] Thus he tended to minimize political change in favor of administrative and economic changes, thinking that the latter would have sufficient appeal in themselves. Though aware that a political spirit was forming, Calonne did not fathom how far it had spread among the French, how deeply it had penetrated minds, and how much it had transformed older attitudes. Ironically, he believed that he had to nurture into being the nation's political consciousness; instead he would permit an opposition to spring to life that would reject many of his reforms and revise others to suit their own design, not that of the Crown or minister. He erred in assuming that his reforms, however beneficent and desired, would easily gain public support and strengthen royal authority. He erred also in impugning to his opponents

[2] AN, K 164, no. 4[2A], fols. 22–23.

[3] For the king's supervision of Calonne's selection of members to the Assembly of Notables, see AN, 297 AP 3 (263 Mi 3), nos. 28 and 29.

the desire to defend their "particular interests" as "privileged," their opposition a refusal to submit their property to regular and equal taxation.

Calonne's initiative in convening an Assembly of Notables to approve reforms provided the forum in which a political culture, hitherto dormant or amorphous, could express itself; in which hopes the minister had aroused and dashed were reshaped into criticisms, claims, and goals made more clear and coherent, more adroit and forceful in contact with the concrete reality of government policies. In the Notables' debates, arguments echoing old plaints yielded to new attitudes and outlooks. "Privilege" ceded to that "national interest" and "patriotic effervescence" that Calonne spied and extolled, and which he now "excited" in a public made wider and more alert as national attention focused on the Assembly of Notables.

I. THE NOTABLES IN OPPOSITION

The 144 members of the Assembly of Notables—seven princes of the blood, fourteen bishops and archbishops, thirty-six "nobles," thrity-eight chief officers of sovereign courts, twelve members of the royal council, twelve deputies of provincial estates, and twenty-five municipal representatives, a social and political elite of prestigious public officials all but a handful of whom were nobles[4]—met for the first time in formal assembly on February 22, 1787. On the following day the controller general presented to them his reform proposals, the first and most important of which were the establishment of provincial assemblies in provinces without estates and a new, uniform tax on all land. Other reforms in an ambitious program included freedom for the grain trade; the elimination of internal trade barriers with tolls on the national frontiers; lower duties on many goods in commerce; reimbursement of the clergy's debt; conversion of the *corvée* (labor service on roads) into a money tax; reform of the *gabelle* (salt tax); and repayment of the public debt at regular intervals.[5] From February until May 1787 the Notables, meeting in seven committees (or bureaux, as they were called) of twenty to twenty-two

---

[4] The category of "noblesse" designated military officers, of whom twenty-eight were also *gouverneurs, commandants en chef*, or *lieutenants-généraux* in provinces, and six were also peers. Among the deputies of provincial estates the clergy, nobility, and third estate each had four representatives. All but two (at most five) of these 144 Notables belonged to the noble order, as determined by a genealogical study based on manuscript sources, printed genealogies, and biographical dictionaries in the Bibliothèque nationale.

[5] For the list of reform projects, see AN, C 1 (2), fols. 201–4, and K 677, no. 135.

members each, debated these issues.[6] The events surrounding the Assembly of Notables have been amply treated by Albert Goodwin and Jean Egret.[7] Here I shall attempt instead to enter into the mental world of the Notables through the record of their working sessions, indicating their perceptions, responses, and objectives as they grappled with the problems the Crown's reform projects unveiled to them. In the course of their work they pieced together arguments and counterproposals which, in sum, afforded little place for privilege but advanced the claims of property and especially of political participation. These goals, linked together, offered a new vision of public life and acquired unprecedented power of appeal and potential for change. A close examination of the Notables' debates, especially on the land tax and provincial assemblies, may substantiate what I suggest was a mutation in elite political culture in the late ancien régime.

A. Fiscal Arguments

The land tax Calonne introduced to the Assembly would replace the *vingtième* with a new, graduated tax on all landed property with no exemptions and in proportion to the wealth produced by the land to a maximum of 10 percent of the product. The controller general sought in this way to eliminate individual inequities but especially the regional disparities by which inhabitants of some provinces paid twice or more the amount of taxes paid in other provinces.[8] The Notables opposed this

---

[6] Each of the seven bureaux was headed by a prince of the blood and had members drawn from each of the categories represented among the Notables.

[7] Albert Goodwin, "Calonne, the Assembly of French Notables of 1787 and the Origins of the 'Révolte Nobiliaire,' " *English Historical Review* (May and September, 1946), pp. 202–34, 329–77; and Jean Egret, *La Pré-Révolution Française, 1787–1788* (Paris, 1962), pp. 5–61.

[8] For the land tax proposal see AN, C 1 (2), fols. 161–76. In the meeting on March 2 with deputies from the seven bureaux, Calonne presented a table with calculations of the disproportionate provincial tax levies which Necker had published in 1784. See Archives des Affaires Etrangères, Mémoires et Documents, France (hereafter, AAE, Mém. et Doc., Fr.), 1402, fol. 117 and also fol. 17v; Pierre Renouvin, ed., *L'Assemblée des Notables de 1787: La conférence du 2 mars* (Paris, 1920), p. 42; Jacques Necker, *L'Administration des finances de la France*, 3 vols. (Paris, 1784), 1: 166–67. Taxes ranged from 12 *livres* per capita (Brittany and Lorraine) to 30 *livres* (the *généralité* of Lyon), the median being 19 *livres* (Provence, Burgundy, the Three Bishoprics) while in the *généralité* of Paris it was 64 *livres* per capita. Most *pays d'élections* were in the higher category and most *pays d'états* or provinces recently incorporated in the kingdom in the lower category. The most outspoken defenders of provincial privilege among the Notables were from provinces in the lower half of this scale.

tax at the same time that they embraced the principle of fiscal equality.[9] For the minister and the Notables, and their contemporaries, equality of taxation had two meanings: the law would no longer exempt from taxes but impose the same tax on all; and taxes would be in proportion to wealth, the actual taxes paid thus weighing more equally on each. Legal equality and proportionality were wed in practice through applying percentages or amounts of taxes graded to assessments of different forms or values of real wealth.[10] Many of the Notables sought to extend the application of fiscal equality, urging that a number of exemptions still remaining cease; that all land—of the clergy, princes, or the Crown, woodlands, houses, parks, and gardens for display of "luxury"—be taxed; that the "privileged" and the wealthiest proprietors pay their full share; and that the poorest pay lower taxes.[11] A few voices, a few declarations, the tacit acceptance of some current tax exemptions were signs

[9] 1st Bur.—AN, C 1 (3), fols. 6 ff., fols. 107v–9, 169v, 4 AP 188, no. 66; 2d Bur.—Bibliothèque de l'Arsenal (BA), MS 3976, fols. 314–17, 376–77, 683–85, 1023 ff., MS 3978, fols. 187 ff., AAE, Mém. et Doc., Fr., 1403, no. 171, Eleutherian Mills Historical Library (EMHL), Greenville, Dela., W2-4712; 3d Bur.—AN, C 2 (6), session of February 28 and following, "Cahier des délibérations," fols. 45, 80 ff.; 4th Bur.—AN, C 2 (6), fols. 9, 86–94, C 4 (11), session of February 27 and following, fols. 24–34, 69; 5th Bur.—AN, C 3 (7), session of February 28 and following, fols. 129–37, 169–70; 6th Bur.—AN, C 3 (7), session of February 28 and following, fols. 23–43, 52–53; 7th Bur.— AN, C 3 (7), session of February 28 and following, fols. 94 ff., 153–56. See also the bureaux' final statements on May 23.

[10] See Calonne's explanation of different tax rates on different qualities of land in Renouvin, ed., . . . *la conférence du 2 mars*, pp. 50–52. For contemporary support of proportional taxes, see *Encyclopédie méthodique: finances*, s.v. "Impôt" (Paris, 1785), 2: 535.

[11] These included: no tax exemptions through ennobling offices (third and seventh bureaux); payment by all proprietors of the money tax to replace the *corvée* (second, third, and fourth bureaux); and no exemption of nobles, clergy, and magistrates from the proposed new capitation tax (first, second, and sixth bureaux). See 1st Bur.—AN, C 1 (3), fols. 10–11, 24–25, 62v–65, 107v, 156, 166–70, BA, MS 3978, fol. 730, and Pierre Chevallier, ed., *Journal de l'Assemblée des Notables de 1787 par le comte de Brienne et Etienne Charles de Loménie de Brienne* (Paris, 1960), p. 28; 2d Bur.—BA, MS 3975, fols. 683, 690, 698 ff., MS 3976, fols. 77–80, 136–65, 301 ff., 332–37, 839–40, 1001 ff., 1016 ff., 1035–36, 1059, 1069, MS 3978, fols. 242, 620–25, 650, 657–59, 684–90, 738, 743, 754; 3d Bur.—AN, C 2 (6) "Cahier des délibérations," fols. 4–11, 45–49, 66, 84–88, and BA, MS 3978, fol. 754; 4th Bur.—AN, C 2 (6), fols. 9, 86–94, 115, C 4 (11), fols. 25 ff., 62, 98–101, BA, MS 3978, fol. 724; 5th Bur.—AN, C 3 (7), fols. 28, 32–35, 54–58, 87–89, 172–80, C 3 (10), no. 19, fols. 6–18; 6th Bur.—AN, C 3 (7), fols. 6–8, 34 ff., 51–65, BA, MS 3978, fols. 745–47; 7th Bur.—AN, C 3 (7), fols. 27, 42 ff., 51–55, 101–12, 134–38, 144–54, BA, MS 3978, fols. 743–47.

that privilege still had its defenders.[12] But support for tax equality far outweighed the defense of privilege by the evidence of the Notables' debates.

Privilege—fiscal exemption—by 1787 had been circumscribed and its material benefits diminished. The *taille* on the nonprivileged, mainly peasants, remained in reduced form even in the Crown's reform program (and the Notables urged further decreases). Yet since 1749, when the *vingtième* tax was introduced, the law curtailed privilege. For almost half a century nobles in France, the Notables among them, had been paying a tax on the land they owned or on noble land, as Betty Behrens convincingly demonstrated. These taxes may have increased less than did their rents as proprietors and their gains from selling surplus crops at rising prices, as Emmanuel Le Roy Ladurie has argued. Influence, underassessments, and other stratagems may also have reduced the share of taxes they paid, making the *vingtième* disproportionate in weight. For that reason Calonne, in 1787, sought to replace it with a new land tax. Yet the proportion of direct taxes on the land rose during the eighteenth century while the proportion of indirect taxes declined, as the evidence of Peter Mathias and Patrick O'Brien indicates. The land tax in France in the last decades of the ancien régime outweighed the land tax in Great Britain.[13] In little over a generation that tax which had been episodic became permanent, and from almost nothing climbed, in the letter of the

[12] Four out of seven bureaux tacitly accepted the Crown's proposals to exempt clergy, nobles, and magistrates from the new capitation tax and the money tax replacing the *corvée*. Nor did the Notables question the financing of poor relief from the *taille* tax, from which they were legally exempt. The arguments of three Notables in defense of fiscal privilege are documented: Le Blanc de Castillon (*procureur-général* of the Parlement of Aix) and Angran d'Alleray (*lieutenant-civil* of the Paris Châtelet) of the second bureau (BA, MS 3976, fols. 419–23, 428–29), and Joly de Fleury (*procureur-général* of the Paris Parlement) in the first bureau (Bibliothèque nationale [BN], fonds Joly de Fleury, MS 1040, fols. 251 ff., 271–86, 293).

[13] Betty Behrens, "Nobles, Privileges and Taxes in France at the End of the Ancien Régime," *Economic History Review*, 2d ser., 15 (November 1963): 451–75; G. J. Cavanaugh, "Nobles, Privileges and Taxes in France: A Revision Reviewed," *French Historical Studies* (Fall 1974), pp. 681–92; Emmanuel Le Roy Ladurie, "Pour un modèle de l'économie rurale française au XVIII siècle," *Mélanges de l'Ecole Française de Rome: Moyen âge, temps modernes* 85, no. 1 (1973): 11–12; Peter Mathias and Patrick O'Brien, "Taxes in Britain and France, 1715–1810: A Comparison of the Social and Economic Incidence of Taxes Collected for the Central Governments," *Journal of European Economic History* 5, no. 3 (Winter 1976): 601–50. Marcel Marion (*Les Impôts directs sous l'Ancien Régime principalement au XVIII siècle* [Paris, 1910], p. 120) calculated that direct taxes in France in 1789 were 40 percent of the total tax receipts.

law, to 5, 10, and in some years (since 1781) 15 percent of landed income. Those who paid felt a newly heavy burden, even if they were paying less than their full share. Already taxpayers in part by 1787, the Notables were not primarily concerned with defending fiscal privilege or opposing fiscal equality as they debated the land tax reform.

They were much more aware that a larger public might share their concerns and favor their efforts.[14] The tax on land in France fell on many more social groups than that in England. Both those who owned and those who cultivated the land had to pay. And ownership of land was widespread in the late eighteenth century, extending the range of taxation to the nobility who owned 20–25 percent of the land, the bourgeoisie who owned 30 percent, and the peasantry who owned about 40 percent (the clergy owned the remaining 10 percent of the land).[15] The mode of assessment and the structure of ownership assured that diverse groups bore the load of the land tax. In cutting back on privilege by extending taxation from commoners to nobles, the Crown inadvertently strengthened its adversaries. Over the long run it helped bring nobles and commoners together against the land tax both paid, offering to them the opportunity for joint "tax revolt."

The arguments and rhetoric heard in the Assembly of Notables may have been masks dissimulating selfishness in the guise of universality and generosity. Yet the faces they hid were not those of "feudal seigneurs" or Renaissance *gentilshommes* clinging to age-old principles that sanctioned material advantages.[16] Theirs were the faces of landowners with a keen eye for rents, income, and market gains; "proprietors" in the physiocratic image, who aimed to protect the economic resource on which the new tax would weigh and which they and many other Frenchmen owned or worked, the land. Since the 1750s agriculture had been drawn into an expanding network of market exchange, the interests of landowners more directly tied to commercial imperatives at the same time as the writings of the physiocrats and others offered a framework of economic

[14] See the outcry against the heavy tax burden in the 1780s by the author of the article "Imposition" in the *Encyclopédie méthodique: finances* (1785), 2: 529. The article "Impôt" supports the view that the French paid heavier taxes, especially land taxes, taking into account lower per capita income, than did the English (2: 541, esp. n. 1).

[15] Mathias and O'Brien, p. 612; for land distribution in France, see Emmanuel Le Roy Ladurie, *Carnival in Romans* (New York, 1979), p. 29. Peasants paying the *taille* and the *vingtième* or the substitute land tax still bore a heavier burden.

[16] For the nobles' defense of fiscal privilege in the late sixteenth century and in the mid-seventeenth century, see Le Roy Ladurie, *Carnival in Romans*, and R. Mousnier, J.-P. Labatut, and Y. Durand, *Deux cahiers de la noblesse pour les Etats-Généraux de 1649–1651* (Paris, 1965).

analysis.[17] Schooled in practical experience and from contemporary writings, the Notables, almost all of whom were landowners,[18] could respond to Calonne's tax with reasoned arguments, unraveling the baneful economic effects on agriculture of the proposed tax.

"We express our views as large proprietors who want in advance to be assured of disposing of their produce," commented the municipal representative of Strasbourg and former ambassador to the American states, Gérard, the lone voice in his bureau supporting the minister's proposal for tax payments in kind. His colleagues objected that paying in produce would prove inefficient and expensive and recommended instead money payments.[19] Through Gérard's words the Notables appear ill disposed to yield to the government in taxes the crops that were fetching steadily higher prices in the market. The author of the *Mémoires secrets* offered another interpretation. "The great seigneurs have especially opposed a land tax in kind, because they are in the habit of negotiating a set money tax, and thereby of escaping an equal apportionment of the tax, which makes true patriots wail."[20] Few wails entered into print in 1787, but there was much applause for the Notables' resistance to the new tax. Within four days of the start of debate, the controller general agreed to payments in money rather than produce for the land tax, and attacks shifted to another front.

The Notables next insisted on a land survey to determine the actual value of land, rather than the rent rolls that Calonne proposed; a land

[17] Pierre Goubert, "Société traditionelle et société nouvelle. II. Les groupes dominants: Les rentiers du sol," in *Histoire economique et sociale de la France, 1660–1789*, ed. F. Braudel and E. Labrousse (Paris, 1970), 2: 578–89, and Emmanuel Le Roy Ladurie, "De la crise ultime à la vrai croissance, 1690–1789," *Histoire de la France rurale*, vol. 2, *L'Age classique des paysans, 1340–1789* (Paris, 1975), pp. 159–599.

[18] All but eight of the Notables bore titles or had patronyms identifying them as landowners. Archbishops and bishops in the Assembly derived their income from the land, and most were descended from landed noble families.

[19] AAE, Mém. et Doc., Fr., 1402, fol. 38v; Loménie de Brienne in Chevallier, ed., *Journal de l'Assemblée de Notables*, pp. 3–12. For criticisms of a tax in kind in the Constituent Assembly, see René Stourm, *Les Finances de l'Ancien Régime et de la Révolution*, 2 vols. (Paris, 1885), 1: 114–21; and, among historians, see Jean Meuvret, "Comment les français du XVIIIe siècle voyaient l'impôt," *Etudes d'histoire économique* (Paris, 1971), p. 306, Gabriel Ardant, *Théorie sociologique de l'impôt*, 2 vols. (Paris, 1965), 1: 212–14, 407–12, and "Financial Policy and Economic Infrastructure of Modern States and Nations," *The Formation of National States in Western Europe*, ed. Charles Tilly (Princeton, N.J., 1975), pp. 182–83.

[20] *Mémoirs secrets pour servir à l'histoire de la république des lettres en France, depuis MDCCLXII jusqu'à nos jours* (1787), 34: 236.

survey, they claimed, was a more accurate method for assessing taxes since rents do not always reveal the true value of land. Theirs is a unique example in the eighteenth century of members of a landed class favoring *cadastres* for the purpose of tax assessments.[21] Yet land surveys would serve a double purpose: they were a means for assuring more equitable taxes and also promised security against frequent and repeated tax increases. Once the land was evaluated and taxes assessed accordingly, it was expected that the amount paid would remain unchanged for almost a generation (twenty to thirty years), freeing the land of added burdens and relieving the owners of anxieties.[22] The lengthy procedure of a land survey, one may speculate, might also have been a tactic to delay more accurate taxation; to the controller general, the many years required to complete a nationwide *cadastre* (and the costs of the operation) were sufficient reasons to reject the proposal in the hopes of obtaining immediate tax reform.

Successful in gaining money payments, set back on the land survey, the Notables now moved to other, more persistent arguments. "In all my days, I have never heard so much talk of gross product, net product, original and annual capital investment, rights of property," wrote the physiocrat Dupont de Nemours to the marquis de Mirabeau on March 6. (Dupont, as secretary of the second bureau headed by the comte d'Artois, knew well what the Notables were discussing.)[23] Drawing from the arsenal of physiocracy, the Notables rejected Calonne's proposal that taxes be assessed on the gross product of the land, recommending instead the "net product" as the base for taxes. Deducting the costs of cultivation (the "frais" and "avances") would, better than rent payments, permit taxes to be proportioned to differences in the fertility and productivity of the land, more fertile land requiring fewer costs and less fertile land incurring heavier costs of cultivation. Taxes on the "net product" would also leave untaxed the capital invested in agricultural improvements, which in turn yielded greater incomes through more sales of produce and higher land values, thus promoting greater agricultural production. As

[21] In the 1760s and 1770s the Parlement of Dijon opposed a *cadastre* (Pierre de Saint-Jacob, *Les Paysans de la Bourgogne du nord au dernier siècle de l'ancien régime* [Dijon, 1960], p. 335, n. 3). For Italian examples, see Renato Zangheri, "I catasti," *Storia d'Italia* 5, I (Turin, 1973): 761–806, and Luigi Dal Pane, *La finanza toscana degli inizi del secolo XVIII alla caduta del granducato* (Milan, 1965), chap. 5.

[22] In his *Compte rendu au roi* (1781), Necker referred to his order that once land estimates were completed, assessments for the *vingtième* should remain unchanged for twenty years (p. 63).

[23] EMHL, Winterthur MSS, ser. A, W2-279, fols. 46–47.

landowners, the Notables also accepted enthusiastically the minister's proposal for free trade in grain, a "most perfect" law, exulted one of the bureau. In a reversal of physiocratic teaching, but expressing views shared by Adam Smith and Jacques Necker, they objected that taxes weigh exclusively on the land and insisted they be equally apportioned on other forms of wealth, especially on the riches of "capitalistes" (that is, financiers) and *rentiers*, untouched by Calonne's land tax. Credit and speculative operations of financiers also drew their ire for the injuries caused to agriculture. High rates of interest for loans yielded greater profits than from the land, draining money from the countryside, contracting the market for land and depressing its value, while reducing employment opportunities for the rural population. The royal government should lower its rate of interest and make investments in landed property equally profitable.[24]

As the land already bore the major weight of taxes, the Notables launched their heaviest attacks against any increase in the land tax. Calonne's reform was to them the latest attempt to extract 40–50 million *livres* more from the land. Try as he might with intelligence and charm to explain that additional revenue would come from more accurate and equitable assessments and not from higher tax rates, the Notables saw only the final sum, greater than current tax yields.[25]

The original project specified set rates of taxation on the produce of the land (varying from one-twentieth on the most fertile lands to one-fortieth on the least productive lands) whose yield would vary as production increased or decreased. In years of good harvest the government would benefit through increased revenue, in years of poor harvest taxpayers would be cushioned and pay lower sums. Total government revenue, proportioned to national production, was not fixed in advance each year nor was the tax limited in time. Such a mode of assessment, known as a *taxe de quotité*, and its unlimited duration were fiscal innovations in the ancien régime, required in the Crown's view to meet constant and

[24] Renouvin, ed., . . . *la conférence du 2 mars*, passim; BA, MS 3978, fols. 724–32; 1st Bur.—AN, C 1 (3), fols. 6, 12, 19v, 24–25v, 30v–31, 160–72; 2d Bur.—BA, MS 3975, March 13, fols. 405–86, 513 ff., 532 ff., 544, 556 ff., 598–606, 616 ff., 633–39, 643–51, 678, 681 ff., 690 ff., 706–7, and March 21 and 23, MS 3976, fols. 915–18, 1023 ff.; MS 3978, fols. 187 ff., 478 ff., 609 ff., 643–49, 683–88; 3d Bur.—AN, C 2 (6), "Cahier des délibérations," fols. 7, 18–26, 68–69, 88; 4th Bur.—AN, C 2 (6), fols. 9–12, 18, 26–36, 115, C 4 (11), fols. 16–25, 62, 71–72, 100; 5th Bur.—AN, C 3 (7), fols. 17–28, 34, 53 ff.; 6th Bur.—AN, C 3 (7), fols. 2–12, 51; 7th Bur.—AN, C 3 (7), fols. 16–17, 26, 42–45, 145–46, 158–61, and C 4 (13), fols. 14, 45, 81, 113–21.
[25] Renouvin, ed., . . . *la conférence du 2 mars*, pp. 45, 53, 55.

rising financial needs.[26] A tax at a fixed rate whose sum varied annually and which was unlimited in time had only one meaning to the Notables: open-ended, constantly rising taxes on the land inviting government waste. It was, moreover, an arbitrary tax, the per capita sum not certain and fixed but varying each year, and the taxpayer, who would not know in advance how much he had to pay, could easily be the victim of unscrupulous tax collectors. Not the minister's scheme, expenses determining revenue and the taxpaying capacity of the nation setting the level of taxes, but the traditional practice of determining the needs of government in advance and limiting public expenses to definite and known needs was the Notables' alternative.[27]

Exact tax payments for individuals and exact tax revenue for the government, they argued, should be set in advance annually, each province allotted its levy, in turn each parish, and within the parish each taxpayer (in proportion to his income from the land and not exceeding 10 percent). The individual would not be responsible just for his own tax payment determined automatically by the proceeds of his land, as with a *taxe de quotité*. All the taxpayers having to pay a repartitional tax would be collectively responsible for paying the amount assigned to the parish, any individual paying less than his prorated share causing others to pay more. Villagers in their assemblies would be more vigilant in preventing underassessments and underpayments, and in opposing increases in the parish levy whose effects would raise taxes on each and all. The "invisible hand" of a repartitional tax, the single taxpayer protecting his own interests, would promote the interests of all and guarantee low and equal tax payments (in proportion to landed income). From year to year this tax would not change, especially would it not increase as production

[26] The *vingtième*, designed as a variable tax, had become a fixed tax (Marion, *L'Impôt sur le revenu*, pp. 201–2, 208).

[27] The physiocrat marquis de Mirabeau some years earlier criticized "a *fluctuating* tax scale" (abbé E. Lavaquery, *Le Cardinal de Boisgelin 1732–1804* [Angers, 1920], p. 124). Arguments similar to those of the Notables were also expressed by the Parlement of Bordeaux in the 1760s (William Doyle, *The Parlement of Bordeaux at the End of the Ancien Régime, 1771–1790* [New York, 1974], pp. 222–24) and in the *Encyclopédie méthodique: finances,* s.v. "Impôts" (1785), 2: 535, 537. The English ambassador, reporting to his government on the proposed tax reform, commented that Calonne was "laying down as a principle (however extraordinary it may appear) that it is not from economy that resources are to be expected but from an augmentation of the revenues . . ." (*Despatches from Paris, 1784–1790*, ed. Oscar Browning, 2 vols. [London, 1909], 1: 176). The Notables expressed ideas current in their day.

increased; improvements on the land and new cultivation would not be penalized but would remain untaxed, offering an incentive for greater agricultural output. In the words of the fifth bureau, only a repartitional tax conformed to the principles of "just and enlightened" government. This "best of all possible" taxes was not the vision of the Notables alone; the French revolutionaries adopted a repartitional tax, which succeeding generations of Frenchmen perpetuated until 1914.[28]

B. An Alternative Financial Program

A tax on land nonetheless should be a last resort. Before deciding on a new tax, the deficit should first be determined. Calonne's speech at the opening session on February 22, alluding to a deficit of 80 million *livres,* then his revelation at a special meeting on March 2 of an even higher deficit of 112 million *livres,* shocked the Notables. After four years of peace, why should the government be so short of funds? They could only suspect wrongdoing, and determined to uncover the truth. Their investigations carried them amid the confusions of government finance. Each of the seven bureaux arrived at different and uncertain estimates of the deficit, higher than Calonne's and as high as 140 million *livres,* from which they concluded that the royal treasury spent and wasted too much money.

"Our news consists of making the king work at economies, as one makes the people work for revenues," wrote one of the Notables, the archbishop of Aix.[29] He and other Notables turned their energies, during the last month of the Assembly's work, to budget cutting, drawing up detailed lists of reductions for the several households of the royal family

[28] 5th Bur., AN, C 3 (7), fol. 168; 3d Bur., AN, C 2 (6), "Cahier des délibérations," fols. 79–81; Loménie de Brienne in Chevallier, ed., *Journal de l'Assemblée des Notables,* pp. 7–10. An unspecified minority in the second bureau did favor a *taxe de quotité* (BA, MS 3976, fol. 993). For contemporary views and policies similar to the above, see Turgot-Dupont de Nemours, "Mémoire sur les municipalités, Septembre 1775, au Roi," in *Carl Friedrichs von Baden Briefleicher Verkehr mit Mirabeau und Du Pont,* ed. Carl Knies (Heidelberg, 1892), 1: 257, 259, 277, 282; Ardant, *Théorie sociologique de l'impôt,* 1: 200–204, 218–32, 463, 473–80; Georges Freche, "Compoix, propriété foncière, fiscalité et demographie historique en pays de taille réelle (XVIe–XVIIIe siècles)," *Revue d'histoire moderne et contemporaine* 18 (July–September 1971): 321–53, see 337; Marion, *Les Impôts directs,* pp. 44, 45, n. 1, 108–9, 160, 169, 327–34, 370–71; Jean Villain, *Le Recouvrement des impôts directs sous l'ancien régime* (Paris, 1952), pp. 279–82; and Adam Smith, *The Wealth of Nations,* ed. Edwin Cannan (London, 1961), 2: 350–51.

[29] AN, M 788, no. 92, fol. 1.

and for the ministries and administrative departments.[30] The king's brothers, Provence and Artois, who presided over the first and second bureaux, promised the Notables they would be more thrifty in the future. Marshals and military commanders recommended large cuts in appropriations for the armed services, along with higher pay for the common soldiers. All the bureaux urged the greatest reductions in the budgets of the war and navy departments and favored fewer and lower royal pensions and gifts. Less spending would make tax increases unnecessary, with happier effects for taxpayers. It was not quite that the Notables thought, in the old way, that the king had to live off "his own," the income from his domains. Ignorance bred by political exclusion of the demands the treasury had to meet, the "sweet" delusion Necker fostered (since the publication of his *Compte rendu* in 1781) of a surplus of royal funds, and the perennial instincts of taxpayers led them to believe that in times of peace, with income from existing taxes, there was no need for additional revenue, no needed public services to provide requiring constant outlays which inflation made even more expensive. If after inefficiencies and waste in government operations were eliminated and expenditures were cut a deficit remained, loans rather than taxes should make up the difference, as loans weighed less heavily at the moment on taxpayers.[31] If taxes were still necessary, then three bureaux, and possibly two others,

---

[30] See the meetings of the bureaux from April 26 on. For the debates on financial reforms and budget controls, see 1st Bur.—AN, C 1 (3), fols. 107v–9, 115–18, 151v, 164v; 4 AP 188, no. 66; Gérard, AAE, Mém. et Doc., Fr., 1402, fols. 66v, 73v; comte de Brienne, AN, 4 AP 188, nos. 13–14–38, 21, 46–47–48, 64–65 and in Chevallier, ed., *Journal de l'Assemblée des Notables,* p. 27; 2d Bur.—BA, MS 3976, fols. 320 ff., 448–55 ff., 472 ff.; MS 4546 fols. 74–75; AAE, Mém. et Doc., Fr., 1403, fol. 171; Loménie de Brienne, BN, nouv. acq. fr. 23615, fols. 177–86, 195, Public Record Office (PRO), (London), PC 1/125, X. 1/7470, fols. 276 ff.; Archives départementales, Meurthe-et-Moselle (hereafter, AD, M.-et-M.), W 1101 (6), "Journal particulier ou Mémoire sur l'Assemblée des Notables . . . ," Coeurderoy, Président, Parlement of Nancy, fols. 46 ff.; 3d Bur.—AN, C 2 (6), "Cahier des délibérations," fols. 50–56, and archbishop of Aix, "Mémoire sur la suppression des caisses intermédiaires," fols. 91–106; 4th Bur.—AN, C 2 (6), fols. 98–103, C 4 (11), fols. 39–55; 5th Bur.—AN, C 3 (7), fols. 129–37, 148–54, 160–62, 181; 6th Bur.—AN, C 3 (7), fols. 32–47, 63–68; 7th Bur.—AN, C 3 (7), fols. 94–130. Necker's *L'Administration des finances de la France* (1784) is filled with recommendations for government economies.

[31] 2d Bur., BA, MS 3976, fols. 294–95; 5th Bur., AN, C 3 (7), fols. 152–53; 7th Bur., duc de Cröy, AN, C 5 (15), no. 16, fol. 2. The author of the article "Impôts" in the *Encyclopédie méthodique:finances* (1785) favored loans instead of new taxes (2: 546).

reluctantly accepted a stamp tax, a vexatious impost but less burdensome to the poor than a land tax, recommending in addition higher duties on transactions involving the wealthy and high officeholders.

Economies, loans, and a stamp tax, the Notables convinced themselves, would suffice to remove the current deficit. Continued economies in the future would permit the debt to be paid off and the budget balanced, at which time a number of taxes, especially the existing land tax, could be reduced and ultimately eliminated.[32] So they envisioned in practice the principle they held of the "true character" of a tax, in the words of Loménie de Brienne, archbishop of Toulouse and member of the second bureau before becoming minister: ". . . that of being established only in just proportion with needs, of growing, diminishing, and ceasing with them [i.e., needs]."[33]

Government revenue in the future would come from the stamp tax, the tobacco monopoly and postal system, customs levied on the national borders, and perhaps other individual taxes. Industry and commerce would be lightly touched by remaining taxes. The poor would benefit. The *taille* and taxes on consumption would be reduced or eliminated; and the salt tax would be replaced by a money tax, no tax increase assured by retaining current although unequal regional levies for the *gabelle* while eliminating forced sales, investigations, confiscations, manhunts, and imprisonments.[34] "Capitalistes," *rentiers, anoblis,* and officeholders would pay the stamp duty. And especially would the land bear a light tax or no tax. The Notables would weigh down on those considered the economic and social "parasites" of their society, those whose wealth and investments in the public debt did not advance economic production, as well as those

[32] Coeurderoy, AD, M.-et-M., W 1101 (6), "Journal particulier . . . , 1787," fols. 57–62 and AN, C 3 (8), no. 14. The Notables were not unique in wanting to eliminate the debt; in 1788 the government in Tuscany would begin to liquidate its public debt (Furio Diaz, *Francesco Maria Gianni, dalla Burocrazia alla Politica sotto Pietro Leopoldo di Toscana* [Milan, 1966], pp. 218 ff.).

[33] AN, C 2 (6), "Cahier des délibérations," fol. 19. See also 1st Bur.—AN, C 1 (3), fol. 169v; 2d Bur.—BA, MS 3976, fols. 314–17, 376–77, 1023–25 ff.; 3d Bur.—AN, C 2 (6), "Cahier des délibérations," fols. 80–87; 4th Bur.—AN, C 2 (6), fol. 9, C 4 (11),-fol. 69; 5th Bur.—AN, C 3 (7), fols. 169–70; 6th Bur.—AN, C 3 (7), fols. 52–53; 7th Bur.—AN, C 3 (7), fols. 153–56.

[34] 1st Bur.—AN, C 1 (3), fols. 38v ff., 56; 2d Bur.—BA, MS 3975, fols. 745 ff.; 3d Bur.—AN, C 2 (6), "Cahier des délibérations," fols. 18–22; 5th Bur.— AN, C 3 (7), fols. 84–89; 7th Bur.—AN, C 3 (7), fols. 51–55; Bibliothèque mazarine (BM), 2406, "Gabelle, mémoire." The Crown's project on the *gabelle* is in AN, C 1 (2), fols. 309–38.

having high posts and status, so as to relieve landed property.[35] It was as if they were willing to submit to taxes the titles and offices they enjoyed to spare the land they owned. They would gain materially, paying less were the land tax reduced or ended than they would pay in higher stamp taxes or a money tax replacing the *gabelle*. They would also gain in other ways. In opposing the new land tax, the Notables spoke not only for the special interest of the privileged few—nobles, high clergy, and officials like themselves who owned land. Theirs was a fetching program of no tax increase and lower taxes on the land that also touched a more general interest of the many in France who owned or cultivated the land and who also feared having to pay higher taxes. In advancing their interests, they tied theirs to the interests of others and expected in turn the gratitude and support of that public.

II. From Opposition to Taxes to Political Opposition

The Notables were not the first nor were they the last group of "politicians" who sought political gain from opposing taxes. They had the instincts of politicians because for years they had engaged in public affairs, and as public officials the king named them to the Assembly. As military governors and commanders in provinces, chief officers of the sovereign courts, deputies of provincial estates, heads of municipal governments, archbishops and bishops, some of them had carried out programs to repair or build roads and bridges, to set up manufactures, poorhouses, or nurseries.[36] They had tasted the delights and frustrations of exercising public authority and learned what their "constituents" wanted or feared. No higher taxes, no new taxes were the desires of individual Notables

[35] For similar criticisms in England of holders of the public debt, see J. G. A. Pocock, *The Machiavellian Moment: Florentine Political Thought and the Atlantic Republican Tradition* (Princeton, N.J., 1975), chap. 13. (Jonathan Dewald kindly brought this to my attention.)

[36] For the exact membership in the Assembly of Notables see Sec. I above. For the activities of some of these Notables, see abbé G. Courmary, *Loménie de Brienne à Toulouse (1763–1788)* (Albi, 1935); abbé E. Lavaquery, *Le Cardinal de Boisgelin, 1732–1804* (Angers, 1920); and François-Xavier Emmanuelli, *Pouvoir royal et vie régionale en Provence au déclin de la monarchie: Psychologie, pratiques administratives, defrancisation de l'intendance d'Aix, 1745–1790*, 2 vols. (Lille, 1974), 1: 100–103; Paul Le Cacheux, "Le chartrier de Belbeuf et les archives des procureurs généraux du Parlement de Normandie à la fin du XVIIIᵉ siècle," *Bulletin de la Société des Antiquaires de Normandie* 53 (1955–56): 10–15; Paul Bisson de Barthélemy, *L'Activité d'un procureur-général au Parlement de Paris à la fin de l'ancien régime: Les Joly de Fleury* (Paris, 1964); and Jean Yver, "Une administration municipale 'orageuse' à Caen à la fin de l'ancien régime: La mairie de M. de Vendoeuvre," *Mémoires de l'Académie Nationale des Sciences, Arts et Belles-Lettres de Caen*, n.s., vol. 6 (1931).

before 1787 who voiced the sentiment in their provinces.[37] Their ardor
to resist tax increases mounted during the weeks of deliberation in the
Assembly, among other reasons also to disprove the cynics who in news-
sheets, cartoons, and doggerel depicted the Notables as easy prey to the
Crown's requests for more money.[38] They also had to inform the audience
beyond their halls of their opposition to taxes, "leaking" to the public
news of their sentiments and resolutions, to remove any blemish on their
reputation and to gather the fruits of public sympathy and support for
their program and their leadership. The Notables courted the favor of
the public whom they wanted as "silent partners."

Lower taxes on the land was a financial program and a political weapon,
one of several ways by which the Notables shifted from a "tax revolt"
to a "political revolt." In their first meetings they dealt directly with a
political issue, the Crown's project to establish provincial assemblies.
From the last day of February when they began to debate the land tax
until the last meeting on May 23, they debated largely financial issues.
Yet their arguments, criticisms, and demands were a heady mix of finance
and politics. Overtly combative and obstreperous on financial matters,
especially the land tax, they were more reticent and diffident when directly
confronting political authority, snipping away at parts rather than attacking
at the source, as if they did not want at once to deny the king's majesty.
Nevertheless, under cover of financial objectives or of modest, particular
changes, their efforts added up to a program whose effect would be to
transform the structure of government and transfer power in the state.

A. Public Consent, Control, and Knowledge

In defending property against a new land tax, the Notables turned quickly
to a political argument: the need for consent. Without consent to taxation
the king, collecting a permanent tax, would forcibly deprive his subjects
of part of their property. Only consent guaranteed freedom of property
and of individuals and groups. This historic refrain they sharpened. It
was no mere rhetorical invocation or cover for corporate interests — they
indicated several means by which consent might be made real.

---

[37] The archbishop of Aix in AN, M 788, nos. 2^8, 2^{10}, unnumbered dated "à
Aix, 29 janvier 1783," nos. 2^{11}, 2^{13}; *procureur-général* of the Parlement of
Grenoble in Jean Egret, *Le Parlement de Dauphiné et les affaires publiques dans
la deuxième moitié du XVIIIe siècle*, 2 vols. (Grenoble, 1942), 2: 146–47; the
comte de Stainville, military commander in Lorraine, as reported by Coeurderoy
in AD, Meurthe-et-Moselle, W 1101 (1), "Journal du Président de Coeurderoy
(18e siècle)," fol. 187.

[38] See esp. *Mémoires secrets*, vol. 34, and *Correspondance secrète inédite
sur Louis XVI, Marie Antoinette, la cour et la ville de 1777 à 1792*, ed. M. de
Lescure, 2 vols. (Paris, 1866), vol. 2.

Opposition to a *taxe de quotité* and support for a repartitional tax were crucial political acts. To the Notables Calonne's fixed-rate tax, viewed as a financial tool for unlimited tax increases and government waste, also offered the possibility for the complete emancipation of the government from the limited financial constraints that existed, and the final entrenchment of absolutism by means of a tax unlimited in amount and in time. Assured of expanding revenues "perpetually" and automatically as agricultural production rose, the Crown would no longer have to ask its subjects for more taxes, listen to their complaints in exchange for their assistance, or solicit their consent to a new tax which remained a principle in jurisprudence and an indirect practice through registration of tax edicts in the sovereign courts and their acceptance by the provincial estates. In reverse, a repartitional tax joined political virtues to financial benefits. It guaranteed the taxpayer against wanton tax increases by giving the local community closer control over taxation. Villagers gathered in their parishes would declare their income and, knowing each other's worth, control the assessments of all who held land in the neighborhood. Tax increases that would raise the parish levy on all, not just the taxes paid by some, would assure stronger collective resistance. And the provinces, through existing estates and new assemblies, would appoint the tax collectors. Local surveillance of assessments, collection of taxes, and responsibility for a communal tax would permit local communities, the parishes and provinces, to take over the functions exercised by agents sent from Versailles and to check the central government's power to tax.[39]

Controls on global taxation would accompany local controls on taxation. The Crown could not project anticipated expenses to determine revenue but must set taxes to the level of its known needs and collect these taxes only for a limited number of years.[40] If the sum became insufficient, or at the end of the stipulated period of time, the government would be obliged to turn to its subjects, justify its expenses and needs, and expose its financial practices. Its freedom of action would be limited in proportion to its fixed resources in taxes. Instead of a "perpetual" tax, a measure of public control over royal finances would be "perpetuated." "No taxation without consent" lay at the heart of the Notables' demand for a repartitional tax.

---

[39] Renouvin, ed., . . . *la conférence du 2 mars*, pp. 3–10; 2d Bur.—BA, MS 3978, fols. 242–43, MS 3976, fols. 430–31; 5th Bur.—AN, C 3 (7), fols. 166–68; conference of May 9, AN, C 2 (6), "Cahier des pièces relatives au procès-verbal," fols. 19–23, BA, MS 3976, fols. 383 ff.; Loménie de Brienne in AN, C 1 (3), fols. 121v–25, and BM, 2406, "Vues générales sur l'impôt territorial."
[40] 3d Bur., AN, C 2 (6), "Cahier de délibérations," fols. 79–81.

Their victory came on May 9 when, following Calonne's dismissal one month earlier, the new minister Loménie de Brienne accepted the form of a repartitional tax which he had urged as a member of the Assembly. One witness, Dupont de Nemours, grasped the political significance of this decision which he believed would elude historians. The financial rule that revenues be proportioned to expenses, rather than the reverse, and the sum be limited in advance—what he called the "English principle"—introduced a new "constitutional maxim" that, in his view, would "change totally" the system of royal government in France. The monarchy would become a "republic," the king a "magistrate decorated with the title and honors of royalty, but perpetually obliged to assemble his people and to ask them to provide for his needs, for which public revenue will be, with this new national consent, perpetually insufficient." The deficit would persist and become greater as year after year money would lose value while government needs would not diminish. The political prospect he foresaw displeased Dupont:

The prince cannot therefore dispense with assembling the nation from time to time and explaining again the insufficiency of the means given to him to pay for all the state's expenditures. A beautiful occasion for *demagogues,* who seek reputation and fortune, and who profit from the repugnance of all people for taxes, a beautiful occasion to cry *economies,* to diminish *the civil list of the prince* and to have a king and public security as cheaply as possible. [Original italics][41]

In the first weeks of the Assembly the Notables argued against a "perpetual" tax, seeking to impose periodic control through consent to taxes. In the last weeks, from the end of April to May 23, they set out to introduce annual controls over government expenditures.[42] Shocked at the confusion in government accounts, the difficulty of calculating expenses, and the existence of a deficit greater than Calonne had estimated, they were intent not to throw good money after what seemed like bad money. Against what they considered to be waste, inefficiency, profiteering, and corruption in the Crown's finances, they directed their attacks and applied their remedies. On the initiative of the archbishop of Aix, the bureaux drew up a series of proposals to reform the structure and practices of the royal financial administration, which included eliminating venal offices and unauthorized loans and payments, drafting itemized

[41] Dupont de Nemours to the baron Edelsheim, July 11, 1787, in *Politische Correspondenz Karl Friedrichs Von Baden, 1782–1806,* ed. Bernhard Erdmannsdörffer (Heidelberg, 1888), 1: 273–74.

[42] See n. 30 above, esp. the memoir of the archbishop of Aix, AN, C 2 (6), "Cahier des délibérations," fols. 91–106.

budgets for the ministries and the royal family, and consolidating the many royal treasuries into one. Their ostensible purpose, to reduce current expenses and avert recurrent deficits so as to lower taxes, would be accomplished by introducing more rational and efficient operations, more bureaucratic organization in government finances—along with greater public control over the bureaucracy.[43]

New spending procedures that the Notables proposed would curb the Crown's financial activities and require it to transfer some functions to other public bodies. A single royal treasury would consolidate the many treasuries scattered across the country, the latter no longer needed since the provinces would assume the administration of taxes. Provincial authority and the activities of members of provincial administrations in public finance would increase. At the center, public supervision of royal finances would be introduced. More rational methods in financial administration, such as the Notables recommended, entailed government submission to the expressed views of its subjects. Budgets published annually and a citizens' committee to audit government accounts, which the Notables insisted on, were devices aimed at opening wider the secrets of royal finances to continuous public scrutiny. Their financial effectiveness may be doubted. Individuals turning page after page of the annual budget, or nonprofessionals examining reams of financial requests and accounts of expenditures twice a year, could hardly contain government spending. Their political significance is undoubted. Published budgets and public auditing raised expectations, in the words of the first bureau: ". . . the most important . . . , the most fruitful in happy effects, is publicity. . . ."[44] These demands testify to a welling desire in the public to know and control the activities of government.

That urge to know which the Notables embodied in specific proposals was impelled by undercurrents of thought revealed in certain themes and words repeated in their debates. The workings of government, they argued,

[43] Bureaucratic practices were introduced in the French financial administration after the Assembly of Notables (John Bosher, *French Finances 1770–1795, from Business to Bureaucracy* [Cambridge, 1970], chap. 11). Some parlements in the 1760s urged a few of these changes (Jean Egret, *Louis XV et l'opposition parlementaire 1715–1774* [Paris, 1970], pp. 123–25). Calonne had indicated his intention to establish a single treasury, but was dismissed before he presented to the Notables his projected financial reforms (AN, C 1 [2], fol. 203; AN, 297 AP 3 [263 Mi 3], no. 91, fol. 3v; AN, 297 AP 3 [263 Mi 4], no. 97).

[44] BA, MS 3976, fol. 436. Lafayette repeated this demand for publicity (MS 3976, fols. 457–60). A finance committee of individuals not in the royal administration differed from the financial council composed of administrators introduced in 1787; on financial councils in the eighteenth century, see Michel Antoine, *Le Conseil du Roi sous le règne de Louis XV* (Paris, 1970), bk. 2, chap. 3.

were "covered" by "obscurities," "mystery" ("scandalous mystery"), a "veil" ("a perfidious veil"), "barriers" which imposed "secrecy of administration," especially on financial operations. "Light" instead had to pierce through, "the eyes of the people" had to penetrate into the activities of government, permitting the public to exercise the power of "observation" so as "to know" and to gain "knowledge." The ubiquity of the unknown in government aroused a mounting passion to learn about the source of those problems for which the public was being asked to pay and which could only be abated by information and access. So the Notables demanded evidence, financial accounts to determine the deficit with exactitude, government records to establish its origin and those responsible. Even the *lieutenant-civil* of Paris, Angran d'Alleray, who usually shuddered at the prospect of any slight change in existing institutions and practices, dismissed as unbelievable the government's response that it could not provide a clear assessment of the current financial situation—since even bankers are able to do so in one day—or that the Notables would be unable to understand the complicated calculations. Members of the Assembly in a meeting with the controller general warned that the Notables "must themselves be capable of undeceiving the public. . . ." From these springs of sentiment came the belief that frequent and constant publicity was a virtual solution.[45]

B. Against Bureaucracy

A "revolution of rising expectations" was taking a political course. The Notables' sense of their distance from and ignorance of government bred suspicion that impelled their quest for knowledge and also for changes in the system of governance. "All administration which remains secret cannot complain if it is suspected . . . ," wrote the archbishop of Toulouse, Loménie de Brienne, over ten years before he became a member of the Notables. Distrust, at all times, lent weight to rumors of "intrigue," of the secret machinations of ministers and courtiers, queens and royal mistresses. In 1787 the French again detected "intrigue" in the maneuvers of the controller general Calonne, who sold or exchanged royal land cheaply to speculators,[46] who tried to raise the government's credit with its lenders in anticipation of new loans, and whose dismissal was attributed

---

[45] BA, MS 3978, fols. 187 ff., MS 3976, fols. 225, 419 ff.; AN, C 2 (6), "Cahiers des pièces relatives au procès-verbal," *compte-rendu*, meeting of March 2, fol. 8, and Renouvin, ed., . . . *la conférence du 2 mars*, p. 69.

[46] For criticisms in the second bureau of the controller general's involvement in exchanges of royal lands with speculators, see BA, MS 3975, fols. 888–93, MS 4546, fols. 48–49; and Chevallier, ed., *Journal de l'Assemblée des Notables*, pp. 39–42, 118–19 (and also pp. 126–33).

to the personal hostility or ambition of ministers or Notables. Distance and ignorance now also spawned other accusations with more enduring effect. Constantly rising taxes, an unexplained deficit in peacetime whose upper limit kept rising, could only be proof of "disorder" in financial administration, responsibility for which lay with the minister in charge, the controller general, and his agents. A decade after Loménie de Brienne had warned that secret operations bred suspicion, the archbishop gave vent to those he harbored, unleashing a tirade of criticism against the single authority of the finance minister: ". . . everything is concentrated in the sole will of the controller . . . everything winds up in the office of the controller, sole and supreme arbiter of everything. What vexations, injustices, . . . exactions does this frightful regime not produce, this arbitrariness always purchased . . . ?" The underlings of the finance minister he attacked more vehemently: "The *commis* do everything, give direction to everything, depending upon whether they are honest or paid by interested parties. . . . Everything is instructed, extracted, judged by the bureaux." Then followed, in its eighteenth-century version, the image of the king displaced from authority, not by favorites but by bureaucrats:

. . . they no longer examine, discuss or regulate in Council the receipts, expenses, or accounts. The interested parties do it, the *commis*, the controller. The controller puts these in his briefcase, has the king sign them, then they are taken to the chancellor who signs them. . . . Thus the king only knows what the controller wants to say to him in their face-to-face working sessions. . . . everything [is done] by rule of the Council which the Council never deliberated and which are still the work of *commis* who at their own pleasure set the course of the *King's action* by means of the arbitrary and false expression *the King being in his Council*. [Original italics]

The numbers of these all-powerful agents also multiplied in recent times: ". . . what were 7 to 8 departments under the abbé Terray [in 1770] are now 25 or 30." Loménie's stark conclusion followed: "From that the dreadful Bureaucracy that exists. . . ."[47]

---

[47] "Memoire de M. L'Ar. de T. 1787 concernant les finances," found among the Calonne papers, PRO (London), PC 1/125, X. 1/7470, fols. 276 ff. This memoir, with certain changes in wording and the deletion of personal names, was published by Jean-Louis Carra (*Un petit mot de réponse à M. de Calonne, sur sa requête au roi* [Amsterdam, 1787], pp. 53–67), who claimed that he wrote and presented it to the Notables in February 1787. In a renewed attack on Calonne (*M. de Calonne Tout Entier, tels qu'il est comporté dans l'administration des finances, dans son commissariat en Bretagne, etc.* [Brussels, April 1788]), Carra states that Calonne attributed this memoir to the archbishop of Toulouse (p. 3). The arguments in this memoir, in particular the demands for financial order, an end to excessive spending, and the establishment of a financial council to control expenditures, fit in with the known views of Loménie de Brienne and

Royal agents—the *commis* in the *contrôle générale,* intendants, tax assessors and collectors in the provinces—conjured for the Notables an unknowable bureaucracy controlled from afar and inherently wasteful, inefficient, and arbitrary. The *commis* do too much and keep knowledge within their small circle, even excluding the king. The intendants and other provincial agents also do too much but have insufficient knowledge of the area and people they administer. Government agents had other demerits. Appointed officials sought only personal advantage, to rise higher in the administration, which they obtained not by demonstrating ability or merit but by gaining the favor of those above them; venal officers were impelled by a mercenary spirit. All were little attached to their functions or places. In its concluding declaration, the third bureau of the Assembly of Notables fulminated against the workings of a remote, centralized administration:

> The government does everything at great cost, because it is far from the place where its agents carry out, with its authority, their long and expensive operations. There is not one enlightened minister who believes he can, from the midst of the court and the capital, supervise the agents that he employs and direct local researches. The necessary operations, for the apportioning of taxes, presuppose knowledge that varies according to the place and that cannot be acquired from far away. This knowledge does not belong to only one man or to a single class of men. . . .[48]

The remedy was not to put the king back at the center but to create many centers of governance. In place of bureaucracy, there should be more self-government and involvement of the public. In contrast to intendants and other agents of the central government, who know and care little of the place in which they operate, those living in the province and community alone have "a local knowledge of the means of amelioration in each province . . . ," said the prince de Robecq (despite his profession of royalist sympathies at the outset of the Assembly).[49] Local people performing the tasks of local government have both the understanding

---

foreshadow the reforms he introduced when he became principal minister later in 1787.

[48] AN, C 2 (6), "Cahier des délibérations," fol. 82. For similar hostility to "clerks, . . . administrators, . . . men in place, . . . ministers of the second or third order" among the lower classes see Jean-Louis Vissière, "La culture populaire à la veille de la Révolution d'après le 'Tableau de Paris' de Mercier," in *Images du peuple au dix-huitième siècle,* Centre Aixois d'Etudes et de Recherches sur le Dix-Huitième Siècle, Colloque d'Aix-en-Provence, 25–26 octobre 1969 (Paris, 1973), p. 127.

[49] BA, MS 3975, fols. 1031–32, 1103–4, 1145.

and the will to do a better job. Loménie in his memoir and the Notables in their debates criticized with the animus of "outsiders" who now insisted on being included in the operations of power.

C. Local Participation and Provincial Autonomy

A share in public authority, a part in making policy and carrying out law regularly were recurrent themes and reiterated demands of the Notables, expressed in ways both old and new.

Claims to "privilege" for the clergy and the provincial estates voiced among the Notables took on altered meaning. "Privilege" became a bridge to "consent," invoked not as exemption from the law or special benefits in the law but as a general right to discuss, approve, and execute the law. The clergy, the Notables agreed (including the archbishops and bishops among them), should pay the land tax as other Frenchmen did, equally, in proportion to their income from the land; but they should not be compelled, as the Crown proposed, to sell their seigneurial income to redeem their debt without first meeting in their assembly to give their consent.[50] The provinces, they argued even more ardently, must submit equally to the same tax law while maintaining their privileges. So long as all the land and each taxpayer paid a proportionate share uniformly calculated to the income of the land (and not exceeding 10 percent), provinces could be permitted different forms of tax administration. Those provinces with estates (the *pays d'états*) should retain their right to consent to, apportion, and collect taxes, "their receivers general or particular [paying] the sums into the Royal Treasury without using any government

---

[50] 1st Bur.—AN, C 1 (3), fols. 11, 156v; 2d Bur.—BA, MS 3978, fols. 685–86, MS 3976, fols. 1004–16, Loménie de Brienne in BN, nouv. acq. fr. 23615, fols. 341–81 ff.; 3d Bur.—AN, C 2 (6), "Cahier des délibérations," fols. 7–9, 66; 4th Bur.—AN, C 2 (6), fol. 17; 5th Bur.—C 3 (7), fols. 28, 31; 6th Bur.—AN, C 3 (7), fols. 5–6; 7th Bur.—AN, C 3 (7), fol. 24, C 4 (13), fol. 31. The Venetian ambassador reported on the Notables' decision: "As to the clerical debt the ecclesiastical lands must be subjected to the operations of the provincial assemblies [i.e., property evaluation and tax assessments], as the lands of other citizens. They reserve for the next assembly of the clergy the liberty to demand the conservation of their form [collection of taxes], and against the violation of property which would be the result of a forced sale of its lands." Archivio di Stato, Venezia, *Dispacci degli Ambasciatori in Francia*, Senato III (Secreta), no. 262, fol. 178. Clerical assemblies in the eighteenth century defended the right of "don gratuit" but along with clerical exemption from regular taxes (Michel C. Peronnet, *Les Evêques de l'ancienne France*, 2 vols. [Lille, 1977], vol. 2, bk. 3, chap. 1).

agents. . . ."[51] And if the taxes of some provinces continued to be lower than those of other provinces, no Notable from the lower-taxed regions, such as Brittany, Burgundy, Provence, and Lorraine, who were the most outspoken advocates in the Assembly of provincial privilege, would ask their fellow Bretons, Burgundians, Provençals, and Lorrainers to pay higher taxes.[52]

Provincial privilege the Notables also interpreted universally. The privilege of the *pays d'états* should not be exclusive to them. They should become the rights of all the provinces. The third bureau, led by the archbishop of Aix, Boisgelin, whose origins in Brittany and career in Provence steeped him in the tradition of provincial privilege and autonomy,[53] expressed this view forthrightly. The practice of *abonnements*, to negotiate with the Crown to determine the sum of taxes and to assess and collect taxes, which since the 1750s the *pays d'états* did for the *vingtième*, should be extended to all the provinces: "The provinces, the communities, the taxpayers, will be *abonnés* from one end of the kingdom to the other. The privilege which the kings have sworn to maintain will not be destroyed. They will become common to all citizens, as the beneficent laws which conserve the natural rights of men. . . ."[54] *Abonnements* was the springboard for the Notables to claim fiscal autonomy for all provinces.

Autonomy not limited to taxes but also in general administration quickly became their objective. From the first days of their meetings, as they debated the Crown's project to establish assemblies in provinces where there were no estates, all the bureaux demonstrated their intent, step by small step, to transform the assemblies the government designed and to give to the provinces effective powers of self-government.

The provincial assemblies were an "absolute benefit," said Castillon, a Provençal magistrate and member of the second bureau, if certain changes were adopted, making the assemblies fit the pattern of the provincial estates.[55] The Notables were virtually unanimous. The functions

[51] BA, MS 3978, fol. 650, and Loménie de Brienne's statement, fols. 457–59; AN, C 2 (6), "Cahier des délibérations," fols. 4–5. See also BA, MS 3978, fols. 684–85, 727; EMHL, W2-4712; AN, C 3 (7), fols. 28–29, 172–74; Renouvin, ed., . . . *la conférence du 2 mars,* p. 48.

[52] See n. 8 above.

[53] See my article, "Paths to Political Consciousness: The Assembly of Notables of 1787 and the 'Pre-Revolution' in France," *French Historical Studies* 13, no. 3 (Spring 1984): 323–55.

[54] 3d Bur., AN, C 2 (6), "Cahier des délibérations," fol. 83. *Abonnements* became more frequent after the ouster of controller general Machault in 1754.

[55] BA, MS 3975, fols. 545–46.

the Crown assigned to the assemblies and their powers were insufficient.[56] These were to evaluate property for the land tax and apportion the tax, to administer public works projects and poor relief, and to inform the government of their communities' needs and views and suggest programs. The assemblies would be mere channels of consultation, with little means to exercise their few responsibilities.

Instead, the assemblies should apportion and collect the land tax, using their own agents, not the assessors or collectors sent from Versailles. Disarmingly, the archbishop of Aix stated: ". . . the provinces do not believe it is too dear to buy the advantages of a provincial administration by assuming the costs of collection. . . ."[57] Indeed, the Notables thought local tax collection would be cheaper, the savings returned to each province for its use or to permit tax reductions. The revenue from the land tax would also be used locally, the assemblies allocating part of the funds to finance their own programs. Other jurisdiction the Crown assigned to the assemblies should be extended, giving them greater authority, for example, over public works projects, with agents subordinate to them or of their own choice, the king and ministers exercising only remote control. Uttering words the Crown forbade, several bureaux demanded that the assemblies be "executive" or "legislative." The third bureau insisted on calling them "provincial administrations" rather than "provincial assemblies," by the shift in word attributing to the provincial institutions full and active administrative powers.[58]

In succeeding weeks, as the Notables discussed reform after reform, time and again they tried to give to the assemblies a role in implementing the reforms, one by one adding to their functions and broadening their powers: to modify, approve, or carry out the reforms in general,[59] and specifying the programs they should oversee, such as redemption of the

---

[56] On the provincial assemblies, see 1st Bur.—AN, C 1 (3), fols. 5–56, 157, 162, Gérard, AAE, Mém. et Doc., Fr., 1402, fols. 123–36; 2d Bur.—BA, MS 3975, fols. 544–46, 960, 1031–53, 1150, MS 3976, fols. 1016–69, MS 3978, fols. 30–60, 160–67, 624–82, MS 4546, fols. 2–3, 73; 3d Bur.—AN, C 2 (6), "Cahier des délibérations," fols. 3–26, 45–87, 101–3, "Cahier des pièces relatives au procès-verbal," fol. 24; 4th Bur.—AN, C 2 (6), fols. 6–19, C 4 (11), fols. 97–102; 5th Bur.—AN, C 3 (7), fols. 11–12, 33–38, 70, 90–91, 176–78; 6th Bur.—AN, C 3 (2), fols. 6, 14; 7th Bur.—AN, C 3 (7), fols. 27, 45–55, 79, 85, 135, 156–67, meeting of April 17, and C 4 (13), fol. 38.

[57] AN, C 2 (6), "Cahier des délibérations," fol. 101.

[58] 2d Bur.—BA, MS 3978, fols. 42–43, 60, 978 ff.; 3d Bur.—AN, C 2 (6), "Cahier des délibérations," fols. 3–4, 22, 59, 65; 7th Bur.—AN, C 3 (7), fols. 5–6, 50–51.

[59] All the bureaux.

clerical debt,[60] free trade in grain,[61] the national customs union,[62] administration of the royal domains,[63] and responsibility for administering poor relief.[64] Without explicitly making the claim, the several bureaux moved in the direction of conferring on the assemblies varying degrees of authority over all taxes, new and old.[65] The assemblies should also serve as guardians of the royal treasury, receiving reports of annual tax receipts and reductions in the deficit so as to assure future tax cuts, particularly in the land tax.[66]

Onto the emerging structure of provincial assemblies most of the bureaux sought to attach greater or lesser degrees of financial and general administration, consultation on policy, and executive and legislative authority. The third bureau expressed openly the thought implicit in the decisions of almost all the bureaux: the assemblies were so important that any new tax would have to await their establishment and approval.[67] With use, the assemblies might gain greater importance and induce further changes in government, as an unidentified memorandum among the papers of the seventh bureau suggested: "an establishment indifferent in its infancy, upsetting for administrators in its adolescence, dangerous for sovereigns, useful for the nation in its virility, and the wisdom of its maturity can prepare a revolution in the constitution that will stamp out despotism, which hides itself until the present under the cloak of the monarchy."[68]

The Notables' ambitions for the provinces centered on the assemblies. They would gain the functions and powers shorn from the royal government—from the tax assessors and collectors, the administrators of bridges and roads, especially the royal intendants. Claims to a public role for the sovereign courts or for the nobility, familiar in the past—in the

[60] First bureau.

[61] Seventh bureau.

[62] The third, fourth, and seventh bureaux, which also proposed consulting the assemblies for future changes in tariffs.

[63] The second and seventh bureaux.

[64] The third and seventh bureaux.

[65] These included the land tax, the money tax to replace the *corvée*, the money tax the Notables proposed to replace the *gabelle*, the reformed *taille*, excise taxes, and the new stamp tax.

[66] The second, third, fifth, and seventh bureaux.

[67] 3d Bur., AN, C 2 (6), "Cahier des délibérations," fols. 75–76. On the provincial assemblies, see Pierre Renouvin, *Les Assemblées provinciales de 1787: Origines, développement, résultats* (Paris, 1921). A few sovereign courts (the parlements of Rouen, Grenoble and Bordeaux, and the *cour des aides* of Paris) earlier had urged the establishment of provincial estates (Doyle, *The Parlement of Bordeaux*, pp. 227–28).

[68] AN, C 4 (13), fols. 248v–49.

uprisings of the sixteenth and seventeenth centuries and in the polemics of parlementary courts in preceding decades—were peripheral issues in 1787.[69] The new assemblies, together with the existing provincial estates, would be the effective organs of local self-government. Composed of socially diverse bodies of landowners, in Calonne's scheme, or of clergy, nobles, and third estate officeholders, as the Notables envisioned and the Crown conceded, they would draw their members from a public that extended beyond nobles and magistrates and who were also residents, proprietors, and public officials in the provinces. With broader powers and local representation, provincial assemblies and those in districts and parishes would provide better government, in the words of the third bureau: "It is for the provincial assemblies to give the rules, it is for the communities to follow and execute them. Each community must itself make its land assessment under the inspection of the provinces; each community charged with the cost of an operation of interest for all its inhabitants will carry it out more economically and with greater exactitude, and the tax will be apportioned more accurately without being increased."[70]

The appeal of local rule was its cheapness, and especially the power it would confer, collectively and individually: for the local regions, the power to do almost as they willed, and for individuals, to wield a portion of that power. The historic desire of the upper classes to enter into and become the government could find satisfaction with authority brought nearer and made theirs to exercise. The millennial desire of the lower classes to be left alone and not pay or pay little taxes, to feel lightly the weight of authority, could be answered by the image of a government that taxes and commands at a distance.[71] Under the banner of local rule each could read its own meaning, and the two could meet.

---

[69] A. Lloyd Moote, *The Revolt of the Judges: The Parlement of Paris and the Fronde, 1643–1652* (Princeton, N.J., 1971); Roland Mousnier, "Pourquoi Etats-Généraux et Etats provinciaux ont-ils joué un si faible rôle pendant la Fronde?" *Parliaments, Estates and Representation* 1, pt. 2 (December 1981): 139–45; and Egret, . . . *l'opposition parlementaire.*

[70] AN, C 2 (6), "Cahier des délibérations," fol. 82. For an analysis of the Notables' motives in requesting provincial assemblies composed of the three orders rather than simply of landowners, see my paper "*Vote by Order:* The Discourse of the Elite at the End of the Ancien Régime," delivered at the Consortium on Revolutionary Europe in Charleston, S.C., February 1983, and printed in the *Proceedings of the Consortium on Revolutionary Europe.*

[71] See Yves-Marie Bercé, *Croquants et Nu-Pieds: Les soulèvements paysans en France du XVIe au XIXe siècle* (Paris, 1974). Georges Lefebvre pointed out

D. A Public Role in National Government

From the provinces the Notables turned their attention to the nation. A sense of the need to coordinate the autonomous activities of the provinces, though not expressed as such, emerged from their discussions. Uniform laws would preserve the national framework the monarchy had created and within which the provinces would operate autonomously. In the words of the second bureau, "in everything which will not alter universality in the contribution, and equality in the apportionment, the rights and privileges of corps and of provinces will be maintained in their integrity."[72] These laws, national in scope, at the same time would express the nation's will. Calls for national consent through a superior institutional process, episodic or marginal in the past, were now repeated.[73] Indirectly and circumspectly, the Notables staked a claim to public participation in national affairs, even to a form of national assemblage. Rarely did they pronounce such principles. More often these views were implicit in their responses to the frustrating constraints on their investigations of government operations or the confusions and irregularities they uncovered. In rhetoric they were still diffident before the royal majesty; in act they were set in a contest with royal power.[74]

The Assembly was convened as a consultative body, but instead of performing as loyal councillors—farmyard animals selecting the sauce

the local inhabitants' appreciation of financial autonomy in Flanders (*Les Paysans du Nord pendant la Révolution Française* [Bari, 1959], p. 172).

[72] BA, MS 3978, fol. 650. See also AN, C 2 (6), "Cahier des pièces relatives au procès-verbal," *compte-rendu*, meeting of March 2, fols. 7–9, and Renouvin, ed., . . . *la conférence du 2 mars.*

[73] See n. 69 above and J. Russel Major, *Representative Government in Early Modern France* (New Haven, Conn., 1980); Miriam Yardeni, *La Conscience nationale en France pendant les guerres de religion (1559–1598)* (Louvain, 1971); Roland Mousnier, *La Plume, la faucille et le marteau, institutions et société en France du Moyen Age à la Révolution* (Paris, 1970), pp. 57–92; E. Carcassonne, *Montesquieu et le problème de la constitution française au XVIIIᵉ siècle* (Paris, 1927), pp. 406–36, 448–67; François Furet and Mona Ozouf, "Deux légitimations historiques de la société française au XVIIIᵉ siècle: Mably et Boulainvilliers," *Annales: Economies, sociétés, civilisations*, no. 3 (May–June 1979), pp. 438–50; Dale Van Kley, *The Damiens Affair: The Unravelling of the Ancien Régime, 1750–1770* (Princeton, N.J., 1984), chap. 4 (my thanks to the author for permitting me to read his work in manuscript form); and Keith M. Baker, "French Political Thought at the Accession of Louis XVI," *Journal of Modern History* 50 (June 1978): 291–95, 298–303, and "A Script for a French Revolution: The Political Consciousness of the abbé Mably," *Eighteenth-Century Studies* 14 (Spring 1981): 235–63.

[74] BA, MS 3978, fols. 82–83, 94–95.

with which they would be eaten, as a caricature of the day depicted them[75]—the Notables fast became prosecuting attorneys. They asked questions, requested information—facts and figures on government activities—and investigated the problems and policies that required reforms. They threatened, decorously, not to act on the land tax until they had the information with which they could decide.[76] Their probes were attempts at surveillance and control. In turn, they jostled at the controls the Crown placed on them. They were invited as individuals but acted as spokesmen—of their corporations (the clergy, the courts) but also of their provinces. All the Notables from Alsace, Lorraine, and the Three Bishoprics joined forces (aided by a "lobbying" effort from their provinces) in objecting that the customs union setting tariffs on the national frontiers would harm their region's close economic ties with countries to their east.[77] The second bureau sought unsuccessfully to organize provincial blocs (which the Crown prohibited).[78] With greater success they stretched the right given to them to "advise," to include the act to "modify," and they insisted on discussing not only "the form" but also "the substance" of each reform project.[79] Prefiguring attitudes and behavior that would soon become widespread but were still exceptional in 1787, several audacious members of the second bureau tried to introduce issues not included in the royal program (such as civil rights to Protestants and reform of the criminal law), arguing that the Assembly had no limits to its rights to discuss and propose: ". . . all the public welfare is within the competence of the Notables," affirmed Nicolai, the president of the Paris *chambre des comptes*.[80] In demanding government records they claimed responsibility to inform the public. In proposing counterprojects or new laws and refusing government measures, they were imposing their claim to consent, adapt, or veto and experimenting with the right to initiate.[81]

---

[75] C. B. A. Behrens, *The Ancien Régime* (London, 1967), p. 168.

[76] On similar demands by parlementary courts for financial information see Egret, . . . *l'opposition parlementaire*, pp. 99 ff.

[77] AAE, Mém. et Doc., Fr., 1402, fols. 144–46v, 268 ff., 295 ff.

[78] BA, MS 4546, fols. 31–32, MS 3975, fols. 368–69, 394.

[79] 2d Bur.—BA, MS 3978, fols. 187 ff., MS 3976, fols. 225, 419 ff.; 4th Bur.—AN, C 4 (11), fols. 22–27, 46; AN, C 2 (6), "Cahier des pièces relatives au procès-verbal," *compte-rendu*, meeting of March 2, fol. 8; Renouvin, ed., . . . *la conférence du 2 mars*, p. 69.

[80] BA, MS 3967, fols. 1094–1102. The first bureau rejected the duc de la Rochefoucald's similar proposals (Gérard, AAE, Mém. et Doc., Fr., 1402, fol. 98).

[81] Among these initiatives were a money tax to replace the *gabelle*, a citizens' committee to audit government expenditures, and reforms in the financial administration: 1st Bur.—AN, C 1 (3), fols. 34v–56, 107v–18, 151v, 164v–165, AN,

They were employing the practices of a legislature and invoking the prerogatives of representatives, transforming the Assembly of Notables into a "national assembly" (as contemporaries called it).

The model of a single national assemblage which their meetings introduced into French public life led the Notables to express the wish that the precedent be repeated in the future and at regular intervals. Within five years, recommended the seventh bureau, to verify that financial accounts were in order and to perform a broader mission: "to come to agreement . . . again on the most suitable measures for the good of his [Majesty's] service, the glory of his reign, and the happiness of his subjects."[82] At the same time the Notables realized that their institution had a flaw: they were appointed, not elected, and in fact did not represent and could not decide for the nation. They claimed to be representative and legislative when they challenged the Crown for information and attempted to block new laws or to initiate laws by their counterproposals. They abjured their representative role and legislative power when they refused to approve the government's reforms, especially the land tax. Their seeming ambivalence was in fact a double tactic for a single purpose. The constraints the Crown placed on their functions, which they often refuted, were also their excuse for conferring magnanimously the larger role of consenting to laws and representing the nation onto another, more effective political body.[83] Their assumed powerlessness was their greatest power to force the monarchy, in order to obtain needed funds, to seek the full and formal consent of the nation.

On the form or process for expressing the national will their ideas were not exact or uniform.[84] At times several of the bureaux merely

---

4 AP 188, no. 66, Gérard, AAE, Mém. et Doc., Fr., 1402, fols. 66v, 73v, comte de Brienne, AN, 4 AP 188, nos. 13–14–38, 21, 46–47–48, 64–65, and in Chevallier, ed., *Journal de l'Assemblée des Notables,* p. 27; 3d Bur.—AN, C 2 (6), "Cahier des délibérations," fols. 91–106; Loménie de Brienne in BN, nouv. acq. fr. 23615, fols. 177–86, 195 and PRO (London), PC 1/125, X. 1./7470, fols. 276 ff.

[82] AN, C 3 (7), fols. 123–24, May 11; see also fol. 96, May 2.

[83] 2d Bur.—BA, MS 3978, fols. 242–43, 430–31, MS 3975, fols. 842, 915, MS 3976, fols. 847–58, 944–45, 960–61, 1043, MS 4546, fols. 56, 73; 3d Bur.—AN, C 2 (6), "Cahier des délibérations," fol. 63; 7th Bur.—AN, C 3 (7), fol. 71.

[84] On national representation, see 1st Bur.—AN, C 1 (3), fols. 71, 163v–64; 2d Bur.—BA, MS 3978, fols. 242–43, 430–31, MS 3975, fols. 842, 916, 999–1000, 1008, 1035–36, MS 3976, fols. 847, 856, 959–60, Loménie de Brienne, BN, nouv. acq. fr. 23615, fols. 188–89, 197; 3d Bur.—AN, C 2 (6), "Cahier des délibérations," fols. 83–87; 4th Bur.—AN, C 4 (11), fols. 28, 38–39; 5th Bur.—AN, C 3 (7), fols. 108, 169; 6th Bur.—AN, C 3 (7), fols. 48, 51; 7th Bur.—AN, C 3 (7), fols. 71, 96, 123–24. Sovereign courts had invoked the

favored reinforcing and extending the existing system of registering laws in the sovereign courts along with their approval in the provincial estates and in the new provincial assemblies, a scheme which accentuated a decentralized system of public authority. A single institution which most completely embodied the national will was the sentiment expressed in all but one of the bureaux, two of them suggesting the outlines of such a national body. A confederal design was one proposal. The third bureau, in its final declaration, recommended that the provincial estates and assemblies send delegates to a national body that would vote on taxes. Ineluctably the members of that body would move to assume broader powers, as the Notables had done and as the comte de Brienne, member of the first bureau, foreshadowed in the initial sketch of a confederal system: "The minister . . . will be obliged to give an account each year to the king in the presence of the deputies of the provincial estates and assemblies of the use of the funds entrusted to him, and he will present the projects for new laws as well as for the reform of old ones to be examined by the members of the provincial estates and assemblies if the king judges it appropriate."[85]

The national institution that the overwhelming number of Notables invoked time and again in their debates and resolutions was the estates-general. The seemingly innocuous measure for long-term leasing of the royal domains brought to the minds of the members of the second bureau (whose minutes are the most detailed and rich in information) the historical memory of the estates-general: the sole legitimate vehicle for national consent, said the hitherto reticent mayor of Limoges; its enactments superior in authority to the royal will, stated a royal councillor (and future royal minister), Laurent de Villedeuil. Only an estates-general could give the nation's consent to alienating the royal domain, to new taxes, to a tax increase, to an unlimited and perpetual tax. The Notables' references to an estates-general became calls for an estates-general as their words filtered through talk and print to the public.[86] Lafayette, in one of the final sessions in the Assembly of Notables, was not the first

---

authority of the estates-general in the 1770s (Egret, . . . *l'opposition parlementaire*, pp. 126–27, 190). The most recent calls for an estates-general came in 1782 and 1783 from the Parlement of Besançon (Marion, *L'Impôt sur le revenu*, pp. 230–31), and in January 1785 from the Parlement of Bordeaux (Doyle, *The Parlement of Bordeaux*, pp. 211–13).

[85] AN, 4 AP 188, nos. 64–65, fol. 6 (also fols. 1, 4–5, 8); see also Chevallier, ed., *Journal de l'Assemblée des Notables*, p. 27.

[86] *Despatches from Paris . . .* , ed. Browning, 1: 181, and *Journal historique et politique des principaux événéments du temps présent ou esprit des gazettes et journaux politiques de toute l'Europe* (1787), 1: 561.

nor would he be the last to suggest that in five years, with financial order restored and the provincial assemblies operating regularly, the king should convoke "an assembly truly national." ". . . the estates-general . . . ?" asked the comte d'Artois in a tone of reproof. ". . . This was precisely the object of his request," answered Lafayette, "and beseeched Monseigneur to inscribe it as expressing the view of convoking the Estates-General of the kingdom. . . ."[87] Distance permitted contemporaries to embellish the collective memory of the estates-general, ascribing to it a role and authority never clearly exercised in the past but which satisfied current aspirations.

*   *   *

The Assembly of Notables seemed to end in stalemate between the Crown and its opponents. Yet certain reforms the Notables accepted and certain modifications the government accepted became new policies: free trade in grain, a national customs union, the substitution of a money tax for the *corvée*, reductions in government expenses, and changes in its financial practices. More important, from the spring of 1787 the French had before them a political design which became the public's. An estates-general elected and legislative, provincial assemblies representative and administrative, taxes fixed in amount and in time: a program for participation in local and national government, and for lower taxes and consent to taxes, emerged from the Assembly of Notables. In defending landed income, not fiscal privilege, against the effects of the proposed land tax, the Notables touched the interests of many in France—nobles and commoners, owners and cultivators of the land. In demanding greater self-government through new institutions of public authority in provinces and in the nation, not power in the name of the clergy, magistracy, or nobility, the Notables stirred the ambitions of a broader range of social groups either excluded from existing corporate activity or whose ambit was narrowly local; provincial *gentilshommes* and urban "notables," in particular, faced the agreeable prospect of entering into provincial government and engaging in national affairs.

III. CONCLUSION

The criticisms and claims that the Assembly of Notables shaped into a program were yearnings at once contemporary and centuries old. Opposition to taxes and demands for consent and participation were persistent undercurrents in European history expressed in learned treatises, customary

---

[87] BA, MS 3976, fols. 959–60. The wording is different in the *Mémoires, correspondance, et manuscrits du Général La Fayette* (Brussels, 1837), 1: 213.

beliefs, and revolutionary acts and manifestos.[88] Peasants protesting tax collectors sent from afar, cities clinging to their municipal autonomy, provinces invoking historical privileges, and nobles, magistrates, and parliamentarians insisting on controlling and sharing in the decisions of their king were the other side of the seemingly inexorable development of the modern state. Within this broad tradition was a range of variations, each example bearing the features of the culture and language of its time, its geographical setting, and its social place. The Notables in 1787 echoed and gave renewed vigor to sentiments already long-lived and commonplace, and to which they added their imprint. They introduced into an older pattern themes that marked changes with previous demands and contributed to a new revolutionary tradition. A contrast with the opposition to the introduction of an earlier tax reform, the *vingtième* in 1749, may underscore the key points in the mutation of political culture among the elite in the late ancien régime which the Assembly of Notables exemplified.

Clergy, provincial estates, and parlementary magistrates opposed the *vingtième,* a tax of 5 percent on the income of all lands.[89] Defense of fiscal privilege—exemption from regular taxes—was explicit in the arguments of the clergy, grounded on divine right and corporate rights.[90] Church and provincial estates (Brittany and Languedoc in particular) similarly defended their respective rights to consent to payments to the Crown and to assess and collect the levy through their own agents. But no spokesmen of the clergy proposed to extend the Church's right of consent through the "free gift" (*don gratuit*) to other orders, nor did the

---

[88] R. R. Palmer, *The Age of the Democratic Revolution: A Political History of Europe and America, 1760–1800,* vol. 1, *The Challenge* (Princeton, N.J., 1959); I. Leonard Leeb, *The Ideological Origins of the Batavian Revolution: History and Politics in the Dutch Republic 1747–1800* (The Hague, 1973); and Simon Schama, *Patriots and Liberators: Revolution in the Netherlands 1780–1813* (New York, 1977); Pauline Maier, *From Resistance to Revolution: Colonial Radicals and the Development of American Opposition to Britain, 1765–1776* (New York, 1972); and Gordon S. Wood, *The Creation of the American Republic, 1776–1787* (Chapel Hill, N.C., 1969). For the "longue durée" of this political culture, see Conrad S. R. Russell, "Monarchies, Wars and Estates in England, France, and Spain, c. 1580–c. 1640," *Legislative Studies Quarterly* 7, no. 2 (May 1982): 205–20; and Teofilo Ruiz, "Oligarchy and Royal Power: The Castilian Cortes and the Castilian Crisis, 1248–1350," and H. G. Koenigsberger, "Why Did the States-General of the Netherlands Become Revolutionary in the Sixteenth Century?" *Parliaments, Estates and Representation* 2, no. 2 (December 1982): 95–101 and 103–111, respectively; and Yves-Marie Bercé, *Révoltes et révolutions dans l'Europe moderne* (Paris, 1980).

[89] See Marcel Marion, *Machault d'Arnouville: Etude sur l'histoire du contrôle général des finances 1749 à 1754* (Paris, 1891).

[90] Peronnet, *Les Evêques de l'ancienne France,* 2: 765–72.

provincial estates attribute the right of consent they claimed for their respective province to all provinces in France. The Paris Parlement offered more elaborated and updated arguments against the *vingtième,* a number of which reechoed in the Assembly of Notables.[91] They decried not the denial of fiscal privilege but the heavy burden of taxes on the land and their harmful effect on agriculture. Their sympathies went to all those on whom taxes would weigh most heavily: noble landowners and peasant cultivators burdened by the tax on land, small shopkeepers and poor consumers bearing the weight of indirect taxes. Reduced government spending, strict financial controls, and limits on the amount and duration of taxes, which they proposed, would permit lower taxes. To oversee financial reforms and control the Crown's financial practices, the Paris court sought to give responsibility to the magistrates in the kingdom, who would become guardians over the royal government. The Paris judges and the clergy especially differed. The Church supported fiscal privilege, while the court, silent on privilege, proposed financial measures that anticipated the Notables' arguments. Yet all the opponents of the *vingtième*—clergy, provincial estates, and parlement—advanced their claims within the similar structure of traditional corporate institutions. The clergy and the estates aimed to preserve financial autonomy each already enjoyed, and the parlement tried to extend the authority of the courts in financial affairs. At mid-century opponents of the royal government had as their vision a "monarchie temperée des corps."

Forty years later the Notables drew from the fund of ideas of their predecessors. Yet particular practices and policies that were similar— opposition to a land tax, insistence on government economies and financial controls, even consent to taxes—were cast in an institutional framework and language, and had objectives, that differed profoundly. Fiscal privilege found no place in their final program, even the clerical members' accepting equality of taxation. The centuries-long divide between those who paid taxes and those who were exempt could now be bridged, and attention could be concentrated on reducing taxes on the land. Controls over government revenue and expenditures and consent to taxes would not be the exclusive prerogative of the clergy, magistracy, and handful of provincial estates but would be exercised by the general public through elected assemblies and representatives from the parish to the province, and ultimately for the nation at large. The Notables attached their fiscal and

---

[91] See Jules Flammermont and Maurice Tourneaux, *Remontrances du Parlement de Paris aux XVIIIᵉ siècle,* vols. 1–2 in *Collection de documents inédits sur l'histoire de France,* vol. 33, pt. 1, pp. 397–403, and vol. 33, pt. 2, pp. 112– 30, 222–31, 243–56, 294 ff., 327 ff., and 361 ff.

political goals to concrete yet broadly based policies and institutions; gave to their cause the imprint of a national identity which linked the efforts of diverse groups and places into a unified network with cohesive force; and expressed their claims in a language of universal application. The opposition they inaugurated, the political culture they voiced, had potentially wide appeal. The public that made this program its own introduced further changes as group after group in the nation sought its place in new institutions for consent and participation.

A significant transformation in attitude and outlook among the elite in the late ancien régime seems undeniable.[92] What prompted such a change is debatable.

"At the end of the eighteenth century," a phrase heard now and then in the debates of the Notables, suggests a conscious awareness that theirs was an age whose values and objectives differed from those in earlier times and required new practices. Were they alluding to the age of the Enlightenment? Parallels abound between arguments heard in the Assembly of Notables and those found in the writings of physiocrats and *philosophes*, including Necker.[93] Glossing over discordancies and inconsistencies, they put together a mosaic of contemporary ideas and common opinions in favor of reduced, universal, and proportional taxation, the elimination of the *corvée* and the *gabelle*, free trade and legal equality, economies and reforms in government finances, and public knowledge, control, and participation in government. Parallels may also be seen between the debates of the Notables and the pronouncements of the Paris Parlement on the *vingtième*, before Enlightenment culture became dominant. Influence came from more than one source; ideas were appropriated in various ways and worked their way indirectly. That "national" spirit Calonne had in mind and the Notables evidenced gained strength from the spread of Enlightenment culture among the elites, but it was also an outgrowth of national integration which royal power and actions advanced.

The Notables' arguments were not a reasoned discourse on government composed in solitude but their response to the immediate problems of public administration as these suddenly became known to them, and which gave priority to practical measures of action. Budget deficits rather than the principles of sovereignty were directly at issue, but the practices of sovereignty imposed themselves in their discourse and emerged changed. Their response was also the fruit of reflection, however hasty under the

---

[92] For a recent statement on the changed character of the nobility see Guy Chaussinand-Nogaret, *La noblesse au XVIIIᵉ siècle, de la Féodalité aux Lumières* (Paris, 1976).

[93] See in particular Necker's *L'Administration des finances de la France*, 3 vols. (Paris, 1784).

daily pressure of their working sessions. If Enlightenment ideas at times gave direction, provided a certain content, and supplied the language for their criticisms and claims, these did not operate as a direct literary influence but helped to confirm attitudes already in mind and to articulate those changes toward which the Notables were groping, which they believed were necessary to overcome problems the government faced, and which satisfied their interests and yearnings.[94] Enlightenment ideas, the practical needs of public policy, and individual or group ambitions converged in the Notables' demands for fiscal equality, lower taxes on the land, and participation in government.

"The end of the eighteenth century" alluded also to a time of peace of which the Notables were keenly conscious. The French involvement in the American war ended in 1783, a war that had been fought far from the territory of France. The Notables' shock at the request for more taxes after four years of peace betrayed more than the traditional belief that the king had a legitimate need for taxes only in time of war. Peace introduced its own dynamic, impelling the French to change the terms of an "implicit social contract" underlying the ancien régime.[95] Mutual obligations between subjects and ruler in a society with a monetary economy and institutionalized monarchy, such as eighteenth-century France, involved an "exchange" of taxes and political authority in a network of more or less tacit assumptions.[96] The peaceful time in which they lived was altering the conditions for "exchange," and obligations they once were willing to accept no longer satisfied. Absolutism at its beginning imposed political obedience and passivity in return for protection; the conditions of foreign and civil warfare in the sixteenth and especially seventeenth centuries made such protection a necessity, forcing the king's subjects to yield a portion of political autonomy in return for the security that greater royal authority afforded. In the eighteenth century, since the end of Louis XIV's reign, war had not devastated much of the land of France or wreaked havoc directly on the lives of most Frenchmen.[97] Two generations of relative internal peace dissolved from historical memory the sense of need for the protection absolutism offered in exchange for yielding political autonomy and public involvement in political activity.

---

[94] Furio Diaz, *Filosofia e politica nel settecento francese* (Turin, 1962), connects the *philosophes'* political arguments to the events and disputes of their day.

[95] The term comes from Barrington Moore, Jr., *Injustice, the Social Bases of Obedience and Revolt* (New York, 1978).

[96] Marcel Mauss, "Essai sur le don. Forme et raison de l'échange dans les sociétés archaiques," *Sociologie et Anthropologie,* intro. by Claude Lévi-Strauss (Paris, 1950), pp. 145–279.

[97] Mousnier, *La Plume, la faucille et le marteau,* pp. 248–53.

To give to the king obedience and the material means for authority that taxes signified now required that the king permit freer public activity and yield a portion of power to his subjects—that participation instead of obedience be exchanged for taxes. The peace that absolutism promised, when it came, denied the premises for its continued practice.

Peasant Grievances and Peasant Insurrection: France in 1789*

John Markoff

INTRODUCTION

The articulate intellectuals of revolutionary parties often leave us voluminous documents laying out their principles, their strategy and tactics, and their often esoteric differences; the leaderships of revolutionary regimes commission official histories, hold press conferences, and embody their views in legislation. The student of these producers of words rarely lacks for sources. Research into the views of the less famous participants in revolution usually requires more imaginative use of more recalcitrant sources and sometimes involves reasoned speculation without any source at all. One vehicle is statements of others about the outlook of the anonymous, obscure, and sometimes illiterate. Thus the records of the courts and police of the old regime (and sometimes the new) may be combed for interrogations or court testimony of members of the popular classes; administrators' reports and legislators' speeches are examined for their claims about the outlook of their less prominent countrymen; popular songs of the revolutionary epoch, iconography, or clothing styles are examined for what they reveal (or what we hope they reveal) of popular states of mind.

Beyond such imaginative uses of data we find the technique of plausible attribution. From our research into the forms of peasant action (do they seize land, attack tax collectors, or converge on local markets?) we make reasoned guesses about their desires. But it is difficult to make such imputations with much certainty in more than a rather crude way. (If they only go after tax collectors, they probably have tax grievances, but are they royalists or republicans—or is it possible that they couldn't care less?) Alternatively, researchers may explore the social matrix that nurtures revolt and attempt reasoned guesses about motivations under the circumstances. (If they only revolt in times of famine, one is unlikely to be far off in seeing hunger as a spur.)

Thanks to the existence of the *cahiers de doléances,* in the instance of the French Revolution, one may proceed more directly, for tens of thousands of

* This study draws on a data file initiated by Gilbert Shapiro and developed in collaboration with him. I am grateful for the comments of John Marx, Susan Olzak, George Taylor, and Charles Tilly on an earlier draft. -

This essay originally appeared in the *Journal of Modern History* 62 (September 1990).

rural communities left us a record of their grievances as the Old Regime crumbled about them. If we must acknowledge certain limitations to these documents, we also may recall their great strength: within a period of weeks, virtually every rural community in France drew up a statement of complaints about the world in which they lived and of their hopes for a better future. If one cannot take these texts as a transparent cross section of communal aspirations but must recognize the likelihood that they are often dominated by the views of the better-off inhabitants, it would, nevertheless, be difficult to exaggerate the value of a reasonably uniform sounding of the dominant rural strata throughout the country.

These documents shall be explored in this article by means of a content analysis that has been described in detail elsewhere.[1] Briefly, the code for a given demand consists, first, of a designation of the subject of the grievance. Since this ordinarily was an institution, such as the church's finances or the salt tax, I refer often to this part of the code as its "institution" as well as its "subject." Second, a code specifies a predicate, or the action demanded (e.g., the abolition or reform of the subject). Since the code guide provides over twelve hundred institutional categories, which can be combined with over fifty action codes, the language provides a variety of over sixty thousand grievances that can be expressed.

The action codes are usually ordinary verbs of the sort to be found in grievances and demands in many historical situations. Some are relatively precise, such as "reestablish," "abolish," "maintain," "equalize," or "simplify," whereas others are deliberately vague, in order to capture the diffuse character of some of the texts. For example, we have a code for the demand that somebody merely "do something about" a subject.

The code for the subject of the grievance, its institutional or problem area, is somewhat more complex: it is organized as a four-level hierarchy. The first level of the hierarchy represents major institutional categories of eighteenth-century France:

0	Miscellaneous
1	General
C	Constitution
E	Economy
G	Government
J	Judiciary
R	Religion
S	Stratification system

[1] John Markoff, Gilbert Shapiro, and Sasha R. Weitman, "Toward the Integration of Content Analysis and General Methodology," in *Sociological Methodology, 1975*, ed. David Heise (San Francisco, 1974), pp. 1–58.

Each of these categories is divided into subcategories that, in turn, are further subdivided into still finer divisions that are again subdivided one last time. A demand concerning the widely loathed salt tax, the *gabelle,* for example, would be encoded as G TA IN GA, representing, in turn, government, taxation, indirect taxes, and *gabelle.*

About forty thousand parish documents were drawn up, some twenty-five thousand of which have survived and are cataloged; over fifteen thousand have been published. A sample of these documents was chosen in two steps. We first selected a sample of *bailliages* and then selected parishes within those *bailliages.* We used as a sampling frame the collections published by the Commission de Recherche et de Publication des Documents Relatifs à la Vie Economique de la Révolution, to which we added collections published by departmental committees set up by the national commission. We arrived at a selection of some forty-six *bailliages* with at least ten parish documents. We studied the representative character of this group of *cahiers* by investigating whether *bailliages* with many parish *cahiers* published by the commission were significantly biased with regard to the events of the Revolution or the social structures of the Old Regime. We also examined possible biases in the set of all published parish *cahiers* as well as the full body of extant manuscripts. Such studies were carried out for a large number of variables. The most important bias is a tendency for the parish documents of electoral districts with larger towns to have survived more frequently than parishes in less urban districts. There are also a few other biases that are closely related (in the sense that they are associated with town size), but these are few and small. More important, the publications of the commission turn out to be at least as good a sample as the far larger body of all surviving documents. The discipline of the commission's standards seems to have been instrumental in bringing about this happy result.[2] The easily available documents that have been published in the official series in the twentieth century, therefore, constitute a good sample of the parish *cahiers* of 1789.

From each *bailliage,* we selected at random between ten and twenty rural parishes, amounting to 748 *cahiers* in all.[3] But if the full sample of 748 parishes seems fairly representative of rural France, one cannot be as confident that regional subsamples are similarly representative. The sample was designed for national estimates of parish opinion, particularly with an eye

---

[2] The evaluation of the representative character of surviving manuscripts and of published *cahiers* is taken up in detail in Gilbert Shapiro, John Markoff, and Silvio R. Duncan Baretta, ''The Selective Transmission of Historical Documents: The Case of the Parish *Cahiers* of 1789,'' *Histoire et Mesure* 2 (1987): 115–72.

[3] In other words, we did not code town *cahiers* nor did we code parish *cahiers* of a *bailliage* if the commission published fewer than ten.

to comparisons with the nobles or urban elites.[4] But the sample is more problematic as a basis for claims about rural opinion in particular regions,[5] especially in regions only represented by a relatively small number of *bailliages,* such as those in which actions directed against taxation took place, to take up an example pertinent to this article. Peasants burned toll collection stations in *bailliages* other than our forty-six. Ideally, we would like to be able to make confident claims about rural grievances in regions where peasants rose against taxation on the basis of those *bailliages* among our forty-six in which antitax insurrections took place. The justification for tolerating an imperfect sample is the significance of the concerns being raised, but the results reported here should be regarded as tentative.

We shall be asking whether areas marked by insurrection in the spring and summer of 1789 had grievances that differed from those expressed in more peaceful regions. We shall inquire as well whether regions characterized by different sorts of rural disturbance differed in the complaints of the spring. I drew upon the existing literature to locate the electoral districts where various forms of rural disturbance took place.[6] I recorded incidents of a public and

---

[4] For example, John Markoff, "Peasants Protest: The Claims of Lord, Church and State in the *Cahiers de Doléances,*" *Comparative Studies in Society and History* 32 (1990): 413–54.

[5] See the reservations expressed by Timothy Tackett, "The West in France in 1789: The Religious Factor in the Origins of the Counter-Revolution," *Journal of Modern History* 54 (1982): 739.

[6] Sources for the events: Georges Lefebvre, *La grande peur de 1789* (Paris, 1970); Michel Vovelle, "Les troubles sociaux en Provence de 1750 à 1792," in *De la cave au grenier: Un itinéraire en Provence au XVIIIe siècle: De l'histoire sociale à l'histoire des mentalités,* ed. Michel Vovelle (Quebec, 1980), pp. 221–62; Guy Lemarchand, "Les troubles de subsistances dans la généralité de Rouen (Seconde moitié du XVIIIe siècle)," *Annales historiques de la Révolution française* 35 (1963): 401–27; Ph.- J. Hesse, "Géographie coutumière et révoltes paysannes en 1789: Une hypothèse de travail," *Annales historiques de la Révolution française* 51 (1979): 280–306; Fernand Evrard, "Les paysans du mâconnais et les brigandages de juillet, 1789," *Annales de Bourgogne* 19 (1947): 7–121; Nikolai I. Karéiew, *Les paysans et la question paysanne en France dans le dernier quart du XVIIIe siècle* (Geneva, 1974); Félix Mourlot, *La fin de l'Ancien Régime dans la Généralité de Caen (1787–1790)* (Paris, 1913); Yves-Marie Bercé, *Croquants et nu-pieds: Les soulèvements paysans en France du XVIe au XIXe siècle* (Paris, 1974); Jules Viguier, *La convocation des états généraux en Provence* (Paris, 1896); Henri Dinet, "Quelques paniques postérieures à la grande peur de 1789," *Annales de Bourgogne* 48 (1976): 44–51, "Les peurs de 1789 dans la région parisienne," *Annales historiques de la Révolution française* 50 (1978): 34–44, "Recherches sur la grande peur dans la Bourgogne septentrionale: La peur de Bernon," *Annales de Bourgogne* 50 (1978): 129–73, "Craintes, brigandages et paniques inédits des années 1789–1791," *Annales historiques de la Révolution française* 53 (1981): 304–16, "L'année 1789 en Champagne," *Annales historiques de la Révolution française* 55 (1983): 570–95; Henri Diné, *La grande peur dans la généralité*

collective character in which a group formed and took some action. An anonymous letter threatening a lord was not counted, but a crowd threatening a lord to extract some concession was. Failures to pay taxes were not counted, but attacking a tax-collection point was. Implicitly challenging the seigneurial regime by silently evading payments was not counted, but burning the lord's records was.

In the forty-six districts from which the sample was drawn, most incidents fell into four categories:

Antiseigneurial events.   This rubric covers attacks on the lord's person or property, public and explicit repudiations of the lord's rights, and destruction of symbols of seigneurial authority. In the forty-six *bailliages* studied here, the spring and summer of 1789 saw the seizing or plundering of châteaux, the killing of the lord's pigeons (enjoyed under the *droit de colombier*), the collective hunting of game (forbidden under the lord's monopoly), the coerced restoration of confiscated firearms, and the forced repayment of fines levied for illicit hunting.

Antistate events.   These were attacks on the physical facilities or personnel of the central government. In the areas and time frame studied here there were incidents in which groups threatened the agents of the tax-collection system or assaulted either the collection points or the offices of some part of the tax apparatus, most commonly the *aides* (the tax on alcoholic beverages).

Subsistence events.   A variety of actions involved attempts to secure food in the face of the severe shortage that followed the disastrous harvest. The incidents included invasion of public storage facilities, searches of homes for grain, insistence that merchants sell at acceptable prices, seizure of grain convoys, or attacks on hoarders.

The Great Fear.   This was a widespread rural panic in which peasant communities sought arms and leadership to defend themselves against a nonexistent attack from bandits, townsfolk, aristocrats, or foreign armies. These remarkable events grew from the atmosphere of tense expectancy, confrontation, and uncertainty that marked the disintegration of the familiar institutions of the Old Regime. The food riots of town and country; the attacks on the lords' estates; the birth of urban militias; the mysterious, threatening,

---

de Poitiers, juillet–août, 1789 (Paris, 1951); Roger Dupuy, *La garde nationale et les débuts de la Révolution en Ille-et-Vilaine (1789–Mars 1793)* (Rennes, 1972); Ch. Huot-Marchand, "Le mouvement populaire contre les châteaux en Franche-Comté (juillet 1789)," *Annales Franc-Comtoises* 16 (1904): 193–204; and Henri Sée, "Les troubles agraires dans le Bas-Maine en juillet, 1789," *Annales historiques de la Révolution française* 2 (1925): 528–37. This list only includes studies that discuss at least one incident not mentioned in any of the others. Locating place names in *bailliages* was possible through the magnificent maps in Armand Brette, *Atlas des bailliages ou juridictions assimilées ayant formé unité électorale in 1789* (Paris, 1904).

and ineffective movements of royal troops; the tension between the representatives of the Third Estate and the king in Versailles; the taking of the Bastille;
the threatening bands of hungry strangers in which the distinction between
bandits and beggars could not easily be drawn—all took on fantastic shapes in
the flow of excited rumor.[7] Instances of countermobilization against imagined
dangers were counted under this heading.

The forty-six *bailliages* were classified according to whether or not any of
the four types of incidents occurred from March through August 1789.[8] More
than one type, of course, could occur. The Great Fear touched Neufchâtel-
en-Bray, for example, where there also had been searches for grain in April,
July, and August. In such cases a *bailliage* was assigned to both categories.[9]
Although Lefebvre regarded the Great Fear as generally quite separate from
antiseigneurial action, he points to regions where peasants, mobilized against
phantoms, subsequently turned on real opponents. If there is an antiseigneurial component, the *bailliage* is so coded as well. In other words, a *bailliage*
with rural action oriented to rumored invasion was classified under the Great
Fear; if that action is also in one of the other categories (usually antiseigneurial), it was classified there as well.[10]

A limitation of depending on the published literature is that incidents will
be missed if they have been overlooked by historians. A chief reason for
restricting this study to public and collective acts is precisely to reduce this
problem. The nonconfrontational tactic of just not paying taxes or tithes or
seigneurial rights was no doubt more widespread than the dramatic and violent
clash and arguably ultimately more important in understanding the trajectory
of the revolutionary legislation, but it is also more hidden from research and
only skimpily described in existing literature. We will never be able to map
the passive noncompliance with seigneurial dues, the anonymous threatening
letters, the furtive destruction of seigneurial property in the middle of the

---

[7] Lefebvre, *La grande peur de 1789.*

[8] A number of other incidents took place in the forty-six *bailliages* that fall outside
of these categories, but they were too few or too idiosyncratic to enter the statistical
analysis to follow.

[9] The available documentation does not always permit confident assignment of an
incident to one of these categories exclusively. For example, Anatoly Ado's survey of
rural disturbances includes many incidents in which an invasion of a château or
monastery includes the public seizure and consumption of food or drink. It would be
foolhardy to draw a hard-and-fast line between the search for food in the cellars of a
suspected hoarder and the humiliating ritual in which the lord is compelled to the
exercise of hospitality on behalf of his menacing visitors. See Anatoly V. Ado,
*Kret'ianskoe dvijhenie vo frantsii vo vremiia velikoi burjhuaznoi revoliutsii kontsà
XVIII veka* (Moscow, 1971).

[10] This procedure means that some documents are counted under more than one
rubric in the statistical tables below. Hence the sums of the numbers of documents on
which particular figures are based will add up to more than the 748 *cahiers* studied.

night, and the menacing insults that pervaded France. But we can be far more confident that frightened onlookers and anxious administrators have recorded the zones of widespread public confrontations of peasants and lords and that these have entered the research of historians. It is clearly established, say, that major subsistence disturbances in Hainaut and Cambrésis broke out in early May and took the form of searches of monasteries; or that the last third of July in Franche-Comté was marked by a determined antiseigneurialism.[11]

A second limitation to this study is the difficulty of unambiguously associating an event with a specific parish. An event took place in a parish, to be sure, but it is clear that the participants often came from farther off. I chose to explore the *cahiers* of parishes near an incident: the tabulations represent the outlook of rural opinion in *bailliages* where various forms of action occurred. It is sometimes possible for a historian to get closer to the actual participants in insurrection through eyewitness accounts of slogans and demands or police interrogations after the fact. While one may be closer, however, one is also restricted to a narrower glance. No study of police records would reveal whether regions of insurrection have unusually many demands, for example, because a comparison with quieter regions is required. We are looking here for the regional relationship, if any, of broad currents of rural opinion and rural insurrection.

PEASANT OUTLOOK AND PEASANT ACTION

We are not especially concerned here with the relationship of rural circumstances and the forms of insurrection, a significant but collateral subject,[12] but with the bearing, if any, of expressed grievances on uprisings. We will not deal, for example, with whether regions in which food prices were especially high were especially prone to revolt, but we will investigate whether revolts tend to take place in regions where complaints about prices were particularly notable. The extensive comparative literature on peasants and revolt leads us to the most diverse expectations, even on such fundamental matters as whether we expect regions whose insurrectionary communities mobilized

---

[11] Of course, the only way we might know for sure if the existing historiography has missed major zones of insurrection would be through a meticulous sifting of archives, for which Jean Nicolas's research in progress on 1661–1789 is a valuable model. Such a study of the revolutionary period would surely locate smaller scale, briefer, and localized incidents that have not as yet entered our overall sense of the mosaic of revolt. See Jean Nicolas, "Les émotions dans l'ordinateur: Premiers résultats d'une enqûete collective" (paper presented at a round table at the University of Paris VII, October 24, 1986).

[12] For the use of some of the present data to that end, see John Markoff, "Contexts and Forms of Rural Revolt: France in 1789," *Journal of Conflict Resolution* 30 (1986): 253–89.

against different targets to differ in their complaints. To frame the presentation of the evidence of the *cahiers,* I shall sketch the polar images suggested by two of the more imaginative approaches in recent years. If we follow the analysis developed by James Scott, we are led, I believe, to expect that peasants whose mobilization assumes quite distinct forms would differ little in their central concerns.[13] But should we turn to the work of Jeffery Paige we would be inclined to look for a set of coherent political visions that are systematically associated with different targets of rebellion.[14]

The aspect of Scott's innovative work that deals with the relation of grievance and action suggests the likelihood of very little systematic association of a highly elaborated rural political program with a particular mode of action, for three reasons. First of all, for Scott, the immediate concerns of peasants are both limited and utterly fundamental. The core of rebellion is a threat to subsistence. Although the trigger may be a poor harvest, an increasingly rigid tax system, or the decline of a genuine patrimonialism on the part of the local landlord, and although the broader roots may well be the encroachment of the market or the state, the central peasant concern is to fend off catastrophe. Similarly threatened peasants take part in movements of quite diverse intentions so long as they appear to deal with the fundamental subsistence issues.

Second, risk-averse peasants do not rise merely out of grievance but out of a complex calculus in which the likelihood of repression and the perceived opportunities for success weigh quite heavily. Moreover, less risky alternatives to rebellion (persuading a landlord to meet traditional obligations, say) are generally preferred. Since the sense of grievance is but one element here, the distinction between peasants who manhandle a lord and those who burn a tax-collection headquarters is as likely to be their sense of opportunity or of risk as it is to be their views of lords and tax collectors. In the third place, this calculus of risk and opportunity may shift with great rapidity at a time of collapse of the apparatus of repression. In this light, rural grievances voiced in March may serve little to illuminate the actions of July and August. Fourth, and finally (and in part a consequence of the foregoing), even in great revolutions (and Scott invokes the French Revolution, among others) coherent, elaborate revolutionary visions are unusual. Ordinary participants are motivated by very down-to-earth matters—but the struggle for a larger share

[13] James C. Scott, *The Moral Economy of the Peasant: Rebellion and Subsistence in Southeast Asia* (New Haven, Conn., and London, 1976), and *Weapons of the Weak: Everyday Forms of Peasant Resistance* (New Haven, Conn., 1985).

[14] Jeffery M. Paige, *Agrarian Revolution: Social Movements and Export Agriculture in the Underdeveloped World* (New York, 1975). What follows is a highly selective use of Paige and Scott, both of whom have developed models of peasant contention with many ramifications, most of which lie outside the present inquiry.

of the crop or a higher wage may nonetheless crack the foundations of the old order and open the way for the visionary. The difference in outlook between peasants who rise and those who do not may well be in their assessment of risks, not in the greater radical consciousness of the one and the more limited goals of the other.

The pertinent aspects of Paige's argument may be stated quite succinctly. The conditions of rural life foster a coherent understanding of the social world and of the extensiveness of change that serves rural interests. If some twentieth-century peasants embrace the cause of revolutionary socialism, it is not, as for Scott, because their limited but fundamental concerns lead them toward a national leadership with much else on their minds of no great moment to their rural adherents. Rather, under certain land-tenure arrangements, peasants recognize that their interests lie in a restructuring of property relations, that this implies a new form of state, and that this in turn implies a protracted war against the imperialist guarantors of the local social order. Paige's peasants, in short, participate in a broad social vision, and those who engage in land invasions or stage agrarian strikes, who join revolutionary guerrilla forces or attempt to impede the local bankers, are engaged in different actions because they understand their interests in deeply different ways.

A somewhat similar debate permeates the historiography of the Revolution. On the one side stand those who see the country people acquiring a broad critique of the Old Regime, although there is the greatest disagreement on the mechanisms that cemented that critique. Lefebvre stressed rural resistance to a feudal reaction in which the lords were tightening the screws.[15] Tocqueville emphasized the suppression of the lord's genuine services at the hands of the greedy state that provided fertile soil for the propaganda waged against privilege at the end of the Old Regime.[16] Labrousse suggested that rising rural literacy was opening the way to some version of Enlightenment thought.[17] Hilton Root has recently pointed to rural communities participating with lawyers in suing the lords as the proving grounds for an antiseigneurial discourse.[18] On the other side, George Taylor, in a provocative reading of the parish *cahiers,* argues for an intense localism, largely immune from political

[15] See, e.g., Georges Lefebvre, *The Coming of the French Revolution* (New York, 1947), pp. 112–24.

[16] Alexis de Tocqueville, *The Old Regime and the French Revolution* (Garden City, N.Y., 1955).

[17] Fernand Braudel and Ernest Labrousse, *Histoire économique et sociale de la France,* vol. 2, *Des derniers temps de l'âge seigneurial aux préludes de l'âge industriel (1660–1789)* (Paris, 1970), p. 729.

[18] Hilton Root, *Peasants and King in Burgundy: Agrarian Foundations of French Absolutism* (Berkeley, 1987).

issues and certainly impervious to any broad critique, whether Enlightenment or otherwise.[19] William Doyle has taken up this view of the Revolution and doubts the intellectual capacity of the peasantry to formulate a general critique of "feudalism," let alone anything else, and Eugen Weber has made a vivid, if intensely debated, case for a continuing rural isolation until late in the nineteenth century.[20]

Actions

We may ask, first of all, whether regions characterized by different forms of rural turbulence differed from each other in their general attitude toward the institutions of the Old Regime and, even more pointedly, whether they differed markedly from the regions without significant rebellions. We may approach this in several distinct ways. Do the *cahiers* of insurrectionary districts show a marked tendency to call for the outright abolition of existing institutions or practices, while the more peaceful zones call for their continued existence? We may get at this by exploring the frequency with which "abolish" and "maintain" appear in our data. Or are certain forms of peasant action perhaps associated with more moderate demands for change that we may summarize under the label of reform?[21]

Sometimes we conceive of a revolutionary mentality as embodying not merely a hostility to the existing order but a vision of a new one. We may inquire whether rebellious zones in general (or the areas that engaged in particular forms of rebellion) were peculiarly prone to call for the establishment of new institutions. We also often conceive of a revolutionary vision as implying a series of calls for action rather than vague grumbling and unformulated resentment. We may ask whether the quieter zones are especially likely to have statements that express hostility to existing institutions

[19] George V. Taylor, "Revolutionary and Nonrevolutionary Content in the *Cahiers* of 1789, an Interim Report," *French Historical Studies* 7 (1972): 479–502.

[20] William Doyle, *Origins of the French Revolution* (Oxford, 1980), p. 198; Eugen Weber, *Peasants into Frenchmen: The Modernization of Rural France, 1870–1914* (Stanford, Calif., 1976). For the debate, see Charles Tilly, "Did the Cake of Custom Break?" in *Consciousness and Class Experience in Nineteenth-Century Europe,* ed. John Merriman (New York, 1979); Eugen Weber, "*Comment la politique vint aux paysans:* A Second Look at Peasant Politicization," *American Historical Review* 87 (1982): 357–89; Melvin Edelstein, "L'apprentissage de la citoyenneté; participation électorale des campagnards et citadins (1789–93)," in *L'image de la révolution française,* ed. Michel Vovelle (Paris, 1989), 1:15–25.

[21] Concretely, I counted as reform proposals those that urged the elimination of abuses; the improvement, clarification, standardization, simplification, or modification of an institution; that an institution be supervised or placed under the control of another; that its working be rendered fairer; that its boundaries be altered; or that some of its aspects (but not all) be abolished.

unaccompanied by specific proposals (in our code: "unfavorable"). And, for that matter, is a similarly diffuse positive evaluation ("favorable") distinctive of any of our regions? We also tend at times to think of revolutionary demands as general ones, reflecting a national outlook and not a provincial or local one. (This is an important element in George Taylor's contention that the parish *cahiers* are most definitely "nonrevolutionary.") We may measure the frequency with which grievances are quite explicitly presented in a regional or provincial scope ("in Brittany") or a local one ("in our village") and see if such tendencies are indeed more characteristic of quiet areas.

Finally, we may ask whether the deeper thought that some would argue accompanies a more serious consideration of social problems is reflected in a greater complexity of expression. We may search our data for complex grievances not readily reducible to our simplified structure. In particular, statements that relate demands in a hierarchy ("if it proves impossible to simply abolish seigneurial dues, we would accept the principle of indemnification of the lord"), that pose alternatives ("either expel the Jews from the kingdom or assimilate them to the status of the other inhabitants of France"), or that make one action contingent upon another ("if the lords will actually exterminate the wolves that harass us, they may retain their monopoly on the right to hunt") we may characterize as "complex" demands. Is greater complexity of expression a tendency of the insurrectionary zones?

Table 1 presents some evidence. The figures for each column concern those *bailliages* in which incidents of particular sorts took place (or in which no incidents were discovered). We see, for example, that 18.9 percent of all grievances in our sample of parish *cahiers* from those *bailliages* with no large risings called for the abolition of an institution.[22] The clear message of table 1 is that there are no strong differences among regions in the actions demanded. Insurrectionary zones are a bit more likely to want to establish new institutions and less likely to call for reform of existing ones; they are more likely to have more complex demands; and they are less likely to see themselves as addressing regional or local issues as well as less likely to express formless hostility. But these differences are quite small. By any criterion of meaningfulness it would be hard to contend that regions with different sorts of risings (or without them altogether) differed much in the actions they demanded. Even though most of these differences are in the direction consistent with the usual images of a radical mind-set, their size is generally tiny.

[22] Since *bailliages* differ in size, we recognize that the twenty parishes randomly selected in a *bailliage* with three hundred represent more of France than the twenty from another *bailliage* with only thirty. In estimating a national figure in all tables in this paper, we weighted the contribution of each of our forty-six *bailliages*. As weights we used the total number of a *bailliage*'s parishes divided by the number in our sample.

TABLE 1
ACTIONS DEMANDED: PERCENTAGE OF GRIEVANCES

	EVENTS IN *Bailliage,* SPRING–SUMMER, 1789				
	No Large Risings	Antiseig-neurial Events	Antistate Events	Subsis-tence Events	The Great Fear
Abolish	18.9	16.6	13.7	17.0	17.3
Maintain	.9	1.4	1.2	1.0	1.1
Reform	27.1	22.1	22.7	24.6	25.3
Establish	11.8	14.8	15.5	14.3	15.1
Unfavorable ...	13.4	10.6	12.7	11.1	10.0
Favorable	1.5	1.5	2.1	1.6	1.6
Replace	.9	1.3	1.3	1.3	1.4
Local	11.3	7.2	9.1	10.1	7.8
Provincial	2.8	1.7	2.5	1.7	1.6
Complex	3.9	5.1	5.4	4.8	4.6
Number of grievances...	9,928	3,565	3,452	9,072	13,506

The strongest point of distinction—and not a very strong one at that—is in the geographic scope of the concern, not with the action as such. Regions without risings were more likely to have their sights on their own parishes rather than the national scene (i.e., there are more demands that say "in this parish"). If the peaceful areas are more parochial, the antiseigneurial disturbances come from the least parochial of all. One would hardly, on the basis of these small, even minuscule, differences, venture the general proposition that peasant uprisings are striking for their occurrence in areas where the documents show a greater national consciousness. But perhaps there is an important set of concerns for which this is indeed the case and which accounts for the pattern exhibited.

A particularly sensitive sector of their world is revealed by the parishes' responses to the demands for payments made on them by state, lord, and church.[23] Table 2 shows a strong tendency for areas with risings to be less likely to restrict their complaints about the lords and the church to their own immediately experienced world. Especially noteworthy in this regard is the low proportion of local grievances about the seigneurial regime emanating from precisely those areas that rose against the lords. So the tendency to see material burdens merely from the vantage point of "our parish" rather than as issues to be addressed far more broadly is more characteristic of districts

---

[23] A subject pursued in Markoff, "Peasants Protest" (n. 4 above).

TABLE 2
PAROCHIAL SCOPE[a] OF GRIEVANCES CONCERNING
MATERIAL EXACTIONS:
PERCENTAGE OF DOCUMENTS

	EVENTS IN *Bailliage*, SPRING–SUMMER, 1789				
	No Large Risings	Antiseigneurial Events	Antistate Events	Subsistence Events	The Great Fear
Taxation	9.1	7.8	8.9	8.1	7.3
Seigneurial rights	21.1	7.4	23.4	14.1	13.0
Clerical payments	33.8	19.7	23.3	16.4	16.6

[a] Demands that explicitly say "in our parish," "in our village," or the like.

without risings. Yet even here the distinctions ought not to be overdrawn; taxation issues are rarely local in scope anywhere.

If we think of "revolutionary" as an adjective that might characterize a state of mind and attempt to measure it by looking at the propensity to abolish existing institutions, to eschew mere reforms, to be loath to maintain elements of the existing order but eager to establish new ones, to be sparing with vague condemnations of the present but to have formed specific calls to action, we would have to conclude that the documents suggest that regions with and without risings (let alone regions with different sorts of risings) differed little (although those slight differences are consistent with one's image of a revolutionary outlook). But we see a glimmer of a more subtle distinction: in some crucial matters, the zones of rebellion are also zones in which a sense of burdens as those of the peasantry of France and not just of our neighbors and cousins seems evidenced in our texts. Are there other ways in which the scope of rural concern might have differed from one zone to the next?

Quantity

Perhaps the single most compelling figure would be the sheer number of grievances. Are action-prone regions those in which there are simply more demands? Table 3 shows this most clearly to have been the case: the turbulent areas all had more complaints than the peaceful ones and the regions of antiseigneurial actions were the most visibly aggrieved of all.

One hypothesis one might propose at this point is that it is the sheer quantity of grievances rather than the characteristics of those grievances that is critical. Those regions that write longer texts, thereby approaching more closely the extended discussions that characterize the *cahiers* of the more powerful, are

TABLE 3
GRIEVANCES PER DOCUMENT

	EVENTS IN *Bailliage*, SPRING–SUMMER, 1789				
	No Large Risings	Antiseigneurial Events	Antistate Events	Subsistence Events	The Great Fear
Mean per document ...	35.8	54.2	49.1	41.6	42.1
Number of documents ...	285	68	70	243	340

those whose people rose in 1789.[24] We may inquire as to whether it is the possession or the expression of more grievances that is the crucial factor. That is to say, is it the experience of a greater number and variety of burdens that promotes insurrection — or is it the capacity to come to an agreement with one's fellow villagers on a larger list of complaints? The first possibility would be consistent with those scholars who see a fairly direct linkage of burdens and revolt; the second is more in accord with those who stress organizational resources and for whom the capacity to achieve unity, the agreement to agree, may well be what the lengthier documents are indicating.

Before embracing such a line of inquiry, however, let us explore further whether the larger number of demands in the rebellious zones (and, among those zones, the larger number in the antiseigneurial regions) are uniformly distributed. We already know that there is not much difference in the actions urged from one zone to the next. We have not, however, established whether the larger number of demands in regions of rebellion means that those regions have more demands on every subject or whether they are particularly prone to have grievances on certain topics; the same may well be asked for the areas in which different sorts of risings took place.

Institutions

Table 4 presents the proportion of documents in each zone that have at least one grievance in any of fifty-three broad categories.[25] These categories could certainly be more finely divided (and we shall present a more fine-grained

---

[24] The mean number of demands in the general *cahiers* of the Third Estate is 233.9; for the nobility the figure is 157.9.

[25] Employing the terminology sketched earlier, we are using the second level of our code hierarchy here.

TABLE 4
SUBJECTS TREATED IN PARISH *Cahiers*: PERCENTAGE OF DOCUMENTS

	EVENTS IN *Bailliage,* SPRING–SUMMER, 1789				
	No Large Risings	Antiseig-neurial Events	Antistate Events	Subsis-tence Events	The Great Fear
Miscellaneous	1.1	1.3	3.5	3.4	2.7
Foreign policy	0	0	0	0	0
Non-Catholics	11.8	0	0	0	.2
Colonies	0	0	0	0	0
Local	23.7	24.2	26.7	21.8	21.0
General	0	0	0	0	0
Posts	8.9	4.7	2.4	5.1	5.2
Public welfare	17.3	35.7	34.2	30.9	29.5
Public health	7.2	2.6	8.1	2.1	2.4
Public safety	3.7	4.9	5.0	5.4	4.5
Education	11.0	22.0	13.3	11.5	12.7
Public works	4.0	2.3	6.8	3.4	2.0
Stratification in general....	3.9	17.7	9.9	9.5	9.3
Stratification— miscellaneous	.4	0	0	0	0
Seigneurial regime	75.0	80.0	68.6	72.3	72.3
Mobility	9.5	32.4	23.3	19.3	18.6
Economic-class relations ..	.5	0	0	0	0
Government— miscellaneous	.6	4.0	.7	2.3	1.9
Government finances	29.2	50.4	40.8	38.7	39.6
Taxation	98.0	100	100	99.6	99.5
Military	28.2	46.7	48.1	48.9	45.1
Administrative agencies ...	54.5	42.4	38.1	29.9	34.4
King.....................	27.1	36.6	49.6	35.0	37.4
Regional and local govern- ment	57.2	62.9	75.9	63.7	64.9
Justice—miscellaneous	0	0	0	.5	.3
Justice in general	29.3	41.2	48.9	44.1	42.0
Due process	18.0	41.6	32.0	31.0	33.0
Courts	46.6	72.8	69.9	64.3	66.5
Criminal prosecution and penalties	7.5	19.4	15.4	15.8	14.2
Civil law and procedure ...	31.1	39.2	22.5	30.8	29.6
Legal professions	24.6	35.8	35.4	35.2	34.5
Enforcement agents of court	57.9	30.2	19.7	18.2	27.4
Religion—miscellaneous ..	.2	1.3	1.6	0	.6
Religion in general	0	0	0	0	0

	EVENTS IN *Bailliage*, SPRING–SUMMER, 1789				
	No Large Risings	Antiseig-neurial Events	Antistate Events	Subsis-tence Events	The Great Fear
Clergy	32.4	60.4	47.6	52.6	52.5
Morality	6.7	13.0	12.4	14.4	11.3
Church organization	16.3	19.6	25.1	18.6	19.3
Church finances	8.5	24.6	28.3	15.2	18.7
Tithe	47.1	53.6	80.6	59.0	53.4
Church-state relations	5.3	18.3	11.1	9.5	9.6
Economy—miscellaneous..	0	2.6	3.3	0	.9
Economy in general.......	38.0	35.6	32.8	20.4	25.3
Agriculture..............	89.1	74.0	87.9	79.6	77.0
Industry.................	24.2	10.9	11.2	14.4	11.2
Finance	13.9	5.3	15.4	9.2	8.0
Commerce	66.5	56.0	54.6	46.0	46.2
Transportation...........	63.1	73.2	70.4	68.8	68.5
Constitution—					
miscellaneous	0	3.0	0	3.0	1.8
Constitution in general	1.2	7.7	7.7	8.4	7.1
Political liberties..........	1.7	5.3	7.9	5.5	4.4
Estates-General	33.1	59.6	49.5	44.9	51.0
Powers of the monarch....	2.9	1.1	7.7	6.1	5.6
Powers of the nation	5.5	4.5	4.2	3.6	4.4
Number of documents.....	285	68	70	243	340

analysis below on a number of points), but this broad, overall picture is already highly informative.

The aggregate effect is again one of similarity. Regions that experienced insurrections in various forms and peaceful regions alike had no interest at all in foreign affairs or colonial issues, paid scant attention to personal liberties, eschewed general discussions of religion, showed some concern for a miscellany of strictly local matters, showed considerable interest in commerce and transportation and rather more in agriculture, and were virtually certain to complain about taxes. The difference in the proportion of documents taking up some subject in the quieter areas from the proportion in the insurrectionary zone with which they differed most is under 10 percent in half the categories. The greatest percentage difference among the four insurrectionary zones is under 5 percent in a bit under half the categories.

Let us examine those subjects for which there is a consistent difference between quiet and turbulent areas. There are eleven subjects for which the difference between the quiet zone and the rebellious zone with which it differs least is at least 10 percent. In the majority of these instances it is the rebellious zones that are more likely to have the grievances: "public welfare," "military," "justice in general," "due process," "the courts," "clergy," "Estates-General." But in the cases of "non-Catholics," "administrative agencies of the government," "enforcement agents of the courts," and "commerce," discussions of these issues are associated with an absence of insurrection. The greater number of grievances in the zones of insurrection, then, does not mean a greater number of grievances of all sorts. By taking up "public welfare" the rebellious zones seem more attuned to issues of poverty; by discussing the Estates-General they show more involvement with the national political crisis (perhaps paralleling the greater national scope of their grievances); by attention to the courts and the clergy they take major national institutions to be significant in their lives. But the more peaceful areas have their own special areas of grievance. This may come as a bit of a surprise. That many grievances or serious ones might fuel revolt is hardly startling (although the delineation of the precise grievances involved might yield the unexpected). But that some grievances actually seem to dampen unrest is by no means a commonplace.

To pursue the matter further we need greater precision. Which aspects of "public welfare" are relevant here and which aspects of military affairs? The presence of three judicial topics seems to indicate a generally greater concern with the structure of justice among rebellious peasants; is this concern diffused across all matters dealing with the legal system or is it sharply focused on particular matters? (We see that at least the issue of "enforcement agents of the courts" is quite distinct since it depresses rebellion.) And what, specifically, about the Estates-General is more salient where peasants rebel than where they do not? As for commerce, we note that in general, economic issues seem more likely to be taken up in the *cahiers* of peaceful regions: while the differences are smaller than in the case of commerce, the discussions of agriculture, of industry, and of finance as well as general discussions of economic affairs are all more common, on the whole, in the quiet zones. Is there something about economic issues that militates against uprisings?

My procedure was to subject a finer classification of French institutions to the sort of analysis presented in table 4. The starting point was the eleven rubrics that have already revealed differences, although hardly enormous ones, between peaceful and turbulent areas. To these were added the other economic categories, since these appear similar to "commerce." And since "taxation" comes up in almost every parish *cahier,* this category, too, was subdivided to see if specific aspects of taxation are addressed in more quiet or more rebellious areas. Rather than present all the numbers thus generated, I present only those concerning more specific institutions for which there is a difference of at least 10 percent between the peaceful zones and at least three of the four insurrectionary zones. Table 5 displays the results for those institutions the discussion of which is associated with insurrection, while table 6 displays the corresponding data for institutions in some way linked to the absence of rebellion.

Among specific existing taxes, we see that it is the *taille* and *capitation* that seem especially associated with rebellion. In areas where country people attacked the personnel or facilities of tax collection, the *cahiers* tend to consider establishing new taxes and discuss organizational aspects of the tax system. This certainly departs from an image of unthinking fury. In addition, if taxes are more carefully considered in regions where peasants attacked them most visibly than they are in zones with other forms of rising, the differences on this score between all the zones of rebellion and the peaceful areas are indeed substantial. Where peasants and rural artisans mobilize at all, they have thought more seriously about the burdens imposed upon them by the state.

TABLE 5

FINER ANALYSIS OF INSTITUTIONS MORE COMMONLY
DISCUSSED IN ZONES OF REBELLION: PERCENTAGE OF DOCUMENTS

	EVENTS IN *Bailliage*, SPRING–SUMMER, 1789				
	No Large Risings	Antiseig- neurial Events	Antistate Events	Subsis- tence Events	The Great Fear
Taxation:					
Capitation	7.6	24.1	32.4	23.7	22.9
Taille	13.3	27.4	33.9	30.5	33.2
New taxes	33.7	46.2	51.8	45.6	51.5
Tax administration	27.0	44.9	67.5	45.7	45.9
Estates-General:					
Composition of assembly.	4.6	20.4	12.6	22.1	17.9
Voting	7.2	21.5	19.4	22.6	20.5
Regular sessions	9.5	24.2	36.3	28.2	29.1
Judicial matters:					
Laws	11.2	29.7	32.6	24.5	25.6
Procedure	14.7	25.0	29.6	26.8	24.4
Due process in general	7.5	25.1	18.9	16.9	18.6
Church:					
Lower clergy	22.1	47.8	32.6	35.5	38.6
Benefices	4.5	17.9	22.1	12.9	14.7
Mobility criteria:					
Posts and career lines	6.9	27.9	17.2	17.0	11.8
Military:					
Militia	23.1	45.4	44.3	43.5	42.1
Number of documents	285	68	70	243	340

TABLE 6
FINER ANALYSIS OF INSTITUTIONS LESS COMMONLY
DISCUSSED IN ZONES OF REBELLION: PERCENTAGE OF DOCUMENTS

	EVENTS IN *Bailliage*, SPRING–SUMMER, 1789				
	No Large Risings	Antiseig- neurial Events	Antistate Events	Subsis- tence Events	The Great Fear
Administrative agencies:					
Water and Forests.......	42.5	8.1	13.0	10.5	10.8
Enforcement agents of courts:					
Priseurs	55.6	25.3	15.0	12.1	21.5
Economic matters:					
Price or availability of any commodity.......	28.8	13.0	6.0	8.0	9.1
Price or availability of wood...............	18.8	2.6	1.7	.5	1.9
Miscellaneous aspects of agriculture	18.8	6.4	5.2	8.4	6.9
Communal rights	61.7	29.2	24.7	17.6	21.0
Tolls, customs..........	54.1	41.8	36.9	26.3	30.1
Number of documents.....	285	68	70	243	340

The same general observations apply as well to several other aspects of the agenda of the insurrectionary areas. The zones of insurrection are more apt to raise some of the broad issues characteristic of the *cahiers* of the more affluent: political demands about the nature of the coming Estates-General, attention to judicial and clerical matters, and mobility issues.[26] These are all matters far more widely discussed in the general *cahiers* of the Third Estate and nobility than in the parish *cahiers* as a whole.[27]

Risings were rather more likely as well among communities that had embraced some of the political or other long-range issues of the more affluent. The mobility issues are particularly interesting in this regard since it is hard to see attainment of high office or ennoblement as rural concerns at all. Recall that in the crucial areas of seigneurial rights and church dues, the *cahiers* of the rebellious zones show more by way of a national orientation and thereby resemble the urban notables in this way as well. While George Taylor has pointed to the narrowness of vision of the parish *cahiers* in general, we note

[26] Under the mobility rubric we include grievances about criteria for attainment of high office (in the government, judiciary, church, or military) and issues of ennoblement.
[27] Markoff, ''Peasants Protest.''

here that the *cahiers* of the rebellious zones are somewhat less narrow.[28] Ought we to see these tendencies as the result of some long-term developmental process that raised the level of political consciousness of a portion of the countryside? Or should we see here an outcome of the immediate crisis in which nobles and urban groups waged a campaign for the hearts and minds of the country people and perhaps persuaded some assemblies to embrace essentially urban concerns as their own?[29] Whatever their source, however, it is hard to see in any of these differences the critical explanation of regional differences in the propensity to revolt. Neither the nature of those grievances more common in rebellious zones nor the size of the differences from the peaceful areas leads one to think that it is in their expressed grievances that we can find the key to explaining the presence or absence of rural revolt.

In exploring the grievances characteristic of insurrectionary regions, thus far there have been no big surprises. That a large number of grievances or grievances of an exceptionally serious character might fuel revolt will surprise no one. It is more noteworthy that some grievances actually seem to dampen unrest: the peaceful areas have their own special grievances. What can this mean? If some grievances are facilitators of revolt, are others suppressors? And if so, why?

Examine table 6 where we present grievances more common in the zones of no rebellion. What is striking here is how much larger some of the regional differences are than those displayed in table 5. Compared with table 5, generated by a search for facilitators of revolt, we are here rather more successful in our search for suppressors. Note how strongly concern with the administration of water and forests, with communal rights, with certain aspects of the indirect tax system, and with the supervisors of court-sponsored auctions are linked to the absence of risings. The inhibitory effect of certain grievances, particularly in the area of communal rights, is so striking that something beyond merely calling attention to this inhibition is called for. I offer an admittedly highly speculative suggestion: that the appearance of certain grievances in the *cahiers* indicates a divided community; that the insurrections of the early revolution were fostered by fairly unitary communities; and, therefore, that threats to such unity reduced the capacity for mobilization. I shall first present the case that some grievances derive from divided communities.

[28] Taylor, "Revolutionary and Nonrevolutionary Content in the *Cahiers* of 1789" (n. 18 above).

[29] Along the lines of the latter possibility, thinking of the town lawyers who were so active in writing and distributing brochures, in circulating to the countryside models for *cahiers,* and sometimes in assisting villagers in drafting their documents, it might be the case that those rural communities that were particularly open to such influence were thereby likely to take on the unusual attention to judicial matters that were clearly highly salient for legal professionals.

Consider first the issue of communal rights. By virtue of these practices, fences might be barred, animals of any members of the community might graze on common land or on the stubble one was required to leave, and crop rotation or even agricultural technology might be mandated. Few matters, indeed, were more bitterly divisive within the rural community. Historians have debated for some time just what the lines of division were. Some have proposed that the more well-to-do wanted to abandon these practices in order to be free to enclose their own fields, choose their own crops, decide on the dates of planting and reaping, hire whatever labor they wanted, and carry out the work on their land to their own taste and profit. Others have suggested that it was precisely the better off who were most able to profit from the existing collective constraints by grazing their large numbers of cattle on the obligatory fallow of others (or even renting this right to commercial stockraisers). Some scholars think the poor favored these rights by virtue of which they were not restricted to their own meager plots for grazing their underfed animals; while according to others, the desperate land hunger of the landless led them to desire a division of the common land so that they had at least something. In one particularly ingenious speculative discussion, it is suggested that it was the "middle" peasant who favored the preservation and even the extension of collective rights: the rich wanted them abolished to pursue their individual dreams of entrepreneurship and the poor had too little to make any use of them and preferred individual title to a bit of land, while the in-between peasants had enough resources of their own to benefit from the additional resources that were held in common but not so much that emancipation from collective regulation of economic life would be a good deal.[30]

What seems beyond doubt is the sheer fact of communal division. There were peasants who opposed some or all of these collective rights and others who supported them. When revolutionary legislatures with an individualistic bent ultimately came to grapple with communal holdings, they found a formidable challenge in the passionate commitments on both sides in rural France.[31] What all the foregoing suggests is that where the issue of communal rights was vigorously alive and pursued with sufficient energy so that one or

---

[30] Georges Lefebvre, "La révolution française et les paysans," in *Etudes sur la Révolution française*, ed. Georges Lefebvre (Paris, 1954); Albert Soboul, *Histoire de la Révolution française* (Paris, 1962), 1:61–63; Florence Gauthier, *La voie paysanne dans la Révolution française: L'exemple de la Picardie* (Paris, 1977); Alfred Cobban, *The Social Interpretation of the French Revolution* (Cambridge, 1964); Ado (n. 9 above), pp. 192–93; Root (n. 18 above); Marc Bloch, "La lutte pour l'individualisme agraire dans la France du XVIIIe siècle," *Annales d'histoire economique et sociale* 2 (1930): 329–81, 511–56; Kathryn Norberg, "Dividing Up the Commons: Institutional Change in Rural France, 1789–1799," *Politics and Society* 16 (1988): 265–86.

[31] The rural divisions are nicely surveyed in P. M. Jones, *The Peasantry in the French Revolution* (Cambridge, 1988), pp. 124–66.

another village faction got its own position inserted into the *cahier,* it may well be that we have a strong indication of a community sufficiently divided to be unable to take action against a common enemy.[32]

If it is correct that discussions of communal rights indicate a community divided along class lines, then an understanding of other suppressors may follow as well. Returning to table 6: the price of wood is particularly likely to be an issue precisely where communal rights are in question, for access to wood was one of the most contested arenas. Communal claims to scavenge for fuel and to graze animals in the forests; the lord's claim to woodlands, newly invoked to sell timber to the rapidly growing towns whose construction industry and fuel demands made wood prices skyrocket; ironmasters seeking charcoal; and a state concerned over conservation to sustain the building of warships—all were locked in bitter conflict. This conflict probably often divided the well off from the poor. Similarly, the Water and Forests Administration—frequently discussed in quiet zones and little noted in rebellious areas—was most likely to make its presence felt in questions of forest use. Where such questions had arisen and the royal official stepped in (or was invited in), the *cahier* registered complaints—my conjecture—and the divided community did not have the unity to sustain an insurrectionary mobilization in 1789.[33]

It is a slight extension of this line of argument to other economic issues as well, for the community often contained both those poised to seize market opportunities as well as those who expected to suffer if collective claims—on artisanal industry, on the movement of goods, on the transport of food—went by the wayside. Glancing again at table 4, we see "industry" and "commerce" as suppressors. We also see in table 6 that price issues generally are more tied to no rising than to any form of rebellion, even food riots. If price issues are signs of hardship for those whose marketable surplus is small, bringing up price issues in the *cahiers,* I have argued, marks a lack of unity. Apparently, here, the organizational weakness had more of a suppressing effect on insurrection than the sense of hardship did on promoting it.

---

[32] The parish *cahiers* themselves only rarely give glimpses of internal divisions. Validation (or invalidation) of the inferences drawn here would require exploration of records of the parish assemblies, which is not only an extensive project but still might not answer the question.

[33] Hilton Root shows that in Burgundy the Water and Forest Administration often acted on the petition of the well off who sought to replace a system that had an equal division of communally owned wood among all taxpayers by a system that favored those with higher taxes. A village minority thus hoped to circumvent the village assembly (and sometimes succeeded). The Water and Forest Administration, then, most directly entered the lives of villagers when village solidarity was violated. It is not clear whether one may take this to be a national phenomenon (Root, pp. 112–23).

Grievances concerning tolls and customs duties, characteristic of the urban notables, probably occurred precisely in those peasant communities whose upper stratum was endeavoring to improve its market position.[34] Such communities, if our supposition is correct, may have been sufficiently torn by something on the order of class conflict to inhibit insurrectionary solidarity.

The court agent whose mention is so clear a sign of regional peace in 1789 is the *priseur,* whose grim task it was to seize and auction off the meager possessions of bankrupt rural families. It is easy enough to see why these agents' actions — and their fees — would lead to widespread detestation. It is surprising, therefore, to discover that this animosity is concentrated in peaceful areas. I do not believe that our knowledge of this important bane of village France permits any very confident interpretation. Was the *priseur,* perhaps, a figure particularly evident in communities divided along economic lines? Someone, after all, was buying the cooking pot or two, the old chest, and perhaps a stray piece of furniture.

The entire argument rests on seeing the inclusion of grievances in *cahiers* as political acts rather than simple compendia of the complaints of individual participants in the parish assemblies. It is hard to imagine the *cahiers* as mere aggregations of individual demands. The widespread hardships of 1789 are well known, yet the immediate economic crisis and its most visible symptom, the price of grain, receive far less discussion in the parish *cahiers* than many other subjects. Subsistence disturbances were far more widespread until the new harvest than antiseigneurial or antistate events, yet subsistence issues occupy far less space in the rural documents than do the seigneurial rights or taxation. What was put in those documents was the result of an act of will.[35] If communities throughout France failed to complain about such clear sources of suffering as shortages and prices, it is hard not to search for an explanation (even a speculative one, if we must) concerning why such complaints were so scarce.

If it is at least plausible (if hardly proven) that grievances that inhibited insurrection may well have emanated from communities divided along class lines, what is the plausibility that the risings of 1789 were the work of united communities? The ambitious attempts at a synthesis of the rural experience of revolution by Anatoly Ado and, more recently, by P. M. Jones propound an

---

[34] Ninety-three percent of the general *cahiers* of the Third Estate take up customs duties and governmental tolls.

[35] This is a wholly separate issue from the hoary question of external influences on the parish *cahiers.* Whether or not a seigneurial judge, a parish priest, or an urban attorney played an untoward role in shaping the thinking of the village assembly, the insertion of grievances into the documents was still a decision, not an automatic enumeration of individual complaints.

overall model consistent with such a view.[36] For both authors, rural mobilization might be the outcome either of a community united against a common opponent or of a struggle within that community—with the former more characteristic of the early Revolution. The collapse of the old order cemented village solidarity against external threats, particularly from the lords but also from the agents of the state and bourgeois property holders. With the struggle against the lords won, the tensions within the rural community boiled over: issues of communal rights and of acquisition of property seized from king, church, and émigrés, conflicts over citizenship qualifications, and divisions over the Revolution's religious legislation all came to the fore. One may suggest, moreover, that the urban struggles of radical factions for national power eventually created potential urban allies for radical village factions that were not present initially. Village Jacobinism required a new organizational network. In this model, then, the Revolution saw both sorts of conflict, but it was temporally structured: the early rural struggles were not internal to the village community, while the later ones were.

Is there any evidence that uprisings early in the Revolution were the work of united communities? Jones's recent book suggests evidence of two sorts. First, we have some indications of the participants in rural actions during the early stages of the Revolution. Second, we have some indications of the victims of those actions. While the evidence is admittedly fragmentary and of geographically narrow scope, it is extremely suggestive. It appears, first of all, that there was a broad range of community participants in those events during the early stages of the Revolution, including independent *laboureurs*, day laborers, and rural artisans. Rural activism was not limited to a single economic stratum. Rural uprisings early in the Revolution seem to have drawn on the spectrum of socioeconomic categories. And, second, to the extent that one can identify persons as targets of rural actions, the early revolutionary period does not seem to have had peasant victims: the victims were lords and lords' agents, state officials, clerics, bourgeois proprietors, and merchants. Again, this is what one would expect of a rural community at war with external enemies, but it is thoroughly inconsistent with a civil war within the village.[37] There is also some evidence that communities with a strong tradition of organizational autonomy were particularly prone to seize the opportunities presented by the collapsing Old Regime to engage in collective action. I have in mind particularly the explosiveness of the Mediterranean

---

[36] Ado, pp. 120, 159, 192–93; Jones, *The Peasantry in the French Revolution*, pp. 124–66.

[37] The most systematic such study, on which Jones relies heavily, is Jean Boutier, "Jacqueries en pays croquant: Les révoltes paysannes en Aquitaine (décembre 1789–mars 1790)," *Annales: Economies, Sociétés, Civilisations* 34 (1979): 760–86. Clearly, more work needs to be done on the social location of rural conflict.

South beyond what seems explainable by economic circumstances, literacy, or urban proximity.[38] That is to say, a previously developed capacity for organizational unity seems to have fostered mobilization in the early Revolution. (In such a model, groupings within the village might later come to mobilize against each other, particularly if they found urban allies, in the course of the Revolution.)

Perhaps, then, divided communities were peaceful through paralysis in 1789, although they may have come to be explosive later. Thus, indicators of division in the *cahiers* would also be indicators of a communal structure not prone to revolt in 1789. I have, assuredly, offered a most speculative account. But why else would grievances about communal rights as well as other economically sensitive matters so consistently inhibit revolt? (To the charge that we do not really know enough about the micropolitics of France's villages in revolution to confirm or refute such a thesis, I would have to assent.)

DIFFERENTIATING INSURRECTIONARY ZONES

Let us now turn to whether grievances differentiate among zones characterized by different sorts of insurrection. If we are searching for evidence that there is a direct connection of views and actions, we should, I imagine, look for something like the following: *(a)* zones of antiseigneurial events will be more likely to have antiseigneurial grievances; *(b)* zones of antistate events will be more likely to have antitax grievances; and *(c)* zones of subsistence events will be more likely to have grievances about prices, food, or scarcity.

But we may also inquire whether such grievances about fairly immediate material conditions have been generalized or are embedded in a mesh of wider concerns. We shall ask the following: *(a)* Are communities in antiseigneurial zones particularly likely to complain about privilege of which the lords' claims form a part? Do they share the sense, later embodied in the National Assembly's discussions of August 11, 1789, of a "feudal regime" (although not necessarily using such a term) of which payments to the church as well as the lord are a central part? *(b)* Are communities in antistate zones hostile to agents of distant authority above and beyond the apparatus of tax collection? Are they particularly likely to be concerned with state structures? and *(c)* Are communities in zones of subsistence events especially likely to discuss issues of immiserization, so immediate in 1789? Are they especially likely to raise longer-term questions of economic growth? As for the Great Fear, there is no obvious link on the level of ideas between anything in the *cahiers* and that remarkable form of action some months later.

I present data on these matters in table 7 and will occasionally refer back to pertinent figures in earlier tables. The record appears mixed. Antiseigneu-

---

[38] Markoff, "Contexts and Forms of Rural Revolt" (n. 11 above).

TABLE 7
GRIEVANCES PER DOCUMENT ON SELECTED SUBJECTS

	EVENTS IN *Bailliage*, SPRING–SUMMER, 1789				
	No Large Risings	Antiseig-neurial Events	Antistate Events	Subsis-tence Events	The Great Fear
Seigneurial rights	3.26	7.28	3.39	4.82	4.26
Tax administration	1.81	2.22	3.35	2.19	2.00
Tax advantages	1.09	1.53	1.44	1.10	1.24
All grievances concerning taxes	7.64	10.18	9.87	7.86	8.52
Prices...................	1.14	.48	.85	.51	.43
Mobility	.24	1.15	.71	.58	.59
Regional and local govern-ment	1.80	2.76	3.18	2.36	2.31
Casuels and tithe	1.11	1.87	2.96	1.93	1.63
Religion (all grievances)...	2.45	5.41	5.95	4.12	4.30
Administrative agencies (including tax adminis-tration)	3.26	3.09	4.09	2.74	2.62
Government finances......	.69	1.35	.93	.85	.96
Poor relief...............	.30	.98	.80	.61	.67
Free trade	.32	.21	.23	.24	.22
Economic matters (other than communal rights) ..	8.26	6.40	7.54	5.81	5.67
Number of documents	285	68	70	243	340

rial zones do spawn grievances about the seigneurial regime. Antistate zones are prone to grievances about tax administration, but if we consider tax privileges or all tax grievances, it is actually the antiseigneurial zones that are a bit ahead. As for grievances about food, shortages, provisioning, prices, there is simply no relationship whatsoever with subsistence events. Although subsistence disturbances were far more widespread in 1789, grievances on subsistence issues are far less common than grievances on the exactions of lord or state. Indeed, if anything, as we have seen, such grievances are apt to be associated with the absence of risings altogether. The most noteworthy thing about complaints of scarcity, in fact, is how few there are in light of the severe hardships in much of the country in 1789.

If we move beyond the search for the most direct linkages between expressed grievances and forms of action—beyond seigneurial rights, the claims of the state, and the fear of hunger—the picture gets even less clear cut. In some ways the antiseigneurial zones appear somewhat more permeated with a far-reaching agenda for reform: they are more likely to raise issues of mobility and privilege, they are even more likely to discuss tax privileges than their fellows of the antistate zones, and they are a bit more concerned with issues of poor relief. We saw earlier, in table 5, that they are more likely to address the balance of power among the three orders at the Estates-General. They are more concerned with many judicial issues (table 4). But they are not consistently the most likely to complain about the church as one might have expected: the tithe, clearly associated in the *cahiers* of the Third Estate with the "feudal" past, is plainly more salient in the antistate zones.[39]

While the antistate zones are, unsurprisingly, more prone to complaints about specific taxes (table 5) and, for that matter, about the administrative aspects of the tax system—though not about issues of tax privilege—they are not much more concerned than other regions with most other facets of government. They are rather more concerned with regional and local government; and they are more likely to refer to the king (table 4)—generally a statement of praise for the beneficence of Louis XVI. As for government finances, one would think this a simple extension of taxation concerns. (We include under this rubric issues of government borrowing and debt repayment as well as concerns for the accountability of finance officials and open disclosure of their activities.) Yet such topics are more likely to be expressed in the antiseigneurial zones.

For their part, not only are districts with subsistence events not especially prone to complain of scarcity, they are not unusually concerned about issues of freedom of the grain trade, one of the debated policies most intimately connected with subsistence events.[40] Nor are they more involved with issues of the poor, with beggars, or with artisanal unemployment than other zones. And even excluding communal rights that we have considered at length earlier, grievances concerning economic policy are less frequent in areas that experienced subsistence events than in most other zones (and, most pointedly, less numerous than in areas unmarked by any kind of large movement).

And what can one say of the Great Fear? I have been unable to locate anything in the parish *cahiers* that predicts this spectacular summer panic or, rather, that distinguishes the zones of the Great Fear from other forms of mobilization. Nor do there appear to be any particular grievances that suppress it without at the same time suppressing all forms of rural activism.

We do not find much of what we would expect if the choice of rural action were intimately linked to a worldview. Antiseigneurial actions do seem tied to

[39] The association of payments due the church and payments due the lord, evident in the National Assembly's dramatic decrees of August 4–11, had been evident already in the Third Estate documents of the spring, a subject on which I shall elaborate in future publication.

[40] Steven L. Kaplan, *Bread, Politics and Political Economy in the Reign of Louis XV* (The Hague, 1976).

the expression of antiseigneurial sentiment and antistate actions, although with less consistency, to antitax sentiments. But the ties are not overwhelmingly strong ones, subsistence events are not tied to the specific strength of subsistence grievances, and the Great Fear seems tied to nothing at all by way of the expression of sentiment. And this is to consider only the narrowest of visions. Lacking even that, there is no point in hunting for a broad vision that goes along with food riots or summer panic. The antiseigneurial zones, however, do evidence a fairly consistent concern with societal privilege, judicial arbitrariness, and political representation. It seems fair to see these latter zones as demonstrating some of what the conquering bourgeoisie would likely have taken to be the most advanced forms of political consciousness. These were the village communities whose agenda most resembled that of the upper reaches of the Third Estate. The antistate zones evince something by way of a general concern over the government, most notably in their focus on regional and local structures of power; but again, their distinctiveness in this regard can hardly be said to be overwhelming, and it is certainly not consistently supported in other ways.

Lessons

What lessons, if any, have we learned about insurrection and grievances in 1789? What does all this suggest about the capacity for insurrection of the French peasantry at the beginning of the Revolution—and what does it suggest as promising areas for further investigation? Most important, we saw that the differences between communities engaged in different forms of action are narrow and hardly overwhelmingly strong. Why?

One might attempt to argue that at critical historical junctures, in which old structures of constraint are disintegrating, even relatively small differences in outlook might have large consequences for behavior. Perhaps this helps us understand the decision to kill the lord's pigeons, say, or to burn a barrier at which tolls were collected; but it plainly helps us not a whit as far as food riots and the Great Fear are concerned.

On present evidence, more plausible, I should think, is the likelihood that the spring and summer of 1789 —and several years beyond— constituted a juncture of rapidly changing constraints and opportunities, in which targets of insurrection were often targets of opportunity. Areas of insurrection do appear to be areas with rather more wide-ranging demands and with *cahiers* that also more closely approximated the concerns of the elites. Some might hold these peasant communities to be models of a relatively advanced rural political consciousness. Yet we have seen that such facilitators of revolt as grievances about the seigneurial regime were less effective in promoting revolt than were several other grievances in suppressing it. To whatever extent, moreover, that particular grievances may have been a vital fuel for the social upheaval, those particular grievances had far less to do with shaping the form that revolt took. While there was a tendency for tax and seigneurial targets to be related to the grievances of the spring, often even these were not so related. And we have seen that subsistence events are utterly unrelated to the intensity of subsistence grievances in the spring. As for the Great Fear, it developed from the political context of the summer and is in no way, our data show quite clearly, related to political positions assumed only a few months before. This is not to say that either subsistence events or the Great Fear took place in a vacuum. Subsistence events are clearly connected to the availability of food. Louise Tilly argued that throughout the eighteenth century it was around the roads and towns — that is, the arteries along which grain convoys moved and the hubs of the provisioning system — that conflicts over grain occurred.[41] The Great Fear, too, tended to take place near large towns and major roads, but, unlike other forms of conflict, it was also highly concentrated in regions of low literacy as well as in wine-producing areas.[42] So there was a structure: food riots near food, rural panic near the roads the imaginary invaders might travel. But the grievances of the spring do not illuminate these events at all.

The evidence presented here underscores the rapidity of events and in that sense supports George Taylor's view that the Revolution cannot be seen as the working out of projects already embodied in the *cahiers*. Between spring and summer much had altered. The entire political context had changed. And in rural France one should never forget the seasons. The harvest was not only the time for bringing in the sheaves but also for preparing to pay in kind to church and lord, and it was the time of some taxes as well. Ado has stressed the relationship through 1792 of the seasonal patterns of exaction and insurrection.[43] Perhaps rural intentions voiced in the *cahiers* of the spring shifted according to the calendar as well as through the intervening drama of riot and repression.

Although rural ideas played a role, the whole thrust of our analysis has directed us toward constraints and opportunities.[44] The data also seem to

---

[41] Louise A. Tilly, "The Food Riot as a Form of Political Conflict in France," *Journal of Interdisciplinary History* 2 (1971): 23–57.

[42] For more on the regional structures that nurtured different forms of rural action in 1789, see Markoff, "Contexts and Forms of Rural Revolt."

[43] Ado, pp. 163, 230.

[44] Other studies suggest the relationship of rural attitudes expressed in the *cahiers* to rural events in the Revolution to be far from straightforward. Paul Bois and Charles Tilly both examined *cahiers* of pro- and counter-revolutionary areas in western France, with somewhat different results. Tilly found the *cahiers* of areas of southern Anjou

underscore the soundness of the direction taken by recent sociological investigation into social movements: opportunities to act and the perception of the balance of benefits and danger as well as organizational capacities are now rather widely taken as the grist to be worked through the analytic mill. The exploration of the intertwining of such matters with each other (and sometimes with felt grievances) now dominates the field.[45] Thus we see here that the inhibiting effect of grievances that seem unlikely to be voiced by a united community was far more dramatic than the encouraging effect of any grievance we have found.

Yet the antiseigneurial movements are associated with an outlook that has some resemblance to that of the urban notables. The antiseigneurial zones are unique in embedding the narrowest definition of their insurrectionary concerns within broader issues. They are not merely unusually prone to take up the structure of privilege rather broadly, with their focus on tax privileges, the distribution of power in the coming Estates-General, and mobility issues, but they are also particularly concerned with the clergy, with education, and with a variety of judicial issues. They are also unusually unlikely to be of restricted, parochial scope when it comes to material burdens.

Why should antiseigneurial activism in 1789, uniquely, be set in regions whose assemblies addressed broad questions of the institutional structure of France? Two rather different, though perhaps complementary, answers suggest themselves. The first stresses the degree to which the seigneurial regime was intimately bound up with so many other institutions. It was linked to the church through the extensive seigneurial rights held by individual and corporate ecclesiastical lords (dues owed to a monastery, say), through the intermingling and sometimes outright confusion of *champart* and tithe (the former a portion of the crop owed a lord who might be lay or ecclesiastic, the latter a portion of the crop owed to a tithe collector who might, in the course of the ages, have

---

that accepted the Revolution to be more open to change in general and more hostile to the lords in particular, suggesting a greater receptivity to the programs of the revolutionary legislators. In the Sarthe, Paul Bois also found continuity, but of a quite different sort: those areas whose rural communities were hostile to threatening outsiders, the lords and the clergy in particular, were those who rose against the new external threat posed by the revolutionary authorities of the towns. See Charles Tilly, *The Vendée* (Cambridge, Mass., 1964), pp. 177–86; Paul Bois, *Paysans de l'Ouest: Des structures économiques et sociales aux options politiques depuis l'époque révolutionnaire dans la Sarthe* (Le Mans, 1960), pp. 189–219.

[45] Mayer Zald and John McCarthy, *The Dynamics of Social Movements: Resource Mobilization, Social Control and Tactics* (Cambridge, Mass., 1979); Anthony Oberschall, *Social Conflict and Social Movements* (Englewood Cliffs, N.J., 1973); Mayer N. Zald and John D. McCarthy, eds., *Social Movements in an Organizational Society* (New Brunswick, N.J., 1987); Karl-Dieter Opp, "Grievances and Participation in Social Movements," *American Sociological Review* 53 (1988): 853–64.

become a lay lord), and through the religious ritual surrounding lordship so frequently encapsulated in the lord's right to a particular favored bench in church. It was linked to the judicial system through the seigneurial courts, which, where still functioning in the eighteenth century, constituted the lowest rung of the complex judicial hierarchy (and in some places, more than the lowest rung).[46] It was linked to the whole structure of power and privilege through the lords' (now often contested) claims to tutelage over village communities and through the many public acknowledgments of the deference due a proper lord. In this light, it is perhaps not surprising that where country people rose against their lords they also had a revolutionary agenda that transcended these immediate targets.

Yet could one not make a similar case for the institutional centrality of taxation or provisioning policy? Zones of antitax or subsistence events, however, see no such generalizing in their documents. This observation suggests that we look for social mechanisms that might have carried the sense of institutional linkage in a way unique to the seigneurial regime. Hilton Root's recent *Peasants and King in Burgundy* suggests a possible nexus. Royal administrators seeking to strengthen the financial standing of the peasant communities on which the tax structure of the Old Regime rested and an abundance of urban lawyers seeking nontraditional clients had for quite some time been supporting rural challenges to the lords' claims. Rising numbers of peasant-initiated lawsuits whose attacks on the seigneurial regime were becoming increasingly broad were the result. Thus, at least for Burgundy, a rising antiseigneurial village activism was developed in alliance with local officials and attorneys.[47] With such a background, would it be surprising that the peasantry of antiseigneurial zones had taken on some of the social concerns of lawyers and administrators? This process, which antedated the struggle for the allegiance of the countryside that marked the electoral campaigns of 1789, may explain why the *cahiers* of these zones carry an ideological baggage of a sort that one is tempted to call bourgeois. Indeed, if one follows Root's argument, the very achievement of a unitary community, which the evidence presented here suggests was so critical to sustaining any sort of mobilization in 1789, was significantly abetted by the agents of the French monarchy.

[46] T. J. A. Le Goff, *Vannes and Its Region: A Study of Town and Country in Eighteenth-Century France* (Oxford, 1981), p. 279.

[47] While we do not yet know if the syndrome Root describes fully characterizes the kingdom as a whole, it is at least clear that the upsurge in the quantity of lawyers was a national phenomenon. (See Richard L. Kagan, "Law Students and Careers in Eighteenth-Century France," *Past and Present*, no. 68 [1975], pp. 38–72.) The incentives leading *intendants* and their subordinates to support peasant antiseigneurialism would also seem to be widespread.

But although antiseigneurial areas have their points of distinctiveness, the more striking implication of the data is how similar are the parish *cahiers* of all regions. It would have been difficult to predict peasant actions from peasant grievances.

The data, then, suggest that the opportunities of the moment and the capacity to mobilize seem more important than do differences in felt grievances in explaining the differences in rural action. Parish assemblies that adopted many demands in their *cahiers,* however, were more likely to take action (although some specific demands were inhibiting). Were these the districts whose people suffered the most? Perhaps, but the matter is far from certain. A *cahier* was not usually a mere compendium of the grievances of individual villagers. It was a collective political act, a joint statement of a community. A lengthier document does not necessarily mean an unusually high level of experienced distress. It may mean that, but it surely indicates an unusually high capacity to reach agreement on a series of public assertions. Communities that could agree on fifty articles were demonstrating a far greater capacity for action than those that could only agree on a handful.

The argument at points has an uncomfortably high element of speculation. Two centuries after France's rural people contributed to making France difficult to govern, we still do not know nearly enough about village politics under the Revolution.[48] Research on the detailed nature of economic change has proved enormously fruitful; may I suggest that an increased knowledge of the microstructures (and microconjunctures?) of local politics is likely to be at least equally important for comprehending what happened in 1789?

[48] Some examples: Raymond Collier, "Essai sur le 'socialisme' communal en Haute Provence," in *Actes du 90e Congrès national des sociétés savantes* (Paris, 1966), 1:303–33; P. M. Jones, "*La république au village* in the Southern Massif Central, 1789–1799," *History Journal* 23 (1980): 793–812; T. J. A. Le Goff and D. M. G. Sutherland, "The Revolution and the Rural Community in Eighteenth-Century Brittany," *Past and Present*, no. 62 (1974), pp. 96–119; Thomas F. Sheppard, *Lourmarin in the Eighteenth Century: A Study of a French Village* (Baltimore, 1971); Patrice L.-R. Higonnet, *Pont-de-Montvert: Social Structure and Politics in a French Village, 1700–1914* (Cambridge, 1971); Jean-Pierre-Jessenne, *Pouvoir au village et révolution: Artois, 1760–1848* (Lille, 1987).

The Monarchy and the Procedures for the Elections of 1789

François Furet

Elections are, as a rule, the poor relations of French Revolution historiography. It is as if historians believed that the revolutionary period possessed a dynamism quite independent of the mechanics of elections, even that it obeyed the opposite logic of insurrection rather than that of regulation. Thus, for example, the municipal, departmental, and legislative elections of 1790, 1791, and 1792 still await systematic studies, whereas popular movements, the clubs, and the sections have been the object of a good number of works throughout our century.

The elections of the spring of 1789 are admittedly in a somewhat different category. If they were not the event that inaugurated the Revolution, since the revolt of the Commons against the royal injunctions in June of that year deserves that credit, they were nevertheless the precondition of that revolt. The deputies chosen in the March and April vote were the same men who would take possession of national sovereignty, so the election itself may borrow some of the glory of the founding event. The assembly of the Estates General, a traditional procedure of the old monarchy, also introduced the Revolution. It unwittingly effected the transfer of power from what was to become the "Old Regime" to what was not yet the Revolution.

The assembly took place, however, at a moment when these two concepts did not yet exist—precisely because it was this transfer of power that was to constitute them. This explains the ambiguity of the brief period between January and April of 1789, during which the juridical and political machinery that would effect the passage from one to the other was instituted. It was a moment that belonged to neither category; and because it harbors the secrets of continuity it clouds the image of a 1789 composed of an end and a new beginning. The problem this moment poses for historians is not so much to understand the rupture between the ancien régime and the Revolution as it is to grasp how the ancien régime, through the Estates General, produced the Revolution.

This essay originally appeared in the *Journal of Modern History* 60, suppl. (September 1988).

It is no longer enough to scrutinize the famous *cahiers de doléances* for a hypothetical state of opinion in France on the eve of the great events. These texts, whatever their documentary value, constitute only static evidence of French attitudes and ideas at the end of the winter of 1789. They say nothing—nor could they possibly say anything—about the men, the institutions, and the mechanisms that so rapidly assured the passage from absolute monarchy to the sovereignty of the people. The historian must instead look beyond the *cahiers* to the election itself—to the choice of deputies—and to the preceding juridical provisions for the election, which were so ardently debated because they involved the stakes of power and a lasting change in public law. It is to this latter aspect of the elections of the spring of 1789 that these remarks are directed.[1]

The institution of the Estates General had been part of the French monarchical tradition since the end of the Middle Ages, and the kings of France made frequent use of it between the fourteenth and the sixteenth centuries. Its purpose was to unite around the monarch, when he so desired, the "representation" of the kingdom, which was charged with the task of assisting him with advice and counsel. The term "representation"—one of the most interesting in politics, ancient or modern—is to be understood here in its older sense. It touches the very nature of traditional French society, in which the individual existed only through the groups to which he belonged or the organic units of which he was a part: family, community, corporate bodies, social orders, all defined by rights that were both collective and individual since the privileges of the group were shared by all its members. The social universe was thus made up of a pyramid of corporate bodies that had received their places and their titles from history and from the king of France, according to a hierarchy that reflected the natural order of the world. The "representation" of this social universe before the king thus was realized quite naturally from the bottom up by condensation from one layer to the next. An upper level "represented" a lower one by embodying it; by virtue of its superior position it took over the identity of the lower level. Furthermore, the king of France, at the very peak of the pyramid, subsumed and incarnated all the groups that made up "the nation" in one body of which he was the head. His

---

[1] The essential work on juridical procedures for the election of the Estates General of 1789 is Armand Brette, *Recueil de documents relatifs à la convocation des Etats Généraux de 1789*, 4 vols. (Paris, 1894–1915). A summary of the question can be found in Jacques Cadart, *Le régime électoral des Etats généraux de 1789 et ses origines (1302–1614)* (Paris, 1952).

consultation of the "Estates" had no other object than to ratify once more the unity and identity of society and his governance.

Within this conception of society, the process of "representation" was intended not to develop a common political will on the basis of the interests or the desires of individuals but to express and transmit, from the bottom to the very summit, the demands (by definition homogeneous) of the various bodies in the kingdom. This is why this process was linked to the binding mandate by which all communities sent to higher levels, and on up to the king, deputies who were charged not with representing them in the modern sense of the word but simply with being reliable spokesmen for their desires. Just as such delegates were necessarily stripped of all personal initiative by a binding mandate, so also the assemblies of the Estates General that they formed were invested neither with sovereignty nor, in particular, with power to govern or legislate. Even if, under special circumstances, they should happen to take part in the elaboration of certain ordinances or edicts, the king remained sole legislator for the kingdom, both as author of the laws and as dispenser and guarantor of privileges. The meeting of the Estates General, an exceptional procedure designed to present to the monarch the sentiment and the counsel of his realm, took place when called for by the government. It lasted only as long as the king desired, and the recommendations it formulated were enacted at his pleasure.

The regulations covering the convocation of the Estates General had never had a fixed form. The same was true of rules governing electoral procedures, the right to vote, and the number of electoral districts and deputies. A systematic history of the Estates General (which does not yet exist) would offer an excellent illustration of the ancien régime's characteristic inability—either in spite of or because of its incessant legislative activity—to establish regular institutions and fixed rules of public law.[2] (Tocqueville returned often to this theme, seeing in it one of the origins of the tabula rasa of the Revolution.) When the decision was taken in July 1788 to call the Estates General for the purpose of consulting them on ways to resolve the crisis in the kingdom, there were, by definition, neither regulatory texts nor a body of doctrine that

[2] The most recent such history can hardly be called satisfactory. It is Georges Marie René Picot, *Histoire des Etats-généraux, considérés au point de vue de leur influence sur le gouvernement de la France de 1355 à 1614,* 5 vols. (Paris, 1868). The best recent summary on the subject is Ran Halévi, "Modalités, participation et luttes électorales en France sous l'Ancien Régime," in *L'explication du vote: Un bilan des études électorales en France,* ed. Daniel Gaxie (Paris, 1985), pp. 85–105.

could help the royal administration define how the elections should operate. The problem of documentation was even more acute because the absolute monarchy had deliberately allowed consultation procedures to fall into disuse since the early seventeenth century. This meant that if the jurists of the king of France wanted to find, if not a doctrine, at least a juridically valid precedent, they had no choice but to return to the Estates General of 1614. This most recent meeting was already nearly two centuries distant; none of its records remained, and it had very nearly disappeared from oral memory as well. A victim of its own practices, the absolute monarchy possessed no heritage, no tradition that would have enabled it to consult opinion according to incontestable forms; it was responsible for having destroyed that heritage and that tradition.

Thus, by decree of the Council of State on July 5, 1788, the king invited his subjects to send to the court "memoranda, information, and clarifications" on the holding of the Estates.[3] The crown made special efforts to ensure the participation of the learned societies, paying homage to the academies that prompted the sarcasm of Tocqueville, who expressed surprise that a topic of the sort would be put up for competition.[4] In the last decades of the eighteenth century, however, the problem of the vote and of political representation (in the modern sense this time) had indeed become philosophic questions debated by scholars, as demonstrated, for example, by the works of Condorcet.[5] If tradition was mute, unclear, remote, or obliterated, philosophy could answer in its place—and the monarchy asked it to do so!

After two centuries of experience in democratic practice, no government in the world would launch with this kind of innocence into a problem with such vast consequences as the practical details of nationwide elections. But the point is that the French monarchy lacked such experience. It was faced with a new, already dominant spirit and an ancient, underregulated institution, and it trusted the new spirit to

[3] Decree of the council July 5, 1788, in Brette, 1:23–25.

[4] Alexis de Tocqueville, *L'Ancien Régime et la Révolution*, vol. 2, chap. 1, "La constitution du pays mise au concours comme une question académique" (The constitution of the country set up as a contest topic like an academic question), vol. 2, in his *Oeuvres complètes* (Paris, 1952), 2:105.

[5] It is widely known that Condorcet thought of all of social life as founded in the rational exercise of the right to vote and that he attempted to elaborate a science of decisions taken by means of votes. See, in particular, his *Lettres d'un bourgeois de New-Haven* (1787), *Essai sur la constitution et les fonctions des assemblées provinciales, où l'on trouve un plan pour la constitution et l'administration de la France* (1788), "Sur la forme des élections" (1789).

inhabit the ancient institution. Not that things had that blueprint-like simplicity since a good many political intrigues were involved in the decisions. The royal entourage was attempting to settle its score with the privileged, who were guilty of having set off the revolt, while Necker, the most popular minister if not the most influential one, was prudently exploring paths toward monarchy in the English style. In the two key texts of December 27, 1788, and January 24, 1789, however, and in all the documents concerning the organization of the approaching Estates General, the general economy of thought and decision making is commanded by that dialogue between the new spirit and a lost tradition it has taken over but not destroyed.[6]

This new spirit was not simply an abstraction, an expression of the reason at work within the history of what the eighteenth century called the march of civilization. It was incarnate in an effervescent public opinion for which the doubling of the Third Estate's representation was a minimal but capital demand, a symbol of the promotion of the middle class following transformations in the economy, in society, and in mental attitudes, and an announcement of its collective ambition. But on September 25, 1788, the highest juridical authority in the realm, the Parlement of Paris, pronounced in favor of strict respect for the forms observed in 1614.[7] This strict respect was incompatible with (among other things) the territorial limits of the kingdom, which had changed since the beginning of the seventeenth century. Moreover, it annulled the political benefit of the convocation by making it unpopular. This led Necker and the king to decide to ask the advice of the "Notables" once again. In the council's decree of October 5 convoking them, Louis XVI demanded respect for "ancient usages," but he introduced a nuance: "in all regulations applicable to the present time."

But precisely what portion of those regulations was applicable— supposing that they were ascertainable? On November 6, when Louis XVI called on the Assembly of the Notables for their advice on the matter, Necker, opening the session, underscored the change that had taken place since 1614 and enumerated the principal reasons for it:

---

[6] The December 27, 1788 report is on preparations for the electoral regulations (Jacques Necker, *Rapport fait au Roi, dans son Conseil, par le ministre des finances*). The electoral code of 1789 is entitled *Règlement fait par le Roi pour l'exécution des lettres de convocation*. These texts have been published by both Brette and Cadart, among others. All of the documents on the organization of the Estates General are available in Brette.

[7] In the decree recording the Declaration of September 23 that announced the meeting of the Estates General.

The considerable increase in specie has introduced something like a new sort of wealth, and the immensity of the public debt shows us a numerous class of citizens closely tied to the prosperity of the State, but by bonds unknown in the old days of the monarchy. Commerce, manufacturing, and the arts of all sorts, reaching levels inconceivable in past times, today bring life to the kingdom by all the means that derive from active industry, and we are surrounded by valuable citizens whose labors enrich the State and to whom the State, in just recompense, owes esteem and confidence.[8]

The Director General of Finance thus set the deliberation on electoral procedures—in particular, the decision on doubling the Third Estate's representation demanded in so many political pamphlets—within a philosophy of history that bears easily recognizable signs of the idea of progress as it had been elaborated during the second half of the century. The development of the economy and of trade (what contemporary Scottish thought called "commercial society") dignified labor and broadened the base of citizenship. It was accompanied by an "increase in Enlightenment," which is to say a decline of traditional prejudices. By this the minister referred to the force of public opinion—the expression of reason in history and an integral part of the entire process since it was public opinion that lent that process meaning through the idea of the universality of modern man. Reliance on the procedures of 1614 was thus weakened, not only because they were uncertain (in this connection, Necker told the Notables, "you will surely wish that principles of general equity serve, at least as interpreters, for obscure things"), but also because they were anachronistic: "You will also weigh, in your wisdom, what should be the influence of an interval of nearly two centuries, during a period in which political and moral opinions have undergone the greatest revolutions."[9]

In point of fact, through the principles of "equity" Necker intended to advance not only the idea of the doubling of the Third Estate, but the idea of proportionality in the ratio of the represented to their representatives.[10] The two propositions were not unconnected since they were both justified by recent social and economic transformations.

[8] *Archives parlementaires,* 1:393.

[9] Ibid., p. 394.

[10] Necker advances this idea by means of an example, which was constantly repeated during the deliberations of the Notables and is reiterated in his report in December: "You will examine, for example, if it is proper that the *bailliage* of Gex, composed of twelve thousand inhabitants, [and] that of Auxois, which has forty thousand, have, as in 1614, the same vote and the same influence as the *sénéchaussée* of Poitou or the *grand bailliage* of Berry, even though these two districts contain today, respectively, six hundred thousand and three hundred thousand [persons]" (ibid., p. 395).

Putting the first of these into effect was to have greater impact on events after the deputies of the three orders were fused into the National Assembly in June. But the second was the more revolutionary in the intellectual order of things. Indeed, even if proportionality appeared limited for the moment to the elections of the Third Estate, it was inseparable from the idea of representation in the modern sense since, in seeking to establish a stable relationship between every representative and the number of his electors, it relied on the concept that all individuals bore equal rights in the formation of political power and a "national" assembly.

Furthermore, as we read the deliberations of the Notables, who were of course in great majority noble, the most surprising thing is not that they were, generally speaking, hostile to the doubling of the Third Estate and to innovations.[11] What is astonishing is that they devoted so much comment to the idea of a need for proportionality between the population of a constituency and the number of its deputies. The Second Bureau, for example, presided over by the comte d'Artois, deliberated on these two questions at length, and the king's own brother analyzed the advantages of proportionality:

The lord comte d'Artois, imbued with impressions of all that is just and useful, desired to register important observations on a proportion that seems necessarily to result from principles of justice and public utility. It is impossible to avoid palpable astonishment at the sight of the enormous disproportion that gives to *bailliages* composed of twelve thousand inhabitants the same representation as to six hundred thousand citizens contained within the electorate of one single *bailliage*. It is difficult to reconcile this apparent contradiction with the equality of the powers and the suffrages of every citizen, which forms the essence of the Constitution of a national assembly.[12]

It would not be difficult to multiply quotations of this sort, taken from an assembly of the cream of the French aristocracy. The hearing given to arguments contrary to their final decisions on the doubling of the Third Estate and proportionality between electors and elected shows how unsure the majority of these "Notables" were of the indefeasibility of their rights. Furthermore, when it came to a discussion of voting procedures within the Third Estate, this assembly of the privileged favored universal suffrage by a large majority and without distinguish-

[11] Only the First Bureau of the Assembly of the Notables, following the comte de Provence, accepted the doubling of the Third Estate (by thirteen votes against twelve). The five other bureaux rejected it, either by fairly clear majorities or unanimously (for the Fourth and Fifth Bureaux).

[12] *Archives parlementaires,* 1:417.

ing between the right to elect and the right to be elected—a distinction, of course, that was to be characteristic of legislation of the Revolution.

Necker's report of December 27 on the preparation of the electoral regulations was thus able to show a similar reliance on the "spirit of the times." Called back to power more by opinion than by the crown, the administrator-philosopher finally found occasion to bring into play his ideas on the need to have elected assemblies representative of society's needs participate in power. The Protestant financier, who remembered his defeat in 1781, knew better than anyone that the nobility and *les Grands* had to be catered to (even more in their egotism than in their interests, as he intelligently noted in *De l'administration des finances*).[13] This explains the contradictory nature of his text, halfway between tradition and innovation, although not in the sense of offering a political compromise on each of the points under discussion. What happened instead was that certain questions were treated in a spirit of innovation and others were abandoned to tradition—or, rather, to the idea that was held of that tradition. Two spirits inhabit Necker's text, but they are simply superimposed on one another with no attempt at synthesis.

These two spirits are asserted, one after the other, from the outset of the report. The first was based on the precedent of 1614; the second, on public opinion. On the level of principles, opinion was the more important since it led Necker to the fundamental recommendation that the number of deputies of the Third Estate be proportionate to the population represented. For Necker, "there is but one opinion in the kingdom on the need to apportion, as much as it proves possible, the number of deputies of each *bailliage* to its population; and since one can, in 1788, establish this proportion on the basis of certain knowledge, it would evidently be unreasonable to neglect these means of enlightened justice in servile imitation of the example of 1614."[14] With their indirect homage to the efforts of the *intendants* and their services to gather statistics, these few lines say it all: the supremacy of opinion, drawing its unanimity from knowledge and from justice; and a political representation of the modern type, founded at once on the equal rights of individuals and

[13] Necker, *De l'administration des finances de la France* (Paris, 1784), 1:250–51: "One can . . . without offending the most respected privileges, sometimes come to terms with them. It is the distinctions of status in France that form the most ardent object of interest. One is perhaps not annoyed to have them favor pecuniary combinations, but, when ideas of superiority are handled tactfully, the most lively sentiment is satisfied."

[14] Jacques Necker, *Rapport fait au Roi*, December 27, 1788, *Archives parlementaires*, 1:490.

on technical and administrative rationality. The rejection of "servile" imitation of the precedent of 1614 is also noteworthy. Through its minister, the monarchy itself opposed reason and justice to tradition.

The recommendation to double the Third Estate was based on similar thinking. On this point—the most burning question in contemporary debate on the national scale—Necker first prudently listed the partisans of the two theses. This parallel enumeration, however, showed the incomparable superiority, in prestige and in numbers, of the innovators' camp since in the final analysis it included, along with a minority of the Notables and the nobility, "the public desire of that vast part of your subjects known under the name of Third Estate."[15] Finally, for good measure, the minister invoked "that muted murmur from all of Europe that confusedly favors every idea of general equity." This was a way of throwing onto the balance of the royal decision the key argument (which was to have such a brilliant career in nineteenth-century thought) of the irreversibility of history. History versus tradition: this opposition shows to how great an extent the French crown, contrary to what Burke later wrote, had ceased to refer to a traditionalist vision of the Constitution of the realm to open the way ostensibly to reform but in fact to a subversion of its own spirit and tradition.[16] The need for change advocated by the minister was governed less by a desire to tinker with institutions than by a sense of the necessity of history.[17]

At the same time that it made this capital shift in the idea of representation, in favor of the Third Estate and in the name of the progress of civilization, Necker's report of December 1788 insisted more strongly than ever on the separation of the three orders in the consultation that was to open and in the assembly that was to follow it. In theory, this would annul the doubling of the Third Estate since as long as the orders were to meet separately the two more privileged orders would maintain their advantage over the third, whatever the number of deputies in each order might be. It is interesting to note that this separation of the orders was perceived more clearly and recommended[18] much more categor-

[15] Ibid., p. 491.

[16] In his *Reflections on the Revolution in France* (London, 1790), Edmund Burke considers that by calling the Estates General the French monarchy sought to restore its "Constitution."

[17] Necker's thoughts on this matter, which were both original and profound, merit study. As with Guizot, Necker the philosopher fell victim to the failure of Necker the politician. I intend to return to this question.

[18] Notably through the idea that each of the orders could choose its deputies only from among its own members.

ically than in the sixteenth century or in 1614, when the assemblies at the *bailliage* level had often mingled nobility and Third Estate.[19] At the very moment that royal authority was demanding (at least implicitly) a democratic conception of the vote within the Third Estate, it was also reinforcing (even beyond its own tradition) the aristocratic nature of that vote.

This vital contradiction can be found throughout the regulatory provisions for the organization of the elections, as established by the decree of January 24.[20] On the one hand, over and above the total separation of the orders, the regulations appealed to tradition, insisted on an assembly conceived as simply counseling the king, prescribed that city dwellers meet "by corporations and trade companies," and increased the number of special cases and exemptions in the name of acquired privilege. Above all, the document kept the traditional procedure of the *cahier de doléances,* the register of grievances that purportedly presented the unanimous desires of each community, a procedure inseparable from the idea of the binding mandate and incompatible, as Augustin Cochin clearly saw, with any sort of public electoral competition in a modern sense.[21]

On the other hand, however, the text of January 24 (which was also prepared by Necker) appealed to the "spirit of the times" and to the evolution of mental attitudes and underscored the need for making representation in the *bailliages* as closely proportional to their population as possible. Its stated objective was "an assembly representative of the entire nation."[22] The entire set of provisions worked out in the January text and the documents that followed it demonstrate a desire to establish a "fixed" principle and to organize the consultation of all the (male) inhabitants of the realm by ensuring that every adult French male inscribed on the tax rolls be an elector.[23] As Michelet clearly saw, in 1789 the French people, the peasantry at their head, were for the first time in history to make a massive entry into a political election.[24]

[19] See Roger Chartier and Denis Richet, eds., *Représentation et vouloir politique, autour des Etats-généraux de 1614* (Paris, 1982).

[20] *Archives parlementaires,* 1:544–50.

[21] Augustin Cochin, *Les sociétés de pensée et la démocratie: Etudes d'histoire révolutionnaire* (Paris, 1921). See my comments on this work in François Furet, *Penser la Révolution française* (Paris, 1978, 1983) (*Interpreting the French Revolution,* trans. Elborg Foster [Cambridge, New York, and Paris, 1981]).

[22] *Archives parlementaires,* 1:544.

[23] All of the documents that followed the January text can be found in Brette (n. 1 above).

[24] J. Michelet, "Elections de 1789," in his *Histoire de la Révolution française,* bk. 1.

Furthermore, no distinction had been made between the right to elect and the right to be elected. Any individual having access to the electoral assemblies—that is, any adult French male on the tax rolls—acquired the opportunity to present himself for election by his fellow citizens. If we combine this nascent political equality with the adjustment of the number of seats to the population of the *bailliages,* the electoral code of Louis XVI—at least, as it concerned the Third Estate—was comparable to an election in a French *arrondissement* today, complicated, however, by the various levels of elections leading from the parish to the seat of the *bailliage.*

For a better and more detailed grasp of this extraordinary mixture of the aristocratic and the democratic in the electoral provisions of 1789, we need to return to the case of the city of Paris *intra muros.* In many regards, Paris escaped the common law, but it was no less subject to this contradiction than other *bailliages.* The electoral procedures particular to Paris illustrate, *a contrario,* the most salient and widespread feature of this contradiction.

Electoral operations in the *prévôté* and *vicomté* of Paris "within the walls" were preceded by bitter polemics over procedures for the consultation—Chassin has traced the *mémoires* and counter *mémoires* that flew back and forth.[25] Everyone agreed that Paris should be endowed with a regime of common law, given the exceptional importance of the capital of the kingdom, but beyond that, everyone had his own solutions to propose and positions to defend. A *mémoire* and a *consultation* typical of enlightened urban opinion appeared December 12, 1788, signed by eleven lawyers (Target among them). For the first time, it suggested that:

If one eliminates the persons under twenty or twenty-five years of age from the 700,000 or so individuals who make up the population of Paris, barely one-half of that number will remain. This half will be reduced to one-fourth, at most, when women are also removed. Next, no matter what respect one may wish to show for the rights of humanity in general, one is obliged to acknowledge that there is a class of men who, by the nature of their education and the sort of work to which their poverty obliges them, are also bereft of ideas and of will and [who are] incapable, on this occasion, of participating in a public project. If one also subtracts, as one should, all those who live in Paris without being born French or having become so by letters of naturalization, and if then one calls to the assemblies only those French-born males of fixed residence in Paris who pay a head tax [*capitation*] of at least six livres, it is credible that the number of voters will be reduced to 50,000 individuals.

[25] Charles-Louis Chassin, *Les élections et les cahiers de Paris en 1789,* 4 vols. (Paris, 1888–89).

This text goes on to propose that elections be held in Paris in the *assemblées de quartier* (ward assemblies) and with no distinction between the three orders on the basis of an overriding membership in the *Commune* and enjoyment of the rights defining it.

It was also in the name of the *Commune* that the city government—the Hôtel de Ville—demanded the right to summon the city's qualified voters to the ballot boxes. However, the municipal oligarchy combined this appeal to its historic rights with a fundamental concession to the new times. In January of 1789 the *quarteniers* (aldermen) and the *officiers* of the capital renounced their traditional privilege of choosing the city's Notables and its deputies. Although they accepted the *assemblées de quartier,* ward assemblies that were to choose electors who would in turn elect the deputies, they insisted on their inalienable right to convoke the representative assemblies of the ancient *Commune,* all orders joined. This claim met with opposition from the Châtelet and its chief, the *prévôt* of Paris, who as the king's representative was the only person empowered to convoke the male inhabitants of the city, by orders, as expressly stipulated in the regulations of January 24. As a result, the king's *officiers de justice* had the upper hand in the entire process of calling the Estates General.

Between the Hôtel de Ville and the Châtelet, the king, faithful to the principle of centralization, decided in favor of the latter. What had he to fear, for that matter, from a municipal oligarchy that had been at his beck and call for more than a century? The regulation of March 28, to be sure, accorded Paris a self-contained electoral district with its own assembly explicitly separate from the General Assembly of the *prévôté.* It also recognized the right of the *prévôt* of the merchants' guild (i.e., the right of the Hôtel de Ville) to call together the Third Estate and to preside over the choice of the electors who would then go on to the assembly of the *prévôté.* But it was the *prévôt* of Paris who was to oversee the redaction of the *cahiers* and the election of the deputies of each order. At this decision, the *prévôt* of the merchants, Le Peletier de Morfontaine, resigned, and Louis XVI, with no further ado, replaced him with Flesselles.

A new and final regulatory document appeared April 13 to interpret the March 28 decree. It set out detailed electoral procedures for Paris. Only the clergy remained subject to the common law defined by the January 24 text. The nobles were no longer called directly to the general assembly of the *bailliage* (or, given the special case of Paris, of the city) as they were in the rest of the kingdom. Like the clergy and the Third Estate, they were to meet first in twenty primary assemblies, by place of residence, to elect their deputies to the General Assembly of

Paris and, eventually, to draw up first-level *cahiers*. The dispositions concerning the Third Estate departed from the January text as well. The sixty *arrondissements* were each to meet in primary assemblies within the ward that were charged with sending deputies to the city-wide meeting, which would, finally, elect the Paris representatives. Furthermore, article 13 of the April 13 text (retaining a suggestion of the December *mémoire*) restricted the summons to holders of university degrees, to incumbent office-holders and commissioners, to holders of masterships (*lettres de maîtrises*) in the arts and crafts, and failing all these, to all men who paid a head tax of at least six livres. Voting requirements in Paris thus mingled status and money, and they were noticeably more selective than in the provinces, where simple listing on the tax rolls assured the right to take part in the community's discussions. They excluded a large portion of the potential electoral body, although in the absence of documentation on tax rolls and socioprofessional status, it is difficult to estimate numbers precisely.

The crown's provisions for electoral procedures in Paris were thus somewhat contradictory. They lent a hand to the separation of the three orders but within an exceptional and supposedly communal electoral constituency defined solely by the urban privileges of the *bourgeois de Paris*. But they also set up electoral districts in which the golden rule of modern democracies—one man, one vote—pertained, even though this new rule was not pursued to its logical conclusion. In the nobles' assemblies the rule discriminating between the right of enfeoffed nobles and nonenfeoffed nobles to represent themselves, introduced in the general electoral code of January 24, was retained in the April document. For the Third Estate, setting a fiscal threshold theoretically implied dismantling the hierarchy of the "Estates," but in reality tax requirements were instated in addition to that hierarchy rather than replacing it. Except for the university, which obtained the right to meet and to choose deputies "as a body," Parisian commoners did in fact meet without respecting the traditional solidarities of profession and status, grouped on a purely administrative basis into sixty districts set up for that purpose. This was a revolution in itself in comparison with 1614.

The royal administration thus achieved a last and triumphant compromise with a society of orders and corporative bodies. In one of its final *règlements* it sketched out something resembling a modern electoral law, intermixed, however, with traditions and concessions. It was doubtless too new for the old that it contained and too old for what was new in it.

The same could be said of the convocation of the nobility. To be sure, the nobles deliberated apart, in conformity with tradition and with the dispositions of the electoral regulations of January 24, and enfeoffed nobles had the privilege of directly representing themselves. The meticulous cleavages of traditional society lay in just such distinctions. By the decree of April 13, however, Parisian nobles were no longer called directly to the assembly on the *bailliage* level, as in the rest of France. They were obliged to meet in primary assemblies, just like the clergy and the Third Estate, to elect deputies to the *bailliage* and, if they were so moved, to draw up detailed preliminary *cahiers*. The April 13 decree set up twenty constituencies to this effect. Thus Parisian nobles were deprived of the electoral privilege of direct participation in the elaboration of the overall *cahier* for the *bailliage*, a privilege that their order enjoyed throughout the realm. They were subjected to the same law as the Third Estate and, like it, were divided into local electoral districts. Although the vote by orders expressed respect for traditional statutes, the principle of preliminary division into districts showed signs of egalitarian electoral law. The vote by primary assemblies was a first step toward breaking up the order of the nobility, a threat that did not pass unnoticed in the twelfth "department," that of the temple, where the nobles protested "against the form of the convocations of the nobility, who should deliberate only as a body."[26] Even the king's own brothers, monsieur and the comte d'Artois, had to participate, just like ordinary esquires, in an assembly of the first "department."

The Parisian clergy met and voted in accordance with the procedures defined by the text of January 24. Thus there were to be primary assemblies of the chapter of Notre-Dame, of the various collegiate churches, and of clergy attached to the city's parishes. (The latter had to be at least twenty-five years of age, to have taken major orders, to hold no benefices, or to be among the lower ranks of the cathedral chapter or in the collegiate churches.) The monks and nuns of Parisian monasteries and convents also had their primary assemblies. The clergy in public institutions—seminaries, schools, and hospitals—were excluded by law, but they managed to find a place on the electoral rolls for the parish clergy. The decree favored the representation of clerics tied to the high clergy, in the sense that no age limit and no requirement of having taken major orders was demanded of the canons, the lower clergy attached to the chapter, or monks, whereas access to the as-

[26] Archives Nationales, B^{III} 113.

semblies of the lower echelons of the secular clergy was subjected to restrictions. Furthermore, unlike the nobility or the Third Estate, the clergy in Paris was summoned, as everywhere in France, to meet in the traditional places of their ministry, canons in their chapter houses, priests in the parish houses of the fifty-two parish churches in Paris (under the vigilant eye of the *curé*), and regular clergy of both sexes in the many mother houses of their orders. Thus, only the order of the clergy in Paris participated in the electoral operations of the spring of 1789 in a manner respecting tradition and in conformity with its privileges and its hierarchy. It was to show proof of this fidelity in its grievances, what is more, to a much greater extent than was true in the other two orders.

The clergy also drew up its grievances in an infinitely more traditional manner. The regulations of January 24 did not provide for the redaction of *cahiers* at primary assemblies of the clergy any more than for beneficed clergy, the bishops, or the nobles, who were all called in person to the assembly on the *bailliage* level. What might seem logical for the individuals—*curés,* benefice holders, bishops, nobles—who would have an opportunity to express themselves at the *bailliage* assembly of their order is more surprising when we find it in the primary assemblies of the clergy, who were by this token stricken with a *diminutio capitis* in relation to the assemblies of the Third Estate. Article 21 of the January 24 text speaks only of "memoranda and instructions [to be] put in the hands of the deputies or the appointed proxies, who are to present them for all reasonable consideration on the occasion of the redaction of the general *cahier.*" The term *cahier de doléances* does not appear, as it does in articles 23 and 24, which made this a duty of assemblies of the Third Estate.

The clergy's opportunity to express itself electorally thus seems all the more restricted, comparatively speaking, because voting conditions for the other two orders were brought up to date by the text of April 15. On the one hand, the nobility met at a preliminary stage, just like the Third Estate, in the local constituencies and could draw up *cahiers* on that level. On the other hand, corporations and guilds were not permitted to hold Third Estate assemblies, and the voting qualifications were defined on the dual basis of residence and payment of taxes, which took Parisian commoners out of the framework of traditional society to make modern voters of them. Their *cahiers* were all the more representative of their general interests.

The nobility and the Third Estate in Paris consequently received the means of expression of a modern democracy, even if such means were in contradiction with the preservation of the dichotomy that kept them separate. Only the clergy continued to express itself uniquely through its traditional heads.

A similar distinction was made at the level of the choice of the deputies. The regulations of January 24 maintained significant inequalities among the clergy. Chapters could choose one deputy for every ten voters, but their lesser members could choose only one-twentieth of their number. The communities of monks and nuns could elect one person per community, regardless of the number present at the assembly. Parishes could pick one deputy for every twenty voters. Oddly enough, protest against this regulation came for the most part from the canons, who were the most generously treated by the law. The nobility and the Third Estate, on the other hand, were ruled by the arithmetic of modern elections. The nobles had the right to send to the *bailliage* one-tenth of the number present at their assemblies. For the Third Estate, where the regulations ideally provided for five hundred voters per district, the general rule in urban assemblies was one deputy per hundred voters.

In this manner, the French monarchy mingled respect for precedent and democratic innovation in the organization of a consultation that it had intended as an embodiment of the spirit of tradition and the spirit of geometry. What is astonishing is not that the crown did its best, here and there, to remain faithful to its own past—the structure of society by orders was part of the very nature of the monarchic system— but that it juxtaposed three consultations, kept more carefully apart than ever and corresponding to the three orders of the realm, with a general implementation of modern democratic principles. It was as if what the monarchy retained of the traditional vision of power and of society was simply destined to give the conflict between the aristocratic and the democratic principles a purity that was already revolutionary.

It is more in conformity with historical truth, however, to suppose more innocence on the part of the actors in this prologue. What gives this sort of interregnum between the ancien régime and the Revolution its exceptional limpidity is not the autonomy or the will of what was still the government of the realm. Its luster comes, to the contrary, from the old monarchy's reflection, for one last time, of society's ambiguities and of the "spirit of the times." The crown decided on the recalling of the Estates General without realizing that although the ancien régime had a past, and even a very long past, it had never had a representative tradition. It had never had any true tradition at all in the English sense of common law. Incapable of reconstructing an institution over this void, it ceded on the two flanks that its history and its epoch offered—to aristocracy and to democracy. At the very moment that the monarchy recognized that the nobility lay at its own core and separated it from the nation, it gave the Third Estate the means to embody that nation and to rally it. The monarchy not only bequeathed democracy to the Revolution. Before it died, it constituted democracy and offered it its perfect scapegoat.

REVOLUTIONARY
POLITICAL CULTURE

The Crowd and Politics between *Ancien Régime* and Revolution in France*

Colin Lucas

There is temerity in discussing a subject already burdened with the weight of scrutiny by several generations of historians, sociologists, and psychologists—"impudence" was the word that came to Richard Cobb's mind at the thought of reconsidering the riots and *journées* of revolutionary Paris.[1] More than temerity, it would be folly to pretend to encompass in one article a phenomenon so diverse in its forms and manifestations. This article seeks first to emphasize some of the elements of continuity between the crowds characteristic of the *ancien régime* and the Revolution. On this basis, it may then be possible to underscore some original characteristics of crowd behavior that were fostered by the Revolution. Finally, the paper discusses some of the ways in which the revolutionaries tried to cope with the crowd. In sum, the intention here is to sketch how the crowd was part of the political culture of the Revolution.

There was not, of course, just one type of crowd in the French Revolution—no more than in any other period of history.[2] The simple aggregation of human beings in a single place—perhaps going about their business, as in a market, or gathered to stare at some incident— is only a crowd in the purely descriptive sense of a density of people. Even when a gathering of people ceases to be or from the outset is not a passive agglomerate of individuals, such an active crowd takes distinct forms and behaves in distinct ways. It is common to distinguish between, for example, festive crowds, audience crowds, panic crowds,

* I wish to thank my colleagues at Smith College, who allowed me the time to begin thinking about this subject, as well as faculty and students at York University (Canada) and the University of Maryland who discussed an earlier version of this article. The article has also benefited from the debate at the conference on "The Political Culture of the French Revolution" held at Oxford in September 1987, and another version appears in its proceedings, *The Political Culture of the French Revolution* (Oxford: Pergamon Press, Ltd., 1988). The present version is published by permission of Elsevier Science, Ltd.

[1] R. C. Cobb, *The Police and the People* (Oxford, 1970), p. 92.

[2] Mark Harrison, "The Ordering of the Urban Environment: Time, Work and the Occurrence of Crowds, 1790–1835," *Past and Present*, no. 110 (1986), pp. 134–68, rightly cautions against confusing "the crowd" and "riot."

and aggressive crowds. Each is distinguished from the others partly by occasion and context and partly by behavior. Possibly what most clearly distinguishes a crowd from a mere aggregate of human beings is a shared sense of purpose in being assembled together along with some sense that this purpose is to be achieved collectively, either by acting collectively or else simply by being gathered together. This is what we may term the "purposive" crowd. Certainly, individuals gathered at a market have for the most part a common purpose of buying goods; but it is only when they become aware that such goods can only be obtained in a satisfactory manner by collective action that they become a purposive crowd. This is what distinguishes a market dispute watched by large numbers of people from a market riot. The participants in festive crowds, audience crowds, and so on share a common sense of why they are there and an understanding that their being there collectively has a different meaning from being there individually.

It is self-evident that the purposive crowds of the *ancien régime* were equally present during the Revolution. No historian would question the essential continuity between the *émotions* and *séditions* of the *ancien régime* (even those occurring during the relative tranquillity of the eighteenth century before 1789) and the turbulent events of the decade 1789–99. It is evident in the market riots and *taxations populaires*; it is evident in the crowds' frequent recourse to rituals that differed little from those of the sixteenth or seventeenth centuries. There are strong echoes of earlier peasant wars in the rural disturbances of the Revolution, from the *jacqueries* of its earlier years to the endemic turbulence of its later years—we see the same methods of action, the same targets, often the same geography, and even, frequently, the same leading figures whom Yves-Marie Bercé identified as "troublemakers" in earlier times (nobles, priests, mayors, veteran soldiers, and craftsmen).[3] Credulity, myth, rumor, panic, fear, and notions of hoarding, speculation, and plots were as potent incitements of popular wrath before 1789 as they were afterward. The tolling of the *tocsin* mobilizing a local population against the troops of counterrevolution or against the republican soldiery, against brigands or against *gendarmes*; the mobilizing capacity of supposed written documents, such as the "king's orders" invoked in peasant disturbances in 1789 or the "missive written in letters of gold" alluded to in southern religious disturbances in 1795–96; the importance of women in food riots; the role of young unmarried men in collective disturbances; the habit of placing women and young chil-

---

[3] Y.-M. Bercé, *Revolt and Revolution in Early Modern Europe* (Manchester, 1987), pp. 64–81.

dren in the front line of an aggressive crowd—none of these (or many other) characteristics of crowd behavior in the Revolution were new. This is not to suggest that patterns of crowd behavior in the late eighteenth century merely reproduced those of the early modern period—but it is to stress that these patterns were still strongly anchored in the habits of earlier times analyzed by historians of both France and England.[4]

Those historians who have directly addressed the question of the crowd in the Revolution have not, of course, denied some elements of continuity. Yet, while acknowledging the indispensable destructive power of the crowd and emphasizing the importance of quite traditional economic issues in mobilizing it, they have tended to concentrate on a single phenomenon: the "revolutionary crowd." Such an approach is epitomized by George Rudé's *The Crowd in the French Revolution,* which is in fact concerned only with the revolutionary crowd of the great Paris *journées.* Indeed, elsewhere Rudé explicitly rejects the notion that any form of crowd other than the "aggressive" type was significant in this context.[5] For him, the aggressive and political crowds are coterminous, and the revolutionary crowd is largely defined as one aware of the political issues of the Revolution and consciously intervening to act upon them.

It does not diminish the importance of Rudé's work if we emphasize how fuzzy his concepts are in some respects. For one thing, they depend on a particular definition (and a very modern one at that) of what is political. Rudé accords prerevolutionary eighteenth-century movements only a cursory glance: he concedes only a kind of rudimentary political quality to Parisian disturbances around the Parlement and considers rural disturbances to have been entirely marked by "political innocence."[6] Such an approach comes dangerously close to identifying "political" with an awareness of and commentary on high politics. Moreover, within the Revolution itself, Rudé's definition of the revolutionary crowd is confined in practice to popular collective action to radicalize the Revolution (despite a rather awkward chapter on Vendémiaire, perhaps intended to show how popular opinion supported the Convention). This definition is curiously at once elastic and re-

[4] See P. Slack, ed., *Rebellion, Popular Protest and the Social Order in Early Modern England* (Cambridge, 1984); N. Z. Davis, *Society and Culture in Early Modern France* (London, 1975); J. LeGoff and J.-C. Schmitt, *Le Charivari* (Paris, 1981).
[5] G. Rudé, *The Crowd in History* (London, 1964), p. 4.
[6] Ibid., pp. 19–32, 47–50.

strictive. On the one hand, it leads Rudé to include a discussion of the gathering at the Champ-de-Mars on July 17, 1791, which was not a crowd of the same order as the others he chooses: the report of the *commissaires* of the Municipality stated categorically that "there were groups of people without there being a definite crowd."[7] On the other hand, it leads him to exclude entirely (except for Vendémiaire) crowd actions that clearly display an awareness of the political issues of the Revolution and that constitute a conscious attempt to intervene but that do not operate to radicalize it—for example, the anti-Jacobin crowds at Lyon and Marseille in 1793 or the various popular resistances to the Revolution such as *chouannerie,* some aspects of the White Terror, religious riots, and so forth. Here a value judgment about what is "revolutionary" denies validity to any other form of crowd action, even when it can be classed as "political" in Rudé's own usage of the word.

These premises betray a further ambiguity. It is axiomatic that the crowd as a collective actor in the Revolution antedated the appearance of the sans-culotte movement. Yet, while we should acknowledge that the Parisian popular movement was born out of the lessons learned through Parisian crowd action, the popular movement's relation to the crowd is in fact ambiguous, and Soboul's study did little to clarify it.[8] Rudé tends to equate sans-culottes with the crowd; however, it seems too simplistic to propose that these radical militants' political consciousness, which was revolutionary in the sense of propounding permanent change through action on the structures of power, directly expressed in articulate form a consciousness possessed by the crowd.[9] Clearly there was a relation between *sans-culottisme* and the crowd; equally clearly, a new political consciousness, or at least a modified consciousness, came to inhabit the crowd during the events of the early Revolution. Precisely what that relation was and, indeed, just how revolutionary the crowd was are questions that bear much closer analysis—closer, regrettably, than space limitations allow in this article.

If we turn back to Georges Lefebvre's 1934 study of revolutionary crowds, we find a discussion that is in some ways more sophisticated.[10] Lefebvre is, for example, less restrictive in his definition of the crowd.

[7] A. Mathiez, *Le Club des Cordeliers pendant la crise de Varennes* (Paris, 1910), p. 140.

[8] A. Soboul, *Les Sans-Culottes Parisiens en l'An II* (La Roche-sur-Yon, 1958).

[9] G. Rudé, *The Crowd in the French Revolution* (Oxford, 1959), p. 207.

[10] G. Lefebvre, "Foules Révolutionnaires" in his *Études sur la Révolution Française* (1934; reprint, Paris, 1963), pp. 371–92.

He is ready to include a wider range of crowds as worthy of attention and he discusses different types of market riots and rural disturbances as well as the *journées*. Furthermore, he elaborates a concept of "the sudden mutation of the aggregate into a revolutionary gathering," an idea recently reformulated by Jacques Beauchard as the transition from the "atomized crowd" via the "crowd in fusion" to the "organized crowd."[11] Lefebvre posits that this mutation is the product of some external event "which awakens affective feelings." His study is valuable because it stresses the importance of examining numerous types of crowds as actors in revolution rather than just the classically defined political crowd. It is valuable also because it stresses that all crowds can potentially intervene in the process of revolution and, finally, because it directs our attention both to this moment of metamorphosis—in particular, to the manner in which exterior events act on the "affective feelings"—and to the degree of transformation involved. The notion of "affective feelings" introduces a further stimulating point in Lefebvre's analysis. The existence of a crowd supposes, he argues, the prior existence of a collective mentality. On entering the "aggregate," the individual escapes from the pressure of the small social groups that provide the context of his daily life and becomes receptive to "the ideas and feelings which are characteristic of wider collectivities to which he also belongs."[12] It is clear in context that Lefebvre is in fact thinking of receptivity to notions of "the nation" or to more general social interests such as those of the poor. As we shall see shortly, it is possible to interpret this receptivity in a different way.

However, at this point, Lefebvre's argument ceases to be productive. His definition of the revolutionary crowd is fundamentally the same as that of Rudé—the crowd that acts to protect and radicalize the Revolution. By a prior collective mentality Lefebvre essentially means the growth of political consciousness; and even if, in an aside, he admits that this collective mentality feeds off popular memory—"off a very ancient tradition"—he nevertheless discusses it in terms of the political education offered by the elections and the *cahiers*, the events of June–July 1789, and so on. For Lefebvre, as for Rudé, the purposive crowd in the Revolution is the one that assembles for a revolutionary purpose; its purest expression must be the Parisian section demonstrations of 1793. Lefebvre too regards 1789 as a rupture in the history of popular behavior. But by taking another look at the prerevolutionary crowd,

---

[11] Ibid., p. 373; J. Beauchard, *La Puissance des Foules* (Paris, 1985), pp. 89–103.
[12] Lefebvre, p. 379.

we may redirect Lefebvre's analysis and understand the crowd's transposition into the revolutionary environment.

* * *

It is possible to argue that a prime feature of the *ancien régime* purposive crowd was its ability to act as a representative. I do not mean to suggest that all crowds in all situations inescapably had a representative function, but that, as an extension of its collective character, the crowd easily acquired the function of representing the community whose members composed it. This representation was more emblematic or virtual than formal or direct. Usually not all the members of the community entered any particular crowd, and it did not implement a policy debated and determined by the community, though some forms of rural contestation both before and during the Revolution could come close to that. Nonetheless, by its public and collective character the crowd established and drew on a rapport with those members of the community who observed it without participating directly in it. The representative nature of purposive crowds is evident, for example, in the prevalence, in disturbances, of youth groups, exclusive by definition yet clearly representative of collective community attitudes in practice; in the fact that, as Steven Kaplan has noted, local officials frequently conceded some tacit legitimacy to groups involved in market disturbances; and in the recurrent presence in such crowds of figures from outside the *menu peuple*.[13] Indeed, spectators were not merely an inescapable part of crowd action; rather, they were indispensable. They constituted an audience crowd alongside the acting crowd, and they were rarely indifferent to the actions of the crowd. At times, they verged on participation—the classic example is the scene at the Bastille on July 14 where, according to one observer, there was gathered "an immense crowd of citizens, assembled mostly out of sheer curiosity," and when, as the victorious crowd surged back up the rue Saint-Antoine with its prisoners, an "inconceivable number of women, children, [and] old people . . . seemed to burst out of the windows of the houses crying: *There they are, the villains! We've got them!*"[14] More usually, they observed and commented. Of course, the crowd frequently overstepped the limit of community acceptability at some point, and there-

[13] S. Kaplan, *Bread, Politics and Political Economy in the Reign of Louis XV*, 2 vols. (The Hague, 1976), 1:191–98.
[14] J. Flammermont, ed., *La journée du 14 Juillet 1789: Fragment des mémoires inédits de L.-G. Pitra* (Paris, 1892), pp. 13, 22.

fore not all that it did can be deemed a community-endorsed gesture. But it is equally clear that the crowd usually claimed and frequently achieved a representative status, just as it is clear that spectators were usually aware of this claim, which they either supported tacitly or openly or else rejected at some point, often intervening either directly or indirectly to check or reprove actions.[15]

The characteristic localism of the eighteenth-century crowd also reinforced this representative quality. Localism was inherent in disturbances in villages or small towns, but, even where geographically wider movements were involved, the separate identities of groups from different communities appear to have been maintained. To take examples from the Revolution itself, it is clear that, in the antiseigneurial attacks that could move crowds over a radius of ten or more miles, groups from individual villages tended to remain distinct within the multitude. As the crowd passed each village, the inhabitants of that village were incited to join in with a cry addressed collectively: "the people of . . . have to join with us"; witnesses in subsequent judicial inquiries frequently described such crowds simply by listing the villages from which they were composed.[16] Similarly, the predominant localism is visible in the anti-Jacobin disturbances in the Midi in 1795 and 1797 when a crowd from a particular village or small town would travel to murder someone from its own community while leaving other victims untouched for the crowds that would come from their own particular communities. Such a pattern was not confined to small localities. Urban disturbances in provincial towns during the Revolution frequently involved definable *quartiers,* whether as the locality of a riot or as an attack by one *quartier* on another. Among the many examples were the patterns of disturbances affecting La Carreterie and La Fusterie at Avignon, or the Plan d'Olivier and Le Boutonnet at Montpellier, or the different *quartier* identities of the *chiffonistes* and the *monnaidiers* at Arles. Even when one can attach socioeconomic characteristics to such patterns, they are far from being the only or indeed the dominant factor.[17]

---

[15] Y. Castan, *Honnêteté et relations sociales en Languedoc 1715–1780* (Paris, 1974), provides an excellent introduction to these themes in collective behavior.

[16] A good example may be seen in the inquiry into the 1792 disturbances in the southern Drôme (Archives Départmentales [hereafter referred to as AD] Drôme L 196).

[17] See C. Lucas, "Résistances populaires à la Révolution dans le sud-est," in *Mouvements populaires et conscience sociale,* ed. J. Nicolas (Paris, 1985), pp. 473–85.

As for Paris, despite the fluidity of the population both socially and geographically that has been noted by Daniel Roche, one can still discern the same feature.[18] David Garrioch has recently demonstrated convincingly the primacy of neighborhood in Parisian sociability.[19] Crowd action was remarkably limited topographically inside the city, even during the Revolution. Leaving aside market riots, one can see this, for example, in the riots over child kidnapping in 1750. Despite the multitude of disturbances and the wide diffusion of the rumor that caused them, the incidents were localized and separate; the participants seem to have been people living close to each incident.[20] Similarly, the disturbances of August–September 1788 were closely confined to the area around the Parlement, principally the Place Dauphine and the Pont-Neuf. Only very late in the events was the crowd drawn out toward the residence of the *commandant du guet* near the Porte-Saint-Martin and the Hôtel de Lamoignon in the Faubourg Saint-Germain. Although the evidence is scanty, it seems that here again the crowd was composed predominantly of people from the neighborhood. The few arrested were from the vicinity or from just across the river, and the best contemporary account confirms the crowd's local character and describes a clear example of the rapport between the crowd and the spectators—between those in the street and those in the houses and shops giving onto it.[21] Similarly, in the Réveillon riot in the Faubourg Saint-Antoine, few people from outside the immediate vicinity intervened.[22] Even the Bastille crowd was heavily localized: 70 percent of the "Vainqueurs de la Bastille" resided in the Faubourg Saint-Antoine.[23] Although this event did draw participants from a wider area, the inhabitants of the Faubourg Saint-Antoine and the Faubourg Saint-Marcel formed quite distinct entities, each providing itself with its own leader (the *brasseurs* Santerre and Acloque).[24] Indeed, it is significant

[18] D. Roche, *The People of Paris* (Leamington Spa, England, 1987), esp. pp. 55 and 69.

[19] D. Garrioch, *Neighbourhood and Community in Paris 1740–1790* (Cambridge, 1986).

[20] E. J. F. Barbier, *Journal historique et anecdotique du règne de Louis XV,* 4 vols. (Paris, 1851–57), 3:124–55. See also A. P. Herlaut, "Les enlèvements d'enfants à Paris en 1720 et en 1750," *Revue historique* 139 (1922): 43–61, 202–23; A. Farge and J. Revel, "Les règles de l'émeute: L'affaire des enlèvements d'enfants," in Nicolas, ed., pp. 635–46.

[21] [Joseph] Charron, *Lettre ou mémoire historique sur les troubles populaires de Paris en Août et Septembre 1788* (Londres, 1788).

[22] Rudé, *The Crowd in the French Revolution* (n. 9 above), p. 38.

[23] R. Monnier, *Le Faubourg Saint-Antoine, 1789–1815* (Paris, 1981), p. 122.

[24] Flammermont, ed. (n. 14 above), p. 13.

that in the confusion of the early moments people from the Faubourg Saint-Antoine should have been able to recognize Elie and to know that, as an "officier de fortune" in the Régiment de la Reine, he would know what to do; it is equally significant that Elie, understanding that he would also have to direct people who did not know him, immediately returned home to put on his uniform.[25] These two Faubourgs continued throughout the Revolution to have separate crowd identities, Saint-Antoine even developing its own spokesman in the person of Gonchon. But, though they were less visible, one may reasonably expect other quarters to have retained at least elements of their own identities. Certainly the section demonstrations of 1793 were by their very essence quarter-based. The instinct to identify oneself by group appurtenances was a prevalent one. For instance, when in July 1791 the Cordeliers Club tried to organize a mass demonstration-march from the Bastille to the Champ-de-Mars under one banner, the other clubs all insisted on marching under their own banners; similarly, the work of preparing the Champ-de-Mars for the Fête de la Fédération in 1790 was not a mass effort with all the classes mingled together but rather one in which each trade remained distinct, each displaying its own banner.[26]

One can argue, therefore, that the eighteenth-century crowd enjoyed a particular, functional relationship with its community and that it characteristically remained rooted in locality and neighborhood. Even in the urban context and even in the great events of the Revolution, a large crowd should probably be seen as an agglomeration of crowds rather than as a single mass.

It is important to define more closely the community that, I suggest, the eighteenth-century crowd represented and to which it related. Community must not be understood as merely a neighborhood defined topographically, although this is an indispensable element. The idea of community also contains a notion of collective awareness—an awareness of belonging to a collectivity that provides the context for one's social existence and sociability. Social differentiation and individual ranking are not abolished, but they are placed within the coherence of a wider collectivity. Community is a constituent of identity and a referent of behavior. It represents a context of existence and provides a guide to living in society. Thus, if community connotes a physical sense of proximity, it also connotes a moral sense of collective norms of

---

[25] Ibid., pp. 3–4.
[26] Mathiez, *Le Club des Cordeliers pendant la crise de Varennes* (n. 7 above), pp. 125–26; L.-S. Mercier, *Le nouveau Paris,* ed. P. Bessand-Massenet (Paris, 1962), pp. 20–22.

conduct, as it were a moral proximity of shared assumptions about the relationship between the individual and the group. It is well known that the all-embracing form of community visible in the early modern period was subject to considerable stress and defection by the time of the later *ancien régime*.[27] Elite groups no longer participated in the festive manifestations of collective culture; elite culture and popular culture were diverging, as were the value systems they articulated. It was much more rare to find people from outside the world of workshop, street trade, and *menu peuple* in the crowd; property owners became more uncomprehending and more quickly frightened of the crowd. The community, in the sense we have adopted, was fast becoming defined in terms of social structure, fast becoming the popular community; in turn, the values it embodied were becoming what historians like to term "traditional" as opposed to "modern." However, if we take Paris as the place where traditional solidarities can be supposed to have decayed the most, the community evidently remained of paramount importance to the mass of ordinary people at the end of the *ancien régime*, even if the quarters were less inward-looking and parochial than they had been a hundred years earlier. Arlette Farge and David Garrioch give countless examples of the way in which the individual appealed to the community and measured his or her place and reputation by reference to it.[28] For the individual, the community constituted a defense and a tribunal; and, by thus regulating itself, the community was able to conserve and perpetuate itself.

Nonetheless, the divorce between the popular community and the elites was not complete. Before 1789, the bourgeois and professional man in Paris and other cities was still caught in the web of community and to some extent still acquiesced in it. As Daniel Roche emphasizes, fear and understanding, even sympathy, were perfectly compatible reactions on the part of contemporary observers.[29] The elites were capable of virtually colluding in some sorts of disturbances, for example, grain riots.[30] The crowd, in turn, called on them to participate—for instance, crowds enlisted half-consenting local figures of standing in their actions—partly, at least, in order to reaffirm the community identity. Indeed, during the Revolution, elite groups were quite capable of speaking to the crowd in the language of the popular community, as

[27] Garrioch, pp. 205–56, reviews the changing nature of the Parisian neighborhood community in the eighteenth century.

[28] Ibid.; A. Farge, *La vie fragile* (Paris, 1986). See also R. Phillips, *Family Breakdown in Late Eighteenth-Century France* (Oxford, 1980), pp. 180–95.

[29] Roche (n. 18 above), p. 46.

[30] Kaplan (n. 13 above), 1:196.

they did in the religious disturbances and during the Thermidorian Reaction. Yet such figures could only manipulate the crowd if they adopted that language. The crowd did not act out of deference; not just any noble could lead peasants in the *chouannerie* simply by reflex of ancient superiority.[31] The standard contemporary official interpretation of riot in terms of instigation by outside agents and leaders from a higher social class was as unsound for the Revolution as it is for the *ancien régime*. The crowd tended to generate its own leaders, and these leaders could change as the direction of an event changed.[32] Stanislas-Marie Maillard's leadership was born in the Bastille crowd; that of Pierre-Augustin Hulin did not long survive his attempts to save victims of that crowd. Indeed, a classic example is provided by the attack on the Invalides: the governor "came in person, had the gate opened, and spoke to the people. For the most part, they accepted what he said; only one man objected and said that any delay represented a new danger, and instantly the crowd rushed into the Hôtel."[33]

It is not at all surprising, therefore, to find people from socially diverse backgrounds in the crowds analyzed by George Rudé. This was natural enough. Yet social cleavages within the community remained indeterminate, and the crowd expressed the ambiguity of these social relationships very well. Joseph Charron's contemporary classification of collective behavior in Paris at the end of the *ancien régime* into "*peuple,* public, populace, *canaille*" was an awkward contemporary attempt to render the complex reality of this evolving relationship.[34] What Charron's account of the events of August–September 1788 in Paris does show very clearly is the ambiguity surrounding the crowd. He notes that "the middling class" ("la classe mitoyenne") enjoyed the noisy turbulence of ordinary street effervescence and was perfectly ready to flip a coin to a street urchin knowing that it would be used to buy fireworks and bangers. He shows that many householders around the Place Dauphine were ready to set lights in their windows in some kind of complicity with the street crowd but that a few refused, "wanting to set themselves apart, or ignoring the proprieties." The crowd returned the next evening to break the windows of the recalcitrant. "Proprieties" clearly implied a tacit recognition of

[31] See, e.g., D. Sutherland, *The Chouans* (Oxford, 1982), pp. 167–94.
[32] See Farge, pp. 314–18.
[33] Jean-Sylvian Bailly, *Mémoires de Bailly,* 3 vols. (Paris, 1821–22), 1:373–74.
[34] Charron (n. 21 above). Compare J. Kaplow, *The Names of Kings* (New York, 1972), p. 158. Roche, pp. 36–63, provides an interesting discussion of other attempts at classification.

the legitimacy of the crowd and a proper colluding solidarity; yet the outright refusal of some to collude was a symptom of the growing detachment of the "middling class." In turn, the reaction of the crowd reflected its instinct to enforce an inclusive community. However, once the festive aspect present in almost every *ancien régime* popular crowd got out of hand, the "middling class" took fright and endorsed the intervention of the *guet*. However, the *guet* behaved in a heavy-handed manner, provoking pitched battles, the burning of guard houses, and finally government mobilization of the *gardes françaises*. At this point, the property owners ("the public," in Charron's terms) intervened to defuse the situation. "The public felt that it was important not to congregate, and the populace . . . withdrew without complaint." Thus, this "public" was clearly still able to assert its community membership and to persuade the crowd; yet, once again, it could only do so provided it did not cut across the crowd's own perceptions and values, for Charron points out that the crowd dispersed because it "respected [the *garde française*] with whom it had never been in conflict." Indeed, the "populace" continued its hostility to the *guet,* culminating in another pitched battle. This left "the public indignant . . . and the *honnêtes gens* anxious." When, finally, the *guet* assaulted a group engaged in perfectly innocent conversation, "all the *honnêtes gens* rose at the news of these acts of inhumanity and demanded vengeance."[35]

In sum, Charron portrays a complex relationship of both tension and collusion between the crowd and the social groups on the edge of the community that the crowd represented. More than that, he reveals how these social groups accorded the crowd a certain legitimacy that did not arise, in this case, out of some sense that the crowd was serving a grander political design of the elites. However, the ambiguity of this relationship was to be laid bare in the Revolution. We may argue that the Revolution hastened the process of separation of the elites from the popular community, from its claims and its values. The crowd's action in the Revolution may be seen as instrumental in accelerating the alienation of the propertied classes from the popular community.

The crowd was peculiarly fit to be the organ of popular representation precisely because, while retaining its local, rooted quality, it stood outside the formal structures of the community. It abolished the hierarchies and relationships in the society of the neighborhood and asserted the commonality of the members of the community in their undifferentiated membership in the crowd. The crowd was in a sense

[35] Charron, pp. 21, 34, 55, 56.

the community temporarily reformed. It was perhaps as close as one could get to the philosophers' ideal of society in the state of nature. It released its members from their established condition, it granted them relative anonymity, and it assembled them in a new association outdoors, on the street and in the squares. In order to exist, the crowd had to be outside (or, on occasion, in the space provided by some large public hall). This location was also essential in that it confirmed the crowd's character as the community reformed, for it involved the voluntary occupation of public space—a space not confined and defined by a particular activity but, rather, neutral by virtue of its accommodating many different activities and individuals. Indeed, the crowd disliked being confined and thus defined: if it entered a closed space in pursuit of a victim, it nearly always took him outside to deal with him, even if this merely involved throwing him out of the window.[36] It is striking that the crowd at the Hôtel-de-Ville on July 14 took all its victims outside, none being killed inside; similarly, the prison massacres of 1795 (as distinct from murders by a few men) all involved extraction of the victims and their death outside.[37] In contrast, the crowd was always suspicious of enclosed, hidden spaces: one need only remember the fears of the July 14 crowd about the cellars of the Bastille and hidden subterranean passages, or the fears about the Paris prisons that led to the September Massacres.

The crowd articulated what the members of the community had in common. It transcended the particular interests of corporate bodies, trades, workshops, and so on, not to mention individuals, and it could thus express a value system that underpinned popular attitudes. The crowd simplified conscious attitudes, emphasizing the common ground of values and codes of conduct that formed the mental basis of popular social attitudes. It put a premium on the assumed and culturally instinctive bases of conduct rather than on rationalized attitudes to complex facts of a changing world. The consciousness of the crowd was, therefore, always likely to be more "traditional" and more coherently simple than that of individuals. If we are looking for Lefebvre's "affective feelings," for the "idea and feelings which are characteristic of wider collectivities to which [the individual] also belongs," for the

[36] The murder of the police agent Labbé during the kidnapping riots of 1750. is a good illustration (Farge, pp. 312–17). Farge's description of the role of the landlord's agent, who controlled the crowd by urging it to take Labbé outside, is another example of how a person can lead a crowd only by speaking to its own assumptions and patterns of behavior.

[37] C. Lucas, "Violence thermidorienne et société traditionnelle," *Cahiers d'histoire* 24 (1979): 3–43.

collective mentality that preexists the crowd, then it is here that we must look. It is this liberation of the traditional reflex that poses the principal problem of the crowd's transposition into the revolutionary environment and informs the whole question of its relation to revolutionary politics.

The crowd, then, was the means through which the *peuple* expressed its collective identity and its values,[38] regulated its relationship with authority and the conduct of public affairs, asserted and defended its place in society, and imposed its collective values on deviant members within its own community. In a very direct sense, therefore, the representative and regulatory crowd was the natural organ of the people. Its members were too weak to have a significant effect as individuals on authority—whether state, social, or economic—but collectively they could express their judgment and defend their interests. In this sense, the crowd invaded the public space not just physically but also morally and politically.

The most direct and obvious expression of this function was the crowd's application of the moral economy in the marketplace, as defined by E. P. Thompson and demonstrated in the French context by Steven Kaplan and William Reddy, among others.[39] For us here, the significant point is that the crowd represented the community, for it stated and acted on its right to enforce the moral economy and to reprove, call to order, and even punish authority that failed to fulfill its obligations. Such acts were perceived as legitimate both by the crowd and by many of those who observed it in the *ancien régime*. This pattern is also visible in a wide spectrum of other relationships with authority. The eighteenth-century crowd acted against agents of government on a whole range of issues in exactly the same terms. The people were not passive accepters of authority, nor were they in a state of permanent hostility to it. Both David Garrioch and Arlette Farge demonstrate how quick Parisians were to have recourse to the *commissaires de police* in matters as diverse as domestic disputes, commercial dishonesty, or disorderly behavior. Public authority had a function in ordering the community, which its members recognized as

[38] There are many similarities between the situation described here and eighteenth-century England as presented by E. P. Thompson in "Patrician Society, Popular Culture," *Journal of Social History* 7 (1974): 381–405, and "Eighteenth-Century English Society: Class Struggle without Class?" *Social History* 3 (1978): 133–65, although Thompson's preoccupation (especially in the second article) is rather different from the one here.

[39] E. P. Thompson, "The Moral Economy of the English Crowd in the Eighteenth Century," *Past and Present*, no. 50 (1971), pp. 76–136.

necessary, even though there were compelling unstated rules governing
an individual's appeal to public authority, especially in smaller societies.[40] Yet, at the same time, people were equally quick to resist and
reprove initiatives that stepped outside what was deemed to be legitimate and necessary action. The limits on authority were anchored in
a popular system of values that authority could at times override by
force, but which the community guarded through the crowd. Just as
the community policed its own members by a judicious dosage of de-
rision, *charivari,* physical assault, and even death, so it policed its
policers by much the same methods. Rather than the law courts, it was
the crowd that was the eighteenth-century answer to the ancient question, "Quis custodet custodes?" Accounts of eighteenth-century
"émotions" make it clear time and again that it was the behavior, real
or suspected, of agents of authority that was the outside event that
mobilized the crowd, the key to Lefebvre's "sudden mutation." We
need refer only to the examples we have already used: in the 1750
kidnapping riots, it was the rumor that police agents were responsible
that brought the crowds out, and it was exclusively the police who
were attacked; similarly, the August–September 1788 gatherings only
degenerated into a riot when the *guet* attacked the crowd, to which
the crowd responded by attacking the guard posts, whereas it left the
garde française alone (at least until the very end of the events) because
it had not thus misbehaved; on July 14, the sequence of events at the
Bastille is important because the crowd did not attack until it was fired
on, and the reproach leveled against those who were massacred was
that "they were said to be artillerymen, they were said to have fired
on the people."[41] For his part, Charron, the chronicler of the August–
September disturbances, was quite clear that there were rules about
how to handle the crowd: "It is not the number of men which overawes
the public . . . ; it is the confident bearing of the soldiers, the discipline
and above all the moderation of their behavior. . . . The *gardes françaises* found themselves unhappily obliged to use force; but there was
no need to harry these unfortunates so closely that they could not
escape; for, even when it deals its blows, justice must still be justice.
It bears another name when it leaves nothing but despair and death to
those whom it punishes."[42] Clearly, there was more here than a simple
tactical precept and, as we have seen, equally clearly the "public"
agreed with him.

[40] Castan (n. 15 above), pp. 69–105.
[41] Bailly, 1:84.
[42] Charron, p. 34.

The crowd observed, commented, judged. It was inescapable, therefore, that the crowd's action should contain a discourse of justice; this
was a function of its sense of the legitimacy of its action. The perception
of the people exercising justice was profoundly anchored in *ancien régime* popular perceptions. This was why the crowd had recourse so frequently to acts that echoed or parodied state justice. Hence, the
propensity of crowds to hang unpopular figures in effigy; hence, the Parisian crowd's habit of going to the Place de Grève, not just as a necessary large open space but also as the site of public executions. The
crowd could make mistakes, but it does not appear that the eighteenth-
century mob was characteristically blind.[43] Choice rather than accident
is the answer to the question posed by any historian of eighteenth-century
violence as to why this individual rather than another fell victim. The
victim of a crowd was usually someone who was known to have infringed the rules or, more rarely, someone whose known previous behavior made it likely that he had. It seems rare indeed that someone fell
victim by mere virtue of his social position or public post. This feature
is visible as much during the Revolution as before it. To cite some random examples, peasant crowds attacked only selected seigneurs, and
there were untouched châteaux in every troubled area; in 1791 and 1792,
there were dozens of nobles in châteaux around Lyon and in the central
Rhône valley indulging in unwise talk and maintaining unsavory friend-
ships, yet Guillin du Montet and the marquis de Bésignan were singled
out for mass attack precisely because they had a long history of tyrannical abuse of the peasantry, compounded by intemperate behavior just
prior to the riot; the disturbances of the 1795 White Terror in the south
are simply incomprehensible without analyzing the selective nature of
the crowd action.[44]

Even if I limit my remarks to the *ancien régime* for the moment, the
exercise of justice is an act of power, an attribute of majesty. By exercising justice, by deliberately endowing it in many cases with the
forms of the execution of royal justice, by exercising it in public and
often in the very site of royal justice, the crowd was in fact laying claim
to some portion of public power and erecting its own codes alongside

[43] Kaplan (n. 13 above) notes the measured quality of market violence
(1:191).

[44] P. Vaillandet, "Le premier complot du Marquis de Bésignan," *Mémoires
de l'Académie de Vaucluse*, 2d ser., 35 (1935): 1–40; "Notice sur Guillin du
Montet," *Revue du Lyonnais* 3 (1836): 476–97; AD Rhône 9 C 13; C. Lucas,
"Themes in Southern Violence after 9 Thermidor," in *Beyond the Terror*, ed.
G. Lewis and C. Lucas (Cambridge, 1983), pp. 152–94.

those of the state. This is, of course, to overstate the matter by developing unduly implications that were certainly unperceived by the *ancien régime* crowd. The relation between the crowd and public power was more complex and, until the Revolution, amounted at most to a kind of coexistence. In absolutist theory, the Crown alone occupied the public space, and it ruled over individuals who owed it unquestioning obedience.[45] In practice, however, this public space was constantly invaded by the population in the shape of the crowd, which exercised definable functions of regulation and disapproval. In this sense, the crowd was political under the *ancien régime*, even if its action rarely surpassed a very localized and specific reproach that did not constitute a direct threat to state power. Through the crowd, the people regulated, checked, and ultimately limited (albeit loosely) the exercise of state power in matters that directly affected the details of their lives.

We may extend this notion of space a little further. Just as the royal state controlled the public space of power, so it controlled the physical public space of highways, streets, and squares. If the crowd invaded the public space, it was trespassing in both political and physical terms. This physical space was marked by a geography of public power: in Paris, the Place de Grève, the houses of the *commissaires,* the Hôtel-de-Ville, the hôtel of the *commandant du guet* and that of the *prévôt des marchands,* the prisons, the *octroi* houses, the Palais, the Châtelet, the Bastille—and the pattern was repeated in any provincial center. The crowd went out of its way to respect this geography, parading its effigies to the appropriate public building, dragging the broken bodies of *archers* and *mouches* to the house of a *commissaire,* carrying the debris of guard posts to the Place de Grève. As the crowd receded from this physical and political public space, so the power of the state flowed back into it, as symbolized by the reappearance of *archers* and police agents, the judicial inquiries, arrests, trials, and public punishments. The relationship between the crowd and the royal state was fluctuating and to some extent ritualized, and the crowd could establish no lasting hold on either physical or political space. This was partly because of the evanescent nature of the crowd itself; but it was also because the crowd, as representative of the community, sought only to regulate state power and not to substitute its own. It was a relationship recognized by both sides. The crowd did regulate itself both in the specificity of its choice of victim and by attempting to prevent

---

[45] See R. Koselleck, *Le règne de la critique* (Paris, 1979).

actions that infringed its own codes.[46] For its part, the repression carried out by the state, for all its spectacular quality, was measured and highly ritualized.[47] Both sides knew they had to respect and fear each other. And each side disguised the relationship in a mutual discourse of goodness: the popular assertion of the goodness of the king, on the one side, and the royal assertion of the goodness of the people, on the other.

In this context, the appearance of the Palais-Royal as a focus is significant. In 1780, the duc d'Orléans ceded the palace to his son (the future regicide), who opened the gardens to the general public. This was a privileged area that the police could not enter.[48] For Parisians it became, therefore, a public space outside the state, a space that could be entered and occupied permanently. At the same time, a host of cafés opened up under the arcades where the politically active elite critics of the regime met. The Palais-Royal became a junction between the much newer political action of the educated speechifiers in the cafés around the edge and the much older political action of the crowd swarming in the central gardens. It was this fusion that Arthur Young described in 1789 in his portrayal of the coffeehouses, which were "not only crowded within, but other expectant crowds are at the doors and windows, listening *à gorge déployée* to certain orators, who from chairs or tables harangue each his little audience."[49]

We must note one final incarnation of the crowd in the public space under the *ancien régime*. This is what Arlette Farge has recently termed the "crowd assembled" (*la foule conviée*).[50] This was the crowd that assembled to witness the great public acts of state power—processions, *entrées*, public functions of officials from *gouverneurs* down to munic-

---

[46] Thus, e.g., the rioter at the Parisian *barrières* who stopped a thief (Rudé, *The Crowd in the French Revolution* [n. 9 above], p. 49); the crowd ransacking the Hôtel de la Police on July 13 scrupulously kept away from the first floor apartment where the wife of the *lieutenant de police* was; every item of value on Berthier's body was handed in; in October, the women policed the Hôtel-de-Ville to keep out thieves who only got in once they had left for Versailles (Bailly [n. 32 above], 1:356 and 2:124). The same feature is visible at the time of the September Massacres when a person caught stealing a handkerchief from a corpse was immediately killed (J. M. Thompson, *English Witnesses of the French Revolution* [Oxford, 1938], p. 194).

[47] See, e.g., S. Hardy's account of the aftermath of the May 3, 1775 riots in Paris printed from his manuscript *Mes Loisirs* in V. S. Ljublinski, *La Guerre des Farines* (Grenoble, 1979), pp. 305–50.

[48] J. Godechot, *La prise de la Bastille* (Paris, 1965), pp. 78–79.

[49] A. Young, *Travels in France*, ed. C. Maxwell (Cambridge, 1950).

[50] Farge (n. 28 above), pp. 201–58.

ipal councils, and, above all, executions. At such times the crowd was invited into the public space, once again as a representative, to bear witness to the display of public power and, by its acquiescence, to restate the submission of the subjects. In practice, of course, the crowd was being solicited as much as convoked; it was a participant as well as a witness. Royal authority needed the stylized adherence of the crowd before which it paraded its majesty. The parade would make no sense without its public and without that public's acquiescence or approval. There was a fine line between acquiescence and approval, and to solicit either one admitted the possibility of its opposite—rejection and disapproval. The crowd, therefore, could potentially break out of the stylized role assigned to it, commenting and hence regulating. The authorities were acutely aware of this possibility and observed the reactions of the crowd attentively. The crowd did indeed comment. It could express approval by cheers and good humor; but even that could be a hostile act if the approval was for some person or institution of which the royal government disapproved. It could remain indifferent and silent, hostile, therefore, to the act it was called on to approve. It could jeer and boo, resort to verbal and, eventually, to physical violence. The crowd assembled was a necessary but dangerous public for the state.

Therefore, whether noisy or silent, the crowd was a definable actor in the play of *ancien régime* politics. It was a critical public that existed before the elite critics of the *ancien régime* broke out of the private world of salons and academies. Some authors have characterized this crowd as "prepolitical" or as effecting "primitive political gestures."[51] This is really to use the politics of the Revolution as the touchstone. Yet it does raise the question of how the politics of the crowd adapted to the revolutionary context and to what degree they were transformed. The contention here is that there is a direct continuity between the functions of the prerevolutionary crowd and the functions of the crowd in the Revolution, between the value system the crowd articulated before 1789 and its development thereafter.

* * *

As far as Paris is concerned, the disturbances of August–September 1788 were the last to be framed almost exclusively in the classic terms I have described. This is true not only in their development as a reaction to repressive behavior by agents of authority and in the crowd's re-

[51] Kaplow (n. 34 above), p. 153; Kaplan (n. 13 above), 1:194.

course to the ritual execution of the effigies of authority figures held guilty; it is true also in their relation to the Parlement, whose dismissal provided the original context of the gatherings and whose return in September amid cheering crowds constituted the last act of these events. It is as well not to overemphasize the significance of the crowd's affection for the Parlement, to anticipate its meaning in the light of 1789. On the one hand, crowd support for the Parlement was an old phenomenon, dating from beyond the Jansenist controversy to the Fronde; on the other, the crowd's chants of "Long live the Parlement" on its return were accompanied by cries of "Prosecute Dubois" (the *commandant du guet*), thereby revealing the center of its preoccupations and, perhaps, the main significance that it now accorded to the return of the law court. Nonetheless, one other note was sounded. Charron emphasizes the wide unanimity of the reaction to the news of Necker's recall: "it was the *Peuple* which expected advantageous consequences from the return of M. NECKER; it was the *Public* which caused the Bourse to rise again because of its expressions of confidence; it was the *Populace* which carried his effigy in triumph on long staves which it got from the quays; it was the *Canaille* which forced passers-by to shout: Long live M. Necker."[52] Beneath the accustomed rituals, the crowd was displaying not merely a knowledge of the broad lines of high politics (normal enough in Paris) but also a sense that a particular policy in government was in its interests.

Quite how popular consciousness developed to this point must be a matter for more extensive discussion than space allows here. As far as the Revolution is concerned, George Rudé is certainly correct to identify the process as an interplay of "inherent" and "derived" ideas, although his sense of "inherent" ideas is quite different from the one here.[53] In terms of background, one of the most stimulating suggestions is that of Steven Kaplan, who sees the effect of the free grain trade experiments of the 1760s and 1770s and the decade of grain riots that accompanied them to have been to instill the notion that, beyond the traditionally identified hoarders and speculators, it was the government—indeed, the king himself—that was deliberately acting against the people and violating its fundamental responsibilities.[54] Certainly, in 1788, Charron found quite absurd the notion that people did not know what was going on; in his view, even if they had not been in-

---

[52] Charron (n. 21 above), p. 57.
[53] G. Rudé, *Ideology and Popular Protest* (London, 1980), esp. pp. 27–37, 104–16.
[54] Kaplan (n. 13 above), 1:395–96.

structed by elite debates, they clearly understood that economic conditions were the consequence of government policy. "Do not believe that crude minds lack energy when they communicate with each other. . . . If [the populace] rationalized its discontent, if its anxieties were well founded, then it necessarily had to participate in the events."[55]

We can see here one way at least in which a profound shift in consciousness was being prepared. It was a shift toward identifying popular interests as being in opposition not simply to acts by individual authority figures that infringed the community's rules but also to the government itself. It prepared popular consciousness to make choices about government and to identify itself with the Tiers État. It was in this ground that were rooted those agencies of revolutionary education normally cited by historians—pamphlets, orators, the elections, the *cahiers,* the assemblies for petitioning in June and July 1789, and so on. Yet the impact of elections and assemblies in 1789 on popular opinion is not straightforward. If it is true that the Crown was inviting the population into the public space of politics, it was trying to do so in a restrictive and controlled manner. Above all, an electoral assembly was not well suited in form or content to popular political expression; moreover, the poorer sections were excluded from much of the process and, in the towns, at best atomized into corporative assemblies that emphasized sectional rather than community interests. In 1789 and beyond the crowd provided a far more potent education as it acted out its traditional functions of expressing a sense of injustice and of providing the instrument for regulation and for obtaining redress. Certainly, even in the earliest moments of the Revolution, the crowd underwent a remarkably rapid evolution. In September 1788, it still personalized its comment in the cry of "Long live M. Necker"; in the Réveillon riot (April 1789) it added to that shout the abstract slogan of "Long live the Third Estate." Yet the very traditionalism of the Réveillon riot, both in its conduct and in its central meaning (after all, Réveillon and Henriot were being reproached for infringing community norms), poses the probably unresolvable question of what the crowd meant by the Third Estate. To what extent did it then, or indeed ever, mean to represent by this term (and subsequently by "the nation") anything more than the community and its values—a predominantly traditional perception, vaguely informed by a sense of its wider applicability culled from and couched in language supplied by the elite revolutionaries? William Sewell's suggestive work reveals that even for

[55] Charron, p. 14.

the sansculottes the important changes wrought by the Revolution in their attitude toward work and trade identity served to emphasize "their collective loyalty to a moral community" and to leave untouched "the moral collectivism of the prerevolutionary corporate mentality."[56] If, as Sewell says, that moral community had by 1793 become the one and indivisible republic, how substantively different were the perceived attributes of that republic from those that popular assumptions deemed necessary to good order and fair dealing in the prerevolutionary society?

The events of July 1789 illustrate many of these themes. Even leaving aside the matter of prices, which was such a powerful mobilizer, there was much about these events that was entirely traditional.[57] The response to the dismissal of Necker was the predictable one of parading his bust and that of Orléans (thought to have been exiled also) and forcing people to doff their hats. It was the Royal-Allemand's firing on this crowd that began the disturbances just as, as we have noted, it was firing from the Bastille that sparked the assault. Certainly the power of Necker's dismissal to produce the crowd's reaction is further evidence of the evolution of consciousness that we have discussed, while the crowd's reaction to the troop movements shows the actualization of the latent sense that the royal government was hostile to the popular interest. Yet the crowd's punitive action was in the traditional mode of attacks on specified individuals in retribution for specific conduct. We have already mentioned the deaths of de Launay and soldiers taken at the Bastille. It is equally clear in the case of Jacques de Flesselles, who had promised weapons but produced a chest full of old linen, who wrote a damagingly sybilline note to de Launay, and whose whole public conduct during the troubles was visibly suspect. Both J.-F. Foulon and his son-in-law L. B. F. Berthier were accused in classic terms of starving the people: Foulon was ritually decorated with a necklace of nettles and a bunch of thistles

---

[56] W. H. Sewell, *Work and Revolution in France* (Cambridge, 1980), pp. 92–113. Lynn Hunt and George Sheridan have argued that the lack of popular defense of the corporations under the Revolution and the deviation of popular attention toward revolutionary politics contradict Sewell's thesis ("Corporatism, Association, and the Language of Labor in France, 1750–1850," *Journal of Modern History* 58 [1986]: 822). This is less surprising if one sees both corporations and popular revolutionary politics as expressing the same basic value system.

[57] The analysis of the events of July 1789 in the following pages is based on the account given by Bailly ([n. 33 above], vols. 1 and 2). Although this account was drawn up around February 1792, it is extensively based on the *Procès-Verbal des Electeurs* to which it adds other material.

"to punish him for having wanted to make the people eat hay"; and, as for Berthier, "They brought bad bread [which he was thought to have put on sale], and the people attributed all its misfortunes to M. Berthier."[58] Furthermore, the deaths of Foulon and Berthier in particular were very carefully presented as acts of justice: in Foulon's case, the crowd in the Hôtel-de-Ville insisted on having an ad hoc court of lawyers set up then and there to try him, and he was placed on a low stool before the council table—obviously, the *sellette* of a regular court—until the crowd got impatient. And, as we have said, they (like de Flesselles) were taken out of the Hôtel-de-Ville to the Place de Grève just as were the condemned criminals of the *ancien régime*.

The crowd action in July was essentially reactive. It was engendered by panic and its motive was fundamentally self-defense. One cannot discern in the crowd, as distinct from the electors and their allies in the National Assembly, any demand for the withdrawal of the troops or any programmatic statements about sovereignty and the relation between National Assembly power and royal power. If we mean by "revolutionary" the design of effecting a permanent change through the reorganization of power as distinct from remedying an immediate grievance perceived in isolation or punishing an individual in authority, then the July crowd does not appear revolutionary. The consequences of its action were, of course, profoundly revolutionary. By acting in the same direction as the National Assembly, it brought to fruition a permanent reorganization of power. But that is not the same thing as having that end in mind. By reacting against the royal troops in a more extended but nonetheless essentially similar version of a time-honored gesture, it helped to expel an already retreating royal power from the public space. But that does not mean that the crowd did not assume that royal power would flow back into that space in the normal course of events.

However, beneath the conventional quality of these gestures lay important new implications. The crowd invaded public space in the double sense defined earlier, but it did not encounter constituted royal power as in earlier times: royal power was in dissolution and, with the defection of the *gardes françaises,* there remained only the physical geography of *ancien régime* power and isolated agents of a dying authority. Instead, the crowd encountered the electors, emerging and claiming power within these very events. The interplay between the crowd and the electors around the remnants of *ancien régime* official-

[58] Bailly, 2:110, 118.

dom and the constitution of a new authority was extremely complex, a phenomenon of simultaneous fusion and separation. Early in these events, de Flesselles "desired to exercise no authority other than what would be given him by the inhabitants of the capital; and by acclamation all those who were there appointed him head [of the executive of the town council]."[59] It is debatable exactly which inhabitants he had in mind: most likely the electors, but the scene took place at the Hôtel-de-Ville in front of "the multitude assembled there" and it was the crowd that had demanded that de Flesselles be called to the Hôtel-de-Ville. The nomination of Jean-Sylvain Bailly as mayor and the marquis de Lafayette as commander of the *milice* on July 15 was even more visibly a mass affair involving both electors and the crowd. Part of the legitimacy of the new authority in the capital undoubtedly derived, therefore, from its acceptability to the crowd. This was an important step.

Other events at the Hôtel-de-Ville allow us to observe more closely this simultaneous fusion and separation of the crowd and the elites, of government and the governed, that characterizes the July crisis. Throughout the crisis (including the murders of Foulon and Berthier on July 22), the crowd was the compelling presence in the Hôtel-de-Ville. For a time, the crowd abolished the distinction between its occupation of the public space of power, outside in the square, and the interior seat of government authority: it had rendered the hidden area of power permeable, for the crowd inside was but the extension of the crowd gathered outside. Indeed, it demonstrated its fury when the committee withdrew to another room behind closed doors, saying that "they were working in secret there, out of sight of the citizens, in order to betray them."[60] Furthermore, the extraordinary popular triumph accorded to Elie after the fall of the Bastille (he was brought to the Hôtel-de-Ville, put up on the council table, crowned like some Roman emperor surrounded by prisoners and by the silver, flag, and great register of the Bastille) was a direct statement of popular power within the very seat of constituted authority.

Yet, at the same time, occupying the interior seat of power clearly constrained the crowd's behavior. It retained a sense of limits on its ability to act, an indefinable sense that within the Hôtel-de-Ville a legitimacy other than that of the crowd held sway. This is visible in the events surrounding the death of Foulon. The crowd in the Hôtel-de-Ville demanded justice. However, it was persuaded by Bailly's ar-

[59] Ibid., 1:346.
[60] Ibid., 1:380.

gument, based in the assumptions of the elites' revolution, that Foulon had to be judged by due legal process, which it was essential to maintain in order to protect the innocent, even though, he conceded, there was a prima facie case against Foulon. The crowd refused to wait for referral to the ordinary courts and tried to force the electors to appoint a court— yet it was still ready to accept the electors' legalistic point that they had no power to appoint judges. At this juncture, the crowd tried to constitute a court itself. However, it did not choose men from its own ranks but, rather, elite figures with public functions: two curés, an *échevin* and a former *échevin*, a *juge-auditeur,* and even, under the pressure of the electors, a *procureur du roi,* and a *greffier.* It was only with the procrastination of these figures that the crowd reverted to its traditional behavior and above all to its traditional space of action by taking Foulon outside onto the Place de Grève.

The Foulon incident clearly demonstrated the limits on the revolutionary nature of the July crowd. However strong the discourse of justice in its action, it could not escape the notion that justice was normally a function of state, properly exercised in the state's forms and by the social elites. The function of the crowd was still to enforce that responsibility and, if the elites failed or refused to assume it in a particular case, to substitute its own justice in its own forms for that case. There was no attempt to effect a permanent substitution, nor indeed any real consciousness that the fount of justice lay in the people. This argument notwithstanding, the experience of July 14 was undoubtedly significant in actualizing shifts in popular perceptions. For one thing, if justice is an attribute of majesty, so too is pardon. Whereas the *ancien régime* crowd had often shouted for pardon on the Place de Grève, it had never obtained it; here, in the famous scene where Elie pleaded for the lives of prisoners at the Hôtel-de-Ville, it exercised that right. The revolutionary notion of the majesty of the people was given here a popular connotation that elite revolutionaries probably did not mean by the phrase. More important, no one reflecting later on the July events could fail to understand that the crowd's action had effected permanent change. Bailly, who thought that these great changes had already been achieved by the National Assembly, nonetheless acknowledged that this was only understood by the legislators and "enlightened minds"—"The Bastille, captured and demolished, spoke to everyone."[61]

To what extent did crowd behavior in the subsequent few years continue to display these same patterns? To what extent did it develop the transformations and resolve the ambiguities I have noted in the

[61] Ibid., 1:390.

July crisis? It is, of course, easy to emphasize the continuities. Some of the examples I have used in my discussion of the *ancien régime* crowd already make the point. Even in Paris, the sugar riots of January 1792 and the soap riots of 1793 did not transcend at all the character and discourse of the most traditional price disturbances.[62] Moreover, the nature of the punitive reaction and the rituals of popular justice remained much the same. One has only to think of the September Massacres with their deliberate institution of popular tribunals—although these massacres do point to other features, as we shall see. One principal motivation of the crowd's attack in September 1792 was still the perception that constituted authority was failing in its obligation. Exactly the same pattern can be seen in the contemporaneous murder of J. L. Gérard at Lorient. He was murdered only after the crowd had failed to persuade the municipality to deal with him, and then the murder was committed in the classic fashion on the town square, followed by a ritual parade of his dismembered parts.[63]

One of the major complications in evaluating the development and transformation of crowd action is the appearance of organized crowds, assembled for some purpose of revolutionary politics under the direction of militants. As Michel Vovelle has emphasized, the organized crowd of this nature was a phenomenon distinct from the spontaneous crowd of the early Revolution.[64] The political education of the popular militants who directed and focused such crowds took place in the clubs and sections even more than in the street. In practice, it is extremely difficult to identify the authentic voice of the crowd behind the spokesmen and the petitions claiming to present its case.[65] I have posited that the crowd liberated the traditional reflex by articulating what the members of the community had in common; it is likely therefore that the crowd always understood the meaning of its actions and of its spokesmen's words more precisely than did those spokesmen. Yet this does not preclude important transformations having occurred in its action and above all in its political function.

It is clear, in the first place, that the crowd swiftly articulated a perception that the *peuple* in the social sense of the popular classes

[62] A. Mathiez, *La vie chère et le mouvement social sous la Terreur* (Paris, 1927), pp. 35–48, 146 ff.; J. Godechot, "Fragments de mémoires de Charles-Alexis Alexandre sur les journées révolutionnaires de 1791 et 1792," *Annales historiques de la Révolution française* (1952): 148–61.

[63] R. M. Andrews, "L'assassinat de Gérard, négociant lorientais," *Annales historiques de la Révolution française* (1967), pp. 309–38.

[64] M. Vovelle, *La mentalité révolutionnaire* (Paris, 1985), pp. 70–75.

[65] See, e.g., Cobb (n. 1 above), p. 86.

was coterminous with the *peuple/nation*. Even in a provincial town like Nogent-le-Rotrou a price-fixing crowd could cry "Long live the Nation! The price of corn will go down!"[66] And crowds were quick to identify as enemies categories of people defined in terms of the politics of the Revolution, especially émigrés and nonjuring priests. To cite random examples, a crowd stopping the transport of grain at Choisy-au-Bec feared that this grain was on its way to émigrés; at Lorient, Gérard had been suspected of shipping arms to the émigrés; the September Massacres rested on a particular perception of nonjuring priests.[67] The ability of the crowd to adduce and act on such considerations constituted a significant extension of its behavior. Similarly, the electrifying effect of the war crises of 1792 and 1793 was profoundly different from the superficially similar defensive reflex in July 1789. Even if we consider only the theme of justice and regulation, it is evident that the definition of what sort of behavior constituted infringement of the norms had undergone a dramatic extension. It was these kinds of transformations in the perceptions of the spontaneous crowd that elaborated the traditional reflex that we have defined and moved beyond it. They laid the foundation for the crowd's availability to section organizers in the set pieces of 1793, for, as we have said, the crowd was not easily manipulated by outsiders whose exhortations did not coincide with its own canons.

Nonetheless, these transformations were not as clear-cut as they might appear. Significant though it must be that the crowd could articulate a condemnation of general categories of enemies, it is not evident that it acted entirely in consequence. When confronted with individuals, the crowd did not exact retribution any more indiscriminately than it had done under the *ancien régime*; the quality of being an émigré or a refractory priest does not appear often to have been a sufficient motivation for violence against persons. I have already used examples from the Revolution to show the personalized nature of retribution. The September Massacres provide another case in point.[68] Although the mobilizing factors and the definitions of "enemy" were of the evolved type, the crowd clearly took pains—and, in some cases, lengthy pains—to distinguish between individuals, liberating some and killing others. Certainly, the fact that the only sentence was death distinguishes the course of the September Massacres from the quite varied structure of punishment to which the *ancien régime* crowd had

---

[66] Mathiez, *La vie chère et le mouvement social sous la Terreur*, p. 103.
[67] Ibid., p. 62; Andrews.
[68] P. Caron, *Les Massacres de Septembre* (Paris, 1935), pp. 27–54; 413–45.

recourse (and that was also employed in the much more traditional events of the White Terror of 1795 in the south); this serves to emphasize how much the crowd had come to see counterrevolution as a heinous crime against the community. Nonetheless, there was a substantial number of ordinary criminals among those killed. This was not the accidental product of the blind mob: the element of deliberate selection applied in these cases too. Moreover, this happened elsewhere—for example, the crowd that murdered counterrevolutionaries at Aix-en-Provence in early 1793 also strung up a couple of thieves and a rapist, while in 1797 at Lyon, a byword for political massacre, the crowd murdered three thieves deemed inadequately sentenced and shortly afterward drowned a *chauffeur* in the Saône.[69] The fact is that the crowd did not clearly distinguish between counterrevolutionary crime and crime *tout court* in a scale of values still anchored in the prerevolutionary mentality. Even if some of the Suisses captured at the Tuileries on August 10, 1792 were massacred on the spot, the crowd also dragged many of them the not inconsiderable distance to the Place de Grève to execute them there.[70] In sum, the popular perception of counterrevolution appears to have been assimilated into a traditional structure of values and responses just as much as, if not more than, it testified to a new political awareness concerning the issues of the Revolution.

The most important of all the factors transforming the action of the crowd was the emergence of a clear sense that, in order to obtain redress of grievance, it had to go beyond agents of authority to put pressure on the seat of power. As we have seen, this sense was present in only the most confused form in July 1789. In October 1789, it was already very much more visible.[71] Whatever the indefinable role of agitators, this was certainly a spontaneous crowd event. It was a traditional crowd movement in its preoccupation with bread, in the prominence of women in a disturbance over bread, in its perception of the king's role as the provider of bread, and in the crowd's forcing Maillard to lead it to do what it wanted to do. But it was new in its specific invasion of both seats of national government—the royal palace and the Assembly—rather than merely the seat of municipal government. It was new in its deliberate securing of the person of the king as a permanent, political solution to a perennial problem rather than a tem-

[69] AD Bouches-du-Rhône L 3043; B. J. Buchez and P. C. Roux, *Histoire parlementaire de la Révolution française*, 40 vols. (Paris, 1834–38), 37:289.

[70] M. Reinhard, *La chute de la royauté* (Paris, 1969), p. 584.

[71] A. Mathiez, "Étude critique sur les journées des 5 et 6 octobre 1789," *Revue historique* 67 (1898): 241–81; 68 (1899): 258–94; 69 (1899): 41–66.

porary solution provided by a *taxation populaire* and by punishment of some delinquent local agent of authority. In these terms, it is October rather than July that appears the more significant event in shaping the revolutionary crowd.

Of course, October did not achieve an immediate and complete transformation in crowd habits. It still resorted to *taxations* and attacks on traditional objects of fury; even in 1793, it still put pressure more readily on the city government than on the Convention. Nonetheless, the lesson of October prepared and was reinforced by that of August 10, 1792. August 10 was the first really organized *journée*. It was promoted by radical politicians, and the politicized *fédérés* from outside Paris played a prominent part as well. As a result, the intentions of the Parisian *peuple* around this event are not entirely easy to read. It was once again the firing of the troops on the crowd that provoked it to storm the palace. It is remarkable that the crowd in the September Massacres made no serious attempt to go near the Temple, and that there was no crowd intervention in the Convention's debates on the king. The crowd watched the king's execution in absolute silence, only breaking into cheers when his head was held aloft. The king's death, arguably one of the most revolutionary acts of the whole period, was accomplished without the intervention of the crowd (even as the "crowd assembled" its behavior was ambiguous and its approval post hoc); it was the last episode in the struggle between the power of the elites and that of the monarchy.

The problem of assessing the true relation between the crowd and organized political action—even in 1793, its most potent year—is well illustrated by the Parisian disturbances of March 9–10, 1793, which saw both the breaking of the Girondin presses and what is usually presented as an attempted insurrection against the Convention under the aegis of a number of clubs. In fact, quite distinct elements were involved. On the one hand, the previous days had seen substantial popular agitation when workers from different trades prepared to gather in considerable numbers in order to demand a reduction in the price of foodstuffs. There had also been talk that "without any doubt . . . , people will march on the central market next Friday." On the other hand, it was volunteer soldiers (possibly no more than fifty of them) who broke the presses, and it was again volunteer soldiers and *fédérés* who paraded menacingly through the Convention. The talk about the sovereign people and the need to act all took place in some section assemblies and clubs, and it was aimed at the *fédérés* and volunteers.[72]

---

[72] A.-M. Boursier, "L'émeute parisienne du 10 Mars 1793," *Annales historiques de la Révolution française* (1972), pp. 204–30.

Nonetheless, there were great demonstrations around the Convention in 1793.[73] Their organized quality was not incompatible with the way in which the action of the spontaneous crowd had developed. The crowd may not have followed the ramifications of sovereignty involved when one of its spokesmen said (to pick up a phrase from June 1792) "the people is here; it awaits in silence a reply worthy of its sovereignty."[74] It may not have understood in detail *Enragé* and militant sansculotte ideas about the regeneration of society, permanent economic regulation, and direct democracy. But it surely did understand at least that the seat of government could be invaded and that the holders of state power could be pressured into adopting measures that ensured more than temporary solutions to popular problems. To this degree, the Parisian crowd was by now revolutionary.

The proof of this is to be found not so much in the organized crowd of 1793, but in the spontaneous crowd, deprived of its leaders, during the Germinal and Prairial Days in 1795.[75] In the face of appalling hardship, it resorted not to the traditional methods of *taxation* and attacks on suspected hoarders, nor even to pressuring the municipal authorities; it turned directly to invading the Convention, and its cry of "Bread and the Constitution of '93" explicitly linked a whole permanent organization of power to the resolution of its problem. Yet, at the same time, the Germinal and Prairial Days also demonstrate the limits on the crowd's capacity for revolutionary action. In practice, once it had invaded the Convention, it did not really know what to do with the power it had gained. It depended entirely on the rump of radical deputies taking charge and providing it with detailed measures to enforce. It had no real concept of revolutionary substitution, no sense that its own power could somehow be permanent—only that the Convention could be forced to enact favorable measures whose permanence was guaranteed mostly by a naive view of the binding character of a constitution. In this respect, the crowd had not moved far beyond July 1789. Although temporarily overawed in 1795, the Convention was no longer constrained by the double jeopardy of invasion and provincial insurrection as it had been in 1793.

* * *

In order to complete our discussion of the crowd in the political culture of the Revolution, we need finally to examine briefly the attitude

---

[73] See M. Slavin, *The Making of an Insurrection* (Cambridge, Mass., 1986).
[74] Reinhard, p. 323.
[75] See the account of 1 Prairial in Buchez and Roux, 36:314–70.

of the revolutionary elites to it. During the arduous transition from the *ancien régime* to the Revolution, the crowd and the elites coexisted uneasily in the public space of power vacated by the monarchical state. At moments, groups committed to the revolution of the National Assembly were prepared to call on the street. Thus, for example, when news of the *séance royale* arrived at Lyon, members of the *Cercle des Terreaux* on the balcony of their club incited a riot among "the people and some young men of the bourgeoisie" in the street below who, after forcing illuminations and maltreating the *prévôt des marchands,* ended up by destroying the *barrières.*[76] But such a direct appeal was extremely rare and the *Cercle des Terreaux* had probably not measured the likely consequence of its enthusiasm. Certainly, the good bourgeoisie of Lyon quickly brought out the *milice bourgeoise* to control the disturbances, and several weeks later they marched out to repress quite brutally the rural disturbances in the region.[77] Indeed, one of the principal "revolutionary" consequences of crowd action in mid-1789 was to stimulate the crystallization of bourgeois revolutionary authority, a process involving the creation of new municipal governments and national guards that were intended to control the crowd. Even in Paris, it is quite clear that the prime motivation of the electors was the question of public order more than Necker and the royal troops. As early as July 11, they were petitioning the National Assembly for a *garde bourgeoise* on the grounds that the presence of the troops was provoking "popular emotions"; as we have seen, they authorized the taking of arms in large part because of the armed crowds already in the streets, and they instructed electors to go to "the guard posts of the armed citizenry to request them, in the name of our country, to desist from any sort of crowd or violence." The first act of the permanent committee was to organize the *milice* and to forbid crowds. For Bailly, there were no two ways about it: "by their courage and activity, the electors saved the city of Paris"—and he did not mean from royal counterrevolution.[78]

For a short while, the crowd and the revolutionaries stood side by side in the arena vacated by the royal state. What better illustration than an incident on July 15 described by Bailly?[79] A long procession wound from the Tuileries toward the Hôtel-de-Ville, comprising the *guet,* the *gardes françaises,* officials of the *prévôté,* electors, members of the National Assembly, and the *milice parisienne,* all under the gaze

[76] A. Brette, "Journal de l'émotion de Lyon (29 Juin–5 Juillet 1789)," *La Révolution française* 33 (1897): 556–63.

[77] *Rapport de l'expédition des citoyens de Lyon dans la province du Dauphiné* (n.p., 1789).

[78] Bailly (n. 33 above), esp. 1:330, 348.

[79] Ibid., 2:18–19.

of a large, cheering crowd—in other words, it was a demonstration in quite traditional form of the fusion of old and new agents of authority under the control of the new revolutionary power and a claim for recognition and endorsement by the crowd assembled. Suddenly, the procession encountered "a sort of triumph" in which a *garde français* crowned with laurel was being escorted in a cart by another large cheering crowd. The first procession joined in the plaudits of the second without ever quite knowing who the man was. By later 1789, however, the revolutionary authorities had largely completed their occupation of the public space of politics and they had inherited the functions of the *ancien régime* state. The enactment of martial law in the aftermath of the October Days enshrined the contradiction between the legal revolution of the elites and the popular revolution of the crowd.

Inheriting the functions of state power, it is hardly surprising that the new authorities should also have inherited much of the *ancien régime*'s relationship with the crowd. Yet, here too, there were significant transformations. Of course, eighteenth-century men of property feared both the crowd and monarchical power; they tended to fear the latter more than the former until the last decade of the century, when fear of the crowd came to dominate. In France, the crowd's behavior in 1789 appalled the more conservative even among moderate reformers—Mallet du Pan exclaimed in the *Mercure de France,* "The Huns, the Harudes, the Vandals, and the Goths will appear neither from the North nor from the Black Sea, they are in our midst"; the abbé Morellet confessed that "from this moment on [July 14] I was struck with fear at the sight of this great but hitherto disarmed power . . . a blind and unshackled power."[80] By 1792, such attitudes had spread to less obviously conservative figures: Thomas Lindet wrote in March 1792 from Normandy, under the impact of *taxation* riots, "We are in a state of war. . . . Verneuil has opened its gates to the enemy."[81] This eighteenth-century vision of the crowd as ignorant, dangerous, uncontrollable, and actuated by murderous passions had by 1795 overwhelmed any more sophisticated perceptions in the minds of the propertied advocates of the legal revolution.

Before then, however, such simplifications were by no means the rule. However much propertied revolutionaries would have liked to expel the crowd from the public space of politics, this was really not

---

[80] *Mercure de France,* August 8, 1789; André Morellet, *Mémoires de l'abbé Morellet sur le dix-huitième siècle et la Révolution,* 2 vols. (Paris, 1821), 2:4.
[81] A. Montier, ed., *Correspondance de Thomas Lindet pendant la Constituante et la Législative* (Paris, 1899), p. 337.

possible, even in the *ancien régime* mode of limiting it to spasmodic appearances. It was not just that the course of the Revolution gave it repeated opportunities and stimulants to act. It was more that, on the one hand, even moderate revolutionaries had to accommodate the fact that in 1789 the crowd had been instrumental in preserving the Revolution and, on the other, radical revolutionaries in particular understood that it could play that role again. Beyond that, their own discourse on sovereignty prevented the revolutionaries from having precisely the same relationship with the crowd as had the old monarchical state. The word *peuple* was extraordinarily ambiguous because of its double meaning: Jacques-Guillaume Thouret pointed this out at the very beginning, in the debate of June 15, 1789 on what to call the Third Estate, when he rejected the Comte de Mirabeau's suggestion of "Representatives of the French People" on the grounds that despite "the noble and general meaning of the word *people,* if this word is taken in the sense which limits it to the great mass, then it is without dignity and, thus confined, it might designate not the whole Third Estate but its nonenlightened part."[82] The difficulties in maintaining the distinction were immediately apparent: on July 16, while Mirabeau was rebutting Jean-Joseph Mounier's opposition to a call to dismiss the ministry with the phrase "you forget that this people, against whom you erect the limits of the three powers, is the source of all powers," Moreau de Saint-Méry (president of the electors) was pointing to the enormous cheering crowd witnessing the king's visit to Paris, saying, "And that, Sire, is the people whom some have dared to vilify."[83] Even if the exercise of political functions was reserved for active citizens until 1792, all individuals by virtue of their rights were participants in sovereignty. There was always the nagging point that the crowd did somehow claim a legitimacy, and those who increasingly came to organize this crowd certainly made that claim. It was no casual shift of language that transformed Gonchon, who first appeared before the National Assembly as "the orator of the Faubourg Saint-Antoine," into "the orator of the people."[84]

Various strategies beyond simple physical containment were available. One early example was the regulation of the right of petition by the decree of May 10, 1791, which, confining this right to individual signed petitions, sought to atomize the crowd. Another strategy was

[82] Quoted by Bailly, 1:148.

[83] Ibid., 2:37; *Discours de M. Moreau de Saint-Méry, président de MM. les Electeurs, au Roi* (n.d.).

[84] V. Fournel, *Le patriote Palloy; l'orateur du peuple, Gonchon* (Paris, 1892).

the National Guard. Although until the fall of the monarchy it was restricted to active citizens, it overlapped in its lower ranks with the social stratum out of which much of the crowd came. When all adult males entered the guard in 1792, it was recruited from the same population as the crowd. Like the crowd, the guard took its members out of their daily context and gave them a collective identity. But it also organized them in a hierarchy that was dominated even after 1792 by men of some substance and put them in the service of public authority. It was, then, the antithesis of the crowd; in a sense, it was the crowd organized to control the crowd. Yet, its ambivalent nature was demonstrated time and again by its refusal to repress the crowd and by its involvement in Parisian *journées*.

The most elaborate strategy was to develop the *ancien régime* device of the "crowd assembled." Mona Ozouf has demonstrated the richness, diversity, and pervasiveness of the revolutionary festival that flowered beginning with the great Fête de la Fédération of 1790.[85] The revolutionaries developed the notion of the "crowd assembled" far beyond anything that the *ancien régime* had envisaged. The *fête* incorporated the crowd into the revolutionary political process and at the same time sterilized it. The popular collective instinct was harnessed; the crowd was assigned a function; it was instructed in the meaning that the revolutionaries gave to the Revolution; it was taught proper revolutionary behavior, so to speak. Nonetheless, the "crowd assembled" still retained in one important respect the function it had had under the *ancien régime*. The "passion for open space"[86] that characterized the revolutionary *fête* was not simply an echo of popular habits; it was a deliberate assertion of the state's occupation of the double physical and political public space. The crowd was still being called on to endorse the power of the state. It could, therefore, still withhold acquiescence as it had done in the past: the inhabitants of the Faubourg Saint-Marcel, for example, simply refused to turn up to the festival in memory of Simoneau, the murdered mayor of Étampes, in 1792.[87] The revolutionaries needed this endorsement even more urgently than did the monarchy. Public executions also were still a statement of power and a demand for acquiescence as they had been before the Revolution. Indeed, the revolutionaries sought to make this even more explicit and

[85] M. Ozouf, *La fête révolutionnaire 1789–1799*; see also, L. Hunt, *Politics, Culture, and Class in the French Revolution* (London, 1986), pp. 52–86.

[86] Ozouf, p. 151.

[87] Godechot, "Fragments de mémoires de Charles-Alexis Alexandre sur les journées révolutionnaires de 1791 et 1792" (n. 62 above), pp. 164–67.

to educate the crowd out of its confusion between ordinary criminality and counterrevolution (which reduced the significance of its endorsement) by separating the two types of execution: executions of criminals remained on the Place de Grève, and political executions hovered between the Place du Carousel and the Place de la Révolution until they were moved to the Barrière du Trône Renversée in Prairial Year II.[88] The government still paid close attention to the reactions of the crowd at executions: one can positively hear the sigh of relief in the police reports on the execution of Jacques-Réné Hébert, and the acclamations at the death of Robespierre were widely commented on.[89] Indeed, the removal of the guillotine to a more remote corner of Paris in the face of the growing lassitude of the public was a sure sign that the Montagnard government was losing support or, as Saint-Just put it, that "the Revolution is frozen." It was a significant symbol of the Thermidorians' desire to criminalize the radical Revolution that the guillotine returned to the Place de Grève from Thermidor Year II to Prairial Year III.[90]

These examples from the Montagnard period demonstrate that the Jacobins had no less difficulty in relating to the crowd than did their revolutionary predecessors. Whatever their plans for the *peuple* and its place in revolutionary politics, the spontaneous crowd did not figure among them. The Jacobin Club's reaction to the sugar riots of January 1792 was to call to order the "women citizens of Paris who, for some sugar, [violate] the most sacred rights of property."[91] In this respect, radicals shared the basic premise of more moderate revolutionaries; their way of accommodating the crowd was but an elaboration of the moderates' perspective. Since one could not avoid either the presence of the crowd or the contribution it made to the Revolution, the solution to the problem was to distinguish between crowd actions—to appropriate some of them to the revolutionaries' cause by defining them as good and to condemn the rest as misguided, criminal, the product of manipulation by enemies of the good cause, or merely infantile. In this way, the revolutionaries were able to carry forward the definition favored by the *ancien régime* that violent crowds were the product of ill-intentioned leaders; they were thus able to accept their own fear of

[88] G. Lenôtre, *La guillotine pendant la Révolution* (Paris, 1893), pp. 249–76.

[89] On Hébert, A. Schmidt, *Tableaux de la Révolution française*, 3 vols. (Paris, 1867–70), 2:186.

[90] Lenôtre, p. 276.

[91] Mathiez, *La vie chère et le mouvement social sous la Terreur* (n. 62 above), pp. 46–48.

the crowd while at the same time rationalizing the inescapable fact of crowd violence by lauding it whenever it appeared to operate in accordance with the Revolution as it was defined by any particular revolutionary group. One early example of this process was the invention of the *Vainqueurs de la Bastille*. We have noted the ambivalent attitude of the revolutionary elites to the July crowd. By instituting the *Vainqueurs de la Bastille* through a formal designation of individual heroes after an inquiry and awards of pensions and medals, the National Assembly appropriated the act, disassembled the crowd into heroic individuals, and sanctified their action, thus rendering it safe.

Robespierre's commentary on the insurrection of August 10 shows how radicals could develop this approach. Robespierre made the classic distinction between the crowd as the majestic instrument of sovereignty and the crowd as an irresponsible, unruly destroyer:

In 1789 the people of Paris rose in a tumultuous fashion to repel the assault of the Court, to free itself from the former despotism rather than to conquer liberty, the idea of which was still confused and whose principles were unknown. Every sort of passion was involved in that insurrection. . . . In 1792, the people rose with imposing coolness to avenge the fundamental laws of its ravished liberty, to return to their duty all the tyrants who conspired against it. . . . It exercised its recognized sovereignty and displayed its power and its justice in order to safeguard its safety and its happiness. . . . The solemn manner in which it proceeded in this great act was as sublime as were its motives and its objectives. . . . This was no meaningless riot stirred up in the shadows; matters were discussed in the open, in the presence of the people; the day and the plan were posted. It was the whole people which was making use of its rights.[92]

The message is clear: this was an orderly, open, mature political act without 1789's frightening qualities and absolutely without relation to the riotous crowd as commonly defined. It was therefore a safe, welcome, legitimate act, an act of justice. This text provides an indispensable commentary on Robespierre's oft-quoted private notes from mid-1793, where he wrote, "The internal dangers come from the bourgeois; in order to defeat the bourgeois, we must rally the people. . . . The present insurrection must continue . . . the people must ally with the Convention and the Convention must make use of the people."[93] For Robespierre, the only good crowd was an organized crowd, directed toward specific revolutionary goals under the leadership of the

---

[92] *Le Défenseur de la Constitution*, no. 12.
[93] *Papiers inédits trouvés chez Robespierre . . . supprimés ou omis par Courtois*, 3 vols. (Paris, 1828), 2:13–16.

radical elites in the Convention. However, the experience of 1793 revealed how unreliable even the organized crowd was. The inception of the Terror was the final appropriation of the crowd, the substitution of state violence for crowd violence. As Danton said, "let us be terrible so that the people does not need to be."[94]

The Germinal and Prairial Days proved to the Thermidorians and the propertied inheritors of *ancien régime* state power, who they represented, that the legal revolution could not coexist with the crowd. Further, they proved that there was no need to accommodate the crowd. Despite the transformations we have tried to analyze, the crowd had failed as an instrument of popular intervention in and regulation of the elites' exercise of power. The era of the property owners' unadulterated fear of the "dangerous classes" and their complete exclusion from politics by a repressive state had begun. The experience of the crowd in the Revolution had provoked the final defection of the bourgeoisie from a culture based in notions of community. In this domain, the rupture with the eighteenth century began in 1795, not in 1789. As for the crowd, it fell back immediately into the highly traditional forms of market riot, protection of community norms, itemized reproach of individual infringements, and resistance to the innovating state that litter the provincial history of the Directory. This was the prelude to the long drawn-out agony of traditional popular protest, which was to be relieved only by the brief flares of the early 1830s and the turn of the mid-century.

[94] Buchez and Roux (n. 69 above), 25:56.

The Second Estate in the Constituent Assembly, 1789–1791

Alison Patrick

Among conventional versions of modern French history, few can be more generally accepted than that of noble hostility to the Revolution of 1789. The legend is straightforward enough. Under the *ancien régime,* a rising bourgeoisie, unfairly excluded from status and promotion, became bitterly resentful of privilege that it did not share. Faced with a threat to its domination, the nobility blindly resisted the government's reform programs and so forced the calling of the States-General. In 1789 the stubborn resistance of the aristocratic Second Estate killed the last chance of peaceful change and pushed the Third Estate into revolution; and after Bastille Day the noble emigration began, symbolizing the counterrevolution that forced the revolutionaries to move, reluctantly but unavoidably, further and further to the left. This is, at least, the story familiar to those who sympathize with revolutionary aims. Those of a different ideology may wish to reverse the perspective to make the nobility the predestined victim of a subversion it could not control, but, either way, the antagonism between the nobility and the makers of a new order has until recently been taken for granted.

During the past twenty years, revisionist historians have been undermining these dogmas in a number of ways. It has been argued that what was developing under the *ancien régime* was not a growing confrontation of ambitious bourgeoisie and exclusivist *noblesse* but, rather, a conflated elite with a common interest in wealth and prestige of the traditional kind whose members would have been happy to adapt old structures to new circumstances; what brought on the revolution was not noble obstinacy but an almost accidental political crisis.[1] Chaussinand-Nogaret has claimed that in 1789 the *noblesse* in general was resigned to change and that the resistance of the noble deputies at Versailles was in fact a betrayal of their constituents' intentions; he argues further that some deputies indeed recognized this at the time and did their best to avoid the "sterile opposition" of an "outmoded squabble" that delayed, but could not prevent, the logical nineteenth-century amalgamation

This essay originally appeared in the *Journal of Modern History* 62 (June 1990).

of elites.[2] A line is drawn between these forward-looking liberals of the Constituent, more in touch with the majority of their own electorate, and the blinkered conservatives sitting with them who were trapped by circumstances and their own (perceived) social interests into a struggle in which they were bound to be defeated.[3] Chaussinand claims both that the liberal minority of the Constituent's *noblesse* were on the side of the future, as the nineteenth century would show, and that in the early Revolution there was no such thing as "noble resistance" per se, since in the Constituent Assembly the nobles were divided against themselves and in the country at large were more inclined to go with the tide than to spend their energies on futile opposition.[4] This fits with Higonnet's claim that "the prospect of a durable reconciliation of bourgeois and nobles . . . was implicit in the fabric of French social life."[5] The accord failed in 1791, says Higonnet, for "ideological reasons," and he refers elsewhere to the bourgeoisie's "mistakes."[6] This line of argument has the effect of turning the nobility into a more or less passive element in the political situation. It is the bourgeoisie that is responsible for the developing confrontation, and traditional assumptions about the *noblesse* are said to conflict with the evidence.

More is involved in these claims than the mere documentation of their plausibility, though this too may present problems—for example, the alleged "liberalism" of the noble electoral assemblies in 1789 may not be as widespread as Chaussinand-Nogaret would suggest.[7] A central issue is that of image: if the nobility was not solidly counterrevolutionary, why did it so quickly get that reputation?

To examine the outlook and behavior of the entire French *noblesse* would be a mammoth task even if there were agreement on its demographic boundaries, and such an examination would end anyhow by raising the same problems; even if one has established, as Greer did long ago, that 95 percent of the nobility did not emigrate, what did the existence of the 5 percent signify to contemporaries?[8] But if one is in search of the origins of an image, it should be profitable to look carefully at those who in 1789–91 were perfectly placed

[2] G. Chaussinand-Nogaret, *The French Nobility in the Eighteenth Century*, trans. W. Doyle (Cambridge, 1985), pp. 172, 173.

[3] Ibid., p. 170.

[4] Ibid., chap. 7.

[5] P. Higonnet, *Class, Ideology and the Rights of Nobles during the French Revolution* (Oxford, 1981), p. 81.

[6] Ibid., p. 90.

[7] In 1789 the members of the Marmande noble delegation separately searched their consciences and got little help from their constituents; P. de Cazenove de Pradines, "En un temps d'illusion . . . 1789. Correspondance du bureau d'Agen avec le secrétaire de l'assemblée de la noblesse de Marmande," *Revue del'Agenais* (1971): 181–217.

[8] D. Greer, *The Incidence of the Emigration in the French Revolution* (Cambridge, Mass., 1950), p. 70.

to supply one, that is, at the members of the Second Estate, chosen by the *noblesse* itself to act as its representatives. As Chaussinand-Nogaret points out, we have at present no detailed knowledge of the general behavior of this group of deputies.[9] After the end of June 1789, the three Estates dissolved into a general body whose divisions have been defined by historians in other terms—as when, for example, a social analysis of the deputies divides the First Estate between the Second and the Third.[10] Yet the mental horizons which had once divided the Estates did not cease to exist, nor need contemporaries have been mistaken in identifying common values; even if, for obvious reasons, such bonds were most evident among the clergy, they might operate elsewhere as well. It should be illuminating to analyze the participation of the deputies of the Second Estate as a group in the parliamentary labors of 1789–91. How many of them took part in what kind of activity, how many withdrew, how far these were replaced, and how the record compares with that of deputies from the other two Estates are questions that can be answered. We may ask also how many deputies took some formal share in the organization of the Assembly, what kind of share it was, and, finally, what happened to the most conspicuous of the image makers when the session was over. There were leading nobles who accepted change, says Chaussinand-Nogaret, but how much change, and how was their activity perceived by others? (One may remember here his opening definition of the nobility as "the kingdom's Jews . . . perceived as alien, and easily enough as antagonistic.")[11] "The behaviour of nobles," says Higonnet, "was in a sense irrelevant to their fate."[12] I will argue that the actions of nobles in the Constituent Assembly seem likely to have had something, at least, to do with the public image of their Estate as a whole and thus with the fate that followed, and that there are ironies about the achievements of the actively revolutionary among them, whose contribution to the revolutionary cause was indeed significant.

The evidence to be examined relates to the fluctuations in the numbers of the different Estates between June 1789 and September 1791, to the participation of the deputies in the committees and *bureau* of the Constituent, and to the later public activity of those members of the Second Estate who in 1789–91 had made themselves especially conspicuous on the side of revolution. It must be stressed that this study is not concerned with day-to-day political debates. The emergence after June 1789 of a vocal and organized

[9] Chaussinand-Nogaret, p. 170 and elsewhere.

[10] J. M. Murphy, B. Higonnet, and P. Higonnet, "Notes sur la composition de l'Assemblée constituante," *Annales historiques de la Révolution française* 47 (1974): 322.

[11] Chaussinand-Nogaret, p. 1.

[12] Higonnet, *Class, Ideology and the Rights of Nobles during the French Revolution*, p. 7.

right-wing opposition, largely though not entirely drawn from the former privileged Estates, has recently been very well documented by Timothy Tackett, whose evidence goes far to reinforce traditional ideas of noble attitudes and adds considerable depth to our understanding of revolutionary anxieties.[13] What can be added to his account is a review of the behavior of the deputies of the Second Estate as members of a body that had an enormous amount of work to do over and above participation in political argument. A minority of well-known noble liberals are known to have worked hard, and this made the image of the nobility as a whole contradictory and confusing, but how much did they do, and how much did others help them?

At present we know little. We do know that the loyalties even of noble "revolutionaries" grew steadily more suspect. In the autumn of 1793, the Convention excluded noble soldiers from all command posts in the armies of the Republic—a decision that helped to bring the liberal ex-*constituant* Beauharnais to the guillotine.[14] This sharpening distrust of nobles as nobles, irrespective of apparent individual attitudes or conduct, is for Higonnet derived from "opportunism . . . concessions to the 'plebs' by the supposedly egalitarian bourgeoisie at the expense of supposedly reactionary nobles."[15] Again, the nobles themselves fall into the background; but questions should be asked about the starting point of this distrust, and one might as well begin at the beginning. In 1789–91, the French electorate was keeping an eye on its deputies. The existence and formal boundaries of the Second Estate had been sharply enough defined by the electoral proceedings of 1789.[16] In the French community, from early November 1789, there were no more Estates, but this did not mean that nobles would automatically be accepted as part of a common mass. They had been sent to Versailles to represent a social category, and their behavior might be seen as significant.

* * *

In their analysis of the membership of the Constituent, Murphy and the Higonnets have considered collectively all the deputies who entered the Assembly during its two-and-a-half-year life, *suppléants* included, excepting

[13] I am much indebted to Timothy Tackett, who has kindly made available to me the text of his forthcoming article, "Nobles and Third Estate in the Revolutionary Dynamic of the National Assembly, 1789–1790," which has allowed me to add a new dimension to an argument already prepared.

[14] July 1794 saw also the execution of General Aoust, son of a *ci-devant* marquis (in 1794 a Montagnard *conventionnel*) who had sat with Beauharnais in the Constituent. Cf. J.-P. Bertaud, *La Révolution armée* (Paris, 1979), p. 153; and A. Kuscinski, *Dictionnaire des conventionnels,* 4 vols. (Paris, 1916–20), s.v. "Aoust."

[15] Higonnet, *Class, Ideology and the Rights of Nobles during the French Revolution,* p. 91.

[16] Doyle (n. 1 above), p. 152.

from the total only Salm-Salm, Arberg, and Maujean, whose elections were annulled by the Assembly itself.[17] This procedure, which makes it simpler to handle the data, creates a body that never existed as a whole, since *suppléants* and those they replaced were, of course, never present at the same time. In addition, the deputies elected by the first two Estates of Béarn and those of the kingdom of Navarre refused to sit, those elected by the nobles of Provence never completed their application to do so, and the colonial deputies only gradually dribbled in.[18] The Constituent's original membership suffered other modifications because some deputies died or resigned and were replaced, because defects in the *suppléant* system meant that men resigning could not always be replaced by *suppléants* from the same Estate as had originially been intended, and because *suppléants* were not always willing to sit when called upon.[19]

Brette's exhaustive survey of the *constituants* lists a total of 1,219 deputies, including those from Arles, Arches et Charleville, and Bassigny-Barrois who were admitted by special Assembly resolutions (one deputy each),[20] and seventeen colonial deputies elected *sans distinction d'ordre*. This gives 302 First Estate deputies, 289 Second, and 611 Third, a total from which one should deduct the men who never sat—the eight Provençal nobles; the one cleric, one noble, and two commoners from Navarre; and the two clerics and two nobles from Béarn—sixteen in all. In mid-1789 the formal numbers of the Estates were thus 299, 278, and 609, respectively. In the months that followed, membership went down and up again as deputies disappeared and were replaced. The process is difficult to trace exactly. Death dates are known, but resignations are trickier, since the available record sometimes shows the date of resignation and sometimes only the date of replacement, and some deputies simply faded out without formally resigning, so that no precise departure date existed and, among other things, it was impossible to replace them. A rough pattern has been arrived at by grouping the defectors according to the month in which their resignations (or other causes of absence) certainly took effect, thus taking into account the latest possible date of effective membership.[21]

[17] Murphy, Higonnet, and Higonnet (n. 10 above), pp. 321–23.

[18] A. Brette, *Les Constituants* (1897; reprint, Geneva, n.d.), pp. 184, 143, 161, and 187–93.

[19] There was absolutely no uniformity in the *suppléant* system: Paris with forty deputies chose thirty-five; Bourges with sixteen deputies chose four; Libourne, like thirty others of the nearly two hundred *bailliages*, chose none at all. (Ibid., pp. 6–7, 39, 68.)

[20] Ibid., pp. 186–87.

[21] There may have been more departures than have been allowed for, but it would not be easy to be sure; when does leave become de facto resignation? And extended leave, e.g., from military duties, was easy to get at the time. (In 1790 Lacombe

TABLE 1

CONSTITUENT ASSEMBLY: DEPUTIES QUALIFIED TO SIT THROUGHOUT WHOLE SESSION

Total listed by Brette...		1,219
Less:		
Never admitted to Assembly	16	
Election annulled by Assembly	3	
Admitted by special resolution of Assembly (no Estate specified)..	3	
Colonial deputies	17	
Died during the session.......................................	28	
Theoretical total, September 1791........................	67	1,152
Distributed among the three Estates:		
First Estate (11 deaths)......................................	282	
Second Estate (2 deaths)	275	
Third Estate (15 deaths).....................................	595	
Total...	1,152	

Two preliminary points may be made. (1) The inquiry is into the behavior of the Second Estate, not into that of all the nobles in the Constituent. In the First Estate there were forty-six noble bishops as well as other noble clergy; at least six members of the Third Estate gave their titles of *noblesse* on the electoral returns; and there are indications that a number more of the Third Estate deputies were of noble origin. Should not a survey of noble behavior include these nobles too? The reply must be that it was the Second Estate alone which had been elected by the *noblesse* to represent the *noblesse* and which should thus be the prime source for any noble image. Whatever the social background of some of its members, the First Estate was a clerical body, and the Constituent's Left made one of its gravest blunders by failing to recognize the importance of spiritual convictions that cut across social boundaries. Such deputies cannot be amalgamated with their secular colleagues even if the colleagues concerned are of the same social origin. As far as the Third is concerned, those nobles who had chosen to sit there had already made a choice that divided them from other members of their order, and it would only confuse the analysis to put them back in a category from which they had decided to remove themselves. (2) For a consistent comparison of the collective behavior of the three Estates, we may exclude from

---

Saint-Michel, technically with his regiment in the Nord, was in Albi helping to administer the Tarn.) The departures taken into account have been those officially noted by the Constituent itself, an unambiguous minimum. On the evidence, a very high proportion of the original deputies were still around in June 1791, and no one has alleged a large-scale flight after Varennes.

TABLE 2
CONSTITUENT ASSEMBLY: WITHDRAWALS, JULY 1789–SEPTEMBER 1791

	July 1789 to January 31, 1790	February 1, 1790 to May 31, 1790	June 1, 1790 to September 30, 1791	Listed July 1791	Total
First Estate....	22	4	3	12	41
Second Estate	25	13	23	17	78
Third Estate...	17	4	7	5	33
Total.........	64	21	33	34	152

analysis, besides those elected *sans distinction d'ordre,* those who entered the Assembly at some point after its establishment and those who for reasons outside their own control could not remain through till the end.[22] This is because latecomers were unequally handicapped in the competition for office and because it is difficult to estimate the contribution of those who had to leave prematurely. Rates of resignation for the different orders, on the other hand, derive from the options of the deputies, and note has been taken of these.

The discussion is thus confined to those deputies who were qualified to sit throughout the session, all of whom could theoretically have taken part in any of the Assembly's activities, had they wished to do so. The deductions from Brette's list are not very numerous, as table 1 shows. The deaths had been almost entirely among men from the clergy and the Third Estate, leaving the nobility almost untouched.

We now come to other losses, which were a different matter and can serve to introduce the discussion of differences between the Estates. Over the whole period, 152 of the 1,152 deputies under consideration chose to leave the Assembly—118 by formal resignation and thirty-four by the de facto absence of which, in July 1791, the Assembly made a formal note.[23] This was hardly a high proportion; in percentage terms, it meant that nearly 87 percent of those present in 1789 were still entitled to see themselves as members in the summer of 1791. The pattern of the losses is shown in table 2.

It seems that the withdrawals of late 1789 were no myth, though their scale has been exaggerated. This was the period when the largest number of deputies took fright. Not surprisingly, it was also the period when the Assembly recognized the possibility of a *suppléant* problem and thus enabled

[22] Some delegations (e.g., Brittany [Brette, pp. 170–81]) were, of course, incomplete.

[23] The deaths and resignations are listed by Brette on pp. 275–79. On pp. 279–80 he lists the 1791 absentees. The dates used are his.

special elections in the Langres, Verdun, and Sarreguimes *bailliages* to fill places that otherwise would have been left vacant; even so, by the end of the year, six permanent vacancies did exist.[24] But they were the only ones. All the other gaps had been filled, and this seems the more significant in that the (comparatively) sizable departures of 1789 had no sequel. From the end of January to the end of May 1790, there were twenty-one resignations, ten of which took effect during May, and during the rest of the Assembly's lifetime only another thirty-three in all. Even if we add the thirty-four absentees noted in the summer of 1791, the total seems small. But it did not affect all parts of the Assembly in the same way.

For the Third Estate the resignations, such as they were, were concentrated in the latter part of 1789. (The only Third Estate *suppléants* entering the Constituent before late September 1789 had been called up because deputies had died.) It seems natural that the defeat of the *monarchiens* should have brought withdrawals in its wake—Mounier (replaced on December 30) was of the Third, after all. But even Mounier's protest could not attract much of a following from the Third, and later withdrawals were negligible. It may even be significant that, of the total of thirty-three Third Estate resignations, one in four was of a man with some kind of commercial or industrial interest: one glassmaker, one ironmaster, six *négociants* of one kind and another, plus the *directeur* of the Limoges Mint; perhaps the reasons for the low representation of commerce and industry in the Constituent are simpler than historians have supposed.[25] The five who simply faded out by July 1791 were four lawyers and a doctor, of whom there seems little to be said. (In June 1790, Viguier spoke up for Toulouse-Lautrec, an errant colleague arrested as a suspect in Toulouse, something which provides suggestive background for his own later withdrawal; a couple of his colleagues appear as signatories of the Tennis Court Oath; and that is all the mark that any seem to have made on the Constituent's proceedings.) All these figures are very small. Of the Third Estate deputies of 1789 still living in 1791, nearly 95 percent were still sitting.

The clergy had more defections, but not many, and, except among the bishops, three-quarters of the resignations came early. What apparently did not happen was any general clerical repudiation of parliamentary duty. Three-quarters of even the bishops continued to sit, and almost all the vacancies created by clerical resignations were duly filled by clerical

---

[24] The two Bazas vacancies remained because the *suppléants* did not arrive; for Chaumont-et-Vexin, Guéret, Strasbourg *ville*, and the *dix villes impériales*, no suitable *suppléants* existed (ibid., pp. 278 [list] and 63, 96, 146). For Langres, Sarreguimes, and Verdun, ibid., pp. 88, 153, 158, and note the errata, pp. 306–7.

[25] For a valuable survey of Third Estate deputies, E. LeMay, "La composition de l'Assemblée nationale constituante: Les hommes de la continuité?" *Revue d'histoire moderne et contemporaine* 24 (1977): 340–63.

suppléants, insofar as these were available. Deputies might strongly and repeatedly oppose changes brought about by the use of the Constituent's authority, but there was little visible attempt to reject the mechanism that made that authority effective. To the contrary, in fact.

A clerical deputy objecting to the Civil Constitution of the Clergy had a range of choices. He could resign his seat and attack the assembly from outside; few did this. He could nominally remain a deputy but in fact retire to the provinces to engage in subversion, as the cardinal de Rohan did; one of the things complained of by de Rohan's enemies was that they could never find him.[26] But de Rohan's choice of action was even more unusual. Or he could stay in the Assembly and speak his mind, as Maury and others did. Finally, he could add to his parliamentary activities the pamphleteering and letter writing by which opinion outside the Assembly might perhaps be swayed. Since vehement opposition to the Assembly's decisions could be seen as counterrevolutionary, either of the latter two choices created awkward problems for the Constituent's radicals, who found themselves tied by principle. They could not easily shut up Maury and his allies, though they tried, and they found it hard to establish the proper response to indignant reports from the provinces that so-and-so, though a deputy, was circulating propaganda against the Civil Constitution. Did right-wing deputies retain the right to disagree, or did they not? It was difficult to argue that they did not,[27] though this in turn raised awkward questions about the definition of basic revolutionary principles and the duties of the citizen; before the Constituent dissolved, it had become possible for zealous local officials to remove a nonjuror from secular office as a communal *procureur* because of his failure to take the clerical oath.[28] But meanwhile, 84 percent of the clerical deputies of 1789 showed by their continuing presence that they were willing to remain participants in the parliamentary process.

For the Second Estate it was different, and the difference is striking even if the figures have been overstated by legend. It was no accident that half of the 1791 "absentees" were nobles. Eleven of these noble "absentees" have

[26] Cf. the proceedings when the Constituent formally indicted him in April 1791: *Archives parlementaires* XXIV (April 4, 1791), p. 554 (hereafter A.P.). When in 1790 he had been under fire, his exact whereabouts had not been clear (A.P. XVII [July 30], p. 437).

[27] Note how long it took to get action against Cardinal de Rohan, despite the outrageous behavior referred to above. Cf. the report on Dufresne, nonjuring deputy and curé of Le Mesnil-Durand, Archives nationales (A.N.) D XIX ᵇⁱˢ 22:238:21–23, letter, Lisieux commune to Comité des recherches, with attachments; both priest and commune were heartbroken over an intractable dilemma.

[28] *Archives départmentales* (A.D.) Maine-et-Loire 1L357ᵇⁱˢ, *Rapport des commissaires Villier et Boullet . . . 5 mai–9 juin 1791,* case of the *procureur* of Doué (May 17).

TABLE 3
CONSTITUENT ASSEMBLY: NET IMPACT OF TOTAL LOSSES ON MEMBERSHIP,
JULY 1789–SEPTEMBER 1791

Deputies remaining in First Estate............................	(− 20)	262
Deputies remaining in Second Estate	(− 48)	227
Deputies remaining in Third Estate	(− 7)	588
Total...	(− 75)	1,077

parliamentary records that seem completely blank, but even if one assumes that all of them had in fact dropped out in 1789, there were still more withdrawals from the Second Estate after early 1790 than there were before, and this pattern was distinctive. Moreover, those affected by it could be conspicuous; three princes and six dukes abandoned their seats. It seems symbolic that the first deputy to resign from the Constituent (July 21, 1789) was the comte de Damas d'Anlézy, *seigneur* of many places and *maréchal de camp,* and the last (August 16, 1791) was the comte de Sainte-Aldegonde d'Aimeries, colonel of the Royal-Champagne cavalry, *gentilhomme de Monsieur*—and *Monsieur,* of course, had emigrated in June. By July 1791 the roll call of absentees could only reinforce an already obvious point, now given an extra edge in that seven of the newly listed defectors came from the endangered Rhineland area.[29]

The highest number of noble replacements came in May 1790 and continued arriving into the summer, but the dribbling away of the nobility was steady, and it is hard overall to relate it convincingly to particular events. The total turnover of membership for the Second Estate should have been more than 28 percent, but the Second also suffered more than the others from delinquencies among the *suppléants,* so that losses were not made good and its overall numbers suffered. By the time the Constituent dissolved, the combined impact of deaths, resignations, and officially attested withdrawals had produced a total of seventy-five empty seats, forty-one of which should have been filled by nobles; in addition, seven nobles who had resigned had been replaced by *suppléants* from the other Estates. The larger number of noble resignations had given defects in the *suppléant* system a greater impact on the Second Estate than was felt elsewhere in the Constituent (see table 3).

But as Chaussinand-Nogaret would point out, to examine only the defections from the Assembly is to tell only half the story. If dukes and princes withdrew, dukes and princes remained. Lally-Tollendal and de

[29] Brette, pp. 275, 279; for Alsace, pp. 146–49. The electorates of Haguenau and Wissembourg retained, from their nominal total of six deputies, only Hell of the Third Estate.

Mortemart and d'Aguesseau might retire, but the La Rochefoucauld clan of two dukes, an archbishop, three bishops, and a *vicaire-général* did not. The paradox of the Second Estate was that although it had the highest proportion of resignations, the highest proportion of voluntary absences, and the highest number of delinquent *suppléants,* it also had among its members some of the busiest deputies in the assembly, and the heavier a deputy's responsibilities, the more likely he was to be a noble rather than a commoner or a priest. At this point we must turn from the Constituent's membership to examine the framework of its legislative activities.

* * *

To cope with its large and complex body of business, the Constituent developed a large and complex body of committees, each created as the need arose—the first on June 19, 1789 and the last on October 15, 1790. Obviously, the first committees needed were organizational—someone had to check the deputies' credentials, devise a few elementary procedures, look over the drafting and so on—and were also large, with forty or even sixty members. But organizational concerns were, of course, only a beginning, and part of the unavoidable further scope of the Assembly's activity is suggested by the creation, also on June 19, of a *subsistances* committee and of the twin *rapports* and *recherches* committees, which might handle matters of subversion. By August, the creations had moved on from a constitution and a finances committee, both still large, to become concerned with the church, the feudal regime, the judicial system, and the criminal law, and thence to agriculture and commerce, Crown lands, the army and the navy, pensions, taxes, colonies, the debts of the Old Regime, and the huge intractable problem of destitution. (Given all the publicity about the Bastille, the *lettres de cachet* committee came strangely late, not until December.) By mid-1790 it was impossible to evade problems of foreign relations, and the Avignon committee was swiftly followed by the diplomatic committee. Finally, late in 1790, the deputies came to grips with public health and with the now nagging worry of the currency (*assignats, monnaies*). By this time, naturally enough, the now very numerous committees were on average very much smaller. Yet an attempt to spread the workload by rotating the membership of *rapports* and *recherches* had foundered, and it was becoming clear that committee membership was like membership of the Assembly's regularly renewed *bureau:* it was not for everybody.[30]

---

[30] For committee membership, A.P. v.I. plus published archives and the D series in the Archives nationales. Committees of unknown membership (*emplacement*) or entirely derived from other committees (Comité central de liquidation, Comité central) have been excluded. The drift of the evidence was consistent. Any committee member elected who almost immediately resigned (e.g., Phélines, Comité de constitution, February 2, 1790) has been ignored.

Theoretically, there might have been a specific committee duty for almost every deputy. By the time the session ended, over eleven hundred committee posts had had to be filled, and in addition there had been the need to find occupants for nearly 250 short-term periods of presidential or secretarial office in the *bureau*. In looking at the amount of work to be done and who did it, it seems realistic to recognize that some posts were occupied only fleetingly while the whole structure was settling down; but even so, there was still a total of about nine hundred effective committee posts plus the *bureau* offices which, although only briefly held, were both prestigious and burdensome. Clearly, there was a great deal to do. But unlike its successor, the Legislative Assembly, the Constituent had no initial rule of one man, one job, and when a decree in this sense was passed, as it was at a fairly early stage, it was not enforced.[31] All the committee work and most of the offices in the *bureau* fell to about 40 percent of the deputies, and within this already limited grouping there were some startling concentrations.

The committees did vary somewhat in character. Membership in one of the big organizational committees might mean little but that a man had somehow been pushed forward in the early days of the session. At a later stage, most such committee members can have had very little to do, and many of them remain very obscure, perhaps not least because the large numbers on the organizational committees were dogmatically divided among the three Estates on a 1:1:2 basis, which may have produced some arbitrary filling up. Again, the constitution committee was reorganized three times in three months, and among its early members there are some deputies hardly sighted again; and the *rapports* and *recherches* committees, reorganized by deliberate intent five and six times, respectively, within a few months, ended with a high proportion of the relatively unknown, left in permanent office by the unheralded abandonment of initially frequent elections.[32] If, however, one looks at the general pattern of committee membership, it seems, first, that the structure originally adopted for the organizational committees was quickly abandoned, and, second, that what happened to the *rapports* and *recherches* committees was more or less accidental, though one would like to know why the outcome was permanent. The final structure of the constitution committee was far more typical. Like almost every other committee in its final form, apart from those just mentioned, this ended with a majority of members who held one or more

---

[31] A.P. VIII, p. 434 (decree); and A.P. XI, pp. 266–67 (brushing aside of an attempted enforcement). Le Chapelier, who argued that to debate the issue was a waste of time, was himself a pluralist.

[32] The last reorganization of *rapports* was on June 7, 1790 and of *recherches*, April 26. The major reorganization of the Comité de constitution took place on September 12, 1789, after which the only changes were the addition of a group to work on local boundaries (November 30, 1789) and the creation of the *révision* group.

posts elsewhere as well. Some committees—the Comité d'Avignon, the Comité Diplomatique, the Comité des lettres de cachet are striking examples—were entirely staffed by pluralists. Indeed, by the time the diplomatic committee was chosen, in the summer of 1790, every man selected to sit on it was already heavily committed elsewhere. This can hardly have been accidental. It reflected a habit noticeable also in the *bureau* elections, where all but four of the sixty-three presidencies and more than half the secretaryships went to pluralists. The concentration of office in the hands of a comparatively small group, well entrenched before mid-1790, meant, among other things, that incoming *suppléants* were in general unlikely to have much influence on the drift of opinion, since their late arrival limited their chances of access to a committee structure whose main features had become visible before the end of 1789.[33] So too with colonial deputies. The two Monnerons were co-opted to the colonial committee as local experts, but the general structure of that committee, which overlapped significantly with that of the naval committee, had been decided before most of the colonial deputies arrived, and it remained substantially unchanged.

The personnel of the committees was significant because this was the arena in which so much of the permanent work of the Constituent was done. In narratives of 1789–91, most attention naturally goes to the great political issues—the royal veto, the franchise, the Civil Constitution of the Clergy, the clerical oath, the final form of the Constitution—that acted as catalysts for the formation of political groups and forced many deputies to crystallize their principles. This is where Tackett has concentrated his attention and has demonstrated the development of political groups with different attractions for the different Estates.[34] But political controversy was not the Constituent's sole occupation; and how definitive were any of its outcomes? By contrast, the reduction in the number of capital offenses was a landmark in criminal legislation. Committees dealing with Crown lands, the system of customs duties, the judicial system, or the debts of the Old Regime went doggedly ahead with their work, dismantling an inherited institutional structure and (with less bitter confrontation and with rather more consensus than over overtly constitutional issues) laying at least a foundation on which a new one might be built. The debates in the full Assembly, from which decisions on such matters finally emerged, were the culmination of a task largely carried out somewhere else.

---

[33] One exception to this rule was Roederer, who did not arrive from Metz until late October 1789 (Brette, p. 276), but who was among the original members of the Comité des contributions publiques and was an important influence: cf. K. Margerison, *P.-L. Roederer: Political Thought and Practice during the French Revolution* (Philadelphia, 1983), chap. 3. But Roederer was a member of the Society of Thirty; see below.

[34] Tackett (n. 13 above).

Nor was this the whole of the committees' work. As soon as any new piece of legislation was sent out to the provinces for implementation, mail began to flood back to Paris. The exact meaning of a decree was not always clear; there could be questions concerning which it was not specific and situations for which it did not provide; would the Constituent please elucidate? In February 1790, Grégoire told his colleagues that there were too many inquiries for all of them to be resolved by full Assembly debate. He asked that the committees be given delegated authority to provide not decisions—that would be wrong—but advice.[35] Thenceforward, in practice a committee spoke in the Constituent's name, for a decree could mean whatever the committee said it meant, and it was seldom useful to look any further. Whether a plea for further or different action ever reached the Assembly was a matter for the discretion of the committee, to which such requests were automatically referred and which made whatever recommendation it chose. As Merlin de Douai irritably told one correspondent, the Assembly did not like amending its decrees.[36]

There were also problems of revolutionary security. The *recherches* committee had an even more delicate task than most, in that to it was referred the mass of correspondence about the suspicious characters, doubtful communications, and rumored conspiracies that were the daily fare of revolutionary France, especially in frontier areas. (It was this committee that was told several times, well before Varennes, of a rumor that aristocratic counterrevolutionaries were plotting to kidnap the king; the apparent currency of this rumor does at least make the Assembly's later endorsement of it more intelligible.)[37] It was valuable for the Assembly to know what rumors were circulating, as well as to try to keep in touch with the facts, and *recherches* was a tool to this end. It was perhaps unlucky that its final makeup was almost accidental and, on the whole, far from distinguished. We do need to know why the Legislative Assembly later decided that it would not create a *recherches* committee, and here the experience of the Constituent cannot be wholly irrelevant.

In view of the importance of the committees' work and what has been said about the composition of the assembly as a whole, it might have been expected that their membership, and more especially their pluralist member-

---

[35] A.P. XI (February 5, 1790), p. 436.

[36] See P. Caron, ed., *Les comités des droits féodaux et de législation et l'abolition du régime féodal* (Paris, 1907), pp. 738–39, for an example of committee rigidity at work.

[37] For the rumor about the king, A.N. D XIXbis 33:344:13, letter, Bochard to Gauthier (Comité des recherches), June 1, 1791. For obvious reasons, this was in a "secret" file.

ship, would be strongly biased toward the Third Estate. Certainly the First
Estate was somewhat unevenly represented in proportion to its numbers, and
the Third Estate was overrepresented, supplying 63 percent of all the deputies
with any significant committee service and nearly 60 percent of those with
three or more appointments. But this is not the oddest phenomenon. For
purposes of comparison, it will be simpler to keep in mind the original
numbers of the three Estates in 1789, since modifications in these are, of
course, related to the problem of participation. The deaths were too few to
have much impact on the whole picture. Let us recall that the original figures
(colonial deputies excluded) were: First Estate, 299 (25.2 percent); Second
Estate, 278 (23.4 percent); Third Estate, 609 (51.3 percent).

We may look first at the purely organizational committees, which were
drawn from the three Estates in more or less appropriate proportions, and note
those who, having served here, never did anything else. Next comes a
category of those who missed out on these first, formal duties but were chosen
for a single committee of a later creation, and then one of those who combined
the two roles to make up the most modest group of pluralists (see table 4).

Here the Third Estate seems to be the least likely to be stranded in the
organizational backwaters with little else to do and the most prolific supplier
of deputies devoting themselves to some specific but limited task other than
organization; the number of such men and the small proportion of priests
among them are quite striking. In all three Estates the proportion of
single-committee to two-committee deputies was about the same, and at each
level of responsibility the balance between the Estates was about the same, for
what that is worth, if anything—after all, apart from the figures in the second
column, the numbers involved are small. But if fewer than one in four of these
rank-and-file deputies had begun to multiply his obligations, what of the real
pluralists? How many were they, and how heavily laden with tasks?

TABLE 4
COMMITTEE MEMBERS: FIRST GROUPS

	ORGANIZATIONAL ONLY		ONE COMMITTEE, NONORGANIZATIONAL		TWO COMMITTEES	
	Number	%	Number	%	Number	%
First Estate......	21	46.6	28	12.5	13	15.2
Second Estate ..	6	13.3	44	19.6	16	18.8
Third Estate.....	18	40.0	152	67.8	56	65.8
Total...........	45	99.9	224	99.9	85	99.8

TABLE 5
COMMITTEE MEMBERS: SECOND GROUPS

	THREE OR MORE POSTS		FOUR POSTS		FIVE OR MORE POSTS	
	Number	%	Number	%	Number	%
First Estate	9	11.7	3[†]	9.1	1[†]	6.7
Second Estate.........	22	28.6	13	39.4	7	46.7
Third Estate	46	59.7	17*	51.5	7[†]	6.7
Total	77	100.0	33	100.0	15	100.1
Total committee places held by deputies.........	289		157	85		

NOTE.—Although the figures are too small for statistical significance, those indicating potential noble influence are striking, especially as they leave the same impression as the record of elections to the Assembly's *bureau* (see p. 245).

*Five of these were of noble family.

[†]One of these, in each group, was of noble family. Dupont de Nemours of the Third Estate, recently ennobled, has been included in the Estate which elected him.

Table 5 shows that the three busiest deputies in the Constituent were each elected to seven committees. Dupont de Nemours, ennobled in 1783[38] and elected for the Third Estate, was the only one of the three to resign all but one of his posts when it became official policy that he should do so. The other two spectacular pluralists were Alexandre de Lameth and the baron de Menou, both of the Second Estate.

Of the whole body of the Constituent, fewer than two-fifths did any committee work at all, and within that proportion, three in five sat on one committee only; another one in five sat on two committees. Near the top of a rather sharply defined pyramid were thirty-three deputies with 157 committee posts between them, and at the apex were fifteen deputies with a total of eighty-five posts. Here we reach the paradox of the Second Estate. The greater the concentration of office in the hands of individuals, the more likely it was that those individuals would be drawn from the (depleted) ranks of the nobility. Dupont, elected by the Third Estate, might, nominally at least, limit his activities, taking note of assembly policy; Menou and Lameth saw no need to do so. Like the duc d'Aiguillon and the marquis de Lacoste of their own order, like Rabaut Saint-Etienne and Barnave and Dubois-Crancé from the Third, they seem to have held office as they chose and for as long as they chose.

[38] D. Wick, "A Conspiracy of Well-intentioned Men: The Society of Thirty and the French Revolution" (Ph.D. diss., University of California, Davis, 1977), p. 228.

It may be argued that committee membership in itself does not necessarily mean very much, that what is important is the real activity of individuals rather than mere formal office, which could have been largely a residual tribute to status. There were certainly some almost unknown deputies— Herwyn, for example, or Roussillou—who made themselves extremely busy in a very unobtrusive way, the membership of a single committee being more than enough to keep them occupied.[39] Nor is there any doubt about the activity of Robespierre, who sat on no committees at all. The problem is complicated by the fact that even for well-documented bodies like the Comité de mendicité or the Comité d'agriculture et de commerce, it is not easy to trace individual contributions in much detail.[40] One can say, however—and this seems significant—that as the pluralist system became more and more evident, the committees were simultaneously getting smaller, so that there was less and less room for the relatively idle, and that there is additional evidence to suggest that the minority of deputies elected (for whatever reason) to committee office were active in other ways as well.

For example, a survey of evidence from the *Archives parlementaires* gives the impression that during the session there were two to three hundred deputies who participated more or less significantly in the debates.[41] A few of these, of whom Robespierre is the best known, sat on no committees. For the others, speech making ranging from the periodic to the perpetual was backed by committee membership and frequently also by some share of the work of the *bureau,* the members of which in their turn were nearly all committee members. The mechanism looks self-reinforcing, and it was rare indeed for a deputy to be as prominent as was Robespierre and still achieve nothing more than a single secretaryship.[42] However much or little the pluralist committee members might contribute to the committees to which they were elected, the committees regularly included members from the same core of very active deputies, whose dominance became increasingly evident.[43] Many busy committee members made relatively few speeches (note here the sporadic

[39] F. Gerbaux and C. Schmidt, eds., *Les Procès-verbaux des Comités d'agriculture et de commerce de la Constituante, de la Législative et de la Convention,* 4 vols. (Paris, 1906–10). Volume 1 gives details of the attendance at every meeting. Herwyn was a very devoted secretary.

[40] From Gerbaux and Schmidt, as above, one gains an impression of the general committee discussions but no access to the mass of work that obviously went on between the meetings.

[41] The index in A.P. v. XXIII, despite idiosyncrasies, gives a fairly consistent impression of deputies' relative activity.

[42] This was on June 21, 1790. Ramel (e.g.) finally reached the *aliénation* committee, but nothing developed for Robespierre.

[43] Attendance at the Comité d'agriculture went up and down, with about a third of the members being really central; see Gerbaux and Schmidt, eds., vol. 1, passim.

appearances of *rapporteurs* like Le Peletier) and voluble pluralists presumably were selective in their committee attendances, but there is evidence that they were expected to take their multiple obligations seriously; though Barère carried the major responsibility for *lettres de cachet*, he assumed cooperation from Mirabeau, Castellane, and Fréteau despite their duties elsewhere, and Dupont continued to follow up his particular interests on the agriculture committee long after he had severed his official connection with it.[44] Given the unavoidable overlapping of the Constituent's concerns, there were advantages in (e.g.) the network of memberships tying the constitution committee to virtually every other major committee of the Assembly, just as the acquaintances and experiences gained by Liancourt during his spell on *finances* should have been useful to him in his magisterial career as chairman of the Comité de mendicité.[45] On the whole, the more numerous the intersections of experience, the more the assembly had to gain, since there was much to be learned about the complex task of drafting legislation and very little time to learn it in. The price of experience was the creation of what one critic called *une véritable aristocratie* conducting the nation's business—a metaphor more literally accurate than he may have realized.[46]

Two contrasting points can be made about the network of committee membership. The first is that it is easy to overlook the diversity of those who were drawn into participation, a diversity of political attitude as well as of social and geographical origin. The thirty-three deputies who sat on four or more committees included a couple of dukes at the (social) head of a significant group of nobles; it also included, as well as Rabaut Saint-Etienne and Dubois-Crancé, Dauchy, the postmaster son of a country innkeeper. One is not surprised to find that Dauchy had been a revolutionary "from the first hour,"[47] but the Constituent got him into varied company; for example, he sat with two other commoners on an *impositions* committee whose other members were six nobles and Dupont de Nemours, whereas the *assignats* committee, another of his interests, seems to have been wholeheartedly plebian. The *agriculture et commerce* committee, a third commitment of Dauchy's, has left a record of the way in which a wide range of talents and backgrounds could be profitably used. This was where two merchants,

---

[44] Cf. A.N. D V 4, letter signed "Mirabeau *ainé, 21 7bre*" (1790?), and the content of A.N. D V 6, *Registre du comité des lettres de cachet contenant ses lettres et ses réponses.* Cf. Gerbaux and Schmidt, eds., 1:570 (October 8, 1790), for the reference of a problem to Dupont, although he had formally left the committee in July.

[45] He was one of the original members of the huge finances committee. The date of his retirement from finances is not clear.

[46] Foucauld on January 31, 1790; see Brette (n. 23 above).

[47] *Biographie nouvelle des contemporains,* 20 vols. (Paris, 1820–25), s.v. "Dauchy."

Roussillou and Goudard, could be put to work on customs duties and trade barriers, where Hell could advise on canals and communications and the marquis de Boufflers could advise on inventions, where Herwyn could investigate free ports, the marquis de Bonnay could present the first legislation on uniform weights and measures, and Meynier could help the vicomte Heurtault de La Merville with the massive toil on the new *code rural*.[48]

The *agriculture* committee records are unusually detailed, but even a passing glance at the personnel of any committee illustrates the great variety of those willing to share the tasks of the early Revolution. The Right was not merely obstructive and the Left did not do all the work. A 1791 pamphlet claiming to list right-wing deputies has a surprising number of names traceable on the committee lists; some of them, like de Bonnay, certainly dropped out, but not before they had done useful work, while others like de Virieu and Milet de Mureau seem active by any criterion.[49] Consider de Batz and d'André, both later of some right-wing notoriety. De Batz's membership on the Comité de liquidation had a strong element of self-interest, but he does seem to have worked quite hard as well on an important committee concerned largely with technical financial matters. D'André sat on three committees, including the Comité diplomatique; he was four times president of the assembly, and his speeches and interventions fill three and a half pages in the index to the debates.[50] All this is a long way from de Batz's desperate tattered Pimpernel plotting to save the king from the guillotine or from d'André's shabby intrigues propped up by the British Treasury in the late 1790s, or, for that matter, from Virieu's 1793 death outside Lyon as the leader of a royalist revolt.[51] In 1789–91, these were deputies making visible contributions to the work of legislation, apparently without reluctance. It is unprofitable to deal with revolution in terms of stereotypes, deducing a man's whole public career from his known political preferences. For the achievements of the early Revolution, what seems more significant is the apparent widespread acceptance of what might loosely be called "bourgeois" assumptions about the bases of adequate government. The Comité de l'aliénation des domaines nationaux, on

[48] Gerbaux and Schmidt, eds., 1:569–81, showing the division of a day's business among the members (October 8, 1790).

[49] *Liste par lettres alphabétiques des députés du coté droit, aux Etats-Généraux, au mois de septembre 1791* (Paris, n.d.). This includes Lablache, elected to five committees. Cf. P. Koldy, "The Right in the French National Assembly, 1789–1791" (Ph.D. diss., Princeton University, 1967), which inter alia lists Boufflers with the Right (app., p. 307). Whatever Boufflers's political views (he emigrated in 1792), he had been very useful on the Constituent's Comité d'agriculture.

[50] Cf. A.P. XXXIII for index entries for both men.

[51] *Nouvelle biographie générale*, 23 vols. (Paris, 1855–66), s.v. "Virieu."

TABLE 6
JACOBIN CLUB: COMMITTEE MEMBERSHIP (Deputy Members, September 1790)

Number of Posts Held	Non-Jacobins	Jacobins	Total
One committee.................	229	40 (17%)	269
Two committees	65	20 (30%)	85
Three committees..............	19	10 (37%)	29
Four committees	10	7 (44%)	17
Five or more committees.....	5	10 (66%)	15
Total.........................	328	87 (21%)	415

which nobles and commoners sat together, completed a whole series of complex accounting tasks in tidying up the inheritance of the Old Regime.[52]

Our first point, then, is about breadth of participation. Even if the majority of the deputies did not become involved in the committees, a very considerable number did, and a large body of quite varied individuals worked very hard, whether they belonged to one committee or to several.

The second point is of a different sort and requires a return to the figures, bearing in mind Tackett's comments on the significant influence of the Jacobin Club, the Murphy/Higonnet information about "liberal nobles," and Daniel Wick's list of those members of the Society of Thirty who became States-General deputies.[53] The Jacobin Club was certainly important as far as numbers went (see table 6). As Tackett points out, its actual membership was never very large, and its own list of September 1790, at the end of the period of committee formation, seems to cover only about 160 deputies, *suppléants* included. However, in view of the length of time over which the committees had developed and the fact that Jacobin influence had taken time to develop, the figures are noteworthy;[54] and there is more behind them than may at first appear.

[52] A.N. D XI 1 illustrates some of this activity.

[53] P. Higonnet, "Les députés de la noblesse aux Etats-généraux de 1789," *Revue d'histoire moderne et contemporaine* 20 (1973): 230–47; Wick, "A Conspiracy of Well-intentioned Men" (n. 38 above), pp. 342–47.

[54] These figures are derived from A. Aulard, *La société des Jacobins*, v.1 (Paris, 1889), pp. xxxiv–lxxxi, and may slightly understate the reality. I have used them because the date is significant (the last committee was created in October) and because they represent the Jacobins' own perceptions. I have excluded from my committee calculations, as before, the essentially short-term posts that greatly inflate the total and of which the Jacobins picked up a good many. But cf. Tackett (n. 13 above), n. 114. Faulcon, who thought one had to belong to a club to get an appointment, may well have been another deputy annoyed at the increasing monopoly of the pluralists; there were plenty of Jacobins, and others, without appointments—what about Robespierre, after all?

On any criterion, the Jacobin Club was a very active body of men devoted to political issues, whom the club provided with valuable opportunities for becoming acquainted, the meetings of the Constituent being so large that it was difficult for isolated individuals to make a sustained impression. For success in committee elections, it was obviously important to be known to as many colleagues as possible, and the Jacobin Club offered a convenient locus for this. Not unnaturally, the club's membership seems to have been drawn overwhelmingly from the Third Estate, with only a very small scattering of deputies from the clergy or the nobility. There were some inactive club deputies and others who did no more than speak their minds occasionally when they really had something to say, but a high proportion of club members, perhaps 50 percent, achieved committee posts worth having, and others were elected to short-term office or to the *bureau,* or both.

Given that in the club's membership the ratio of Third Estate to privileged-order deputies (the two Estates taken together) was on the order of six to one, or probably rather more, the Estate background of leading Jacobin committee members is interesting (see table 7). A possibly significant subfactor is emphasized if we look in detail at the table of the thirty-three leading pluralists (table 8). Jacobins are marked with the symbol #.

Just over half of these very busy deputies were Jacobins, but the Jacobin representation was not exactly dominated by the Third Estate, since seven of the seventeen Jacobin deputies had been elected for the *noblesse.* In addition, of the sixteen leading committee members who were not on the 1790 Jacobin membership list, three came from the First Estate, seven from the Second, and six from the Third, and the three clergy were all of noble birth. The significance of noble background rather than merely Jacobin affiliation is confirmed by the fact that the loosely associated "liberal nobility" and the almost entirely noble Society of Thirty, each with very small representation in the Constituent at

TABLE 7
JACOBIN COMMITTEE MEMBERS: ORIGINAL ESTATES

	ESTATES		
NUMBER OF COMMITTEES	First	Second	Third
One..............................	1	2	37
Two	2	4	14
Three............................	1	1	8
Four	0	2	5*
Five or more...................	0	4	6†

*Two of these were of noble family.
†One of these was of noble family.

TABLE 8

CONSTITUENT ASSEMBLY: PLURALISTS

Deputy	Estate	Age	Occupation	Electorate	"Liberal Noble"	Society of Thirty
Seven committees:						
Dupont*† ....Third	Third	50	*Savant*	Nemours		x
#A. de Lameth*† ....Second	Second	29	Soldier	Péronne	x	x
#Menou*† ....Second	Second	39	Soldier	Tours	x	x
Six committees:						
Fréteau*† ....Second	Second	44	*Parlement*	Melun	x	
#Gaultier† ....Third	Third	50	*Avocat*	Clermont-Ferrand		
Talleyrand*† ....First	First	34	Bishop	Autun		x
La Rochefoucauld......Second	Second	46	*Savant*	Paris-ville	x	x
Five committees:						
#Aiguillon† ....Second	Second	28	*Officier*	Agen	x	x
#Barnave*† ....Third	Third	28	*Avocat*	Dauphiné		
Dubois-Crancé† ....Third	Third	43	Soldier	Vitry-le-François		
#Mirabeau (noble)* ....Third	Third	40	Pamphleteer	Aix	x	
#Rabaut*† ....Third	Third	46	Pastor	Nimes		
#Régnier† ....Third	Third	46	*Avocat*	Nancy		
Lablache ....Second	Second	50	Soldier	Dauphinée	x	
#Lacoste† ....Second	Second	?	Soldier/Diplo-mat	Charolles	x	
Four committees:						
#Barère† ....Third	Third	34	*Avocat*	Bigorre		
Bureaux de Pusy*† .....Second	Second	39	Soldier	Vesoul	x	
Castellane† ....Second	Second	31	Soldier	Chateauneuf-en-Thymerais	x	x
Dauchy*† ....Third	Third	32	Postmaster	Clermont-en-Beauvoisis		
#Defermon*† ....Third	Third	37	*Procureur*	Rennes		
#A. Duport*† ....Second	Second	30	*Parlement*	Paris-ville	x	x
#Gossin ....Second	Second	45	*Officier*	Bar-le-Duc		
#Laborde de Méréville (noble)† ....Third	Third	Young	*Seigneur*	Etampes		x
Le Chapelier*† ....Third	Third	35	*Avocat*	Rennes		
#Sillery† ....Second	Second	52	Man of letters	Reims	x	
#Treilhard (noble)*† ...Third	Third	47	*Avocat*	Paris-ville		
Tronchet* ....Third	Third	53	*Avocat*	Paris-ville		
Virieu* ....Second	Second	35	Soldier	Dauphiné	x	
Allarde ....Second	Second	37	Soldier	St.-Pierre-le-Moutier		
Bonnefoy ....First	First	41	Cleric/writer	Riom		
Coulmiers (noble)......First	First	?	*Abbé*	Paris-hors-les-murs		
Malouet ....Third	Third	49	*Officier*	Riom		
#Vieillard† ....Third	Third	33	*Avocat*	Coutances		

#Member of Jacobin Club.
*President of Assembly.
†Secretary.

large, had major representation at this summit of the committee pyramid. Of the society's twenty-eight deputies, eight are here to be found.

The impression of a very strong imprint from the Society of Thirty specifically, as well as from the liberal nobility generally, is not misleading. Only two of the twenty-eight society deputies mentioned above failed to find a place on some committee; nineteen sat on at least two, and twelve sat on three or more. Of the eighty-nine "liberal nobles," fifty-nine (almost exactly two-thirds) saw committee service. For such small groups, this seems astonishing. *Bureau* offices showed the same influence, and this was especially marked in the crucial first weeks of July–August 1789 when three of the five presidents and twelve of the eighteen secretaries came from the Society of Thirty. As the debates went on, the deputies broadened their acquaintance and the struggle for domination began, with the result that a wider pool of talent was drawn on but, nevertheless, between mid-January and mid-September 1790 there were only five presidents not clearly of noble status, and two of these were Dupont and Sieyès of the Society of Thirty. Tackett notes Thomas Lindet as saying in November 1790 that "the aristocracy no longer has an influence, it seems to me, on the choice of Assembly officers."[55] Since Alexandre de Lameth was elected president on November 20 and d'André on December 21, this must have been a political rather than a social judgment. (It is true that from this point on the secretaries were mostly, though not entirely, from the Third.) Of nineteen presidents in 1791, ten were noble, the last of these being Broglie on August 13, and the last secretary elected, Target, was of the Society of Thirty, which overall had supplied more than a quarter of the presidents and more than one secretary in nine.[56]

The detailed committee records suggest that only five committees—*recherches, rapports, règlement de police, assignats,* and, surprisingly, the Comité féodal—had no one from the Society of Thirty; in contrast, the Comité diplomatique had three society representatives out of seven, with Barnave its only commoner. Some specific political foci became evident: for example, the de Lameths and Duport shared twelve committees between them, with minimal overlap, providing an implicit statement of calculated influence and personal priorities.[57] From another angle, and bearing "Jacobin" influence in mind, it is noticeable that the Comité de constitution took in no new blood after 1790, that all its then-members had been elected to one or more other committees before the end of 1789, and that when the *révision*

---

[55] Tackett, n. 137.

[56] For the office bearers, Brette (n. 18 above), pp. 283–86 is the easiest source.

[57] They had no taste for social problems (*salubrité, mendicité*), nor for knotty practical problems (Crown lands, feudalism, *assignats*); there is a pattern in what they would engage in, as a group, and what they left alone. The lack of overlap is very striking indeed, and suggests deliberate policy.

subcommittee was added in September 1790, all of its members had already been prominent a year or more earlier. On this subcommittee there sat men whose 1789 political differences had seemed unbridgeable: Clermont-Tonnerre (removed from the parent committee after the *monarchien* defeat in 1789) alongside Pétion, Buzot, and Barnave. The other members included Alexandre de Lameth, so that three of the seven came from the Second Estate. Turning to more technical areas, we find Le Peletier of *législation criminelle* acting as *rapporteur* for a body which in its final form had five noble members out of seven. Of course, numbers are not everything, and in any case there were committees like *assignats* or the Comité féodal where the hard work was patently being done by commoners, or *lettres de cachet* where it was shared; but Liancourt on *mendicité* and Heurtault de La Merville on *agriculture et commerce* are but two reminders of the powerful impact of strong chairmanship, and both men happened to be nobles.[58]

What are the possible sociopolitical implications of all this? It would be nonsensical to argue that the Constituent's revolutionary achievements were little more than a vehicle for a series of power plays by an ambitious noble faction using its "liberalism" as a front. To stress the post-1789 importance of the nobility is perfectly consistent with McManners's long-ago observation of a group of nobles, largely Parisian, who had no need to fear change because they were well equipped to deal with any challenge it might offer and who were therefore interested in larger opportunity rather than in mere defense of the status quo.[59] (Daniel Wick has given a twist to this argument by pointing out that what some prominent members of the *noblesse* were getting from the status quo, in money or prestige, was not really very much.)[60] This does not convert the operations of 1789–91 into a mere attempted aristocratic confidence trick, nor does it make the revolutionary remodeling of French institutions a mere modification of the *ancien régime*. The guiding principles of men like Castellane, Liancourt, or Le Peletier rejected not only the institutional framework of the past but also some of the basic assumptions that supported it. But neither does it mean that there was a standard "revolutionary" attitude in which liberal nobles were, for all practical purposes, indistinguishable from bourgeois.

---

[58] One wonders if anyone but Liancourt would have had the self-confidence, not to say arrogance, to co-opt to an official Constituent committee, apparently on his own authority, a selection of outside experts who were not deputies at all. C. Bloch and A. Tuetey, eds., *Procès-verbaux du Comité de mendicité de la Constituante, 1790–1791* (Paris, 1911), pp. x–xi.

[59] A. Goodwin, ed., *The European Nobility in the Eighteenth Century*, 2d ed. (London, 1967), chap. 2 by J. McManners, who brilliantly evokes the conflicting varieties of *noblesse*.

[60] Wick, "A Conspiracy of Well-intentioned Men," pt. 2, and cf. his "The Court Nobility and the French Revolution: The Example of the Society of Thirty," *Eighteenth-Century Studies* 13 (1979–80): 263–84; Tackett, n. 131.

One might argue that the rejection of the *noblesse* as inherently counter-revolutionary, which was beginning to develop by the end of 1791, was based partly on prejudice deriving from the Constituent's noisy Right, partly on ignorance and a false identification of all nobles with a small minority of *émigrés*, and partly on the general discrediting of the constitutional monarchists that affected most of the ex-*constituants*. Here the very enthusiasm with which some nobles had adopted a (now unfashionable) revolutionary policy would tell against them, as it told against the commoners with whom they had been associated, but because nobles were easily identifiable, they would be unreasonably separated out as having a distinctive counterrevolutionary attitude. The problem with this argument is that among the most conspicuous members of the Constituent Assembly there do seem to be differences in the way that nobles, as against commoners, responded to the crisis of 1791–92.

In 1792, the massive electoral rejection of ex-*constituants* is well known. Of 1,290 surviving deputies from the Constituent, *suppléants* included, eighty-three reached the Convention: eight from the First Estate (including six constitutional bishops), seven from the Second Estate, and sixty-eight from the Third. Of these, two from the Second Estate and six from the Third were *suppléants*, so that the success rate of the noble deputies of 1789 was meager indeed. Our elite thirty-three pluralists, half of them after all Jacobins, were more committed to the hard work of revolution than any other group of *constituants;*[61] what happened to them when they were again faced with crisis?

In mid-1791, fifteen of the seventeen Jacobins joined the Feuillants, Gossin and Vieillard being the only abstainers.[62] Some drifted back to the parent club; others did not. If we look at the later response of the whole thirty-three to the collapse of the constitution they had helped to create, the record is revealing. Mirabeau had died in the spring of 1791, still trying to rescue the monarchy. In 1792, Louis XVI was dethroned. Dupont went into hiding after vainly struggling to protect his king. Lameth emigrated. Menou had already returned to the army, and he stayed there to become in due course a Napoleonic staff general. Fréteau resigned his post as a judge and withdrew from public life; Gaultier became (again) *maire* of Clermont; Talleyrand emigrated; La Roche-

---

[61] Tackett's list of the twelve leading Jacobins, based on the debates, includes only five of the seventeen Jacobins burdened with massive committee work, suggesting that the two activities were complementary, though they overlapped considerably. Mirabeau and Adrien Duport, both noble, are on both lists. Cf. Tackett, n. 131.

[62] *Liste des membres de l'Assemblée nationale (séants aux Feuillants) fondateurs et membres de la Société des Amis de la Constitution . . .* (n.p., n.d. [Paris, 1791]). This purports to be a list of those who have removed from the club's premises to sit elsewhere. It has 365 names, but gives the impression it was casting its net rather wide—e.g., it includes La Rochefoucauld, who was certainly not on the Jacobins' 1790 list, though he had had Breton Club associations in 1789. Nor is it easy to envisage La Fayette as a 1791 Jacobin.

foucauld resigned his presidency of the Paris department, tried to withdraw to the country, and was lynched. Aiguillon emigrated. Barnave, living in the country away from politics, was arrested in August 1792 and executed in 1793. Dubois-Crancé, back in the army, was elected to the Convention, as was Rabaut Saint-Etienne. Régnier, Lablache, and Lacoste all retired. Barère, Defermon, Sillery, and Treilhard all reached the Convention, where Sillery (the only Second Estate deputy from the thirty-three to be reelected) was executed in 1793 as a Girondin. Bureaux de Pusy, Laborde de Méréville, and Malouet all emigrated; Castellane resigned his colonelcy and went home; Dauchy and Gossin became departmental officials in the Oise and the Meuse respectively; Le Chapelier went under cover (and was ultimately executed) after being wrongly listed as an *émigré;* Duport became a fugitive who finally emigrated; Tronchet acted as an official defender of Louis XVI; Virieu was ultimately killed in the rebellion, as we have seen; and the others retired into invisibility.[63]

The general contrast in destiny is plain enough in that, among these thirty-three most conspicuous deputies, only one of the *émigrés* was a commoner (Le Chapelier's English visit had been genuinely for business),[64] while only two of the reelected (Sillery and Treilhard) were nobles. It might be argued that nobles were more likely than commoners to feel so threatened that they had to emigrate and that nobles were not reelected because there was unfair prejudice against them. However, it was Malouet's political attitude that endangered him and caused him to emigrate,[65] and there were political reasons for La Rochefoucauld's murder, doubtless intensified by his rank but existing independently of it.[66] Among our thirty-three deputies in 1789–91, the nobles, on average, turned out more royalist than the commoners, and after the monarchy fell their behavior was more often open to criticism. It was, of course, not a total contrast. The Third Estate too had its royalists, but that was not the point; the trouble was that the Second Estate needed republicans to even the score, and these were not very noticeable. For example, the thirty-three included nine soldiers, Dubois-Crancé and eight nobles. Whatever personal reservations these might have had, in 1792 France

---

[63] See *Dictionnaire de biographie française* (Paris, 1933–), for Dupont, Fréteu, Gaultier, Aiguillon, Castellane, Allarde, and Coulmiers; Kuscinski, *Dictionnaire des conventionnels* (n. 14 above), for Barère, Sillery, Treilhard, Dubois-Crancé, Rabaut, and Defermon; the *Biographie nouvelle des contemporains* and the *Nouvelle biographie générale* for the rest, except Vieillard (information kindly supplied by Mme. E. LeMay), and Le Chapelier and Malouet (S. F. Scott and B. Rothaus, eds., *Historical Dictionary of the Revolution,* 2 vols. [Westport, Conn., 1985]). Lacoste has been classed as diplomat rather than as soldier.

[64] Scott and Rothaus, eds., vol. 2, s.v. "Le Chapelier."

[65] Ibid., s.v. "Lameth."

[66] *Nouvelle biographie générale,* s.v. "La Rochefoucauld."

was at war and threatened with invasion and soldiers, noble or otherwise, who were committed to a new France could be expected to see its defense as their first duty. In 1792 Menou and Dubois-Crancé (until his reelection) remained in the republican army. The remaining seven did not. Castellane resigned his commission, Lablache and Allarde disappeared, Virieu became embroiled in counterrevolutionary plotting, and the others left France. From the republican point of view, the record of this group of soldiers was: one counterrevolutionary rebel (Virieu), two deserters to the Austrians (Lameth and Bureaux de Pusy), three absences from duty (Lablache, Castellane, and Allarde— admittedly, Lablache was over fifty), and an *émigré*, Aiguillon. Menou's patriotism could hardly balance such an account.

Among the very nobles who in 1789–91 had been most committed to the new order the radicals could find by 1793 a good deal of material to reinforce an antinoble stereotype. Daniel Wick notes that "most of the *noblesse d'épée* in the Society of Thirty had emigrated by 1793 and therefore avoided the anti-aristocratic bloodbath of the Terror."[67] The death toll among our major pluralists does suggest that it was safer to leave France than to stay, and at least as risky to be a commoner as a noble: La Rochefoucauld was lynched and Virieu killed in action, but the two men executed as a direct result of their Constituent service were both commoners (Le Chapelier and Barnave), and the three executed in the feuds of 1794 were one noble (Sillery) and two commoners (Rabaut and Gossin). But if antinoble prejudice was the issue, the existence of conspicuous *émigrés* can only have encouraged distrust and made a bloodbath more likely. The *émigré* Liancourt would not plot against his country's republican government; nevertheless, in 1792 he had given Louis XVI money and offered him sanctuary and in August he abandoned an army command to emigrate.[68] The nobles of the Convention, even if headed by eight *ci-devant* marquises and Philippe Égalité, could fairly be seen as renegades from a social group whose prominent leaders had different loyalties.

For most of the outstanding contributors, the considerable noble share in the great reforms of the revolution came to a jarring halt when a final choice between monarchy and revolution had to be made. To accept revolution in 1789, or even 1791, was not necessarily to accept the 1792 Republic. The consequence was clear. If in 1792 a former revolutionary should choose to reject the Republic, why should republicans bother to distinguish him from others who had shown their colors rather earlier? Once a man was on the wrong side of the frontier, what was there to choose between the marquis de La Fayette and the prince de Condé or, for that matter, between the duc de

[67] Wick, "A Conspiracy of Well-intentioned Men," p. 326.

[68] J.-D. de La Rochefoucauld, C. Wolikow, and G. Ikni, *Le duc de La Rochefoucauld-Liancourt, 1747–1827* (Paris, 1980), pp. 212–17.

Chartres and his relatives Artois and Provence? Historians have drawn distinctions among the motives of successive waves of *émigrés*. Contemporaries did not necessarily do so, and assumptions about the motives of noble *émigrés* were not made only by the republican French; for example, the British government subsidy preserving many refugees from destitution was not paid to laymen of military age.[69] An *émigré* like Lameth, fleeing for his life, would feel the revolutionary condemnation to be unfair, but it could be replied that by deserting the revolutionary cause, whatever its 1792 political form, he had chosen his own fate. Menou met no threat; nor (in 1792) did Sillery.

One can illustrate the fatal ambiguity of the Second Estate's image by looking at three of its deputies, two somewhat obscure and the third very well known. Clermont Mont-Saint-Jean, a colonel of *chasseurs* from the Savoyard border, brought a series of dubious activities to a climax in the summer of 1792 when he claimed that he could not be classed as an *émigré* because he was not really French; his family had property on both sides of the frontier and his brother lived permanently in Savoy. The departmental authorities politely pointed to his acceptance of office in the Constituent as sufficient evidence of citizenship and took appropriate action.[70] Clermont had never actually abandoned his Constituent post, but he had moved with suspicious regularity between Paris and the frontier and had issued in August 1790 an *Exposé des principes* arguing that the greatest threat to the public lay in a collapse of executive power.[71] In 1792, his behavior could only reinforce a local image of noble soldiers already unfavorable enough.[72] A notable number of the potential *émigrés* coming before the Ain officials that summer were nobles who seem to have underestimated the perceptiveness of the administration.[73]

Clermont fits the classic pattern of the counterrevolutionary nobility. However, as evidence that nobles should not be classified en bloc, we have someone less flamboyant who reached his post in the Constituent in June 1790, the month in which nobility was officially abolished. (At this time, noble resignations were on the rise and some *suppléants* were failing to arrive.) He sounds conservative enough, describing himself merely as a *seigneur* living in eastern France, and his name was old-fashioned: Alexandre-Anne-Antoine-Marie-

[69] K. Berryman, "Great Britain and the French Refugees, 1789–1802" (Ph.D. diss., Australian National University, Canberra).

[70] A.D. Ain L81, pp. 59–61, May 9, 1792; for an earlier instance of Clermont in trouble, see A.N. D XIXbis 16:175 (4) (December 1790).

[71] Clermont de Mont-Saint-Jean, *Exposé des principes et de la conduite . . . addressé à ses commettans . . .* (Paris, 1790).

[72] A.N. F1^a401 has two letters describing the Ain's situation. In 1792 two noble *commandants* had emigrated within six months, the second taking with him the plan of campaign and all the maps.

[73] Series of cases in A.D. Ain L81 (May–June 1792).

Gabriel-Joseph François de Mailly marquis de Chateaurenaud. Mailly's only distinction as a *constituant* was a secretaryship in the closing months of the session, but he did not afterward abandon public life. He became departmental president of the Saône-et-Loire and in 1792 was one of the eighty-three ex-*constituants* to become *conventionnels*. In January 1793 he was one of thirty-one among the eighty-three to refuse the king a single vote; he joined the Jacobin Club and accepted the Montagnard regime; in 1795 he moved on into the legislature of the Directory, being one of a group of about fifty deputies elected to the States-General who maintained unbroken public service right through from the early Revolution into the Directory—a very select group indeed, who may be seen as among the most devoted politicians in revolutionary France.[74]

Unluckily for his caste, it was not a man like Mailly who was likely to attract attention in 1792. Alexandre de Lameth *was* likely to attract attention. Like La Fayette, in 1792 he was publicly committed to the wrong side, and after August 10 he escaped arrest by following La Fayette into the Austrian camp. What would be remembered here was not the real danger from which Lameth was taking refuge but the attitude which had brought him under threat plus his willingness to find shelter with the enemies of revolutionary France.[75] If two of the most famous liberal nobles of 1789–91 could openly engage in such desertion–and La Fayette tried to take his army with him—there was little hope of avoiding angry generalizations for which there was far too much apparent justification. Lameth and Clermont fitted the stereotype. Mailly did not, but who would think this significant?

* * *

The contradictory image of the Second Estate in the Constituent raises the problem of the relationship in the minds of potential revolutionaries between political framework and social content, as well as that of the commitment of liberal nobles to the changes that they were so eager to promote. For very many French, the gains of the early Revolution were fundamental, and members of the Second Estate made a disproportionate contribution to the legislation that embodied them. Such men were willing to lend themselves to massive changes. The price they were willing to pay for maintaining these was another matter. When the institution of monarchy was challenged, most of the noble leaders of the Constituent put traditional loyalties first, narrowing the gap dividing

---

[74] Kuscinski, *Dictionnaire des conventionnels* (n. 14 above), s.v. "Mailly." Treilhard and Rochegude were similar. From the leadership of 1789–91, Treilhard was the only "liberal" noble continuously in politics through to the Directory; there was no one from the Society of Thirty. Eight "liberal" nobles resigned from the Constituent before the session ended.

[75] Scott and Rothaus, eds. (n. 63 above), vol. 2, s.v. "Lameth."

them from the conservatives of 1789 and blurring all distinctions in a common image of treason to the revolutionary cause. The men involved were not very many, but they had made themselves uncommonly conspicuous and from the revolutionary point of view they had been the most hopeful element of their caste; taking the behavior of the Constituent's Second Estate as a whole, what was left if these men defected? It is hard to see as unreasonable the conclusions that might be drawn from their conduct—conclusions that might, however, be used as rationalizations for other kinds of antagonism, with tragic results. Among the Constituent's nobles, the range of political attitudes was possibly wider than it was among the commoners, but republican political classifications were crude. What the republicans thought they had recognized—and this was the heart of the tragedy—was the existence of what the twentieth century would call "objective counterrevolution." It seemed in 1792 that to secure the gains of 1789–91 the monarchy itself must now be sacrificed, and those who could not accept this were moving into the same camp as those who wished to preserve the *ancien régime:* "He that is not with me is against me." There was no solution to this problem, and for public figures the caste mark of counterrevolution was hard to evade.

A postscript may be added. During the Directory years, about a hundred ex-*constituants* reappeared in Paris as deputies, sometimes disastrously, sometimes with considerable influence. La Revellière endured, and Reubell, and Grégoire battling to salvage the constitutional church, and Sieyès busy with intrigue. About half of them had soldiered on as *conventionnels*. In the whole four years from 1795 to 1799, the ex-Constituent total included only six *ci-devant* nobles; few such men would engage in republican politics, and by late 1797 Heurtault de La Merville was their only incoming representative. In 1799 he could watch Sieyès, survivor from the Society of Thirty, bringing to an end the revolution they had both helped to launch. Loyal to the lost image of the Constituent's liberal nobility, Heurtault went home and gave up politics.[76]

[76] For those elected, A. Kuscinski, *Les députés au Corps législatif, Conseil des Cinq-Cents, Conseil des Anciens de l'an IV à l'an VII* (Paris, 1905), pp. 345–92; for Heurtault, *Nouvelle biographie* and A. Robert, *Dictionnaire des parlementaires* (Paris, 1889). A rough count makes the (surprisingly low?) total of ex-*constituants* 114, including fifty-four *conventionnels*. About a dozen of the 114 had their careers cut short at *fructidor*, after which Madier and Boissy d'Anglas were deported; fewer than fifty of the rest still seem to have been sitting in 1798–99. The political experience of the Directory's politicians in general is currently being analyzed.

War and Terror in French Revolutionary Discourse (1792–1794)

Mona Ozouf

It has been said that when the French go off to war, they do so with greater hate for each other than for the enemy. Such a statement may be disputed. But it is less easy to dispute the period during which that French tradition began to arise—that is, the French Revolution. Here once again a founding event, the Revolution forced the nation to confront both an internal and an external war. How was it possible to shatter the efforts of a Europe united against France while at the same time holding firm on the domestic front? This unforeseen difficulty gave rise to a lasting division of France into two parts.

Was the Terror a response to such a formidable situation? It is easy to understand how some historians have been tempted to think so and have even found comfort in arguing strongly for the affirmative. The Terror, an unassimilable event of French Revolutionary history that has been the subject of an immense quantity of apologetic studies,[1] becomes less striking if it is viewed as inseparable from the war—wedded, in other words, to exceptional circumstances. To consider only the Terrorist side of this marriage would then be to limit one's vision to the point of precluding any understanding of the operation of the whole. Such is the classic criticism leveled by Seignobos against Taine's history of the Revolution.

The question—To what extent was the Terror a response to the war situation?—is indeed an excellent test for classifying historians of the Revolution. On one side, there are those who believe with Esquiros that "the regrets and complaints engendered by the Terror must tumble before

---

[1] No one shows this better than Quinet: "There is something extraordinary and quite unparalleled about these years: on the one hand, an ideal city of happiness and justice, an age of gold written on the threshold; on the other hand, to put this ideal into practice, an implacable nemesis. One could say that, in order to bring its ideas into the world, the eighteenth century uses the force of the sixteenth century. Two ages coexist, monstrously united: the sentimental logic of Rousseau takes as its instrument the axe of Saint-Bartholomew's Day. . . ." See Edgar Quinet, *Le christianisme et la Révolution française* (Paris, 1845), p. 349.

This essay originally appeared in the *Journal of Modern History* 56 (December 1984).

a word as sharp and inflexible as an axe: it was necessary."[2] Galvanizing this group of historians is a repugnance against admitting the contingent into the history of a Revolution that must be thought of as an indivisible whole. On the other side, those who question the necessary link between the war and the Terror are grouped together behind a banner brandished as early as 1795 by Benjamin Constant: "It is my purpose," he said, "to show that the Republic was saved despite the Terror."[3]

Within this second group, the opposing point of view is often criticized— as by François Furet in *Interpreting the French Revolution*[4]—for using in its interpretation of revolutionary events the same language as the revolutionary actors themselves, thereby producing a history that is more incantatory than explanatory. The research for the following article was prompted by this latter assertion. To find out whether it is indeed the subjective sense of the participants that has won out in the conventional historiography, I have gone back to the discourse of the Revolutionaries who enacted, excused, or rationalized the Terror. My goal has been to ascertain the relative importance attributed in their decisions to the two wars, foreign and civil; to discover, in other words, what role these war dangers played in revolutionary language.

It must be recognized, however, that the nature of the link between War and Terror, often rather casually asserted, is not at all clear. Is it a link of causality? And if so, in what direction is that causality exerted? From war to terror, or from terror to war? Or is it rather a synchronic connection, terror being to war what a mountain is to a valley—that is, another way of seeing and of naming? Such questions, and the difficulties to which they give rise, require commentary before we can proceed to the heart of the matter.

The course leading from war to terror is the most commonly encountered: it can be found from Thiers and Mignet to Mathiez. From this perspective, terror was a misfortune in response to another misfortune, a response to tragedy. The actions of the Terror are examined in the light of the great extenuating circumstances of foreign invasion and civil war; it is under-

---

[2] Esquiros pursues the metaphor to the end: "The French Revolution was not only an event, but a harvest of ideas. Every harvest needs its scythe. The French Revolution needed the Terror." See Alphonse Esquiros, *Histoire des montagnards*, 2 vols. (Paris, 1847), 2: 393.

[3] Constant balked particularly at intellectual acceptance of the Terror: "The evil done by the Terror would become irreparable if ever the principle were established that terror is necessary toward the middle of every revolution that has liberty as its object." See Benjamin Constant, *Des effets de la Terreur* (n.p., Year V [1796]), p. 78.

[4] François Furet, *Penser la Révolution française* (Paris, 1978), pp. 13–109.

stood as a frantic, desperate reaction to a twofold aggression. Thus the Revolution moved from military defeat to terror.

The causality hypothesis also follows a second course, one which leads from terror to victory. Terror here is no longer a response; it is an anticipation, an instrument which revivified the people and galvanized patriotic sentiment. It was through the authority of the guillotine that the people marched off to the front or crushed domestic conspirators. This idea of a miraculously functional kind of terror is found in Joseph de Maistre, for whom it was a "supernatural" means invented by the infernal genius of Robespierre to break the momentum of the coalition, and hence requiring no further extenuation.

These two versions of the causality hypothesis—most of the time poorly distinguished from each other, it may be added—are clearly not mutually exclusive. Both may be put forth simultaneously, as by Albert Soboul.[5] In his view, terror, at first an improvised response to defeat, once organized became an instrument of victory. Thus Soboul stresses that "terror was so strictly related to the national defense that it suffered from each military setback" (terror here is part of and not autonomous from war). But he also asserts in the same paragraph that the terror that was provoked became in turn a cause in its own right and with its own consequences. It was the Terror which made possible the *levée-en-masse,* the requisitions, the Maximum, and the nationalization of the war industries. Thus the Terror was both response and anticipation.

In placing the two interpretations together haphazardly, one may easily overlook the fact that they differ in emphasis. For the first, the emphasis is on resignation, while for the second it is on a triumphalism of the will. From time to time historians will suddenly shift from one emphasis to the other, abruptly moving from the misfortune of the times to the fortune of the means. It is this shift toward the second emphasis which jars the sensibility of historians hostile to the Terror. Michelet felt that if it was the perpetrators of the September Massacres who energized the army and formed the vanguards at Jemmapes and Valmy—if, in other words, terror was transformed into victory—then this was a sorrowful confession to make. The same sense is found in Albert Sorel: "If by some stroke of misfortune one should be so shortsighted and so narrowminded as to see nothing but these two objects—a scaffold and an army, a government which exterminates and heroes who give their lives—and if one derives the one from the other, then one ends in the paradoxical position of

[5] Albert Soboul, *La civilisation et la Révolution française* (Paris, 1982), p. 375.

attributing to the most debasing of tyrannies France has ever known the most magnificent achievement of the French spirit."[6]

What separates versions of the causality hypothesis is the degree of lucidity and willfulness each attributes to the revolutionaries in setting up the Terror. The entire polemic between Louis Blanc and Edgar Quinet acknowledged the operation of a purely reactive impulse only at the outset of the Revolution. At that early stage, every revolutionary act was clearly a response to some aggression, either internal or external: "In response to the ouster of the Girondin ministry came the 10th of August; to the taking of Verdun, the September Massacres; to the league of kings, terrorism."[7] Threatened, provoked, and winded, the Revolution retaliated with insurrection or terror (we should note in passing that Quinet at that point viewed the two as identical, blind reactions of despair, and did not yet distinguish between them). Then came the day when such reprisals were organized into an invention stamped with the names Saint Just, Billaud-Varenne, Robespierre—men who strove to systematize the irrational component of terror. At this point, it was not at all a matter of a determined relationship—the necessity behind the revolutionary reprisals came to an end, for Quinet, somewhere in the middle of 1793—but rather a question of premeditated initiative. And that initiative was all the more unfortunate in that it did not bring about the victory it had promised.

According to Louis Blanc, on the other hand, the Terror was precisely anything but a "system," since there can be no system unless there are men who desire it in its entirety.[8] By radicalizing the idea of system, by feigning to believe that a system must be enacted as a whole (How is it conceivable that people could have gotten together and said: "Alright now, let's invent a system, let's chop off some heads"?), Blanc sought to ridicule Quinet's analysis. For his part, he maintained that the Terror, begotten of the perilous conditions of the moment, was, in consequence, either simply endured by those who brought it into existence or else accepted as a last resort in the accomplishment of a greater good: "France conceded to the necessity of centupling its strength and energy by concentrating them."[9] Yet despite the vehemence of their mutual rebuttals, Louis Blanc and Quinet are perhaps not as far apart as they themselves imagined. When Quinet wrote that the leaders of the Terror were not possessed of the spirit of the Terror, was this not a way of saying that

---

[6] Albert Sorel, *L'Europe et la Révolution française,* 9 vols. (Paris, 1885–1911), 2: 531.

[7] Edgar Quinet, *La Révolution,* 2 vols. (Paris, 1865), 2: 182.

[8] For Blanc's fullest discussion of Quinet and the Terror, see Louis Blanc, *Histoire de la Révolution française,* 2 vols. (Paris, 1868), pp. xiv–xvii.

[9] Ibid., p. xvi.

they did not completely realize what they were doing, that they did not completely want what they wanted? When Louis Blanc wished to make the revolutionary debate incarnate in personalities, was this not a recognition that individual temperaments had their role to play in the events? In short, the Terror depicted by Louis Blanc was less unaware of itself than he claimed, while Quinet's Terror was less consciously contrived than he believed. Between full shadow and broad daylight, between men completely manipulated and men who are nothing but manipulators, any number of degrees can be imagined.

Nevertheless, whatever one may think of the possible psychological variations between lucidity and blindness, these two ways of articulating Terror and War as if they were two hands of the same clock (one preceding or following the other as the case may be) have one point in common: they distinguish between a time for terror and a time for war and are therefore both subject to chronological verification. Yet such verification works rather poorly. Whichever historiographical version is taken—terror follows defeat/terror precedes victory—can readily be opposed with contrary examples. At times terror followed victory (at Lyons and Nantes, for example, the Terror appeared well after the end of the civil war), and at times it preceded defeat (far from having brought the Vendée to its knees, the Terror there engendered a second uprising). On the one hand, it is no longer possible to maintain that a confused, desperate sort of terror blindly arose from the exposure of the nation to danger. On the other, it is difficult to go on singing patriotic couplets in praise of *la force coactive* (i.e., the guillotine) and its miraculous cure for the country's ills. Quinet masterfully underscored the weakness of the second perspective: "The Great Terror showed up almost everywhere after the victories. Shall we pretend that the former produced the latter? It would indeed be necessary to do so if we wish to go on contending that the Terror was necessary to bring about the Republican victories that preceded the Terror. . . ."[10]

Does this mean that any and all links between war and terror are thus discredited and invalidated? The answer is clearly negative, for the two may be seen in an inclusive rather than a successive relationship. If the Revolution is a "Great Whole," as Quinet put it sarcastically, it encompasses not only all forms of war, civil or foreign, but all forms of defense as well: defense against rebellion, or against treason, or against any possible conspiracy. Terror enters into this arsenal of defense, no longer as a consequence but as an aspect of war, and therefore inseparable from it. Hence the success of Robespierre's "nothing more" phrases in the

[10] Quinet, *La Révolution. Cinquième édition, revue et augmentée de la critique de la Révolution*, 2 vols. (Paris, 1868), 1: 31.

language of Revolutionary historiography—"Terror," he said, "is *nothing more* than prompt, severe, inflexible justice"[11]—phrases which have been transmitted intact from Louis Blanc to Albert Soboul. In the mind of the former, for example, "terrorism was *nothing more* than the bloody side" of the revolutionary dictatorship; for the latter, "it was *nothing but* an aspect" of the civil war.[12] Compared to the discourse of causality, this discourse of identity has certain advantages. First, it is exempt from chronological verification. Second, it dispenses with the need to confront the Terror directly, since the latter is always seen as something other than itself. Third, it claims a panoramic vision of the Revolution. Just as the man seeking an explanation of evil would have it, according to Leibniz, if he could imagine the universe in its totality, so the man capable of seeing each and every aspect of the Revolution would integrate the Terror logically and aesthetically into the best of all possible revolutions. From this perspective, the evil of the Terror is indeed nothing more than the effect of a shortsighted, narrow-minded, or else partial vision. It is the product of *mal/veillance* in the double sense of the word, as malevolence and mistaken vision.

These are the problems, the subject of 200 years of debate by historians of the French Revolution, that I wished to test by examining the official discourse of the revolutionaries themselves, that is, by seeking to determine the importance the foreign and civil war had in their pronouncements on terror. For this purpose, I have selected three sample sections of the *Moniteur,* corresponding to one month each: the first after the September Massacres, from September 2 to October 2, 1792; the second from August 20 to September 20, 1793, when the Convention inaugurated the legal Terror; the third from 27 *floreal* to 27 *prairial* of the Year II, when the Great Terror was being put into place. I am aware of the disadvantages of a sample of this kind, particularly in that it throws a comparatively stark light on the scene of the Convention while leaving the provinces and the pro-Consular terror in obscurity. Nevertheless, these disadvantages are balanced out by the unity of the source. In a relatively homogeneous discourse, it should be possible to identify the stages by which the discourse

---

[11] Robespierre, "Discours sur les principes de morale politique qui doivent guider la Convention dans l'administration intérieure de la République," in *Réimpression de l'ancien Moniteur . . . depuis la réunion des Etats-généraux jusqu'au Consulat (mai 1789–novembre 1799),* 32 vols. (Paris, 1840–47) [henceforth cited as *Le Moniteur*], 19: 404. For Robespierre, this was a stylistic habit; see, e.g., the same report: "[La terreur] est moins un principe particulier qu'une conséquence du principe général de la démocratie appliquée aux plus pressants besoins de la patrie."

[12] Blanc, *Histoire de la Révolution française,* p. xvi; Soboul, *La civilisation et la Révolution française,* p. 375.

of "circumstance" took root, to determine whether and by whom the Terror was equated with a response to national peril, to characterize the important moments and locate convergences. Finally, it should become clear to what extent the historiography of the French Revolution has indeed been dominated by the initial rationalization of the Terror offered by the revolutionary actors themselves.

*   *   *

The history of the September Massacres seems almost to have been invented to illustrate the first version of the causal hypothesis, namely, the sequence defeat→terror. On September 2, when the news of the fall of Verdun arrived in Paris (four days earlier, the Longwy disaster had been announced), "popular tribunals" sprang up in the prisons and the massacres began. Still authoritative, Pierre Caron's study of the respective responsibilities for the September Massacres emphasizes the mildness of the government's reaction (including that of the Justice Ministry, at the time headed by Danton).[13] Caron minimizes the guilt of the members of the Commune, who were not very active in the popular tribunals; he finds no conclusive evidence of Marat's or of Pétion's participation; and he taxes most of the leaders at the most with acquiescence motivated more by cowardly realism than by heartfelt conviction. The final explanation Caron gives of this first Terror—which was too spontaneous to be considered as Terror by Benjamin Constant[14]—stresses the moral contagion of fear. The September Massacres — triumphant expression of the belief that the right to judge as one sees fit is inherent to sovereignty— were like an urban version of the Great Fear. And the fear derived from the military disaster: "The influence the war situation had on the relations of the French one to another was never more clearly evident in the course of the Revolution."[15]

Does the official discourse show any support for such an interpretation? In fact, it is a discourse of shame, in which the shock produced by the eruption of blind violence can be distinctly felt in the words of the revolutionaries. The first speech of Interior Minister Roland is telling: "Yesterday was a day over which it may be best to throw a veil."[16] The image

[13] Pierre Caron, *Les massacres de Septembre* (Paris, 1935), pp. 261–63.

[14] "Individual outbreaks of disorder, calamities that are frightful—but momentary and illegal—do not constitute the Terror. It exists only when crime is the system of government and not its enemy, when the government orders it rather than combats it" (Constant, *Des effets de la Terreur*, p. 35).

[15] Caron, *Les massacres de Septembre*, p. 470.

[16] *Le Moniteur*, 13: 611–12. In his letter of September 3, 1792, Roland used the word "terror," but in order to attribute it to the activities of the Court, which "long since prepared, awaited only the hour to accomplish all treasons, to unfurl over Paris the standard of death and to reign there by Terror" (*Le Moniteur*, 13: 611).

of the veil was well chosen. It came up later in the account given of the Orléans prisoner massacre, which "every wise man would prefer to cover with a veil," and was also to be used by Pétion.[17] The fact was, everyone wanted above all to avoid having to come up with a complete account of what had happened.

Yet an account had to be given, no matter how succinctly. And it is striking, first and foremost, in the uncertainty of its characterization of the phenomenon it was describing. There was not yet a "Terror" in the singular, but rather several "terrors." During the session of September 1, the very one in which it was announced that the enemy was at the gates of Paris and that Verdun, the last defense, would be unable to hold out more than eight days, Vergniaud expressed his fear that "panic-engendered terrors . . . inspired by the emissaries of counterrevolution" might break out and "paralyze our strength."[18] The following day, even before city officials had come to announce that crowds were forming in the prisons and throats were being slit at Les Carmes, Vergniaud again voiced his fear in a superb speech. France, he said, no longer had to fight "kings cast in bronze" but rather "kings surrounded by powerful armies." But the French had less to fear from the latter, he argued, than from the "panic-spawned terrors"[19] which the kings were so adept at provoking by distributing gold by the handful. Thus these "terrors" were still not organized into a single whole. They attained the dignity of the singular only as a spectacle of terror played out in the prisons: the event was a drama directed by an invisible hand, in which the participants, mere actors, did not really know what they were doing.

In such circumstances it is easy to see why the event was interpreted in terms of constraint, not freedom. The September Massacres are the zero point of revolutionary lucidity. The official account of what happened on Sunday, September 2, emphasized a series of chance occurrences which produced the spark. The resistance of sixteen prisoners who were being transferred, the accidental firing of a pistol, the cry of an anonymous citizen: "Let them all die!"—these formed the powder trail leading to the crime. Those who did the massacring were seen as "men deceived by imagination . . . prey to a terrible, first reaction."[20] The sequence of their acts did not form any coherent program. The report of the special commission of the National Assembly on September 19 stressed this

---

[17] See Pétion's speech of September 6: "Allow me to throw a veil over the past; let us hope that these distressing scenes will not recur" (*Le Moniteur*, 13: 635).

[18] Ibid., 13: 596.

[19] Ibid., 13: 600.

[20] Ibid., 13: 614.

point: "A just and good people can never conceive of the idea of a system of disorder and murder which would sully the Revolution."[21]

Hence the only justification for the September Massacres was to be found in the signs of sensitivity and hesitation shown by some of the witnesses to these horrible events, signs which in a sense were supposed to balance out the brutality. As early as the first night, reports of Commune commissaries point to mitigating anecdotes, to "interesting traits" (to use the expression of the times). Haste there may have been, but there *was* a court; prison records concerning the prisoners' crimes *had* been taken into account in some cases; and the dead *had not* been stripped of their belongings. Roland was later to come back to this point: in taking vengeance, he argued, the French people still harbored within them a "kind of justice," and they were filled with joy when "they were not called upon to punish." In short, the horrors of the September spectacle could be "lightened" if "all the motives attenuating the violence or the brutality are taken into consideration."[22] It thus becomes clear just how much the hard-sought justification was moral, and how little it appealed to expediency.[23]

What is striking, indeed, is the tenuousness of the link suggested between the massacres and the dangers facing the country. It was no doubt the evil intentions of enemies craftily and stealthily manipulating the collective psyche that propelled the massacres; hence the true culprits were the kings. Despite this conviction, the sense that the country was in danger was notoriously absent from this first rationalization of the Terror. In the immediate report made by a committee of the Commune, there was not a word about the military defeats or the enemy invasion. Throughout the month of September, the idea of appealing to perilous circumstances made little headway, either at the Convention or, more surprisingly, at the Jacobin society, where it took another month before the defensive argument viewing the massacres as a response to defeat was to take form.[24] Only at that point did the idea of the two fronts begin faintly to appear, with its theory of an internal front stripped thin of its defense (and thereby exposed to the scheming of traitors) as a result of

[21] Ibid., 13: 739.

[22] Ibid., 13: 682. See also, e.g., Guiraud: "In exercising its vengeance, the people also rendered its justice" (ibid., 13: 603).

[23] The official account in *Le Moniteur* makes this clear: "If the justice of the people was terrible, it nevertheless gave free rein to its joy when it was not obliged to punish. The innocent were set free and carried off in triumph. Minor offenders were brought to see the expiring criminals, and this spectacle of terror preceded the moment of their liberation" (ibid., 13: 614).

[24] See Bazire's speech of November 4 (ibid., 14: 403).

the departure of patriots for the external front. Such an idea, although it was later to gain a large following, was still in the throes of birth in September 1792.

The sequence defeat→terror, so obvious to Caron in the September Massacres, is thus only very indirectly suggested in the official accounts of that event. As for the sequence terror→victory, it is totally absent. Did the massacres succeed in "frightening off the traitors"? The speeches point at times to such a possibility. But—and this proves that the speeches treated the idea only rhetorically—a warning was added: the disorders, if allowed to continue, would lead to a paralysis of the war effort. Pétion clearly mentioned the joyous enlisting of men into the army; yet he presented it as the counterpart of, if not the consolation for, the massacres and never as a result of them.

If then we put together the various characteristics of this discourse of shame, we find nothing or almost nothing of the future rationalization of the events. The September Massacres, an eruption of barbarous behavior in a people reputed to be naturally gentle and innocent—an enormous incongruity, then—profoundly troubled the men of the Revolution. The massacres whispered to a few of those men—to Danton and Robespierre, who were in agreement on this from the first days of the Convention— the idea of an organized and therapeutic Terror, a way of purging the irrational component of the terrors. Though it was true that the massacres constituted an immediate response to the news of military defeat and to the proximity of the enemy, they did not yet lead the Convention to reflect on their relationship to the war, and the idea of viewing them as a measure for preserving the public safety would have been horrendous. The September Terror then is a shadowy area, full of "bitter pictures" best not examined too closely. A year later, things were to have changed considerably.

*   *   *

To reopen the *Moniteur* of the following year, between August 20 and September 20, 1793, is to enter the most dramatic period of the Revolution. Although by the end of the summer the federalist insurrection was practically stamped out, the news of the fall of Toulon into the hands of the English on August 27 threw the French people once again into a state of collective anxiety. There was an immediate sense of impending danger in the feverish days when the *sans-culottes* came to the Convention to impose far-reaching measures of national defense (mass conscription, which was to give the republican armies an advantage of numbers) and extensive use of terror (the Law of Suspects, in particular). The chronological proximity of the two series of measures (separated only by a few weeks) and the fact that they were both enacted in a highly charged atmosphere, and despite the misgivings of the majority, by a Convention under pressure from the Paris Commune, lead naturally to the conclusion that they were mutually interconnected. (It took all the bad grace of a historian like Albert Sorel, for example, to continue to maintain that the national defense was carried out without the Mountain and even against it, through what he called the "natural" efforts of the French nation.) My purpose then will be to find out whether the de facto concurrence was a perceived, desired, and rationalized convergence. When the Convention passed the measures concerning national defense, was it with the Terror in mind? When the Terror measures were passed, was it with the war in mind? To answer such questions, we have at our disposal a wide range of texts, for the sessions were rich in contradictory speeches. The Convention was no longer in a state of shock, as in the fall of 1792; nor was it yet reduced to the paralyzed silence of spring 1794.

When, in August 1793, the Convention was debating the national defense measures, did the Terror form part of the debate? This first question is the easiest to answer, and in the negative. In the speeches on the war, one can certainly find the mobilizing theme of the amalgamation of all the wars, civil and foreign, into a single, gigantic aggression. Barère put it eloquently: "The Republic is now but a great city under siege."[25] In such circumstances, even the least civic action is an act of national defense. The entire nation is absorbed in participation in the war effort. Young men will fight at the front; married men will attend to the food needs of the army; the women will care for the wounded while the children shred linen for bandages; and the elderly will be carried to public squares to whip up the patriotic ardor of the young soldiers, spread hatred for kings, and preach the unity of the Republic. But in this rather unalarming picture of a busy and almost joyous nation, there is not the slightest reference to the need to keep watch and to punish. The generalized war necessitated generalized measures—a collective life galvanized by the demands of the public safety—but the Terror does not seem to enter into it.

When, a few days later, on the other hand, the Convention debated the legislation of the Terror, was it in reaction to the war? This question is not as easy to answer, for in the dramatic, event-filled inaugural day of the Terror, September 5, 1793, at least two acts must be distinguished.

The first opened at the Convention that morning. Several groups, fewer in number than had been expected, came in from the Commune and from the Sections with claims dealing mostly with food problems. The internal enemies of the State noted in Chaumette's speech were indeed in league

---

[25] Ibid., 17: 475.

with the tyrants of Europe; but these enemies were exclusively identified as hoarders, people who kept their grain from market and brought the distribution of foodstuffs in the country to a standstill. The measures put forward by Chaumette had a simple aim—to prevent famine—and straightforward means, conjoining war and the Terror.[26] A revolutionary army combing the countryside would seize the wealth of the land and its inhabitants by force, using the authority of the instrument trundled behind it—"the fatal instrument which cuts cleanly and in a single blow through both conspiracies and conspirators' lives."[27]

Supported by Billaud-Varenne (originator of the war metaphor, "We are in the gunroom, we must act"), opposed by Romme, Jean Bon Saint-André, and Bazire (who dragged their feet), the proposal was first softened and transformed by Danton, ostensibly "to take advantage of the sublime élan of our people pressing around us."[28] A revolutionary army had to be formed at once, and each soldier given a gun; working men had to be paid to attend their Sections twice a week (meetings of the Sections were thereby limited to two a week); and, lastly, the functioning of the Revolutionary Tribunal had to be improved so that each day "an aristocrat, a scoundrel shall pay for his infamy with his head."[29] Danton's solution to the problem of channeling the flood of terrorism is interesting in several respects: first in its silence concerning the war; next in its sleight of hand regarding the food problem; then in its rather rhetorical allusion—"*an* aristocrat, *a* scoundrel"—to political prisoners. Finally, it should be noted that Danton refused to link the revolutionary army to the Revolutionary Tribunal. While the first needed to be created, the second simply required that its functioning be improved.

Everything changed as the Jacobin delegation arrived at the Convention, marking the start of the second, and decisive, act of the story unfolding that day. The Jacobins also dreamed of a revolutionary army which would drag the guillotine around in its baggage train, but they forgot that its purpose was to ensure plentiful food supplies and reserved it simply for punishing "all traitors."[30] What does that last phrase mean? It referred

[26] Chaumette well understood the logic of the position into which this measure cast the revolutionaries: "No more quarter, no more mercy for traitors. Let us throw up between them and us the barrier of eternity . . ." (ibid., 17: 580).

[27] Ibid.

[28] Ibid., 17: 583.

[29] Ibid. The measure to pay for attendance at Sections was opposed by those (Romme, e.g.) who had "such a lofty conception of the Revolution that they found repugnant the idea that it would be necessary to pay the people to attend the sections" (17: 584).

[30] Ibid., 17: 586.

not only to the entire body of noblemen (a "class" which was seen as collectively guilty, particularly because of its war treasons) but also to the federalists, including Brissot, Vergniaud, and Gensonné, to whom one Section was to add Veuve Capet. But what is striking in the Jacobin discourse is the vigorous reduction of the plural to the singular: the "treasons" were viewed as sprouting all from the same tree. This totalizing effect was accentuated when the Jacobin proposal was taken up again by the extremists of the Convention. Drouet demanded that the blood of the culprits be shed without too much concern for judicial procedure (the Revolutionary Committee, he said, "should not have to give its reasons") and without excessive attention to "philosophical considerations" ("You are called brigands," he said, "let's be brigands for the good of the people").[31] He even went so far as to express the wish that all political prisoners should feel the threat of further September-like massacres. Amidst the commotion stirred up by this speech—the Convention's stormy applause broke off Thuriot's speech numerous times as he reminded Drouet that "it is not for crime that revolutions are made"[32]—Barère barely had time to catch his breath before presenting his rationalization for the Committee of Public Safety.

What exactly did this rationalization consist of? The speech which, as in the words of an obscure Jacobin that were taken up by Barère, "made Terror the order of the day"[33] in essence presented Terror as a response to the "terrors" spread by the Royalists, particularly in the prisons. The Royalists had announced a great "movement" within Paris, a euphemism which everyone understood as meaning that the massacres would start up again. So the Royalists would indeed get the "movement" they had announced, not through the spasms of illegal vengeance but by means of a special tribunal. In other words, they would get Terror in the singular and not in the plural.

This retaliatory Terror, both legal and organized, was nevertheless conceived neither as a response to famine (the latter, according to Barère, was a phantom born of the ill-intentioned imagination of the Royalists) nor as a response to war (to which Barère made a single, oblique allusion in saying that the Revolution had to be given the power to expel, at least from their military functions, those persons rendered suspect by their habits, corporate loyalties, and prejudices). In other words, little importance was attributed to the perilous circumstances of the moment. In fact, the list of suspects drawn up by Merlin de Douai on September 17

---

[31] Ibid., 17: 588.
[32] Ibid.
[33] Ibid., 17: 591.

also paid little attention to those perils: to the old litany of suspects—emigrants, foreigners, civil servants stripped of their positions—Merlin de Douai added only a single extra verse, namely, "the partisans of tyranny and federalism and the enemies of liberty."[34] A rather elastic definition, to be sure—one which would encompass the rebels of Lyons and Toulon, and the Vendéens—but at the same time too vague to suggest that the terrorist measures were specifically directed at the hotbeds of civil war.

Thus the revolutionary discourse of September 1793 simply juxtaposes—far more than it links—the necessities of war and those of the Terror. No one at the Convention presented the Terror as anticipating the armies' victories or as a necessary response to military failure. Its most explicit purpose seems to have been to provide a proper, acceptable channel for the revolutionary torrent. On the other hand, the discourse of the Jacobins—with its identification of all forms of "treason" as one—was already showing traces of a different justification for the Terror which was to emerge in full force in the spring of 1794.

*　　*　　*

Skipping over several months to *prairial* of the Year II, we obviously come to a moment of immobility in the Revolution. The power of the Committee of Public Safety over the Convention was total, and the opposition press had completely disappeared. Since *germinal,* there was no longer a revolutionary army, and the popular societies of the Sections were steadily disappearing. Abroad, the Revolution seemed to have won out. Robespierre's long report on the national celebrations during *floreal* Year II was given in an atmosphere of exaltation over the recent victories of the Convention. Preparations for the Celebration of the Supreme Being were being organized around the idea, or illusion, that the Revolution was finally over.

This radiant month of *prairial* was nevertheless the month in which the Terror gained its greatest momentum, the month in which Couthon wrenched from the Convention his series of harsh measures designed to free the Revolutionary Tribunal from paralysis—by eliminating the right of the accused to legal defense, by dropping the requirement that material proof be produced, and by granting the greatest possible importance to moral certainty. It is therefore the month of *prairial* which poses the most formidable problem for those whom François Furet has called the "circumstance historians." They have resolved the problem in very different ways, sometimes arguing that Robespierre was physically exhausted, at other times that the two attempts on his life at the beginning of *prairial*

[34] Ibid., 17: 680.

had profoundly disturbed him. That month, all the debates at the Convention were punctuated by discussions of these assassination attempts: popular societies declared their indignation; repeated medical reports were given on the health of the worthy locksmith who deflected the would-be assassin's pistols away from Collot d'Herbois; and Robespierre himself, in a dramatic speech no doubt orchestrated in advance for maximum effect but no less profoundly experienced, expressed the feeling that his days were numbered.

What interests us here is the way in which the official rationalization of the Terror had shifted since the previous fall. In an assembly where the number of men daring to propose amendments or postponements could be counted on the fingers of one hand, only the big brass were still vocal: Barère and Robespierre on 7 *prairial*, Couthon on 22 *prairial*, Robespierre again on 24 *prairial* (this was to be his last speech before *thermidor*) when he came to defend Couthon's bill and to sweep away the last timid hesitations of the Assembly. I shall consider these speeches as a whole. For while it is true that they all bear the personal stamp of the individual speakers and that a certain division of labor can be perceived—Barère always speaking as a specialist in foreign policy, Couthon as a technician, and Robespierre as a metaphysician—they all follow the same logic.

It was in the name of "the energy which in these last weeks has given us the means to vanquish our foreign enemies by putting a stop to the daring enterprises of our internal enemies"[35] that Couthon demanded the *prairial* measures. In doing so, of course, he placed these demands within the system leading from Terror to Victory. But it was no longer possible to pretend that the Terror was a response to defeat. News of cannons seized, troops routed, masses fleeing, and cities taken punctuated the speech of Barère on 4 *prairial*. "Their artillery has fallen into our hands, their satellites have fallen before us," claimed Robespierre on 7 *prairial*.[36] The expression "panic-stricken tyrants" was on everyone's lips. Hence it is impossible to argue that the Terror was the energy of despair.

But—and this is the interesting point in the *prairial* speeches—the announcement of military victory was not an announcement of the victory of the Revolution. Why? Because kings, in their defeat, react desperately, in any way they can, falling back on murder and internal terror when they are no longer in a position to make use of their armies. Thus the equation, republican defeat→republican terror, has to be abandoned for the equation, royal defeat→royal terror. The killing of the Convention's

---

[35] Ibid., 20: 695.
[36] Ibid., 20: 588.

members, according to Couthon, was the last resort of "governments begotten by crime."[37] Here it is the very triumph of the Revolution which brings about the criminal plots of the tyrants and necessitates a counter-terror. It was Couthon's role to put it with *prairial* logic: since each Republican victory throws the tyrants into a new rage, the Republic is all the more endangered with the news of each victory. This wild logic even led him to contend that the Revolution would not have had to defend itself from such misfortune had "Hébert, Danton, Fabre d'Eglantine and Chabot won out"[38]—if, in other words, the Revolution had lost out. Robespierre gave his own personal twist to this idea at the Jacobin Club: "I said two months ago: if we beat our enemies, if we foil the conspiracies they have hatched by corruption, then we shall be assassinated."[39] The idea that the Revolution would be more endangered the more it triumphed implied the logical impossibility of ever halting the Terror.

Yet a demonstration of this was only possible by redefining the war. That summer of 1793, the war was the concurrent presence of internal and external enemies (the "two fronts" already adumbrated during the September Massacres). But it was not yet the universalized and ubiquitous war we would hear of in *prairial*. There was no longer a limited theater of operations since, as Barère put it, the English were everywhere: in the Alps and the Pyrénées, at the Convention, in Ardèche, Lozère, and Orléans, aided by countless spies and using a thousand disguises. The ubiquitousness of the war meant the ubiquitousness of the Revolution's enemies. In examining the list of the enemies of the People drawn up by Couthon, one sees that of the eleven categories of suspects, only three were defined in express relation to the war, one of them directly (those who had betrayed the Republic in commanding the armies) and the other two indirectly (those who had supported the enemies of France, and those who had abetted the tyrants' activities).[40] The other eight categories nonetheless singled out men who were at war against the Revolution, even if their "war" was discernible only in their "moral depravity," an elastic expression which provoked from the crushed Convention one of

---

[37] Ibid., 20: 544.

[38] Ibid.

[39] Ibid., 20: 579 (speech of 6 *prairial*, Year II); see also the speech of 7 *prairial:* "Surrounded by their assassins . . . I cling to a fleeting life only from love of the *patrie* and the thirst for justice. . . . The more they hasten to end my career here below, the more I wish to hasten to fill it with actions useful to the happiness of my fellows. I shall at least leave them a testament that will make the tyrants and their accomplices tremble. I shall perhaps reveal frightful secrets that a kind of cowardly prudence would have led me to conceal" (20: 588).

[40] Ibid., 20: 697.

its rare moments of protest. In this intellectual drifting in which the imaginary held sway over the real, what could have been more telling than Couthon's indignation when someone dared remind him that Robespierre's would-be assassin was from Puy-de-Dôme and thus a compatriot? Only England, cried Couthon amidst the applause of the Assembly, could have "vomited up such a monster."[41] So the locksmith from Auvergne found himself a naturalized Englishman, as would be the case for all the "factions." The ubiquity of the combat and its combatants explains rather well Robespierre's propensity for "setting aside the facts," to quote Rousseau's famous phrase. As the Revolution was being constantly attacked, the theme of external danger could be treated rhetorically. As in the case of the Celebration of the Supreme Being, the words, "the only hope of the foreigner," were henceforth to be read under the allegorical figures, Atheism, Ambition, Egotism, Discord, and False Simplicity.[42]

It is understandable that this discourse should no longer need to distinguish between the different factions and instead should lump them all together into the faction of Indulgence, the faction which was "the patron and support for all others."[43] Such was indeed the end result of the gigantic undertaking of identification in the terrorist discourse. The undertaking can be interpreted in a circumstantial fashion: at the moment when the Revolutionary Tribunal was going to take terrible measures, it was obviously the "faction of indulgence" above all—the faction that had left its memories and ramifications within the Convention—that had to be eradicated. Yet it is also possible to see here something more than a simple series of measures linked to the immediate situation. The question everyone asks himself under a terrorist regime—"When will all this come to an end?"—was the very question to which "the faction of indulgence" demanded an answer. Indulgence sees the various aspects of an individual, offsets faults with virtues, and acts with intention, a process which is opposed to the very essence of Jacobinism if it is admitted that the latter tears down the barriers between the private and the public and acknowledges no right whatsoever to interiority.

Once the external and the internal factions were identified as one, not war but crime was at the center of the official *prairial* discourse. This explained why the Republic was not saved (and could not in fact have been saved), since the essence of the Republic lay not in victory but in virtue. To understand this, we must listen to Robespierre, who gave the

[41] Ibid., 20: 544.
[42] See "Plan de la fête à l'Etre Suprème, qui doit être célébrée le 20 prairial, proposé par David et décrété par la Convention Nationale" (ibid., 20: 653).
[43] Ibid., 20: 695.

most significant speech of all. In his last address to the Convention, he denounced the very use of the word "Mountain." As any demarcation between individuals was forbidden, he said, there could be no Mountain in a country where a pure People reigned.

But on 7 *prairial,* Robespierre was heard to doubt whether a pure People could possibly exist. Was the virtue of the French people sufficient to save the country? No, for there were two "peoples" in France. On the one hand, there was the mass of citizens, "pure, simple, thirsting for justice, the friend of liberty"; and on the other, a "pack of factious traitors and intriguers, the blabbering charlatans and fakes who show up everywhere, who criticize everything, who take over the tribunes."[44] One consequence of the character of this second People, these scoundrels, foreigners, and counterrevolutionaries, was that eradicating them was difficult, if not impossible. In opposition to the social oneness was this plurality, this divided, fragmented "pack" of scoundrels constantly reappearing out of its own ashes. (Poisonous plants, Barère called them, which could never quite be rooted out completely.) A second consequence was the continued presence of a curtain between the French people and its representatives: a curtain which could not be totally removed, and whose mere existence represented a major failure for Jacobin thought, which dreamed of perfect psychological and social transparency and could not imagine that the popular will could be divided without criminal intervention.

*   *   *

To conclude the study of these texts, if we go back to the question of the extent to which the discourse of the historians of the French Revolution has been dominated by that of the revolutionaries themselves, we can see more clearly both their additions and their dependence, and that it was not at all a question of modeling one discourse on the other.

The additions? I hope it is clearer now that an entire line of French historiography, from Louis Blanc to Mathiez and Soboul, has inflated the degree to which the Terror was a direct response to the contingencies of national defense. To the men of the Revolution, the Terror appeared expedient only insofar as it saved the country from a less controllable type of terror. Here, then, historians have drifted considerably away from the discourse of the Revolution. Essentially, this drift is a result of the definition of Jacobinism (cherished throughout the nineteenth and twentieth centuries) as a policy of public safety, the French proclivity for dreams filled with images of threatened borders, of an endangered nation, of the miracle performed by a strong central power. This is a

[44] Ibid., 20: 589.

kind of romanticism of energy, which can indeed be found in revolutionary thinking about the war, but much less in the rationalization of the Terror. It was more posterity than the Revolution itself that linked War and Terror.

On the other hand, the conventional historiography has adopted the specifically Jacobin identification of external and internal enemies, and hence the belief in a generalized war. The first consequence of this is that the Terror is seen as striking only those alien to the national family, like a gust of wind shaking the bad fruit from a tree and leaving the good, to use Garnier de Saintes's expression. The second is that the Terror is seen as consubstantial with the Revolution—*nothing but* one of its aspects—and that the former has to be accepted unless the latter is rejected. Robespierre's question has been endlessly repeated: "Do you want a revolution without revolution?"

The paradox is that in using this second language without criticizing it, in extending the first, and in putting the two rather haphazardly together, many historians hardly seem to have seen the contradiction between them. For the first discourse places the Terror as best it can within a history: whether bearing the burden of the past or the palpitations of the future, the Terror is nevertheless seen as transitory. The second, on the contrary, sets the Terror outside chronology in an eternal present, as if it were an interminable spiritual war, impossible both to lose and to win.

Ideologies and Social Revolutions: Reflections on the French Case*

William H. Sewell, Jr.

This article was inspired—perhaps I should say provoked—by Theda Skocpol's *States and Social Revolutions.*[1] I believe that her book deserves the general acclaim it has received as a model of comparative historical analysis and as a brilliant contribution to the sociology of revolutions. But I also believe that Skocpol's treatment of the role of ideology in revolution is inadequate. This article begins by developing an alternative to Skocpol's conception of ideology, then demonstrates how this alternative conception can help to illuminate the history of the French Revolution, and concludes with some suggestions for future comparative studies of revolutions.

Skocpol's goal in *States and Social Revolutions* is to specify, by means of a comparative historical analysis, the causes and the outcomes of the three great social revolutions of modern times: the French, the Russian, and the Chinese. She analyzes revolutions from what she terms a "non-voluntarist, structuralist perspective,"[2] emphasizing three fundamental structural relations: (1) between classes (especially landlords and peasants), (2) between classes and states, and (3) between different states in international relations. To summarize a very complex and subtle argument, Skocpol sees a particular combination of conditions as being conducive to social revolution: (1) well-organized and autonomous peasant communities, (2) a dominant class of absentee agricultural rentiers who are highly dependent on the state, and (3) a semibureaucratized state that falls behind in military competition with rival states. When these three conditions are present, as they were in different ways in France, Russia, and China, the result can be social revolution—a breakdown of the state, a peasant uprising, a transformation of class relations, and, eventually, a massive consolidation of bureaucratic power in a new state.

One of Skocpol's most important contributions to the history and sociology of revolutions is her approach to the problem of multiple causation. All serious analysts agree that the causes of revolutions are complex. But in the face of this complexity they usually employ one of two strategies: a "hierarchical" strategy of asserting the primacy of some type of cause over the

* I would like to thank Keith Baker, Richard Eaton, Dale Eickelman, Neil Fligstein, Peter Machinist, Sarah Maza, William Reuss, Renato Rosaldo, Theda Skocpol, and Norman Yoffee for comments on earlier drafts. An earlier version of this article was presented at the American Historical Association meetings in Los Angeles in 1981.
[1] Theda Skocpol, *States and Social Revolutions: A Comparative Analysis of France, Russia, and China* (Cambridge, 1979).

[2] Ibid., p. 33.

This essay originally appeared in the *Journal of Modern History* 57 (March 1985).

others, or a "narrative" strategy of trying to recount the course of the revolution in some semblance of its real complexity. The trouble with both the usual strategies is that they are, literally, insufficiently analytical. The narrative strategy discusses different causal features of the revolutionary process only as they make themselves felt in the unfolding of the story. Consequently, causes tend to get lost in a muddle of narrative detail and are never separated out sufficiently to make their autonomous dynamics clear. The problem with the hierarchical strategy is that while it successfully specifies the causal dynamics of one factor, it tends to subordinate the roles of other factors, either treating them only as background (as most studies of revolution have done with the problem of the international setting) or conflating them with the chosen causal factor. Here the obvious example is the way that Marxist theories of revolution have tended to view the state as simply an expression of class power, rather than as a distinctive institution with its own interests and dynamics.

Skocpol's strategy is to insist that causation is a matter of "conjunctural, unfolding interactions of originally separately determined processes."[3] Although I might prefer "autonomously determined" to "separately determined," I believe that Skocpol's strategy is an inspired compromise, one that combines the best features of both the usual approaches while avoiding their faults. It appropriates the conceptual power of the hierarchical strategy and applies it to not one but several causal processes; but it also appropriates the narrative strategy's emphasis on sequence, conjuncture, and contingency. By proceeding in this way, Skocpol manages to specify the distinct causal contributions of class, state, and international structures and processes to the outbreak and outcome of revolutions, while at the same time respecting the unique and unfolding concatenation of causal forces in each of the revolutions she studies. I have nothing but admiration for the way she solves the problem of multiple causation. My quarrel with her is that she has not made her causation multiple enough—that she has not recognized the autonomous power of ideology in the revolutionary process. In her account, ideology remains conflated with class struggle or state consolidation, just as the state has usually been conflated with class in Marxist theories of revolution. One of the tasks of this paper is to trace out the autonomous dynamics of ideology in the case of France, and to indicate how ideology fit into "the conjunctural unfolding of interacting processes" known as the French Revolution. But doing this, as I hope to demonstrate, does more than add one more "factor" that can account for some portion of the change that took place. It also leads to a fundamentally different conceptualization of the process of revolution.

Skocpol systematically rejects ideological explanations of revolution. Her principal argument for doing so is that the ideologies of revolutionary leaders serve as very poor predictors of "revolutionary outcomes." As she puts it, "any line of reasoning that treats revolutionary ideologies as blueprints for revolutionary outcomes cannot sustain scrutiny. . . . " Leaders "have typically

---

[3] Ibid., p. 320, n. 16.

ended up accomplishing very different tasks and furthering the consolidation of quite different kinds of new regimes from those they originally (and perhaps ever) ideologically intended."[4] This is true, of course, and it certainly is sufficient ground for dismissing any argument that the ideology of revolutionary leaders provides a sufficient explanatory blueprint for the regimes that emerge from revolutionary struggles. But Skocpol goes on to make the entirely unwarranted conclusion that ideologies are of *no* explanatory value. "It cannot be argued," she writes, "that the cognitive content of . . . ideologies *in any sense* provides a predictive key to . . . the outcomes of the Revolutions."[5] This is an extreme position and a very difficult one to sustain, even for so careful and systematic a thinker as Skocpol. One example will suffice to make this clear. A glaring difference between the outcomes of the French and Russian Revolutions was that private property was consolidated in France and abolished in Russia. Can this difference be explained without taking into account the different ideological programs of the actors in the French and the Russian Revolutions? In one of the most awkward and least convincing passages in the book, Skocpol attempts to do so. But she cannot explain the contrast without introducing ideology surreptitiously, in the guise of "world-historical context." She assures us that because "there were no world-historically available models for state-controlled industrialization" at the time of the French Revolution, "no communist-style, mass-mobilizing political party could consolidate state power."[6] In Russia, by contrast, "there were world-historically available models of state control over industries."[7] In other words, socialism, an ideology invented in the nineteenth century, was not available in 1789 but was well-known by 1917. This is an obvious truism, but it does point toward something important about the difference between the French and Russian Revolutions. The leaders of the French Revolution, to the last man, not only were not socialists, but were adherents of a particular "world-historically available model" (that is, an ideology) in which private property figured as an "inalienable natural right." Similarly, the Bolsheviks, since long before 1917, had been passionately committed to a quite different "world-historically available model," which featured the collectivization of the means of production. In short, Skocpol's invocation of differing world-historical contexts turns out to introduce, although in a highly obfuscated form, the crucial difference between French and Russian revolutionary ideologies.

This obfuscation marks a sharp departure from the usual lucidity of Skocpol's argument. Similarly, her steadfast denial of the importance of ideology marks a departure from her otherwise rather catholic explanatory strategy. For example, when she determines that class antagonisms and struggles cannot by themselves explain the outbreak or the outcomes of revolutions, she does

[4] Ibid., pp. 170–71.
[5] Ibid., p. 170. Emphasis mine.
[6] Ibid., p. 234.
[7] Ibid., p. 235.

not conclude that they are of *no* explanatory value. Rather, she incorporates them as one of several important factors that *together* explain the outbreak and consequences of social revolutions.

What accounts for this uncharacteristic and unsatisfactory treatment of ideology? I suspect that Skocpol's refusal to include ideology in her explanatory package derives from her rejection of naive voluntarist theories of revolution. To admit that ideologies have a strong causal impact on revolutions would appear to give people's conscious intentions a much more significant role in the revolutionary process than Skocpol thinks they deserve. Although I would allow a somewhat greater role than Skocpol does for conscious choice, I think her distrust of naive voluntarist explanations is well placed. What I dispute is that building ideological factors into the explanation necessarily entails a surrender to naive voluntarism.

Although Skocpol is concerned to give a "structural" explanation of revolutions, her own account of ideology has not taken into account the (broadly speaking) "structuralist" mood that has come to dominate recent thinking about ideology. Theorists as diverse as Louis Althusser, Michel Foucault, Clifford Geertz, and Raymond Williams, to name only a few, have shifted the emphasis from highly self-conscious, purposive individuals attempting to elaborate or enact "blueprints" for change, to the relatively anonymous and impersonal operation of "ideological state apparatuses," "epistemes," "cultural systems," or "structures of feeling."[8] For these theorists, the coherence and the dynamics of an ideological formation (under whichever title) are sought in the interrelations of its semantic items and in their relation to social forces, not in the conscious wills of individual actors. Ideologies are, in this sense, anonymous, or transpersonal.

Ideology, then, should be conceived in structural terms. However, I hesitate to use Skocpol's term "nonvoluntarist." Ideological utterances, like all other forms of social action, require the exercise of human will. To say that an ideology "is structured" or "is a structure" is not to say that it is inaccessible to human volition, but that ideological action is shaped by preexisting ideological (and other) realities. All social structures (of which ideological structures are a subcategory) are, as Anthony Giddens has pointed out, "dual" in character.[9] That is, they are at once constraining and enabling. They block certain possibilities, but they also create others. Ideological structures undergo continuous reproduction and/or transformation as a result of the combined willful actions of more or less knowledgeable actors within the constraints and the possibilities supplied by preexisting structures. It is, consequently,

[8] Louis Althusser, "Ideology and Ideological State Apparatuses," in *Lenin and Philosophy* (London, 1971), pp. 123–73; Michel Foucault, *The Order of Things: An Archaeology of the Human Sciences* (New York, 1970), and "What Is an Author?" in *Language, Counter-Memory, Practice: Selected Essays and Interviews*, trans. Donald F. Bouchard and Sherry Simon (Ithaca, N.Y., 1977), pp. 113-38; Clifford Geertz, *The Interpretation of Cultures* (New York, 1973); Raymond Williams, *Marxism and Literature* (Oxford, 1977).

[9] Anthony Giddens, *New Rules of Sociological Method* (London, 1976), p. 161.

not quite right to speak of ideological structures as "nonvoluntary" or "non-voluntarist," since both the reproduction and the transformation of these structures are carried out by a very large number of willful actors. Ideological structures are, however, anonymous. The whole of an ideological structure (with its inevitable contradictions and discontinuities) is *never* present in the consciousness of any single actor—not even a Robespierre, a Napoleon, a Lenin, or a Mao—but in the collectivity. An ideological structure is not some self-consistent "blueprint," but the outcome of the often contradictory or antagonistic action of a large number of actors or groups of actors. If anonymous ideological structures in this sense do not seem quite parallel to the "nonvoluntarist" state, class, and international structures analyzed by Skocpol, this is because, in my opinion, she has a far too reified conception of social structure. State, class, and international structures are in fact characterized by the same anonymity, duality, and collectivity as ideological structures. They, too, are reproduced and/or transformed by willful actors, acting within the constraints and possibilities imposed by preexisting structures, not by some reified extrahuman forces. By defining ideology in structural terms, and by de-reifying class, state, and international structures, all four types of structures can be encompassed by a single, consistent conceptual framework.

It is necessary, then, to replace Skocpol's somewhat naive voluntarist conception of ideology with a conception of ideology as an anonymous and collective, but transformable, structure. But this is not the only way in which Skocpol's conception of ideology must be revised. Ideology must also, as most recent theorists have insisted, be understood as constitutive of the social order. While agreeing, in one way or another, that social being determines consciousness, recent theorists would also insist that consciousness simultaneously determines social being. Ideology must be seen neither as the mere reflex of material class relations nor as mere "ideas" which "intellectuals" hold about society. Rather, ideologies inform the structure of institutions, the nature of social cooperation and conflict, and the attitudes and predispositions of the population. All social relations are at the same time ideological relations, and all explicit ideological discourse is a form of social action. What all of this suggests is a very different and far more complex object of study than Skocpol takes up in her fairly cursory discussions of revolutionary ideology. It is not enough to treat ideology as a possible causal factor explaining some portion of the change wrought by revolution. If society is understood as ideologically constituted, then adding ideology to the account will also mean rethinking the nature, the interrelations, and the effects on the revolution of state, class, international, and other structures. Moreover, the replacement of one socio-ideological order by another also becomes a crucial dimension of the change that needs to be explained, one no less important than the replacement of one class system by another or one state apparatus by another.

I believe that a view of ideology as anonymous, collective, and as constitutive of social order is not only superior to Skocpol's view of ideology but actually more consonant with a structural approach to revolution. This is a contention that cannot be demonstrated by theoretical argument alone. I will therefore try to demonstrate it briefly in practice by sketching an account of ideological change in the French Revolution.

THE IDEOLOGY OF THE OLD REGIME

As usual, any account of the French Revolution must begin with the Old Regime. The ideological foundations of the French Old Regime were complex and contradictory. The complexities and contradictions were of two distinguishable types: those internal to the traditional ideology of the French monarchical state, and those introduced during the eighteenth century by the new Enlightenment ideological discourse.

The traditional ideology of the Old Regime was itself made up of disparate materials arising out of various discourses in different historical eras. It was composed of feudal, Catholic, constitutional, corporate, and juristic elements, fused only imperfectly in a sometimes precarious absolutist synthesis under the centralizing monarchs of the seventeenth century. To characterize a highly complex set of ideas very briefly, this synthesis pictured society as a set of privileged corporate bodies held together by the supreme will of a semi-sacerdotal king.[10]

The units of the kingdom were not individual subjects, but corporate bodies of widely varying kinds—including the three estates of the realm, the provinces, the chartered cities, trade guilds, universities, academies, religious orders, chartered companies, and numerous bodies of magistrates. Privilege was the key to the corporate conception of the social order. Privilege, in the seventeenth or eighteenth century, had a meaning very close to its etymological roots: "private law" (from the Latin *privus* and *legum*). Each of the corporate bodies that composed the state had particular indemnities, advantages, customs, and regulations—in short, a set of laws peculiar to itself—that set it apart from the rest of the population. It was these privileges that defined it as a distinct corporate body and gave it a definite place in the state. Left to themselves, these diverse corporate bodies would inevitably fall into disunity. Concerned above all with maintaining their privileges against the claims of rivals, the corporate bodies were bound to quarrel among themselves over jurisdiction and precedent. It was the royal will that welded them together into a unified state. The various corporate bodies were themselves only subordinate members of the political body of the state. The king, as head of this body, kept a proper balance between the members by regulating and adjudicating privilege and by maintaining the rightful hierarchy. In contrast to the partial and self-interested concerns of the subordinate corporate bodies, the king was concerned with the welfare of the state as a whole. Because his

---

[10] See esp. Roland Mousnier, "Les concepts d'ordres, d'états, de fidelité, et de monarchie absolue en France de la fin du XVe siècle à la fin du XVIIIe siècle," *Revue historique* 502 (April–June 1972): 289–312; and William H. Sewell, Jr., "Etat, Corps and Ordre: Some Notes on the Social Vocabulary of the French Old Regime," in *Sozialgeschichte Heute, Festschrift für Hans Rosenberg zum 70. Geburtstag*, ed. Hans-Ulrich Wehler (Göttingen, 1974), pp. 49–68.

was the only truly public will, it was by rights absolute. The king was the supreme legislator, the font of justice and honor, and the embodiment of the majesty and glory of the state.

The king's position of supremacy was justified largely on religious grounds: the monarch ruled by "divine right." He was placed in his position by the will of God, and was owed obedience as God's representative.[11] The king's extraordinary quasi-sacerdotal quality was made evident in the royal coronation ritual—the French call it the *sacre*—which marked the king's elevation to his high office.[12] One of the crucial phases of the ceremony was the anointment of the king's head and body with chrism (holy oil) miraculously preserved from the original seventh-century *sacre* of Clovis. Thereafter, the king took communion, receiving not only the consecrated host of the layman, but the consecrated wine normally reserved to the priest. The king was, in fact, the only layman in the realm who ever took communion "in both species," as it was called. These two holy substances, the chrism and the consecrated wine, raised the king forever from the ranks of laymen, transforming him into an earthly representative of divine power and providing him with a priestly aura. It was this God-given power that made the king's will supreme in the state. Corresponding to this intimate relationship between spiritual power and public authority at the pinnacle of the political order was a pervasive intermingling of secular and religious idioms at all levels of society. Such corporate bodies as trade guilds and cities had their own patron saints whose feast days were celebrated with appropriate pomp and display, and the ritual of most corporate bodies included common masses and worship. Moreover, the entry of a person into a corporate body normally involved the swearing of a religious oath. In this sense, the bonds that united members of a corporate body were spiritual as well as legal, just as the royal power that welded all the corporate bodies into a single state was spiritual in origin.[13]

This ideology was intimately linked with the institutional structure of the French state. As Tocqueville long ago observed, the Old Regime state was composed of several distinct historical layers—a feudal layer dating from the early middle ages, a corporate layer dating from the rise of cities, guilds, and estates in the high middle ages, a magisterial layer dating from the proliferation of venal office in the sixteenth and seventeenth centuries, and a bureaucratic layer dating from the administrative centralization of Richelieu and Louis XIV.[14] Each of these successive forms of the state had superseded, but not abolished, the earlier forms. Thus, the officials of Louis XIV could establish the hegemony of the central government over feudal seigneurs,

---

[11] The definitive statement of this theory was by Bishop Bossuet. Jacques Benigne Bossuet, *Politique tirée des propres paroles de l'Ecriture sainte*, ed. Jacques Le Brun (Geneva, 1967).

[12] G. Père, *Le sacre et le couronnement des rois de France, dans leurs rapports avec les lois fondamentales* (Paris, 1922).

[13] This is set forth more systematically in Sewell, "Etat, Corps, and Ordre."

[14] Alexis de Tocqueville, *The Old Regime and the French Revolution*, trans. Stuart Gilbert (Garden City, N.Y., 1955).

chartered cities, provinces, and assorted bodies of magistrates, depriving them of much of their public power. But it could not do away with them entirely.[15] The beauty of the idea of privilege was that it brought together all of the diverse rights and duties of these established institutions under a single operative concept, one that simultaneously gave state recognition to their autonomy within their own sphere and limited them to the role of quasi-private, partial bodies. It rendered the whole range of established institutions dependent on the king—cast as the guarantor of privilege—while leaving the direction of the state entirely in his hands.

It is important to recognize, however, that the absolutist state and its ideology, while greatly enhancing the power of the king, nevertheless embodied a historic compromise. The price of the king's theoretically absolute power was his recognition of the privileges of preexisting institutions. He had the power to regulate and adjudicate privileges, and, as the head of the state and the font of honor, to create new institutions and to grant new privileges. He also had the formal power to abolish privileges as well as to create them, but this power was severely circumscribed in practice. Any wholesale abolition of privileges by the king would violate his own raison d'être and thus jeopardize his "absolute" power. The corporate ideology of the absolute monarchy rendered it absolute only within a system of essentially fixed privileges.[16]

The retention of corporate privileges, however residual under the reign of a powerful monarch such as Louis XIV, was of crucial importance for the politics of the eighteenth century. Under the far less effective Louis XV and Louis XVI, bodies whose powers had been diminished almost to the vanishing point by Louis XIV could return to vigor and claim broad public functions. Thus the eighteenth-century parlements were able to use their right of remonstrance to assert (not always successfully) an important role in royal legislation. And in the ultimate crisis of 1787–89, the king found himself forced to call the Estates General, an old corporate institution with a claim to very broad public powers. Under the firm hand of Louis XIV, the internal contradictions of the corporate monarchical ideology were not salient. But in times of crisis or weakness of royal power, the suppressed claims of corporate bodies could burst forth and challenge the absolute supremacy of the king.

The internal contradictions of the corporate monarchical ideology were complicated by the development of the new centralized royal administration. The relation of the administration to the monarchical ideology was highly paradoxical. On the one hand, the idea of corporate privilege was a crucial device for one of the administration's most important tasks: subordinating all institutions to the royal will. Moreover, the king's ability to create the centralized administration depended on his extraordinary position as ruler

[15] Skocpol's discussion of this pattern is excellent (*States and Social Revolutions*, pp. 52–54).

[16] See Roland Mousnier and Fritz Hartung, "Quelques problèmes concernant la monarchie absolue," *Relazioni del X Congresso Internazionale di Scienze Storiche*, 6 vols. (Florence, 1955), 4:1–55.

by divine right. The rational and centralized royal administration was in a sense the highest expression of the supremacy of the royal will over the defective and partial wills of the myriads of corporate bodies. On the other hand, the corporate ideology of absolutism could not give a coherent account of the structure of the administrative system, whose officers, far from becoming a privileged corporate body, instead remained royal servants, revocable at the will of the king, and whose purposes and activities tended to undermine the particularism intrinsic to the corporate view of society. It was in the context of a monarchical state whose practices were expanding beyond their own ideological foundations that the ideology of the French Enlightenment emerged.

The Enlightenment contradicted the ideology of the monarchical state in both of its essentials. First, where the monarchical ideology saw divine spirit as the ultimate source of the social order, the Enlightenment insisted on a purely naturalistic account of the world. Social order was derived from natural phenomena, and was to be understood in terms of the operation of natural laws. Second, where the monarchical ideology pictured society as composed of a multitude of particular corporate bodies, each with its own specific privileges, the Enlightenment insisted on the universal applicability of reason to human affairs. It had scorn for all privilege, no matter how ancient or venerable. Considered as a body of abstract doctrines, the Enlightenment appears as a direct assault on the ideology of the French monarchical system.

Yet few contemporaries regarded it as such. In fact, the new Enlightenment ideas, vocabulary, metaphors, and prejudices were adopted rapidly and enthusiastically by the social and economic elites of the Old Regime, the very groups who had the greatest stake in the existing system. The Enlightenment became the compulsory style of the most exclusive and prestigious Parisian salons and won many converts in the upper circles of the army, the magistracy, the royal bureaucracy, the Court nobility, and even the Church. It was embraced with particular fervor by certain members of the royal bureaucracy. Although many bureaucrats continued to conceive of state and society in traditional terms, there was a strong affinity between the bureaucracy and the Enlightenment. Enlightenment notions of reason and natural law provided bureaucrats with a fully elaborated discourse in terms of which they could justify their attempts to promote administrative uniformity and abolish entrenched privileges. The epitome of the Enlightenment bureaucrat was Turgot, whose distinguished administrative career was capped by a brief term (1774–76) as controller general (head administrative officer of the crown), when he attempted wholesale legislative abolition of privileges.[17] But even after Turgot had been driven from office and most of his innovations reversed, his successors continued to pursue a less radical version of his reform program. It is perhaps

[17] On Turgot and his ministry, see Douglas Dakin, *Turgot and the Ancien Regime in France* (London, 1939; reprint, New York, 1965); Edgar Faure, *La disgrace de Turgot* (Paris, 1961); and Keith Michael Baker, *Condorcet: From Natural Philosophy to Social Mathematics* (Chicago, 1975), pp. 55–72.

not surprising that royal bureaucrats, whose position and mission lacked any coherent justification within the terms of the corporate monarchical ideology, should have adopted the Enlightenment so enthusiastically. But at least the terminology of the Enlightenment was embraced by the leading defenders of corporate privilege as well. The Parlement of Paris, in its blistering remonstrances against Turgot's reform edicts, laced its rhetoric with appeals to nature and reason.[18] In fact, in the last two decades of the Old Regime, virtually all shades of political opinion drew, to a greater or lesser extent, on the Enlightenment idiom.[19]

By the end of the Old Regime, the French political system did not have a single ideology. Rather, it had two sharply divergent yet coexisting ideologies that differed not only in their policy implications, their modes of thought, and their pictures of society, but in their ultimate metaphysical foundations. The ideology of the Enlightenment was, of course, elaborated largely in opposition to the corporate monarchical ideology. It is therefore tempting to characterize the corporate monarchical ideology alone as the true ideology of the Old Regime and to see the Enlightenment as a proto-revolutionary force, a powerful solvent of Old Regime principles that was already at work within the very integument of the Old Regime state. But this would be to read history backwards. The corporate monarchical ideology and the Enlightenment ideology were *both* working parts of the Old Regime as it existed in the 1770s and 1780s. Since these ideologies differed on so many points, it is fair to say that there was an ideological contradiction at the core of the state. But there is no reason to believe that the contradictions weakened the state or hastened its fall. There is, after all, no necessary connection between the ideological consistency and the stability of states. The admirably stable British state of the eighteenth and nineteenth centuries was hardly famous for its ideological consistency. One could even argue that the coexistence of corporate and Enlightenment ideologies contributed to the stability of the Old Regime French state; that the smooth functioning of a state structured in this particular way was actually enhanced by the simultaneous availability of both corporate-monarchical and rational-universal principles. But even if one admits that the split ideological personality of the Old Regime state was bound to give way eventually to some more coherent ideological formation, it certainly need not have led to a revolution. Elements of the two ideologies might have been combined in any number of stable amalgams, just as they were in so many European states in the nineteenth century.

IDEOLOGY AND THE REVOLUTIONARY CRISIS

The Old Regime state was thrown into crisis by impending bankruptcy, not by its split ideological personality. But once the crisis had begun, ideological

[18] These remonstrances are available in Jules Flammermont, ed., *Remontrances du Parlement de Paris au XVIIIe siècle,* vol. 3 (Paris, 1898).

[19] See Keith Michael Baker, "French Political Thought at the Accession of Louis XVI," *Journal of Modern History* 50 (June 1978): 279–303. The mixing of corporate and Enlightenment language and ideas among the provincial elites of the Old Regime

contradictions contributed mightily to the deepening of the crisis into revolution. The crisis was propelled by two overlapping but distinguishable politico-ideological processes: the disintegration of the absolutist synthesis and the development of a radical Enlightenment program. The central issue around which both of these ideological processes revolved was the calling of the Estates General.

In order to resolve the financial crisis, the king had no alternative to imposing far-reaching reforms that would abolish many hitherto sacrosanct privileges — especially the nobility's and the clergy's exemptions from taxation. But to do this meant to revoke the implicit compromise on which the absolutist synthesis rested — the guarantee of corporate privileges in return for renunciation of corporate claims to public authority. Any foreseeable resolution of the financial crisis was therefore certain to rupture the existing mode of government. The question was whether it would do so to the benefit of the king's powers or to those of the privileged corporate groups. In the event, the weakened king could not impose reforms against the resistance of the privileged groups. Instead, they forced him to call the Estates General, which was the supreme embodiment of corporate power.[20] The Estates General was composed of representatives of the three estates of the realm: the Clergy, the Nobility, and the Third Estate. According to ancient constitutional principle, the king could not impose new taxes without its consent, and it in turn could demand redress of grievances from the king before consenting to new levies. The "absolute" monarchs of the seventeenth and eighteenth centuries had, of course, imposed new taxes repeatedly without calling the Estates General; in fact, the Estates had not met since 1614. But like all the other political powers of corporate bodies, which its existence had both epitomized and protected, the Estates General had never been abolished in principle, only suspended in practice. Its calling in 1788 marked the end of absolutism and the consequent resurgence of the corporate claims so long suppressed by the absolute monarchs.

Nowhere was the ideological character of the revolutionary crisis so clearly displayed as on the question of the Estates General. After all, in 1788 the Estates General had only an ideological existence. As a functioning institution it had disappeared in 1614. The necessity of reviving the Estates General was an *ideological* necessity. In order to unify their resistance to the king and give it a coherent justification, the insurgent parlements, assemblies of notables, and provincial estates had to call for restitution of the only body with a powerful claim to represent all corporate interests simultaneously. But the revival of a long absent institution meant that it had to be reconstituted from scratch. After nearly one and three-quarters centuries, there were no living memories of an Estates General and no precedents sufficiently au-

---

is massively documented in Daniel Roche, *Le siècle des lumières en province: Académies et académiciens provinciaux, 1680–1789*, 2 vols. (Paris and The Hague, 1978).

[20] The best account is Jean Egret, *La pré-révolution française, 1787–1788* (Paris, 1962); English trans., *The French Prerevolution, 1787–1788* (Chicago, 1977).

thoritative to determine its composition and procedures. In these circumstances it is hardly surprising that the way in which this phantom institution was to be fleshed out became the topic of an immense and unprecedented ideological debate.

If the calling of the Estates General was determined by the logic of disintegration of the absolutist ideological synthesis, the ensuing debate was dominated by the emergence of an Enlightenment alternative to the increasingly disjointed corporate and absolutist discourse. While the Estates General was obviously corporate in its external form, the calling of the Estates could also be interpreted in Enlightenment terms — as a consultation of the national will or as an invitation to revise the social contract. Moreover, since the electorate was supposed to formulate and discuss its grievances for the meeting of the Estates, censorship was suspended. This lifting of the usual limits on political discourse was greeted with an avalanche of pamphlets and newspapers advancing theories and proposals of every description. The most influential of the pamphlets was the Abbé Sieyès's *What Is the Third Estate?* which mounted a thorough and passionate attack on the whole system of privilege, denouncing the aristocrats as enemies of the Nation and arguing that the Assembly of the Third Estate was in fact a fully sovereign National Assembly.[21] Thus, by the time the Estates General met, in May of 1789, a fundamental recasting of the state in Enlightenment terms was already on the agenda, and many of the Third Estate representatives were inclined to see their estate as the germ of a National Assembly rather than as a subordinate part of an ancient corporate body.

Up to the crisis of 1787, the ideology of the Old Regime had been characterized by a twofold but apparently stable contradiction: a contradiction between a dominant absolutist and a subordinate corporate conception of the state, and a second contradiction between this absolutist synthesis and the ideology of the Enlightenment. The royal bankruptcy and the ensuing crisis led to a disaggregation of this complex and contradictory ideological formation into its elements — absolutist and corporate ideologies that were groping for satisfactory self-definitions in the new circumstances, and an Enlightenment revolutionary ideology whose proponents were now searching to recast the political world in its mold. The crisis of the Old Regime state liberated Enlightenment ideology from its ambiguous partnership with absolutism and made possible an attempt to reorder the state fundamentally in Enlightenment terms. The drift of events over the spring and summer of 1789 continued to undermine the plausibility of the corporate and absolutist alternatives, while enhancing that of the revolutionary alternative. The Third Estate's arrogation of the title "National Assembly," the Tennis-Court Oath, the defection of "patriot" nobles and clergy to the National Assembly, the taking of the Bastille and the consequent municipal revolutions, the spreading peasant revolts: each of these familiar events increased the supremacy of the revo-

---

[21] Emmanuel Joseph Sieyès, *Ou'est-ce que le Tiers Etat?* ed. Roberto Zapperi (Geneva, 1970).

lutionary Enlightenment ideology over its rivals. But it was not until the night of August fourth that they were finally swept from the field.

The night of August fourth was the crucial turning point of the Revolution both as a class struggle and as an ideological transformation. These two aspects of the night of August fourth were intimately linked. By decreeing the end of the seigneurial system, the National Assembly was recognizing the peasants' victory over the feudal lords, attempting to satisfy the peasants and thereby win their firm adherence to the Revolution. But the reforms of August fourth dismantled much more than seigneurialism. Thanks to a combination of astute planning on the part of the patriot faction and a wave of magnanimous radicalism that swept over the deputies, the Assembly abolished the entire privileged corporate order. The way in which this happened is significant: privileges were renounced amid joyous weeping by those who had been their beneficiaries. Great seigneurial landowners proposed abolition of seigneurial dues, representatives of the clergy offered up their tithes, representatives of the provinces and the cities renounced provincial and municipal privileges, and so on. The result was a holocaust of privilege. By the morning of August fifth, the entire array of corporate institutions and the privileges that had fixed their place in the state had been formally annihilated. What remained was the uncluttered Enlightenment ideal of equal individual citizens governed by laws that applied to all and represented by a National Assembly that expressed their general will.

The specifically ideological component of the night of August fourth must be emphasized. This component can be seen above all in the enthusiasm that swept through the Assembly. By early August, the National Assembly had been living a deep ideological contradiction for nearly three anguished months. It had embarked on the construction of a new political order based on Enlightenment political theory, yet it had done so within the shell of a theoretically absolute monarchical regime and surrounded by a privileged corporate society that contradicted the Assembly's enunciated principles. It had consistently taken whatever steps were necessary to protect its position against the king, but it had so far held back from any systematic attack on the old social system—partly out of fear, partly out of regrets for an old order that had treated most representatives well, and partly out of sheer prudence. It was, of course, the exigencies of the peasants' class struggle that dictated abolition of seigneurial privileges. But this first breach in the system of privilege led immediately to a sweeping abolition of privileges that were by no means threatened by the peasant rebellion. Once the Assembly was forced to destroy one complex of privileges, it was moved forward by an overwhelming urge for ideological consistency and destroyed them all. The mood of the Assembly on the night of August fourth—the transports of lofty emotion, the tears of joy—reveal the meaning of its actions. It was at last forsaking the murky paths of ideological compromise and stepping forward into the clear light of revolutionary purity. By annihilating privilege, the Assembly was declaring the nation to be genuinely transformed, cutting it loose from its decaying moral and metaphysical moorings and setting it on a firm course of reason and natural law. The representatives' rapture in the midst of these events is understandable: they were participating in what seemed to them a regeneration of the world.[22]

The regeneration was metaphysical as well as institutional. When the Assembly destroyed the institutional arrangements of the Old Regime, it also destroyed the metaphysical assumptions on which they had been based. No longer was the social order derived from divine will operating through the media of king, Church, religious oath, and common worship. The destruction of privilege meant the destruction of the entire spirit-centered conceptual world from which privilege had derived, and its replacement by a new natural world. On the night of August fourth the accent was on destruction of the old institutional order, but the Assembly swiftly followed with a solemn Declaration of the Rights of Man and Citizen, which set forth the metaphysical principles of the new order—"the natural, inalienable, and sacred rights of man." The Assembly's first priority after the night of August fourth was to formulate a proper metaphysical foundation for the state. Only after this had been accomplished did it begin the long and arduous task of writing a new constitution.

Skocpol, of course, recognizes the central importance of the night of August fourth. It was then, above all, that Marx's "gigantic broom" swept away the "medieval rubbish" that had hitherto cluttered the French state.[23] The problem is that she reduces August fourth to an outcome of the peasant revolt. She fails to recognize that it was a crucial turning point in two quite distinct revolutionary processes: a class process of peasant revolt and an ideological process of conceptual transformation. Its role was very different in the two processes. The night of August fourth began the *closure* of the peasants' class struggle. By assenting to the destruction of the seigneurial system, the National Assembly legitimized and effectively quieted the peasant revolt. While the peasants remained restive for some time, refusing to pay their former lords the fees enacted by the Assembly for redemption of seigneurial dues, and often resisting the payment of taxes as well, the peasant problem dwindled steadily in significance. It was essentially terminated in 1793 when redemption payments were abolished.

The role of August fourth in the ideological transformations of the French Revolution was very different. August fourth marked the end of one ideological dynamic—the tension between Enlightenment and corporate monarchical principles. But it also inaugurated another: the elaboration of Enlightenment metaphysical principles into a new revolutionary social and political structure. The peasant revolt contributed mightily to the destruction of the Old Regime. It dictated the destruction of seigneurialism and it made the country ungovernable—thus paralyzing the Old Regime state and giving the National As-

---

[22] This interpretation of the night of August fourth was originally worked out by Keith Baker and myself in a course on the French Revolution which we taught jointly at the University of Chicago in 1973. Detailed accounts are Patrick Kessel, *La nuit du 4 aôut 1789* (Paris, 1969); and Jean-Pierre Hirsch, *La nuit du 4 aôut* (Paris, 1978).

[23] Skocpol, *States and Social Revolutions*, pp. 183–85.

sembly the opportunity to assume power. But after August 1789, the peasant revolt had only a limited role in determining the shape of the new regime and the nature of the conflicts that drove the Revolution forward. These were determined by a quite different array of forces, including the pressures of international war and the need to consolidate state power which Skocpol rightly emphasizes. But the conflicts were also shaped crucially by the metaphysical and ideological redefinitions that occurred in August and September of 1789. These created a new framework of rhetoric and action and a new set of political issues that dominated the subsequent unfolding of the Revolution. This ideological dynamic, which Skocpol's account of the Revolution misses, will be the subject of the following section.

THE ELABORATION OF REVOLUTIONARY IDEOLOGY

The developmental dynamics of revolutionary ideology changed drastically when the Enlightenment idiom became the dominant idiom of government. One of the remarkable features of the night of August fourth was the unanimity of the Assembly's actions, a unanimity that lasted through the adoption of the Declaration of the Rights of Man and Citizen. As long as Enlightenment principles were viewed essentially in opposition to the corporate-monarchical principles of the Old Regime, they seemed uniform and consistent. But once the corporate-monarchical ideology was driven from the field, the contradictory possibilities inherent in the Enlightenment began to emerge. The ideology embraced by the National Assembly on August fourth and then enshrined in the Declaration of the Rights of Man and Citizen was highly abstract and general. It was, thus, less a blueprint than a set of architectural principles that could be applied to the construction of quite different sociopolitical orders. The ideological dynamics of the Revolution arose out of the elaboration of practical plans from these abstract revolutionary principles. It would be impossible, in a brief paper, to recount the ideological history of the French Revolution—and pointless besides, given the vast existing scholarship on the subject.[24] Instead, I will try to indicate four important general features of the Revolution's ideological dynamic: first, the progressive radicalization of ideology from 1789 to 1794; second, the production of rival ideological variants; third, the ideological restructuring of a vast range of social life;

[24] The great general histories of the Revolution include Albert Mathiez, *The French Revolution* (New York, 1964); Georges Lefebvre, *The French Revolution*, 2 vols. (New York, 1964); and Albert Soboul, *The French Revolution, 1787–1799*, trans. Alan Forest and Colin Jones (New York, 1975). See also, Crane Brinton, *The Jacobins* (New York, 1930); M. J. Sydenham, *The Girondins* (London, 1961); J. M. Thompson, *Robespierre and the French Revolution* (London, 1952); Albert Soboul, *Les sans-culottes parisiens en l'an II: Mouvement populaire et gouvernement révolutionnaire, 2 juin 1793–9 thermidor an II*, 2d ed. (Paris, 1962); the central section of this book has been translated into English as *The Parisian Sans-Culottes in the French Revolution, 1793–1794* (Oxford, 1964); Albert Mathiez, *Girondins et Montagnards* (Paris, 1930); *Etudes robespierristes*, 2d ed., 2 vols., (Paris, 1927); and *La réaction thermidorienne* (Paris, 1929).

and, finally, the emergence of politically crucial but quite unanticipated ideological outcomes.

Radicalization

The progressive radicalization of the Revolution from 1789 to the Terror of 1793–94 is one of the most familiar features of French Revolutionary history. Here Skocpol essentially accepts the now dominant interpretation which sees the outbreak of international war as the crucial factor leading to the Terror.[25] According to this interpretation, the exigencies of war—enforcing conscription, assuring supplies for the troops, maintaining discipline in the sometimes balky provinces—gave an advantage to the "Mo ntain" (the radical faction in the National Convention), which alone was willing to adopt the extreme measures necessary to save the Revolution. The result was the emergence of a virtual dictatorship by the Convention's Committee of Public Safety, staffed by Montagnards, with Robespierre as its leading figure. At the same time, the war crisis also fueled radicalization by mobilizing the sans-culottes— the common people of Paris—whose fanatic republicanism was colored by economic grievances against the rich. The sans-culottes and the Mountain forged an uneasy but powerful alliance, with the insurrectionary sans-culottes repeatedly purging or intimidating the moderate faction in the legislature, while the Mountain passed legislation guaranteeing low bread prices and permitted the sans-culottes to harass the wealthy. As long as the war crisis continued, the sans-culottes, the Mountain, and the Committee remained united. But with the definitive victories of the French armies in the spring of 1794, this radical alliance came apart, and in the end Robespierre was abandoned by the sans-culottes and was executed by vote of his erstwhile collaborators in the Convention. According to this interpretation, the radicalization of the Revolution resulted from a particular conjuncture of class struggles and legislative struggles under the goad of the war emergency.

Although the period of the Terror was also a period of tremendous ideological radicalism, most historians have treated ideology either in instrumental terms— as an arm of factional struggle—or as a reflection of the actors' class positions. Recently, however, François Furet has put forward a new interpretation of the ideology of the Terror that replaces the conventional class and political dynamic with an internal ideological dynamic. In *Penser la Révolution française*,[26] Furet denies the conventional explanation that the Terror was a response to the national peril,[27] and denies that class interests played a decisive role in revolutionary struggles for power.[28] Instead, he sees the Terror as developing inevitably out of the ideology of the Revolution. The revolutionaries had

---

[25] Skocpol, *States and Social Revolutions*, pp. 185–93. On the effects of the war on radicalization, see, e.g., Lefebvre, or Soboul, *The French Revolution*.

[26] François Furet, *Penser la Révolution française* (Paris, 1978), trans. Elborg Forster, as *Interpreting the French Revolution* (Cambridge, 1981).

[27] Furet, *Interpreting the French Revolution*, pp. 61–63.

[28] Ibid., p. 51.

borrowed from Rousseau a highly abstract notion of popular sovereignty which insisted on the unity of the general will. Furet points out that this notion of the general will could not be sustained without its Manichean double: the idea of an "aristocratic plot." If a united popular will did not always manifest itself clearly in the cacophony of revolutionary debate, this was not because of a real disunity, but because of the lies and deceptions of the people's enemies, who wished to restore the Old Regime by treachery. Given the primacy of this abstract notion of the unified people's will, dissent was understood not as a normal fact of political life, but as a plot, a manifestation of treason against the people and the Revolution, and dissenters had to be destroyed to maintain the virtue—indeed the very existence—of the revolutionary state. According to Furet, the Terror was generated by a continuing dialectic between the notion of the general will and the aristocratic plot, and was implicit in revolutionary ideology from the beginning. Although the Terror developed through the "circumstances" of the war and attending political struggles, its dynamic was essentially internal and ideological.[29]

In sharp contrast to Skocpol, Furet insists on the collective and anonymous character of this ideological dynamic. He goes to some length, for example, to argue that Robespierre's personal characteristics are irrelevant to his role in the Revolution. Robespierre was a dominant figure not because he was "the incorruptible," nor because of his unique political talents, but because he succeeded in "becoming an *embodiment*" of revolutionary ideology.[30] Revolutionary ideology itself, not Robespierre, was the significant historical actor. "The Revolution," as Furet puts it, "would speak *through* him. . . . He was the *mouthpiece* of its purest and most tragic discourse."[31] The discourse of the Jacobins during the terror, thus, was not a voluntary creation of Robespierre, or Saint-Just, or Marat, or any other revolutionary leader, but the completion of a semiotic circuit already operating since the summer of 1789.

This account of the radicalization of the Revolution marks an important advance. Its insistence on the anonymity of the ideological dynamic supplies a crucial corrective to Skocpol's interpretation. But it is marred by an extreme causal monism. For Furet, the ideological dynamic was not just autonomous, but absolute. Political power having been "vacated by the traditional authorities" in 1789,[32] it was not a class or a party but an *ideology* that seized power. "The Revolution," according to Furet, "placed the symbolic system at the center of political action";[33] it established "a world where mental representations of power governed all actions, and where a network of signs completely dominated political life."[34] From 1789 to 1794, ideology broke loose from social moorings, and its dynamic utterly dominated over social

[29] Ibid., p. 63.
[30] Ibid., p. 56.
[31] Ibid., p. 59, 61; emphasis mine.
[32] Ibid., p. 43.
[33] Ibid., p. 51.
[34] Ibid., p. 48.

and political existence. Class, warfare, and political factionalism were not constraints shaping ideological developments, but mere grist for the ideological mill. Not until the Thermidorian reaction did civil society reemerge with "its unwieldiness, its conflicting interests, and its divisions."[35] This claim that 1789 established a kind of semiotic despotism transcending all social constraints is untenable. Instead of demonstrating how the ideological dynamic interacted with class struggles, the international system, political alliances, and the exigencies of state building, Furet lapses into a causal monism worthy of the most economistic of Marxists. Surely an adequate explanation of the radicalization of the Revolution must admit *both* that class struggles and the exigencies of war pushed the Revolution to ever more radical measures, *and* that the nature of these measures and the way in which struggles and exigencies were interpreted and acted upon were largely determined by the structure of revolutionary ideology.

Ideological Variants

While the general drift of revolutionary ideology from 1789 to 1794 was certainly in a radical direction, this was the outcome not of some necessary elaboration of inherent tendencies, but of a succession of sharply contrasting rival ideological variants. These variants were elaborated by different political factions, each of which sketched out a different blueprint from a common set of revolutionary principles. There were Constitutional Monarchist, Girondin, Jacobin, and sans-culotte variants of revolutionary ideology—and, subsequently, Thermidorian and Napoleonic variants as well.

Each of these variants was developed in opposition to some other variant or variants. They consequently underwent continuous revision according to the vicissitudes of factional struggle. None of the factions ever succeeded in holding the field unchallenged, not even—perhaps least of all—the Jacobins. This, of course, meant that no faction was ever in a position to impose its own ideological blueprint on state and society. Thus, the question Skocpol poses as a test of the effect of ideology in the French Revolution—Does the Jacobin ideology accurately predict the outcomes of the Revolution?—turns out to be a very poor test. Even if it were possible in principle for a revolutionary group successfully to impose its ideological blueprint on a society (and I do not for a moment believe that it is) neither the Jacobins nor any other faction in the French Revolution held power long enough or firmly enough to have done so. The reshaping of state and society was the outcome of an evolving struggle between political factions, each of which was attempting to construct society according to its own evolving plan.

Each variant of revolutionary ideology can be conceptualized as a systematic transformation of existing rival variants. Thanks to the work of Albert Soboul, this process of transformation can be demonstrated most clearly for the sans-culottes.[36] The sans-culottes had two class-based predilections that colored

---

[35] Ibid., p. 78.

[36] Soboul, *The Parisian Sans-Culottes;* and Walter Markov and Albert Soboul, eds., *Die Sansculotten von Paris, Dokumente zur Geschichte der Volksbewegung, 1793– 1794* (Berlin, 1957).

virtually all of their thought and actions: a hostility to the rich that arose from their relative poverty, and a collectivism that, as I have argued elsewhere, derived from the corporate or guild values of the prerevolutionary urban *menu peuple*. The sans-culottes' transformations of revolutionary ideology can be seen, for instance, in their notions of "aristocracy" and of "the aristocratic plot." In the discourse of the Constitutional Monarchists, the distinction between "the aristocracy" and "the people" was above all legal: "aristocrats" were those who had privileges that separated them from the common people and the common law. In Girondin and Jacobin discourse, the distinction became increasingly political: "aristocrats" were those who opposed the Revolution, or who opposed the radicalization of the Revolution. The sans-culottes, while accepting both of these prior notions, added important nuances of their own: "aristocrats" were also the rich, who lived better than they and cared more about their gold than about the republic; or the haughty, who put on airs, wore breeches instead of the baggy trousers of the common people, wore powdered wigs, or spoke in a "distinguished" fashion.[37] The sans-culottes, in joining the common campaign against "aristocrats," redefined them in a way that reflected their own class resentments. A similar transformation took place in the sans-culottes' notion of the aristocratic plot. The Girondins and Jacobins alike attributed all types of political opposition and administrative difficulties to the aristocratic plot. But for the sans-culottes, the aristocratic plot was also responsible for high prices of foodstuffs. Aristocrats were systematically withholding grain from the market in order to starve out the patriotic sans-culottes and reduce them to slavery.[38]

The sans-culotte conception of the aristocratic plot was based on a distinctive conception of the economy. The economic policy of all revolutionary governments, whether headed by Constitutional Monarchists, Girondins, or Jacobins, was to establish free trade in all commodities and to leave individuals free to pursue their own self-interest—thereby releasing the natural laws of political economy whose operation would lead to prosperity and universal well-being. The sans-culottes opposed the establishment of free trade, but they based their agitation on an equally naturalistic political economy of their own. According to the sans-culottes, nature was bountiful, providing sufficient food to assure the subsistence of all. If prices rose so high as to reduce the people to hunger, this could only be the result of speculation by evil aristocrats, who hoarded grain in order to enrich themselves and to starve the true patriots. To ensure proper circulation of nature's bounty, it was necessary to institute price controls and to enforce them by a policy of terror against speculators.

The sans-culottes also transformed the revolutionary conception of property to make it fit with their conception of the economy. The Jacobins and Girondins saw property as the absolute possession of individuals, who were free to

[37] Soboul, *The Parisian Sans-Culottes*, pp. 19–23.

[38] Ibid., pp. 53–68. This idea was, in fact, a politicized version of the idea of a *"pacte de famine"*—a famine plot—which was already widespread among the popular classes during grain shortages of the Old Regime. Steven L. Kaplan, *The Famine Plot Persuasion in Eighteenth-Century France* (Philadelphia, 1982).

dispose of it as they saw fit. But the sans-culottes saw proprietors—especially proprietors of foodstuffs—as mere trustees of goods that in the final analysis belonged to the people as a whole.[39] Hence the people had the right to set prices at a level that would assure the subsistence of all. This view of property owners as trustees was closely related to a view of elected officials as "man-datories." The sans-culottes reduced the notion of political representation almost to the vanishing point. As opposed to the Girondins, who saw the individual citizen's chief role as casting a vote to choose members of a representative body, who would then rationally determine the general will and enact it into law, the sans-culottes believed that the people as a whole, acting through their local sectional assemblies, should constantly, collectively, and unanimously express their general will, maintaining continual surveillance over all their "mandatories" and immediately replacing those who deviated from the general will. Just as proprietors were continuously responsible to the whole of the people for the good and honest management of the means of collective subsistence, so the "mandatories" were continuously responsible for the correct expression of the collective will.[40] In both cases the sans-culottes were suspicious of mechanisms that alienated power from the direct control of the people, and they utilized terror as the means of enforcing what they saw as the general will.

This sketch makes it clear that the ideology of the sans-culottes was distinct from that of other revolutionary factions. But it also demonstrates that the sans-culotte ideology was constructed out of the same terminology and the same essential set of concepts: popular sovereignty, natural law, the general will, representation, virtue, property, aristocracy, the people. The ideologies of the sans-culottes, the Jacobins, the Girondins, and all other factions were each transformations of one another; they were formed in the continuing dialogue and conflict of mutual struggle, shaped out of common materials by the strategic choices, the presuppositions, and the interests of each faction. They can be seen as distinct but related explorations of the possibilities— and the constraints—inherent in the structures of French Revolutionary ideology.

Ideological Restructuring of Social Life

French Revolutionaries of all factions were acutely aware that the whole of social life was infused with ideological significance, and were therefore de-termined to restructure society from top to bottom and across the board. Indeed, I would insist that this totality of revolutionary ambition be included as part of any meaningful definition of "social revolution." The French,

---

[39] William H. Sewell, Jr., *Work and Revolution in France: The Language of Labor from the Old Regime to 1848* (Cambridge, 1980), pp. 112–13; and Soboul, *The Parisian Sans-Culottes,* pp. 464–67.

[40] Soboul, *The Parisian Sans-Culottes,* p. 109. For an analysis of the Girondin concept of representation, see Keith Michael Baker, *Condorcet: From Natural Philosophy to Social Mathematics* (Chicago, 1975), pp. 303–16.

Russian, and Chinese Revolutions were "social" not only because they included revolts from below and resulted in major changes in the class structure, but because they attempted to transform the entirety of people's social lives—their work, their religious beliefs and practice, their families, their legal systems, their patterns of sociability, even their experiences of space and time. Of course, the collapse of the Old Regime state made reforms of many social institutions imperative. The peasant uprisings had shattered rural property relations of the Old Regime; the events of the summer of 1789 had destroyed discipline in the army; and on the night of August fourth the National Assembly had abolished the tithes and tax privileges of the clergy and had dismantled the old legal and administrative system, with its venal magistrates and its widely varying municipal and provincial privileges and customs. The revolutionary legislators therefore had no choice but to elaborate reforms for all of these institutional sectors. Moreover, the exigencies of state consolidation and class struggles set important limits on how these reforms would be structured. The new system of rural property, for example, could not recognize seigneurial rights, and the new legal system could not be administered by magistrates whose purchased offices conferred nobility. Yet, as I will attempt to demonstrate, the particular shape of the reformed institutions was largely determined by revolutionary ideology.

Moreover, the revolutionaries were by no means content to reform only those areas of social life where the collapse of the Old Regime had destroyed existing institutional arrangements. Their revolution recognized a new metaphysical order; wherever existing social practices were based on the old metaphysics they had to be reconstituted in new rational and natural terms. This involved legislative intervention into many institutional spheres and social practices that had survived the upheavals of 1789 intact and whose continuation would have posed no threat to the consolidation of the revolutionary regime. Two examples were enactment of a new system of weights and measures and adoption of a new revolutionary calendar. The new metric system replaced a confused welter of local weights and measures with a uniform system based entirely on decimal calculation and facts of nature. The meter, the unit of length, was set at exactly one ten-millionth of the distance from the North Pole to the equator. Zero degrees and 100 degrees temperature were defined by the freezing and boiling points of pure water at sea level. Other measures were derived from these. The liter was defined as 100 cubic centimeters; the gram as the mass of a cubic centimeter of water at the melting point; the calorie as the quantity of heat required to raise a cubic centimeter of water one degree in temperature; and so on. Where the old systems had been arbitrary, clumsy, heterogeneous, and based on the tyranny of local custom, the new system measured out the world in terms at once uniform, rational, easily manipulable, and based on immutable facts of nature.[41]

[41] Legislation on the metric system is reprinted in John Hall Stewart, *A Documentary Survey of the French Revolution* (New York, 1951), pp. 503–6, 555–60, 754–58. How serious the legislators were about exact correspondence with nature is demonstrated

If the metric system was intended to impose a new naturalistic conception of quantity, the revolutionary calendar was intended to transform the population's experience of time. Except for the names of the months, which were Roman, the old calendar was entirely Christian. The years were counted from the birth of Jesus; the week of seven days was terminated by a day of worship; each day was associated with a different saint; and the yearly round of seasons was marked by religious festivals: Christmas, Lent, Easter, the Assumption, All Souls, and so on. The very passage of the days, thus, was a continuing reminder of the cosmic drama of Christianity. The revolutionary calendar, which was introduced in 1793 and remained in use for thirteen years, wiped out all this Christian symbolism. The "French Era" was proclaimed to have begun at the autumnal equinox on September 22, 1792, which coincided with the proclamation of the French Republic. Years were thenceforth to be numbered by their distance from this beginning, rather than from the birth of Christ. Weeks were increased to ten days, with each day denominated by its number—Primidi, Duodi, Tridi, and so forth, up to Decadi, the day of rest, which now came every ten days rather than every seven. (The Republic was, among other things, a speed-up.) Three Decadis (also the term for the ten-day week) made up a revolutionary month, and the remaining five days each year were set aside as a Republican festival, called the *sans-culottides,* to commemorate the patriotic deeds of the sans-culottes. The months were named for their natural climatic characteristics: Vendémaire, Brumaire, and Frimaire, the months of vintage, fog, and frost (September 22–December 20); Nivose, Pluviose, and Ventose, the months of snow, rain, and wind (December 21–March 20); Germinal, Floréal, and Prairial, the months of germination, flowers, and meadows (March 21–June 18); and Messidor, Thermidor, and Fructidor, the months of harvest, heat, and fruit (June 19–September 16). Finally, each day of the year was given the name of a plant (turnip, chicory, heather), of some other product of nature (honey, cork, beeswax), or of an animal (hog, ox, cricket), just as each day under the old calendar had been the day of a particular saint. The Decadis, the days of rest, were named for implements of labor that were used the other nine days to transform natural objects into useful goods—pickaxe, shovel, mattock, and so on.[42] This revolutionary calendar established an entirely new framework for reckoning the passage of time, one that was based on, and therefore called to mind, nature, reason, and virtuous republican deeds.

Reforms of weights and measures and of the calendar were only the beginning of the revolutionaries' wide-ranging attempts to recast the social order—and indeed the physical order—in the new metaphysical mold. The revolutionaries reformed educational and scientific institutions. They eliminated earlier forms of address, substituting the universal terms *citoyen* and *citoyenne* for the

---

by the law of 19 Frimaire, Year VIII (December 10, 1799) where the previously decreed length of the meter was lengthened slightly to fit the latest measurements of the meridian (p. 757).

[42] Ibid., pp. 507–15.

hierarchy of status-bound terms from the Old Regime. They redefined marriage as a purely civil contract, rather than a sacrament, and therefore permitted divorce. They made birth, marriage, and death civic rather than religious events, and required that they be duly enregistered by the civil authorities. They changed the punishment meted out to criminals, among other things making decapitation the universal form of capital punishment rather than an exclusive privilege of the nobility. The list goes on and on. These reforms absorbed an enormous amount of the revolutionaries' energy and made significant contributions to the overall pattern of revolutionary outcomes. And they are incomprehensible except as a result of revolutionary ideology.

If many of the revolutionary reforms seem to be explicable in purely ideological terms, ideology also had a role in shaping even those reforms which were powerfully influenced by class struggles and struggles for consolidation of the state. One example is the reform of territorial administration. The provinces, which were the units of territorial administration under the Old Regime, were stripped of their sundry privileges on the night of August fourth. Before long, however, the provinces themselves were abolished and replaced by new units called departments. Unlike the provinces, which varied from immense and internally differentiated territories such as Languedoc or Burgundy to tiny and homogeneous ones such as Foix or Aunis, the departments were drawn up to be approximately equal in size and population. The uniformity of the departments was motivated in part by the goal of state consolidation; homogeneous territorial units made possible a simpler and more efficient state apparatus. But the motivations were also ideological. The geographic uniformity of the departments reiterated and established the equality and uniformity of citizens' rights everywhere in the French nation. Moreover, the new departments were named for natural features of the territory—the High Alps, the Low Alps, and the Jura; the Seine, the Garonne, the Loire, and the Moselle; the Moors, the mouths of the Rhone, the North Coast, Land's End, and so on.[43] The administrative units of the French state were henceforth "natural" divisions of the territory, not an accumulation of dynastic accidents.

The role of ideology was equally important in the National Assembly's disastrous attempt to reform the Church. On the night of August fourth, representatives of the clergy renounced tithes and tax privileges, thus necessitating important reforms in Church organization. But it was by no means inevitable that these reforms would drive the Church into counterrevolution. The reform of the Church revolved around three issues: finances, church government, and oaths.[44] The financial issues were the most practically exigent, but also gave rise to the least controversy. Since tithes had been abolished, some new means of supporting the clergy had to be devised. The Assembly's solution was to make clergy paid state officials. This new demand on the

---

[43] Ibid., pp. 137–41.
[44] For an excellent brief discussion of these reforms, see M. J. Sydenham, *The French Revolution* (New York, 1965), pp. 74–78.

public budget was more than compensated for by expropriation of the Church's vast landholdings. Since the old taxes were virtually uncollectible and new taxes had not yet been imposed, sale of Church lands was the only practical means available to the state to finance the costly reforms of the early Revolution. The expropriation of Church land was accepted with surprisingly little protest— in part, perhaps, because the state salaries for parish priests were considerably more generous than their prerevolutionary earnings.

Reforms in Church government were derived more from ideological than from practical political necessity. Their essential features were a redefinition of parishes and episcopal sees to make them correspond to the communes and departments of the new civil administrative system, and the provision that priests and bishops, like other governmental officials, were to be elected by popular suffrage. The reasoning of the National Assembly on this issue is clear enough: if priests and bishops were to become public servants, they should be chosen by the same methods as legislators, judges, mayors, and councilmen. This proposal posed serious problems for priests, however, since it seemed to require an obedience to popular will that contradicted their obedience to bishops and the pope. Reforms of Church government, therefore, threatened to drive a wedge between the Church and the Revolution in a way that expropriation of Church lands did not.

The issue that precipitated an open break, however, was the far more abstract, purely ideological, issue of oaths. This issue went straight to the core of the metaphysical transformation of 1789. The religious vow or oath had been an essential metaphysical constituent of Old Regime society. An oath was a crucial part of the royal coronation; guild members swore an oath upon entering the body of guild masters; it was the vows taken in ordination that transformed laymen into members of the First Estate. These oaths were sworn to God, and were therefore permanent; as the metaphor put it, they made an indelible impression on the soul of the swearer. It was largely through the medium of religious oaths that spirit structured the social order of the Old Regime. The Revolution based the social order on reason and natural law rather than divine spirit, on dissoluble contracts rather than permanent religious oaths. It therefore could not tolerate oaths that claimed to establish perpetual obligation or that recognized an authority superior to the French nation. Thus it dissolved all monasteries and convents and released monks and nuns from their "perpetual" vows. (It was this same impulse that led to making marriage a purely civil and dissoluble contract rather than a sacrament.)

Finally, the National Assembly, in 1791, imposed a civic oath—a kind of public vow of adherence to the social contract—on all priests. The civic oath was a simple and superficially innocuous affair: "I swear to be faithful to the Nation and the Law, and the King, and to maintain with all my power the constitution of the kingdom."[45] The problem was that it seemed to a majority of the clergy to contradict the oath of obedience to ecclesiastical

---

[45] Stewart, p. 233.

authority, and therefore ultimately to the pope, which they had sworn upon ordination. They therefore refused to take the oath, were suspended from their parishes, and were driven either into exile or into open defiance of the Revolution. The attempt to impose the civic oath on the clergy was one of the greatest political disasters of the Revolution. The alienation of the clergy, whose prestige and influence in many rural parishes was enormous, also alienated much of the rural population. It created a continual source of disorders—clandestine masses, baptisms, and marriages performed by nonjuring priests, riots when "constitutional" priests were introduced into parishes, and so on. In the west of France, these conflicts led to the famous Vendée rebellion of 1793, which plunged the Republic into civil war at the same time that the allied monarchical forces were advancing on Paris.[46] The attempt to reform the Church, hence, set in motion one of the major dynamics that led to political polarization, radicalization, and the Terror. More clearly than any other episode of the Revolution, perhaps, it demonstrates the importance of ideology as a determinant of the course of Revolutionary history.

Unanticipated Ideological Outcomes

It should be clear by now that the content of revolutionary ideology is crucial to any adequate explanation of the course of the French Revolution. But this does not exhaust the role of ideology in the Revolution. Enlightenment political ideology was itself transformed by the struggles of the Revolution, and among the most important (indeed, world-historically important) outcomes of the Revolution were certain new ideological discourses. Like many of the political outcomes Skocpol discusses, these ideological outcomes were shaped by the exigencies of revolutionary struggles, and therefore were not and could not have been foreseen by revolutionary actors.

One of the most important ideological products of the Revolution was the idea of revolution itself. Before 1789, the meaning of the word "revolution" in political discourse, was, in the words of the Académie Française, "vicissitude or great change in fortune in the things of the world." As an example of its use the dictionary gave the following sentence: "The gain or loss of a battle causes great revolutions in a state."[47] A revolution was, thus, any sudden change in a state—anything from a fundamental reordering of a state's constitution to the mere loss of a battle or fall of a ministry. Before 1789, the word also had connotations of recurrence. The political philosophers of the age were fond of observing that all states are subject to revolutions in the course of time—that is, to unforeseeable changes in fortune, in circumstances, or in their constitutions. Revolution, as the word was used in the Old Regime, was a recurring fact of political life, an inevitable result of the instability of all human institutions.

It was the events of 1789 to 1794 that introduced the modern notion of revolution to the world. Revolution came to mean not any sudden change in

---

[46] The best account is Charles Tilly, *The Vendée* (Cambridge, Mass., 1964).

[47] *Le dictionnaire de l'Académie françoise*, 2 vols. (Paris, 1694).

the affairs of the state, but something much more specific: the overthrow of one government by the people and its replacement by another government. Revolution was henceforth inseparable from the exercise of popular sovereignty. (It is only in the context of this definition that the modern distinction between revolution and coup d'état makes sense.) Before 1789, a revolution was something that happened to the state—it was unpredictable, a kind of chance occurrence that was bound to happen now and again, but not something that could be foreseen and planned for. The decisive interventions of the Parisian people during 1789—the taking of the Bastille in July of 1789 and the removal of the king from Versailles to Paris in the "October days"— were in fact quite unplanned; they were revolutions in the old sense. But they gave rise to a concept of popular insurrection that made possible deliberate and concerted uprisings later—the Revolution of August 10, 1792 that deposed the king, and the insurrection that purged the Girondins from the Convention on June 2, 1793.

After 1789, revolution became something that people did to the state consciously and with forethought. This new concept of revolution had an enormous impact on subsequent history. Protecting the state against revolution became one of the cardinal concerns of governments, and, at the same time, some people became self-conscious planners and fomenters of revolution. Before 1789 there could be revolutions, but the nouns "revolutionary" or "revolutionist" did not exist. It was only after 1789 that self-conscious revolutionaries made their entrance onto the stage of the world and, consequently, into the world's dictionaries. Skocpol rightly points out that both states and revolutionaries have vastly overestimated the latter's powers. With rare exceptions "revolutions are not made; they come."[48] But there can be no denying that the idea of revolution as a planned event has transformed politics—not only in France, but in the entire world.

Another crucial ideological discourse produced by the French Revolution was Nationalism. The idea of the nation was central to the political theory of the Revolution from the beginning. Originally it was bound up with the theory of the social contract. The nation was the body created by the social contract. Its bonds of solidarity were voluntarily created and were maintained by formal political and legal institutions. Sieyès's definition of the nation was typical: "a body of associates living under common laws and represented by the same legislature."[49] This conception of the nation suffered from one very serious weakness: it was highly abstract and rational, and therefore proved incapable of inspiring passionate emotional commitment to the state on the part of the mass of citizens. This was a crucial problem once war began, since the government had to motivate the citizens to take up arms and risk death in defense of the Revolution. The traditional focus of emotional

---

[48] Skocpol, quoting Wendell Phillips, *States and Social Revolutions*, p. 17. The Iranian revolution has made Skocpol question the universality of this claim. Theda Skocpol, "Rentier State and Shi'a Islam in the Iranian Revolution," *Theory and Society* 11 (1982): 265–84.

[49] Sieyès, p. 126.

loyalty to the state had been the monarch. But the king was already in disgrace and in virtual captivity when the war broke out in 1792; he could not serve as a symbol of loyalty to the Revolution. In their attempts to raise the ardor of the populace, the revolutionaries made plenty of appeals to the social contract, the law, liberty, and the constitution. But on the whole these proved less effective than invocations of the *Patrie*.

"*La Patrie*" was a complex notion. Originally signifying the land where one had been born, during the eighteenth century it came to be linked to the idea of liberty. To be a "patriot" by 1789 meant not only to love one's native country but to love liberty as well.[50] The *Patrie* was, consequently, an ideal emotional symbol of the revolution, associating the primordial loyalties of birth with the revolutionary regime and revolutionary ideals. Over time, however, the *Patrie* or Nation came to be defined increasingly in terms of land and blood. An example was the emergence of the idea that France was endowed with "natural frontiers" (the Alps, the Mediterranean, the Pyrenees, the Atlantic, the Channel, and the Rhine)—an idea that led the French Republic to annex the entire West Bank of the Rhine with its vast German- and Flemish-speaking population as an integral part of France. But the definition of the nation in terms of land and blood went farthest in Germany, where French nationalism and French domination led to an explosion of nationalist thought and agitation, and where the liberal connotations of the nation were much less salient. In Germany the nation could be thought of as a primordial fact of nature prior to all social contracts or constitutions. For example, by 1813 the German nationalist Josef Görres could speak of the "common tie of blood relationship" that "united all members of the nation. . . . This instinctive urge which binds all members into a whole is the law of nature and takes precedence of all artificial treaties. . . . The voice of nature in ourselves warns us and points to the chasm between us and the alien."[51] As this quotation makes clear, the form of nationalism that became ubiquitous in the nineteenth and twentieth centuries was already present by the end of the Revolutionary and Napoleonic wars.

Two features of this emerging nationalist discourse should be stressed. First, for all of its contrast with the political ideas of the Enlightenment, it, too, was based on the Enlightenment's naturalistic metaphysics. It defined the nation and citizenship in terms of the natural substances land and blood, and it conceived of the loyalty of the national land and blood as natural. Second, it had no notable theorists. It was an anonymous discourse that arose out of the demands of the situation and the possibilities of preexisting ideology rather than being formulated systematically by some theoretician.

---

[50] Jacques Godechot, "Nation, patrie, nationalisme et patriotisme en France au XVIIIe siècle," *Annales historiques de la Révolution française* 206 (1971): 481–501; Robert R. Palmer, "The National Idea in France before the Revolution," *Journal of the History of Ideas* 1 (1940): 95–111.

[51] Quotes in Hans Kohn, *Prelude to Nation-States: The French and German Experience, 1789–1815* (Princeton, N.J., 1967), pp. 294–95.

Nationalism and the new concept of revolution were certainly two of the most significant unanticipated ideological outcomes of the French Revolution, but they were not the only ones. The concepts of political terror and of what Marxists eventually dubbed the "vanguard revolutionary party" were both produced in the years 1789 to 1794. Conservative political thought was a product of the Revolution no less than revolutionary political thought. The horrifying example of the French Revolution was the inspiration for the theories of Burke, Bonald, and de Maistre, and for the conservative political regimes of all the European states of the Restoration era. Socialism, as I have argued elsewhere, must be seen as a somewhat more distant response to the social and ideological changes introduced by the French Revolution.[52] The French Revolution also produced a new consciousness of history and a new concept of the social order; it stands at the origin of modern social and historical thinking.[53] The French Revolution was an ideological event of the first magnitude. If anything, its ideological outcomes were even more important than its class or state-building outcomes.

CONCLUSION

What implications does this account of ideology in the French Revolution have for the comparative analysis of revolutions? I think it suggests four things. First, that ideology plays a crucial role in revolutions, both as cause and as outcome. Second, that to understand this role, we must adopt a much more robust conception of ideology than Skocpol's — one that treats ideology as anonymous, collective, and constitutive of social order. Third, that this conception makes it possible to analyze ideology in a fashion consonant with Skocpol's "structural" approach. And fourth, that such an analysis suggests hypotheses that could profitably be investigated comparatively. The first three propositions I shall take as sufficiently demonstrated. The fourth needs some elaboration.

Although the specific ideological developments of the French Revolution cannot be expected to recur elsewhere, the French case suggests a number of things to look for in other revolutions. Did other old-regime states contain such deep ideological contradictions? (Perhaps the existence of a reforming bureaucracy in old-regime Russia or of western-educated officials in old-regime China were signs of this kind of contradiction.) Were political crises more likely to develop into social revolutions where such ideological contradictions existed? How common were metaphysical revolutions of the sort that occurred in France in August of 1789? (The tremendous artistic and cultural ferment that followed the Bolshevik Revolution certainly suggests something of the kind in the Russian Revolution.) Were revolutions that included such metaphysical transformations likely to be more radical or more

---

[52] Sewell, *Work and Revolution in France.*

[53] Here it is significant that the first uses of the term "social science" were in France in the 1790s (Keith Michael Baker, "The Early History of the Term 'Social Science,' " *Annals of Science* 20 [1969]: 211–26).

social than those that did not? Under what conditions did revolutions generate a large number of ideological variants? What determined the extent to which revolutionaries attempted to restructure a wide range of social life? How commonly did such attempts lead to resistance that crucially affected the course and outcome of the revolution? (Collectivization of agriculture in the Soviet Union appears on the surface to be such a case.) How did the struggles and exigencies of the revolution lead to the development of unanticipated ideological discourses? Why did some revolutions (such as the Russian) lead to an extended ideological freeze, while others (such as the French and the Chinese) led to the continued production of new ideological variants for decades after the apparent consolidation of the revolution? Such questions are no less susceptible to comparative study than the questions Skocpol asked about old regime state and agrarian structures, international pressures, peasant uprisings, and processes of state consolidation. They certainly belong on the agenda for future comparative histories of revolution.

Cultural Idioms and Political Ideologies in the Revolutionary Reconstruction of State Power: A Rejoinder to Sewell

Theda Skocpol

It is a rare pleasure in intellectual life to have one's work confronted in a simultaneously appreciative and challenging fashion. I am indebted to William Sewell for offering an analytically sophisticated and historically grounded critique of the way *States and Social Revolutions* addresses the problem of ideology.[1] He rightly points out that I treated the issues too cursorily and relied upon a notion of ideologies as deliberate blueprints for change that leaves untouched many of the ways in which ideas may affect the course of revolutions. Sewell offers instead "a much more robust conception of ideology . . . that treats ideology as anonymous, collective, and constitutive of social order."[2] According to Sewell, this way of understanding ideology is consonant with the overall structural analysis of *States and Social Revolutions,* and it can guide us toward wise questions and answers about the role of ideological transformations in the French Revolution and beyond.

If *States and Social Revolutions* "provoked" Sewell to write the preceding article, his able discussion has in turn encouraged me to think through more carefully how the analysis of ideologies should—and should not—be incorporated into future historical and comparative work on revolutions. Perhaps surprisingly, given my reputation for "structural determinism," I shall suggest that we need a less "anonymous" approach than Sewell advocates. I certainly agree with Sewell that culture is "transpersonal," but I want to register profound reservations about the use of anthropological conceptions of cultural systems in analyzing the contributions made by cultural idioms and ideological activities to revolutionary transformations.

A Nonintentionalist and State-centered Approach to Revolutions

Few aspects of *States and Social Revolutions* have been more misunderstood than its call for a "nonvoluntarist," "structuralist" approach to explaining social revolutions. "Nonintentionalist at the macroscopic level" might have been a better way to label my approach. For the point is simply that no single acting group, whether a class or an ideological vanguard, deliberately shapes the complex and multiply determined conflicts that bring about revolutionary

---

[1] Theda Skocpol, *States and Social Revolutions: A Comparative Analysis of France, Russia, and China* (Cambridge, 1979).

[2] All quotations from Sewell from William H. Sewell, Jr., "Ideologies and Social Revolutions: Reflections on the French Case," in this issue.

This essay originally appeared in the *Journal of Modern History* 57 (March 1985).

crises and outcomes. The French Revolution was not made by a rising capitalist bourgeoisie or by the Jacobins; the Russian Revolution was not made by the industrial proletariat or even by the Bolshevik party. If the purpose is to explain in cross-nationally relevant terms why revolutions break out in some times and places and not others, and why they accomplish some changes and not others, we cannot achieve this by theorizing as if some grand intentionality governs revolutionary processes. This point was (and is) worth making, because much social-scientific and historiographical work on revolutions is pervaded by untenable intentionalist assumptions. Sewell and I apparently agree that these misleading assumptions need to be rooted out.

Rather than seeking to ground the causes of social revolutions and their outcomes in hypostatized interests or outlooks, *States and Social Revolutions* focused on "structures," or patterned relationships beyond the manipulative control of any single group or individual. Such social structures, understood in historically concrete ways, give us the key to the conflicts among groups that play themselves out in revolutions, producing results outside of the intentions of any single set of actors. Yet, of course, social structures—such as landlord-peasant relationships, or ties that bind monarchs and administrative officials—are not themselves actors. They are, as Sewell rightly says, both enabling and constraining, and they are produced and reproduced only through the conscious action of the concrete groups and individuals that relate to one another in the relevant patterned ways. Since the historical case studies of *States and Social Revolutions* are replete with groups acting for material, ideal, and power goals, it should be apparent that I never meant to read intentional group action out of revolutions—only to situate it theoretically for the explanatory purposes at hand.

While the nonintentionalism of *States and Social Revolutions* has frequently been misunderstood or misrepresented, the book's substantive theoretical message has been more obvious to readers. Class structures and conflicts, I argued, are not the only or the basic "structural" keys to revolutionary causes or outcomes. Analysts need to focus more directly on the international relationships of states to one another, and on the relationships of old-regime rulers and revolutionary state builders to dominant and subordinate classes. Class conflicts as such, especially conflicts pitting peasants against landlords and existing agrarian property relations, certainly entered into the processes of revolution in France, Russia, and China. But one must constantly focus on the direct and indirect interactions of class struggles with the primary conflicts in these revolutions—the conflicts surrounding the breakdown of the administrative and coercive organizations of the old-regime monarchical states, and the subsequent, often highly protracted conflicts over the kinds of new state organizations that would be successfully consolidated in the place of the prerevolutionary regimes. Thus, in France, peasant revolts in 1789 both grew out of and accelerated the collapse of monarchical absolutism. And rural property relations—indeed, all property relations in revolutionary France—were practically and legally transformed from 1789 through the Napoleonic settlement, not only according to the vagaries of class struggles but also in relation to the needs, opportunities, and constraints faced by successive sets of political leaders seeking to reconstruct the French polity and the administrative and military apparatuses of a centralized national state.

REVOLUTIONS AS IDEOLOGICAL REMAKINGS OF THE WORLD

Perhaps it was unfortunate that I was so preoccupied in *States and Social Revolutions* with reworking class analysis in relation to a state-centered understanding of revolutions. As a result, I did less than I might have done to rework in analogous ways an alternative strand of theorizing about social revolutions—one that sees them not as class conflicts but as ideologically inspired projects to remake social life in its entirety.

One modern scholar who takes this approach is Michael Walzer. He defines revolutions as "conscious attempts to establish a new moral and material world and to impose, or evoke, radically new patterns of day-to-day conduct. A holy commonwealth, a republic of virtue, communist society—these are the goals revolutionaries seek."[3] Walzer explains varying revolutionary outcomes by analyzing the relationships between the classes that revolt against old regimes and the ideologically inspired vanguards that attempt to use terror to construct revolutionary utopias under their own hegemony. In his view, some modern revolutions—the ones he likes better, such as the English and the French—have resulted in "Thermidor," in which the revolutionary class was able to depose the ideological vanguard. Others—especially communist-led revolutions in countries with peasant majorities—have resulted in the permanent institutionalization of vanguard power through continuing moralistic and coercive efforts to remake the world according to an ideological vision.

Sewell also understands the essence of revolution as an ideologically inspired attempt to remake all of social and cultural life. Witness his description of the night of August 4, 1789: "The representatives' rapture . . . [was] understandable: they were participating in what seemed to them a regeneration of the world." Sewell clearly joins the historical actors he describes in this perception. "The regeneration was metaphysical as well as institutional," he says. From August 1789 on, the French peasantry, one class apparently not gripped by Enlightenment ideas, drops out of the story of the French Revolution, which thenceforth becomes in Sewell's telling "the elaboration of Enlightenment metaphysical principles into a new revolutionary social and political structure." To be sure, various factions and social strata, from the Constitutional Monarchists to the Girondins to the Jacobins to the sansculottes, continue to contend. But they are simply elaborating different ideological variants from a shared set of revolutionary principles. For August 4, 1789 "marked the end of . . . the tension between Enlightenment and corporate

---

[3] Michael Walzer, "A Theory of Revolution," *Marxist Perspectives*, no. 5 (Spring 1979), p. 30.

monarchical principles," and from then on the "Enlightenment idiom became the dominant idiom of government," creating "a new framework of rhetoric and action and a new set of political issues that dominated the subsequent unfolding of the revolution."

It is worth underlining how and why Sewell's understanding of revolution as an ideological remaking of the world contrasts to Walzer's intentionalist version of this perspective. Sewell does not claim that a particular ideological vanguard took control on August 4 and tried to remake France after that. His argument is more "impersonal," "anonymous," "collective" than Walzer's. Because Walzer's theory of revolutions is so thoroughly intentionalist, he is forced to designate a particular group as the carrier of the ideological project to remake the world in each revolution. For France, he designates those Jacobins who conducted the Terror. But what are we then to do with the other political leaderships and groups that made ideological arguments in the French Revolution? According to Sewell, what came to the fore in August 1789 was a new ideological idiom, a new set of principles of discourse and action, under the aegis of which many contending groups then proceeded to wage political struggles. In contrast to Walzer, Sewell's approach has the important advantage that we can talk about contending and successive "ideological variants" developed by different groups of actors.

THE DISADVANTAGES OF AN ANTHROPOLOGICAL UNDERSTANDING OF CULTURAL SYSTEMS

But Sewell's approach also has important drawbacks, centering on the unconvincing attempt he makes to portray August 1789 as *the* ideologically pivotal moment of the French Revolution. If Sewell's understanding of ideology improves upon Walzer by allowing for many groups to elaborate related ideological discourses, it suffers in being unrealistically totalistic and synchronous. This reflects what I will label Sewell's "cultural system" understanding of ideology. As he puts it, ideology is "constitutive of social order," and "if society is understood as ideologically constituted," then "it is not enough to treat ideology as a possible causal factor explaining some portion of the change wrought by revolution." Instead, "the replacement of one socio-ideological order by another . . . becomes a crucial dimension of the change that needs to be explained" for any given revolution.

Who thinks about cultural meanings in this way? Who treats culture as "constitutive of social order"—which means fusing into one concept both social relations and meaningful discourse pertaining to a social world holistically conceived? Anthropologists, of course. Their fieldwork experiences and disciplinary tasks have given a certain plausibility to this conception. For they have immersed themselves in the social activities and the talk of strange communities for relatively short periods of time and then come back to tell Western academics what they learned. Analysis of cultural systems has been their way to do this. Lately, due above all to the inspired writing and broad intellectual influence of Clifford Geertz, anthropological approaches to cultural analysis have been seeping into neighboring disciplines.[4] No discipline has been more eager than history to borrow, adapt, and deploy Geertzian approaches to cultural analysis.[5] And William Sewell, himself profoundly influenced by Geertz, has been one of the most able agents of this cross-disciplinary intellectual movement.[6]

Dangerous pitfalls lurk when students of complex, changing, highly stratified sociopolitical orders rely upon anthropological ideas about cultural systems.[7] It is all too easy to suppose the existence of integrated patterns of shared meanings, total pictures of how society does and should work. Given the impossibility of face-to-face fieldwork contact with diverse societal groups acting and arguing in real time, there is an inevitable temptation to read entire systems of meaning into particular documents—such as the Abbé Sieyès's *What Is the Third Estate?* Most risky of all, one is tempted to treat fundamental cultural and ideological change as the synchronous and complete replacement of one society-wide cultural system by another. Thus: on the night of August 4, corporate monarchical political culture was swept from the field and the logic of the Enlightenment took over.

TOWARD A MORE HISTORICALLY GROUNDED APPROACH

The influence of "the Enlightenment" on "the French Revolution" is hardly a new historiographical topic; generations of historians (and others) have weighed in on this question and no doubt will continue to do so.[8] As I survey the ongoing debates, certain substantive conclusions seem tentatively established and particular ways of posing the issues seem more fruitful than others. Surely the whole drift of research and debate has been away from any inclination to conflate the Enlightenment—a transnational intellectual movement dealing with basically metaphysical issues—with the French Revolution as a series of social and political conflicts that occurred in only one of the many nations affected by, and contributing to, the Enlightenment.[9] Many cultural changes

[4] For a widely read statement of this approach, see Clifford Geertz, *The Interpretation of Cultures* (New York, 1973).

[5] See Ronald G. Walters, "Signs of the Times: Clifford Geertz and the Historians," *Social Research* 47 (Autumn 1980): 537–56.

[6] See the discussion of history and cultural anthropology in William H. Sewell, Jr., *Work and Revolution in France* (Cambridge, 1980), pp. 10–13.

[7] I do not mean to imply that anthropologists cannot do an excellent job of analyzing ideologies in complex societies. An exemplary piece of work on cultural idioms and ideological variants in a revolutionized nation is Michael M. J. Fischer, *Iran: From Religious Dispute to Revolution* (Cambridge, Mass., 1980). My remarks here are in part an attempt to conceptualize the kind of approach Fischer uses so that it can be generalized to other historical contexts.

[8] A (somewhat dated) overview of generations of historiography on this topic appears in William F. Church, ed., *The Influence of the Enlightenment on the French Revolution*, 2d ed. (Lexington, Mass., 1974). Recent scholarship includes the important works by Keith Baker and Daniel Roche cited by Sewell. See also the useful discussion in Robert Darnton, "In Search of the Enlightenment: Recent Attempts to Create a Social History of Ideas," *Journal of Modern History* 43, no. 1 (March 1971): 113–32.

[9] See Roy Porter and Mikulas Teich, eds., *The Enlightenment in National Context* (Cambridge, 1981).

that occurred in France around the time of the Revolution might well have occurred in one way or another anyway; thus a careful analyst has no warrant to attribute them to "revolutionary" anything. Meanwhile, the particular versions of Enlightenment ideas elaborated in Old Regime and revolutionary France were affected by the political institutions and conflicts of the time, just as the politics was influenced by Enlightenment ideas. Yet there was no simple fusion of Enlightenment and politics. Given the nature of Enlightenment thought itself, there hardly could have been. Again and again, intellectual historians have pointed out the variety of implicit and explicit political views held by the *philosophes,* including Rousseau, and have underlined their reluctance to prescribe any particular political reforms or institutional arrangements.[10] Sewell knows all of this, and reports some of it. But does he realize how problematic these realities make his attempt to turn "Enlightenment principles" into a governing "ideology" that could structure political arguments and actions in revolutionary France from August 1789?

Historians, sociologists, and political scientists are not well served by supposing that sets of ideas—whether intellectual productions or cultural frameworks of a more informally reasoned sort—are "constitutive of social order." Rather, multiple cultural idioms coexist, and they arise, decline, and intermingle in tempos that need to be explored by intellectual and sociocultural historians. At any given time, cultural idioms are drawn upon by concretely situated actors as they seek to make sense of their activities and of themselves in relation to other actors. To be sure, it will make a difference which idiom or mixture of idioms is available to be drawn upon by given groups. Indeed, the very definitions of groups, their interests, and their relations to one another will be influenced by cultural idioms. But the choices and uses of available idioms—and the particular potentials within them that are elaborated—will also be influenced by the social and political situations of the acting groups, and the tasks they need to accomplish in relation to one another.

I prefer to reserve the term "ideology" for idea systems deployed as self-conscious political arguments by identifiable political actors. Ideologies in this sense are developed and deployed by particular groups or alliances engaged in temporally specific political conflicts or attempts to justify the use of state power. Cultural idioms have a longer-term, more anonymous, and less partisan existence than ideologies. When political actors construct ideological arguments for particular action-related purposes, they invariably use or take account of available cultural idioms, and those idioms may structure their arguments in partially unintended ways. Yet they may also develop new ideological arguments in response to the exigencies of the unfolding political struggle itself. By thus separately conceptualizing "cultural idioms" and "ideologies," one can hope to attend to the interplay of the nonintentionalist

[10] Arguments along this line appear in Darnton; Alfred Cobban, "The Enlightenment and the French Revolution," pp. 305–15 in *Aspects of the Eighteenth Century,* ed. Earl R. Wasserman (Baltimore, 1965); and Norman Hampson, *The Enlightenment* (London, 1968).

and intentionalist aspects of ideas in revolutions much as I tried to do in *States and Social Revolutions* by examining class and state structures in relation to the goals and capacities of acting groups.[11]

Substantively speaking, the analysis of cultural idioms and ideologies in social revolutions deserves treatment analogous to the analysis of class relations and class conflicts: both phenomena must be studied in relation to the central drama of the breakdown and rebuilding of state organizations. Sewell asserts that a huge range of reforms introduced by French revolutionaries "are incomprehensible except as a result of [Enlightenment] revolutionary ideology." I do not agree (and I am not even exactly sure what this statement means). Although many reforms were indeed conceptualized in the light of certain understandings of Enlightenment ideals, the reforms figured in ongoing political struggles and typically helped (as much as possible in given circumstances) to strengthen the authority of the French national state in relation to the Church and particular private groups ranging from the wealthy and privileged to local communities. How, for example, could we understand the introduction of the revolutionary calendar—a reform that Sewell labels "purely ideological"—outside of this political context?

From the foregoing perspective, issues of political ideology in the French Revolution need to be approached somewhat differently from the way Sewell approaches them. Enlightenment principles were only one of the various cultural idioms that coexisted in France from the Old Regime through the Revolution, and there certainly was never any pivotal moment at which the Enlightenment became embodied in an overarching political ideology (or even a system of ideological variants) that took over French politics. The Old Regime itself (as Sewell acknowledges at points and forgets at others) was not associated with a single overarching ideological system. Within ruling circles, corporatist, Catholic, and absolutist principles coexisted with various borrowings from the Enlightenment; and popular groups had their own "little cultures," blends of even more diverse elements tied to particular localities and occupational communities.

After a decade of ideologically passionate revolutionary struggles, moreover, eclecticism continued to prevail in the official imagery of the French new regime. Napoleon deliberately melded together bureaucratic personnel and symbols from all political factions under the aegis of a highly generalized French nationalism. Unlike Sewell, I see no basis for attributing "nationalism" (even unintentionally) to some Enlightenment-inspired cultural code, and it

---

[11] Although he does not use the terminology I offer here, an example of the kind of analysis I have in mind appears in Alvin Gouldner, "Stalinism: A Study of Internal Colonialism," pp. 209–59 in *Political Power and Social Theory*, vol. 1, ed. Maurice Zeitlin (Greenwich, Conn., 1980). Marxism is treated as a cultural idiom that predisposed all of its adherents against viewing the peasantry as an autonomous or modernizing force. Then Gouldner shows how Stalinist ideology, forged under particular Russian circumstances in the 1920s, took the *potential* antipeasant bias in Marxism to a violent extreme. Gouldner also discusses how, under very different circumstances of political struggle in relation to Confucian cultural legacies, the Chinese Communists came to see the peasantry in a more positive light as objects of revolutionary persuasion.

seems to me that the most important ideological fact about Napoleonic rule was precisely its deliberate amalgamation of nationalism with contradictory strands of revolutionary political symbolism in order to help stabilize a bureaucratic-authoritarian state without the aid of an hegemonic political party.

As for the struggles of the revolution itself, the early leaders used shifting combinations of corporate-representational and Enlightenment ideas to challenge, first, monarchical absolutism and then "privilege." They also seem to have fashioned a quite new conception of unified national-popular sovereignty that grew from the exigencies and opportunities of the initial political struggle itself—a conflict pitting assemblies of elected representatives against the monarch. From the summer of 1789 onward, as Sewell rightly says, many of the deliberately planned institutional changes were influenced by (various readings of) the thought of the Enlightenment. But we need to ask pointed questions about how and through precisely whose efforts this happened—and with what varying degrees and kinds of success.

From the time of the initial elections to the Estates General, the revolutionary process itself was bringing to the fore strategically located leaders who were prone to draw inspiration from various readings of Enlightenment ideas. More than in most social revolutions, political leaders in the French Revolution engaged in continuous talk about reconstructing institutions. This was, after all, a revolution unusually centered in the urban politics of elected assemblies, dominated by lawyers and other literate elites. The research of George Taylor has given us clues to why this pattern of political organization gave unusual leverage to Enlightenment-inspired politicians.[12]

But we should not make the mistake of assuming that the talkers and the legislators could ever straightforwardly shape outcomes according to Enlightenment principles. After all, some of the most moralistic attempts to apply Enlightenment principles — such as the revolutionary calendar and the Cult of the Supreme Being—failed to become permanently institutionalized. The "logic of the Enlightenment" will not tell us why. Nor will it tell us why successive leaderships in the French Revolution understood the political potentials of Enlightenment ideals quite differently. Instead, for each phase of the Revolution, we need to examine the possibilities for consolidating various forms and functions of state power and consider how those possibilities interacted with the specific ideas and modes of political action available to particular groups.[13]

Throughout the Revolution, not only various readings of Enlightenment precepts but other existing and emergent stands of meaningful discourse were repeatedly mobilized for political purposes. These included corporatist-representational ideas deployed by Constitutional Monarchists; traditional norms of social solidarity and "just prices" used by the *sans-culottes* and by peasants

---

[12] George Taylor, "Revolutionary and Nonrevolutionary Content in the *Cahiers* of 1789: An Interim Report," *French Historical Studies* 7 (Spring 1972): 479–502.

[13] In addition to Taylor, see the discussion of the political adaptation of Rousseau's ideas by Brissot, Robespierre, and Saint-Just in Norman Hampson, "The Enlightenment in France," pp. 48–52 in Porter and Teich.

engaged in a variety of struggles against high prices, dues, tithes, and taxes; and Catholic and monarchical principles advocated by the Vendean rebels and other counterrevolutionaries. Emergent conceptions of national sovereignty and rights were elaborated both by the French and by their diverse foreign antagonists in the unending European wars of this period. With all of these ideologically self-conscious forces at work, the French Revolution's "outcomes" obviously cannot be attributed simply to the efforts made by Paris-centered assemblies and vanguard committees to apply in practice their Enlightenment-influenced conceptions of societal regeneration. Sewell would agree with this point. But neither can the outcomes be attributed to the impersonal working out of the logic of an impersonal Enlightenment cultural code.

Instead, the outcomes of the French Revolution—ranging from private property to administrative rationalization to the Concordat with the Catholic church—were nonintentionally shaped by the interactions of all of the intentionally mobilized political discourses that figured in the conflicts to displace and replace the Old Regime. A full analysis of the many ways that cultural idioms figured in the political arguments of the French Revolution, as well as in the shaping of its complex and contradictory outcomes, requires attention to much more than just Enlightenment discourse treated as if it were a cultural system "constitutive of social order." It requires that we examine very concretely the consciousness and talk of particularly situated acting groups, and that we take seriously the essentially political tasks they were trying to accomplish during the Revolution. From this perspective, Enlightenment discourses—plural—emerge as important idioms, but not the only idioms, used in the political ideologies developed by revolutionary state builders in France from 1789 until the collapse of the Terror. Recognizing this, we can do a more historically grounded job of explaining the culturally conditioned choices of these conscious actors—and a better job of explaining the successes and failures of their ideas and arguments within the overall context of multiple cultural idioms and contending ideologies that constituted the ideational aspect of the French Revolution.

FROM THE FRENCH CASE TO COMPARATIVE STUDIES

Sewell suggests at one point that the "totality of revolutionary ambition," the will to "transform the entirety of people's social lives—their work, their religious beliefs and practice, their families, their legal systems, their patterns of sociability, even their experiences of space and time"—"be included as part of any meaningful definition of 'social revolution.' " In my view, this would impose a misreading of the French Revolution, an inappropriate conflation of the Enlightenment and the Revolution, onto a concept that needs to allow more room for the analysis of variations across modern history. In any given revolution, there may well be actors struggling to reconstruct social life as a whole in moral, even metaphysical terms. But rather than assume this by definition, we need to understand why and how such efforts have played more prominent roles in some social revolutions—such as the French Revolution and in the contemporary Iranian revolution, for example—than in others—such as the Mexican revolution.[14]

Epochal and transnational intellectual transformations—such as the Enlightenment and the proliferation of modernist and militant-traditionalist discourses within contemporary Islam—do not in and of themselves "cause" social revolutions to happen. But they probably do independently affect the scope of transformations that revolutionary politicians attempt to institute when they rise to state power amidst ongoing social revolutions. The political organizations available to contending leaderships in revolutions also affect the scope of transformations attempted. Groups organized in Leninist fashion are especially prone and able to act as totalitarian vanguards in Walzer's sense. And I have already suggested that the French Revolution gave unusual opportunities for planning sociopolitical reconstructions to assemblies of legislators. But there have been modern social revolutions, such as the Mexican, fought out primarily by contending armies rather than by Leninist parties, militant clerics, or well-read legislators. Partly as consequence, I would hypothesize, these revolutions have allowed less political space for moralistic efforts to remake all of social life. The reconstruction of national politics as such, drawing upon and melding together strands from cultural idioms appealing to various social forces in the revolutionary alliance, has been the primary ideological accomplishment of such nonmetaphysical social revolutions.

Sewell concludes his essay with some tantalizing suggestions of questions about ideology that belong on the agenda for future comparative studies of revolutions. Although I would not frame all of the queries in quite the same way, I agree wholeheartedly that the time has come for *comparative* analysts—not just students of single revolutions—to probe the patterns of interrelation among cultural idioms, political ideologies, and the politics of revolutionary transformations. Comparative history is just as useful for pinpointing unique patterns as it is for teasing out causal regularities.[15] It may turn out that patterns of culture and ideology are causally unique to each revolution, but that would not make them the less significant. As a comparative historical

---

[14] On the Mexican case, see John Dunn, *Modern Revolutions* (Cambridge, 1972), chap. 2; and Walter L. Goldfrank, "Theories of Revolution and Revolution without Theory: The Case of Mexico," *Theory and Society* 7 (January–March 1979): 135–65.

[15] See Marc Bloch, "A Contribution towards a Comparative History of European Societies," pp. 44–81 in *Land and Work in Medieval Europe: Selected Papers by Marc Bloch*, trans. J. E. Anderson (1928; New York, 1967); William H. Sewell, Jr., "Marc Bloch and the Logic of Comparative History," *History and Theory* 6, no. 2 (1967): 208–18; and Theda Skocpol and Margaret Somers, "The Uses of Comparative History in Macrosocial Inquiry," *Comparative Studies in Society and History* 22, no. 2 (April 1980): 174–97.

sociologist who has analyzed causal regularities in modern social revolutions, I continue to believe that struggles over the organization and uses of state power are at the heart of all revolutionary transformations. Yet each revolution has its own idioms of politics, and these must be deciphered with the aid of the best strategies of cultural analysis we students of society—historians, anthropologists, sociologists, and political scientists alike—can devise.

COUNTERREVOLUTION

The West in France in 1789: The Religious Factor in the Origins of the Counterrevolution*

Timothy Tackett

The problem of the west in France has long held a peculiar fascination for students of French history. The great rural uprisings and cycles of guerrilla warfare after 1792 in large segments of Brittany, Anjou, Maine, lower Poitou, and lower Normandy,[1] the open popular rebellion against a Revolutionary regime which saw itself as the embodiment of popular sovereignty, were major elements in the origins of the Reign of Terror and contributed to the political instability of later governments through the end of the Directory. There were, to be sure, other areas of the country in which significant counterrevolutionary movements occurred. And the west itself was by no means monolithic in its attitudes. Nevertheless, in no other sector of France did the rural opposition movement begin in earnest so early, spread so widely, and attain such a degree of violence, intensity, and organization. In no other sector did it produce such a lasting collective memory. The distinctive character of the west in its political and cultural reactions to national events would endure as an important theme in French history throughout the nineteenth and much of the twentieth centuries.[2]

The debate over the causes of the *Vendée* and the *Chouannerie* has been nearly as long and impassioned as the debate over the origins of

* I wish to express my appreciation to Gilbert Shapiro and John Markoff for providing access to their data on the *cahiers de doléances* at the University of Pittsburgh, and to Robert McIntyre for his assistance in the analysis of the data and the preparation of the maps. My thanks also to those who have read and offered criticisms of earlier drafts of this article, especially Donald Sutherland, Jack Censer, Claude Langlois, T. J. A. Le Goff, and Robert Forster.

[1] For purposes of the present study, the west has been defined, in terms of the extent of counterrevolutionary activity, as the *départements* of Côtes-du-Nord, Morbihan, Ille-et-Vilaine, Manche, Mayenne, Sarthe, Loire-Atlantique, Maine-et-Loire, and Vendée.

[2] See especially André Siegfried, *Tableau politique de la France de l'Ouest sous la Troisième République* (Paris, 1913); and Paul Bois, *Paysans de l'Ouest*, abr. ed. (Paris, 1971). On the varying degrees of counterrevolution and the pockets of republicanism in the west, see also Roger Dupuy, *La Garde nationale et les débuts de la Révolution en Ille-et-Vilaine* (Rennes, 1972); Claude Petitfrère, *Bleus et blancs d'Anjou (1789–1793)*, 2 vols. (Lille, 1979), and Michel Lagrée, *Mentalités, religion et histoire en Haute-Bretagne au XIXe siècle* (Paris, 1977)

This essay originally appeared in the *Journal of Modern History* 54 (December 1982).

the Revolution itself.[3] After decades of increasingly sterile jousts between left and right, Catholics and anticlericals, a significant breakthrough emerged in the early 1960s out of the local studies of Paul Bois and Charles Tilly—and to a lesser extent, those of Marcel Faucheux—into the social and economic background of the counterrevolutionary movements.[4] For Bois and Tilly, it was ultimately the relative degree of economic integration between towns and rural areas, the process of modernization or "urbanization" of certain segments of the country population which provided the key for understanding the rebellions. But whatever the success of the two authors in forging and hammering their theses into position within their respective microcosms of the *départements* of Sarthe and southern Maine-et-Loire, and whatever the importance of both works as veritable discourses on method, difficulties seemed to arise when attempts were made to save the models for application to the west as a whole. Various critics have pointed both to the regions of rebellion within the west where the modernization models did not seem to apply and to the areas elsewhere in the kingdom where economic conditions seemed strikingly similar to the Vendée and where, nevertheless, no uprisings occurred. Equally disconcerting were several apparent discrepancies between the explanations of Bois and Tilly—as to the role played by rural artisans in the engendering of the rebellion, for example.[5] But the publication of these seminal works also helped stimulate a wave of new research and new hypotheses. Of particular importance is the thesis recently developed jointly by T. J. A. Le Goff and Donald Sutherland which would attach counterrevolutionary activity in the west, above all, to the specific forms of land tenure and to the rural distribution of wealth prevalent in these regions.[6]

[3] On the major traditional arguments see Charles Tilly, *The Vendée* (Cambridge, Mass., 1964), pp. 6–9.

[4] Works cited above. Also, Marcel Faucheux, *L'Insurrection vendéenne de 1793, aspects économiques et sociaux* (Paris, 1964).

[5] See, for example, Harvey Mitchell, "The Vendée and Counterrevolution: A Review Essay," *French Historical Studies* 5 (1967–68): 405–29; Claude Mazauric, "Vendée et Chouannerie," *La Pensée* 124 (1965): 54–85; Barrington Moore, *Social Origins of Dictatorship and Democracy* (Boston, 1967), pp. 92–101; Richard Cobb, "The Counter-Revolt," in *A Second Identity* (London, 1969), pp. 111–21; book review of Tilly and Faucheux by Maurice Hutt in *The English Historical Review* 81 (1966): 408–410; and Donald Sutherland and T. J. A. Le Goff, "The Social Origins of Counterrevolution in Western France," *Past and Present*, in press.

[6] See the article by Le Goff and Sutherland cited above and their recent monographs: T. J. A. Le Goff, *Vannes and Its Region in the Eighteenth Century* (Oxford, 1981); Donald Sutherland, *The Chouans: The Social Origins of Popular Counterrevolution in Upper Brittany* (Oxford, 1982). See also Harvey Mitchell,

Although each of the writers in question has been conscious of the broader problem of counterrevolution throughout the west, virtually all of their inquiries have been pursued in the context of individual local studies. Clearly, one of the goals of future research will be to begin working toward the broader perspectives of a regional analysis, to discover what it was that made the west as a whole different from the generally pro-Revolutionary provinces further to the east and south—the provinces of Ile-de-France, Touraine, Orléanais, Berry, and upper Poitou (referred to here as the Parisian Basin and the center).[7] In all probability, any satisfactory solution to this question will have to take into account a wide variety of social, economic, demographic, cultural, and political factors. But if such a comprehensive synthesis can come only in the future, a useful overview on one critical aspect of the problem may already be feasible: the regional analysis of church structures and religious culture.

In point of fact, none of the newer accounts neglects the religious issue—even though, in the view of the authors, the ultimate factors distinguishing the rebellious from the patriotic zones are economic in nature. Both Bois and Tilly stress the importance and power of the parish clergyman within the society of the future counterrevolutionary areas. Both attribute this in large measure to the curé's position in the structure of local society, to his key role as a social and cultural elite, to his function of providing the sole symbolic center for community cohesion within the dispersed hamlet society. But in what way was the clergyman's position in the west any stronger than in the many equally dispersed and non-modernized areas outside the sector of the west: in Sologne or Limousin, or upper Normandy, for example? In fact, Bois and Tilly diverge rather sharply in the answers which they give to this question. The latter accepts the suppositions of earlier writers such as André Siegfried and Gabriel Le Bras that the peasants of the Vendée were more pious than those in the future republican areas, that the veritable "Eucharistic frontier" cutting across western France, so well identified for the nineteenth century, already existed prior to the Revolution. The intense clericalism of the Vendée, then, could be directly linked to a higher degree of re-

---

"Resistance to the Revolution in Western France," *Past and Present* 63 (1974): 94–131; T. J. A. Le Goff and Donald Sutherland, "The Revolution and the Rural Community in Eighteenth-Century Brittany," *Past and Present* 62 (1974): 96–116.

[7] For present purposes, the Paris Basin has been defined as the *départements* of Oise, Seine-et-Oise, Seine-et-Marne, Seine, and Eure-et-Loir; the center has been defined as the *départements* of Loiret, Yonne, Loir-et-Cher, Indre-et-Loire, Vienne, Indre, Cher, and Nièvre.

ligiosity.[8] Paul Bois, on the contrary, seriously puts in doubt the existence of any such regional differences in religiosity before 1789. For Bois, the striking nineteenth-century dichotomy in the Sarthe between a pious west and an increasingly indifferent east represented an ideological polarization born of the Revolution itself, arising out of what were fundamentally political options fashioned by specific sets of economic interactions. If the ecclesiastical oath of 1791 became such an important issue for the rural population in the west, it was above all because it served as the convenient occasion for a kind of referendum on the Revolution in general as it was perceived at that point in time.[9] In the final analysis, most other recent historians have tended to line up behind Bois on this question. Such seems generally to be the position of T. J. A. Le Goff who, however, would also contest the enormous importance given to the clergy as the single organ of solidarity and sociability in the hamlet society of the *bocage*.[10]

But there is an additional dimension to the problem. Although no historian has overlooked the issue of the religious perceptions of the rural classes in the west, very little treatment has been given to the religion of the lay elites in the western towns. Clearly, if we are to understand the specific cultural chemistry of this area in a regional perspective, we must examine the nexus of interaction between town and country in the religious sphere, as Bois, Tilly, Le Goff, and Sutherland have already done in the economic and political spheres. It will be necessary to learn much more about the opinions of these urban notables in comparison to their counterparts elsewhere in the kingdom.

It is the purpose of the present study to bring together a certain amount of new evidence on the religious and ecclesiastical character of the west— evidence which was, in large part, unavailable to previous scholars — and to suggest that prior to the Revolution the religious configuration of this area was indeed distinct from that in much of the rest of the kingdom; and that this particular religious culture may have been an important contributing factor to the counterrevolutionary tendencies throughout so much of the west after 1792.

[8] *The Vendée*, pp. 100–103. On the nineteenth and twentieth centuries, see Siegfried, *Tableau politique*, p. 363; Gabriel Le Bras, *Etudes de sociologie religieuse*, 2 vols. (Paris, 1955–1956), 2: 526–45; and, more recently, Fernand Boulard, "La Pratique religieuse en France, 1802–1939: Les Pays de Loire," *Annales E. S. C.* 31 (1976): 761–801.

[9] *Paysans de l'Ouest*, esp. pp. 23–27, 91–97, 282–94, 307–11.

[10] Especially lucid in this regard is the article by Le Goff, "L'Ouest se bat-il pour la foi?" in *2000 ans de christianisme*, 9 vols. (Paris, 1975), 7: 132–138; also *Vannes*, pp. 222–223. See also Faucheux, *L'Insurrection vendéenne*, 94–95, 126–130; and François Le Brun, *Parole de Dieu et Révolution* (Toulouse, 1979), pp. 32, 37, and notes.

THE STRUCTURAL BASIS OF RURAL CLERICALISM IN THE WEST

Perhaps in the future someone will devise a means of assessing the relative intensity of religious beliefs under the Old Regime and the extent to which those beliefs genuinely modified actions. But such a generalized test has yet to be found.[11] It seems clear that everywhere in France, in the center as in the west, the rural inhabitants, beset by the same overpowering threats to their health and their crops and their mental well-being, sought answers and solace in a supernatural that was more or less impregnated with Christianity; and in a sense, all were indeed religious. What evidence exists for the Old Regime would also suggest the near universal fulfillment in most of rural France of the Church's basic minimal requirements of the "Easter duties"—confession and communion at least once a year.[12] While certain historians have pointed to the vigorous mission campaigns in the seventeenth- and eighteenth-century west—by Grignion de Montfort and others—too little is presently known of the activities and relative success of the similar efforts carried out concurrently in the center and the Parisian Basin to allow for any meaningful conclusions.[13] To date, no one has successfully responded to Paul Bois's challenge to prove the presence of a "Eucharistic frontier" existing prior to the French Revolution. But there is another, more viable approach to the comparative assessment of religion. If we look not at the ambiguous category of "piety," but examine rather the regional ecclesiastical structures, we discover that the west was strikingly different from the center and the Parisian Basin and that such differences may well have had effects on the relative position and status of the clergy and, ultimately, on the lay conception of religion itself within the rural communities. The distinctive peculiarities of the Church in the west can be identified

---

[11] Note that the study of the clauses in wills to gauge religious piety as used by Michel Vovelle, *Piété baroque et déchristianisation en Provence* (Paris, 1973), can be employed only with difficulty in many parts of the west because of differing legal codes: Philippe Goujard, "Echec d'une sensibilité baroque: Les Testaments rouennais au XVIIIᵉ siècle," *Annales E. S. C.* 36 (1981): 26–43.

[12] Le Bras, *Etudes*, 1: 275–76.

[13] Both Tilly and Faucheux make reference to the missions in the Vendée: *The Vendée*, p. 103; and *L'Insurrection vendéenne*, p. 95. For Brittany, see La Goff, *Vannes*, p. 246; Claude Langlois, *Le Diocèse de Vannes au XIXᵉ siècle* (Paris, 1974), pp. 72–94; and Alain Croix, *La Bretagne aux XVIᵉ et XVIIᵉ siècles* (Paris, 1981), pp. 1211–46. See also the introduction and conclusion by Louis Pérouas to *Mémoires des missions des Montfortains dans l'Ouest (1740–1779)* (Fontenay-le-Comte, 1964). On missions in the Parisian zone see Jeanne Ferté, *La Vie religieuse dans les campagnes parisiennes* (Paris, 1962), pp. 196–230; and Jean Mauzaise, *Le Rôle et l'action des Capucins de la province de Paris dans la France religieuse du XVIIᵉ siècle*, 3 vols. (Lille, 1978).

in three separate but related areas: the distribution of Church wealth, the rural density of the clergy, and the patterns of clerical recruitment.

As estimated from the ecclesiastical tax rolls of 1760, the relative wealth of the Church in the west varied considerably from section to section, with Normandy among the wealthiest in the country, Brittany among the poorest, and most of the remaining provinces only somewhat better off than the nation as a whole.[14] The unifying characteristic of the region may have been the proportion of this wealth controlled by the parish clergy. Thus, in a sample of Old Regime dioceses of the center and the Parisian Basin, the curés held only about one-fourth of the total diocesan revenues—the remainder going to bishops, priors, canons, and monastic houses—while the corresponding ratio in the west ranged from one-third to almost three-fifths of the total.[15] As a result, the curés of the region were, on the average, among the wealthiest of the entire kingdom and received substantially higher revenues than their colleagues to the east and south. There was, to be sure, a very considerable range of revenues, from below 500 *livres* to over 6,000 *livres* per year in 1790.[16] Yet the infamous *portion congrue*, the fixed-money salary owed

---

[14] Calculations are based on the declared revenues for all benefice holders within the "Clergy of France" assembled for each diocese by the *agents-généraux* of the clergy: "Pouillé de 1760": A.N., G[8]*, 516–532. The declarations are unreliable for the absolute values of individual benefices, but have been found relatively accurate for the proportionate revenues and distribution of wealth. The median diocesan wealth index was 108 livres per square kilometer. In Normandy the diocesan index ranged from 153 to 313 livres; in Brittany, from 50 to 99 livres; in Maine and Anjou, from 134 to 138 livres; in Lower Poitou, 80 livres.

[15] For the diocese of Tours, the curés controlled 25 percent of the diocesan wealth; for Orléans, 29 percent; for Paris, 24 percent; for Reims, 24 percent. But in the diocese of Le Mans, 45 percent; Coutances, 58 percent; Vannes, 39 percent; Angers, 34 percent; Bayeux, 41 percent (A.N., G[8]*, 516, 522, 525, 526, 527, 529). The lengthy analysis required to obtain these proportions precluded a systematic calculation for all dioceses.

[16] Samples have been taken in a number of dioceses or districts to determine the net declared revenues of curés in 1790, usually the most accurate figures available for the Old Regime. Thus, net curé revenues in the *bailliage* of Cotentin were 2275 livres per year; in the district of Laval, 2195; in the diocese of Nantes, over 2000; in the district of Cholet, 1857; in the western Sarthe, between 2100 and 2300; in the Loire-Inférieure, 2897; and in the *département* of Ille-et-Vilaine, 1417. Compare these to areas further east and south: about 1000 in the district of Les Sables d'Olonne; 943 in the *bailliage* of Bourges: 1159 in the *département* of Saône-et-Loire (four districts); 1288 in the Charente (former dioceses of Angoulême and Périgueux); and 1094 in the *bailliages* of Auxerre (Emile Bridry, *Cahiers de doléances du bailliage de Cotentin*, 3 vols. [Paris, 1907–1912], passim; A. D. Mayenne, L 1436; Charles Berthelot du Chesnay, "Les Prêtres séculiers dans la Haute Bretagne," unpublished *thèse d'état*, University of Rennes

to curés by nonresident clerical tithe owners, that institution so decried in all of the *cahiers de doléances* of 1789, was in fact relatively rare in most zones of the west.[17] In many cases, the rural parish clergymen collected revenues superior to those of the town-dwelling clergy, including some canons and priors. Whenever the laity in the west pictured the typical country curé, the image had to be that of a wealthy ecclesiastical gentleman with a large farmhouse, substantial landholdings, and the secured income in kind of the tithes. In the hands of other clergymen—monks or canons or even bishops—such wealth was invariably deemed excessive by the country people, and considerable hostility was aroused when local tithe payments were siphoned off to the cities for the accounts of such nonresident ecclesiastics. Yet similar complaints against the parish clergy were altogether rare.[18] Not only did the curés and *vicaires* perform

---

(1973), pp. 441–42; Faucheux, *L'Insurrection vendéenne*, pp. 80, 86–87; A. D. Sarthe, L 339–350 (for Doyennés, in the west, of Brûlons, Fresnay, Sillé-le-Guillaume, and Vallon; and, in the southeast, of Oisé, La Chartre, and Le Château-du-Loir); Alphonse Jarnoux, *La Loire leur servit de linceul* (Quimper, 1972), pp. 400–404; Armand Rébillon, *La Situation économique du clergé à la veille de la Révolution dans les districts de Rennes, de Fougères et de Vitré* (Rennes, 1913), passim. Alfred Gandilhon, *Cahiers de doléances du bailliage de Bourges* (Bourges, 1910), passim; A. D. Saône-et-Loire, 1 L 8/107, 110, 113, 116; J. Nanglard, *Pouillé historique du diocèse d'Angoulême*, 3 vols. (Angoulême, 1896–1898), 2: 14–430; Charles Porée, *Cahiers des curés et communautés ecclésiastiques du bailliage d'Auxerre* (Paris, 1927), passim. It is not clear if the revenues for Loire-Inférieure are net or gross. If the latter were the case, the net revenues would be a few hundred livres less, certainly still above 2000. Revenues for 1790 are as yet unavailable for lower Brittany, but it is possible that curés' incomes there were lower than in other parts of the west: Le Goff, *Vannes*, p. 258.

[17] On the approximate percentage of curés on the *portion congrue*, see Claude Léouzon Le Duc, "La Fortune du clergé sous l'ancien régime," *Journal des économistes*, 4ᵉ série 15 (1881): 228–230. Portions of the west had the lowest congruist rates in France: 13 percent in Maine; 5 to 23 percent in the dioceses of lower Normandy; 10 percent in Anjou; 8 percent in lower Poitou. In Brittany they varied from 7 percent to 28 percent in Finistère, Morbihan, Loire-Inférieure, and Ille-et-Vilaine, but were very much higher—well over 50 percent—in Côtes-du-Nord. In the center, the rates vary from about 22 to 40 percent. In the Parisian Basin, from about 12 to 30 percent.

[18] Charles Girault, *Les Biens d'église dans la Sarthe à la fin du XVIIIᵉ siècle* (Laval, 1953), pp. 372–91, 397, 400; Henri Marion, *La Dîme ecclésiastique en France au XVIIIᵉ siècle et sa suppression* (Bordeaux, 1912), pp. 195–207; Pierre Gagnol, *La Dîme ecclésiastique en France au XVIIIᵉ siècle* (Paris, 1910), pp. 356–424; Bois, *Paysans de l'Ouest*, p. 308. On the high standard of living and comfortable life-style of the curés in the west, see Girault, pp. 372–391; M. E. Viviers, "La Condition du clergé séculier dans le diocèse de Coutances au XVIIIᵉ siècle," *Annales de Normandie* 2 (1952): 3–27; Sutherland, pp. 201–204.

important day-to-day services for the villagers, but most of the revenues they received remained in the parish. In fact, within a society where wealth was an important element of status, the particular economic structure of the Church in the west greatly enhanced the prestige, the "notability" of the resident parish clergy as a group.

In the second place, compared to the provinces of the center, the southwest, and much of the Parisian Basin, there was a substantially greater visibility of the clergy in the rural parishes of the west. To be sure, the regional clerical density, the number of secular and regular clergymen as a ratio of the total population in each diocese, was probably lower in the west than in France generally.[19] The critical difference was not the overall density of clergymen—which would include monks, mendicants, canons, etc., largely concentrated in the towns—but the actual presence of priests in the country communities. Thus, besides the curé or rector—as he was called in Brittany—there seems to have been an average of one *vicaire* or more per parish in nearly all of the western *départements*. In addition, there were commonly other nonparish clergymen residing locally with the corps of *vicaires* and curés—chaplains, *habitués*, *prêtres libres*, and the like. By contrast, in almost all of the Parisian Basin, the center, and as far south as Guyenne, a rural nonparish clergy was virtually nonexistent and *vicaires* were to be found only in every third or fourth parish at best. (See Figure A.[20])

The significance of these regional differences in the nature of the clerical presence should not be underestimated. One of the central objectives of

---

[19] The total male clerical density in 1790, including seculars and regulars, was about twenty-seven per 10,000 inhabitants in the *département* of Vendée; twenty-five per 10,000 in Finistère; twenty-four in Morbihan; twenty-six in Sarthe; thirty-seven in the former diocese of Avranches: Yves Chaille, "Livre d'or du clergé vendéen," *Archives du diocèse de Luçon*, nouvelle série 32 (1960): 5; Daniel Bernard, "Le Clergé régulier dans le Finistère en 1790," *Bulletin de la société archéologique du Finistère* 64 (1937): 105; "Le Clergé séculier dans le Finistère en 1790," *Bulletin diocésain d'histoire et d'archéologie, diocèse de Quimper et de Léon* 40 (1941): 104; Augustin Cariou, "La Constitution civile du clergé dans le département du Morbihan," *Mémoire de la société d'histoire et d'archéologie de la Bretagne* 45 (1965): 59–88; Charles Girault, *Le Clergé sarthois face au serment constitutionnel de 1790* (Laval, 1959), pp. 12 and 34; Jean Bindet, "Le Diocèse d'Avranche sous l'épiscopat de Mgr. de Belbeuf," *Revue de l'Avranchin* 46 (1969): 45–48, 54–55, 61. For France as a whole, if we assume a population of 27 million and a total of 115,000 male clergymen, the rate was forty-three per 10,000 inhabitants. Faucheux, *L'Insurrection vendéenne*, pp. 70–73, found a higher overall density in the republican regions, but his calculations included canons, regulars, etc.

[20] This and the following two maps (Figures B and C) are based on an analysis of the clergy of the Revolution alive and receiving government pensions in 1817.

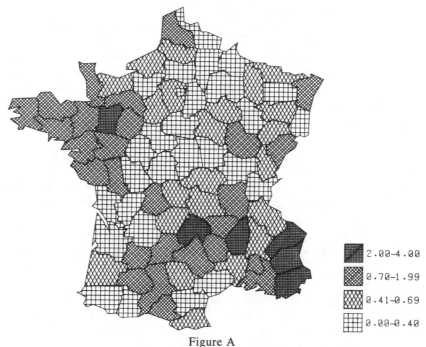

2.00-4.00

0.70-1.99

0.41-0.69

0.00-0.40

Figure A
Ratio of *Vicaires* to Curés (i.e., Parishes)
by *Département* of Residence Among Survivors of 1817

the Catholic Reformation, as it was implemented in France by the bishops during the seventeenth and eighteenth centuries, was to disengage the priest from all lay activities (economic, sexual, or recreational) and to create a model in which the clergyman's identity would be shaped by his attachment to the Church hierarchy and ecclesiastical society rather than to the secular society.[21] The very existence of the microsocieties of clergymen in the western communities, where two or more priests were

---

They originally appeared in T. Tackett and Claude Langlois, "Ecclesiastical Structures and Clerical Geography on the Eve of the French Revolution," *French Historical Studies* 11 (1980): 352–370. They are reproduced here with the permission of the Editor of *French Historical Studies*. On the non-parish clergy residing in the villages in certain parts of the west, see ibid., pp. 353, 362.

[21] See Dominique Julia, "Le Prêtre au XVIIIᵉ siècle, la théologie et les institutions," *Recherches de science religieuse* 58 (1970): 521–34; and "Discipline ecclésiastique et culture paysanne aux XVIIᵉ et XVIIIᵉ siècles," in *La Religion populaire. Colloques internationaux du centre national de recherche scientifique* 576 (Paris, 1980): 199–209.

present, invariably facilitated the maintenance of this Catholic Reformation ideal. Though on occasion the relations between ecclesiastics in the same parish were far from cordial, still the presence of other clerics living together in the same community and frequently in the same rectory, the possibility of mutual surveillance or emulation, the existence of a miniature local hierarchy subordinated to the authority of the curé, all must have strengthened the *esprit de corps* and helped reinforce the general sensitivity to ecclesiastical authority. While the reform of the clergy had been pursued in central France as vigorously as in the west, the very nature of the priestly order in these villages made it more difficult to maintain the sense and the reality of clerical separation. Here, the solitary priests, residing for decades relatively alone in the midst of the peasantry, deprived of daily contact with ecclesiastical society, were probably far more dependent and vulnerable in their relations with their flocks.[22]

The contrasts in clerical presence between the west and the center were paralleled by markedly differing patterns of clerical recruitment.[23] First, though the overall recruitment ratio (the number of men entering the clergy in proportion to the population) was not unusually strong compared to that of the kingdom as a whole—and in no way stood out as it would in the nineteenth century—it was nevertheless distinctly greater than that of the center and the Parisian Basin. Second, there is a good indication that vocations to the clergy were stable or even increasing in many western dioceses in the later eighteenth century—at the very time when they were declining in most of the kingdom and dropping precipitously in the center and in Paris. Third and perhaps even more significant, the priests in much of the west originated massively from rural communities, while the majority of those entering the clergy just to the south and east usually came from the towns. (See Figure B.) There were, it is true, other areas in France with strong rural recruitment, but the western clergy was especially unusual in that a larger proportion—over 50 percent in several dioceses—probably came from agricultural milieus, most likely from the more prosperous landholding peasantry. Thus, toward the end

---

[22] The origins and evolution of these regional differences over time is uncertain. Note, however, that already in the mid-seventeenth century, the diocese of Chartres in the Parisian Basin had relatively few *vicaires* and *habitués* compared to the diocese of La Rochelle, most of which was in lower Poitou: Louis Pérouas, *Le Diocèse de La Rochelle de 1648 à 1724* (Paris, 1964), pp. 194–196; and Robert Sauzet, *Les Visites pastorales dans le diocèse de Chartres pendant la première moitié du XVIIᵉ siècle* (Rome, 1975), pp. 115–121.

[23] On the regional and chronological patterns of clerical recruitment described in this paragraph, see Tackett and Langlois, "Ecclesiastical Structures"; see also Tackett, "L'Histoire sociale du clergé diocésain dans la France du XVIIIᵉ siècle," *Revue d'histoire moderne et contemporaine* 26 (1979): 198–234.

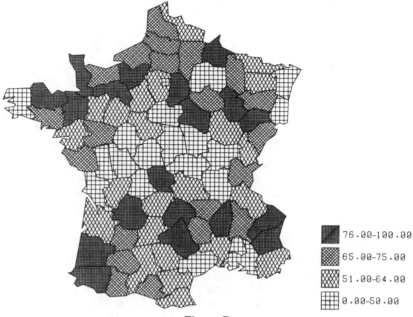

76.00-100.00

65.00-75.00

51.00-64.00

0.00-50.00

Figure B
Percentage of Pensioners Born in Rural Areas
(by *Département* of Origin)

of the Old Regime, at least 54 percent of the clergy in the region of Vannes, 64 percent in the diocese of Tréguier, well over 50 percent in the west of the diocese of Le Mans, and perhaps 75 percent in lower Normandy came from probable agricultural milieus, compared to approximately 12 percent near Paris and well under 10 percent in the Orléanais, in the Saumurois, and in the region near Niort.[24]

[24] Tackett, ''L'Histoire sociale,'' pp. 209–216, 227. The data for the diocese of Le Mans concern the *archidiaconé* of Passais and are based on research conducted jointly with Alex Poyer in the *insinuations ecclésiastiques* for 1779–1788: A. D. Sarthe, G 405– 409. For the Saumurois, see Louis Gallard, ''Le Clergé saumurois de 1789 à 1795'' (D.E.S., University of Poitiers, 1960), p. 104. For the Paris region, Jacques Staes, ''La Vie religieuse dans l'archidiaconé de Josas à la fin de l'ancien régime'' (Thèse, Ecole des Chartes, 1969), pp. 288–289. On Vannes, see Le Goff, *Vannes*, pp. 250–251, where it is clear that the figures given for clergy of peasant origins are only minimums. For Tréguier, Georges Minois, ''Les Vocations sacerdotales dans le diocèse de Tréguier au XVIIIe siècle,'' *Annales de Bretagne* 86 (1979): 53. Included as being of ''probable agricultural milieus'' are not only those from families of *laboreurs*, *vignerons*, etc., but also those from rural villages with parents calling themselves *marchands*

Such contrasts in recruitment trends throw additional light on the social position and role of the parish clergy in the different regions. Although motivation for entering the clergy in the eighteenth century was undoubtedly complex, the substantial numbers of vocations from agricultural milieus in the west are probably indicative of a society in which the clergy commanded relatively greater respect and prestige.[25] But there was another dimension to the question. The heavier rural recruitment in the west meant, through the effects of supply and demand, that the parish priests there were primarily local men and that a large proportion were from the same rural and/or peasant backgrounds as their parishioners.[26] Many, in fact, were from precisely those wealthier peasant elite families which stood to dominate the local social and political life. Whatever the ultimate origins of these distinctive trends in clerical recruitment, they could be viewed in the context of the eighteenth century as both cause and consequence of the generally higher clerical status in the west. To the east, on the other hand, a greater proportion, sometimes even the majority of parish clergymen, were outsiders to their parishioners, imported from elsewhere to compensate the insufficiency of priests in the rural areas: outsiders who came from the towns rather than the countryside and often from other dioceses or provinces altogether. (See Figure C.[27]) From unknown families, little or even totally unfamiliar with local customs and dialects, they invariably had greater difficulty integrating themselves into the village community. The bishops in these regions would themselves

---

or giving no specific professional title: see above article for the justification of this procedure. Note, however, that exceptionally high recruitment from agricultural milieus did not obtain everywhere in the west. The proportion was only about 30 percent in southwestern Maine. Unfortunately no systematic sources on clerical family origins have yet been located for Anjou and lower Poitou. The figures given by Yves Chaille, *Livre d' or du clergé vendéen* (Luçon, 1964), p. 6, sometimes used by historians, refer to only seventy of 655 non-noble priests in the *département* of Vendée in 1791 and are certainly biased in favor of non-peasant families.

[25] See Louis Pérouas, "Le Nombre des vocations sacerdotales est-il un critère valable en sociologie religieuse historique aux XVIIᵉ et XVIIIᵉ siècles," *Actes du 87ᵉ congrès de sociétés savantes* (Paris, 1963) pp. 36–40; Vovelle, *Piété baroque*, pp. 214–228; Tackett, "L'Histoire sociale," pp. 201–203, 206–208.

[26] "Local" is to be taken in the sense of originating in the same *département* or Old Regime diocese. It was rare that a priest served in his parish of birth (e.g., only 5 percent in Sarthe in 1790). It is not surprising that Tilly found only 23 percent of the priests in the Mauges originating from the canton in which they served: *The Vendée*, p. 105.

[27] The same general pattern is conveyed by the partial evidence of the geographic origins of the clergy serving at the end of the eighteenth century: Tackett, "L'Histoire sociale," pp. 223, 229.

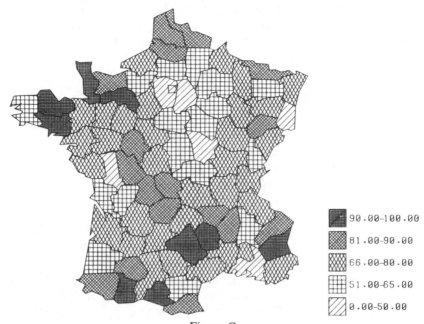

90.00–100.00

81.00–90.00

66.00–80.00

51.00–65.00

0.00–50.00

Figure C
Percentage of Pensioners Born in the *Départements*
in Which They Were Residing in 1817

commonly complain of the deleterious effects on their dioceses from this large influx of "foreign" priests into local parish posts.[28]

Thus, there is a strong suggestion that differences in church structures and career patterns between the west and the center had important ramifications for the presuppositions of both clergy and laity as to the place and power of parish priests within rural religion and culture. It was not simply that the priest provided a principal unifying element for the scattered hamlet society in the west. There were, as has been shown, many other areas of France, including large sections of the center, where similar patterns of population dispersion existed. The difference was rather in the relative economic wealth of the parish clergy in the west, in the priests' local visibility, in their close connections with rural elite family networks: factors which combined to give them a stronger rural-based presence and prestige than perhaps anywhere else in France.

[28] See, for example, Staes, "La Vie religieuse," p. 276; and Guy Mandon, "Les Curés en Périgord au XVIIIᵉ siècle" (Thèse de 3ᵉ cycle; Bordeaux, 1979), pp. 48–49.

Much has been written in recent years on the "clericalization" of Catholicism in France, born of the efforts of the post-Tridentine Church to make the priest a far more integral and dominant force in the practice of religion than ever before. In an attempt to reform or suppress various popular religious activities increasingly viewed as dangerous or "superstitious," the bishops of the seventeenth and early eighteenth centuries strove to impose ever greater clerical control over all aspects of the religious life and moral values of the population. In some areas of France these attempts gave rise to a veritable clash between the "new" religion of Tridentine inspiration and an "older" religion of the countryside with its emphasis on the direct intercessory powers of the saints and various communal expressions of religion in which the presence of the priest was viewed as peripheral or unnecessary.[29] Though it would be difficult to prove conclusively, it is interesting to speculate that the peculiarities of ecclesiastical structures in the west may have made this area particularly well adapted for the acceptance and interiorization of a "clericalized" religion. Perhaps it was the superior status of the curé and his assistants in the cultural symbolism and the lines of social power, coupled with a keener sentiment of ecclesiastical society on the part of the priests themselves, which gave the Counter-Reformation concept of the clergyman such a tenacious hold in the west on both priest and parish alike. But in the center and in the Parisian Basin, the situation was substantially different. Although there were sections—notably near Paris—where the clergy as a whole was stronger in both numbers and wealth than in the west, such strengths were essentially urban in character. For the country people of these regions, who watched a greater portion of their tithe payments being carried away from the village to unknown clergymen, who viewed the solitary and modestly endowed local priest as an outsider, and who, perhaps for this very reason, experienced little enthusiasm for sending their sons into the Church, the rural clergy invariably seemed more distant and somewhat alien. It is possible that the newer conception of the priest was never really integrated into the social and religious mores of the population of these zones. At any rate, by the later eighteenth

---

[29] Within the extensive recent literature on popular religion and the effects of the Tridentine reforms, see Jean Delumeau, *Le Catholicisme entre Luther et Voltaire* (Paris, 1971); and *La Mort des pays de Cocagne* (Paris, 1976); Robert Muchembled, *Culture populaire et culture des élites dans la France moderne, XVe–XVIIIe siècles* (Paris, 1978), esp. pp. 255–272; Robert Mandrou, "Clergé tridentin et piété populaire," *Actes du 99e congrès de sociétés savantes* (Paris, 1976), 1: 107–117; Marie-Hélène Froeschlé-Chopard, *La Religion populaire en Provence orientale au XVIIIe siècle* (Paris, 1980); Philip T. Hoffman, "Church and Community: The Parish Priest and the Counter-Reformation in the Diocese of Lyon, 1500–1789," (Ph.D. dissertation; Yale University, 1979).

century many parish clergymen of the Paris Basin and the center may have found another, competing model of the parish priest more appropriate and viable for their situation: a newer model of a citizen-priest popularized by writers like Voltaire and Rousseau. It was a scheme which laid far greater stress on the curé's role as a public servant to the community, an educated link to urban society, and the tutor of Enlightened technological change to the peasantry.[30] After 1790, the sharply contrasting positions and images of the priest in his relation to religion and community would be of the greatest importance in the optic by which priests and their parishoners viewed the transformations of the Civil Constitution of the Clergy.[31]

THE TRANSFORMATION OF THE URBAN ELITE IN THE WEST

The distinctive character of rural religious structures in the west is of considerable interest in its own right. But it takes on special significance when juxtaposed with a veritable transformation in religious attitudes among the urban elite of this same region during the latter half of the eighteenth century. In fact, recent research provides us with a number of convergent indicators concerning the changes in values among some segments of this group.

Perhaps no one fact better illustrates the profound chasm between town and country in the evolution of religious commitment than the movement of clerical vocations in the west during the latter eighteenth century. An extrapolation from the age profile of the clergy of 1791 would suggest that between the periods 1757–1771 and 1776–1791 the number of entries into the secular clergy from the rural areas of Maine, Anjou, and Vendée increased by approximately 48 percent. But over the same time span, recruitment from the towns in this region declined 34 percent. It is worth stressing that nowhere else in the entire kingdom was the divergence in recruitment between town and country so great. In the center, by contrast, clerical entries decreased substantially over the same period in both rural and urban areas (by 34 percent and 43 percent, respectively).[32] On the eve of the Revolution, in the west only about 18 percent of new clergymen in the diocese of Coutances, 23 percent in the diocese of Nantes, and 25 percent in the diocese of Vannes came from urban families, and even

---

[30] Tackett, *Priest and Parish in Eighteenth-Century France* (Princeton, 1977), pp. 166–69.

[31] On the appearance of these two ideal types of priests in the oath speeches of 1791, see below.

[32] Based on an analysis of the pensioners' list of 1817, as yet unpublished. See above, n. 20. In the Ile-de-France, rural recruitment rose 10 percent, while urban recruitment declined 3 percent.

smaller percentages could be classified as "notables": officeholders, members of the liberal professions, wealthy merchants, or property owners living off their *rentes*. Such proportions might be compared to the 84 percent in the center diocese of Orléans originating in towns, to the 78 percent in the diocese of Paris, or the 57 percent in the southwestern diocese of Angoulême.[33] The shunning of clerical careers by young men from towns in the west is all the more noteworthy in that career opportunities open to middle-class clergymen were, as we have seen, rather attractive from an economic standpoint.

That this declining interest in clerical careers was related to changing religious values on the part of the urban elites is further suggested by the research of Jean Quéniart into the production and consumption of books among nine important western towns in the course of the eighteenth century.[34] To be sure, an examination of the output of local provincial publishing houses reveals an enormous quantity of religious books — reprints of earlier publications — continuing to come off the presses in the west through the end of the Old Regime.[35] And the analysis of the book collections of members of the elites — nobles and prominent officeholders, for the most part — indicates that the average proportion of religious books possessed by such individuals actually increased through the 1750s. But thereafter and through the decade of the Revolution, there was a brutal change. With very few exceptions — primarily widows and unmarried women — the number of works on religion to be found on the bookshelves of notables declined drastically or disappeared altogether.[36]

The lack of similar extensive research into book holdings in other regions disallows direct comparisons between the west and the kingdom generally or between the nine towns and the surrounding countryside. What does seem clear, however, is that most of the rural inhabitants of the west could not read at all — or were, in any case, unable to sign their names at the end of marriage acts. With the exception of Normandy, the entire region was in a sector of minimal literacy varying from under 40

[33] Tackett, "L'Histoire sociale," pp. 224–225. Also Le Goff, *Vannes*, p. 256. Note also the Breton diocese of Tréguier, where the town-born clerics were only a tiny minority: Minois, p. 54.

[34] *Culture et société urbaines dans la France de l'Ouest au XVIIIe siècle* (Paris, 1978).

[35] Jean Brancolini and Marie-Thérèse Bouyssy, "La Vie provinciale du livre à la fin de l'ancien régime," in *Livre et société dans la France du XVIIIe siècle*, ed. François Furet, 2 vols. (Paris, 1965–1970), 2: esp. p. 27.

[36] Quéniart, *Culture et société*, pp. 225–86. Unfortunately such trends are impossible to follow among members of the "bourgeoisie de talent" (lawyers, doctors, etc.) since their libraries were dominated by the professional books of their trades throughout the century.

percent to under 10 percent for men and everywhere less than 20 percent for women.[37] Moreover, the gap in literacy, or name-signing ability, between town and country was even greater in the western provinces at the end of the Old Regime than in many other provinces. Thus there was a difference of close to or greater than 30 percentage points between the signature rates of Le Mans, Angers, Nantes, and Saint-Malo and their respective *départements* generally. At the same period there were corresponding differences of fourteen points in thirteen southwestern *départements*, only a few points in Calvados, and between five and nineteen points for men in the *département* of Nord. Although data of this kind are clearly in need of further refinement, they provide a crude but suggestive indication of the very substantial cultural dichotomy between town and country in the west on the eve of the Revolution.[38]

Whatever the relative cultural isolation, whatever the strength of religious clericalism and traditionalism in the rural areas, the towns of the west were anything but backwaters to the intellectual currents of the age. Historians, noting the relative sparsity of provincial academies and masonic lodges in the western provinces, have often overlooked the particular importance and concentration of *chambres de lectures* and *sociétés littéraires* in this sector of the kingdom. Beginning in the 1750s and proliferating rapidly in the 1780s, the reading rooms effected, according to Daniel Roche, "a notable transformation of the elites" in this region.[39] By the eve of the Revolution almost every town of any size in the west possessed such an organization, a network that seems to have been at

[37] Michel Fleury and Pierre Valmary, "Les Progrès de l'instruction élémentaire de Louis XIV à Napoléon III d'après l'enquête de Louis Maggiolo," *Population* 12 (1957): 71–92; and François Furet and Jacques Ozouf, *Lire et écrire, l'alphabétisation des Français de Calvin à Jules Ferry*, 2 vols. (Paris, 1977), 1: 13–68.

[38] Quéniart, *Culture et société*, pp. 59–60; Furet and Ozouf, *Lire et écrire*, 1: 230–231, 236. Unfortunately, similar figures have not been found for the center and the Parisian Basin. There were undoubtedly large literacy gaps in other regions, particularly between large towns in the south and the surrounding areas: twenty-six points between Lyon and the *département* of Rhône; thirty-three points between Aix and the Bouches-du-Rhône; but zero points between Manosque and the Basses-Alpes: Maurice Garden, *Lyon et les Lyonnais* (Paris, 1970), p. 450; Michel Vovelle, "Y a-t-il eu une révolution culturelle au XVIIIᵉ siècle," *Revue d'histoire moderne et contemporaine* 22 (1975): 93, 100.

[39] Daniel Roche, *Le Siècle des Lumières en Province*, 2 vols. (Paris, 1978), 1: 63. Roche is referring specifically to Brittany, but the same might be said of Maine and perhaps Anjou. On the distribution of Masonic lodges, see Michel Vovelle, "Essai de cartographie des limites de la sociabilité méridionale à la fin du XVIIIᵉ siècle," *Actes du 96ᵉ congrès de sociétés savantes* (Paris, 1976), pp. 169–171.

least as dense as in any other region of the kingdom. In many respects far more independent and spontaneous than the academies and masonic lodges, and thus potentially more radical in their orientations, the private reading societies were to play an important role not only in the propagation of Enlightenment ideology but also in the politicization of the urban elites during the pre-Revolutionary period.[40]

But if evidence is available as to the active influence of certain aspects of Enlightenment thought and the decline of religious commitment among the urban notables of the west, there remains the problem of probing the specific views of this group on religion and the clergy in comparison with the perceptions of other provincial elites. Fortunately, one approach for such a comparison does exist: an examination of the Third Estate general cahiers of 1789—those statements of grievances, drawn up in the final stage of the electoral process of that year, to be presented directly to the king at Versailles. While there has been considerable debate as to the opinion represented and the influences exercised in the various preliminary cahiers—those written by parishes, guilds, towns, etc.—the general cahiers at the level of the *grands bailliages* pose far fewer problems. There are ample indications of the progressive elimination of the more humble elements of the population through the successive steps of the elections. The assemblies signing the general cahiers were clearly dominated by petty officials, lawyers, and members of the upper bourgeoisie. In Anjou, for example, almost all in attendance were able to sign their names, immediately setting them apart from the general population of the province. Those deputies actually drawing up the cahiers for approval by the assemblies were probably even more elitest, and heavily weighted in favor of the largest towns. Thus, at least five of the nine members of the committee for the cahier of Anjou were residents of Angers, and many items in the final document—especially those concerning the Church—were copied almost verbatim from the cahier of the town of Angers. There was probably also a strong influence exercised by the town notables of Rennes and particularly by the canonist Lanjuinais on the cahier of the *sénéchaussée* of Rennes.[41] Thus, a strong case can be made that the general cahiers of the Third Estate represented precisely

---

[40] Roche, 1: 61–64 and esp. the maps, incomplete but suggestive, of the distribution of *chambres de lectures* in France: 2: 477. See also Augustin Cochin, *Les Sociétés de pensées et la Révolution en Bretagne* (Paris, 1925), pp. 19–21; François Furet, *Penser la Révolution* (Paris, 1978), pp. 58–59; and Michael L. Kennedy, *The Jacobin Clubs in the French Revolution* (Princeton, 1982), pp. 8–9.

[41] Beatrice Hyslop, *A Guide to the General Cahiers of 1789* (New York, 1936), p. 82; Arthur Le Moy, *Cahiers de doléances des corporations de la ville d'Angers*

that group of nonpeasant notables, and especially those from the towns, whose views on religion we wish to examine.

In an effort to explore the critical question of regional variation in the general cahiers, I have made use of the data from two separately conceived cahier analyses: first, a thematic coding of selective grievances originally prepared by Beatrice Hyslop and later adapted by Sasha Weitman; secondly, a content analytical coding of all grievances, directed by Gilbert Shapiro and John Markoff.[42] In many respects, the two sets of data, assembled and coded independently, serve to complement one another—the Hyslop data grouping broader, more historically defined clusters of demands, but limited by the author's specific questions and perspectives; the Shapiro-Markoff data more nominalistic and inclusive of *all* cahier demands, but sometimes requiring a second-stage manual regrouping and recoding for the purposes of the present study. In order to facilitate the mapping and the comparison with Revolutionary and post-Revolutionary data, scores tallied for the various Old Regime electoral districts have been transformed into scores for the French *départements* of 1790 through a weighting

---

et des paroisses de la sénéchaussée particulière d'Angers pour les Etats généraux, 2 vols. (Angers, 1915–1916), 1: cii–ciii, cxlvii–cxlviii, and ccxxxii–ccxxxv; Henri Sée and André Lesort, *Cahiers de doléances de la sénéchaussée de Rennes,* 4 vols. (Rennes, 1909–1912), 1: ciii–cvi; Paul Bois, *Les Cahiers de doléances du Tiers-état de la sénéchaussée du Château-du-Loir pour les Etats généraux de 1789* (Gap, 1960), p. 69 and passim. Note also the assembly of the *sénéchaussée* of Brest which simply accepted the cahiers of the town of Brest in toto, adding only eighteen supplementary articles: *Archives parlementaires, 1ᵉ série (1787 à 1799),* 82 vols. (Paris, 1867–1913), 2: 475. There was a similar dominance of the town of Dinan over the cahier of its *sénéchaussée*: Hervé Pommeret, *Esprit public dans le département des Côtes-du-Nord pendant la Révolution* (Saint-Brieuc, 1921), p. 38. For southern Brittany, see Le Goff, *Vannes,* pp. 143–144.

[42] Both data files were made available to me by Gilbert Shapiro and John Markoff of the University of Pittsburgh. For a description of the methodology and coding procedure used by Shapiro and Markoff, see their articles, written with Sasha Weitman, "Quantitative Studies of the French Revolution," *History and Theory* 12 (1973): 163–191; and "Toward the Integration of Content Analysis and General Methodology," in *Sociological Methodology,* ed. David R. Heise (San Francisco, 1974), pp. 1–57. See also John Markoff, "Who Wants Bureaucracy? French Public Opinion in 1789" (Ph.D. dissertation; Johns Hopkins University, 1972). On the Hyslop-Weitman data file, see Sasha Weitman, "Bureaucracy, Democracy, and the French Revolution" (Ph.D. dissertation; Washington University, 1968). Weitman adapted a manuscript coding originally used in the context of Hyslop's study, *French Nationalism in 1789 according to the General Cahiers* (New York, 1934). Some of her data were published in an appendix of that book, pp. 250–87. For the Hyslop-Weitman file, the data base consists of 207 coded cahiers out of a probable original total of 236—including several written jointly by the Third Estate and one or both of the other two orders. The Shapiro-Markoff data are based on the analysis of 198 of the 236.

procedure based on proportionate overlapping territorial areas.[43] Three different approaches have been used to examine the regional differences in demands concerning questions of the Church and religion. An initial analysis based on the Shapiro-Markoff data file sought to determine quite simply the number of grievances in each general cahier which dealt with religious subjects. How frequently, in their appeals to the king, did the provincial notables make mention of problems concerning the clergy and the practice of religion?[44] When transposed from *bailliages* to *départements* and represented cartographically, the scores reveal a scattering of regions where ecclesiastical questions received especially full treatments, above the average of about twenty-five mentions per *département*. (See Figure D.) Portions of the south, from Gascony to Provence stand out, as do the eastern provinces of Champagne, Burgundy, and Franche-Comté. Nevertheless, by far the most prominent and cohesive cluster of *départements* appears in the west—but a west which, in this case, excludes Normandy and seems to be linked in continuity with the region around Paris. Even a cursory reading of the documents themselves reveals the remarkable differences between the cahiers of such western *bailliages* as Nantes, Le Mans, Rennes, or Anjou—with their lengthy and detailed programs for ecclesiastical change—and those of *bailliages* further south and east, like Saumur, Loudun, Angoulême, Sens, or Semur-en-Auxois, which include, at the most, only five or six grievances on the subject.[45]

Yet if the notables of the west in 1789 concerned themselves more frequently with religious questions than in any other section of the kingdom, what precisely did they say on this score? While a detailed examination in the context of an article would obviously be impossible, the Hyslop-Weitman coding does allow us to create a general aggregate score registering various forms of hostility towards the established Church

---

[43] The procedure for the transformation of scores was devised by Markoff and Shapiro and is described by them in "The Linkage of Data Describing Overlapping Geographical Units," *Historical Methods Newsletter* 7 (1973): 34–46. A special weighting procedure has been devised to account for the few missing cahiers.

[44] Analyzed, in practice, are all grievances coded by Shapiro and Markoff under the general rubric "R" (Religion). This rubric excludes a few types of grievances—e.g., those concerning education and charity, which were monopolized by the clergy—that ideally would also have been included in the count. But the small number of such grievances could scarcely have changed the overall picture. Note that in considering the total number of religious grievances rather than a ratio, I am following the precedent persuasively defended by Gilbert Shapiro and Philip Dawson in "Social Mobility and Political Radicalism: The Case of the French Revolution of 1789," in *The Dimensions of Quantitative Research in History*, ed. William O. Aydelotte et al. (Princeton, 1972), p. 178.

[45] *Archives parlementaires*, 1: 7–10, 38–45, 131–133; 3: 596–598, 644–645; 4: 94–101; 5: 538–550, 723–726, 757–761.

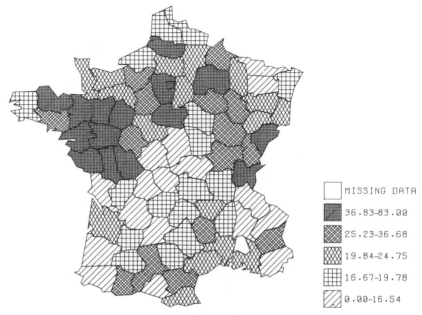

Figure D
Total Religious Grievances in Third Estate Cahiers

☐	MISSING DATA
▦	36.83–83.00
▩	25.23–36.68
▨	19.84–24.75
⊞	16.67–19.78
⧄	0.00–16.54

and its policies. Counted in this tentative measure of ecclesiastical "progressivism" are six sets of grievances: those demanding an end to clerical privilege, a full or partial secularization of key social institutions, a full or partial state control of Church property, an end to the legal and fiscal prerogatives of the papacy within the French Church, the institution of an expanded form of toleration, and a democratization of the Church by giving greater power and status to the parish clergy.[46] From this point of view, the geography of the cahiers presents a somewhat different and generally less coherent picture. (See Figure E.) Several of the southern and eastern *départements* for which the Church was a relatively more common topic of interest were apparently less "progressive" by our definition. Among those regions where lay notables indicated the strongest desire for change of religious and ecclesiastical institutions were the Parisian Basin, the Rhône Valley, portions of the Massif-Central, and once again, the west.´Indeed, the west had not only the highest total ranking—the average composite score per *département*—in France, but

[46] A score of 1 was attributed to a *bailliage* cahier each time one of the designated grievances occurred. The *bailliage* scores were then transformed to *département* scores through the procedure of proportionate areas described above.

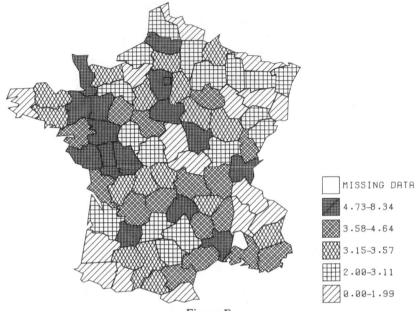

☐	MISSING DATA
▓	4.73–8.34
▦	3.58–4.64
▨	3.15–3.57
▤	2.00–3.11
▧	0.00–1.99

Figure E
Progressivism in Third Estate Cahiers

also the highest on all but one of the six individual sets of ecclesiastical grievances, with the Parisian region itself ranking but a close second.[47] Only on the question of religious toleration did the western *départements* rank low, not, for the most part, because of attitudes of intolerance, but because the issue was seldom raised at all—not suprising in a region where Protestants and Jews were rare or absent.[48]

It will be noted that the definition of "religious progressivism" used here is essentially empirical, formulated by grouping together many of the most common kinds of grievances related to religion and the Church actually found in the cahiers. A third, more teleological confrontation of the problem has been to use the Shapiro-Markoff data in order to measure the degree to which the different cahiers anticipated the Revolutionary reorganization of the Church on fifteen specific reforms embodied

[47] The west, as defined above in note 1, attained an average departmental aggregate score of 5.34. The Parisian Basin had 4.81; the Rhône-Mediterranean region, 4.77; the Massif-Central, 4.13. The lowest was in Alsace-Lorraine: 1.74.

[48] The departmental scores for demands indicating tolerance were at or below average in all *départements* of the west except the Manche. A second score measuring demands registering "intolerance" was also calculated. In the west, only the *département* of Ille-et-Vilaine achieved a high score (well above average) on this issue.

in various decrees passed during the period 1789–1790, especially those of the Civil Constitution of the Clergy.[49] For the kingdom as a whole, the results of this operation are relatively meager. It is clear that the legislation of the Constituent Assembly went vastly beyond the stated wishes of even the most articulate Frenchmen of 1789.[50] Yet the geography of this "degree of anticipation" is, in some ways, even more striking and coherent than for the two previous indices. (See Figure F.) While there is once again a scattering of "darker" *départements*, caused in most cases by solitary, unusually radical cahiers, the strongest anticipation scores are found in an arc extending from Artois south through Ile-de-France and then westward through Brittany—but excluding Normandy. One is again impressed by the continuity of elite opinion across western France from Paris to Nantes, a continuity that stands out in even sharper focus when one considers only the five most radical religious measures to be instituted by the Revolutionary legislature: the suppression of the tithes, of monastic vows, and of the chapters; the sale of Church property; and the lay election of curés and bishops. (See Figure G.) But it also emerges once again that in religious matters, the single most radical area of the entire kingdom—whether as measured by the total anticipation score or by the anticipation of the five most radical demands—was in Maine, upper Brittany, and Anjou, at the very core of the future Vendée-Chouans territory, in an area where 80 to 95 percent of the parish clergy would soon refuse their allegiance to the Civil Constitution.[51]

[49] The grievances scored were as follows: abolish clerical privileges (fiscal, seigneurial, political, judicial, honorific); abolish the regular clergy; sell Church property; change the boundaries of dioceses or parishes; choose curés and bishops by election; open all posts to talent, regardless of class or status; abolish simple benefices; abolish the tithes; abolish the *casuel*; abrogate the existing Concordat with Rome; require residence of all clergy with cure of souls; reduce wealth and income of bishops; provide pensions for sick and elderly priests; give parish clergy greater voice in diocesan affairs; abolish chapters. The initial count was made by hand, using the Shapiro-Markoff data as a guide to all Church-related grievances. This was necessary since the same essential grievances were sometimes coded differently in the data (through errors by coders, the failure to detect different names for the same institution, etc.). Each appearance of any of the designated grievances was scored 2. A partial rendering of any of the demands (e.g., abolish some regular orders, sell a portion of Church lands for state purposes) was given a score of 1.

[50] Thus, demands requesting the suppression of the tithes appeared in only twenty of the 198 Third Estate cahiers coded (10 percent); those for the suppression of the regular clergy in eight of 198 (4 percent); those for the sale of all Church property in five of 198 (3 percent).

[51] The *départements* with the three highest scores in the country on their general anticipation of the Civil Constitution were Ille-et-Vilaine (12.0), Maine-et-Loire (10.9), and Loire-Inférieure (9.9). On the score for anticipation of the most

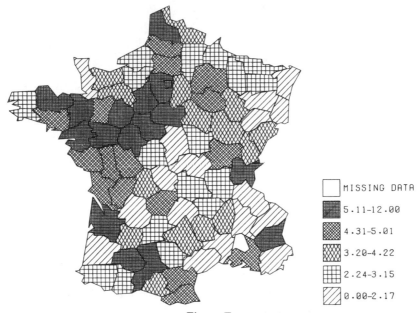

MISSING DATA

5.11-12.00

4.31-5.01

3.20-4.22

2.24-3.15

0.00-2.17

Figure F
Total Demands Anticipating Civil Constitution of the Clergy

The limitations to this preliminary consideration of the *cahiers de doléances* are only too clear. One would like to find the means of measuring the actual language used in making demands, the intensity, the tone—deferential or antagonistic—with which the grievances were formulated. A systematic linguistic analysis of this kind is obviously impossible in the context of the present article and, in any case, would open up a whole new array of interpretive difficulties. An impressionistic reading of the documents for the west, center, and the Parisian Basin reveals that the majority consisted essentially of straightforward demands, not couched in any overtly editorial rhetoric. One is struck, nevertheless, by the strong anticlerical tone of several of the Breton cahiers: that of Rennes with its indictment of the "corruption, intrigue, and despotism" in the nomination of both upper and lower clergy; that of Ploërmel with its condemnations of the "laziness" and "uselessness" of the regulars; or that of Brest, calling for a radical disengagement of the clergy from all temporal affairs—economic, political, and juridical—and an exclusive preoccupation with spiritual matters.[52] But anticlerical remarks are also

radical measures, three of the western *départements* (the same three) were in the top five, and five were in the top eight.

[52] *Archives parlementaires*, 1: 468–469; 5: 382, 542. The two data files used here offer little possibility for a linguistic analysis. The Shapiro-Markoff coding

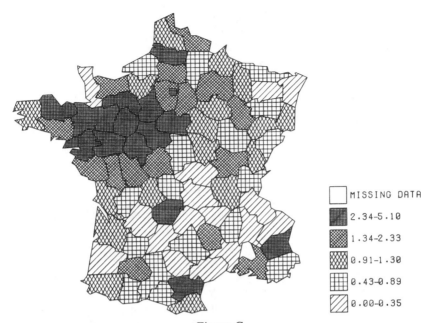

Figure G
Radical Demands Anticipating Civil Constitution of the Clergy

in evidence in certain cahiers of the Parisian region—Etampes, Nemours, and Paris *intra muros*, for example—coinciding, in short, with the previously identified continuum of more radical cahiers from the west to the Parisian Basin.[53]

And one would also hope to be able to compare the opinion of the notables in the general cahiers with opinions at the parish level.[54] While Tilly found no striking differences in religious demands in the various subregions of southern Anjou, Bois showed that the parish cahiers of the western Sarthe were distinctly more critical of the clergy—the regular clergy, for the most part. Yet the opinion represented in these local cahiers is far more difficult to associate with a given social grouping and

scheme does include information on the verb used—the "action" code—and on whether the demand was restricted, softened, emphasized, etc.; but this coding—especially as interpreted by individual coders—appears somewhat vague and impressionistic. Beatrice Hyslop categorized some cahiers as "showing anticlericalism," but it has been impossible to determine the objective criteria for her judgments: *French Nationalism*, pp. 263–4.

[53] Anticlerical tendencies can also be detected in the center in the cahiers of Chatellerault and Montargis.

[54] Shapiro and Markoff have coded the parish cahiers in forty-eight of the approximately 230 *grands bailliages*, but these tend to be clustered together in five or six areas of France and cannot easily be used for regional analysis.

should most certainly not be equated with peasant opinion. There is considerable evidence that a great many of these documents were strongly, even overwhelmingly influenced in their composition by outsiders to the peasant milieu, frequently by the very elite commoners who would later draw up the general cahiers for the bailliages.[55]

A Confrontation of Worlds

In a noted passage of his *Paysans de l'Ouest* Paul Bois describes the remarkable frontier cutting across upper Maine, dividing the west from the fringes of the Parisian Basin:

> With the coming of the great and prolonged upheaval of the Revolution, the manner of feeling and thinking and reacting would not be the same on the two sides of this invisible line which no one could have perceived until then. For in reality, across this vast *bocage*, so uniform in appearance, there lived not one but two different peoples.[56]

For Bois, and for most recent interpreters of the counterrevolution, it was above all a particular constellation of economic and social relationships which gave rise to this dichotomy. It is the hypothesis of the present article, in its examination of the west as a totality, that there was also an independent cultural and religious dimension to the forms of feeling and reacting which separated the two peoples of rural inhabitants; and that the veritable collision of the particular religious conceptions of the westernmost of the two peoples with the strikingly different world view of the islands of the urban cultural elite in that region would be one significant factor in the origins and special character of the uprisings in the west after 1790.

All historians have been aware of the profoundly unsettling effect of the Civil Constitution of the Clergy on the west and of its role in the causal patterns of the counterrevolution. There were, to be sure, variations in oath rates from district to district within this region, and numerous pockets of greater oathtaking as there were pockets of rural republicanism.[57]

---

[55] Tilly, *The Vendée*, pp. 183–185; Bois, *Paysans de l'Ouest*, pp. 91–97. On the composition of the rural cahiers see, for example, Alexandre Onou, ''Les Elections de 1789 et les cahiers du Tiers-état,'' *Révolution française* 26 (1909): 525; Henri Sée, ''La Rédaction et la valeur historique des cahiers de paroisses pour les Etats généraux de 1789,'' *Revue historique* 103 (1918): 929–306; Tilly, *The Vendée*, pp. 165–67. A limited effort was made to hand code a few sets of parish cahiers for ''religious progressivism.'' In general, mean parish scores were extremely low everywhere compared to the *bailliage* cahiers, and the range of regional variation was considerably less.

[56] Bois, *Paysans de l'Ouest*, p. 269.

[57] Dupuy, *La Garde nationale*, map, p. 233.

Yet such local variations tend to fade into insignificance when the west as a totality is compared to the center and the Parisian Basin.[58] Once a large contingent of the clerical corps in the west had been ousted for refusal to comply with the oath to the Constitution, the efforts of administrators to replace them—often with men whom local people perceived to be outsiders—would be met almost everywhere by hostility, even rage on the part of the village population. But the reasons for the massive rejection of the oath in the west, in contrast to its general acceptance in the Parisian Basin and the center, have been far more difficult to resolve. The results of the previous analysis, however, help to shed new light on the question. For both the clergy and the laity, the Civil Constitution represented a frontal attack on precisely that highly clericalized formulation of Catholicism which had been inculcated by the Council of Trent and which, for the combination of reasons described previously, had taken such strong root throughout much of Maine, Anjou, Brittany, lower Normandy, and Poitou. In the first place, the parish clergy, identifying itself to a relatively greater degree with the Church hierarchy, could be expected to be more responsive and submissive to the refusal of the oath on the part of the near totality of the bishops. Indeed, there is a remarkably high correlation in the west, center, and Parisian Basin between the percentage of refractory clergy for each Revolutionary district and the number of *vicaires* per parish—a useful indication, I have argued, of the local sense of "ecclesiastical society."[59] Yet throughout the west, there is also evidence of substantial pressure to reject the oath exerted on the clergy by the lay population. This initial hostility may have reflected, in part, a broad unhappiness with the economic policies of the Revolution. But equally important was the perception that the Civil Constitution was a direct attack on the strongly priest-oriented belief system of the rural inhabitants. The proposed elimination of all local clergymen such as chaplains and *habitués* not assigned to specific pastoral functions;[60] the lay election of curés (not by the parishioners themselves but by the

[58] Considering the regions as a whole for oath percentages as of the summer of 1791, 79 percent of *fonctionnaires publics* had taken and maintained their oaths in the *départements* of the Paris Basin, 75 percent in those of the center, and 29 percent in those of the west.

[59] Within the 134 districts of this sector of the kingdom for which data are available, the correlation coefficient is 0.77. For the 380 districts of the entire kingdom for which there are data, the correlation coefficient is 0.41.

[60] In this light, note the pleas made by an unknown deputy before the National Assembly on January 8, 1791 that a means be found to maintain the *habitués* and chaplains who normally participated in the sacred services in some areas of France. Such priests are said to be especially important for the feast days, and their expulsion, it is argued, will "exciter le mécontentement dans les âmes faibles": *Archives parlementaires*, 22: 81.

outside district electoral bodies); the substantial reduction of the economic position of the parish priest (both by eliminating his landed endowment and by lowering, in most cases, his absolute revenues);[61] the increased control achieved by the civil administration over the local priest: all such measures might easily appear in the rural west as threats to the status of the priest and thus to the very character of religion itself.

It was not simply a coincidence, a question of timing, that made the oath of allegiance to the Civil Constitution of 1791 a central issue in the initial crystallization of opposition towards the Revolution. Commonly, in protesting the Civil Constitution, and in exerting enormous pressure on the local priest to refuse the oath, the country people protested specifically that religion itself was in danger, that the Revolutionaries in the towns were Huguenots trying to convert them to Protestantism. It would be a mistake not to take such statements at face value. For in the context of the religion of the west, the Civil Constitution would indeed "change their religion."[62] In the center and in the Parisian Basin, by contrast, where the priest had already been a far less important figure and where religion in general had probably always been less clericalized, the Civil Constitution was not perceived as effecting the same kinds of major transformations in the character of religion. Indeed, the model of the priest embodied in the new Constitution was not far removed from the image of the citizen-priest, public servant to the community, already popular among many curés. Throughout most of this region the clergy was far less sensitive, often indifferent to the positions taken by the ecclesiastical hierarchy.[63] If the local population took an active interest in the question, it was usually in order to support the new laws. Here the Civil Constitution could much more easily be viewed as essentially a political, administrative document—as it had been, in its original conception, by the majority of the National Assembly. There are, in fact, numerous examples of intense popular pressure exerted on the clergy of these regions not to reject, but to accept the oath of 1791.[64]

---

[61] Because of the formula for determining the annual salaries of the curés after 1790 —1200 livres plus one-half of their Old Regime revenues over 1200 livres— a great many curés in the west would have their salaries significantly cut.

[62] See, for example, Cariou, "La Constitution civile du clergé dans le département du Morbihan," pp. 67–70; Emile Sévestre, *Liste critique des ecclésiastiques fonctionnaires publics insermentés et assermentés en Normandie* (Paris, 1922), p. 343; Le Goff, "L'Ouest se bat-il pour la foi?" p. 137.

[63] This is not to underestimate the possible importance of other factors in the weakness of ecclesiastical authority among the parish clergy of these regions— factors such as the heritage of Jansenism in certain dioceses.

[64] See, for example, Fernand Bridoux, *Histoire religieuse du département de Seine-et-Marne pendant la Révolution*, 2 vols. (Melun, 1953), 1: 89–90; A. D.

As for the clergymen themselves, the differences in self-image between the jurors and the non-jurors can often be discerned in the statements by which they justified their decisions on the oath. While there were invariably numerous exceptions, nevertheless a certain ideal type of oath explanation can be perceived for the two groups. If the refractory clergyman attached the priest primarily to the ecclesiastical hierarchy, the juror would insert him first and foremost within the whole lay community. If the first saw him as a servant of God, the second saw him as the servant of mankind. In the very language that they spoke, the refractory's emphasis on salvation and truth, the constitutional's stress on happiness and utility, the two sides revealed a fundamental confrontation of two world views, of two mental universes.[65]

But there was a further dimension to the conflict in the west, where the position of the urban elite of the Third Estate would intensely exacerbate the situation. To judge by the grievance lists, nowhere in the kingdom were the commoner notables more adamant to bring under attack the more clericalized, "Tridentine" brand of Catholicism, nowhere were they already prepared to advance ideas that would anticipate the Civil Constitution and, in particular, the most radical measures of that legislation. Perhaps it was the very intensity of the surrounding rural clericalism which gave a particular meaning and relevance to the anticlericalism of the Enlightenment, stimulating and intensifying the feelings of the notables towards priests and the priesthood.

A systematic typology of the manner in which national policies were implemented by departmental and district authorities has yet to be attempted. But historians have long been aware of the considerable independence of action assumed by these authorities in their interpretation of the flood of new laws dispatched almost daily by the National Assembly. And there is indication that many of the local officials in the western administrations, chosen from among the same urban elites who had written the cahiers, would soon prove especially impatient, unsympathetic, ex-

---

Millard, *Le Clergé du diocèse de Châlons-sur-Marne, première partie, le serment* (Châlons-sur-Marne, 1903), pp. 362, 376–378; Louis-Victor Pécheur, *Annales du diocèse de Soissons*. Volume VIII. *La Révolution* (Soissons, 1891), p. 413.

[65] Close to 200 oath explanations have been examined in drawing these generalizations. Detailed analyses will be published subsequently. The principal sources are from the four *départements* of Calvados, Seine-et-Marne, Moselle, and Côte-d'Or: Sévestre, *Liste critique*, pp. 303–414; A. D. Seine-et-Marne, L 282–283; P. Lesprand, *Le Clergé de la Moselle pendant la Révolution*, 4 vols. (Montguy-lès-Metz, 1934–1939), vols. 3 and 4; B. M. Dijon, ms. Reinert. Similar conclusions were reached by Louis Pérouas, "Le Clergé creusois durant la période révolutionnaire," *Mémoires de la société des sciences naturelles et archéologiques de la Creuse* 39 (1977): 564–565.

asperated with the religious sentiments of their rural constituencies.[66] The efforts of officials in Maine-et-Loire to forcibly impose juring priests on the population and repress popular pilgrimages has often been recounted.[67] More recently, Alison Patrick has assembled considerable evidence that the administrators of Maine-et-Loire, in particular, and several other western *départements*, in general, were unusually abrasive in their attempts to establish the Civil Constitution, and that this very "style" of administration, in its aggressiveness and lack of sensitivity, was a major element in the origins of the Vendée uprising.[68] For the *département* of Sarthe, Maurice Giraud has given proof of similar attitudes of near paranoia, with officials going well beyond the guidelines of the National Assembly in their vigorous pursuits against non-jurors.[69] It is clear that in many other parts of France where large numbers of refractories were likewise a problem, local governmental leaders were far more conciliatory and patient.[70] Thus, in the spring of 1792, the Ministry of the Interior found that the *départements* of the west were particularly active in drawing up unilateral and technically illegal orders, expelling all refractory priests from their parishes or *départements* or incarcerating them in central locations—long before such measures were embodied in national legislation. Yet there is no evidence that such tactics were commonly used in the strongly refractory areas of the north or the Massif-Central.[71] It is also noteworthy that there was a weak but significant correlation for

[66] This is not to overlook an initial honeymoon at the beginning of the Revolution when anticlerical sentiments were largely smoothed over in the general enthusiasm of national unity, and the gratitude of the middle-class revolutionaries for the contributions of the parish clergy to the events of 1789. It was clearly the confrontation over the Civil Constitution which lay bare the old anticlerical suspicions and impatience.

[67] See, for example, Pierre de la Gorce, *Histoire religieuse de la Révolution française*, 5 vols (1909–1923), 2: 369–381.

[68] Alison M. H. Patrick, "How to Make a Counterrevolution: Department Policy in the Maine-et-Loire, 1790–1793," paper delivered at the Society for French Historical Studies, Pittsburgh, March 1979. My thanks to Alison Patrick for kindly allowing me to refer to her research.

[69] *Essai sur l'histoire religieuse de la Sarthe de 1789 à l'an IV* (Paris, 1920), pp. 188–189, 260, 387–392. Also, for Ille-et-Vilaine, see Sutherland, pp. 249–250.

[70] In Rouergue or in Franche-Comté, for example: A. D. Aveyron L 1937; Jean Girardot, "Clergé réfractaire et clergé constitutionnel en Haute-Saône pendant la Révolution," *Mémoire de la société pour l'histoire du droit et des institutions des anciens pays bourguignons, comtois, et romands* 24 (1963): 126–127.

[71] Such measures were passed in 1791 or 1792 in all of the *départements* defined here as the west, with the exception of Manche. Compared to the ten western *départements* (including Finistère), only nine others in the entire country are known to have taken such measures—primarily in eastern France and across the Midi from Landes to Aude. There is no record of such measures in the north or the Massif-Central, except in Haute-Loire. Conclusions are based on the

the kingdom as a whole between the frequency of religious grievances in the cahiers of the Third Estate notables in a *département* and the proportion of the clergy per *département* refusing the ecclesiastical oath.[72] The action and reaction growing out of a clash of religious world views would soon greatly intensify the violence and counterviolence of a civil war.

But to develop such a perspective is not to attempt to conjure up another unidimensional explanation of the west. The observations presented here draw attention to a complex of attitudinal factors necessary but not sufficient for the outbreak of counterrevolution in wide areas of the west as a whole. Such factors should in no way be construed as providing a mechanical explanation for the uprising valid in a one-to-one analysis of individual parishes. It is also clear that the religious structures and attitudes explored above do not by themselves explain the strikingly sharp religious "frontier" of Gabriel Le Bras and Fernand Boulard. Insofar as can be ascertained, none of those measures found useful in the present discussion—e.g., clerical recruitment, *vicaire*-per-parish ratios, clerical revenues—marked off the stark boundary lines of the Boulard maps, but rather changed by transitional gradations as one traveled from east to west. A polarization after the fact, created by the political conflict itself, still seems the most plausible agent for the sharp honing of the frontiers.

In the final analysis, there can be no denying the importance of economic relations, of patterns of land tenure, of the issue of military conscription as factors in the outbreak of the *Vendée* and the *Chouannerie*. Yet it seems clear that the socioeconomic clashes between town and country were paralleled and greatly reinforced by an independent cultural clash; and that the peculiar constellation of religious structures and attitudes rendered this clash as sharp and pronounced as in any other region of France. And we must seriously entertain the possibility that it was this very religious confrontation which served as a key catalyst in the relative cohesion and unity of so much of the rural west, galvanizing and energizing the diverse and sometimes contradictory patterns of social and economic conflict at the local level.

---

records of the royal government's efforts to put a halt to the "intolérance" of local administrators against refractory clergy: general list drawn up by the Ministry of the Interior: A.N. F[19]311, supplemented by departmental responses to a government circular of March 1792: A.N.F[19]398–481. See also the speech by the Minister of the Interior before the Legislative Assembly, February 18, 1792: *Archives parlementaires*, 38: 627–630.

[72] The correlation by *département* between the percentage of clergymen refusing the oath in 1791 and the frequency of religious grievances in the cahiers was 0.22.

Redefining Revolutionary Liberty: The Rhetoric of Religious Revival during the French Revolution*

Suzanne Desan

In December 1794, in the midst of the French Revolution, the town officers of St. Bris in Burgundy tried to enforce a departmental decree closing the village church. The Catholic villagers responded by gathering en masse before the church doors and demanding the right to assemble peacefully to pray to the "Supreme Being." When the mayor locked the church, he returned the next day to find the doors removed. A second attempt also failed; the villagers pried off the locks, entered, and began to sing psalms and offices despite the absence of a priest. Next they assembled on the front steps and drafted a petition demanding to benefit from "the decree in which the Convention assured them religious liberty." Finally the mayor threw up his hands in despair and conceded that perhaps his persistent Catholic villagers should be allowed to worship publicly. "It is impossible to close the temples," commented the mayor. "The people have decided."[1]

The activism of the religious protesters of St. Bris was hardly unusual, for in the winter and spring of 1794–95 French Catholics launched an energetic and widespread revival of their religion. After the fall of Robespierre when the thermidorean government partially relaxed the laws restricting religious worship, parishioners throughout France seized the keys to parish churches, sang hymns and offices, and petitioned for the right to practice their religion in public. The revival movement involved a cultural clash between the newly created system of revo-

* I would like to thank Laird Boswell, Dena Goodman, Lynn Hunt, and Domenico Sella for their helpful suggestions. An earlier version of this paper was presented at the French Historical Studies Conference in Quebec in March 1986.

[1] Archives départementales de l'Yonne (AD Yonne) L716, Lettre du maire de la commune de St. Bris à "mon ami," 9 nivôse an III (December 29, 1794), and Procès verbal par le maire de la commune de St. Bris, 8 nivôse an III (December 28, 1794); Archives communales de St. Bris (AC St. Bris), Dépôt 583, D2, Procès verbaux de la commune de St. Bris, 11 nivôse au 24 pluviôse an III (December 31, 1794–February 12, 1795).

This essay originally appeared in the *Journal of Modern History* 60 (March 1988).

lutionary rituals and symbols and the traditional, Old Regime, Catholic worldview. In the midst of revolution and political upheaval, the clash was inevitably political as well as religious.

As Michelet wrote in the late 1840s in his *Histoire de la Révolution française:* "Religious or political, the two questions are deeply, inextricably intermingled at their roots. Confounded in the past, they will appear tomorrow as they really are, one and identical."[2] Indeed, this inextricable intermingling of the religious and the political lay at the cultural core of the French Revolution and will be the focus of this article. I will examine lay Catholic activism as a political and religious movement and ask how the context of revolution influenced the political activism of Catholic villagers. I would like to challenge the prevalent assumption that Catholics almost inevitably adopted counterrevolutionary attitudes. On the contrary, many Catholic revivalists in peaceful regions of France not only consistently supported the Revolution but also turned its promises and ideology to their own advantage. Above all, I will focus on the political language used by Catholic villagers: they reinterpreted and appropriated certain aspects of the revolutionary discourse as they demanded the return to free religious practice after the fall of Robespierre.

Catholics in prorevolutionary regions of France were especially likely to combine religious and revolutionary language in surprising ways and to transform and appropriate the language of the Revolution in support of Catholicism. My work is based on the activism of Catholic protesters in just such a region: the department of the Yonne in Burgundy, an area that was religious yet not counterrevolutionary. The Yonne is located in north-central France, mainly in the Old Regime wine-producing province of Burgundy with its northern tip in the wheat-growing province of Champagne. Most of the inhabitants of the Yonne welcomed the early stages of the Revolution. Likewise, almost 90 percent of the local clergy took the oath to the Civil Constitution in 1791, and three-quarters of these parish priests abdicated during the relatively widespread dechristianization campaign of 1794. Although the town of Avallon briefly supported the federalists in 1793 and although the Yonne elected moderate or right-wing candidates to the national legislature in the late 1790s, there was never any serious counterrevolutionary movement in Burgundy.[3] However, when the fall of Robespierre seemed to

[2] Jules Michelet, *Histoire de la Révolution française,* 2 vols., 2d ed. (Paris, 1868), 1:18.
[3] AD Yonne L687–L705. These *liasses* contain various dossiers on the reactions of the clergy of the Yonne to the Civil Constitution and to the abdication

offer hope for a return to the public practice of Catholicism, villagers in the Yonne, as in many other regions of France, demanded en masse the right to public worship. The political and religious activism of Catholics in the Yonne provides a representative illustration of the religious revival in much of northern and central France, including the Bourbonnais, Burgundy, Champagne, Orléanais, Île-de-France, the eastern part of the Loire Valley, and parts of Picardy and Normandy. For although economic and social structures varied widely in these regions, their political and religious configurations shared many elements: these were all regions that did not experience strong counter-revolutionary movements and where Constitutional clergymen were in a majority.[4] Yet these areas, like the Yonne, witnessed a resurgence of Catholicism after the Terror.

The French Revolution fundamentally altered the relationship between religion and politics. In 1789 Catholicism and the monarchy offered each other mutual support. As the official religion of France, Catholicism had a virtual monopoly of public religious expression. By 1794, only five years later, the Revolution had nationalized church lands, closed numerous churches throughout France, and caused most of the clergy to abdicate, go into hiding, or leave the country to escape the anticlericalism of the dechristianization campaign of the year II

---

campaign of the year II. Gustave Bonneau, *Notes pour servir à l'histoire du clergé de l'Yonne pendant la Révolution,* 1790–1800 (Sens, 1900); Michel Gally, "Notices sur les prêtres et religieux de l'ancien archidiaconé d'Avallon," *Bulletin de la Société des études avallonaises* (1898), pp. 13–177.

[4] Archives Nationales (AN) F7 3820, Tableaux des départments qu'on doit considérer comme en état de troubles, et des départements paisibles ou dans lesquels il n'a pas éclaté jusqu'ici des troubles essentiels, Ministre de la Police, vendémiaire an VIII (September–October 1799). This report includes fifty departments, primarily in the northern half of France. The "troubled" departments are mainly in the west, with a few listed in the southeast. "Peaceful departments" are concentrated in the central and northern part of France: Allier, Aube, Cher, Creuze, Indre, Loiret, Marne, Nièvre, Oise, Seine, Seine-et-Oise, Seine-et-Marne, Yonne, Aisne, Meuse, and Moselle. A third group of departments, listed as partially troubled, lie primarily in a band between the west and center, including Seine-Inférieure, Indre-et-Loire, Loir-et-Cher, Pas-de-Calais, Ardennes, Nord, and Somme, among others. The political geography of "peaceful departments" coincides quite well with the geography of clerical loyalty to the Revolution. In all of the above "peaceful departments" (except Moselle), more than half of the clergy took the oath. Oath taking was low in Brittany, Normandy, the rest of the West, the far north and northeast, the Massif Central, and the southwest corner of France. Timothy Tackett, *Religion, Revolution, and Regional Culture in Eighteenth-Century France: The Ecclesiastical Oath of 1791* (Princeton, N.J., 1986), pp. 52–54, 307–66.

(1793–94). In December 1793 Robespierre attempted to temper the dechristianization movement by promoting a bill guaranteeing freedom of religion; however, by the spring of 1794 the public practice of Catholicism had become virtually impossible in most of France. By 1795, church and state were separate by law, a tenuous experiment that would last only seven years. From September 1794 until the promulgation of the Concordat in 1802, the nation did not pay clerical salaries nor was Catholicism in any way officially linked to the French state. Public religious practice in the late 1790s remained severely curtailed; in particular, before the summer of 1795 and after the fructidorean coup d'état in 1797, French Catholics rarely had access to churches.[5] Throughout the thermidorean and Directorial periods, laws prohibited the ringing of bells, replanting of crosses on roadsides, and performing of outdoor festivals, processions, or funerals. Priests wishing to worship were subject to a series of declarations of loyalty to the Republic, yet their legal status remained precarious and unclear. The laws governing the religious practice of clergy and laity alike shifted constantly as the *jeu de bascule* of Directorial politics left its mark on national religious policy.

Moreover, the revolutionary leadership had created a whole cultural system of revolutionary rituals, symbols, and language that aimed at replacing Christianity and reeducating people according to the political ideals of the Revolution. For radical revolutionaries had come to view Christianity as the rival cosmological and moral system that had provided the frame and underpinning of the monarchy and the traditional hierarchical order. As a result, the creators of revolutionary culture developed a rhetoric of opposition: the hierarchy of Catholicism versus the egalitarianism of the Revolution; superstition versus reason; irrational mystery versus revolutionary transparency; a vague supernat-

---

[5] The law of 18 frimaire an II (December 8, 1793) made a promise of freedom of religion and prohibited violence against any cult. The law of 3 ventôse an III (February 22, 1795) guaranteed the freedom of private worship for small groups, but the Republic would not recognize or fund any cult. No bells, processions, or external religious symbols such as crosses were allowed, and churches were to remain closed. Despite its restrictions, this law inaugurated a two-and-a-half-year period of relative religious freedom in France. The law of 11 prairial an III (May 29, 1795) permitted parishioners to reclaim unsold churches, provided that the curé made a declaration of loyalty to national laws. However, immediately after the coup d'état of 18 fructidor an V (September 4, 1797), the newly purged legislature inaugurated a new period of religious repression by resurrecting the campaign of the year II to restrict and enclose public Catholic worship and by tightening laws regarding the clergy.

uralism versus the secular, this-worldly orientation of the Revolution. Despite the profoundly secular emphasis of revolutionary thought, the new political culture took over didactic, sacralizing, and regenerative functions and characteristics which had previously been the exclusive reserve of religion. The revolutionaries appropriated into the realm of political activism and political culture many of the former roles of religion, including the moral formation of human nature, the codification of social relations, and the ceremonial support of the political regime and its ideology.[6] During the late 1790s the Directory and the national legislature continued to support this ideological reeducation of France as they refurbished and promoted the revolutionary calendar and festivals with renewed zeal.

But this modern transformation of politics into a secular, moralizing force that could create a culture independent of religion was not a smooth process. Just as the revolutionaries had sacralized and moralized politics, so too they politicized religion. The Revolution's attempt to replace Christianity with new revolutionary cults and culture would fuel counterrevolutionary movements in certain regions of France, particularly the west and parts of the southeast. Although the conflicts may have been less violent in noncounterrevolutionary areas of France, the issues were no less pervasive and critical. The choice to attend Mass, wear finer clothes on Sunday, or baptize one's child with a saint's name suddenly became a political issue. Religious allegiances and practices became means of playing out political or social conflicts within towns and village communities. Catholics had to develop political methods of reclaiming and maintaining their right to practice publicly.

In this politically and symbolically charged atmosphere, the revival of Catholicism was not solely a direct reaction against the Revolution nor a simple return to past practices. For the most part historians have analyzed the Catholic revival either as an attempt to return directly to the religious practices and structures of the Old Regime or as part of a political reaction against the central government—in short, religious revival as counterrevolution. This historiography, whether written by the left or the right, has essentially adopted the language and the categorizations, if not always the value judgments, of the early revolutionaries. Especially during the debates over separation of church and state at the turn of the century, historians tended to view the Revolution as a monolith, which, depending on the historian's own viewpoint, either freed the French people from the bonds of superstition and

---

[6] Lynn Hunt, *Politics, Culture, and Class in the French Revolution* (Berkeley, Calif., 1984); Mona Ozouf, *La fête révolutionnaire, 1789–1799* (Paris, 1976).

priestcraft or destroyed social bonds and stability and cast Terror into the hearts of all. Catholicism, in turn, was invariably portrayed as unequivocally opposed to the Revolution. Most of these interpretations, whether political or religious in emphasis, stressed a clear-cut opposition between the Revolution and Catholicism as the only point of focus.[7]

A closer look at Catholic religious activism reveals the striking limitations of this traditional assumption that Catholicism and counter-revolution invariably went hand in hand throughout France. For in large areas of France, particularly in the central and northern regions, villagers accepted and even welcomed many aspects of the Revolution, and yet they continued to cling to their traditional religious practices and Christian worldview. Often, lay religious activists found in the political techniques and ideology of the Revolution itself the means to demand their right to worship freely in public. The revolutionary attempt to refashion society, with its peculiar combination of quasi-religious fervor and secular orientation, also opened up the discourse on both political and religious issues. While the revolutionaries had created a political language, ideology, and techniques, which they intended to use for their own goals, the very act of creating a new discourse on power and the sacred threw the floor open for debate and for different uses of their ideology. The revolutionary discourse was not a fixed

---

[7] Several key works on religion during the Revolution written from a Catholic point of view at the turn of the century include Pierre de la Gorce, *Histoire religieuse de la Révolution française*, 5 vols. (Paris, 1912–23), a very useful narrative despite its Catholic bias; Victor Pierre, *La déportation ecclésiastique sous le Directoire* (Paris, 1896); M. Sciout, *Histoire de la Constitution civile du clergé* (Paris, 1891); and Abbé Sicard, *Le clergé de France sous la Révolution*, 3 vols. (Paris, 1912–17). There are numerous works that trace the fate of the clergy in many regions. For the Yonne, see Bonneau (n. 3 above). The principal works written on religion from the revolutionary point of view are F. A. Aulard, *Le Christianisme et la Révolution française* (Paris, 1924), and *Le Culte de la Raison et le culte de l'Être Suprême, 1793–94* (Paris, 1892); and Albert Mathiez, *Contributions à l'histoire religieuse de la Révolution* (Paris, 1907), and *La Révolution et l'Église* (Paris, 1910). Mathiez's books are collections of essays that appeared in article form between 1900 and 1910. Useful recent works that discuss lay religiosity include Olwen Hufton, "The Reconstruction of a Church, 1796–1801," in *Beyond the Terror: Essays in French Regional and Social History, 1794–1815*, ed. Gwynne Lewis and Colin Lucas (Cambridge, 1983); and Claude Langlois and Timothy Tackett, "À l'Épreuve de la Révolution (1770–1830)," in *Histoire des Catholiques en France du XVe siècle à nos jours* (Paris, 1981). These necessarily brief overview essays do not pay much attention to the connections between religious expression and political language and forms of activism.

entity. Not only were the revolutionaries themselves constantly redefining their politics and creating power through rhetoric, but groups
without power could also make use of the revolutionary discourse. It
was open to all.

In fact, revolutionary rhetoric was appealing and powerful precisely
because it had a chameleon-like quality. It could be adopted and transformed by different groups for different uses. In addition, the actual
content of revolutionary ideology by its very nature contained certain
principles that opened the way for ambiguous or oppositional interpretations. In particular, the concepts of popular sovereignty, liberty,
and the general will had especially ambivalent meanings. Catholic activists would use revolutionary arguments for liberty, popular sovereignty, the Constitution, the general will, and freedom of opinion to
defend their right to worship in public. Catholics of the Yonne continued
to rely on forms of protest that they had long used for different purposes, ranging from tax riots against central government officials to
charivari protests against local transgressors to petitions to higher authorities, but religious activists lent greater force to these Old Regime
forms of protest by infusing them in original ways with revolutionary
rhetoric. Moreover, the Revolution's validation of the popular will lent
legitimacy to their demands for religious freedom. An examination of
the political language of Catholic protesters and petitioners not only
helps to illustrate their political techniques, it also reveals popular
attitudes toward the Revolution on a local level as villagers strove to
incorporate innovations in revolutionary ideology into their traditional
belief structures.

* * *

This discourse found its most clear and explicit expression in petitions for freedom of worship. Although petitioning was fairly common
in the Old Regime, its use was limited by the legal and bureaucratic
structures of the royal administration and the seigneurial system. The
power to petition lay primarily in the hands of the notables or syndics
of each village, who petitioned in the name of the village assembly to
bring cases to court or, on occasion, to make a special request from a
seigneur, intendant, or bishop. The Revolution transformed the process
of petitioning when the National Assembly decreed in 1789 that petitioning was a political right guaranteed to all active citizens.[8] A wider
range of people now had the legal right to petition. Furthermore, the

[8] Lettres-patentes du Roi, sur un décret de l'Assemblée nationale pour la
constitution des municipalités, 28 décembre 1789, Article LXII, in *Lois et
Actes du gouvernement, août 1789 au septembre 1790* (Paris, 1834).

new structures of local and national government institutions, the revolutionary guarantees of freedom of opinion, and the ideology of popular sovereignty all gave added value to the voice of the people and to petitioning.

When Catholic villagers in the Yonne formally demanded freedom of worship, by far the largest number of petitions, roughly 40 percent in the Yonne between Thermidor and the Concordat, involved requests for the right to use churches; Catholic villagers also requested the release of priests, the return of sacred objects, the use of rectories, and the right to ring bells and hold processions.[9] Revivalists sent their petitions to municipal and departmental authorities, to the national legislature, and to the Directors. Lay religious activists were keenly aware that numbers meant strength; they used popular assemblies and door-to-door soliciting to gather as many names as possible. In some cases, local leaders of the religious movement, often the village schoolteacher or the *fabriciens,* drew up formal petitions to read to their fellow citizens at a village assembly or to circulate throughout the village. In other cases, the composition and signing of petitions was more spontaneous: it often took place in conjunction with religious ritual or with illegal popular *rassemblements.* For example, in Auxerre on Palm Sunday in 1795 the Catholics who had illegally entered the town cathedral sent a delegation of fifty citizens to the municipality to demand use of their church. Once at the town hall, the protesters "cried out, 'Glory to God! Respect for the Convention and the constitutional authorities! Vive la République!'" The Catholic citizens then presented their demands in a written petition.[10]

Petition signers were predominantly male, were a least partially literate, and in theory had to be heads of household in order for their

[9] Sources for Catholic petitions include (1) AD Yonne: the "police des cultes" records; departmental, district, and municipal deliberations; court records; (2) AN, esp. the F7 (police) and F19 (cultes) series; (3) newspapers: *L'Observateur du département de l'Yonne* and *Journal politique et littéraire du département de l'Yonne.*

[10] AD Yonne L716, Lettre de Leclerc-Racinnes aux citoyens administrateurs de St. Florentin, 7 fructidor an VI (August 24, 1798) and Pétition des habitants catholiques de St. Florentin aux citoyens administrateurs de la commune de St. Florentin, 12 fructidor an VI (August 29, 1798); AD Yonne L710, Procès verbal du Conseil général de la commune d'Auxerre, 9 germinal an III (March 29, 1795); AN F7 4439¹, Lettre des députés du département de l'Yonne au Citoyen Mailhe, Représentant en Mission, 20 germinal an III (April 9, 1795), and Procès verbaux de la commune d'Auxerre, 11 & 13 floréal an III (April 30 and May 2, 1795); Gaston David, "Tableaux de l'histoire d'Auxerre de 1789 à 1817," *L'echo d'Auxerre* 88, pp. 27–29, esp. 27–28.

signatures to be legal. Petitions frequently listed additional names of illiterate villagers who also supported the cause. The social composition of the signers manifested a wide social spectrum and seemed most often to reflect the social composition of the town or village as a whole. Petitioning was not dominated by village elites, nor was the desire for a return to public Catholic practice confined exclusively to poorer members of society.[11] Although women were very often the predominant figures in religious riots, assemblies, and illegal processions, male signatures were invariably more numerous on petitions. Widows, as legal heads of household, also signed petitions. But the existing political and social structures brought about a certain gender-based division in the Catholics' techniques; women were channeled toward illegal forms of activism as their legal means of political expression were more severely limited. Interestingly, however, although women had no legal right to petition, they were politically well versed in the language of revolutionary promises. They frequently used the politicized rhetoric of revolutionary rights when they justified their behavior in riots or when they wrote individual letters to the Directors, national legislature, or local authorities. For example, the women of Vaux who forced their mayor to surrender the church keys in 1795 testified that "since everybody had freedom of opinion, we desired our religion and thought we were authorized to demand the keys to practice it."[12] Paradoxically, the revolutionary discourse and context reinforced certain traditional notions of moral economy.[13]

Finally, religious petitions in the Yonne came from towns and villages of all sizes. Catholics in all ten towns of the Yonne with over two thousand inhabitants submitted written requests, but petitions with revolutionary rhetoric were likewise strikingly widespread in tiny communes throughout this rural department. Not only were rural petitions pervasive; they were also original. No circulation of model religious petitions seems to have taken place and, despite the suspicions of the authorities, priests had very little role in the composition of petitions in the Yonne. Petitions were the indigenous and spontaneous product of local Catholic villagers. The revolutionaries had been notably suc-

[11] Suzanne Desan, "The Revival of Religion during the French Revolution (1794–1799)" (Ph.D. diss., University of California, Berkeley, 1985), pp. 194–207.

[12] AD Yonne L1118, Procès verbaux du comité révolutionnaire d'Auxerre, 18 & 19 nivôse an III (January 7, 8, 1795).

[13] E. P. Thompson, "The Moral Economy of the English Crowd in the Eighteenth Century," *Past and Present* 50 (1971): 76–136.

cessful in some ways in their struggle to politicize the people of the countryside; yet, paradoxically, Catholic peasants and townspeople would turn this political education to their own ends against the visions of the radical revolutionaries.

* * *

The religious activists who petitioned for free use of their churches or for the return of sacred objects did not always intend to make counterrevolutionary demands. On the contrary, they believed that the Revolution itself guaranteed the right to religious freedom. They made their requests within the context, language, and assumptions of the revolutionary discourse on religion, culture, and politics. The petitioners took the revolutionary promises of liberty and popular sovereignty and applied them together with revolutionary political techniques to defend one aspect of their daily lives that seemed threatened to them—the realm of religious practice and belief. They reinterpreted revolutionary concepts to suit their religious convictions and their own conception of freedom. It is important to note that, although religious activists voiced these assumptions regarding the guarantees of the Revolution most clearly in written petitions, the same concepts also found expression in their speeches in village assemblies, in shouts at riots, in testimony at trials, and in threatening placards tacked to liberty trees, parish churches, and town walls. The notion that the Revolution itself was the basis of popular sovereignty, religious liberty, and freedom of belief and expression was more than a rhetorical tactic to appeal to authorities: it was a deep-rooted conviction among people newly educated and formed in the heat of revolution.

On the most general level, religious activists invoked "liberty" as a basic right. After five years of revolution, villagers no longer conceived of "liberty" in the Old Regime sense of "privilege"; rather, it had become for them a natural "right," an inherent characteristic and inalienable possession of mankind. Yet the revivalists sometimes viewed "liberty as a right" in a different light than did the radical revolutionaries. To a villager, "liberty" might indeed mean freedom from seigneurial dues or protection from arbitrary arrest as the revolutionary leaders in Paris expected, but "liberty" could also mean the freedom to dance on Sundays and saints' days or the right to lead a funeral procession through the village streets. "Where then is liberty if we cannot dance whenever we want to? If we are not free, we must cut down the Liberty Tree," declared villagers throughout the Yonne in 1797 according to the *commissaire* of the department. In the spring of 1795 the members of the four sectional assemblies of Auxerre clearly expressed their belief that liberty meant the freedom of conscience and the right to practice whatever religion one wished. They jubilantly announced that now once again "the virtuous citizen is assured the enjoyment of his rights," as they congratulated the National Convention for proclaiming freedom of religion and for putting an end to the attempt by the "enemies of the people to exercise their tyrannical empire even over the consciences [of individuals]." As one anonymous letter writer warned the president of the Council of Five Hundred, the antireligious actions of the government were "contradictory and did not conform to the wishes of the public who have elected you and whose opinion and liberty you must respect. . . . You want to impose tyranny over our thoughts as well as our actions, and [we are] men whom you like to call free." In fact, Catholic villagers frequently became deliberately defiant and stubborn in their claims for liberty of conscience; they seemed on occasion to take illegal actions just to prove that they had the right to defy the government. In 1796, in a brawl with the guardsmen who tried to disband an illegal festival in the town of Saint Georges, one villager made this taunting claim in defense of liberty as a general principle: "People are free to gather every day and amuse themselves; the fair only existed to prove that the citizens were free; there is no law that could change Saint Pierre."[14]

For the most part protesters were more specific in their use of the word "liberty." Most frequently, they referred explicitly to the promise of *liberté des cultes,* "so often and so strongly pronounced by the National Convention," as the villagers of Courgis were quick to point out.[15] The Declaration of the Rights of Man and Citizen, the successive constitutions, as well as various explicit laws, had in fact repeatedly guaranteed this freedom of religious practice. Catholic petitioners, rioters, letter writers, priests, municipal officers, and court witnesses alike referred again and again to this guarantee in a wide variety of contexts as they demanded freedom of public worship. While the citizens of Noyers in 1799, like many other Catholics of the Yonne, cited the *"liberté des cultes"* to assert their right to use the local church,

---

[14] AN F1c III Yonne 5, Compte analytique de la situation du département de l'Yonne, par Collet, commissaire de l'Yonne, thermidor an VI (July–August 1798); AC Auxerre Dépôt 3, 12, Addresse des sections d'Auxerre à la Convention nationale, sans date (c. ventôse an III/February–March 1795); AN C568, Lettre anonyme au président du Conseil des Cinq-Cents, sans lieu ou date (c. fructidor an VI/August 1798); AD Yonne L230, Procès verbal de la commune de Saint Georges, 11 messidor an VI (June 29, 1798).

[15] AD Yonne L712, Pétition de l'assemblée des citoyens de la commune de Courgis à l'administration départementale, sans date (c. early in frimaire an II/November–December 1794).

the inhabitants of Fontenailles likewise based their claim for the return of sacred objects on the "Constitution which allows the freedom of religion."[16] A speaker at a village assembly in Ligny in 1793 gave a classic formulation of the argument: "We have obtained liberty. The principle is incontestable, it is constitutional: this liberty includes the practice of whatever religion we judge appropriate to adopt. The freedom of worship cannot be forbidden—Article VII of the Declaration of the Rights of Man. The commune of Ligny has therefore the right to continue the practice of the Catholic religion if [the inhabitants] think it is good and to follow the religion in which they have been brought up and which their fathers have taught them."[17] This villager's plea for the continued practice of Catholicism combined the revolutionary principle of constitutional liberty with the traditional argument of the "religion of our fathers" in a typical fashion.

Although Catholic activists made claims based on the Revolution's promise of freedom of religious practice throughout the revolutionary era, at certain moments this type of claim became particularly prevalent or opportune. The revivalists were keenly aware of the political tone of different eras of the Directory and they shifted their use of rhetoric accordingly. The law of 3 ventôse an III (February 21, 1795) made a promise of religious liberty and allowed small groups to worship together, although the law did not grant the use of churches and continued to prohibit public practice and public Catholic symbols; on 11 prairial an III (May 29, 1795) the Convention went a step further by allowing parishioners to reclaim unsold parish churches. Inspired by these new promises in the spring of 1795, religious activists referred triumphantly and optimistically to the laws increasing religious liberty. Early in April 1795 the municipality of Auxerre, purged of its most radical leaders of the year II (1793–94), sent a group of spokesmen to appear at the bar of the National Convention to applaud the work of the deputies since the Ninth of Thermidor, "notably the decree which maintains the freedom of religious practice." In the same triumphant mood, a few months later, Citizen Islème from Asquins-sous-Vézelay wrote to the National

---

[16] AD Yonne L715, Pétition des habitants de la commune de Noyers au canton de Noyers, 4 prairial an VII (May 23, 1799); AD Yonne L707, Pétition des habitants de la commune de Fontenailles au district de Saint Fargeau, 19 frimaire an II (December 9, 1793).

[17] Speech given by villager at *assemblée générale* of Ligny, December 11, 1793, as quoted in Michel Valot, "Maître Louis Bouteille, Curé de Ligny," *Bulletin de la société des sciences historiques et naturelles de l' Yonne* 107 (1975): 103–25, p. 108.

Convention that the 11 prairial an III (May 29, 1795) law was "an inexhaustible source of joy for all good citizens. 'Vive la Convention! À bas les Jacobins, les terroristes!' These are the cries repeated by the people who swear their attachment to the great principles of liberty."[18]

In the aftermath of the fall of Robespierre, petitioners used the language of the Thermidorean reaction. They strove to associate the repressive religious policy of the year II (1793–94) entirely with the politics of Robespierre and the Terror. In December 1794 when the municipality of Mont Saint Sulpice appealed for the return of their church bells, they spoke of the bell-removing brigands with a peculiar mixture of religious and Thermidorean rhetoric. "We still *pardon* them for this act of *tyranny* and of *despotism*," proclaimed the petitioners, with the self-righteous assurance of Thermidoreans. The religious activists were quick to warn against a return to the Terror, particularly during the attempt by the Directory to enforce observance of the republican calendar and *fêtes décadaires* following the coup d'état of 18 fructidor an V (September 4, 1797). The religious agitators of Charny who violated the republican festival laws deliberately cried out against the Terror. The *gendarmes* who went to prevent the celebration of a religious festival in Vézelay in the year VI (1797–98) were met with the defiant cry, "Where are your orders? Those are only departmental decrees. We don't give a damn. This won't last long. If we had a flute, we would dance despite you. We are *no longer under the reign of Robespierre*."[19]

Lay Catholic protesters were very conscious of specific laws that guaranteed their religious rights. Sometimes the petitioners made very precise references to laws that had just been passed. A petition addressed to the legislature and to the minister of police by "the citizens of different communes of the department of Yonne" in 1799 formally quoted the most important legislation on religious liberty, including the laws of 3 ventôse an III (February 21, 1795) and of 7 vendémiaire an IV (September 29, 1795) as well as article 354 of the Constitution of the year

---

[18] Procès verbal de la Convention nationale, 16 germinal an III (April 5, 1795), as quoted in M. Légé, "Nicolas Maure," *Annuaire de l'Yonne* (1892), pp. 156–272, 258; AN DIII 304, Lettre du citoyen Islème à la Convention nationale, 17 prairial an III (June 5, 1795).

[19] AD Yonne L712, Lettre de la municipalité de la commune de Mont Saint Sulpice à l'administration départementale de l'Yonne, 14 frimaire an III (December 4, 1794); AD Yonne L217, Procès verbal de Charny, envoyé à l'administration départementale de l'Yonne, 25 brumaire an VII (November 15, 1798); AN F7 7488, Procès verbal des gendarmes à Vézelay, 11 thermidor an VI (July 29, 1798).

III. The petitioners appealed to the legislators to crack down on those who threatened and troubled the freedom of worship and concluded their plea with the observation that no other right of the Constitution was more dear to the people and more sacred for the state than the right to religious freedom. Likewise, the inhabitants of Coulange-la-Vineuse cited several laws and concluded their petition, "Vive la République, vive la Constitution de l'an III!" when they objected to the closing of their church. Not all petitions quoted sections of the laws at such length, but they cited them with great frequency.[20]

Even when they did not have knowledge about an exact law, protesters insisted that they had legal backing. When the women of Toucy marched to the town council on March 22, 1795 to demand the keys of the church "built by their ancestors," three leading women "insisted that there was a decree which they didn't have, but which authorized their actions." Likewise, the villagers of Charny who celebrated an illegal festival accompanied their threats, gestures, and assaults with the claim that the law to observe the republican calendar "was not a law." "They objected continually against the attacks on the Constitution and the free practice of religion," reported the municipal officers.[21] In short, while the composers of petitions more frequently cited specific laws, the leaders of more spontaneous religious uprisings were not as precise in their information. In the heat of the moment, they called on their general sense of certainty that the Constitution, the Declaration of the Rights of Man, and some unspecified laws supported their claim to religious liberty.

[20] AN F7 7585, and AN C568, Pétition des citoyens du département de l'Yonne aux citoyens législateurs, 14 ventôse an VII (March 4, 1799); AD Yonne L712, Pétition des habitants de Coulange-la-Vineuse à l'administration municipale du canton de Coulange-la-Vineuse, 4 vendémiaire an VII (September 25, 1798). See also AD Yonne L710, Pétition des paroissiens de Saint Étienne à l'administration du départment de l'Yonne, sans date (c. nivôse an VIII/ winter 1799–1800); AD Yonne L716, Pétition des Catholiques de Saint-Julien-du-Sault au département de l'Yonne, 23 nivôse an VIII (January 13,1800); AD Yonne L68, Arrêté du département de l'Yonne (regarding petition from Blenne), 13 messidor an III (July 1, 1795); Pétition des citoyens du faubourg Saint Martin d'Avallon à l'administration municipale d'Avallon, 29 messidor an III (July 17, 1795), as quoted in Abbé Giraud, "La Ville d'Avallon pendant la période révolutionnaire d'après les procès verbaux de l'administration municipale," in *Bulletin de la Société d'Etudes d'Avallon* (1910–11), pp. 135–698, p. 475; see also the church use declarations in AD Yonne L706.

[21] AN F7 4439[1], Procès verbal du conseil général de Toucy, 4 germinal an III (March 24, 1795); AD Yonne L217, Procès verbal de la municipalité de Charny, envoyé à l'Administration départementale de l'Yonne, 25 brumaire an VII (November 15, 1798).

In a sense, the exact content and wording of the laws had become less important than their existence as symbols of the villagers' rights. The villager at Ligny who objected to the reading of the decree closing churches by waving an almanac containing the Constitution and by asserting vociferously that this document guaranteed freedom of religious practice may never have read the Constitution, but reference to its written word had become a source of authority. The *commissaire* of the Yonne noted in the winter of 1800 that the law of 7 nivôse an VIII (December 28, 1799) "seemed to have put into the hands of malevolent people a weapon for striking and destroying republican institutions."[22] Interestingly enough, municipal officers also tried to use laws or decrees as concrete symbols. Officials routinely read decrees to rioters, as if the very words of the law, as manifestations of their authority, would convey a power beyond their actual verbal content.

Villagers in some cases misinterpreted laws, either deliberately or inadvertently, in such a way as to give more legitimacy to the religious revival. The law of 7 vendémiaire an IV (September 29, 1795) required parishioners and priests to make a formal declaration *if* they intended to use their parish church; but when they made their church declarations to local municipalities, several groups of Catholics went so far as to suggest that the law *required* them to choose a church. The inhabitants of Gland commented that "they assembled to obey the law which *obliged* them to select a place to practice the Catholic religion," while the Catholics of Butteaux spoke of the law which "*ordered* them to choose a locale for worship."[23] Rumors about laws on religious practice or about speeches given at the national legislature were not always well founded, but they clearly influenced the actions of the villagers. As early as March 2, 1795 the national agent of Préhy complained of the adverse effect of the law of 3 ventôse an III (February 22, 1795), "not yet promulgated, but already known." Rumors about the speech given by the deputy Camille Jordan calling for a return to bell ringing set bells ringing throughout France in the summer of 1797. In early September 1797 the cantonal administration of Épineuil, for example, decreed that local agents should seize bell-tower keys and

---

[22] AD Yonne L714, Procès verbal de la municipalité de Ligny, 6 nivôse an III (December 26, 1794); AN F19 481⁴⁻⁵, Lettre du commissaire de l'Yonne au ministre de l'Intérieur, 9 pluviôse an VIII (January 29, 1800). The law of 7 nivôse an VIII allowed parishioners to reclaim unsold churches once again and simplified the declaration of loyalty required of the clergy.

[23] AD L706, Procès verbal de la commune de Gland, 16 fructidor an IV (September 2, 1796); Procès verbal de la commune de Butteaux, 24 brumaire an IV (November 15, 1795).

bell cords because "many people took the motion made in the Council of Five Hundred on bell ringing as a pretext for violating the law."[24]

In any event, authorities noted that religious activists acted as if the guarantee of *liberté des cultes* was more fundamental than any other national law. The representative on mission Mailhe complained in the spring of 1795 that fanatics and royalists misinterpreted the "humane and philosophical decree on the freedom of religious practice [as a] pretext for persecuting good citizens in the name of heavenly vengeance." The municipality of Flogny complained that no law, no letter from the Minister of Police, no departmental decree—in short, no legal authority—could make any impact on the villagers' insistence on performing "their ancient religious ceremonies with great pomp" on Sundays and holy days; the inhabitants would only respond "that they were free to practice these ceremonies, that no one had the right to force them to change these days." When the department decreed that all church goods be inventoried and returned to the municipality in August 1798, the inhabitants of Flogny immediately took most of the religious objects from the temple, apparently assuming that the promise of *liberté des cultes* gave them the right to take such an action.[25]

* * *

Just as Catholic villagers relied heavily on their own religious interpretation of the liberty promised them by the Revolution, so too they used the ideology of *popular sovereignty* to lend greater authority and certainty to their cause. In the Old Regime, village assemblies had made demands of seigneurs and intendants and had taken these higher authorities to court on occasion. However, the villagers' expectations for success lay entirely in the hands of the justices of various courts. After 1789, the people were able to act on their own in a new way. The Revolution altered popular conceptions of their own political roles, for the Revolution brought both the ideological guarantee of popular sovereignty and the formation of new political structures which, in theory at least, were meant to convey the general will and to insure representation of the masses.

Catholic activists made use of the ideological argument of popular sovereignty in their struggle for the right to practice religion publicly.

[24] AD Yonne L715, Lettre de l'agent national de Préhy au district d'Auxerre, 12 ventôse an III (March 2, 1795); AN F7 7283, Procès verbal du canton d'Épineuil, 22 fructidor an V (September 9, 1797).

[25] AN F7 4439¹, Lettre de Mailhe, représentant en mission, à Maure, représentant du peuple, 7 floréal an III (April 26, 1795); AD Yonne L1407, Procès verbal de la municipalité de Flogny, 17 fructidor an VI (September 1, 1798).

A woman from Joigny tacked a placard to the base of a newly cut Liberty Tree in the summer of 1799:

> Wake up, people of France. No government is as despotic as ours. They tell us, "You are free and sovereign," while we are enchained to the point where we are not allowed to sing or to play on Sundays, not even allowed to kneel down to offer homage to the Supreme Being. . . . After this, *are we sovereign?* Isn't this playing with the people?

In this remarkable document "Suzanne sans peur" went on to criticize the factionalism of the government and the schisms in popular assemblies as well as the national war policy.[26]

The revivalists' interpretation of popular sovereignty was local and communal, rather than national, in its basis. Villagers had no desire to sacrifice their communal support for Catholicism to an abstract Rousseauian general will of the "nation" as a whole, as interpreted by authorities in Paris. In any event, Catholics of the Yonne remained convinced that the majority of French people shared their religious feelings. Sometimes revivalists pointed out that antireligious policy went against the wishes of the population in general, but for the most part villagers gave a concrete and local interpretation of political representation and of the general will. Since they were aware that the will of the majority carried weight, Catholic villagers consistently strove to prove that their desire for public Catholic practice represented the dominant, if not the universal or unanimous, will of the village. The citizens of Noyers based their petition for church use on the Constitutional guarantee of "freedom of religious practice" and insisted that Catholicism was "the religion of the *major part, if not the totality, of the citizens of Noyers.* Since your intention, citizen administrators, is not to deprive your people of their *rights,* (you will please grant us the use of the church). . . . In doing this you will show more and more that you are worthy of fulfilling the honorable office *to which the people have called you.*"[27] The Catholic citizens of Noyers did their best to marshal the arguments of *liberté des cultes,* the rights of the majority, and popular sovereignty. Above all, they specifically reminded the cantonal officers that they were responsible for listening to the demands of the people who had elected them to office.

---

[26] AN F7 3699² and AD Yonne L217, Affiche trouvée à Villethierry au pied de l'arbre de la Liberté, signée Suzanne sans peur, 16 messidor an VII (July 4, 1799).

[27] AD Yonne L715, Pétition des habitants de la commune de Noyers à l'administration cantonale de Noyers, 4 prairial an VII (May 23, 1799).

Petitioners used different tones as they reminded government authorities of their duties to their constituents. The Catholics of Sens simply expressed their confidence that "their magistrates loved and cherished this liberty [of religious practice] as they did, and that they would eagerly seize any circumstance to prove it." The parishioners of Saint Étienne were more direct as they pointed out that returning the cathedral to Catholic practice would illustrate the wisdom of the administrators in "procuring happiness and peace in all that could accord with the glory of the Nation." The *marguilliers* of Saint Lazare in Avallon reminded the municipality that if they met resistance in their commune "they should hasten to do everything necessary to discover the general will [*volonté générale*]," while the Catholics of Champs, according to the municipal officers, broke into the church and "required us [the municipal officers] to represent their cause as one generally held by all." These Catholic citizens of Champs assured the authorities that they had "assembled to pray to God, the Supreme Being, for the conservation of all the goods of the Republic, the preservation of the National Convention, and the protection of the armies," but they also warned them that they "would shed their blood rather than surrender the Catholic religion, which they had always professed."[28]

The petitions of Catholic villagers had power in part because local officials too were aware of the power of popular demands and of the validity of claims based on popular sovereignty. The national agent of Courgis wrote to the Revolutionary Committee of the district of Auxerre that it would be oppressing his villagers to deprive them of their religion; not only were they supported by the Declaration of the Rights of Man, but in addition, "it would be breaking the law of the Sovereignty of the People" to oppose their peaceful assemblies. He was convinced that they could be both Catholic and republican. Town authorities were also afraid of the physical power of the majority. The municipal officers of Pont-sur-Yonne, for example, pointed out to the departmental authorities that they had best grant the Catholic peti-

---

[28] AD Yonne L717, Pétition des habitants de Sens à l'administration communale et au commissaire de Sens, 27 frimaire an VIII (December 18, 1799); AD Yonne L710, Pétition des paroissiens de Saint Étienne (d'Auxerre) à l'administration départementale, sans date (c. nivôse an VIII/January 1800); AD Yonne L711, Mémoire pour la paroisse de Saint Lazare d'Avallon au sujet des cloches contre le conseil général de la commune présenté aux citoyens administrateurs du département de l'Yonne, sans date (c. July 1792); AD Yonne L712, Extrait du procès verbal de la municipalité de Champs, 14 pluviôse an III (February 2, 1795).

tioners use of the local church, lest violence result. The composition of the petition had already coincided with the breaking of laws regulating religious worship.[29] Town officials were painfully aware that, if petitioning failed, villagers might very well turn to more violent means of regaining the use of their churches and the right to worship in public. Government figures found themselves in a delicate and sometimes dangerous position, suspended between popular demands to restore Catholicism and pressures from higher authorities to institute the new revolutionary cults and culture. In the midst of a revolution whose origins and legitimacy were built on popular political activism, whether peaceful or violent, the voice of the people had power.

* * *

The writers of petitions and the participants in religious riots had varied attitudes toward the Revolution. While the Yonne was not a counterrevolutionary region of France, undoubtedly some of the Catholics who demanded free religious practice had counterrevolutionary leanings. Particularly during the crackdown on public worship following the fructidorean coup d'état, some protesters' invocation of their religious rights and liberties seemed to grow more threatening and filled with disillusionment. Some religious activists protested bitterly that if the promises of revolutionary liberty had been broken, then the current law too should be broken. At the very least, Catholic villagers could use illegal symbolic actions to express their disenchantment with revolutionary promises. The disappointed counterrevolutionaries who stripped the bark off the Liberty Tree at Junay left an inscription claiming, "we are destroying the liberty trees because they bear no fruit." Likewise, another poster left on the freshly planted Liberty Tree at Vermenton in December 1797 warned, "You who were supposed to make the peace of the nation, you will die."[30] Furthermore, even those Catholics who were willing to accept many of the ideological and political changes brought by the Revolution still rebelled against the creation of revolutionary cults and calendar as cosmological rivals of Catholicism.

[29] AD Yonne L712, Lettre de l'agent national de Courgis au comité révolutionnaire du district d'Auxerre, 5 pluviôse an III (January 24, 1795); AD Yonne L715, Lettre de l'administration cantonale de Pont-sur-Yonne à l'administration centrale du département de l'Yonne, 15 prairial an VII (June 3, 1799).

[30] AD Yonne L218, Lettre du commissaire de Vézinnes au commissaire de l'Yonne, 21 thermidor an VII (August 8, 1799); *L'Observateur de l'Yonne* 36, 5 nivôse an VI (December 25, 1797).

Yet although Catholic villagers of the Yonne could not accept many of the rituals and symbols of the revolutionary cults, they did not reject the Revolution out of hand. For what was most striking and widespread in the Yonne was the pervasive conviction of religious activists that they could be loyal to both Catholicism and the Revolution. Frequently, petitioners and letter writers sought to disabuse government officials of the deep-rooted conviction that Catholicism equaled counterrevolution and fanaticism. In thermidor an IV (July 1796) one anonymous letter writer, as he appealed to the "citizen president" to give satisfaction to the people by allowing the return of the mass, assured him that he was "among those citizens most loyal to the Republic and most attached to the Roman Catholic, apostolic religion, which according to his opinion could go together very well." Petitioners routinely included assurances that religion would support the moral fabric of the nation and that religion and the Republic were compatible. The petitioners of Courson in the fall of 1794 demanded the right to practice Catholicism "as real republicans, all having sworn to be loyal to the laws of the Republic," and concluded their petition with the postscript, "We demand [the celebration of] offices, all without priests. Vive la République!" As the petitioners of Chablis claimed in 1795, "We wish to be Catholics and republicans and we can be both the one and the other."[31]

Obviously, Catholics' assertions of loyalty to both religion and republic must be taken with a grain of salt, for to a certain extent petitioners no doubt felt compelled to reassure authority figures who were wary of counterrevolution. Yet these proclamations were not only extremely widespread but they also went beyond simple promises of obedience and tranquillity to more explicit and enthusiastic declarations of revolutionary conviction. Sometimes they included expressions of anticlericalism which the revolutionaries would share. Moreover, in many instances Catholics expressed their loyalty to the Revolution in

---

[31] AN F7 7182, Lettre anonyme au citoyen président, 7 thermidor an IV (July 25, 1796); AD Yonne L712, Pétition des habitants de Courson à la municipalité de Courson, 11 brumaire an III (November 1, 1794); AC Chablis, Dépôt 296 1P1, Pétition des citoyens de Chablis à l'administration du district d'Auxerre, sans date (c. ventôse an III/February–March 1795). The demand of the petitioners of Courson is representative of a large number of parishioners who chose to celebrate "lay masses," i.e., masses led by laymen without priests. Catholic villagers supported these lay masses not only because priests were scarce in the late 1790s but also because many Catholics were willing to accept a less hierarchical and less clerical form of Catholic practice. Lay cults persisted even after the Concordat.

actions as well as words. For example, the Catholics of the town of Beine provided a striking example of fidelity to both religion and republic as they reacted in this way to the reading of the Convention's decree of *liberté des cultes:*

The *agent* was interrupted by all the citizens of the assembly, more than 350, with shouts of Vive la Convention! Vive la loi! Vive la République! exclamations repeated so often that it was impossible to bring them to order. . . . They cried that the National Convention . . . had delivered them from slavery and destroyed tyranny, that they . . . intended to assemble in the Temple of Reason only to invoke the Supreme Being and sing hymns and canticles, not to compromise the cause of liberty; they swore to live both as good republicans and Catholics without ministers. . . . As for priests, source of their unhappiness, they didn't want them any more and . . . would turn them in to denouncers.

The villagers went on to make further promises to remain loyal to the Convention and the law, to live as good republicans, even to "pour out their blood for the country and the unity of the Republic." Likewise, in that same winter of 1795 worshipers in Mailly-le-Vineux ardently proclaimed the *liberté des cultes* decreed by the National Convention, claimed that the "temple of the Supreme Being belonged to them," and promised to pray for the armies of the Republic. The *agent national* argued that his fellow citizens were in fact good republicans, except for their religious fanaticism.[32]

* * *

This type of amalgamation of religious and revolutionary discourse was most possible in parts of France that were prorevolutionary and where a majority of the local clergy had accepted the Civil Constitution of the Clergy. In those regions of France where the Civil Constitution had kindled early opposition to the Revolution and where hopes for a union of Catholicism and republicanism had died long before dechristianization, such a combination of revolutionary and religious discourse was less likely. In the "troubled" departments of the West, for example, Catholics likewise petitioned for freedom of religious practice. But while they sometimes referred to the laws guaranteeing specific religious rights and to the constitutional promise of freedom of worship, petitioners in the *chouan* regions of the West not surprisingly were unlikely to assert in words and action that they could be both Catholic and republican. *Chouan* Catholics generally shared the view of the

---

[32] AD Yonne L208, Procès verbal de Beine, 18 frimaire an III (December 8, 1794); AD Yonne L207, Lettre de l'agent national de Mailly-le-Vineux au comité révolutionnaire d'Auxerre, 4 pluviôse an III (January 23, 1795).

radical revolutionary leadership that republicanism and Catholicism were fundamentally opposed to one other; *chouans* tended to see patriots as outsiders and enemies, or even as "devils" or "black-hearted" individuals who were damned.[33] On the other hand, Catholic petitioners who supported Constitutional clergymen or who lived in "bleu" villages in sharply divided departments, such as the Sarthe, Côtes-du-Nord, and Ille-et-Vilaine, were intently anxious to voice their patriotism and republicanism as well as their opposition to the counterrevolutionary behavior of their neighbors.[34] Catholics of the West who had remained loyal to the Republic seemed to view *liberté des cultes* as a particular right earned by their loyalty. In 1796, for example, the Catholic republicans of one village in the Ille-et-Vilaine claimed that when their town was "surrounded by misguided communes, the butt of all the furor of the *chouans,* the commune of Gahard found patriotism . . . to be an invincible wall against its enemies and those of the country." Noting that they had perhaps done more than any other commune for the Republic, these villagers went on to request freedom of religious practice in exchange for all their "sacrifices."[35]

In the West the guerilla warfare against the Revolution, the massive lay and clerical resistance to the Civil Constitution, and the heavily clerical nature of Old Regime Catholicism had all left their mark on the religious requests and petitioning style of the religious activists.[36] In many cases, when petitioners from the West demanded freedom of practice—whether they were *chouan* or not—their petitions took on an almost threatening allure as they declared that Catholics had in fact "fought" to gain religious freedom and that if this freedom were not granted war would return. In 1795 the petitioners of Corlay in the Côtes-

[33] Donald Sutherland, *The Chouans: The Social Origins of Popular Counterrevolution in Upper Brittany, 1770–96* (Oxford, 1982), pp. 255–56, 279.

[34] AD Sarthe L380, Pétition des habitants de Montailler au département de Sarthe, 16 floréal an IV (May 5, 1796); AD Ille-et-Vilaine L445, Pétition des habitants de Guipry et Loudéac à l'administration départementale d'Ille-et-Vilaine, 22 pluviôse an VII (February 11, 1799), and Pétition de Saint Ganton à l'administration départementale d'Ille-et-Vilaine, 26 floréal an VII (May 15, 1799); AN F7 7265, Pétition des partisans de l'église constitutionelle à Lannion (Côtes-du-Nord) au Ministre de la Police, 10 juin 1797 (they used the v.s. dating).

[35] AN F19 1018, Pétition des habitants de la commune de Gahard (Ille-et-Vilaine) au Conseil des Cinq-Cents, 7 messidor an IV (June 25, 1796).

[36] See Tackett (n. 4 above), esp. chap. 10, on the correspondence between refusal of the oath in 1791 and a high density of clergy in the Old Regime, particularly in western France.

du-Nord, for example, belligerently claimed newly won "liberty" for themselves and asserted, "The people armed themselves in order to have religion. . . . Since they only demand what has been given to them by their fathers, you cannot refuse their request."[37] Catholics of the West generally seemed certain that freedom of public worship and, above all, the return of their nonjuring priests were the necessary conditions for local peace and for conformity to the republican government. Not only did the religious activists of the West harp more frequently on the themes of warfare and public tranquillity than did their fellow Catholics of the Yonne, they also placed a much heavier emphasis on the necessary role of the clergy. The petitioners of Rennes summed up the essence of the western revival when they referred to the "obvious truth that the freedom of priests is inseparable from the freedom of religion, and that this is inseparable from public tranquillity, especially in the countryside."[38] This attitude was reflected also in the actions of the departmental and local officials in the West. They moved more gingerly than the authorities in the Yonne and were especially hesitant to take action against returning refractory priests.[39] As one government official of the Calvados commented in 1796, "We promised them liberty and equality, and after that we tyrannized them and denied them religious freedom, which would bring peace to all if we would only grant it to them."[40]

Even in the counterrevolutionary West there were moments during the Revolution when it seemed as if changes in the legal structures of republican government might offer a peaceful solution and religious liberty, particularly in the springs of 1795 and 1797. Above all, in the spring of 1797 when the newly elected moderate and right-wing national deputies staged an attempt to turn around the Revolution from within

[37] AD Côtes-du-Nord, LM5 87, Pétition des citoyens de Corlay à l'administration du district de Loudéac, 8 floréal an III (April 27, 1795).

[38] AD Ille-et-Vilaine L1006, Pétition des citoyens de Rennes et des communes environnantes au Conseil des Cinq-Cents, 11 brumaire an V (November 1, 1796).

[39] AN F19 418, Lettre de l'administration départementale et du commissaire des Côtes-du-Nord au Ministre de l'Intérieur, 13 nivôse an III (January 2, 1795); Raoul Patry, *Le régime de la liberté des cultes dans le département du Calvados pendant la première séparation, 1795 à 1802* (Paris, 1921), pp. 123–24; H. Pommeret, *L'esprit public dans le département des Côtes-du-Nord, 1789–1799* (Saint Brieuc, 1921), pp. 357, 415 ff.; Marcel Reinhard, *Le département de la Sarthe sous le régime directorial* (Le Mans, 1936), pp. 124–25, 568.

[40] AN F7 7192, Lettre de Laneuve au président du Conseil, 11 fructidor an IV (August 28, 1796), as quoted in Patry, pp. 122–23.

the Councils, there was a corresponding campaign in the provinces to use the very structures of the Revolution to act against its political culture and to restore Catholicism. In western towns such as Rennes and Saint Brieuc, petitions with ample references to revolutionary laws and constitutional promises of religious freedom were circulated and gained hundreds of signatures. In contrast to the Yonne, model petitions were sent out to the countryside; some villagers copied these urban-based petitions word for word. The petition campaign was linked to the right-wing leadership of the "honnêtes gens"; priests were some-times instrumental in circulating these petitions and in composing rural ones as well. Petition warfare broke out between factions within towns and villages as anticlerical, left-wing republicans accused right-wing Catholic activists of gathering false signatures in their attempt to "over-throw the Constitution by the Constitution" and to conceal their attack on the Republic "beneath the mask of the religion of humanity and of patriotism."[41]

However, once the fructidorean coup d'état put an end to hopes for a peaceful reconciliation between the government and Catholicism until the coming of Napoleon, petitioners of the West seem to have lost hope in the idea that religion could exist under the Republic. The flurry of petitioning died down amid the general certitude that the republican promises of religious liberty and popular sovereignty were indeed empty. The years VI and VII (1797–99) brought a return of both *chouan* guerilla warfare and the Vendéan civil war. While the West had witnessed cases of republican Catholicism during the Revolution, this combination be-came less and less possible in a region where the "golden legend" of the heroes of the Vendée who had "died for the faith" became etched

[41] Pommeret, pp. 397–99; Reinhard, p. 272; Patry, pp. 137–39; AN F7 7255, Pétition des habitants de Moncoutour (Côtes-du-Nord) aux représentants du peuple, 10 floréal an V (April 29, 1797); AN F7 7263, Lettre du commissaire de Paimpol (Côtes-du-Nord) au Ministre de la Police, 1 messidor an V (June 19, 1797), and Lettre du commissaire des Côtes-du-Nord, 24 prairial an V (June 12, 1797); Pétition (imprimée) des catholiques romains de Saint Brieuc aux deux Conseils, s.d. (c. prairial an V/May–June 1797); AD Ille-et-Vilaine L1006, Pétition des citoyens de Rennes et des communes environnantes au Conseil des Cinq-Cents, 11 brumaire an V (November 1, 1796); AN F7 7262, Pétition des habitants (républicains) de Lamballe au Directoire, 24 messidor an V (July 13, 1797), and Lettre de Mareschal au ministre de la police, 2 thermidor an V (July 20, 1797). Model petitions also existed in the spring of 1795: AD Côtes-du-Nord LM5 86, Pétition des catholiques romains des Saint Brieuc au district, reçu le 22 germinal an III (April 11, 1795); AD Côtes-du-Nord LM5 87, Pétition des catholiques de Pleury à l'administration du district de Loudéac, 29 floréal an III (May 18, 1795).

on the collective memory. The Vendéan and *chouan* resistance left a deeply rooted ideological legacy: throughout the modern period, Catholicism in the West would remain in some sense the prisoner of counterrevolutionary ideology. It became impossible to conceive of religion that was not opposed to any and all forms of republicanism.[42]

In noncounterrevolutionary regions such as the Yonne, on the other hand, persistent confidence in the power of popular demands without recourse to counterrevolution was more pervasive and long-lasting. Well before the hopeful spring of 1797 and even under the severe weight of the postfructidorean dechristianization campaign of 1797–99, Catholics in the Yonne in tiny villages and large towns alike continued to bombard the authorities with their persistent requests for religious liberty, still couched in the revolutionary language of popular sovereignty, the general will, and the promise of religious liberty. Many Catholics in other prorevolutionary regions of France shared this optimism. They might invoke Jean-Jacques Rousseau, the "General Interest," and the "will of the majority of French people," as did some villagers in Nièvre, or they might assert, along with the self-proclaimed "Catholics" and "patriots" of De Griège in the Saône-et-Loire, that the return to Catholicism was "the well-known will of all the communes of the department and of the neighboring departments—in one word, the will of the people."[43] Obviously, regional attitudes toward the Revolution varied, but to view the alliance of counterrevolution and Catholicism as invariably the case throughout France is to take at face value the rhetoric and viewpoint of revolutionary officials. In much of France, Catholic villagers sought to reconcile loyalty to their religion with loyalty to the Revolution. They shared the view of the Citizen Serret

[42] Nadine-Josette Chaline, Michel Lagrée, and Serge Chassagne, *L'église de France et la Révolution: Histoire régionale, l'Ouest* (Paris, 1983), pp. 13, 41, 50–52, 59–60, and 86; Reinhard, pp. 627–30. In his chapter on Rennes, Lagrée gives examples of republican Catholicism in the West, but he also discusses its limitations.

[43] AN F19 1018, Pétition des habitants de Saint Léger de Fougeret (Nièvre) au Conseil des Cinq-Cents, 23 fructidor an IV (August 10, 1796), and Celle de Mèves au Conseil des Cinq-Cents, s.d. (c. messidor–thermidor an IV/July 1796); AN F19 467–68, Pétition de la commune de Griège (Saône-et-Loire) aux citoyens législateurs, s.d. (c. 9 nivôse an IV/December 30, 1795). Multiple examples of petitions with revolutionary language from Catholics in northern and central France can be found in AN F19 398–481 and in various regional histories of Catholicism during the Revolution. A closer examination of those departments that were not counterrevolutionary and yet favored Catholicism would no doubt reveal many more instances of this combination of republican and religious discourse.

Fargeau who protested when the district of Saint Fargeau characterized Catholicism "as fanaticism, which was, they said, the same thing as royalism." On the contrary, he claimed, "The freedom of religious practice is the only way to bring all the individual spirits of the Republic to unity."[44]

Paradoxically, the Revolution opened up surprising and unexpected possibilities for the laity in prerevolutionary regions of France to find within the Revolution itself political techniques and ideology to aid their reestablishment of Catholicism. In effect, the Catholic villagers of the Yonne assimilated those aspects of revolutionary political techniques and language that they could incorporate within their traditional frameworks and belief structures. As they infused their petitions and placards with revolutionary rhetoric and used the political institutions of the Revolution to voice their claims, the religious activists continued to draw as well on traditional forms of protest and to combine religious activism with their political strategies. This fusion of the religious and the political and of the traditional and the revolutionary increased the power of the Catholic revival.

Examination of the language of the religious revival also illustrates the need to reevaluate how the Revolution was received on the local level. The revolutionary discourse was a live entity; the politicians and journalists in Paris and in large provincial cities were not the only ones who struggled to create and control it. Catholic villagers constantly strove to integrate revolutionary innovations into their old traditional patterns of life and assumptions. In doing so, French villagers transformed and reinterpreted the Revolution in an active and dynamic way. They redefined the goals of the Revolution to accord with their religious beliefs and their own conception of freedom. Perhaps the Citoyen Laire spoke with some truth when he commented about the citizens of Yonne, "The French heart may well be republican, but the customs are still monarchical."[45]

The revolutionaries tried to do something radically different: they worked hard to untangle Michelet's "inextricable intermingling" of religion and politics. They sought to separate the religious from the political, or at least to draw a clear-cut dichotomy between Catholicism and the Revolution. But in reality it was not so simple to divide the traditional religious culture from the new secular political culture of

[44] AN F19 481 (4–5), Lettre du Citoyen Serret de Saint Fargeau au Comité de salut public, 15 Messidor an III (July 3, 1795).

[45] Bibliothèque de la Société du Port Royal, Carton Yonne, Lettre de Laire à Grégoire, 21 nivôse an III (January 11, 1795).

the Revolution in the minds and attitudes of the people. Popular attitudes toward the Revolution were not always what politicians in Paris might expect. Would revolutionary deputies understand the thinking of the villagers in the Périgord who had insisted early in the Revolution that their *curé* put a revolutionary tricolor cockade on the host and that he leave the doors of the tabernacle open "so that the good God might be free?"[46] God, too, according to these villagers, should benefit from revolutionary liberty. Religion and revolution might mix in unusual ways. To create a secular political culture entirely independent of religion was not so simple as the radical revolutionaries hoped.

[46] Lettre de Vergniaud, 16 janvier 1790, in Vergniaud, *Manuscrits, Lettres et papiers, pièces pour la plupart inédites,* classées et annotées par C. Vatel (Paris, 1873), as quoted in Ozouf (n. 6 above), p. 151.

"Federalism" and Urban Revolt in France in 1793*

Bill Edmonds

During the spring and summer of 1793 the local authorities in many French towns defied the National Convention. They denounced its subjection before the Paris Commune and the radical clubs and sections of the capital. (*Son asservissement* or *son avilissement* were favorite expressions.) They refused to recognize its authority because, they said, the persecution of the Girondins placed all its members *sous le joug d'une poignée de factieux*. In most cases the defiance went no further than wordy protest and the selective nonapplication of unwelcome decrees. Some local authorities —usually the directories of the departments acting either alone or in concert with districts and municipalities —created unconstitutional committees or commissions to exercise the authority which the Convention was supposed to have forfeited. In some places the defiance reached the stage of armed revolt, with departmental armies being raised and in a few cases actually launched in the direction of Paris. With little regard for the diversity of this movement, historians have customarily labelled it "federalism."

The concept of "federalism" provides an opportunity to investigate provincial responses to three years of revolutionary change in France. It also raises some difficult questions about sociopolitical alignments. Whatever one may think of the much-debated view that a revolutionary bourgeoisie made the Revolution, it is difficult to dispute the proposition that the Revolution materially advanced bourgeois interests. Yet here, at a moment of acute counterrevolutionary threat at home and abroad, some of the most important mercantile communities of France turned against the national government. It is not surprising that the "federalists" have been called counterrevolutionaries but the character and the motives of the "counterrevolutionary bourgeois"—if such they were—remain obscure, as do the factors which differentiated them from those bourgeois elements which were prepared to accept Montagnard government until the war crisis was over. We need to understand "federalism" before we can speak with confidence about the outlook and aspirations of the pro-

* I benefited from comments on an earlier version of this article read to the Australasian Association for European History in 1977.

This essay originally appeared in the *Journal of Modern History* 55 (March 1983).

vincial bourgeoisie at the period when the centralized French republic was being created. This article has been written because the recent efflorescence of research on the Revolution in the provinces makes it possible to tackle these problems at a national level by comparing systematically new evidence from different places, including the most important "federalist" centers.[1] The aim is to use this material to correct some misconceptions about "federalism" which linger on in general accounts of the Revolution, to assess its character and significance, and to explain why it led to revolts in some places but not in others.

I   THE SCOPE OF "FEDERALIST" PROTEST

The claim is frequently made—or mentioned *faute de mieux*—that more than two-thirds of the departments of France were "federalist" in mid-1793, an estimate which provides useful support for the common textbook argument that centralization and the Terror were justified by a vast counterrevolutionary threat.[2] It is, however, wrong. Both Montagnard and "federalist" propaganda naturally exaggerated the extent of the movement to justify stern countermeasures on the one hand and to create expectations of success on the other. But Henri Wallon, who made the only systematic attempt to examine departmental records for evidence of "federalist" commitment, found that even verbal support for the idea of resisting the Convention was apparent in only forty-three departments[3]—certainly

---

[1] Useful regional studies include Alan Forrest, *Society and Politics in Revolutionary Bordeaux* (Oxford, 1975); William Scott, *Terror and Repression in Revolutionary Marseilles* (London, 1972); Gwynne Lewis, *The Second Vendée. The Continuity of Counter-revolution in the Department of the Gard*, 1789–1815 (Oxford, 1978); Martyn Lyons, *Revolution in Toulouse. An Essay on Provincial Terrorism* (Berne, 1978); D. Stone, "La révolte fédéraliste à Rennes," *Annales historiques de la Révolution française* 205 (July–September 1971); M. H. Crook, "Federalism and the French Revolution: The Revolt of Toulon in 1793," *History* 65 (October 1980). Useful older studies specifically concerned with federalism are P. Nicolle, "Le mouvement fédéraliste dans l'Orne en 1793," *Annales historiques de la Révolution française* 13 (1936) and A. Goodwin, "The Federalist Movement in Caen in the Summer of 1793," *Bulletin of the John Rylands Library* 42 (1959–1960).

[2] For example, A. Soboul, *The French Revolution 1787–1799* (London, 1972), p. 317; J. M. Thompson, *The French Revolution*, 2nd ed. (Oxford, 1966), p. 366; J. M. Roberts, *The French Revolution* (Oxford, 1978), p. 53.

[3] H. Wallon, *La Révolution du 31 mai et le fédéralisme en 1793 ou la France vaincue par la Commune de Paris*, 2 vols. (Paris, 1886). Wallon examined the departments listed by Julien one by one. From his account the "federalist" departments may be grouped roughly as follows:
A. Public opposition to the revolution of May 31–June 2: Ain, Aisne, Charente, Côte-d'Or, Dordogne, Doubs, Drôme, Gers, Landes, Lot, Lot-et-Garonne,

evidence of widespread hostility towards the Montagnard seizure of power in Paris, but hardly a national movement of resistance. Among the forty-three, fourteen were involved in military resistance to the Convention.

Even this military resistance seldom amounted to more than token rebellion, with the authorities dabbling in armed revolt but soon lapsing into embarrassed submission. The department of Ille-et-Vilaine is an example. On June 5 the departmental council met jointly with the Municipality and District of Rennes to discuss the expulsion of the Girondins from the Convention. It was decided to send a force against Paris and on the tenth Rennes called on the surrounding departments to help organize it. But when a Central Assembly of Resistance to Oppression was established at Caen the Rennes "federalists" immediately ceased their own efforts to coordinate anti-Jacobin activity in the northwest. Two deputies and a few National Guards were sent to join the Caennais, but the local authorities continued channelling tax money to Paris and recruiting soldiers for the regular army. When it was learned that the royalists had taken Saumur, troops from Rennes were quickly sent to Nantes to join the struggle in the Vendée. In mid-July the Rennais withdrew their support from the rebellion.[4]

Federalism in Toulouse was even less impressive: Jacobins were arrested, illegal authorities were set up, loud protests were made against the actions of the Convention, but little more. Fear of counterrevolution or invasion outweighed fear of Jacobins and *anarchistes*. Toulouse was the main base of both armies fighting on the Spanish front and with French troops falling back on Perpignan in late May it was clear that the southwest would soon be in Spanish hands if Toulouse disrupted the war effort.[5]

More serious acts of rebellion occurred in Caen, Bordeaux, and Nîmes, but after early setbacks the rebels showed little perseverance. About two thousand armed men set out from Caen on July 9 only to be routed six days later near Pacy-sur-Eure by a small detachment of regular troops whose success in a surprise attack was facilitated by the "federalists"

Lozère, Manche, Morbihan, Hautes-Pyrénées, Haute-Saône, Somme, Tarn, Haute-Vienne, Vienne.

B. Unauthorized convocation of primary assemblies, formation of commissions, committees of public safety, etc.: Basses-Alpes, Hautes-Alpes, Aude, Ardèche, Aveyron, Haute-Garonne, Hérault, Isère, Jura.

C. Contribution to "federalist" armed forces: Côtes-du-Nord, Eure, Finistère, Ille-et-Vilaine, Loire-Inférieure, Mayenne, Orne, Sarthe.

D. Armed revolt: Bouches-du-Rhône, Calvados, Gard, Gironde, Rhône-et-Loire, Var.

[4] Stone, pp. 370–385.
[5] Lyons, pp. 41–54.

having indulged immoderately in the local cider. By July 24 all the authorities of the department of Calvados had retracted their declarations of resistance to the Convention and the Assembly of Resistance to Oppression had dissolved.[6] The rebellion of Bordeaux lasted longer and produced a vast quantity of antigovernment propaganda, but the Bordelais army was only four hundred strong and it got no further than Langon, fifty kilometers from Bordeaux. Its demoralized troops melted away on July 24 as the Convention's forces approached. This, and the failure of other "federalist" cities to achieve better success, persuaded the "federalist" Popular Commission of the Department of the Gironde to dissolve itself (August 6). In the sections, however, opposition to the Convention remained strong and it took extensive negotiation by the deputies Baudot and Ysabeau to regain full control of the city.[7] The revolt in Nîmes followed a similar pattern. Having repressed the popular society of Nîmes on June 11, the department of the Gard formally adhered to the "federalist" movement nine days later. A Committee of Public Safety was set up and a few hundred troops were sent to Pont-Saint-Esprit to await the Marseillais force which was marching northwards. But on July 14 they capitulated to General Carteaux and "federalism" in the Gard was finished by the end of the month.[8] Some other towns recruited troops for the march on Paris and so, technically, reached the stage of armed revolt, like Nantes, which sent sixty men to join the "federalist" army in Caen.[9] But their halfhearted efforts were closer to the token "federalism" of Rennes and Toulouse than to the genuine, if unsuccessful, essays in armed revolt undertaken by Caen, Bordeaux, and Nîmes.

The heart of the "federalist" threat lay in three cases of sustained armed revolt. The rebellions initiated by the sections of Lyon, Marseille, and Toulon lasted longer than the others and more force was needed to repress them. Marseille succeeded in raising an army of three and a half thousand men and its forces occupied Avignon on July 7 as they marched towards Paris. Avignon was recaptured by General Carteaux on July 27 but it took two more encounters with the Marseillais army to break the city's resistance.[10] Lyon and Toulon resisted longer still and surrendered only after bloody sieges.[11] The existence of deep hostility towards the

[6] Goodwin, pp. 333–334.
[7] Forrest, pp. 109–180.
[8] Lewis, pp. 63–66.
[9] Wallon, 1:407.
[10] See Scott (n. 1 above), pp. 85–126.
[11] The most complete accounts of the rebellions so far published are Camille Riffaterre, *Le mouvement anti-Jacobin et anti-Parisien à Lyon et dans le Rhône-et-Loire en 1793*, 2 vols. (Lyon, 1912–1926); Edouard Herriot, *Lyon n'est plus*,

Convention in each of these places may be illustrated by a few examples. Whereas most "federalist" cities did their best to avoid hindering the war effort directly, the sections of Lyon successfully opposed the removal of military supplies from the city's arsenal in June even though it was an important supply point for the Alps army, which was daily expecting a Piedmontese offensive.[12] Whereas most "federalist" cities permitted referenda on the constitution voted by the Convention on June 24, Marseille refused outright and the Toulonnais response to the Representatives on Mission who delivered copies of it was to tie them up and drag them to the cathedral, where a Te Deum was celebrated to give thanks for the anti-Jacobin revolution.[13] As is well known, Toulon surrendered to the British on August 28.

II POLITICAL AND SOCIAL CHARACTERISTICS OF "FEDERALISM"—SOME REAPPRAISALS

The "federalists" have suffered the fate of the comprehensively defeated: their conquerors not only conquered them and executed a good many— perhaps 4,500[14]—but have had their version of events accepted by posterity. The Montagnards saw the "federalist" revolts as part of a concerted campaign against the Republic, a campaign inspired by royalism and regional feeling, reinforced by the selfish pride and anti-Parisian sentiment of rich provincial bourgeois and intended to weaken France by imposing on it a complex federal constitution.[15] This Montagnard version is for

---

4 vols. (Paris, 1938–1940); Crook (n. 1 above); Paul Cottin, *Toulon et les Anglais en 1793*, 2nd ed. (Paris, 1898).

[12] *Procès-verbaux des séances des corps municipaux de la ville de Lyon 1787–An VIII*, 6 vols. (Lyon, 1900–1904), 2:296, June 6, 1793; Archives de la Guerre, B³103*, dossier 6; Archives Départementales du Rhône (hereafter AD), 42L33, dossier C (16); *Procès-verbaux du conseil général du département de Rhône-et-Loire*, ed. G. Guigue, 2 vols. (Trévoux, 1895), 2:326 and 396, June 6 and 9; July 1793.

[13] Scott, p. 116; Cottin, p. 80.

[14] Greer counts 3,451 executions during the Terror for sedition in Rhône, Morbihan, Ille-et-Vilaine, Finistère, Calvados, Eure, Haute-Garonne, Gironde, and Bouches-du-Rhône, and for "federalism" elsewhere. Crook estimates that about one thousand executions took place after Toulon's recapture, and one hundred people from "federalist" areas were executed in Paris. (D. Greer, *The Incidence of the Terror during the French Revolution* (Gloucester, Mass., 1966), pp. 144, 148–153; Crook, p. 397.)

[15] See, for example, E.-L.-A. Dubois-Crancé, *Première et deuxième parties de la réponse de Dubois-Crancé aux inculpations de ses collègues Couthon et Maignet*, 2 vols. (n.d. [1794]), 2:106, letter to General Kellermann, June 12, 1793; and 2:112–127, "Proclamation des représentants [. . .] aux citoyens du département de l'Isère" (June 22, 1793); Dubois-Crancé, Albitte, and Gauthier, *Proclamation des représentants du peuple envoyés près l'armée des alpes* (Gre-

the most part misleading, unproven or clearly wrong, yet echoes of it are still to be found in recent writing on the revolutionary period.

To start with, the term "federalist" is misleading. Insofar as the revolts were based on political theory it was not on a theory of "federalism" but on the theory of the Declaration of the Rights of Man and the Citizen, and in particular the right of resistance to oppression proclaimed by article two. The "federalists" said they were resisting the oppression of a Jacobin minority in Paris which had first intimidated the Girondin deputies and then purged them from the Convention. Their rights violated, the people of the departments reclaimed their sovereignty and set up new sovereign bodies whose only specific aim was to found an inviolable, independent national representation—hence the titles of such bodies as the United Departments' Central Assembly of Resistance to Oppression. These were claimed to be temporary innovations to meet an emergency, and so was the projected assembly of departmental representatives in Bourges.[16] If the rebels wanted the restored national legislature remodelled on federal lines they did not say so.

Surprisingly, there is little sign in the rebellions even of anti-Parisian feeling, which has been called "the real meaning of the word [federalism] as it was understood by the Montagnards."[17] Perhaps it was tactical prudence which made the rebel leaders so careful to distinguish the tyrannous Jacobin minority from the mass of oppressed Parisians awaiting liberation.[18] But if anti-Parisian feeling was one motive for rebellion it is odd that the rebels did not try harder to exploit it in June and July. In Lyon, at any rate, the thousands of denunciations collected after the collapse of the revolts provide little evidence that the "federalist" in the street or in the section was hostile to Paris or the Parisians. Even the

---

noble, July 3, 1793), p. 7; J. Julien, *Rapport fait au nom du Comité de surveillance et de Sûreté Générale sur les administrations rebelles* (Paris, 1793).

[16] See Forrest, p. 274; *Procès-verbaux des séances de la commission populaire, républicaine et de salut public de Rhône-et-Loire*, ed. G. Guigue (Lyon, 1899), p. 26; *Lettre [. . .] aux assemblées populaires de Rhône-et-Loire* (Caen, n.d. [July 1793]), Bibliothèque de la Ville de Lyon (hereafter BL), Fonds Coste 4480; Scott, p. 155; Riffaterre (n. 11 above), 1:391–392.

[17] M. J. Sydenham, *The Girondins* (London, 1961), p. 196.

[18] Forrest, p. 168; Goodwin, p. 216; for Lyon, see for example *Rapport au conseil général de la commune de Lyon par l'un des commissaires de section [. . .] à Paris* (Lyon, n.d. [June 1793]), p. 7; *Lettre des commissaires de Lyon à Bordeaux* (Lyon [June] 1793), p. 6; AD Rhône IL375, letter from the editor of the *Journal de Lyon*, J.-L. Fain, to the Provisional Municipality, June 14, 1793; Proceedings of the Sections of Port-Saint-Paul (June 18) and La Croisette (July 7) (strong supporters of the rebellion), AD Rhône 31L21, folder 9 and 31L2, folder 16.

much-resented disparity between low Parisian bread prices and high provincial ones was blamed on the Jacobins, not the people of Paris.[19] In Lyon the only published attacks on Paris *per se* (on its turbulence, its overweening pride, its desire to dominate France, and so on) were in an address from Nantes and in the reprinted speeches of the Girondin deputies. Hostility to Paris was equally unimportant in Toulon.[20]

Certainly it is easy to see why the Montagnards *suspected* the rebels of federalism. Some departments dabbled with Girondin devices which the Montagnards had been denouncing as "federalist" since September 1792—Buzot's idea of a departmental guard for the Convention, for example, and Barbaroux's proposal for a Republic of the Midi in the event of northern France being lost to the Revolution.[21] As Goodwin points out, the rebels' habit of delegating spokesmen to deliberate in central assemblies gave their activities a "federalist" appearance, but this was a matter of tactics rather than political principles.[22] And while sovereignty was certainly divided *de facto* between the central government and various local bodies, this is not conclusive evidence of "federalist" tendencies. It is a symptom of the temporary breakdown of political authority and an inevitable consequence of civil war. "Federalist" was a propaganda label, and an effective one. To attack the unity of the Republic had been declared a capital crime on September 25, 1792, and to advocate drastic decentralization at a time of military disaster could in any case easily be represented as treasonable. The Montagnards had every reason to want their opponents called "federalists," but there is little justification for calling them that now except the convenience of maintaining an established usage.

If the Montagnards' labelling of "federalism" is misleading, so too is their social analysis. Dubois-Crancé, for example, regarded the rebellions as the combined work of former nobles and a new bourgeois aristocracy.[23] Some historians have accepted this verdict[24] but most have hesitated to go beyond the vague suggestion that "federalism" was bourgeois. Recent research enables us to be much more precise. The instigators of rebellion in the great cities were generally well-to-do, but nowhere

[19] *Rapport au conseil général de la commune de Lyon [. . .]*, p. 11.

[20] "Les Nantais à tous les départements de la République" (June 7, 1793); "Précis tracé à la hâte par le citoyen Rabaut-Saint-Etienne" (June 22) in *Registre du secrétariat général des sections de la ville de Lyon*, ed. G. Guigue (Lyon, 1907), pp. 493–537; Crook, p. 394.

[21] Sydenham (n. 17 above), pp. 192–197.

[22] Goodwin, p. 330.

[23] Dubois-Crancé (n. 15 above), 1:106.

[24] For example, G. Lefebvre, *The French Revolution from its Origins to 1793* (London, 1962), p. 266; Soboul (n. 2 above), p. 318.

was there much sign of the old aristocracy. For Bordeaux we have information on the Popular Commission and the Municipal Council which supported it, though not on the militants of the sections. About two-thirds of the "federalists" appear to have been merchants of the grander kind, including one or two of the shipowning magnates.[25] But in other important rebel cities "federalism" had a broader base of social support.[26]

While the main social group in the Lyonnais rebellion was the upper bourgeoisie—rentiers, silk merchants, mercantile brokers, *négociants*, and wealthy professional men[27]—others also played a considerable role. Of the presidents and secretaries in the sections which supported the revolt in May, the occupations of twenty-six have been established. None of these was from the former local aristocracy; thirteen belonged to the upper bourgeoisie; three were merchants of the middling sort. There were also many petty bourgeois (more than a third of the total) and three artisans. The upper bourgeoisie dominated the Provisional Municipality which took over control of Lyon on May 30 and was still more dominant in the Popular Commission elected on June 24. But the roots of Lyonnais "federalism" lay in the sections, and amongst their presidents and secretaries and the members of their *comités de surveillance* were numerous petty bourgeois, clerks, *boutiquiers*, artisans, and silk weavers. So the rebellion seems to have been started and run by men from all levels of the bourgeoisie, with substantial participation by the kinds of people who were *sans-culottes* in Paris. Later, the role of the bourgeoisie and of the prerevolutionary élites became more important as the counterrevolutionary potential of the revolt increased and as the burden of continuous political activity became greater for those who had to keep small businesses and workshops going. (See Table 1.)

In Marseille the social base of federalism was broader still, with popular elements involved alongside the "[socially] middle-ranking group" which predominated among the sectionaries in May.[29] What Vovelle calls the "social ambiguity" of the movement is most clearly demonstrated by his analysis of the 1394 Marseillais prosecuted for "federalism" under the Terror: more than 50 percent were artisans or shopkeepers.[30] Amongst

[25] Forrest, pp. 122–123, 125–127.

[26] Lyons, pp. 51–52; Lewis, pp. 74–76; Scott, p. 11. See also Crook, pp. 391–397 (works cited in n. 1 above).

[27] See Maurice Garden, *Lyon et les Lyonnais au XVIIIᵉ siècle* (Lyon, 1970), pp. 358–360, 363, 368–374, for a masterly analysis of prerevolutionary Lyonnais élites.

[28] See footnote to Table 1, p. 30.

[29] Scott, p. 11; Michael L. Kennedy, *The Jacobin Club of Marseilles, 1790–1794* (Ithaca, 1973), pp. 123–124.

[30] Michel Vovelle, "La Révolution," in *Histoire de Marseille*, ed. Edouard Baratier (Toulouse, 1973), pp. 276–283.

Table 1[28]

	A — "Federalist" Section officials—May		B — Section officials—June		C — Militants		D — All Section officials—May/June–October	
		(%)		(%)		(%)		(%)
1. Nobles, clergy	—		9	(11.5)	10	(7.4)	20	(5.7)
2. Upper bourgeoisie	13	(50.0)	34	(43.6)	55	(40.7)	148	(42.4)
3. Merchants	3	(11.5)	10	(12.8)	31	(23.0)	66	(18.9)
4. Lesser professions, clerks	5	(19.2)	12	(15.4)	7	(5.2)	23	(6.6)
5. Artisans, boutiquiers	4	(15.4)	9	(11.5)	20	(14.8)	55	(15.8)
6. Silk weavers	—		4	(5.1)	10	(7.4)	28	(8.0)
7. Journaliers	1	(3.8)	—		2	(1.5)	9	(2.6)
Total	26	(99.9)	78	(99.9)	135	(100.0)	349	(100.0)

[28] The "section officials" under A and B were presidents and secretaries of section assemblies; the figures under C and D include members of comités de surveillance as well. Many "federalists" slipped through the Terror so that firm occupational identification cannot be made for many in these categories. Those analyzed in column A represent about half of this category, those in B about one-sixth, and those in D at least a third. "Militants" includes those who are known to have held office for at least a month during the rebellion and "section officials—June" includes members of the Provisional Municipality, two of whom were chosen by each of thirty-two sections.

The thirty-two Lyonnais members of the Commission Populaire du Département de Rhône-et-Loire included two former avocats, another lawyer, an ex-procureur, four négociants, a marchand-fabricant de soie, a surgeon, two physicians, a taxation official, a clerk, a bookkeeper, and a stocking weaver. Sources for "federalist" personnel in Lyon: AN AFII, no. 6; AD Rhône 31L1–31L49, 42L13, 42L12, 42L17, 42L19–22, 42L34 dossier A(1), 42L56–42L154 (individual dossiers compiled during the Year II), 42L96–97, 42L99–102, 42L107, 42L109, 42L112–113, 42L116; Archives Communales de la Ville de Lyon (hereafter AC), 1⁴; Secrétariat, ed. Guigue (n. 30 above), pp. 474–475; Antonin Portallier, Tableau général des victimes et martyrs de la Révolution en Lyonnais, Forez et Beaujolais (Saint-Etienne, 1911); Liste des citoyens éligibles aux places municipales de la ville de Lyon (Lyon, 1790); Almanachs de Lyon, 1789–1792.

the sectionaries of Nîmes there was a substantial minority of artisans and in Toulon, while the leadership of the revolt was firmly in the hands of the urban elite, one-third of the *commission municipale* elected by the "federalist" sections in July were clerks, artisans, and dockworkers.[31] Clearly the main "federalist" revolts had substantial support from below, support which is difficult to account for in terms of interpretative traditions deriving from Montagnard propaganda.

Of all the Montagnard accusations, the claim that "federalism" was inspired by royalists is the least justified, but it has been widely accepted.[32] In fact, what we now know about its origins suggests that it emerged from "patriot" sectors of opinion rather than royalist ones. In Marseille many early "federalists" had been active in the Jacobin clubs up to the winter of 1792.[33] In Caen one of the first calls for action against the Convention came from the Jacobin club, which did not repudiate the Paris Jacobins until late May.[34] In Lyon the anti-Jacobin movement began in the popular societies in December 1792 and by April 10 had the support of fifteen of them, nearly half the popular societies of Lyon.[35] By May the focus of anti-Jacobin activity had moved to the sectional assemblies. They were a sounder base for the movement because they had legal status and wide powers under the law of March 21 establishing sectional sur-veillance committees.[36] It may be that as the anti-Jacobin movement spread to the sections its ranks were swelled by crypto-royalists, who are naturally hard to spot. But the fact that the movement began in the strongly republican popular societies and was still flourishing there in mid-April makes it unlikely that it had become a royalist movement by the time insurrection broke out in late May. The evidence from Toulon points to similar conclusions: the leading architect of "federalism" there, the master saddler J. B. Roux, "possessed an impeccable radical pedi-gree," and he was supported by other club members.[37] Royalists took over only in the later stages of the revolts which lasted longest, when their early leaders were left with no choice other than surrendering to an

[31] Lewis, pp. 74–76; Crook, p. 391.

[32] George Lefebvre, *French Revolution*, p. 52; M. J. Sydenham, *The French Revolution* (London, 1969), p. 164; François Furet and Denis Richet, *The French Revolution* (London, 1970), p. 154.

[33] Kennedy, p. 124; Scott, pp. 77–80, 82.

[34] Goodwin, pp. 317, 319.

[35] A. C. Lyon, 1²4, dossier 45, folders 40, 42, 44–46, proceedings of the Club of la Croisette for December 26, 1792, March 13, 17, 20, and 26, and April 1, 3, and 10, 1793.

[36] See S. Charléty, "La journée du 29 mai 1793 à Lyon," *La Révolution française* 39 (October 1900):413.

[37] Crook, p. 386.

intransigent Committee of Public Safety or accepting the aid of royalist navy or army officers who alone were capable of organizing military resistance. But there is no evidence that royalists engineered the "federalist" revolts.[38]

While not as bad as royalism, regionalism and particularism were naturally suspect to good revolutionaries. They had the taint of the Old Regime about them, and it is not surprising to find them included in the Jacobin case against "federalism." This is echoed by many historians,[39] but the evidence to support it is surprisingly scanty. To take the case of Bordeaux first: there had been outcries over royal assaults on the Bordeaux Parlement in the 1770s and 1780s and there had also been strong local feeling against royal economic policy, particularly the withdrawal of the privileges enjoyed by the wine trade and the abolition of the slave trade.[40] No doubt there was a sense of local pride in this great and prosperous trading port, as well as an aspiration to regional leadership, but it is not easy to find evidence which links these things with the rebellion of 1793. If localism and a sense of provincial identity were important ingredients in the "federalist" mentality, the Bordelais "federalists" were remarkably quiet about them. Dislike of the Convention's economic policies and dissatisfaction with their local effects may have fuelled "federalism,"[41] but that does not entitle us to say that regionalism and particularism were causes of the rebellion.

Even though Marseille had no tradition of resistance to Bourbon centralization, a spirit of local pride and independence was clearly manifested there during the Revolution. Some Marseillais held that their city had a particular revolutionary vocation and that it was better fitted to regenerate France than the servile north, which in their eyes began at Aix-en-Provence. Vigorous efforts were made to shock sleepy Provence and sluggish Paris into properly revolutionary postures, and the storming of the Tuileries is only one example of how willingly Marseille shouldered its revolutionary responsibilities. But such thinking characterized the more extreme Jacobins rather than their opponents and particularism was only incidental to the revolt of 1793.[42]

The same can be said for Lyon. Lyon was not yet the center of a regional economy, and the province of the Lyonnais had no tradition of

[38] Scott, pp. 220–223; Crook, pp. 394–395; Riffaterre (n. 11 above), 2:10–94. See also Forrest, pp. 255–257 and Lyons, p. 53.

[39] A. Mathiez, *La Révolution française* (Paris, 1963), p. 375; M. J. Sydenham, *The French Revolution* (London, 1969), p. 166; R. Ben Jones, *The French Revolution* (London, 1967), p. 127; Soboul (n. 2 above), p. 308.

[40] Forrest, pp. 24, 32, 52.

[41] Ibid., pp. 9–10, 18, 32.

[42] Scott, pp. 2–3, 10, 20, and 27–37.

independence. The only living regional traditions in its department of Rhône-et-Loire were those of the Forez and the Beaujolais, and their main expression was the demand for administrative independence of Lyon.[43] Regional autonomy was the last thing Lyon needed, for it was doubly dependent on the national government both to ensure its food supplies, which had to be brought from distant sources through a hostile countryside, and to protect its enormous and vulnerable silk industry. As a trading center which looked abroad and to Paris for its raw materials and markets, Lyon's outlook and interests were international, not regional.[44] Lyon also lacked a living tradition of political independence. Its municipal institutions—its *consulat* and its *milice bourgeoise*—were atrophied by the second half of the eighteenth century and Lyon watched with indifference as the remnants of its autonomy disappeared.[45] The community's main focus of local pride was its wealth and productive capacity and it is hard to see how this could have generated the kind of particularism on which a rebellion might be based.

A relationship between particularism and regionalism has been suspected in some other urban rebellions but evidence of it is equally hard to find.[46] Deep-seated local loyalties undoubtedly existed but to invoke them as part of an explanation of "federalism" is to suggest that it had deep roots in regional history which in reality it lacked.

III   THE POLITICAL ROOTS OF "FEDERALIST" PROTEST

So far the discussion has concerned what "federalism" was not. To discover what it was, it seems reasonable to start with what the "federalists" had to say for themselves. Anyone who is able to face the task of wading through the masses of "federalist" rhetoric which later poured into the archives of the Terror—addresses, oaths, proclamations, manifestoes, calls to arms, denunciations, reports, and programs circulated, reprinted, recirculated, and reprinted again until the whole paper edifice of the united departments' resistance to oppression finally collapsed in late July—will emerge with an image of a "federalist" mentality dominated by the fear of anarchy and the imminent collapse of the social and political order. The imminence of anarchy was the *leitmotif* of "feder-

---

[43] Louis Trénard, *Lyon de l'encyclopédie au préromantisme*, 2 vols. (Paris, 1958), 1:219.

[44] Verninac, *Description physique et politique du département du Rhône* (Lyon, An IX), p. 55; Pierre Léon, "La région lyonnaise dans l'histoire économique et sociale de la France. Une esquisse (XVIᵉ–XXᵉ siècles)," *Revue historique* 237 (1967):43.

[45] Garden (n. 27 above), pp. 494–495; Trénard, 1:18, 20, 30.

[46] Lyons, pp. 13, 42; Goodwin, pp. 314–315.

alism." It recurs endlessly, from the *Manifeste* of the Marseillais to the widely circulated speeches of Grangeneuve, Vergniaud, and Guadet, and the profession of faith of the Club of la Croisette in Lyon: "War on anarchists, war on tyrants, respect for the national representation, for the laws and for lawful authority."[47] Anarchy was a blanket term for whatever threatened the settlement of 1791, the rule of law, the security of property, and the safety of the bourgeois person. Anarchy in its concrete form was what was happening in Paris. In the "federalist" towns in late May the capital was thought to be out of control, a city no longer subject to the rule of law. Fears for property were often voiced: there were rumors of the *loi agraire*, of plots to equalize wealth and to impose massive taxation on the rich.[48] The much-quoted letter written by the anti-Jacobin deputy Chasset on May 15 to the president of the Club of la Croisette in Lyon sums up the worst fears of the "federalists": "It is a question first of our lives and then of our property."[49]

It is doubtful whether fears of social disintegration were so uniformly intense as the rhetoric suggests. There was certainly widespread anxiety, for in the wake of the September Massacres, the execution of the king, and the Law of the Maximum, anyone with property or a twinge of regret for the Old Regime had good reason for anxiety about what was coming next. As well there were grave fears about the damage which was being done to trade by inflation, government intervention, and war. "Federalist" propaganda exploited and exaggerated these fears. The talk of threats to life and property, particularly when addressed to "nos frères des campagnes," was designed to maximize support, just as were the appeals to ancient religious rivalries by the Protestant "federalist" leadership in the Gard.[50] If there had been a widespread conviction amongst the provincial bourgeoisie that they faced a life-or-death struggle, as Chasset's warning implied, "federalism" would have been a much more substantial movement and the "federalist" revolts would have been much more

[47] AC Lyon, 1²4, dossier 45, proceedings of the Club of la Croisette, May 10, 1793. For examples of the anarchy theme in "federalist" propaganda see Forrest, pp. 102 ff.; Kennedy (n. 29 above), p. 127.

[48] Goodwin, pp. 316, 319; Forrest, pp. 94–102; see also Robert Lindet's letters of June 9 and 10 on provincial misconceptions of the situation in Paris (*Recueil des actes du comité de salut public*, ed. F. A. Aulard, 28 vols. [Paris, 1891–1951], 4:497, 510); Riffaterre (n. 14 above), 1:206; *Gonchon aux citoyens de la section des quinze-vingts, Fauxbourg Saint-Antoine* (Lyon, 1793); Jean Schatzmann, "La Révolution de 1793 à Lyon vue par un témoin oculaire, Jean Salomon Fazy," *Annales historiques de la Révolution française* 7 (1940):52; Scott, p. 76; Lewis, pp. 62–65.

[49] Mathiez (n. 39 above), p. 390; Soboul (n. 2 above), p. 318.

[50] Lewis, p. 65.

dangerous than they were. The general state of anxiety in the provinces undoubtedly fuelled the protests and the gestures in the direction of revolt which constituted the most common form of "federalism," but it does not explain why revolts occurred when and where they did.

The same applies to the other main theme in "federalist" propaganda, summed up in the catch-cry "la représentation nationale est violée." There was strong provincial sympathy for the Girondins' struggle against the Parisian Jacobins, the bloodthirsty Marat, the intriguing demagogues Robespierre and Danton, the "tribuns insolents" and "hommes soudoyés" of the street. The Girondin speeches were carefully calculated appeals to opinion in the departments and they did not miss their target, particularly when an able deputy such as Barbaroux combined declarations of political principle with campaigns on behalf of local economic interests.[51] The order for the arrest of twenty-nine Girondin deputies was a shock to an electorate which had recently transferred its reverence for the king to the chosen representatives of the people and which had been taught to regard the persons of its deputies as inviolable. But whether outrage at the expulsion of the Girondins was a prime cause of rebellion (as distinct from "federalism") is doubtful.

This is a point on which views have differed. Mathiez has the revolts "planned and premeditated,"[52] so that violent provincial reaction to the Parisian insurrection becomes the culmination of a long-developing rebel movement. Hampson discovers no plot but emphasizes the local causes of the revolts, again minimizing the significance of the provincial reactions to the purge.[53] Soboul, while acknowledging that "the federalist revolt was a natural extension of the sectional movement of the month of May," says that "news of the insurrection in Paris and the elimination of the Girondin deputies both precipitated the revolt and widened its appeal."[54] Jacques Godechot places still more importance on the impact of the "coup d'état" of May 31–June 2 and sees the revolts as a "resistance movement" to the "fait accompli" in Paris.[55]

The differences of opinion reflect the difficulty of generalizing about the revolts. Particular cases can be cited which seem to fit one version or another. Bordeaux, for example, nicely fits Soboul's. There was nothing

[51] Scott, pp. 94–95.

[52] Mathiez, p. 389.

[53] Norman Hampson, *A Social History of the French Revolution* (London, 1966), pp. 171–175. Crook takes a similar view (n. 4 above), p. 384.

[54] Soboul, p. 317.

[55] Jacques Godechot, *La contre-révolution: Doctrine et action, 1789–1804* (Paris, 1961), p. 233. There is a similar view in R. R. Palmer, *The Age of the Democratic Revolution* (Princeton, 1959, 1964), 2:111.

but bellicose talk from the few Bordeaux sections until the news of Lyon's revolt plus the arrest of the Girondins emboldened the department of the Gironde to convoke a Popular Commission.[56] Rennes and Caen fit too.[57] Marseille, on the other hand, was well along the road to revolt by May 2, when the General Committee of the Sections defied the Representatives on Mission, Bayle and Boisset, who had ordered the dissolution of their Popular Tribunal. It is true that formal defiance of the Convention itself did not occur until June 9, but on May 27 the majority of the sections (which by then effectively controlled the city) refused to accept the Convention's decree of May 15 confirming Bayle and Boisset's order.[58] Lyon's revolt appears at first sight to have been generated by local issues. The immediate aim of the military operation mounted by the sections on May 29 was to overthrow the Jacobin Municipality. But even at this early stage the Lyonnais rebels were flouting the authority of the Convention by imprisoning the Representatives on Mission, Nioche and Gauthier, until they endorsed the provisional regime. And while the anti-Jacobin authorities did not formally withdraw recognition of the Convention until after learning of the purge of June 2, their defiance of the Convention's representatives on May 29 was tantamount to defiance of the Convention itself.[59]

Only in Bordeaux did the Girondins matter enough for the campaign against them to provide a plausible motive for revolt. Five of the eight deputies from the Gironde who are classed by Alison Patrick amongst the Girondin "Inner Sixty" were Bordelais by birth or long residence.[60] Since late 1792 Vergniaud, Gensonné, Bergoeing, Grangeneuve, and Guadet had been bombarding the city with propaganda designed to represent Jacobin successes in Paris as directly threatening to their constituents' interests. Their proscription was called for by the Paris Commune on April 20; two were arrested on June 2 and two more fled. All of them were closely associated with the political, legal, and merchant classes of Bordeaux, who saw in the Girondins' fate a forewarning of their own.[61] For the other "federalist" strongholds, however, there are no

[56] Forrest, pp. 96–108.

[57] Stone (n. 1 above), pp. 369–370; Goodwin, p. 319.

[58] Scott, pp. 88–89, 112–113.

[59] "Rapport fait par C. N. Nioche . . . sur les malheureux événements arrivés à Lyon, le 29 mai 1793," in Dubois-Crancé (n. 15 above), pp. 73–74, 85; *Détail de ce qui s'est passé à Lyon les 28, 29 et 30 mai 1793 (extrait du Journal de Carrier)* (Lyon, n.d. [1793]), p. 15.

[60] See the notes on the following in Kuscinski, *Dictionnaire des conventionnels* (Paris, 1916): Vergniaud, Guadet, Gensonné, Grangeneuve, Boyer-Fonfrède; Alison Patrick, *The Men of the First French Republic* (Baltimore, 1972), pp. 318–319.

[61] Forrest, pp. 88–106.

such powerful links with the Girondins to explain why they should have been more disposed to revolt in protest at their fate than Rouen, Clermont-Ferrand, Orléans, or Tours.

The same problem arises if the revolts are attributed to dissatisfaction over the Convention's performance in general rather than the narrower issue of its treatment of the Girondins. Disillusionment with the Convention undoubtedly prepared the way for revolt. Mathiez is correct in saying that the revolts were prepared weeks before the revolution of May 31–June 2, but they were prepared in the sense that local authorities, sectionaries, and National Guards were disposed to withdraw obedience from the Convention well before revolt occurred, and not in the sense that there was a long meditated conspiracy against it. Those in the Mathiez tradition are right to insist that the rebellions were about national politics from the beginning. Explanations of their outbreak in terms of local conflicts fail to do justice to the depth of provincial feeling against the Convention and its effects on the emergence of the disposition to revolt. The new assembly had been in session for little more than a month when open criticism of its factiousness and its slowness to act became widespread in Marseille.[62] Bitter resentment of the Convention had become evident in other areas, particularly Brittany, by the beginning of 1793.[63] In some "federalist" centers these symptoms appeared later, but when they appeared they reflected the same mentality. On May 10 the mouthpiece of the anti-Jacobin sections of Lyon published and endorsed a strongly worded declaration by the sections of Marseille which attacked not merely the machinations of the Montagnards but the behavior of the Convention as a whole.[64] In Caen, too, the local authorities were convinced by mid-May that the Convention was no longer capable of controlling events.[65] Clearly the campaign against the *appelants* and the revolution of May 31–June 2 did not create the necessary mentality for "federalist" revolt by themselves, though they did generalize it and provide a justification for resistance as well as encouraging more resolute action. Disillusionment with the Convention was not created in late May 1793 but over a long period by what the provinces saw as its inability to rein in the Paris Commune, its factionalism, its failure to produce the promised Constitution, and its acquiescence in *sans-culotte* social demands, most notably exemplified by the decree of the *maximum*. As Sydenham has reminded us,[66] one of the paramount concerns of the revolution of 1789 had been

[62] Scott, p. 60.

[63] Wallon (n. 3 above), 2:393–398, 471–473.

[64] *Journal de Lyon*, May 10, 1793, pp. 313–315.

[65] Goodwin, p. 316; see also Stone, pp. 368–369.

[66] M. J. Sydenham, *The First French Republic 1792–1804* (London, 1974), p. 9.

to establish the rule of law and the supremacy of representative institutions. In 1793 both seemed under threat not only in Paris but in the provinces, where Montagnard deputies were riding roughshod over properly elected local authorities. In this context the rhetoric about anarchy had meaning. The literature of "federalism" is pervaded by the fear that representative government and the rule of law were under threat, and this is the best evidence we have as to the causes of "federalist" protest. But it was a long road from protest to revolt and not many travelled it. Some of the most virulent and widely circulated attacks on the Convention came from places where no rebellion or only token rebellion occurred.[67] Again the question arises, why did hostility to the Convention turn into revolt in some places but not in others?

IV FROM PROTEST TO REVOLT

To account for the pattern of revolt in France as a whole we need to look at a wide range of factors. To start with, it is clear that both geography and the military situation played a part in determining whether concern over events in Paris developed into revolt or was confined to verbal protest. Of the six serious armed revolts none was closer to a theater of war than Lyon. Being close to Paris exposed the would-be "federalist" to the danger of swift retribution, and towns close to the war, like Toulouse, were easily discouraged by the proximity of both French armies and foreign ones. Those in the northwest like Rennes and Nantes had to weigh the iniquities of Jacobinism against the ferocious royalism of the Vendéens. The activities of royalist bands in the Lozère had a similarly dampening effect on "federalism" in surrounding areas.[68]

Geography and accidents of the military situation could work the other way. Because of its location between the "federalist" Breton departments and Paris, Caen became a natural base for the most active "federalist" elements of surrounding areas and a refuge for fugitive Girondin deputies. And because of local shortages there was popular support for a strategy which included diverting grain from the voracious Paris market. The sympathy of the army commander at Cherbourg for the "federalist" cause was also important. When on July 7 he transferred his headquarters to Caen and accepted appointment to command the "federalists," General Wimpffen restored some of the plausibility which their military threats

---

[67] The most notable example is *Les nantais à tous les départements de la République* (Nantes, 1793); see also Wallon, 2:439–524 (Appendices—particularly XXII [Département de la Vienne, June 15, 1793] and LXVII [Département du Jura, June 7, 1793]).

[68] See Lewis, p. 58; Wallon, 2:197, 287.

had begun to lose as the 1,500 volunteers of early June melted away to forty-five on the twenty-fourth.[69]

Except in the case of Caen, geography and military factors help to explain why revolt did not go far rather than why it did. Other factors can be related directly to the hostility towards the Convention out of which "federalism" grew, the most important being Montagnard centralism. The process which tightened the grip of the central authorities on provincial France is well known, beginning in September 1792 with the dispatch of agents by the Ministry of the Interior to recruit national guards for the defence of Paris and to report on the patriotism of the provincial authorities. With their extensive and ill-defined powers, the less circumspect of them became the bane of local administrators.[70] They were followed in increasing numbers by Representatives on Mission, at first mainly to deal with emergency situations, then in the early spring of 1793 to implement the *levée en masse* and other revolutionary measures. Major centers received many such visitations—Lyon had ten Representatives on Mission in eight months, including two visits from Legendre with his butcher's talk and his *sans-culotte* bodyguard Rocher, "un scélérat de moustafa" (as an indignant Lyonnais complained) "avec ses moustaches et son air assassin [qui] vous suit comme licteur oui sans doute comme chez les Romains."[71] The impact of these *commissaires* on local opinion was considerable and so was the irritation generated by their interference in the affairs of communities which had become accustomed to some autonomy since 1790, particularly since some of the intruders made no attempt to disguise their doubts as to the quality of local patriotism.[72] The hostility generated by Montagnard centralizing process naturally focused on the Representatives who enforced it on the provinces, and

[69] Goodwin, pp. 325–328, 341.

[70] See Pierre Caron, *La première Terreur (1792). Les missions du conseil exécutif provisoire et de la Commune de Paris* (Paris, 1950), *passim*.

[71] Anonymous letter to Legendre, March 1793 (BL Fonds Coste, MS 596). The other deputies *en mission* at Lyon before the rebellion were Vitet and Boissy d'Anglas (with Legendre) (September–October 1792); Basire and Rovère (with Legendre) (March 1793); Nioche, Gauthier, Albitte, and Dubois-Crancé (May 1793).

[72] Dubois-Crancé, for example, made no secret of his belief that Lyon was a hotbed of counterrevolution. See *Discours prononcé au club central de la ville de Lyon le 4 mars 1792 par M. Dubois-de-Crancé* (Lyon, 1792) and *Discours sur le siège de Lyon prononcé par le citoyen Dubois-Crancé [. . .] au club des Jacobins, à Paris [. . .]* (Paris, n.d. [An II]. For local reactions to the *missionnaires* see, e.g., *Journal de Lyon*, March 12, 1793, pp. 210–212, and March–May 1793, *passim*; Bibliothèque de Lyon, Fonds Coste, MSS 578, 587, 596, 599, 600 (letters to the deputies, mostly anon.).

it provided a rich source of "federalist" sentiment which was eagerly exploited by the leaders of the rebellion. Analogies were drawn with the tyrants of history, "the thirty tyrants of Athens, the Decemvirs of Rome . . . Nero, Tiberius, the Dukes of Alba, the Inquisitors of Spain and Portugal, and lastly the Dairi of Japan." "Who are these cowardly despots who dare to establish their atrocious dictatorship in the departments, disorganizing the authorities, violating all the laws of justice and humanity, hiring infamous agitators? And they call themselves representatives of the people!"[73]

Another contributing factor was the lack of political sympathy between the Montagnards and the directories of most of the departments. Even though the departmental elections of October 1792 were held under the widened suffrage of the First Republic, there was little change in either the social makeup of the councils and directories or their conservative-to-moderate political complexion.[74] As this lack of sympathy became outright hostility in the spring of 1793, with the Montagnards tightening their grip on national politics and their agents intervening in departmental affairs, the departmental directories became hotbeds of "federalism." Their commitment to "federalism" was an indispensable precondition for "federalist" revolt, for without their sanction the "federalists" had no weapons except the inherent appeal of their cause. A departmental directory could provide the rebels with funds and an administrative apparatus. It could order the *gendarmerie* to support them, could prevent decrees from Paris from reaching people, could give bodies created by the rebels an appearance of legitimacy and, above all, could claim to speak for the countryside as well as for the town. No city could risk being seen to march in a completely different political direction to the rest of its department. Since the smaller towns and villages were seldom interested in "federalism" and often opposed the politics of the *chef-lieu* on principle, the support of the directory was the only way to maintain a semblance of regional unity in anti-Jacobin cause.[75]

But it is not possible to explain the major revolts in terms of the factors mentioned so far. Most of France had moderate departmental directories,

---

[73] *Adresse du peuple de Lyon, à la République française* (Lyon, 1794). p. 3; *Adresse aux armées, aux citoyens et à tous les départements de la République française par les autorités constituées réunies à Lyon* (Lyon, n.d. [June 1793]), p. 4.

[74] See J. Godechot, *Les institutions de la France sous la Révolution et l'Empire* (Paris, 1968), p. 318.

[75] For an account of rural hostility to "federalism" see C. R. Lucas, *The Structure of the Terror. The Example of Javogues and the Loire* (Oxford, 1973), chapter 2. See also Forrest, pp. 118–122.

and most of it was dosed with centralism, but only a small part of it went into "federalist" spasms. It could be answered that some areas were handled much more roughly by the Representatives on Mission, and that these included the cities which Paris was most afraid of, Lyon, Marseille, and Toulon. Yet it was possible for a town to suffer violent incursions from Paris without responding with more than token "federalism." If any Representative on Mission possessed the talents necessary to provoke revolt single-handedly it was Chabot, whose descent on Toulouse in early May was to be remembered with horror years afterwards. He bullied the local authorities, dismissed the *procureur-général-syndic* of the department of Haute-Garonne, expounded his version of Jesus as the first *sans-culotte*, and capped it all with a plan to make Toulouse into a convention center for all the most exalted Jacobins of the southwest.[76] But even Chabot could not produce more than a slight, brief "federalist" fever in Toulouse. The reason is that after their flirtation with "federalism" the Toulousains saw the dangers of being provoked and were able to revert to the resigned acceptance of what happened in Paris, to the *attentisme* which was the most usual provincial response to the political crisis of spring 1793. As Lyons puts it, they knew that "moderation and unity were the best means of neutralizing pressures from outside Toulouse, and of denying any room for manoeuvre to the repressive authorities in Paris."[77]

In the places where serious revolts *did* occur it was the failure to apply this excellent principle of survival which led to the disaster of "federalist" revolt. We need not suppose that they lacked the political guile which other towns used to minimize the encroachments of the agents of centralization. Their problem was that in early 1793 they were *unable* to apply the principles of *attentisme* and solidarity against outsiders as did Rouen, Elbeuf, Bourges, and a hundred other places great and small. They were unable to do so because of the extreme turbulence and polarization of their local politics.

It is in this respect that they contrast most sharply with the less resolute federalist centers. Bordeaux was firmly under the control of the mercantile bourgeoisie, which was not seriously threatened before the year II by the radicals of the *Club National*.[78] In Caen the Jacobin and popular societies were sufficiently moderate to work hand in hand with the local authorities.[79] And in Nîmes there had been a hiatus since late 1791 in

---

[76] Lyons (n. 1 above), pp. 43–45, 47; Kuscinski (n. 60 above), entry on Chabot.
[77] Lyons, p. 41.
[78] See Forrest, chapters 3 and 4.
[79] Goodwin, pp. 317–319.

the bloody round of conflict which had marked the first two years of the Revolution and which was to resume in 1795. The Protestant élite had won temporary political control in 1790 and insofar as it was under challenge from local rivals in 1793 the threat came from Catholic counterrevolution in the adjacent Lozère more than from the ultra-Jacobins, a fact which goes some way towards explaining the halfheartedness of the Nîmois campaign against the Convention.[80]

In Lyon, on the other hand, political antagonisms were acute in early 1793, inflamed by sharp social divisions. As Garden has shown, there were vast differences of wealth between the upper strata of aristocratic and bourgeois families and the mass of the population, the largest section of which, the silk weavers, hovered perpetually on the edge of destitution. Violent fluctuations in the fortunes of the silk industry, combined with the reduction of the master weavers to a condition little different from that of their *compagnons*, led to agitation for guaranteed wages which culminated in a long and violently repressed weavers' strike in 1786.[81] In 1789 the élites attempted an orderly transition to the new political order created by the National Assembly, but they were thwarted by a popular insurrection in February 1790 which forced the local authorities to establish a democratically elected National Guard.[82] Over the next few years Lyon's history became increasingly violent. On two occasions the city was virtually out of control: for three weeks in July 1790, when the *barrières* were destroyed and the *octrois* could not be collected, and for six weeks of violence in autumn 1792 which brought food riots, *taxations populaires*, and two prison massacres.[83] After the formation of a network of popular societies (clubs) in September 1790, the democrats began to loosen the grip of the conservative social élites on local government and on the National Guard.

---

[80] James N. Hood, "Revival and Mutation of Old Rivalries in Revolutionary France," *Past and Present* 82 (February 1979): 113; Lewis (n. 1 above), pp. 61–63.

[81] See Garden (n. 27 above), pp. 175–204, 275–309, 355–387; Justin Godart, *L'ouvrier en soie* (Lyon, 1899), pp. 91–92; Louis Trénard, "La crise sociale lyonnaise à la veille de la Révolution," *Revue d'histoire moderne et contemporaine* 2 (1955):5–45.

[82] For details of Lyon's politics under the constitutional monarchy see Maurice Wahl, *Les premières années de la Révolution à Lyon, 1788–1792* (Paris, n.d.). The political situation in early 1790 is described on pp. 123–132.

[83] For the troubles of 1790 see *Corps municipaux de la ville de Lyon* (n. 12 above), 2:98–152, July 9–27; for those of 1792: AN, F⁷3686⁶, dossier 7, Municipal Council of Lyon to Roland, September 10 and October 26, 1792; F¹¹217, dossier 8, Municipal Council of Lyon to Roland, Minister of the Interior, September 18, 22, and 24, 1792.

But in 1792 the departmental and district administrations and the National Guard were still controlled by men whom many patriots regarded as servants of counterrevolutionary interests.[84] Frustrated, the more advanced patriots rallied to the Jacobin Joseph Chalier, a fervent Robespierrist who advocated a program of terror, encouraged acts of popular justice, and denounced the "aristocratie mercantile" as counterrevolutionary. The widened suffrage enabled Chalier's followers to win a majority on the Municipal Council elected in November, but control of the department and the National Guard still eluded them.[85] They looked to the capital for aid in their war on counterrevolution, and it was forthcoming. During the September troubles came commissars from Paris, one of whom, Laussel, officially a *commissaire-observateur* for the Ministry of the Interior, outraged the then Rolandist Municipal Council by immediately taking the part of the more advanced Jacobins. He later became *procureur* of the newly elected *sans-culotte* Municipal Council.[86] The involvement of the commissars in radical politics culminated in mid-May, when Dubois-Crancé approved the creation of a Revolutionary Army. This was ingeniously planned to have two brigades, the first to prevent counterrevolution in Lyon and the other one to fight it on the battlefields of the Vendée. A committee of Jacobins was to determine who was conscripted into which brigade. But the Lyonnais Jacobins were too badly organized to effect this project quickly. They were overthrown within three days of the first rumors that Dubois-Crancé was coming to their aid with an armed force, a threat which convinced the majority of the sections that the time had come to choose between insurrection and the "dictatorship" of men like Chalier.[87]

[84] See Wahl, pp. 569–593.

[85] See Maurice Wahl, "Joseph Chalier. Etude sur la Révolution française à Lyon," *Revue historique* 34 (1887): 1–30; Takashi Koi, "Les 'Chaliers' et les sans-culottes Lyonnais (1792–1793)," *Annales historiques de la Révolution française* 50 (1978); A. Da Francesco, "Montagnardi e sanculotti in provincia: Il caso lionese (agosto 1792–maggio 1793)," *Studi storici* 19 (1978): 600–626; Herriot (n. 11 above), 2:102, 113–114, 159–161.

[86] AN F¹¹217, dossier 8, Laussel to Roland, September 16, 1792; Vitet (then Mayor of Lyon) to Roland, September 14, 1792; *Corps municipaux de la ville de Lyon* (n. 12 above), 3:383 (November 20, 1792) and 4:250–253 (May 14, 1793).

[87] Of a projected Revolutionary Army of 6,400, only about 400 men had been assembled by May 29 (*Les citoyens de la ville de Lyon à leurs frères* [. . .] *de la République française* [Lyon, n.d.], p. 7); AN AF II 43, Plaq. 339, no. 23, Departmental Council to Garat, May 27, 1793; *Les commissaires des sections de la ville de Lyon réunies en comité les 29 et 30 mai, 1793* (Lyon, 1793), p. 2; *Procès-verbaux de conseil-général du département de Rhône-et-Loire*, ed. G. Guigue, 2 vols. (Trévoux, 1895), 2:309, May 28, 1793.

Two aspects of this history are particularly relevant to the outbreak of the "federalist" revolt. One is that by early 1793 political divisions in Lyon had become deep and intractable. The followers of Chalier freely anathematized all those to their right and they in turn were regarded as criminal fanatics or just plain criminals by Rolandins as well as by the more conservative elements of the upper bourgeoisie. Thus, for François Billemaz, one of the founders of the popular societies in 1790, Chalier was "the author of all the evils which have befallen us in Lyon since he returned from Paris shouting for heads and more heads." As for the Municipality, "of the twenty municipal officers, fourteen are rogues and cut-throats; I forbear to dwell on their incapacity . . . the least of their faults are ineptitude and absolute ignorance, they are all fit for the gallows."[88] None of the contending factions was in a position of dominance, but each had its strongholds. The Rolandins shared control of the department with feuillantine elements, and the latter were also strongly represented amongst the officers of the National Guard and in the law courts; Chalier's followers included not only the bulk of the members of the Municipality but also the judges of the *Tribunal de Commerce* and the *chefs de légion* of the National Guard.[89] It was therefore impossible either for the politically active elements in Lyon to unite in defence of the city's interests or for one group to take command and steer a provident course through the turbulence of 1793. The other main feature of Lyonnais politics in early 1793 was that the Montagnard Representatives on Mission had become regular and active participants in them. This was partly a result of the Convention's understandable concern about the instability of the second city, and partly a response to appeals for help from the partisans of Chalier. Their visits were interpreted as attempts to shore up the position of the Municipality and their behavior reinforced this impression—for example, Legendre's furious rejection of a petition requesting the convocation of the sections and Basire's authorization of a Committee of Public Safety composed of Jacobin members of the department, the District, and the Municipality.[90] Clearly, opponents of the

---

[88] AN F⁷3686⁶, dossier 7, no. 8, Billemaz to Roland, November 29, 1792. Numerous similar accounts of Chalier and his followers in the newly elected municipality are to be found in letters to Roland in ibid., dossiers 7–9, and in AN F¹ª Rhône 8, dossier 1.

[89] Wahl (n. 82 above), pp. 566–568; Herriot, 1: chapters 5 and 7.

[90] [Genet-Bronze, Pelzin, and Badger], *Rapport et pétition sur les troubles arrivés à Lyon, présentés et lus à la barre de la convention nationale, le lundi 15 avril 1793* (Lyon, 1793); *Journal de Lyon*, March 12, 1793, p. 210. (The *Représentants* had the editor of the *Journal de Lyon* arrested soon after the publication of the issue which criticized their behavior—see petition of Carrier, journalist, April 20, 1793 [AN AA 53, dossier 1487, no. 51]).

sans-culotte Municipality would also be opponents of the Montagnard *conventionnels*. It was this which gave federalism its substantial base in Lyon. By May 29 opposition to the Municipality was such that eighteen of thirty-two sections participated in its overthrow.[91] Thus, automatically, they became enemies of the Montagnards and, after June 2, enemies of the Convention itself. The Committee of Public Safety continued to insist that only the restoration of the Jacobin Municipality and the surrender of the rebel leaders could end the "counterrevolution" in Lyon. Garat recorded Robespierre's response to suggestions that a compromise with the Lyonnais might be reached if the Convention ordered new municipal elections: "I understand. You propose to us that we should dismiss a *patriote* Commune; it is against all true principles; the revolutionary government is here to maintain them and not to annihilate them."[92] Consequently, all who had contributed to the overthrow of the Lyonnais Jacobins had reason to support the "federalist" rebellion.

Marseille and Toulon were if anything more turbulent than Lyon between 1789 and 1793, and as in Lyon the main sources of instability were precocious and sustained radical political offensives which mobilized substantial sections of the *menu peuple* in a ferocious struggle with first the local representatives of the crown and the *notables* aligned with them and later, the moderate bourgeoisie. Social divisions, local circumstances, and contingencies combined to produce a pattern of bitter and virtually uninterrupted political conflict out of which a radical Jacobin faction emerged in control of municipal government in the summer of 1792 but then became, as in Lyon, increasingly isolated.[93] In both places the popular reaction to the revolutionary crisis was immediate and violent, with *émeutes* provoked by shortage and high prices in the spring of 1789. In both, popular discontent was soon channelled into support for the *patriote* cause, a new orientation symbolized by the Toulonnais dockyard workers' defiance of orders forbidding the tricolor cockade in their workplace and by the successful campaign for the removal of royal troops from Marseille.[94]

[91] This estimate is based on references to participation by National Guard battalions in the attack on the Jacobin-held Town Hall (*Conseil-général du département de Rhône-et-Loire*, II, 310, May 29, 1793; *Détail de ce qui s'est passé à Lyon les 28, 29 et 30 mai 1793* [AN AF II, Plaq. 339, no. 10]; AD Rhône-42L64, dossier 2; 42L75, dossier Estournal; 42L3, folder 198; AC Lyon-1²3, dossier 31; 1²7, dossier 152).

[92] J. Garat, *Mémoires* (Paris, 1862), p. 248. On the Montagnards' uncompromising attitude towards the oppressors of the Lyonnais patriots, see Herriot, 2:chapters 2, 5–8.

[93] On the isolation of the Jacobins see Crook, pp. 389–390, and Kennedy, pp. 121–125.

[94] Maurice Agulhon, *Une ville ouvrière au temps du socialisme utopique. Toulon de 1815 à 1851* (Paris, 1970), p. 18; Vovelle (n. 30 above), pp. 271–272.

Different factors sustained the revolutionary momentum built up in 1789–1790. In Marseilles the powerhouse of patriotism was the Jacobin Club which, under the energetic leadership of such men as Isoard and Barbaroux, made itself the arbiter of politics not only in Marseille but in much of Provence. Patriotism triumphed early in Marseille but because of the strength of the reactionary nobility in inland Provence, it was never secure and fear of counterrevolution undoubtedly explains much of the aggressive and uncompromising character of the Marseillais revolutionaries and their partiality for preemptive action against potential threats—for example, the capture and demolition of royal forts in the city itself (April–June 1790), raids on nearby aristocratic strongholds like Aix (July 1789 and February 1792), the arbitrary expulsion of refractory priests (July 1792), and, most spectacularly, the disarming of an entire regular army regiment by the Marseilles National Guard (February 1792).[95] By mid-1792 Marseillais revolutionary dynamism had become chronic. Presumed enemies of the Revolution were lynched in the city and throughout the department in July, August, and September. A campaign of abuse against the rich turned into systematic intimidation by means of large-scale disarmaments and a Committee for Forced Loans. In the sectional assemblies, a countermovement grew rapidly in April, but again the anti-Jacobins were thwarted by Montagnard deputies, this time Bayle and Boisset, who had already closed down the moderate assemblies in Aix and now set about levying a force of six thousand men to crush counterrevolution in the Midi. Since their arrival on March 27, these "torrents devastateurs" (as Barbaroux described them) had consistently taken the part of the Jacobin Club against the sections, whose members they denounced furiously, but without apparent justification, as counterrevolutionaries. They became so unpopular that they were forced to withdraw to Montélimar, and from there they continued to fire decrees at the anti-Jacobin sectionaries who had taken control of the city. The sectionaries did not hesitate long when the Parisian insurrection of May 31–June 2 gave them the choice between civil war and letting the local *anarchistes* regain control of Marseille with the full backing of the Representatives on Mission and the Convention.[96]

In Toulon political polarization was rooted in social divisions. Like Lyon this naval port was untypical of eighteenth-century French cities in that a large proportion—at least a quarter—of its working population was employed in a single industry, the royal shipyards known as the Arsenal. And like the Lyonnais weavers, the workers of the Arsenal were miserably paid and united by particular grievances in addition to the

[95] Vovelle, p. 272; Scott, pp. 27–39.
[96] See Scott, pp. 37–112.

usual problems of *la vie chère*. In particular they were plagued by late payment of their wages which the administrators of the Arsenal attempted to palliate by issuing paper credit. This expedient, however, heightened the discontent, for the merchants of Toulon would accept the paper only at a discount. On the eve of the Revolution fear of the Arsenal's workforce was such that a wealthy Toulonnais, the printer Mallard, advanced on one occasion 50,000 livres and on another 60,000 so that their wages could be paid.[97] From the first year of the Revolution Toulon was politically divided between radical patriots and conservatives ("blancs" and "noirs") and by 1791 a radical movement had emerged "which attracted the allegiance of artisans, shopkeepers, and above all, dockyard workers and sailors from the town's great naval base."[98] Against them were grouped the *notables* of the Old Regime and the remnants of the local nobility, many of them outsiders who had come to Toulon as navy or army officers. Amongst the latter, dislike of the Revolution grew in proportion to political consciousness and indiscipline amongst the sailors, which no doubt explains the high proportion of naval officers and engineers in the "federalist" General Committee.

Toulon's history of political violence rivalled Marseille's and Lyon's and surpassed them on July 28, 1792 with the murder of four members of the Var Departmental Council who had been condemned as counter-revolutionaries by the local clubists. The Jacobins took over the municipality in mid-1792 and initiated a series of purges, arrests, and executions. They also cooperated with the Montagnards in pressing the war effort and imposed greater discipline and financial sacrifices on the dockworkers, who were paid in depreciating *assignats* from May 1793. In return they were supported by the Montagnard Representatives on Mission, Beauvais and Baille, whose activities met opposition from anti-Jacobins well before the expulsion of the Girondins from the Convention. The resistance to these "sponsors" of "brigands and assassins" was intensified by mass arrests on May 21 under their authority, and it led directly to the repudiation of the Convention which had unleashed them on Toulon.[99] From the start the rebellion was not just a local affair, a *coup* to oust a radical town council. It was a rejection of the national government which was determined to keep the radicals in office. Anyone who saw himself as likely to be their victim had reason to support political action which would prevent the Convention's writ from running within his city's walls, whether he

[97] On social conflict in Toulon see Crook, pp. 286–396; Agulhon (n. 94 above), pp. 7–19; Norman Hampson, "Les ouvriers des arsenaux de la Marine pendant la Révolution française," *Revue d'histoire économique et sociale* 39 (1961).

[98] Crook, p. 385.

[99] Ibid., pp. 385–387, 393; Cottin (n. 11 above), p. 24.

was a moderate member of a departmental or district directory, of a municipality or a club, whether he had been a partisan of the constitutional monarchy, attended clandestine masses or frequented sectional assemblies suspect to the *sans-culottes*, whether he was a naval officer (in Toulon), a silk merchant (in Lyon), a ship owner (in Marseille), or a personal enemy of some influential Jacobin. The bitter, violent politics of Lyon, Marseille, and Toulon stored up the fears and hatreds on which the rebellions fed. They made it impossible for these communities to put up a united front against the commissars from Paris, and they provided powerful reasons for opponents of the Jacobins to resist the Convention once it became clear that the Representatives on Mission intended to consolidate and increase the power of their enemies.

V "POPULAR" FEDERALISM

My explanation of the major federalist revolts thus centers on the effects of Montagnard intervention in violent and long-standing local political conflicts. Besides being consistent with what we know about the revolts, this approach helps to account for one of their more puzzling features, the substantial popular support they enjoyed. Other factors can plausibly be advanced to explain it, such as the economic dependence of the *menu peuple* on the merchant classes and on the rich in general. Particularly where trade in luxury items like silk was important, the hostility to the rich expressed by Chalier and his like seemed suicidal to artisans whose livelihood had already been damaged by the impact of the Revolution on the church and the nobility.[100] It is also significant that ultra-Jacobins had already controlled Lyon, Marseille, and Toulon for lengthy periods when the "federalist" revolts began to gather force. They therefore took the brunt of popular dissatisfaction with high prices, low wages, and shortages. While subsidies and the *maximum* reduced bread prices in Paris they remained high in the provinces, and the provincial Jacobins' professions of support for popular economic demands led only to disillusionment and hostility when they were not matched by action.

We don't know by what mischance we can't eat bread as good as in Paris . . . now that the people is sovereign and we have sans-culotte municipal officers in whom we place our trust we don't know by what misfortune it happens that the more the price of bread goes up, the worse these rogues make it, what infamy! . . . A baker in rue Gentil called Chabou . . . asked our gallant municipality for permission to bake no more bread but to permit him to make fine brioches . . . our good

---

[100] This factor is stressed in Da Francesco, "Montagnardi e sanculotti" (n. 85 above), pp. 613–615.

municipality has allowed him to make nothing but brioches and in this way the aristocrats have more of them to eat for their luncheon.[101]

On May 26 the Jacobin mayor of Lyon, Bertrand, a merchant who owed his election to the intervention of Basire, Rovère, and Legendre, found that his reputation as a good *sans-culotte* and friend of Chalier carried no weight with a crowd pillaging army stores: "the people seemed to contest all the remonstrances that were put to them."[102]

But popular "federalism" can be understood more fully if it is related to the dissension introduced into provincial popular politics by the agents of Montagnard centralism. The triumph of Chalier's followers in Lyon was achieved at the expense of splitting Lyon's well-established network of popular societies (clubs). From early 1791 the clubs had prospered to the extent that they were able to dominate the city's political life. In the poorer quarters they were genuinely "popular," but they had lent their support to the bourgeois *patriotes* who had initially been grouped around Roland.[103] When Chalier brought the campaign against Roland to Lyon in August 1792 there was resistance to it within the club movement and this began a split which culminated in the collapse of the clubs early in 1793.[104] By then the issue was no longer the fate of Roland, nor even the campaign to expel supporters of the *appelants* from the clubs, but the attempt of Chalier's associates to replace the loose association of "clubs de quartier" which had existed since September 1790 with a single Jacobin club on the Parisian model.[105] Many clubists valued the autonomy of the *clubs de quartier* and resisted the efforts to eliminate them but the Jacobins had enough sympathizers to cause secessions from several *clubs de quartier* and to obtain the adherence of a few to their

[101] BL Coste MS 601, petition of citizen Dubreuil to the Deputies of the National Convention (n.d. [March 1793]). Crook, pp. 387–388, has plentiful evidence of popular discontent with the radical municipal council of Toulon.

[102] AN AFII 43, Plaq. 339, no. 28, communication to the Ministry of the Interior from the Directory of the Department of Rhône-et-Loire, May 25, 1793.

[103] On the social composition of the popular societies, see T. Koi, "Les 'Chaliers' " (n. 85 above), and his thesis of the same title (Thèse de Doctorat, IIIᵉ Cycle, Université de Lyon III, 1975); on their political orientation, Wahl (n. 82 above), pp. 227–299.

[104] *Journal de Lyon*, February 21, 1793, p. 165. The earliest sign of the split was the Club of la Pêcherie's refusal to accept that Roland was a conspirator, which was combined with a declaration that the Club Central of Lyon (controlled by Chalier's followers) would destroy the clubs if it persisted with the campaign against him. (Société populaire of la Pechêrie, resolution of December 9, 1792, AC Lyon, 1²2, dossier 108.)

[105] Da Francesco (n. 85 above), p. 623.

proposal. As the club network disintegrated the anti-Jacobin campaign moved to the sections, in most of which, as we have seen, bourgeois elements were dominant. It was at this point that popular leaders became involved in the nascent federalist movement. The best evidence for this is in the records of the weaving quarter of Port-Saint-Paul, where several of those who had played leading roles in club and sectional politics between 1790 and 1792 became "federalist" militants in 1793, including the weaver Denis Monnet, one of the leaders of the strike of 1786, celebrated as the unmasker of the counterrevolutionary "Lyon Plan" in 1790, a close associate of one of the cofounders of the popular societies, François Billemaz, and a member of the General Council of the Municipality in 1792. With eight other weavers Monnet served on the *comité de surveillance* elected on May 19 by the Section of Port-Saint-Paul in defiance of the Jacobin Municipality and he was still president of the committee in the last month of the rebellion.[106] The participation in the rebellion of people like Monnet becomes comprehensible when it is viewed as a defensive reaction against the intrusion of Montagnard centralism into Lyonnais popular politics, an intrusion which was tearing the clubs apart and breaking up the political framework on which had been built the *patriote* victories of 1790–1792, not to mention numerous political careers which were threatened by the new ultra-Jacobinism of Chalier. Viewing the "federalist" revolt as a political response to the combined threat of Montagnard commissars and local Jacobins makes more sense of its popular component than versions of it as the work of a counterrevolutionary bourgeoisie or an expression of particularist sentiment.

Popular "federalism" in Marseille seems to have had similar origins. Division in the Jacobin society was followed by the departure of the moderates from it in January and February, and as Michael Kennedy observes, it was this which laid the groundwork for the "federalist" rebellion of 1793.[107] As in Lyon, it is probable that the presence of clubists and men from the lower socioeconomic categories amongst the "federalist" sectionaries of 1793 was in large part due to the radical Jacobins' attempts to concentrate power in their own hands, to their

---

[106] AD Rhône, 31L20, 21, 23, Section de la Concorde [Port-Saint-Paul], correspondence and proceedings, January 1790–August 1793. See François Billemaz, *Jugement du tribunal du district de Lyon en faveur du citoyen Denis Monnet, prononcé ensuite du plaidoyer du citoyen François Billemaz, homme de loi, défenseur officieux* (Lyon, 1791); Louis Trénard, "La crise sociale lyonnaise à la veille de la Révolution," *Revue d'histoire moderne et contemporaine* 2 (1955):5–45.

[107] Kennedy (n. 29 above), p. 118.

uncompromising rejection of moderates, and to their increasing disregard of opinion in the sections.[108]

The involvement of former radicals in Toulon's revolt has already been mentioned. There is evidence of a split amongst the clubists early in 1793, of "erosion of the widespread support which had thrust the radicals into office,"[109] and of *sans-culotte* disillusionment with them. The fact that a clubist was the first to be guillotined under the radical regime[110] demonstrates that wayward radicals had as much to fear from the authorities as had counterrevolutionaries, and as much reason to want their former associates removed from office. Substantial sections of the artisan classes in these cities had become politically involved. When the clubs which had been the main agents of this process divided and split, their popular elements did not all follow the Montagnard line. For some the path which began with opposition to the local Jacobins led on to "federalism" and rebellion.

VI   CONCLUSIONS

Recent work on "federalism" provides grounds for questioning some widely accepted views of its causes. There is little to support the view that it was a product of localism or particularism. There is even less evidence that royalism was a significant cause, although where rebellion persisted into the late summer royalists came to acquire considerable influence, having belatedly recognized "federalism's" potential as a weapon against the Republic. As to the political orientation of the revolts, "federalism" is a misleading label which has been loosely applied to cover political phenomena ranging from cautious verbal protest to premeditated armed revolt.

The various forms of "federalism" had common features. There was genuine outrage at the treatment of the Girondins, but the Parisian insurrection was not so much a cause of "federalism" as a convenient justification for resistance to Jacobin centralism which was gathering force anyway. "Federalist" rhetoric uneasily combined the language of popular sovereignty with a legalistic phraseology which reflected an underlying aim—to restore the rule of law and regular administration along the lines laid down in the constitution of 1791. "Federalism" can be understood only if this aim is recognized as central to it. The current preoccupation with the "social" character of the Revolution and with

---

[108] Ibid., pp. 123–125, 159–160; Scott, pp. 115–118.

[109] Crook, "Toulon," pp. 386–387.

[110] Ibid., p. 387. Similarly, Pierre Laugier, president of the Marseille Jacobin Club in January–February 1793, was the first "federalist" to be executed there during the Terror (Kennedy, p. 124).

the minutiae of regional history should not be allowed to obscure the fact that the national political issues about which the Revolutionaries talked so much did in fact matter to them. The definition, distribution, and limitation of political power were of deep concern to the educated in late eighteenth-century France and they were all at issue in early 1793.[111] The division of political and administrative responsibilities between central and provincial authorities had appeared to be settled by the local government legislation of the National Assembly, just as the legitimization of authority had appeared to be settled by the transfer of sovereignty to a national representative body. But this was all thrown back into the melting pot by Montagnard centralism and the Convention's increasing subjection to radical forces in Paris. The shape of the emerging Montagnard dictatorship—with its tightening centralization, its arbitrariness, and its compromises with direct democracy—was abhorrent to those who had embraced (and profited by) the system of government established between 1789 and 1791. "Federalist" protest was extensive because this abhorrence was widespread. But in the final analysis, faced with the risks of civil war, invasion, and counterrevolution, the provincial bourgeoisie abandoned its political principles. Acquiescence in Montagnard centralism at least offered the possibility that direct Parisian intervention in local affairs could be avoided and the local predominance of the *notables* maintained largely intact.

Only where "federalism" appeared in a context of deep-rooted local political violence and instability did serious revolts follow. In Marseille, Toulon, and Lyon successful Jacobin offensives had provoked anti-Jacobin movements based in the sectional assemblies. Long periods of conflict and agitation had politicized the *menu peuple* and some popular elements, rejecting the local brands of radical Jacobinism, were drawn into the "federalist" camp, thus providing it with a comparatively broad social base. In these places the ranks of those who had political differences with the local Jacobins—and hence an interest in the success of the revolts—had been swelled by the intensity of the political struggle. They had much to lose from the policy being followed by the Montagnard Representatives on Mission—the extension and consolidation of the local Jacobins' power by means of revolutionary institutions which could override the only remaining restraints on the local "anarchists," the departmental and district directories. The events of May 31–June 2 in

[111] For a clear discussion of political ideas and disputes in the first year of the Convention—and a case for seeing them as crucial to an understanding of the Revolution—see Sydenham (n. 66 above), pp. 3–25, and the same author's "The Republican Revolt of 1793: A Plea for Less Localised Local Studies," *French Historical Studies* 12 (Spring 1981), pp. 135–138.

Paris made it clear that the Convention would support the Representatives in these policies and reinforced the determination of the threatened anti-Jacobins to persist in their rebellion.

Somewhat paradoxically, the revolts were more serious where the local *notables* were *not* in secure command of the cities. The pertinacity of the major revolts is not attributable to regional peculiarities or separatist tendencies or to the existence of a powerful counterrevolutionary provincial bourgeoisie but to the inability of local élites in three large cities to regulate local conflict within the political framework created by the Revolution. The rarity of such major urban revolts is an indication of the firm grip which the men of property had on local power. In most places they were secure enough to ride out the storm created by the Jacobin–sans-culotte alliance.

A broader question emerges from this analysis. The threat to the Republic from "federalist" revolts has been used since Mathiez as partial justification for the Montagnard policy of Terror. But if the most serious "federalist" revolts were themselves products of a Montagnard policy, that of keeping provincial Jacobins in power no matter how limited their support or how strong the local opposition to them, then the Terror in the great "federalist" centers must be counted as a consequence of the Montagnard strategy of enforcing centralism and political uniformity and not simply as a justifiable response to a crypto-royalist, separatist, counterrevolutionary threat. Perhaps the Montagnards were right to believe that moderates could not be relied upon to keep the cities safe for the Republic or to support the war effort with sufficient vigor and that ultra-Jacobins like Chalier would better serve these purposes. But we cannot assume that they were right to make these judgments. Montagnard Representatives on Mission acted in ways which helped provoke revolts which were later used to justify the Montagnard policy of terror. So any attempt to justify the provincial Terror necessarily involves an assessment of the correctness of the judgments on which Montagnard policy towards the provinces was based, and of the wisdom of pursuing this policy at the risk of civil war.

This essay has attempted to make three main points about the "federalist" revolts. First, it has aimed to show that it took violent shocks from outside combined with unusual local circumstances to move provincial cities from the *attentisme* which they usually adopted as the best defense of their autonomy and tranquillity. Secondly, it has argued that "federalist" revolt should be clearly distinguished from "federalist" protest. Thirdly, it has suggested that the revolts were not a war of the provincial bourgeoisie against Paris and the Revolution, but a defensive reaction against Montagnard centralism, a reaction whose intensity was directly related to the intensity of preexisting local conflict.

The Royalist Press in the Reign of Terror*

Jeremy D. Popkin

The revolutionary *journée* of August 10, 1792, which toppled the French monarchy, also marked the end of the royalist newspapers that had defended the king's cause against the rising tide of republicanism. Leading royalist journalists who had not previously fled the country were either killed or arrested, and the victorious revolutionaries banned all further royalist propaganda.[1] Neither the imprisonment and subsequent execution of the king nor the repressive measures against journalists, however, prevented the reappearance of a royalist press shortly after the September massacres, and some of the papers founded in this period survived well into 1794. Previous historians of the revolutionary press have taken this very survival as proof of these publications' insignificance. Alma Söderhjelm, whose *Le Régime de la presse pendant la Révolution française* remains fundamental for this subject, claimed that these journals "took no part in the fight, the way the aristocratic papers had before August 10, they were neither frank nor outspoken like those papers, they stayed on the sidelines, trying to mask and disguise their opinions as much as possible, and avoid attracting attention."[2] Indeed, some formerly monarchist publications did restrict themselves to a monotonous diet of officially approved news until thermidor allowed them to show their true colors again. But there were

* I would like to give special thanks to Jack Censer, Patrice Higonnet, and William Murray for their comments and advice on this project, and to the helpful staffs of the Bibliothèque nationale, Archives nationales, and Widener Library for their assistance. The Social Science Research Council gave me necessary support for research in France, and Harvard's Center for European Studies provided office space and assistance in completing the writing. Acknowledgment is made to the University of North Carolina Press for permission to use some material from my forthcoming book, *The Right-Wing Press in France, 1792–1800*.
    [1] William Murray, "The Rightwing Press in the French Revolution, 1789–1792" (Ph.D. diss., Australian National University, 1971), pp. 414–29. Although the revolutionary Commune had demanded a law against the creation of new newspapers, in order to keep earlier royalist sheets from reappearing under new titles, as early as August 23, 1792, the Convention did not actually pass a law against royalist propaganda until December 4, 1792. The execution of such prominent royalist journalists as De Rozoi and the fate of others caught up in the September massacres undoubtedly served as a deterrent to some, however. Murray's work supersedes earlier accounts of the counterrevolutionary press in the early stages of the Revolution. See also the section by Jacques Godechot in the collective *Histoire générale de la presse française*, 5 vols. (Paris, 1969), 1:471–85.
    [2] Alma Söderhjelm, *Le Régime de la presse pendant la Révolution française*, 2 vols. (Paris and Helsinki, 1900), 1:229.

This essay originally appeared in the *Journal of Modern History* 51 (December 1979).

also a number of antirevolutionary papers which behaved very differently. If not overtly royalist, like their predecessors, they continually criticized the republican regime, played an active role in the Girondin-Jacobin struggle, and even managed to question some aspects of revolutionary policy until the time of the Hébert and Danton trials in April 1794. Although they did not succeed in turning back the Jacobin tide, they fought a stubborn rearguard action and also helped prepare the way for the resurgence of royalism after thermidor.

After a brief phase of political confusion following August 10, 1792, the history of the royalist press in the Terror went through four phases. From September 1792 until the Girondins' final defeat in the Convention on June 2, 1793, the counterrevolutionary journalists, de facto allies of the anti-Jacobin republicans, enjoyed considerable freedom, and were able to stake out an independent position on many issues. From June to August, 1793, after the Girondins' defeat, the royalist papers still managed to keep up the fight against the Jacobins. From the fall of 1793 onward, however, as the federalist rebellions were crushed, the revolutionary government also forced the opposition press in Paris to mute its tone, although new right-wing papers were founded as late as October 1793. Finally, at the time of the ventôse crisis in March 1794, the surviving cryptoroyalist papers lost the last of their freedom and several journalists were arrested. Even at this point, however, there was no systematic attempt to round up former royalist writers and suppress their papers. A number of them continued to publish, waiting for the renewed opportunities to speak out which appeared after thermidor.

During the open struggle between Girondins and Jacobins which preceded the latter's triumph on May 31, 1793, four loosely linked publications dominated the royalist press.[3] Two of them, the *Quotidienne* and the *Révolution de 92*, began publication on September 20, 1792; the others, the *Journal français* and the *Feuille du*

---

[3] The royalist publications I have chosen to concentrate on in this study were those which were sold openly—indicated by the publication of an address for subscriptions in each issue—and took clear-cut political positions which distinguished them from other papers of the period. There were also some essentially clandestine royalist publications, such as J. Corentin Royou's *Véridique* (October 1792–March 1793), and some whose status is uncertain since so few issues have survived, such as the *Spartiate* and the *Journal chinois*. More numerous were the papers which took at best a very muted right-wing stance between 1792 and 1794 but later swung to the right, such as Suard's *Nouvelles politiques*, Poncelin's *Gazette française* (to judge by the single known copy from its first year and a half of publication), and the *Messager du soir*. Some of these, like the *Nouvelles politiques*, were the continuations of earlier constitutional monarchist publications; others were disillusioned republicans or unprincipled opportunists. I have not included these publications in this study.

Matin, appeared in the second half of November. A fifth paper, less directly connected with the others but close to them ideologically, was also appearing by this date, although it is not clear when it started; this was the *Bulletin national.* The *Feuille du Matin* was the continuation of a well-known royalist paper from before August 10, the *Journal de la Cour et de la Ville,* better known as the *Petit Gautier.*[4] The other four papers were new enterprises, although some of their staffers had been contributors to previous royalist publications. Many of these royalist journalists were young men with no previous careers; others were veteran men of letters whose ambitions had been frustrated prior to 1792 by more talented competitors.[5] For both groups, the plunge into royalist propagandizing at such a perilous moment represented both an ideological commitment and a pursuit of an unexpected professional opportunity. Although they sometimes differed with each other in print, the royalist journalists formed a mutual admiration society, came to each others' defense against republican harassment, and clearly considered themselves a cohesive political group.[6]

A reader totally unfamiliar with the Parisian press during the Revolution might not always have known that these five papers were edited by dedicated royalists who had declared their position publicly before 1792 and were to do so again after thermidor. But few newspaper readers at the time were so naive. Even had they overlooked these five papers' frequent expressions of sympathy for Louis XVI, up to and after his execution, and their constant critique of all phases of the Revolution and the distinctly defeatist tone of their foreign news reports, they could hardly have missed the papers'

[4] The *Feuille du Matin* officially denied any connection with the earlier paper (December 4, 1792), but a closely related royalist publication, the *Avertisseur,* which consisted mostly of classified ads interspersed with occasional propaganda, clearly hinted at the link, which was obvious anyway from the paper's tone and typographical appearance, in its issue of November 29, 1792.

[5] Altogether, I have identified fourteen collaborators involved with these five papers. Only one had edited a paper before August 10, 1792, although ten had been associated with one or more of the earlier royalist publications. Only the *Quotidienne* seems to have been created entirely by journalistic novices. There is some information on these journalists and their previous careers in the memoirs of one group member: Louis-Ange Pitou, *Une Vie orageuse,* 3 vols. (Paris, 1820), 1:72–73, 83–89. See also *Biographie universelle,* s.v. "Rippert," and the anonymous manuscript titled "Journaux Bibliographie" at the Bibliothèque historique de la Ville de Paris (MS 722–33), which consists of notes for an unpublished study of the revolutionary press dating from around the turn of the century.

[6] Typical favorable cross-references are in the *Avertisseur,* November 29, 1792 (for the *Feuille du Matin*), and December 2, 1792 (for the *Journal français*). When Nicole, editor of the *Journal français,* was arrested on January 29, 1793, the other royalist papers all demanded his release (see, e.g., *Quotidienne,* February 2, 1793).

repeated attempts to link themselves with the best-known royalist journals from before 1792. Admittedly, the papers' content was usually not overtly antirepublican in the same way the papers before 1792 and after 1794 were. They usually gave their readers a more or less biased summary of foreign and national political news and, in some cases, a surprisingly detailed picture of Parisian municipal politics. Often, they distinguished themselves from other anti-Jacobin papers primarily by their virulent polemical tone. The ideological assumptions behind their criticism of the Revolution, however, did not always differ noticeably from those of some moderate republicans, although they were always stated in the strongest possible terms. "Jacobins, isn't it true that in your group, atheism, the agrarian law, the murder and abasement of constitutional authorities are openly preached?" the *Journal français* demanded (December 19, 1792). Of the three general issues raised in this attack on revolutionary radicalism, the religious question received the least attention in the papers, especially compared to the prominence it enjoyed in the post-thermidorian counterrevolutionary press. For the most part, the journalists limited themselves to accusations that the revolutionary de-Christianizers were creating a new form of intolerance. They made little effort to prove their general claim that society needed a religious basis.

The royalist journalists were more outspoken in their opposition to social and economic egalitarianism. Although they made no effort to defend the pre-1789 system of social privilege, they drew on familiar eighteenth-century arguments to show the necessity of differences in wealth—arguments also used by some of the Girondins. The *Journal français* admitted that the promise of equality would always be popular, since there were more poor than rich, but "the agrarian law is the true anti-social law: its execution would be the immediate end of society . . ." (December 15, 1792). The paper's editorialist conceded that inequality always produced a certain corruption of *moeurs,* but, for him, this was outweighed by the stimulus it provided to individual enterprise and the resulting progress of civilization (November 27, 1792). In the *Bulletin national,* Gallais, a lively polemicist, vigorously defended free enterprise against the Jacobin effort to impose a controlled economy, and argued for differential rewards according to merit: men might be equal in virtue and patriotism, but "no matter how extensive the system of equality is, talent can never be equalized" (November 10, 1792; July 31, 1793). Such critiques of egalitarianism invariably—and unjustly—assimilated the Jacobin program and the crudest *sans-culotte* agitation. Nevertheless, they drew on the same general body of Enlightenment social thought used by the revolutionaries themselves. Many of the royalist journalists' articles could have been taken directly from texts like Voltaire's article on "Equality" in the *Philosophical Dictionary.*

Closely related to the journalists' defense of inequality was their opposition to radical democracy. As the *Journal français* noted, economic inequality created a large class of poor who could always be stirred up by agitators: " 'Let us have our turn' becomes the general cry, and the pride which mixes with it, identifies love of liberty with refusal to submit to a government whose power is above it" (November 27, 1792). With the September massacres fresh in all minds, the royalist journalists made some of their most telling attacks against political leaders who endorsed popular violence. "We would appreciate it if citizens Da[nton], Ma[rat], and Robes[pierre] would deign to tell us how many killers must be assembled, in order that a murder committed by them ceases to be a crime and becomes an act of the people's justice . . . ," the *Feuille du Matin* wrote (November 27, 1792). Similarly, the papers condemned deputies who bowed to mob pressure in voting to execute the king (*Journal français,* December 28, 1792). The journalists could draw on classical arguments against democracy, and in particular on familiar condemnations of popular fickleness (*Révolution de 92,* January 1, 1793). Sometimes, they also used more topical sources: in August 1793, Gallais published a dialogue refuting the claim that any section of the population could rise up against acts of the national government. Although he used the arguments the Jacobins were employing against the federalist rebels, he gave them a very different twist by directing them against *sans-culotte* claims to a privileged political position (*Bulletin nationale,* August 15, 1793).

Social and political theory interested the royalist journalists much less than the immediate struggle for power between revolutionary factions. In the absence of any genuinely counterrevolutionary movement, the royalist press consistently supported the Girondins against the Jacobins and later backed the Jacobins against the radical *sans-culotte* movement. Up to May 31, 1793, the papers lumped all the radical factions together, claiming that the divergences between Jacobins, Cordeliers, and other groups were more apparent than real. All these factions, the papers claimed, had one common goal: "disorder and complete anarchy" (*Feuille du Matin,* December 10, 1792). There could be' no compromise with them. Although the royalists had to work hard to top the Girondins' own vituperation of their opponents, the *Journal français* achieved some distinction in this vein when it printed a letter urging the assassination of Danton,

Robespierre, and Marat (December 11, 1792). Even as they cheered the Girondins on, however, the royalist papers frequently expressed a well-founded pessimism about the moderates' chances. When rising food prices set off riots in February 1793, the *Journal français* said, "What we found most disgusting, was not the looting, but the imperturbable calm with which the Parisians remained motionless spectators of it" (February 27, 1793), and an earlier article had concluded that even the moderates' dominance in the press would prove meaningless: "It is true that, with pen in hand, we take our revenge, but the sole shadow of a dagger makes us tremble" (December 12, 1792). A more philosophical editorialist, writing in the *Quotidienne*, concluded that the events of the Revolution vindicated pessimistic political thinkers:

> Without a doubt, seeing in our days this rage to destroy, one would be tempted to believe in the existence of an evil principle at work in the universe, with fights in the heart of man, which rejoices in evil, and takes pleasure in the midst of ruins and death. . . . These ideas are not consoling, and if it were demonstrated that the dangerous and antisocial passions are truly the most powerful, the most widely spread among men, certainly, of all principles of government, that which would be the best adapted to our nature, would be that of Machiavelli's Prince, which holds that the science of the legislator tends to hold down subjects by force. [January 25, 1793]

This pessimism about human nature and the strength of the anti-Jacobin opposition did not keep the royalist journalists from disagreeing with their Girondin allies on a number of major issues. Usually, they could not argue openly against republicanism, although they sometimes made their point clearly enough, as in an article on the English Restoration, praising General Monk (*Quotidienne*, April 7, 1793). But they did campaign strongly against the trial and conviction of Louis XVI, in which the Girondins were heavily implicated. The *Révolution de 92*, which gave the fullest coverage of the trial and the surrounding polemics, denied that the Convention had any legal authority to judge the king (January 6, 7, and 17, 1793). Several royalist papers printed long extracts from pamphlets defending the king, together with occasional snide comments about the efforts of men like Necker, who were now trying to get the monarch out of the situation they had, from the royalist point of view, put him into.[7] The journalists warned that the emigré royalist

---

[7] The *Révolution de 92* offered the widest selection of material defending the king, with something on the subject in almost every issue from late November 1792 until the execution. For its attitude toward Necker, who had published a pamphlet defending the king, see the issue of November 19, 1792. The *Quotidienne* gave Necker's work a more positive review on November 21, 1792, and reprinted excerpts from it on November 25 and 27, 1792. On the other hand, the *Journal français* said

movement would be strengthened if the king's brother became free to proclaim himself regent (*Feuille du Matin,* December 20, 1792). After Louis's execution, the *Journal francais* warned that the other European powers would never consent to make peace with a regicide government (January 25, 1793). Other editors openly expressed their personal grief, and the *Quotidienne* risked publishing a verse "Testament de Louis XVI" which ended:

> And I see myself by a faithless people,
> Dragged from the throne to the scaffold.
> Prepared to finish my life,
> O people! I die innocent,
> I pardon you as I expire.
>
> [February 24, 1793]

The papers also printed Louis XVIII's proclamation laying claim to the regency and other reports about the emigré movement (*Quotidienne,* February 25, 1793).

The royalist press also opposed the Girondin policy of spreading the Revolution abroad. As French armies advanced into Belgium, Germany, and Italy, the Girondin papers claimed they were being hailed as liberators, but the royalist press publicized all the evidence of local opposition. The *Quotidienne* printed proclamations from several Belgian cities reaffirming loyalty to the country's traditional institutions (December 3 and 9, 1792), and the *Révolution de 92* claimed that the conduct of French troops in Piedmont had "disgusted all the Italians in the area" and driven them into the arms of the counterrevolution (March 9, 1793). Although their reports were plainly at odds with the version of events given in the Girondin press, their coverage of Belgian reactions to the French occupation paralleled the attitude Dumouriez took in late 1792, when he broke with the Girondin policy of sponsoring French-style revolution in the conquered provinces. The royalist press thus once again followed a policy of supporting whichever republican faction came closest to its own positions on any particular issue.[8] The papers also gave exaggerated accounts of the coalition's military preparations and offered the Austrian version of conditions in parts of French territory occupied by Imperial troops (*Révolution de 92,* March 27, 1793). For the most part, the royalist papers seem to have drawn their foreign

---

little about the trial on the grounds that such editorials would not do any good (December 23, 1792).

[8] For Dumouriez's efforts to publicize Belgian resistance to the French invasion, starting in November 1792, see Marc Martin, *Les Origines de la presse militaire en France à la fin de l'ancien régime et sous la Révolution* (Vincennes, 1975), pp. 163–64.

news from papers printed outside the country, which continued to reach Paris through much of this period, but some of them may have had correspondents, perhaps among the emigré royalists.

Neither foreign news nor defenses of the king succeeded in altering the political balance in Paris. Unlike the Girondin politicians, the royalist journalists apparently realized that their opponents could only be defeated if the papers could ally themselves with a mass movement in the capital itself. Compared with the Girondin press, which concentrated on politics in the Convention, the royalist papers consistently showed greater interest in the grubby but vital details of municipal politics. They provided detailed reports on the Paris Commune, the sectional assemblies, the Jacobins and other clubs, and even the wall posters which played such a role in political agitation.[9] And when an opportunity presented itself, they made a serious effort to challenge the radical domination of this urban political machinery.

The occasion for this royalist dabbling in street politics arose at a critical moment in 1793. As the Convention strove to fend off foreign invasion, cope with Dumouriez's spectacular treason, and appease economic discontent, it suddenly found itself faced with the additional threat of the Vendée rebellion. To meet the revolt, the Convention ordered local governments to raise an emergency levy of troops. In Paris, this task fell to the Commune and the forty-eight sections, where pro-Jacobin agitators were in the midst of a campaign to force the arrest of the leading Girondin deputies. The Commune decided to make the burden of conscription fall most heavily on the city's "white-collar" workers, who had shown both a notable lack of patriotic zeal and an uncanny ability to evade previous draft calls.[10] These "notaries' clerks, clerks of the advocates and lawyers, clerks of the wholesale merchants, the moneychangers and bankers, the

---

[9] The *Révolution de 92* provided the most ample coverage of the Paris Commune that I have found in any Paris paper of the period. The *Quotidienne* also gave considerable coverage of municipal politics and street agitation. One of its periodic surveys of recent wall posters is in the issue of April 23, 1793. By contrast, Girondin papers like Brissot's *Patriote françoise* hardly paid any attention to such lowly forms of political activity.

[10] The Commune's decree of May 1, 1793, ordered the sections to draft men "whose momentary absence will cause fewer inconveniences . . . ," and specified the unmarried office clerks of all public and private enterprises in the capital (Buchez and Roux, *Histoire parlementaire de la Révolution française* [Paris, 1836], 26:333). Chaumette, the Commune's *procureur-générale*, defended this measure on the grounds that these young men from the middle classes had been leaving the burden of military service to the poor, since they had been able to buy substitutes or secure exemptions from previous draft calls: "The poor have done everything long enough; the rich should do something" (quoted in *Révolutions de Paris*, May 4–11, 1793).

speculators, those employed in the government offices . . . ," as Marat characterized them, made up the Parisian *jeunesse*, sons of the middle classes and aspiring young men who hoped an education would enable them to rise above their background.[11]

Leadership for the suddenly threatened *jeunesse* arose from two groups accustomed to a public role: some actors from the Paris theaters, and the journalists active in the royalist press. On May 4 and 5, there were mass rallies in the western part of the city, stronghold of the bourgeoisie, which attracted as many as 1,000 supporters.[12] In addition, politicized members of the *jeunesse* packed several sectional assemblies and ousted their radical leadership. The royalist papers gave this movement generous coverage, often written in the first person, and trumpeted the movement's temporary successes as the start of a counteroffensive against the hated Jacobins. "The sections are de-Jacobinizing themselves everywhere, because the good citizens are finally starting to attend, and to realize that this is the only way to eliminate the root of the evil," the *Journal français* proclaimed (May 10, 1793).[13] Even before this article appeared, however, the more experienced radical militants had regrouped and driven the moderates out of the assemblies they had briefly captured. Although the royalist papers continued to hope that their supporters could regain the initiative until the final defeat on May 31, 1793, their movement had been

[11] Marat, *Publiciste de la République français*, May 7, 1793. Marat's categorization of the group's members is substantially the same as that of the *jeunesse* members themselves. See Georges Duval, *Souvenirs thermidoriens*, 2 vols. (Paris, 1844), 2:10–11.

[12] The first demonstration, on May 4, 1793, was at the Luxembourg Gardens and was led by an actor, Quesnel. According to Georges Duval, 300 attended, but contemporary newspaper accounts give higher figures (Duval, *Souvenirs de la Terreur*, 4 vols. [Paris, 1841], 4:5, 10; *Quotidienne*, May 5, 1793). The following day, there was a larger demonstration on the Champs-Elysée at which Duval says from 1,000 to 1,200 were present. It was dispersed by forces from the more revolutionary sections of the city (Duval, *Souvenirs de la Terreur*, 4:16; *Révolution de 92*, May 8, 1793). Nonroyalist newspapers either ignored these demonstrations or gave them only passing mention; they are referred to briefly in standard works such as Georges Lefebvre, *The French Revolution*.

[13] *Journal français*, May 10, 1793. The prison dossier of one leader of the movement gives a good picture of what actually took place in the assemblies. Isidore Langlois, an activist in the Bonconseil section, had previously been exempt from the draft as a surgical student. On May 4, 1793, he and his friends captured control of the Bonconseil assembly, elected themselves its officers, and drew up an address swearing loyalty to the Convention—then temporarily under Girondin control—which Langlois delivered to that body on May 5. While he was addressing the legislators, however, the section's radicals called in allies from neighboring districts and ousted Langlois's supporters. Langlois fled to a relative's home outside the city, but the other leaders of the movement were arrested (Isidore Langlois, dossier in Archives Nationales [hereafter cited as A.N.] F7 4764).

completely broken. It served, however, as a model for the much more extensive activities of the *jeunesse dorée* after thermidor, culminating in the major right-wing *journée* of 13 vendémiaire IV (October 5, 1795), in which several journalists active in the royalist press during 1793 played leading roles.[14]

Having identified themselves so closely with the Girondins, the royalist papers naturally suffered the consequences of their allies' defeat on May 31, 1793. The fiery *Journal français* was suppressed, and the prolix *Révolution de 92* suffered several interruptions of publication.[15] Unlike their Girondin colleagues, however, the royalists were not physically eliminated. Except for the *Feuille du Matin,* which had apparently ceased publishing before the coup, all the royalist papers managed to reappear before the end of June 1793. The staff of the *Journal français* founded a new paper, the *Correspondance politique,* and openly solicited former readers of their own paper and the Girondin press.[16] Together with the other royalist papers, this publication provided extensive coverage of the federalist revolts around the country and the Vendée rebellion. Although they no longer dared to editorialize against the Jacobins, these papers printed manifestos from the rebel leaders in Normandy, Brittany, and the Midi which stated the anti-Jacobin case for them.[17] Surprisingly, the victorious Parisian radicals, so thorough in their repression

[14] The best account of the *jeunesse dorée*'s activities in the sections after thermidor is K. Tonnesson, *La Defaite des sans-culottes* (Paris, 1959), pp. 90–49, 182–83. On the journalists' role in vendémiaire, see Harvey Mitchell, *The Underground War against Revolutionary France* (Oxford, 1965), pp. 83–87, and Jeremy Popkin, *The Rightwing Press in France, 1792–1800* (Chapel Hill, N.C., 1979).

[15] The last issue of the *Journal français* appeared on June 2, 1793. The *Révolution de 92* was interrupted from June 3 to June 6 and again from June 13 to July 1, 1793, when it resumed publication under the new title of *Journal historique et politique.*

[16] The prospectus for the new paper, issued June 18, 1793, began, "Many papers having been swept away by the revolutionary force of May 31, we have thought it appropriate to substitute ourselves in their place. . . ." Although the authors denied any intention of adopting the banned papers' political line, they specifically mentioned the Girondin papers of Gorsas and Brissot and the royalist *Journal français* and *Révolution de 92* (which resumed publication in its own right soon afterward).

[17] For example, *Correspondance politique,* reports from rebel centers in Normandy (June 19, 1793), Marseille and Bordeaux (June 21, 1793), Marseille and Toulon (June 29, 1793), and the Vendée (July 1, 1793). The *Quotidienne* was forced to suspend publication briefly after printing a proclamation from "the leaders of the Catholic and royalist armies" in the Vendée (June 27, 1793), but soon reappeared and continued publishing news of the federalist revolts, such as an article claiming that the Lyon federalists had abolished the *maximum* and that, as a result, grain was abundant in the city (July 13, 1793). The *Révolution de 92* had published an account of the *journée* on May 31, 1793, which refuted Jacobin claims of a spontaneous, city-wide movement (June 8, 1793). It was temporarily suppressed on June 13, 1793, for reprinting the deputy Lanjuinais's speech defending the Girondins, delivered in the Convention on June 2.

of the Girondins, moved very slowly to bring the royalist press under control. As late as August 18, 1793, the *Bulletin national* was still publishing letters from the federalist rebels in Lyon.

As the federalist revolts were crushed, however, the Paris newspapers gradually abandoned their open opposition to the Convention. Sometimes, a visit from the police gave a journalist time to "think things over," as the *Quotidienne*'s editor put it (August 1, 1793). In other cases, the newspapermen seem to have reached the desired conclusion on their own. Even at this point, though, the former royalist papers remained noticeably nonconformist. The *Bulletin national* openly defended some political figures tried by the Revolutionary Tribunal, even though their fate was already clear.[18] When the *Quotidienne* was finally suppressed on October 18, 1793, it was almost immediately succeeded by a paper called the *Trois Décades,* which continued to distinguish itself from the "patriotic" press. It printed a sardonic account of life inside the revolutionary prisons, and, during the winter of 1794, constantly harped on the grain shortage which was stimulating popular discontent. It also reprinted articles from Camille Desmoulins's *Vieux Cordelier.* Together with the other surviving right-wing papers, the *Trois Décades* sheltered behind Robespierre, once one of its editorialists' leading targets, to oppose the de-Christianization campaign. When the Incorruptible and Danton spoke out against the excesses of the de-Christianization campaign in late 1793, the *Trois Décades* commented that their speeches "are stongly reasoned and shine with beautiful eloquence. One cannot deny that from the philosophic manner in which some overturn cults and pursue their former ministers to intolerance, there is no more than a step. . . ."[19]

Around the time of Robespierre's move against the followers of Hébert and Danton, in March 1794, several cryptoroyalist journalists were also arrested and their papers suppressed. The revolutionary police had been aware of the papers' activities since their inception and had no doubts that they continued to pose a threat, even in their toned-down versions.[20] Gallais, the *Bulletin national*'s editorialist,

[18] For example, a defense of General Custines, in *Bulletin national,* August 20, 1793. Gallais was arrested and the paper temporarily suppressed on September 9, 1793, but the charge against him and the publisher, Bérard, was summed up by an official of the Comité de Sûreté générale in rather vague terms: "These journalists should have, on certain occasions, restrained themselves from reporting certain facts, which might have affected public opinion." Bérard was soon released and resumed publishing under the new title of *Bulletin républicain.* It is not clear how long Gallais remained in prison (Dossier Bérard, in A.N., F7 4594).

[19] *Trois Décades,* articles of 10 frimaire II (November 30, 1793), 11 and 13 plûviôse II (January 30 and February 2, 1794), 9 frimaire II (November 29, 1793).

[20] The police reports printed in Pierre Caron, ed., *Paris pendant la terreur,* 6 vols.

had been arrested in September 1793; now it was the turn of the *Trois Décades'* editor and of Duplain, a newspaper publisher closely associated with the group which put out the *Correspondance politique*. Surprisingly, the dossiers of the arrested journalists give no indication of a systematic effort to suppress the opposition press. The charges against Coutouly, the *Trois Décades'* editor, were based mainly on his association with "the most gangrened aristocracy of his section . . ." before 1792;[21] Duplain was interrogated about differences between the two daily editions of his *Courrier universel,* but no evidence indicated that they had any political implications.[22] Once both men had been jailed, lack of evidence was not enough to save them from the guillotine. But a surprising number of their colleagues either evaded arrest or, more astonishingly, were briefly arrested and then released. It is possible that well-placed bribes helped some of these fortunate souls and accounted for the virtual immunity of the much-denounced *Correspondance politique,* which contrasts strongly with the severe punishment meted out to arrested collaborators on the royalist papers from before August 10, 1792.[23] Even more than police corruption, however, the royalist journalists seem to have benefited from the lack of organization in the Republic's repressive machinery. No single police agency was ever entrusted with the task of rooting out subversive publications to the exclusion of all other preoccupations. The Ministry of the Interior's

---

(Paris, 1910–58), show this clearly. The *Correspondance politique* was denounced as early as September 25, 1793 (Caron, 1:193) and on at least seven subsequent occasions; the *Quotidienne* or its successor, the *Trois Décades,* are mentioned in reports on 4 nivôse II (December 24, 1793) and two subsequent occasions (Caron, 1:382–83). The only other publication which could be considered counterrevolutionary mentioned in these reports after September 1793 was the *Vieux Cordelier* of Camille Desmoulins, which received considerably more attention than the former royalist papers.

[21] Dossier Coutouly, in A.N., F7 4656.

[22] Dossier Duplain, in A.N., F7 4654. The paper printed an express edition for distribution in the provinces and a regular edition. According to Duplain, the higher-priced edition had 1,400 subscribers at the time of his arrest in March 1794.

[23] Rippert, publisher of the *Quotidienne,* was arrested along with his associate Coutouly, but disappeared when his guards let him leave the jail, unescorted, to buy himself a dinner! (Dossier Rippert, in A.N., F7 4774[93]). The accommodating guards were promptly jailed themselves. Lefortier, editor of the *Correspondance politique,* was arrested in March 1794 for printing an article regarded as an attack on the republican armies, but promptly released (Dossier Lefortier, F7, 4774[12]). That bribery may have been involved in such cases is suggested by Pitou's account of how he purchased acquittals in his two trials during the Terror (Pitou [n.5 above], 3:60–63). Murray (n. 1 above), pp. 417–30, indicates that out of eleven journalists, printers, and other collaborators with the pre-August 1792 royalist papers arrested after the fall of the monarchy, ten were guillotined. It may be that the revolutionary leaders were more eager to pay off old scores than to supress the relatively less outspoken papers appearing in late 1793 and 1794.

police agents, for instance, included their reports on the royalist papers with daily rundowns on protests over food prices, Hébertist agitation, and a host of other problems which may well have struck their superiors as more urgent.

Even though many formerly outspoken and presumably unconverted royalists continued to work for various Paris newspapers after March 1794, the revolutionaries could at least be satisfied that they had stopped the publication of right-wing propaganda in the daily press. With the elimination of the *Trois Decades* and the *Révolution de 92*'s cessation of publication, only one of the former royalist newspapers continued to distinguish itself in any way from the common run of the press. This was the *Correspondance politique*, which had replaced the *Journal français*. The gaps in surviving collections of this publication make it hard to follow its career in detail. During the summer of 1793, it doggedly continued to publicize the federalist revolts. Although no copies have survived from late 1793 or early 1794, police agents continued to denounce it regularly for its aristocratic leanings. By April 1794, however, it had become an outspoken supporter of Robespierre. At a time when even pro-Jacobin papers had learned to avoid printing political commentary of any kind, the *Correspondance politique* suddenly began to feature long editorials signed by J. J. Dussault, a minor journalist who had previously written for several apolitical papers and had contributed at least one article to the *Quotidienne* in 1793.[24] Dussault, who had previously covered the Convention debates for the paper, now signed his name to attacks on Hébert and on the Dantonists, an article applauding the execution of the *fermiers généraux,* one endorsing the closing of the popular societies, and a somewhat nuanced article on the various effusions of government-sponsored deism.[25] None of these contained anything likely to offend the Committee of Public Safety, but their mere appearance at a time when hardly any other journalist of any political persuasion was willing to print a personal opinion of any kind is curious.

[24] Dussault had been a young schoolteacher in 1789. He began his journalistic career with the apolitical *Gazette des Tribunaux,* and contributed a signed article to the *Quotidienne* on April 10, 1793.

[25] The article on Hébert can be found in the *Bulletin républicain,* 1 germinal II (March 21, 1794); it had appeared earlier in the *Correspondance politique.* The other articles referred to appeared in that paper on 22 floréal II (May 11, 1794), 5 prairial II (May 24, 1794), and 16 floréal II (May 5, 1794). After thermidor, when Dussault had to account for these articles, he claimed that they had been rewritten without his approval by a Jacobin sympathizer on the paper's staff (*Quotidienne,* 9 fruc. III [August 28, 1795]). This seems implausible, especially since Dussault could easily have stopped lending his name to them if he found that his views were being so drastically distorted.

In June 1794, Dussault published an article which, in retrospect, shows that the *Correspondance politique* was beginning to align itself with the thermidorian plotters in the Convention. Robespierre had just rammed through the law of 22 prairial II, which, among other things, stripped members of that assembly of their immunity from the Revolutionary Tribunal. Two future thermidorians, Tallien and Bourdon de l'Oise, opposed the law in speeches which most newspapers were careful not to publicize.[26] Dussault, on the other hand, wrote an article which, while appearing to deny the existence of divisions within the Convention, actually drew attention to this incident and asked why Robespierre had claimed that a Dantonist faction still existed among the deputies.[27] This article strongly suggests that the *Correspondance politique* had made contact with the thermidorian plotters and was preparing to work with them as the *Journal français* had earlier collaborated with the Girondins. This suspicion is strengthened by the fact that, immediately after 9 thermidor, the *Correspondance politique* became the thermidorians' semiofficial paper. Dussault, who had fallen silent in the last month of Robespierre's dictatorship, was the first to open a press campaign against him after 9 thermidor, and he continued to defend the policies of Tallien, Fréron, and their allies in that paper until he took over Fréron's own paper, the *Orateur du peuple*.[28] He also played a leading role in the *jeunesse dorée,* an organization based on the same social groups as the antidraft movement of May 1793, which initially served as a paramilitary prop for the thermidorian regime before turning against the Convention in 1795.[29] Thus it appears that the alliance between certain royalist journalists and the thermidorian *conventionnels* actually developed before Robespierre's downfall.

After thermidor, the young journalists who had staffed the royalist papers during the Terror quickly resumed their work. The group which had formed around the *Correspondance politique* and the unlucky Duplain's *Courrier universel* began putting out a new, much more overtly royalist edition of the latter paper. After many twists and turns, this paper finally became the basis for the Bertin brothers' *Journal des Débats,* the major royalist paper of the Napoleonic

---

[26] R. R. Palmer, *Twelve Who Ruled* (Princeton, N.J., 1943), pp. 364–66.

[27] *Correspondance politique,* 1 messidor II (June 19, 1794).

[28] Dussault's debunking biography of Robespierre appeared in the *Correspondance politique* on 12 thermidor II (July 30, 1794), and was reprinted as a pamphlet, *Portrait de Robespierre* (Paris, An II [1794]). On his connection with Fréron and the *Orateur du peuple,* see J. J. Dussault, *Lettre de J. J. Dussault au citoyen Fréron* (Paris, An IV), pp. 4–5, and Pitou, 1:96.

[29] On Dussault's leading role in the *jeunesse dorée,* see Duval, *Souvenirs thermidoriens,* 1:264.

period.[30] Despite the execution of its editor, the *Quotidienne* also reappeared, and soon reestablished itself as one of the most important royalist papers. Gallais, whose articles had made the 1793 version of the *Bulletin national* one of the most interesting counterrevolutionary papers, now joined the *Quotidienne,* although his former paper, retitled the *Bulletin républicain,* struggled on into 1795 without him. Two royalist papers of the Terror period—the *Révolution de 92* and the *Feuille du Matin*—did not come back to life after thermidor, although their respective editors both surfaced again with short-lived royalist sheets in 1797.[31] Their place was filled, however, by a swarm of new royalist publications founded in the thermidorian and Directory periods. This wave of counterrevolutionary journalism continued to mount until the republican coup d'état of 18 fructidor V (September 4, 1797) drove the writers underground.

The surviving copies of the royalist papers show what these journalists tried to achieve during the Terror, but they do not indicate exactly what they actually accomplished. There is no doubt that these virulently antirevolutionary papers were bought and read. The frequent denunciations of them in the Convention, the republican press, and revolutionary police reports show that their opponents were thoroughly familiar with them. The papers did have some measurable political impact. They certainly helped stimulate the May 1793 antidraft demonstrations, the largest antirevolutionary protests in Paris before the vendémiaire insurrection in 1795. And, according to at least one account, Charlotte Corday had admitted reading the *Feuille du Matin* and other royalist publications.[32] The exact extent of the papers' readership is unknown, but at the time of his arrest, Coutouly testified that the *Trois Décades* had 1,300 paying subscribers and that he had been printing between 2,500 and 3,000 copies a day of it and a second, less political paper.[33]

The fact that the royalist papers ultimately failed to prevent a Jacobin takeover should not mask their real importance during the Terror. After the fall of the monarchy, those who opposed the

---

[30] The tangled sequence of splits and reconciliations which produced the *Débats* as the final descendant of the *Courrier universel* is unraveled in the anonymous manuscript referred to in n. 5 above (MS 724).

[31] Salles de la Salle, editor of the *Révolution de 92,* put out a paper called the *Aurore* in 1797; Gautier also revived his paper briefly in that year.

[32] According to the *Chronique de Paris* of July 23, 1793, Corday denied having read the Girondin papers, but said she had occasionally looked at "certain sheets which replaced the Petit Gautier and the so-called Ami du Roi." These were probably the *Feuille du Matin* and the *Journal français.*

[33] Dossier Coutouly, in A.N., F7 4656. In separate testimony, the paper's printer gave a slightly lower figure for the two publications' combined press run.

Revolution had lacked any public leadership. Both the journalists and their readers were left groping, but by keeping their publications going, the journalists at least provided the assurance that when circumstances permitted, they would provide their audience with renewed political direction. In this way, even papers which adopted a completely neutral political stance throughout the Terror, such as Suard's *Nouvelles politiques*, helped keep right-wing opposition to the Republic alive. By maintaining communication with a sympathetic public, they ensured the future existence of the right-wing opposition to the regime.

Developments after thermidor show that the Jacobins' failure to root out the royalist press did pose a genuine threat to the Republic. It is therefore somewhat surprising that the revolutionaries were so haphazard in their suppression of the right-wing papers. Although the Committee of Public Safety did improvise a censorship system, its policy toward the royalist press was unsystematic. There was no thoroughgoing effort to track down the contributors to counter-revolutionary papers, and the cryptoroyalist papers continued to print pro-Girondin propaganda even after the Girondins' own publications had been closed down. The reasons for this are not clear. There was some lingering ambivalence about press controls among the revolutionaries, but the punishment meted out to cryptoroyalist journalists who were arrested shows that it did not prevent strong repressive measures in practice.[34] Police corruption and bureaucratic disorganization were probably more help to the journalists than any republican commitment to press freedom. Under these circumstances, a determined group of political zealots could keep up their struggle for a long time before they were completely silenced. The story of the royalist press during the Terror thus throws light on both the opposition to the Revolution and on the way in which revolutionary institutions actually operated.

[34] Although Robespierre had explicitly included press freedom among those rights which a revolutionary government might have to suspend (speech to Convention on April 19, 1793, in A. Soboul and M. Bouloiseau, eds., *Oeuvres complètes,* 10 vols. [Paris, 1939–67], 9:452), the Constitution of 1793 gave this right absolute protection. The Convention hesitated to bring the press under complete control because of a persistent distrust of state-subsidized publications, reflected in a debate as late as 23 ventôse II (March 14, 1794) (Caron [n. 20 above], 1:23).

Patterns of Popular Protest in the French Revolution: The Conceptual Contribution of the Gard*

James N. Hood

Since the Great Revolution, mass political enthusiasm, regardless of its ideology, has usually expressed popular hatred and fear of big businessmen. In France, before the end of the eighteenth century, contrasting groups joined in articulating with unprecedented clarity their common antagonism toward merchants. Inhabitants of the long-established cohesive communities which dominated urban as well as rural society focused their hatred of the rich upon those who had violated tradition by amassing fortunes through trade. The general collapse of authority at the outset of the Revolution suddenly freed their pervasive anticommercial sentiment from customary restraints. The economic disruption which accompanied the Revolution further embittered the masses by threatening their meager livelihood. Appeals to their hostility came alike from dechristianizing popular democrats in Paris and, at the other political extreme, from Catholic leaders of the counterrevolutionary movement in the West, known as the Vendée. Among departments where popular factions supported both extremes during the Revolution, the experience of the Gard illustrates the mainsprings common to both and thereby opens a whole new perspective on popular politics. Comparison of that case with the Revolutionary experience in other regions suggests a correlation of certain social environments with specific political loyalties—a general model which deserves testing in other contexts of time and place.

Drawing on the information collected regarding some ten thousand families under scrutiny in a study of all aspects of local society, the following overview of the background and consequences of the Revolution in the Gard cites a few families and provides a preliminary basis for comparison with the rest of France.[1] In the Gard, the

* Research and writing for this and future publications were made possible by the Woodrow Wilson and Danforth Foundations, the West Virginia University Senate, the Tulane University Council on Research, the American Philosophical Society, and a Charles Phelps Taft Fellowship at the University of Cincinnati. Gwynn Lewis and Daniel P. Resnick made helpful comments. Jonathan S. Harbuck embellished the map.

[1] The generalizations which follow are based on several thousand bundles and registers of manuscripts, most of them deposited in the Archives Nationales in Paris

This article originally appeared in the *Journal of Modern History* 48 (June 1976).

dominant position of merchants and their allies was challenged first by the popular following of militant counterrevolutionaries, such as the clan of Pierre Froment, and later by that of such democrats as Joseph-Antoine Courbis and his friends. As later in the West, traditional leaders in the Gard recently displaced from power—priests and urban oligarchs aiming to restore Throne and Altar to their former authority—aroused the peasants who longed to be self-sufficient. After 1791, in cities of the Gard as in Paris and in much of France, popular democrats aroused an urban populace committed to specialization but displaced by the Revolution and consequently demanding limits on the concentration and power of capital. The old anticommercial faction shared with the new a desire for a strong paternalistic state which would subordinate the power of the rich to the needs of the people. The first advocated a strengthened monarchy, the second a democratic republic. Their opposite constitutional conceptions reflected contrasting social backgrounds which prevented them from cooperating against their common commercial foes.[2]

(hereafter cited as A.N.), the Archives Départementales de l'Haute-Garonne in Toulouse, the Archives Départementales de l'Hérault in Montpellier (cited as A.D., Hérault), and the Archives Départementales du Gard in Nîmes (cited as A.D., Gard). Other manuscript collections which have furnished important information are located in the Archives Diplomatiques du Ministère des Affaires Etrangères, in the Bibliothèque Nationale, in the Bibliothèque Municipale de Nîmes, in the Bibliothèque Municipale de Montpellier, in the Bibliothèque de l'Evêché de Nîmes, and in the Bibliothèque du Consistoire de Nîmes. Since it is impossible to append to this brief overview of many topics a list of all relevant bundles and registers, let alone the numerous documents in each, the following notes furnish details only for those documents specifically described in the text. For manuscripts available in one or more printings, only one edition is cited. For additional citations, see James N. Hood, "The Riots in Nîmes in 1790 and the Origins of a Popular Counterrevolutionary Movement" (Ph.D. diss., Princeton University, 1969), "Protestant-Catholic Relations and the Roots of the First Popular Counterrevolutionary Movement in France," *Journal of Modern History* 43 (June 1971): 245–75, and forthcoming works.

[2] See especially Paul Bois, *Les Paysans de l'Ouest: Des Structures économiques aux options politiques depuis l'époque Révolutionnaire dans la Sarthe* (Le Mans, 1960); Richard C. Cobb, *Les Armées Révolutionnaires des départements du Midi (automne et hiver de 1793, printemps de 1794)* (Toulouse, 1955), *Les Armées Révolutionnaires: Instrument de la Terreur dans les départements, avril 1793–floréal an II*, 2 vols. (Paris and The Hague, 1961 and 1963), *Terreur et subsistances, 1793–1795* (Paris, n.d.), *The Police and the People: French Popular Protest, 1789–1820* (Oxford, 1970), *Reactions to the French Revolution* (London, 1972), and *Paris and Its Provinces, 1792–1802* (London, 1975); Marcel Faucheux, *L'Insurrection vendéenne de 1793: Aspects économiques et sociaux* (Paris, 1964); Harvey Mitchell, "The Vendée and Counterrevolution: A Review Essay," *French Historical Studies* 5 (Fall 1968): 405–29, and "Resistance to the Revolution in Western France," *Past and Present*, no. 63 (May 1974), pp. 94–131; George F. E. Rudé, *The Crowd in the French Revolution* (Oxford, 1959), and *The Crowd in History, 1730–1848* (New York, 1964); Albert Soboul, *Les Sans-culottes parisiens en l'an II* (Paris, 1958); and Charles Tilly, *The Vendée* (Cambridge, Mass., 1964).

I

Political antagonisms in the Gard traditionally arose from cultural contrasts in this extremely diverse region. Formerly known as the Sénéchaussée of Beaucaire and Nîmes, a name commonly simplified by omitting Beaucaire, the Gard lay in the southeast corner of Languedoc, just west of the mouth of the Rhône (see fig. 1). The

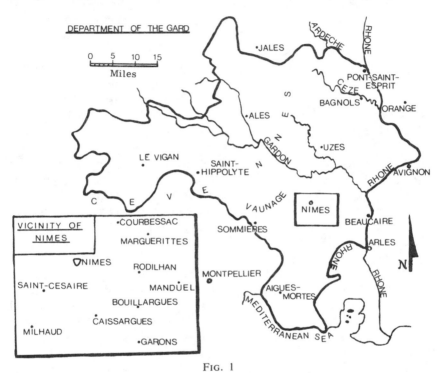

FIG. 1

coastal plain here met the highlands of the Massif Central in a band of barren limestone foothills partly covered by bushy secondary growth called *garrigue*. Transportation on the Rhône and the Mediterranean was easily accessible to inhabitants of the fertile plain south and east of the hills. In addition, the main land route between northern Europe and the Iberian peninsula had always passed through this plain; so had the only one between Italy and Spain. For the people who lived to the northwest, in the foothills and in the mountains called the Cévennes, contact with the outside was more difficult, and even internal communication required extra effort.

Similar terrain encouraged isolation and conservatism, cultural as well as economic, on both sides of the northern border of the Gard, including the Vivarais in the department of the Ardèche. In the Cévennes, to the west, thin soil, summer droughts, and other natural obstacles to general polyculture outweighed the difficulty of transport and made specialization for the market more attractive to the people of the hills than to those of the Mediterranean plain. In the Middle Ages, Cévenols eager to supplement the yield of their cultivation had tanned the hides and processed the wool produced by traditional herding. Later, silk provided them a new raw material to finish for urban merchants. The intractable land of the mountains and foothills encouraged a frugality, reinforced by the network of commercial specialization through which various heresies spread in southern France. This frugality seems to have made the Cévenols exceptionally receptive to doctrines of moral austerity, including those of the Albigenses, the Waldenses, and later the Calvinists. Specialization involved these peasants in the commercial network through which Protestantism first penetrated southern France. Soon Calvinism dominated also farther south, among the peasants of the gently rolling and less specialized Vaunage and of a corridor extending to the sea. During the eighteenth-century spurt in silk production, entrepreneurs in the cities used Protestant towns and villages in the Vaunage and the Cévennes as bases for further colonizing the countryside by extending the textile trades. In this region, Calvinism and commerce clearly reinforced each other.

On the contrary, inhabitants of the Rhône valley and of the eastern Mediterranean plain remained less specialized and overwhelmingly Catholic. Here, despite the proximity of major land and water routes and the occurrence of the internationally famous fair at Beaucaire late each July, many proprietors persisted in a traditional subsistence polyculture relatively isolated from expanding commerce. A great variety of phenomena reflected the contrasts with the west. In 1765, for example, assemblies of the three civil dioceses of the Sénéchaussée showed their different reactions toward commercialization of agriculture: that of Uzès, to the northeast, in contrast with the dioceses of Nîmes and Alès, favored maintenance of communal rights 'of *vaine pâture*. Apart from the extreme north, some proprietors even in the diocese of Uzès made the long-term commitment of land and labor required to specialize in grapes and olives. Particularly after mid–eighteenth century, the exploding industrial population to the west increased local demand for wine and oil from the east. New roads and canals improved access to distant markets, where prices were higher. More proprietors, particularly those nearest markets, risked specialization. Even then, however, entrepreneurs in the east generally supplied not raw materials for industry itself but foodstuffs for the persons engaged in industry.[3] These two contrasting cultural traditions met in a band of territory where the hills tapered off into the plain. In the midst of that zone lay Nîmes, the economic, cultural, and governmental capital of the entire region. By 1789, Nîmes had become the largest city in lower Languedoc and the principal industrial center south of Lyon. Despite the unparalleled industrial boom after 1750, it retained a large population of peasants cultivating land nearby. Consequently, the population as well as the location of Nîmes made it the center of contacts and the focus of misunderstandings between communities extending in opposite directions from the city.

Religious loyalties had provided a traditional focus and added special poignancy to economic and political divisions. In the face of social and economic as well as military persecution, French Calvinists had developed a common identity, which cut across the divisions of occupation and wealth. In areas where Protestants were as numerous and powerful as in the Sénéchaussée of Nîmes, Catholics also developed a special cohesion and sensitivity to reli-

---

[3] In addition to the archival collections cited above, see the following works regarding the economic, cultural, and administrative development of the region: Marc Bloch, "La Lutte pour l'individualisme agraire dans la France du XVIIIe siècle," *Annales d'histoire économique et sociale* 2 (July and October 1930): 329–86, 511–56, and esp. 349; Alexis de Tocqueville, *Oeuvres, papiers, et correspondances d'Alexis de Tocqueville*, ed. J. P. Mayer, 5th ed., vol. 2, *L'Ancien Régime et la Révolution* (Paris, 1952), pp. 253–61; Paul Dognon, *Les Institutions politiques et administratives du pays de Languedoc du XIVe siècle aux guerres de religion* (Paris, 1895); Léon Dutil, *L'Etat économique du Languedoc à la fin de l'ancien régime, 1750–1789* (Paris, 1911), "La Fabrique de bas à Nîmes au XVIIIe siècle," *Annales du Midi* 17 (1905): 218–51, and "L'Industrie de la soie à Nîmes jusqu'en 1789," *Revue d'histoire moderne* 10 (1908): 318–43; Emmanuel Le Roy Ladurie, *Les Paysans de Languedoc*, 2 vols. (Paris, 1966); Tihomir J. Markovitch, "L'Industrie française au XVIIIe siècle: L'Industrie lainière à la fin du règne de Louis XIV et sous la régence," *Economies et sociétés: Cahiers de l'Institut de Science Economique Appliquée* 2 (août 1968): 1620–31, 1690–97; Hector Rivoire, *Statistique du département du Gard*, 2 vols. (Nîmes, 1842), "Notice sur l'industrie de la ville de Nîmes," *Mémoires de l'Académie du Gard*, 1852–53, pp. 268 (misnumbered 291)–97, and "Notice sur Jean Paulet," *Mémoires de l'Académie du Gard*, 1849–50, pp. 65–79; Jean-César Vincens et Baumes, *Topographie de la ville de Nismes et de sa banlieue*, ed. C. Vincens-Saint-Laurent (Nîmes, 1802); Albert Soboul, *Les Campagnes montpelliéraines à la fin de l'ancien régime: Propriété et cultures d'après les compoix* (Paris, 1958); Raymond Dugrand, *Villes et campagnes en Bas-Languedoc: Le Réseau urbain du Bas-Languedoc méditerranéen* (Paris, 1963); Camille-Ernest Labrousse, *La Crise de l'économie française à la fin de l'ancien régime et au début de la Révolution* (Paris, 1944); and the critical comments on Labrousse's interpretation of data by David S. Landes, "The Statistical Study of French Crises," *Journal of Economic History* 10 (November 1950): 195–211, and the subsequent discussion between André Danière and Landes, ibid., 8 (September 1958): 317–44. For further detail and for other secondary sources, see Hood, "The Riots" and "Protestant-Catholic Relations."

gious divisions. Hostility on both sides remained intense throughout the region. It was most bitter in the transitional area which separated the Protestant west from the Catholic east, and it came into clearest focus in Nîmes itself. Generally, Protestants lived apart from Catholics, often in separate villages. Although the sects commingled in the same neighborhoods of cities and market towns, ordinary parlance attached sectarian labels to urban residential areas. Cosmopolitan social mixing without regard for religion rarely went as far as intermarriage, even among the wealthy in Nîmes, for intermarriage, like conversion, still amounted to a rejection of heredity and upbringing.

To be sure, the distinction between Calvinists and Catholics lost most of its theological meaning for those attracted to the rational emphasis on morality which was fashionable among the educated in pre-Revolutionary France. Nîmes had the outward trappings of enlightenment: an academy, a successful comic theater troupe, a weekly newspaper, and several thriving Masonic lodges. Only after 1750, though, had rapid expansion of textile manufacture made the city a major metropolis. Culture and administration had not changed as rapidly. There was no university, no sovereign court, and no seat of an intendancy. The veneer of enlightenment did little to change the attitudes of common people, who persisted in seeing issues of all sorts as aspects of the rivalry between groups which they defined in religious terms. Familiarity with local circumstances rapidly convinced even outsiders that politics around Nîmes was at base a struggle for power between the representatives of two communities with broad popular followings. Social divisions were defined not by voluntary associations with clearly conceived goals but by traditionally hostile religious communities based, even in commercial and industrial circles, upon ancestry and personal contacts.

Religious allegiances interacted with economic development to produce occasional outbursts of physical violence as well as a constant undertone of political friction. Nîmes, with almost one-sixth of the Sénéchaussée's population, was the natural point of convergence for all hostilities. It reflected in microcosm the diversity of the region, religious as well as economic. About one-third of its population was Calvinist—the same proportion as that in the entire Sénéchaussée. Consequently, Nîmes was the most Calvinist among large cities in France and symbolized the exceptional strength of Protestantism in the region. Although thousands of Calvinist merchants, craftsmen, and professionals were scattered in other cities, Nîmes was the only metropolis in France with practicing adherents at all economic levels in every occupation. Here, as in the rest of

France, limits on Calvinists' sale of real estate did encourage Protestants to concentrate their enterprise in commerce, but in Nîmes and most of the Sénéchaussée enforcement of that and other disabilities was sporadic. The crown never was able to apply consistently in this region its legal prohibitions on public worship and holding of office by Protestants.

By the early sixties, the unofficial establishment of de facto toleration as royal policy brought a reduction of violence. Royal administrators restrained the ambitions of both local parties. In the seventies, the crown allowed the legal restrictions on Protestant sale of real estate to lapse. Educated leaders of both religions urged their communities to abandon traditional intolerance and denied the importance of confessional distinctions. During the two decades before the Revolution, Nîmes and its environs witnessed no destructive religious outbursts such as those which royal intervention had frequently catalyzed in the past. However, the reforms of 1787, which enabled Protestants to regularize their civil status, irritated Catholics without removing the disabilities which most annoyed many Protestants. Furthermore, local rivalries maintained tension between the two sects.

The overwhelming influence of Calvinists in commerce made the popular resentment of capitalists, common in much of eighteenth-century western Europe, a basis for the extension of religious hostilities in the Sénéchaussée of Nîmes. The peculiar characteristics of rapid industrial expansion set the context, timing, and tone for many expressions of those traditional hatreds. Entrepreneurs in Nîmes had a particular reason for favoring free trade: the franchises for production and marketing of silk by merchants of Lyon and Tours restricted enterprise in Nîmes and other cities. Since the crown had never strictly enforced the Colbertian quality regulations on silk production anywhere, entrepreneurs in Nîmes had long produced light silk cloth and stockings at a lower price in order to capture the markets which their counterparts in Lyon and Tours had neglected by confining their production to the heavy weaving and fine knitting required by the rules. Further slackening of enforcement after mid–eighteenth century promoted dramatic expansion in the silk trades, especially in centers like Nîmes where most manufacturers produced in contravention of the rules. Late in the century, changing fashions gave Nîmes a positive advanage over other textile centers: world demand moved away from the expensive regulation textile goods, in which Lyon and Tours continued to specialize; and toward cheaper textiles of the sort for which entrepreneurs in Nîmes were famous. Their custom of using inferior or broken raw silk and of preparing it by simpler methods offered competitive advantages which allowed them to succeed spectacularly in expanding foreign markets. While the absence of technical innovations prevented the establishment of large shops, other circumstances encouraged concentration of control in the hands of a few. Advantages of international contacts, economies of large purchases and sales, and vertical integration of production from raw silk through finished goods were all less available to the independent artisans than to the great merchants who provided materials for the numerous pieceworkers in villages, towns, and cities.

Although preliminary signs of contraction appeared earlier, the most serious blow came in 1778, when the Spanish government prohibited the import of foreign silk goods to its American colonies. Dependence on foreign markets made all segments of the silk industry in Nîmes and its hinterland vulnerable, but stocking manufacture declined most rapidly. Domestic commercial contraction and closure of foreign markets due to the war with Britain soon deepened the region's depression. When commercial confidence collapsed during the Revolution, the overwhelming importance of a single group of luxury textile items spelled disaster.

Shrinking markets ruined many small and some large commercial enterprises during the eighties, but a few great merchants extended their control over those unable to survive alone. These capitalists reduced most of the textile gild masters to the level of pieceworkers. Opposition of interests between journeymen and masters declined to insignificance as masters became dependent upon merchants. Royal officials had encouraged concentration of industry in the hands of a few great merchants, mostly Calvinists, whom they considered more efficient. Already in the 1750s they spurned protests from hard-pressed gild masters against abuses by which Protestant merchants ruined small Catholic manufacturers. Catholics also protested that merchants' employment of rural workers represented religious favoritism since most of the expanding cottage industry was located in the Protestant Vaunage and Cévennes. Royal officials responded with the laisser-faire argument that merchants should be free to employ workers in that hinterland, where lower piece rates prevailed. In fact, workers flocked to the city, attracted not only by higher pay but also by better prospects for unemployment relief, which merchants, religious establishments, and city government combined to provide. Many who came to Nîmes in search of temporary employment stayed permanently, despite the higher cost of living and the lack of that agricultural employment with which they would have been able to supplement their incomes if they had remained in their villages. In the 1780s, unstable markets made urban unemployment chronic. The spiraling cost of relief in the city encouraged merchants to try to stop immigration by paying the villagers a higher wage than they paid to workers in Nîmes. Catholics protested that change as further evidence of merchants' preferential treatment of Protestants. Royal officers rebuffed that new complaint, declaring that any worker in Nîmes could move to the Cévennes.[4]

In fact, the lower orders of commerce and industry possessed neither economic class consciousness nor traditional cohesion. Recently uprooted rurals composed most of the industrial labor force in the city. They occasionally expressed their disorientation in unruly conduct but were too closely tied to their employers to develop economic and social solidarity based on common occupation and interests. Dependence on the merchants for relief as well as for wages prevented the workers from conceiving an alternative to the established social order. For many, loyalty to entrepreneurs acquired a personal dimension. Furthermore, Calvinism, by associating a majority of textile workers with the faith of their employers, provided the basis for a commercial solidarity which confirmed the quiescence of the industrial labor force. At the same time, sectarian distinctions intensified, in the minds of formerly independent Catholic gild masters, both a resentment of their employers and a loathing for immigrant workers, mostly Calvinists, who earned the same wage without paying the fees required for entry into the gilds. Regardless of religion or membership in gilds, however, textile workers rarely complained in public. Even when they did denounce Protestant merchants, the workers blamed their misery not upon their employers but upon municipal officers, whom they held responsible for the inadequacy of relief. Equally divided by religious loyalties, many nontextile craftsmen and shopkeepers had also fallen under the tutelage of great merchants. Thus dependence, as well as diversity of religious and geographic backgrounds, prevented workers, artisans, and shopkeepers alike from uniting against their commercial overlords.[5]

---

[4] Phéline, "Observations et avis sur les mémoirs des fesant fabriquer, marchants fabricants, et maîtres ouvriers en bas de la ville de Nîmes," 25 juillet 1782, A.D., Hérault, C.2799, chemise 2.

[5] Note, for example, that in 1779 masons helped extinguish a fire in the house of a textile merchant at the price of fighting off a crowd of *travailleurs de terre* (peasants who owned their own equipment but little or no land) who wanted to see the fire consume the house (undated, untitled petition of Louis Pau and Conilière, received by the Keeper of the Seals, 20 novembre 1790, A.N., D.iv. 29, fol. 704, pièce 4). In 1787 an unemployed silk worker vehemently denounced the municipal officers as less

Throughout their controversies, most inhabitants of the Sénéchaussée in the eighteenth century conceived public affairs in terms of individual personalities, not formal or abstract policies. Sensitive matters, public as well as private, proceeded by oral interchange, of which only spotty hearsay reports remain. But the Revolutionary upheaval provoked a new flood of pamphlets as well as a vastly expanded administrative correspondence. In these, the issues dividing local society appear with unprecedented clarity. In both oral and written statements, leaders expressed their attitudes and policies in traditional categories. Their formalized terminology glossed over the complexity of social divisions, customarily reducing them to a rivalry between Calvinist merchants and Catholic landed interests, each with a popular following. However, almost from the outset of the Revolution, politicians of both contending factions argued that the issues separating them coincided with those under discussion in the capital. They thereby transformed local affairs by placing them in a new and enduring national perspective.

Before 1792, general criticisms of Calvinist merchants emanated not from workers, craftsmen, shopkeepers, or their leaders but from the landed interests associated with the municipal oligarchies. Jacques-Marie Boyer (or Boyer-Brun), who published the weekly *Journal de Nismes* from its beginning in 1786, reflected their views in his infrequent comments on controversial subjects. In August 1787, when that year's bad harvest of raw silk drastically reduced textile manufacture, he advocated freeing municipal and religious charities from the burden of assisting unemployed workers. He invited readers' comments on his proposal for a *caisse de prévoyance* funded by withholding 5 percent of workers' wages—a scheme as unattractive to workers as to employers. Then Boyer devoted the bulk of his next issue to a letter from "a subscriber who is not a manufacturer and who pays 100 livres in capitation." The letter, dated only one day after Boyer's invitation to comment and printed just a week later in the space where he customarily printed his own observations, was probably the work of a friend if not of the editor himself.[6]

This letter presented "an extremely widespread opinion" expressed by "persons infinitely respectable by their birth, by their understanding [*lumières*], and by their zeal for the administration of our city." While the writer claimed to disagree, he explained their

---

responsive than blocks of wood. The original appears in A.D., Gard, C.178; a transposition into standard French appears in A.N., H.1023, pièce 33.

[6] *Journal de Nismes* (9 et 16 août 1787).

argument sympathetically: "Manufactures give the city only a fleeting lustre, at the price of periodic misery terribly burdensome for the citizens. . . . We could live much better without commerce and manufacture. Our produce . . . would still sell at the same price; our rents [*loyers*] would remain as high; our artisans would find the same resources in their industry; and the competition of workers would bring the price of a day's labor back to 12 or 15 sous, as it was formerly, to the great advantage of owners of land."

The anonymous author declared that accepting "this system of political economy" would make unnecessary any discussion of relief for indigent workers. The city should issue passports to all and send them to Spain, where they would be welcomed by the owners of those looms already exported from France. Thereby the city could free itself of "that miserable populace which, after *buying* wheat and wine for 15 or 20 years, now induces us . . . to *give* them bread for six months." Although he rejected that view, the author asserted that more than two-thirds of the five thousand workers in the city were transient journeymen traveling from Nîmes to Lyon, to Tours, or to Avignon in pursuit of work and cheap wine. Those, he argued, had no claim on public assistance, which should be limited to masters of the gilds. Since these true citizens needed relief more promptly than a levy on wages could provide, the anonymous author advocated a surcharge of 40 percent on the capitation for those who, regardless of their occupation, paid more than three livres.

Boyer himself castigated the Calvinist merchants still more explicitly in his propaganda against patriots in 1789 and 1790; however, the most vehement rebukes were written by or for oligarchs of the traditionally dominant faction of the legal profession—the faction which supported the interests of landowners and which had long controlled the administration of Nîmes. Protestants' disabilities in owning real estate and in holding offices had reinforced the association of Calvinism with commerce and of Catholicism with landed property and public functions. The rivalry between wealthy merchants and landowners focused on a prolonged contest for control of the municipal government. That entire controversy revolved around the Froments, the most visibly aggressive family of the entrenched legal oligarchy and the most vocal defenders of landed interests, clerical and secular. For many years its patriarch, Pierre, and one son, François, had held several responsible positions. The father had been municipal registrar (*secrétaire-greffier de la ville*), the son collector of revenues for the canons of the cathedral (*receveur du chapitre*). After more than a decade of contention, lawyers representing commercial interests obtained the conviction of Pierre for juggling the *compoix cabaliste* to the disadvantage of merchants.[7] Then Froment's defenders, who hated merchants for their political aggression, formulated arguments blaming them also for the crowding and misery of the urban populace.

Those merchants send outside the realm to be worked most of the silk which enters the city, with the consequence that, of 30,000 persons who depend on commerce and industry for their subsistence, at least 10,000 have to beg for bread. . . . Their aim has been and still is to place people of their religion at the head of the city. . . . Everyone knows the steps they have taken in neighboring villages to have selected as aldermen [*consuls*] persons sharing their religion. They have just built a hospital and a cemetery without royal permission for that contravention of the laws.[8]

Sieur Perrin sought to allow into the administration only those whom the laws excluded. . . . He allowed only six Catholics in a council of 24.[9]

However, in violation of these customary stereotypes, some Catholic merchants, such as Castor Chas, and lawyers, such as Jean Perrin, played leading roles in the merchants' extension of their political power in the Sénéchaussée of Nîmes after 1770. By 1785, for the first time in a century Protestants and their allies among Catholics were the dominant force in public as well as private affairs. The Protestant merchants' success in politics united against them Catholic clergy, landed proprietors, and the defenders and dependents of both, including inarticulate peasants as well as vocal lawyers. Educated members of both parties in local politics absorbed into their old rivalry the rising national discussion of royal policies. The urgent question of the legal status of Protestants and their church had obvious meaning in the Sénéchaussée of Nîmes. Some conceived it as part of general legal reform. Royal policies in the eighteenth century made the generosity of *philosophes*, even those with explicitly anti-Christian sentiments, seem outstanding to a persecuted minority. Therefore French Calvinists embraced rationalizing and even secularizing reforms which would integrate them into the state as full citizens. Abstract considerations led a few educated Catholics to share Calvinists' enthusiasm at the prospect of reform, but most of the devout awaited an opportunity for a purified Catholic church to reassert its authority over society, especially over Calvinist heretics. Of course, the overwhelming majority of partici-

---

[7] The *compoix cabaliste* was the assessment for the *taille* on personal property.

[8] Unsigned letter to ?, Nîmes, 29 mai 1785, A.N., H.801, pièce 223 or, by another numbering, 145.

[9] *Mémoire pour le sieur Froment* (no publication information), pp. 13–16 (the second 16, pp. 15 and 16 being repeated) and 37.

pants in both religious communities exhibited no interest in national policies unless they anticipated a direct impact upon their own lives.[10]

II

Nevertheless, the vacuum of authority at the center in 1788 and 1789 brought a lull in public manifestations of rivalries between traditional leaders. Alert segments of both factions of the local elite hoped to increase their power through national reforms. Calvinists took the lead in welcoming the convocation of the Estates General, but Catholics were not far behind. Merchants hoped to extend their recent gains; landowners hoped that national reforms would allow them to reverse the expansion of commerce, the extension of merchants' political power, and the hated legalization of Protestant civil status. Most Catholics were not seriously disconcerted even by the selection of the pastor Rabaut de Saint-Etienne and of several other Protestants as deputies for the third estate of the Sénéchaussée of Nîmes, for they felt confident of support from the rest of overwhelmingly Catholic France. During the summer, unanimous calls for reform therefore distracted attention from the contradictory aspirations of Calvinist merchants and Catholic landed proprietors.

Furthermore, the Sénéchaussée escaped the bitterness which issues of noble status aroused elsewhere by 1789. Most noble families surviving the wars of religion, which continued into the early eighteenth century in lower Languedoc, were neither rich nor powerful. Under Languedoc's partially independent administration, fiscal privilege had depended upon the status of the land rather than that of its owner. In some localities, such as Aiguesmortes, most real estate was "noble," but all such land was taxed in a special assessment. Nearly everywhere nobles and other proprietors had allowed the peasants to convert personal dues to contractual money payments. "Feudalism" was therefore not a serious economic issue, and nobles generally behaved like commoners with similar interests. There is no evidence of controversy in the Sénéchaussée of Nîmes over the right to sit in the assembly of the nobility in March 1789. Royal officials reported struggles for control in the general assemblies of the second and third estates. However, the *cahiers* of those two estates reflected the considerable agreement on basic

[10] The entrenched municipal oligarchy resisted the rising political demands of the commercial community by arguing that merchants were ineligible for municipal offices: they were tainted by their commercial activities, most of them were Calvinists, and the remainder were corrupted by social as well as commercial contacts with Calvinists.

principles of national and provincial reform achieved by discussions among the leaders who finally dominated in those two assemblies.[11]

The clergy, on the other hand, acted largely alone. Deep rivalries had long pitted bishops against canons of cathedral chapters, and curés against both. Nevertheless, traditional suspicion made all clerics sensitive to Calvinists' unprecedented influence in the primary and general assemblies of the third estate. Hence, the assembly of the clergy was able to submerge its internal differences and to rally behind a *cahier* which insisted on separation of the three orders. In March, articulate and influential clergymen united against reform because they were the first to see how it benefited the Protestants. Even the curé of Courbessac, who at the beginning of 1789 had agitated against episcopal authority, engaged before the end of the year in anti-Calvinist propaganda. Evidently he assumed that Catholics would reunite against the intensified Calvinist threat. This sort of clerical agitation accelerated the disillusionment of lay Catholics with the Revolution.[12]

Already by fall, national and local developments began to resolve uncertainties of authority in favor of Calvinists and merchants in the Gard. Those changes disillusioned the Catholic landowners' hope that the new order would afford them an opportunity to reassert their power. Many followed the lead of the prominent clerics into active opposition to the Revolution. Merchants extended their authority by gaining control of the new militias from the time of their formation in July. In the city of Nîmes, Castor Chas was able to facilitate that process because he was acting mayor in the absence of Jean Antoine Teissier, baron de Marguerittes, who was in Paris as a deputy to the Constituent Assembly. Furthermore, that Assembly reduced the independence of the church. It placed cities and districts under departmental administrations, subordinating local to regional government, which men with commercial contacts could more easily dominate. It granted full citizenship to religious dissenters, who could henceforth legally hold any public office without feigning Catholicism. Soon Protestants could vote in the elections of state-

[11] E. Bligny-Bondurand, *Cahiers de doléances de la sénéchaussée de Nîmes pour les Etats Généraux de 1789* (Nîmes, 1909), 2:579–606; Roussel to ? (probably Ballainvilliers), Nîmes, 21 mars 1789, A. D., Hérault, C.877; H. Chobaut, "Documents sur les élections aux Etats-Généraux à Nîmes (mars 1789)," unidentified offprint, pp. 363–69, A. D., Gard, Fonds Légal, no. 11.

[12] Bligny-Bondurand, 2:573–79; Joannis, curé de Marguerittes, to Necker, Marguerittes, 8 avril 1789, A.N., BA.57, liasse 141, dossier 6; *Mémoire de la Garde Nationale de Nismes en réponse à l'adresse presentée à l'Assemblée Nationale par les officiers municipaux de laditte ville et signée Boyer, substitut de la commune, chargé par eux de leur défense* (Nismes, 1790), p. 27. Series G of A.D., Gard, abounds with examples of divisions among secular clerics.

employed Catholic priests. The position of Catholicism became the predominant issue, since the Great Fear bypassed most of lower Languedoc and since the decisions of the Constituent early in August 1789 scarcely infringed on the status of nobles in the region. To fervently sectarian Catholics, the reduction of the church's power and independence suggested the Assembly's complicity in the anti-Catholic and antiroyal *ligue* for the establishment of federative republics, which they had equated with anarchy and Calvinism ever since the sixteenth century. A pseudonymous brochure asserted, "To grant Protestants freedom of worship and admission to civil and military offices and honors is an evil which brings no real advantage to you or to the nation but rather exposes both to the greatest disasters."[13]

Popular resentment against the impact of the Revolution provided the Froment clan in Nîmes and persons with similar interests in other cities a long-awaited opportunity to challenge the merchants' control over the new militias, which were now the decisive force in the department. First, François Froment discussed his plans with Louis XVI's brother, the Comte d'Artois, with that prince's court in exile at Turin, and with nobles in upper (western) Languedoc. Then he took the lead in arousing against Protestants the Catholic peasants in the eastern part of Nîmes and in adjacent villages. Here the collapse of wine and oil prices in the eighties had intensified resentment against merchants. Several hundred of these peasants joined the new Catholic companies of the militia. In this locale, Catholic agricultural day laborers (*journaliers*), small independent proprietors (*ménagers*), and numerous peasants on the margin of independence between the two (*travailleurs de terre*) were predisposed to believe the spokesmen for large proprietors who blamed heretics for low prices and agricultural underemployment. All associated unprofitable specialization with Calvinists even where the connection was not direct. A few of the lesser but independent merchants backed Froment, notably several members of the Penitens Blancs, a lay order which maintained close ties with the upper clergy. But most

---

[13] *Pierre Romain aux Catholiques de Nîmes* (n.p., 1790), p. 4. On the parallel to the sixteenth-century *ligue*, see *Nouvelle déclaration et pétition des Catholiques de Nismes* (n.p., 1790), p. 11. That *déclaration* rejected (p. 12) the label "counter-revolutionary" by which patriots designated the Catholic party, but soon after his defeat Froment began to vaunt the plans he claimed to have formulated to overturn the Revolution. He also elaborated the implication of earlier pamphlets that the National Assembly was an agent of Protestants seeking to establish federative republics and urging Protestants to massacre Catholics (*Mémoire historique et politique contenant la relation du massacre des Catholiques de Nîmes les 13, 14, 15, et 16 juin et les réflexions sur les causes qui l'ont amené* [n.p., 1790], p. 55).

Catholic shopkeepers, artisans, and workers dared not antagonize the great merchants by expressing any sympathy they may have felt for Froment's direct appeals to their special grievances against commerce. Several affluent Catholics were among those active against him. Undated pseudonymous pamphlets, such as *Charles Sincère à Pierre Romain*,[14] aimed to pry workers away from their employers by arguing that Protestants showed less consideration for their workers than the American planters for their slaves. Those heretics, the author proclaimed, must be deported from France. François Froment confessed that he had failed to recruit textile workers to serve in Catholic companies of the legion when their employers objected.[15] Yet he succeeded in organizing enough Catholics to threaten Reformed merchants and their allies, who claimed to be patriots because they backed the Revolution. Froment at Nîmes and his imitators at Montauban thereby focused the attention of much of France on those southern cities and their environs.[16]

The Constituent Assembly intended to eliminate the confusion of authority by substituting nationally standardized institutions of local administration for the patchwork of rival agencies which was the legacy of the ad hoc arrangements made in each locality in the summer of 1789. But in areas with factions as clearly defined as those in the Gard, the contest in 1790 for control of the new

[14] No publication information.

[15] *Aux Citoyens de Nismes* (no publication information).

[16] The degree to which their ideology alienated most French Catholics is illustrated by the avalanche of hostile pamphlets, such as the *Adresse des administrateurs du département de Seine et Marne aux citoyens de la ville de Nismes* (Melun, 1790). In May the municipality of Châlon-sur-Saône denounced to the ecclesiastical committee of the Constituent Assembly the propaganda from Nîmes which depicted that Assembly as aiming to destroy the Catholic faith (*Archives parlementaires de 1787 à 1860: Recueil complet des débats législatifs et politiques des chambres françaises*, première série, 82 vols. [Paris, 1867–1913], 15:487). Counterrevolutionaries at Montauban, fifty kilometers north of Toulouse, succeeded in seizing control of their city in May 1790. Testimony later during the Revolution indicates that they were purposely imitating the plan which Froment applied in Nîmes. They, like Froment, hoped to lay the foundation for national counterrevolution ("Projet d'une seconde adresse à l'Assemblée Nationale," certified [8 messidor an 2] by d'Haupilla as having been dictated to him in spring 1790 by the Comte de Sainte Foy at Montauban; also several other documents so certified, A.N., F⁷.3692). In fact, volunteers from Bordeaux as well as the area around Montauban soon arrived to demonstrate that the authorities in control of their communities unanimously opposed the counterrevolution at Montauban. The presence of these militiamen liquidated the municipal administration's ability to act, forced it to release from prison its patriot enemies, and, before the end of May, purged the militia on which counterrevolutionaries' power had depended. In July, the Constituent formally removed from office the administrators of Montauban (Daniel Ligou, *Montauban à la fin de l'ancien régime et aux débuts de la Révolution, 1787–1794* [Paris, 1958], pp. 207–44).

institutions raised traditional rivalries to an unprecedented pitch. The Froment faction and the clergy campaigned by printed pamphlets, as well as by personal contacts, to elect municipal and departmental administrators who would counteract patriot domination of the urban militias. The installation in Nîmes of a new municipal administration, again headed by Teissier, baron de Marguerittes, but now dominated in the lower ranks as well by persons sympathetic to Catholic landed interests, seemed to Froment and his Catholic counterrevolutionaries the first step toward overturning the local impact of the Revolution. As their confidence mounted early in the spring, they dreamed that a victory at Nîmes would awaken the rest of France to the urgent necessity of restoring the old regime. However, the governing council of the militia refused to surrender its authority to the hostile administrators of the city. Merchants, led by Chas, discredited the city council by cutting off the funds for municipal relief. Entrepreneurs assisted the unemployed directly through the new militia, which they themselves continued to control. The absence in 1790 of even the rare complaints which workers had directed against their employers during earlier industrial crises reflects the merchants' success in obtaining public recognition for every sou they contributed.

Finally, the losses which counterrevolutionaries were suffering in the elections of the departmental administration provided the shock which shattered their confidence. The vehemence and bitterness of sentiments on all sides made François Froment certain that the self-styled patriots who were gaining power would repress his movement for restoration of Throne and Altar. Feeling more vulnerable with each passing day, he and about 200 of his most loyal followers responded with force on June 13 to the threats and provocation in which their enemies persisted. In the ensuing battle, they were hopelessly outnumbered. The few who survived depicted their party's action as innocent and unprepared self-defense against an unprovoked and premeditated attack. Patriots justified their own violence by accusing their foes of undertaking a counterrevolutionary coup. Although he later denied it, Froment may well have seen this show of force as a desperate step to revive flagging popular support, hoping that the sudden exhilaration of violent action would ensure the success of a preemptive strike. In the event, patriots exploited the opportunity to butcher not merely every one of Froment's armed men whom they could capture but also many whom they suspected of sympathizing with him and still others against whom they held purely personal grudges.

Patriots devastated their foes so easily and decisively because the

Catholic oligarchs' anticommercial appeal had a narrow popular base. Alongside abjectly dependent textile workers, other artisans and retail merchants, most of them members of trade gilds, customarily defended commercial interests. Even in periods of declining business, the accumulated benefits of decades of commercial expansion tempered the shopkeepers' and artisans' resentment of the wealthy merchants' arrogant control of the city and its environs. The Catholic oligarchs' policy of reducing taxation on real estate by increasing that on other investments drove small entrepreneurs to support the great Calvinist capitalists. Not interested in restoration of a purified Catholic monarchy at Versailles, few tradesmen and retail merchants were tempted to join the attack on the political power of great merchants and their allies in 1790.

The priests and lay oligarchs, knowing that the Calvinist supremacy west of Nîmes would remain impregnable unless counterrevolutionaries obtained help from the east, erred in trusting that the peasants and townspeople in the solidly Catholic Rhône valley would hasten to the aid of beleaguered coreligionists in Nîmes. In fact their anti-Calvinist propaganda seems to have appealed to Catholics only where the two sectarian communities lived and worked side by side. Here competition had kept religious hatred smoldering, but denunciations of merchants attracted only those few who were eager to escape from the commercial nexus. The sectarian split had tended to dichotomize the whole complex of economic, social, and political distinctions. Loyalties based on personal contacts were more decisive than rational interests and convictions in determining who would back counterrevolution.

Struggling to establish a following among those few who were sensitive to their appeals or to their influence, oligarchs displaced from political power in Nîmes flew in the face of national political trends and established a popular movement which became the model for their counterparts throughout the Gard and in the region of Montauban, north of Toulouse. Until the West rose up more than two years later, there was no comparable popular support for counterrevolution. But the limitations on the Catholic counterrevolutionaries' popular support prevented them from gaining control of the Gard. The counterrevolution in western France, based on a parallel resentment of commerce among zealous Catholics who felt that their faith was in danger, diverted national troops from the foreign front for years. In the Gard, the narrow base of the first popular counterrevolutionary movement assured that patriots could repress it promptly and without help from outside.

In sharp contrast, patriots effectively mobilized, except in the extreme north of the department, a broadly based support for the Revolution. As Calvinist leaders had done for a century, patriots insisted that religion was irrelevant to politics. Nevertheless they organized their backers by exploiting personal and commercial ties which, in many cases, paralleled sectarian allegiances. These ties facilitated patriots' efforts to make active allies of the soldiers in the royal Guyenne regiment stationed at Nîmes. The soldiers' egalitarian grievances against the oligarchy of military officers seemed to civilian patriots parallel to their own resentment against defenders of the old regime. Patriots exploited their control of communications to spread reports of events in Nîmes which diverted the few volunteers who were coming from the Rhône valley. At the same time they welcomed to the city volunteers from the Vaunage and the Cévennes who flocked to Nîmes to stamp out the Catholic insurrection. That unruly crowd of armed patriots massacred about 300 persons and pillaged the houses of religious orders and those of many Catholic laymen suspected of complicity in counterrevolution. These excesses embarrassed respectable patriots, who, nevertheless, skillfully managed news of the disorders to discredit their rivals. The landed families which had dominated local politics before 1770, as well as the peasants and priests who had supported them, ceased to be a significant political force around Nîmes. The survivors emigrated, went into hiding, or eschewed public affairs.

In February 1791, public protest recurred at Uzès, the only city in the Gard to experience a disturbance based upon confessional divisions similar to those in Nîmes. By 1791, patriot victories liquidated Catholic political cohesion except in the northernmost reaches of the department. Elsewhere, for several years, any suggestion that religion had political implications associated its author with outlawed counterrevolutionaries, who had to act mainly in secret until 1795. Their most persistent activity was the series of camps held during the next four years at the château of Jalès, located within the limits of the former Sénéchaussée but north of the new departmental boundary. After the clashes at Nîmes and Uzès, Catholics in the extreme north of the department responded to the defeat of their confederates by meeting at Jalès and issuing sympathetic manifestos offering aid to Catholics against their Protestant oppressors. Consequently the insurrection at Nîmes and the echo at Uzès continued to weigh heavily on nervous authorities as they evaluated the reports of subsequent conspiracies in the northern villages which had supported the camps of Jalès since 1790. In June and July 1792 and in September 1794, nonjuring priests such as Claude and Dominique Allier and their lay backers—such as the Comte François-Louis de

Saillant, until a crowd butchered him after his 1792 insurrection—organized Catholics from these villages to attack Protestants, constitutional clergy, military detachments, and civil functionaries. The northeastern extremity of the Gard, as far south as Bagnols, acted politically like the Vivarais, where a conservative Catholic elite retained control throughout the Revolution and Napoleon's Empire. From there and from Avignon, Arles, and western Provence, a network of Catholic agitators continually sent bands of assassins to wreak political vengeance inside the area solidly committed to the Revolution. Repeatedly the local authorities feared a resumption of civil strife like that which had ravaged Nîmes in 1790. But there were no serious consequences for most of the department in 1792, 1793, or 1794.[17]

III

During the early Revolution, the Gard, fractured by competing sects, cultures, and economic communities, had maintained its traditional political division. In 1790 and early 1791, the department's populace had backed two rival elites composed of persons of means. It had excelled in brutal civil strife expressing old hatreds exacerbated by the Revolution. Through the end of 1791 and into early 1792, the Gard remained exceptionally calm, just as it had been in 1789, in contrast with areas where disorders followed the Parisian lead.

The patriots had killed some of the most committed leaders of counterrevolution and had driven the rest into hiding. The survivors who chose to stay in populated areas of the Gard outside the extreme north had to appear to collaborate with the patriot authorities, even if they engaged in clandestine resistance. This remnant of the Catholic elite therefore could not maintain any independent prestige or leadership. On the other side, patriots' cohesion gradually disintegrated in the absence of any credible threat to their control over most of the department. The commercial faction had

[17] In addition to numerous pamphlets in several libraries and the voluminous administrative correspondence scattered through several series in A.N. and concentrated in the immense Series L in the A.D., Gard, see the accounts of these events in the following: Simon Brugal, *Les Camps de Jalès* (Nantes, 1885), reprinted from *Revue de la Révolution* (1884–86), 4:341–62, 424–39; 5:107–21, 405–23; 6:22–37; Marius Tallon, *Le Camp de Jalès: Episode de la Révolution française* (Vienne, 1879); François Rouvière, *Histoire de la Révolution française dans le département du Gard* (Nîmes, 1888–89), vol. 2, *La Législative, 1791–1792*, vol. 3, *La Convention nationale (Le Fédéralisme) 1792–1793*, and vol. 4, *La Convention nationale (La Terreur) 1793–1794*; Charles-H. Pouthas, *Une Famille de bourgeoisie française de Louis XIV à Napoléon* (Paris, 1934).

free rein in Nîmes for almost eighteen months after the victory of June 1790. Headed by Jean-Antoine Griolet, a Calvinist lawyer from Nîmes allied with the merchants, the departmental administration at first kept patriots united by invoking the fear of renewed counter-revolutionary movements. Events such as those at Uzès and Jalès intensified this fear. At the same time, Griolet and his associates continued to work systematically to discredit the religious loyalties which defeated counterrevolutionaries had used. This policy undermined the ideology of Protestant cohesion as well. In those parts of the Gard where Protestants lived, the evaporation during 1791 of all serious Catholic threats removed the challenge which had always tended to hold Calvinists together and had prompted them to rally behind merchants who posed as spokesmen for that menaced religious minority.

Deepening crisis accelerated the movement away from the old doctrinal split and temporarily allowed the more complex issues common to much of France to predominate. Revolutionary politics in the Gard finally entered into phase with those of the capital and most of the nation. The continuing national political crisis, local population movements, and the general economic crisis further undermined traditional popular loyalties to persons of substance or status, including the leaders of both old factions. Throughout a nation threatened by a disloyal chief executive and by his foreign backers, a growing segment of the poor took a political stance expressing their patriotism and their own aspirations. In the Gard, the extreme urban violence of 1790 and early 1791 had led many affluent persons to seek security in the countryside, even if their sympathies lay with the victorious party. In addition, many unemployed textile workers, faced with an abrupt contraction of relief funds, left the cities for their native villages. Nevertheless, the remaining population strained the resources of the cities. Utter dependence on money and trade made the people who lived there especially vulnerable to inflation and to the interruption of commerce. The Constituent Assembly had dissolved the gilds, through which the commercial elite formerly directed artisans' and shopkeepers' self-expression. Even in the countryside, these multiple dislocations threatened the economic security of all but the few who were self-sufficient or wealthy. All these changes make it intelligible that, through 1792, 1793, and 1794, popular anticommercial sentiments ceased to serve counterrevolutionaries and became the principal source of support for radical democrats, who demanded alleviation of the plight of the masses.

In April 1792, a widely circulated rumor convinced peasants, artisans, and shopkeepers alike that a conspiracy was responsible for the shipwreck of national guardsmen on the Rhône, in which many of their neighbors and relatives had drowned. The panic-stricken populace was conditioned by reports of the European powers' preparations to attack France. Apparently these people considered the local disaster a confirmation of subversive plotting, which popular democratic propaganda from Paris imputed to all the rich who did not employ their resources singlemindedly in the nation's service. Many of the disinherited came to agree that all of the well-to-do, including those ostensibly passive, demonstrated counterrevolutionary principles as clearly by their selfish greed as did organizers of counterrevolutionary armed forces by their positive actions.

In this state of excitement, insecure peasants acted decisively, attacking wealthy landlords, most of whom had only remote contact with the great urban merchants. The volunteers who still maintained order for the urban elite could not reach these rural estates promptly enough to restrain the peasants. As if to compensate for their quiescence during the Great Fear of 1789, the rural populace now pillaged or burned about 120 châteaux and country houses. They destroyed coats of arms and other reminders of the old regime, along with the contracts which fixed their money dues to wealthy proprietors, many of whom had not been nobles. Scarcely articulating their ideology except in violence, these peasants apparently blamed their insecurity and distress on those who had prospered, regardless of hereditary title. Throughout the department, the insurgents displayed a remarkably uniform response to signs of wealth, disregarding the religious and economic patterns which divided the department into politically antagonistic zones before 1792 and again after 1794.[18] Peasants soon withdrew from political initiative in the Gard, as those in most of France had done earlier. But, by attacking more successful participants in the market economy, they had set the new pattern of the real struggle for control of the department from 1792 through 1794, which again focused in towns and cities.

An urban radical movement appeared half a year before the eruption in the countryside. A few opulent patriots, dissatisfied with the political and social conservatism of the existing Revolutionary clubs, organized discontented shopkeepers and artisans into new popular societies with much lower annual dues. Some members of the old clubs joined the new societies, maintained membership in

[18] This conclusion is based upon a systematic analysis of the events described by Henri Mazel, "La Révolution dans le Midi: L'Incendie des châteaux du Bas-Languedoc," *Revue de la Révolution* 8 (1886): 142–57, 307–19, 380–91, and 456–69, and by Rouvière, *Histoire*, 2:177–284.

both, and gave educated leadership to the popular movement, which crossed both occupational categories and economic levels within them. In the Gard, as in Paris, some men played leading roles in the radical clubs after entering with great wealth. Some of them had accumulated their fortunes while holding important public offices. The leaders of the popular society (Société Populaire) of Nîmes illustrate this diversity.[19]

Barthélemy Estruc was among the thirty peasants, craftsmen, and shopkeepers who founded the society on November 13, 1791. He and his several brothers who later joined it were stocking makers who paid small sums in taxes. Apparently relatives of one patriot by that name whom the counterrevolutionaries had murdered and thrown into an aqueduct in June 1790, the Estrucs in 1792 signed petitions calling on the local administrators to endorse the governmental and social program of the Parisian Jacobin club. Toward the end of the year, however, their names ceased to appear in the registers of the Société Populaire, as leadership in it passed to men like Joseph-Antoine Courbis.

A lawyer admitted to practice before the Parlement of Toulouse, Courbis had, in 1790, assaulted the counterrevolutionaries, who accused him of showing anti-Catholic feelings but did not label him Protestant. His active role in the patriot club led to the post of chief administrator of the district of Nîmes, and he did not join the Société Populaire until October 1792. Soon he became its president and its most passionate radical firebrand. The Federalists removed him from office, painting him as an opportunist without scruples who had exploited his public power to amass a tremendous private fortune. During the height of the Terror, Courbis was mayor of Nîmes. With the backing of the Convention's representative on mission, he acquired a reputation as the Marat of Nîmes. After Thermidor, a crowd lynched him in his prison cell.

At first the popular societies cooperated with the old patriot clubs and with the administrators who supported them. In Nîmes the new society and the old club joined the directory (executive body) of the department in restoring order and providing relief after a crowd of women publicly protested high bread prices in January 1792. Soon ambitious men, frustrated by exclusion from the inner circle of local authority, began to encourage and exploit popular grievances. They denounced the old club at Nîmes for breaking off relations with the

---

[19] "Registre des délibérations de la Société Populaire de Nismes, du 9 germinal an 2 jusqu'au 30 floréal suivant," Bibliothèque Municipale de Nîmes, MS. no. 362, and "Registre des procès verbaux, délibérations, pétitions, et adresses [de la Société Populaire de Nismes]," A.D., Gard, L.2123.

Jacobin club of Paris in July 1791 in order to correspond with the
Feuillants. They held local administrators up to obloquy as lackeys
of the new "aristocracy," composed of great merchants. In the
spring of 1792 the popular society expressed its alienation from local
authority by entering into regular correspondence with the Jacobin
club. The departmental administration reproached disorderly national guards for failing to stop the pillage and burning of châteaux
near Nîmes in April 1792. The Société Populaire protested indig-
nantly, blaming the excesses, which it admitted, upon the directory's
own failure to order the national guard into action. The popular
society declared that it was understandable to any patriot why the
populace had acted against the estates of such well-known perpetrators of the counterrevolutionary disasters of 1790 as Teissier, the
former mayor, and François Descombiès, Froment's friend and ally
in insurrection. While criticizing the directory's actions, the popular
society took pains to minimize the differences of principle, economic
and political, which separated them from the dominant commercial
party. They rejected as pure slander the directory's charge that the
crowds sought to fix prices.[20]

Faithful to the tradition established by 1789 in the Gard, the two
factions made national politics the first object of public debate. The
directory, along with those of many other departments, deplored the
demonstration on June 20, 1792, by Parisian republicans against "the
hereditary representative of the French people." It demanded
punishment of "crimes against the Constitution."[21] In July, the
Société Populaire of Nîmes sent a detachment to the national federation in Paris in defiance of the local administrators' failure to
cooperate. The popular societies rebuked those officials for demur-
ring and successfully depicted themselves as the only true friends of
Parisian republicans. Nevertheless, the directory proceeded to isolate itself still further by declaring to the Minister of the Interior that
changing the Constitution would be as bad as counterrevolution:
"Two opposed factions exist in the Gard; with different ends and
different means both factions attack the Constitution and spread
disorders. One, aroused by priests and fanatics, sees in the new laws
the destruction of religion; the other, excited by anarchist agitators,
would like to prolong the revolution and change or destroy the new
Constitution."[22]

[20] See the summary of administrative correspondence contained in Rouvière, *His-toire*, vol. 2.
[21] The directories of districts and the municipal administrations seconded these
protests. See, for example, the adherence of the municipality of Nîmes, July 3, 1792,
A.N., DXL.9, pièce 55.
[22] Quoted in Rouvière, *Histoire*, 2:348–52.

Thus moderates and radicals alike in 1792 defined their positions more by innuendo and accusation than by their own positive, coherent programs. They imitated the rhetoric current in Paris, developing arguments by adapting discussions in the capital to local circumstances. Suspension of the monarchy in August forced defenders of the Constitution of 1791 into reluctant republicanism, but they still tried to maintain the Constitution's other principles. They restricted activities of popular democrats, justifying restraints by claiming that behind a deceptive facade of political democracy lurked the threat of economic leveling and anarchy, which would discredit the Revolution and make counterrevolution win out. Democrats, on the contrary, tried to shift discussion away from the social realm, where common fear united property owners against them, to political principles, where their own republicanism had become national policy. Radicals, like their conservative patriot rivals, denounced as counterrevolutionary all opposition to themselves. In particular, the popular democrats argued that all defenders of the Constitution of 1791 (*feuillants*) were really "aristocrats" who should be excluded from the electoral assembly which chose the Gard's deputies to the Convention in September.[23]

At first, democrats succeeded in the elections at that assembly. Then news of the September massacres in Paris swayed uncommitted electors into crediting the conservative patriots' claims that popular societies encouraged anarchy. After that, the assembly chose supporters of the departmental administration. The Société Populaire of Nîmes petitioned the electoral assembly for parity of wages with inflated prices.[24] The society thereby emphasized the economic motives of popular political activity, appearing to substantiate conservatives' claims that the popular societies threatened all persons of means. The consequent reaction against popular democrats allowed conservative republicans to use the elections of November 1792 to consolidate their control of local government at all levels. Of the eight districts in the Gard, only that of Nîmes elected an administration sympathetic to the popular societies.

Before the end of 1792, conservative patriots' consistent endorsement of republican principles complicated democrats' efforts to keep the controversy exclusively on a political plane. In January 1793 the Société Populaire of Nîmes again denounced to the Convention slanderous accusations of social revolution leveled against them: "Those modern aristocrats . . . , doubtless agents of foreign powers

---

[23] See François Rouvière, *Le Mouvement électoral dans le Gard en 1792: Recherches pour servir à l'histoire de la Révolution française* (Nîmes, 1884).
[24] The petition is quoted in Rouvière, *Histoire*, 2:449–50.

. . . , accuse us of preaching redistribution of property [*partage des biens*]. . . . [They] seek nothing less than to oppress the respectable sansculottes.''[25] Despite the firm grip of a departmental administration defending the economic principles of the Constitution of 1791, some signs of criticism appeared in the spring of 1793. On May 20, citizens of one section of Nîmes protested to the full departmental administration that the directory had failed to establish a maximum price for grains, as required by the Convention's decree of May 4. They claimed to seek nothing but work and bread, which only people with hearts of stone could refuse. "The party of the poorest populace [*peuple*] awaits that salutary decree with impatience. It will contribute greatly to save the Republic, whatever egoists, hoarders, and the enemies of equality of rights may say; we do not seek equality of wealth, as they continually preach to the ignorant and imbeciles who listen to them; they paint men who seek the public welfare as brigands, anarchists, and monsters who have no desire but to spill the blood of their richest fellow citizens in order to take their property.''[26]

On June 3 the Directory of the Gard issued an order (*arrêté*) forbidding workers (*ouvriers* or *journaliers*) from assembling "for the purpose of limiting free exercise of industry or of labor by fixing the price of a day's work." Six days later, the directory finally published the decree of May 4 and the maximum prices which it required but limited their application to major cities and warned workers that higher wages would merely increase prices.[27]

Almost simultaneously, news reached the Gard of the purge from the Convention of some of the deputies whom the local ruling elite respected most highly but whom the Montagnards condemned as Girondins who would weaken the state to a federation which could not survive. The Directory of the Gard expressed its displeasure by summoning to Nîmes representatives from the sections of cities throughout the department. Before the end of June the assembly of those representatives declared the Gard in open rebellion against the tyranny of the crowds of Paris. The Montagnards called that assembly's policy federalist, since it undertook to cooperate with other departments, from Bordeaux to Marseille and Lyon, in sending armed forces to restore the liberty of the Convention—just as counterrevolutionaries had dreamed of restoring the king's freedom

---

[25] Quoted in Rouvière, *Histoire*, 3:194–95.
[26] Quoted in Rouvière, *Histoire*, 3:471–73.
[27] The *arrêté* is quoted in Rouvière, *Histoire*, 3:469–70. The limitations on the maximum are noted in Pouthas, *Une Famille*, p. 127, n. 3.

after October 6, 1789. The Gard promised to serve as a strategic link between the Federalists in the east and those in the southwest.[28]

During the Federalist revolt, the social issues separating the two republican parties in the Gard emerged more clearly than ever. A year later, in the interrogation which followed his imprisonment on 19 Thermidor Year II (August 6, 1794), Courbis described Federalists in such a way as to flaunt his own sympathy for sans-culottes. He implied that Federalists had been unscrupulous counterrevolutionary merchants who gained the appearance of a popular following by hiring impoverished thugs to intimidate true republicans. The Federalist authorities of Nîmes detained G. Feydel and Jean Scipion Sabonnadière, who went south on other business for the Convention. These two observers, in reports they wrote during and immediately after the revolt, emphasized that the leaders of the rebellion represented the conservative patriot club. Although commercial interests still dominated that club, Feydel and Sabonnadière claimed that it now united all people of means, including some "fanatics" who had supported counterrevolution in 1790. "The federalists are an aristocracy of merchants [*négociants*] who have accustomed people to consider their wealth the source of the prosperity of the city, while they are really its scourge." Federalists in the Gard based their appeals for support on promises to protect property and order against the threat of the *loi agraire*. They justified suppressing the Société Populaire of the city and the administration of the district of Nîmes, which supported that society, by labeling both "Maratist" and "anarchist."[29]

When the armies loyal to the Convention arrived at Pont-Saint-Esprit and at Orange in mid-July, the Federalist forces of the Gard surrendered without a fight. In the general *sauve qui peut* which followed, the Federalist administrators argued that the entire episode originated in a misunderstanding due to faulty communications. They hastened to support the Convention's representatives on mission, who proceeded to suppress remnants of rebellion in the Midi. Nevertheless, later representatives purged all identifiable Federalists from administrative office. The Revolutionary Tribunal of Nîmes further underlined the social issue which separated Federalists from Terrorists by dispatching to the guillotine persons convicted of hoarding—a crime of which Terrorists could accuse any merchant.

[28] *Procès-verbal de l'assemblée des députés des communes du Gard formée à Nismes, chef lieu du département sur l'invitation des administrateurs* (Nîmes, 1793); *Pièces qui font connaître les Fédéralistes du Gard* (Paris, n.d.).

[29] Courbis's testimony is quoted in Rouvière, *Histoire*, 3:382. Feydel's and Sabonnadière's reports are collected in A.N., F^{1a}.551.

The Terror imposed on the commercial elite and on the remaining landed elite an unprecedented unity which was to mitigate their old rivalry for years to come.

After Thermidor (July 1794), however, the rump Convention began to restrain expressions of the provincial sansculottes' anticommercial passions. In his report of 6 Frimaire Year III (November 26, 1794), Jean-Baptiste Perrin, the Thermidorian Convention's representative on mission, declared that Terrorists who had imprisoned merchants just before the fair at Beaucaire and thereby deprived 8,000 workers of their employment were not friends of the fatherland. "The rich must aid the poor, but that does not justify theft."[30] The opulent leaders of Federalism, defeated a year earlier, now regained the upper hand, still backed by some people who had royalist sympathies and landed interests. Nevertheless, the personnel of local administrations changed only gradually. During Thermidor, socially conservative republicans purged the most demagogic Terrorists from administrative bodies and from the popular societies. Until 1796, late in Year IV, men of modest means retained a large share of the local posts which they had gained by fiat from above in July 1793, but after Thermidor most of them avoided offending the affluent. Those who were less discreet fell victim to new purges.

As late as the spring of 1795, famine again mobilized many sansculottes. In Paris, they protested, by the *journées* of Germinal and Prairial, the socioeconomic and political conservatism of the republicans who dominated municipal and national government. Only after the Vendémiaire uprising of October 1795 did the royalist threat seem grave enough to reunite Parisians who opposed a restoration of the Bourbon monarchy. In the Gard, the Rhône valley, and other parts of the South, by contrast, the White Terror—lynch law inspired by old sectarian, political, and personal hatreds—demonstrated the menace of royalism several months sooner. Again, as in 1790, the sharp traditional fragmentation of society in the Gard placed it in the forefront among regions where Catholic oligarchs, excluded from power for several years, seemed to pose a serious challenge to revolutionaries of all shades, who now increasingly overlooked the issues ·which had divided them in 1792, 1793, and 1794. In the spring of 1790, revolutionaries had rallied as patriots behind the commercial interest which had extended its dominance in 1789 and which proceeded to defeat counterrevolutionaries in pitched battles. In the spring of 1795, with radical democrats already

---

[30] *Réimpression de l'ancien Moniteur,* 32 vols. (Paris, 1858–63), 22:609.

defeated, revolutionaries again united, this time under a republican banner against reactionary royalists. As always, though, national political slogans and labels had various meanings in different places, even within the Gard. Their significance for most people derived from personal contacts and concrete experiences more than from abstract thought.

Surviving members of the commercial families used their advantages of wealth and education to regain dominance in the administration of the Gard. That predominantly Protestant elite tightened its grip under the Executive Directory and retained it without any serious challenge until 1814. Catholic royalists expressed their resentment at the dominance of heretics by continual terrorist harassment, which recalls the Calvinist guerrillas' nettling of the authorities and of the Catholic elite a century earlier under Louis XIV. Thus, after a brief submersion from 1792 through 1794, the inveterate rivalry between Protestant and Catholic communities regained its primacy in the Gard. After Thermidor, their antagonism remained a public issue despite the brief and halting steps by the Convention and the Executive Directory toward disestablishment of religion, freedom of worship, and accommodation of even refractory Catholic priests. By erratic enforcement of policies, which themselves oscillated between toleration and persecution, both regimes exacerbated the bitterness of ardent Roman Catholics in the Gard.

During the Empire, Catholics continued to resent the local Calvinist community's purchase of former Catholic churches from the state for use as Protestant temples. Also, they blamed heretics' influence over the administration for the prohibition of Catholic processions in the region. Napoleon left unimpaired the dominance of the Calvinist commercial community, which mobilized for him the resources of the department. However, he did not appoint any self-proclaimed Protestants to the very highest local posts, judicial or administrative, and he did not completely eliminate the raids by royalist murder gangs operating out of the Catholic north. The emperor's authority and his dual policies of suppressing insurgents and subsidizing both sects again papered over the antagonism between Catholics and Protestants, but their mutual hatred survived unabated, ready to surface again in the White Terror of 1815. Then, as in 1790, the sectarian fissure and related social issues went far to define the Gard's response to the crisis precipitated by the collapse of central authority. The region witnessed renewed civil war, which again attracted national and international attention.[31]

[31] Pouthas, *Une Famille*, pp. 173, 189. Daniel P. Resnick, in *The White Terror and*

IV

Developments after Thermidor show that, despite the profound traumas which accompanied the Revolution and the Empire, the traditional cleavage of the Gard into two popular factions, each obedient to a wealthy elite, remained paramount except for three years. During 1792–94, imported issues took first place, but they meshed poorly with local habits, feelings, and economic relations and lost their supremacy too soon to effect a restructuring of social attitudes which could endure. In that brief period, provincial leaders, imitating Montagnards in Paris, appealed to anticommercialism among all segments of the populace but seem to have succeeded best in forging sustained backing among the marginally independent in the cities. Most of the active sansculottes shared with great merchants an irreversible commitment to the commercial nexus, but they apparently felt that those capitalists were exploiting the Revolutionary economic crisis to deprive them of the last remnants of their independence. While most textile workers remained subservient to great merchants, the combined pressures of inflation, declining business, and food shortages, particularly acute in a region so heavily dependent upon imports, finally made shopkeepers and craftsmen, above all those outside the textile trades, abandon their ambivalent loyalty toward entrepreneurs. Since the political kaleidescope spun at a dizzying pace, the lines of social division were in rapid flux. Opulent men of unrequited political ambition and others who sought fortune as well as fame were eager to lead a popular anticapitalist movement. But they had to grope for a new principle to unite the diverse individuals—drawn from every occupational, economic, social, and sectarian category—who now played an active part in public deci-

the Political Reaction after Waterloo (Cambridge, Mass., 1966), emphasizes the national context of reaction and calls attention to the reports written to Louis XVIII's minister of police in 1815 and 1816 by Eymard, a former prefect in Provence. Located in the Archives Privées and in the F⁷ Series of the Archives Nationales, these reports stress the consistent hegemony of the Calvinist merchants throughout the Gard and especially in Nîmes from the end of the Great Terror to the end of the Empire. In works completed and in a forthcoming volume, Gwynn Lewis uses close analysis of families and clans to offer incisive analysis of the issues, personalities, and background of the crisis of 1815 in the Gard, with special emphasis on the grudges and fears surviving from the Terror as well as from the counterrevolutionary insurrections: Gwynn Lewis, "The White Terror of 1815 in the Department of the Gard: Counter-Revolution, Continuity, and the Individual," *Past and Present,* no. 58 (February 1973), pp. 108–35, "La Terreur Blanche et l'application de la loi Décazes dans le département du Gard (1815–1817)," *Annales historiques de la Révolution française,* no. 176 (avril–juin 1964), pp. 175–93, and "The White Terror in the Department of the Gard: 1789–1820. A Study in Counter-Revolution" (D. Phil. thesis, Oxford University, 1965).

sions and administration. They defined these followers first as citizens, then as consumers, and occasionally even as wage earners.

In provincial cities, social as well as political contests mimicked those in Paris, reflecting the impact of propaganda from the capital as well as basic similarities of urban social conditions, which the Revolutionary economic crisis and the new uniform local administrative framework had further standardized. Sansculottes everywhere demanded strong administrative measures to alleviate misery and to equalize opportunity by eliminating extremes of wealth while upholding the principle of private property. However, the balance of power between the rival factions in the Gard was the reverse of that in Paris. Radical Montagnards in the Convention, collaborating with the Jacobin club, played a leading role in the capital's municipal politics through their influence over the section assemblies; in cities of the Gard, clubs of conservative patriots used similar influence over city sections to retain their control of the department until faced down in July 1793 by troops imposing the will of the capital.

Between 1789 and 1795 leaders at both extremes of the political spectrum exploited popular anticommercialism. They aroused popular support for antithetical policies by blaming the eclipse of their followers' old security upon a commercial elite which, they contended, had sacrificed social responsibility to narrow profit motives. Both extremes aimed to bring the extension of commerce under control by strengthening the central executive and making it more paternalistic. The Gard in 1790 and the West after 1792 suggest that active popular support for one extreme—a powerful Bourbon monarchy purified of those abuses which had led it to err in supporting powerful merchants—was most likely to arise in cohesive traditional communities. That support usually expressed popular resentment of merchants' recent intrusions. By undercutting customary polyculture, the market economy threatened the very integrity of these communities and conditioned them to heed counterrevolutionary agitators. Peasants in areas only superficially commercialized but living in or near commercial centers were first to attack the merchants and remained the principal source of popular support for counterrevolution, later in the West as first in the Gard.[32] Likewise,

---

[32] Paul Bois emphasizes, as decisive to the origins of counterrevolution in the' Sarthe, the resentment of the Revolution among prosperous, independent peasants living in relative isolation from cities before the Revolution. Charles Tilly shows how, in the Maine-et-Loire, resistance to the Revolution centered in less self-sufficient agricultural communities, where the textile industry had recently made significant progress in commercializing the economy. He suggests that, in these areas, the "bourgeois," who took both economic and political advantage of the early Revolution, had not yet established pervasive popular loyalty. In the Gard, the counter-

the experiences of Paris and the Gard from 1792 through 1794 suggest that a program of popular democratic government by a strong unicameral assembly gained its most powerful support among small but independent operators of a shop, a craft, or specialized agriculture. Many of them saw their independence threatened or destroyed in the economic crunch of the Revolution. In their minds, reduction of extreme contrasts in wealth took precedence over customary loyalties.

However, participants in the two popular movements in the Gard emphasized differences between their political goals and overlooked what they shared. Even if they had stressed their common hostility toward merchants, differences of social background and aims would have made a united front impossible: sansculottes were committed to specialization; counterrevolutionaries sought to escape it. Only the commercial interest itself seems to have noted that these popular movements, while advocating opposite constitutional schemes, agreed on the need to reduce merchants' power. Even the merchants conceived the likenesses among their foes in political rather than social terms, labeling their enemies at both extremes "counter-revolutionaries."

The struggle between French royalists and patriots reflected the diversities among the regions where it developed as well as the common popular anticommercialism from which it sprang. In parts of the South, a sectarian cleavage reinforced economic and cultural antagonisms. Reactionaries there succeeded in mobilizing a segment of the populace against merchants two years before their counter-parts in the West. Hatred of wealth in general, though omnipresent, was neither the ostensible nor the central motive. Neither counter-revolutionaries nor their foes formulated a social vocabulary, much less a social program, which was intelligible throughout France. Nevertheless, the emphasis by both of those factions on the most deeply rooted social antagonisms gave followers of established elites a profound commitment—one which inspired perseverance in adversity even to the point of martyrdom.

The struggle between Federalists and sansculottes presents sharp contrasts. In the Gard, a few isolated counterrevolutionaries resisted

revolutionary movement two years earlier seems to have drawn its popular support mainly from peasants to the east, where agriculture had recently become more commercial without any significant penetration by the textile trades. The textile industries had long played an important role in the economy of the Sénéchaussée of Nîmes. But their rural expansion, even when it accelerated rapidly after 1750, occurred almost exclusively in the western part of the Sénéchaussée—a region predisposed by its Calvinism as well as by commercial contacts of long standing to sympathize with the urban merchants and their allies when they extended their political authority over the countryside in 1789 and 1790.

boldly in 1790; Federalists, despite broad support, surrendered in 1793 without firing a shot. By then, of course, events had further demonstrated the futility of resisting the capital, but the most serious weakness of Federalists was the one they shared with their sansculotte foes: the superficiality of the recently defined loyalties to which both appealed. By 1793, in commercial centers of the Gard and much of France, the threat from domestic counter-revolutionaries seemed remote. Consequently, rivalries among those committed to specialization and to the Revolution took temporary precedence. The Revolutionary economic crisis focused attention to an unprecedented degree upon hostilities between rich and poor. Both factions in this new contest formulated their program, which was explicitly economic as well as political, in terms the entire nation could understand. They necessarily employed categories which cut across loyalties to established elites. Both factions lost in depth what they gained in breadth. Even in a capitalist-dominated textile center like Nîmes, their program lacked the deep social roots of old divisions.

While Federalists in the Gard capitulated, those in Lyon, Marseille, Toulon, and Bordeaux resisted. However, that party's greater firmness in those cities outside the Gard may have expressed not a deeper sensitivity to the new social issues but rather an overconfidence based upon exceptional prospects for both foreign intervention and royalist collaboration. Like the shallow commitment of most Federalists in 1793, that of their sansculotte foes collapsed suddenly in 1794. Disillusioned by the Convention's progressive betrayal of their program, which began even before Thermidor, sansculottes protested only briefly and feebly in 1794 and 1795, even in Paris, where they had been strongest.

Of course, resentment of extreme inequities of wealth was not new. Many of the poor always had a latent hatred and envy of the rich. Expressions outside the political framework, in the form of isolated *jacqueries*, occasional brigandage, and urban criminality, maintained fear among the rich. At first the disorders of mid-1789 terrified men of means in Paris and the provinces alike because they suggested a generalization of disrespect for wealth, if not for all private property. In 1790 new evidence of that disrespect appeared in civilian society in several cities and became ever clearer in tensions between soldiers and commissioned officers in the royal garrisons of many cities, including Nîmes as well as Nancy, the site of the great mutiny in August 1790.[33] But civilian society in Nîmes

[33] For an overview, see Samuel F. Scott, "Problems of Law and Order during 1790, the 'Peaceful' Year of the French Revolution," *American Historical Review* 80

and the Gard exemplifies in the extreme the power of traditional political factions, each commanding loyalty from rich and poor alike. Here the chiefs of each faction prevented a general attack on the affluent. They channeled their clients' hostility toward wealth away from themselves and into specific antagonism against the opulent leaders of the other faction. The unique case of the Gard suggests that the context of politics in the old regime in other cities and regions may also have obscured hatred of wealth for a time by mixing it with traditional rivalries which cut across extremes of wealth and poverty. Not until 1792 did the network of provincial societies affiliated with the Jacobin club succeed in making the issue of economic extremes a focus, along with republicanism, of the national political dialogue, isolating that issue from communal loyalties and spreading it to most of France. The crisis of Year II (1793–94) permanently tempered the old division between the two elites in the Gard. Each briefly lost the control which it customarily exercised over the poor of the party it led. Most rich families temporarily united against the poor. After that, the memory of Year II prevented the rich from trusting the poor as unquestioningly as they had before. The Calvinist commercial elite, though now espousing republicanism, continued to fear the lawyers, craftsmen, and shopkeepers who had organized the Terror in the Gard. That elite continued to accept the backing of discreet Catholic landed royalists, who, like merchants, dreaded arbitrary requisitioning and social leveling in the towns and the countryside. As usual, personal loyalties, exceptional economic interests, and anomalous political preferences led several clans to violate this general pattern. As the shock of the Terror began to wear off, old sectarian hostilities regained first place, retaining through the nineteenth century their reorientation around national parties with conflicting political principles—an orientation established at the very beginning of the Revolution.[34]

The persistence of hostility against the wealthy, variously defined in different times and places, illustrates a basic social continuity in the Revolution. That continuity transcends political issues and social traditions and has united revolutionary politics with mass politics ever since. While it thereby illustrates the kernel of truth in

(October 1975): 859-88. On the mutinies at Nancy, see William C. Baldwin, "The Beginnings of the Revolution and the Mutiny of the Royal Garrison in Nancy: *L'Affaire de Nancy, 1790*" (Ph.D. diss., University of Michigan, 1973). Regarding tensions in the Guyenne Regiment at Nîmes, see James N. Hood, "The Riots in Nîmes" (n.1 above) and forthcoming works.

[34] The best recent treatment in English of episodes in Nîmes and the Gard since 1815 appears in David H. Pinkney, *The French Revolution of 1830* (Princeton, N.J., 1972).

economic interpretations of the Revolution, from Barnave through Marx to Soboul, it also shows the risks of oversimplifying the global significance of the Great Revolution. To be sure, the case of the Gard exemplifies great merchants' extension of their political power at the outset of the Revolution. Holding that power against one challenge in 1790, they lost it in 1793 but regained it by 1795. Furthermore, the Revolution did permanently reduce the wealth of the clergy and of the merchants' leading enemies among the laity. However, "feudalism" was scarcely an issue. Extension of merchants' control of local government merely confirmed a pattern two decades old, which depended more on personal ties and royal sympathy toward commerce than on the impersonal power of capital.

Industrial decline coincided with the Empire and the early Restoration and followed the brief revivals of the silk industry in the early 1820s and in the early 1840s. During the industrial crises, many of the wealthy families which had gained control of politics in the Gard at the end of the eighteenth century turned away from the provincial enterprise in which they had made their fortunes. Some left the region, while others sought complete respectability by investing in education and above all in land. The flight of their capital confirmed the decline of economic activity in the Gard—a decline which had begun before the Revolution. Far from encouraging commerce and industry, the Revolution had weakened both. After it, as before, merchants apparently moved into politics most aggressively when their business was poor. Success in politics, symbolized during the Great Revolution by the commercial interest's eventual victories over both counterrevolutionaries and popular democrats, may in the long run have assured a further decay of their business by distracting merchants from private affairs.

The Failure of the Liberal Republic in France, 1795–1799: The Road to Brumaire*

Lynn Hunt, David Lansky, and Paul Hanson

The 18th Brumaire of the first Napoleon never had its Karl Marx. To many contemporaries and most historians, some kind of military intervention seemed inevitable in 1799, and no one, then or since, lamented the passing of a regime consistently characterized as corrupt and ineffectual.[1] Marx himself never mentioned the Directory years when castigating the revolutionaries of 1848 for mimicking the 1789 Revolution, and he evidently considered the Directory part of the "long crapulent depression" that "lays hold of society before it learns soberly to assimilate the results of its storm-and-stress period."[2] For Marx, as for most other commentators, the Directory had nothing in common with the high drama of the Revolution's earlier years.

Marxist historians of the 1789 Revolution implicitly follow the lines of Marx's analysis of 1851 when they get to Brumaire. Albert Soboul, for example, claims that 18th Brumaire brought the revolutionary era to a "definitive close. Consolidation was to succeed upheavals, the social primacy of the propertied classes was to be established once and for all."[3] According to Georges Lefebvre, Napoleon "arranged a temporary reconciliation between the diverse elements of the modern dominant class. This permitted it (under the tutelage of its protector) to shape institutions and codify legislation in its own way, to establish itself in the high positions of the state

* The research for this article was funded by grants to Lynn Hunt from the Institute of International Studies and the Committee on Research of the University of California, Berkeley. An earlier, much shorter paper using some of the research was presented by Hunt at the Fifth Annual Conference of the Western Society for French History in November 1977 at Las Cruces, New Mexico. We are very grateful to Isser Woloch for his many helpful comments on earlier drafts.

[1] As Albert Meynier claimed: ". . . le régime existant en France ne pouvait pas durer; sa chute se produirait tôt ou tard. . . . L'économie publique du pays était ruinée; l'assistance aux malades n'existait plus, faute de fonds. La société était en pleine déliquescence. A cette situation désespérée il fallait un remède extrême" (Les Coups d'état du Directoires, 3 vols. [Paris, 1928], vol. 3, Le Dix-huit brumaire, an VIII (9 novembre 1799) et la fin de la République, p. 88).

[2] Karl Marx, The Eighteenth Brumaire of Louis Bonaparte (New York, 1963), p. 19.

[3] Albert Soboul, The French Revolution, 1787–1799: From the Storming of the Bastille to Napoleon, trans. Alan Forrest and Colin Jones (New York, 1975), p. 547.

This essay originally appeared in the Journal of Modern History 51 (December 1979).

and the administration, and to accelerate the revival of the economy." Yet in its rush for order, the bourgeoisie was hoodwinked; "they expected that he would govern in collaboration with them— but he did not consult them."[4] The bourgeoisie of 1799—like its successor in 1851—found itself compelled to give up political freedom in exchange for economic stability.[5]

Marx's analysis of the Nephew's success rested on an examination of the politics of the Second Republic, and Marx described in colorful detail the battle between parliamentary factions and parties. This "political" history was always set within a broader context of class struggle; nevertheless, for Marx the focal point—especially after the June Days—was the parliamentary battlefield. Marxist historians of the First Republic have paid relatively scant attention to the parliamentary conflicts of the comparable period, 1795–99; because they emphasize the role of the *sans-culottes* in the revolutionary coalition, they naturally concentrate on the period 1792–95. Yet the Uncle's coup did not immediately follow upon the defeat of the *sans-culottes* (just as the Nephew's did not immediately follow the June Days); it only became possible when the majority of deputies themselves gave up on parliamentary government. The road to Brumaire was built by bourgeois politicians.

The government of the First French Republic did not simply break down in November 1799 like a worn-out machine. The main body and functioning parts of the Directory administration were retained by Napoleon, most notably the bureaucratic structures and tax system, and even much of the personnel.[6] Moreover, by the autumn of 1799, some measure of economic prosperity had returned to France, and the danger of invasion had been averted.[7] To be sure, the Directory government still faced many difficult problems at home and abroad, but these were certainly not insurmountable, as the succeeding government was to show. Napoleon did not step in to fill a vacuum at the top; he was invited to intervene by a group of "revisionists" within the government itself who wanted to change

[4] Georges Lefebvre, *The French Revolution,* vol. 2, *From 1793 to 1799,* trans. John Hall Stewart and James Friguglietti (New York, 1964), p. 317.

[5] Compare this to Marx's analysis in 1852: the "parliamentary party of Order . . . declared the political rule of the bourgeoisie to be incompatible with the safety and existence of the bourgeoisie. . . ." (*The Eighteenth Brumaire,* p. 106).

[6] See, e.g., the instructive article by Clive H. Church, "The Social Basis of the French Central Bureaucracy under the Directory, 1795–1799," *Past and Present,* no. 36 (April 1967), pp. 59–72. A useful overview can be found in the chapter "Administration and the 'Conspiracy of Indifference,' " in Martyn Lyons, *France under the Directory* (Cambridge, 1975), pp. 159–73.

[7] A. Goodwin, "The French Executive Directory—a Revaluation," *History* 22 (December 1937): 201–18, esp. p. 218.

the structure of the constitution. By 1799, these men preferred the uncertainties of authoritarian rule to the continuing ambiguities of parliamentary politics. And within the ruling circles and the political classes of the nation, there was no group with the will, the organization, or the following to stop them.

The Brumaire coup seems relatively effortless in retrospect because there was so little resistance to it. Apparently the way had been well prepared. But why did the Revolutionary "notables" agree to give up their liberal republic? Albert Soboul points to a "social fear" which was aroused by the recrudescence of Jacobinism in the Year VII.[8] Yet the Jacobins had been defeated in the legislature in the summer before the coup. According to Martyn Lyons, "it was clear that the chief cause of the collapse of the Directory was the nation's political apathy."[9] But would not apathy just as easily allow the Directory to continue indefinitely in power? Was Bonaparte's success based on "un immense malentendu?"[10]

I

We shall argue here that the Brumaire coup—its possibility and its success—grew out of a fundamental contradiction in the way the Revolutionary notables thought about and acted out their politics. The legislators of 1795 instituted a representative government based on electoral politics, but they were unwilling to accept the consequences of their handiwork, the growth of organized political parties. Using a computer analysis of Directorial deputies as our point of departure, we will describe the parliamentary leaders of the political parties that were emerging during the Directory period. This evidence will help us demonstrate that the development of parties posed a dilemma for the bourgeois republic which, unresolved, directly contributed to its failure. This failure was in the first instance ideological, but ideological in a way that ultimately involved social as well as political considerations. In essence, the republicans of 1795 wanted to establish a liberal republic without accepting the imperatives of liberal politics. The notables of 1795 (the landowning, professional, and commercial bourgeoisie who had benefited from the Revolution) wanted to preserve what they had won in 1789 and 1794; they wanted a government that would be anti-aristocratic and nonpopular at the same time. It is impossible to understand the difficulties facing the Directory politicians without recognizing the importance of each of these ends, for otherwise the policies of the

[8] Soboul, p. 543.
[9] Lyons, p. 234.
[10] Goodwin, p. 218, quoting Albert Vandal.

Republic's leaders seem vacillating and pusillanimous. Key to the maintenance of anti-aristocratic and nonpopular government was the system of annual elections: one-third of the legislative seats came up each year, but the final, direct vote was limited to about 30,000 property owners.[11] This arrangement was meant to insure the dominance of "les meilleurs."[12]

Elections had been the cornerstone of the Revolutionary achievement since 1789, for it was elections that opened up political, judicial, ecclesiastical, and even military careers to talent. Elections were essential to the revolution against privilege, and as a consequence, scuttling them was inconceivable in 1795. Yet the electoral system was also the weak spot in the constitutional structure. Since most adult Frenchmen qualified to vote in the primary assemblies, elections provided a regular opportunity for the mobilization of the popular classes. After 18th Brumaire, the supporters of the coup in the legislature repeatedly harped on the dangers of the annual elections of the past: according to the doctor Cabanis, for example, "annual elections put the people in a fever state at least six months out of twelve. . . ."[13]

If representative government was to be bourgeois, that is, neither aristocratic nor popular, then the national elections had to be "managed" in some way. In short, to accomplish their aims, the notables needed a party system or at least an effectively organized patronage system on the local level. Individual members of the Directory government tried to establish their own personal patronage connections, but the Directory government as a whole failed to organize a center party of its own, and it obstinately refused to countenance the development of any organized opposition. In their minds, no opposition could be loyal if it was based on party organization, for party meant faction or division in the revolutionary, fraternal "communion of citizens."[14] As the moralistic Director La Revellière-Lépeaux claimed, "it was better to die with honor defending the republic and

---

[11] Jacques Godechot, *Les Institutions de la France sous la Révolution et l'Empire,* 2d ed. (Paris, 1968), pp. 460–61.

[12] Boissy d'Anglas made this explicit in a speech given on behalf of the constitutional commission in 1795: "Nous devons être gouvernés par les meilleurs; les meilleurs sont les plus instruits et les plus intéressés au maintien des lois . . . ceux qui, possédant une propriété, sont attachés au pays qui la contient. . . . Un pays gouverné par les propriétaires est dans l'ordre social; celui où les non-propriétaires gouvernent est dans l'état de nature" (*Projet de Constitution pour la République française et Discours préliminaire prononcé par Boissy-d'Anglas, au nom de la Commission des Onze, dans la séance du 5 messidor, an III* [Paris, an III]).

[13] *Discours prononcé par Cabanis à la suite du rapport de la commission des sept* (Séance extraordinaire du 19 brumaire, an VIII).

[14] C. F. Volney, *La Loi naturelle ou catéchisme du citoyen français,* 2d ed. (Paris, an II).

its established government than to perish or even to live in the muck of parties and the playthings of the factious.''[15]

Political parties in fact had been developing in France since the opening of the Estates General in 1789, but they never had been accepted as a natural part of the political process; even the Jacobins of the Year II considered themselves representative of the true interests of the whole nation—or at least of "the people." After 9 Thermidor, Year II, party to most became synonymous with the Jacobins, and to establish their own legitimacy the leaders of the reaction called themselves "a national movement." Boissy d'Anglas, for instance, insisted that "the day of 9 Thermidor was not a party victory, but a national movement which gave back to the people the exercise of its rights and to the Republic its independence."[16] The survivors of the Year II made their distrust of potential political parties explicit in their constitution, article 362: "No private society which concerns itself with political questions may correspond with another, or affiliate therewith, or hold public sessions composed of the members of the society and of associates distinguished from one another, or impose conditions of admission or eligibility, or arrogate to itself rights of exclusion, or cause its members to wear any external insignia of their association."[17]

Under the Directory regime, parties, which generally meant the Jacobins, were feared because they had demonstrated their capacity to mobilize the popular classes. As Boissy d'Anglas declared in the same speech of February 1795, "Domination is a need for them, and the exercise of power an irresistible passion: these scourges of the universe have always profited from the passions and the blindness of the part of human kind that is most numerous in order to satisfy their insatiable thirst for an authority without limits and a deadly celebrity."[18] Or as the Toulousain deputy-on-mission Pérès asserted a month later, the Jacobins had the "extensive connections" and "adroitly distributed affiliations" necessary to "rouse. at their pleasure, the Republic in all of its parts. . . ."[19]

Most historians of the Revolution have taken the antiparty rhetoric of the politicians and administrators to heart and either have ignored

[15] *Memoires de La Revellière-Lépeaux*, 2 vols. (Paris, 1895), 1:379.
[16] *Motion d'ordre contre les terroristes et les royalistes, faite à la Convention Nationale, dans la séance du 21 ventôse, an III, par Boissy-d'Anglas* (Paris, an III).
[17] This is the translation given by Isser Woloch in his *Jacobin Legacy: The Democratic Movement under the Directory* (Princeton, N.J., 1970), p. 17.
[18] *Motion d'ordre*.
[19] *Discours prononcé sur la place de la Liberté à Bruxelles le dix-sept germinal, l'an troisième . . . par Emmanuel Pérès* (Paris, an III).

or rejected any notion of party development in this period.[20] The one major exception is Isser Woloch, who in *Jacobin Legacy* argues that France "nearly did achieve the formation of rival parties during the 1798 election campaign as a consequence of the Neo-Jacobin resurgence."[21] There were three main possible party groupings in Directorial France: the left (Jacobins), which had the best-developed local party structure; the center (Thermidorians and Directorials), which rejected the possibility of its own organization for the most part; and the right (shading into royalists of various colors), which was essentially a parliamentary coalition with diverse and often conflicting local bases.

These three potential party blocs were primarily defined by their views on the nature of the revolutionary settlement. Although there were many possible areas of disagreement, there were three main issues in question: the place of the formerly privileged classes (including the clergy) in the new polity, the strength of the executive, and the relationship of government to the popular classes. There were differences of opinion within each party bloc, but they can be characterized briefly as follows. The right favored the inclusion of the formerly privileged in the polity, it wanted a stronger executive (some wanted a king, of course), and it would severely restrict if not eliminate popular participation. The left insisted upon the exclusion of the privileged classes, it too favored a stronger executive (though never a king), and it would argue for the widest possible popular participation in the polity. There might not have been a center in doctrinal matters if it had not been for the peculiar conditions of Year III politics. But in 1795 there was a center and it was characterized by largely negative political positions: it was worried about the return of the privileged classes (especially the return of a fanatical clergy), it did not want a strong executive (it wanted neither royalty nor "demagoguery"), and it did not want active popular participation (thus it was willing to let most men vote in the first stage of the elections but not in the second). Each potential party bloc had enough doctrinal unity to give it ideological cohesion, at least in opposition to the other two positions.

To become parties, these three groupings had to have leaders, followers, and most important of all, organizations that could forge some kind of national unity out of local groups. The center had a

---

[20] Martyn Lyons, for example, characterizes Jacobinism as consisting of "certain departmental lobbies of deputies, or a series of localized pressure groups, centred on individuals or families. . . ." (p. 224).

[21] Woloch, p. 272.

majority of the seats in the legislature and in the executive Directory, but it never developed a party organization to complement and
ensure its control of the government apparatus.[22] Because the right
and the left devoted considerable energy to the development of local
party structures, they continually threatened the center majority.
Rightists and leftists on the local level had clubs and newspapers,
and on the national level they had recognizable parliamentary leaders. In general, however, the left was better organized and more
coherent, that is, more party-like, than the right. After the 1797
elections, the ranks of parliamentary rightists swelled dramatically,
and they had a center for their policy discussions in the Parisian
Clichy Club.[23] But on both the national and local levels, the right
was unmanageably heterogeneous: conservative republicans, constitutional monarchists, and "pure" royalists often only agreed on
their hostility to the Directory regime. Local rightist organizations
frequently worked at cross-purposes, and the proliferation of various
rightists' newspapers made painfully clear the right's relative lack of
unity and coherence.[24] In contrast, the left's parliamentary base was
never very strong until 1799 because many Jacobins were excluded
from office before they could take their seats.[25] Yet despite official
persecution, the Jacobins enjoyed a relatively long experience with
local political clubs and had in the *Journal des hommes libres* a
single, national political voice.[26]

[22] The work of Jean-René Suratteau is indispensable for the study of this period.
According to Suratteau's figures, 51 percent of the deputies in the Year IV were
moderates or centrists (18 percent were of uncertain loyalty); see J.-R. Suratteau,
"Les Elections de l'an IV," *Annales historiques de la Révolution française* 23 (1951):
374–93, and 24 (1952): 32–62, see esp. the table on p. 47. Suratteau gives slightly
different figures in *Les Elections de l'an VI et le "coup d'état du 22 floréal" (11 mai
1798)* (Paris, 1971), p. 301. After the Year V elections, 45 percent of the deputies
were royalists or counterrevolutionaries, 38 percent were government supporters, 10
percent were Jacobins, and 7 percent were of undetermined loyalties (p. 303). Of the
510 deputies elected in the Year VI—seventy-three too many because of schisms—57
percent were Directorials, 16 percent were of undetermined loyalties, 25 percent were
Jacobins, and only 2 percent were royalist or counterrevolutionary (p. 304). Thus only
in the Year V was there any great threat to the center majority, and even then the
rightist opposition did not have a clear majority of seats. The right never had much
support inside the Directory itself.
[23] For royalist organization, see W. R. Fryer, *Republic or Restoration in France?
1794–97* (Manchester, 1965); and Harvey Mitchell, *The Underground War against
Revolutionary France: The Missions of William Wickham, 1794–1800* (London, 1965).
[24] Jeremy David Popkin, "Enlightened Reaction: The French Rightwing Press under
the First Republic, 1792 to 1800" (Ph.D. diss., University of California, Berkeley,
1977).
[25] Woloch claims that "Lacking a tangible center, and assuredly without a parliamentary nucleus of any significance, the Jacobin party consisted of autonomous
local political clubs linked by the democratic press and by indirect ties of common
outlook and background" (p. 274).
[26] Max Fajn objects to Woloch's characterization of the *Journal des hommes libres*

To meet the threat posed by rightist and leftist mobilization, the Directory government cultivated a variety of techniques for influencing elections. It conducted propaganda campaigns against the "extremists," it dispatched special agents to the departments with lists of approved candidates and facilitating funds, and it encouraged its agents to promote schisms in the electoral assemblies (this it did in both 1798 and 1799.)[27] When these more subtle methods proved insufficient, the Directory redressed the electoral balance by fiat. A few months after the right won most of the seats up for election in 1797, the three moderate republican Directors—La Revellière-Lépeaux, Reubell, and Barras—mounted a coup against the rightists in the Councils with the aid of General Augereau, Napoleon's emissary. The majority in the Councils promptly agreed (September 4–5, 1797/18–19 Fructidor, Year V) to annul the elections in forty-nine departments, to exclude 177 deputies, and to sentence sixty-five men to deportation to Guiana, including fifty-three deputies and the two right-leaning Directors, Carnot and Barthélémy.[28] After the Jacobin resurgence in the 1798 elections, the Directory and its parliamentary supporters acted before the new deputies could take their seats. Using as its justification the fact that there had been many schisms in the electoral assemblies, the outgoing legislature voted to exclude 121 newly elected deputies, most of whom were excluded as "anarchists" or "terrorists" (the coup of May 11, 1798/22 Floréal, Year VI.[29] The Fructidor and Floréal coups showed that the shrinking center majority in the executive and the legislature would cooperate to compel the continuation of a moderate republican regime—by armed force if necessary.

This cynical electoral manipulation could not succeed in the long run. Even after the coups of 1797 and 1798 there were 140 deputies on the left and 110–20 deputies on the right still sitting in the Councils.[30] And the annual elections scheduled for the spring of 1799 offered the "factions" another occasion to improve their position. A

---

as a clearinghouse of information for the Jacobins, yet he offers no evidence that is compelling (*The "Journal des hommes libres de tous les pays," 1792–1800,* Studies in the Social Sciences, no. 20 [The Hague, 1975], pp. 73–74). Woloch provides interesting evidence for links between the Jacobin press in Metz and Vatar's *Journal* in "The Revival of Jacobinism in Metz during the Directory," *Journal of Modern History* 38 (March 1966): 13–37, p. 30.

[27] Agents were sent to the departments under the pretext of checking the state of the roads and planning the placement of customs barriers. The development of this kind of electoral preparation is described in Suratteau, *Les Elections de l'an VI.*

[28] For a description of the coup, see Meynier (see n. 1 above), vol. 1, *Le Dix-huit fructidor, an V (4 septembre 1797).*

[29] Suratteau, *Les Elections de l'an VI.*

[30] Ibid., p. 446.

few administrators within the Directory government had begun to realize the importance of organizing the center.[31] Through its regular agents in the departments, the Central Commissioners, the Directory gathered information on public opinion and tried to push the candidacies of scores of hand-picked moderates. Its efforts came too late to be effective: only 61 of the 143 candidates recommended by the Directory won seats. Once again, the government's agents fostered schisms in departments dominated by the opposition, but this time the Councils decided to validate the elections of almost all of the regular assemblies.[32] The moderate deputies categorically rejected the administration's attempt to organize the electorate. As the parliamentary veteran Pérès proclaimed in the Council of Ancients, "je suis épouvanté, je vous l'avoue, de l'influence que tant et tant de commissaires cherchent à exercer sur les élections du peuple."[33] Pérès would support the Bonapartist solution a few months later.

II

The rightists of 1797 and the Jacobins of 1798 and 1799 did not represent political parties in the modern sense of the term, if only because their organization was not—in the circumstances, could not be—permanent. Still, the Directorial coups of Fructidor, Floréal, and Brumaire provide us with the opportunity to examine the core of party leadership in the legislature and to compare the leaders of the right and the left with the majority of moderate deputies. For the purpose of this comparison, we have singled out the fifty-four deputies (including Carnot, a former deputy), scheduled for deportation as supposed royalists on 19 Fructidor, Year V; the eighty-four deputies excluded as presumed Jacobins on 22 Floréal, Year VI; the fifty-nine deputies expelled from the Council of Five Hundred after the coup of 18th Brumaire, Year VIII; and a random sample of deputies who sat in the Councils between 1795 and 1799.

[31] Information gathering had become systematic by the Year VII. In that year, the Central Commissioners of the departments received printed forms from the Minister of the Interior which were entitled "Etat nominatif des membres des administrations municipales, avec des renseignements sur leur partiotisme, leur moralité, leurs opinions et leurs capacités" (Marcel Reinhard, *Le Dèpartment de la Sarthe sous le régime directorial* [Saint Brieuc, 1936], p. 373.

[32] Relatively little is known about the elections of 1799. For a brief account of the elections, see Meynier, vol. 2, *Le Vingt-deux floréal, an VI (11 mai 1798) et le trente prairial an VII (18 juin 1799)*, pp. 186–201.

[33] *Rapport fait par Pérès (de la Haute-Garonne) sur la résolution du 6 prairial relative aux doubles élections de l'assemblée primaire du canton d'Anvers* (Séance du 11 prairial an 7) (Paris, prairial, an VII).

In terms of pre-Revolutionary occupation, there was no great difference between the party leaders on the right and the left and the rest of the deputies.[34] Almost all of them came from the educated, property-owning classes, and most of them (two-thirds to three-quarters) were lawyers or professionals. There were a few clergymen, soldiers, and merchants in almost every political group, but virtually no representatives of the lower classes.[35] Like their predecessors in the Constituent Assembly and the National Convention, the vast majority of Directorial deputies—whether from the right, left, or center—were middle-aged men who represented urban France in disproportionate numbers (see tables 1 and 2). Yet, within the Directorial Councils, there were some intriguing differences: the leading rightists were significantly more urban (and more Parisian) in background than any other group.[36] The leftists purged in Floréal and Brumaire appear to form two distinct groups: the Brumaire deputies were on the whole more urban in background and younger than the Floréal deputies. Moreover, the Brumaire Jacobins included in their ranks a substantial proportion of deputies from outside metropolitan France (the annexed territories, the colonies, and Corsica). Evidently, the older, and perhaps more notorious, left was eliminated first in 1798, and the younger, less experienced left was only eliminated when Napoleon made his bid for power.

A comparison of the political backgrounds of the deputies demonstrates that most of them—again regardless of political affiliation—

---

[34] We have chosen not to include a table with a breakdown of pre-Revolutionary occupations because it was impossible to determine a significant proportion of them: in our random sample 26 percent of the occupations were unknown, and the figures for the deputies identified as rightist or leftist were even higher (ranging from 32 to 48 percent).

[35] The pre-Revolutionary occupations of the Directorial deputies were much the same as those of the deputies to the Constituent Assembly and the National Convention (Edna-Hindie Lemay, "La Composition de l'Assemblée Nationale Constituante: Les hommes de la continuité?" *Revue d'histoire moderne et contemporaine* 24 [July-September 1977]: 341–63). For the Convention, see Alison Patrick, *The Men of the First French Republic* (Baltimore, 1972), esp. pt. 3.

[36] It should be noted that our information for the Floréal Jacobins is considerably weaker than that for any other group. This is because many of the Floréal Jacobins never actually took their seats; they were excluded beforehand. Hence there is much less information about them in the biographical dictionaries. Nothing leads us to believe, however, that this seriously distorts our conclusions. Ten of the Fructidor rightists were born in Paris as compared to one of the Floréal Jacobins and none of the Brumaire Jacobins. The right appears less urban if we consider the deputies who were simply excluded from the councils: in a random sample of one-third of this group, 37 percent came from towns under 5,000 in population; 23 percent from towns between 5 and 15,000; and 41 percent from towns over 15,000 in population (excluding the 6 percent unknowns). The excluded rightists (as opposed to those scheduled for deportation) were also a bit older: 23 percent were fifty and over.

TABLE 1

PRE-REVOLUTIONARY RESIDENCES OF DIRECTORY LEGISLATORS (all Figures in %)

Town Size	Fructidor Rightists[a] (N = 54)	Floreal Jacobins[b] (N = 84)	Brumaire Jacobins[c] (N = 59)	Directory Sample[d] (N = 200)	Constituent Assembly[e] (N = 648)	National Convention[f] (N = 749)
Under 5,000	24	62	23	50	48	61
5,000–15,000	18	6	27	19	27	9[g]
Over 15,000	57	30	35	25	25	30
Outside France	2	2	15	6	...	...
Total (unknowns excluded)	101	100	100	100	100	100
Unknowns	6	44	19	6	...	1

NOTE.—We have followed the procedure described in Alison Patrick, *The Men of the First French Republic* (Baltimore, 1972), p. 255; birthplaces have been used only where no other evidence was available. Biographical information was taken principally from Adolphe Robert, Edgar Bourloton, and Gaston Cougny, *Dictionnaire des parlementaires français*, 5 vols. (Paris, 1889–91); and Auguste Kuscinski, *Les Députés au Corps legislatif, Conseil des Cinq Cents, Conseil des Anciens, de l'an IV à l'an VIII* (Paris, 1905).

[a] The list of men purged on 19 Fructidor, Year V, was taken from the *Réimpression de l'Ancien Moniteur*, 15:1419 (24 Fructidor, Year V). We have analyzed fifty-four men scheduled for deportation: eleven members of the Council of Ancients, forty-two members of the Council of Five Hundred, and the Director Carnot. Of the twelve nondeputies scheduled for deportation, only Carnot satisfied two essential criteria: he had been a deputy previously, and at the time of the coup he held a major governmental position.

[b] Jean-René Suratteau found individual reasons for expulsion for 116 deputies. He divides them into four categories: "jacobins," "royalistes ou contre-révolutionnaires," and "directorialistes" (*Les Elections de l'an VI et le "coup d'état du 22 floréal"* [11 mai 1798] [Paris, 1971], annex Z, pp. 370–82.) We have separated the eighty-four deputies listed as "jacobin" from the thirty-two others.

[c] We have analyzed the fifty-nine deputies from the Council of Five Hundred who were listed as excluded in the *Réimpression de l'Ancien Moniteur*, 19:200 (21 Brumaire, Year VIII).

[d] We generated the random sample using a random number table and Kuscinski, pp. 345–92.

[e] Edna-Hindie Lemay, "La Composition de l'Assemblée Nationale Constituante: Les hommes de la continuité?" *Revue d'histoire moderne et contemporaine* 24 (July–September 1977): 341–63, table 9.

[f] Patrick, p. 255.

[g] Patrick's categories are somewhat different: (1) towns over 15,000: (2) *chefs-lieux* under 15,000 or 15,000 plus towns known to be of 10,000 or more: and (3) other places.

TABLE 2
AGE DISTRIBUTION OF DIRECTORIAL LEGISLATORS

Age in 1795 (Years)	Fructidor Rightists (%)	Floréal Jacobins (%)	Brumaire Jacobins (%)	Directory Sample (%)	Constituent Assembly[a] (%)	National Convention[b] (%)
Under 30	12	2	6	5	3	7
30–39	31	33	64	35	29	39
40–49	45	48	25	37	35	35
50–59	8	15	4	18	24	16
Over 60	4	2	2	5	9	3
Total (unknowns excluded)	100	100	101	100	100	100
Unknowns	6	45	10	8	6	0
Mean age (years)	41	43	37	43	...	...

NOTE.—Categories and sources are the same as those for table 1.
[a] Age in May 1789.
[b] Age in January 1793.

had made their political careers in the Revolution and not before (see table 3). There were fewer former Old Regime officeholders in the Directorial legislatures (13 percent) than in either the Constituent Assembly (49 percent) or the National Convention (27 percent).[37] Not surprisingly, there were even fewer Old Regime officeholders (both Floréal and Brumaire) and more holders of local Revolutionary offices (Brumaire) on the left than there were on the right and center.[38] Moreover, a closer look at the parliamentary right shows that the less known rightist deputies (those simply excluded from the Councils in Fructidor, Year V) were more tied to the Old Regime (30 percent had held Old Regime offices) and less experienced in national parliamentary politics (only 9 percent sat in a Revolutionary legislature before the Year V and three-fourths of these sat in the Constituent) than those rightists singled out for deportation.[39] Still, many rightists had participated in the Revolution on the local level, and by the mere fact that they had not emigrated, they showed some acceptance of constitutional, representative government.[40]

Three examples, though they may not be entirely "typical," may make these general characteristics more vivid. One of the leaders of the young and urban right was Denis-François Moreau de Mersan, who was only twenty-eight when he was elected to the Council of Five Hundred in the Year IV. Born in Paris, Mersan was the son of a *procureur* who practiced in the Parlement. As a young partisan of the Revolution, Mersan was elected *procureur-général syndic* of the Loiret department in 1790. After being elected to the legislature from the Loiret in 1795, however, Mersan was excluded on the grounds that he had instigated popular agitation against the National Conven-

---

[37] Our figure of 13 percent should be taken as an approximation because it comes from a sample and because information on the Directorial legislators is on the whole less complete than that available for the Constituent Assembly or the National Convention. For the deputies to the Constituent, see Lemay, p. 345. For the deputies to the National Convention, see Patrick, p. 260. We have combined Patrick's figures for lawyers holding official posts and civil servants.

[38] The low figure for local revolutionary experience among the Floréal Jacobins cannot be considered accurate because there is virtually no information on the political background for almost half of them. Those who had held seats in previous national assemblies did not escape the attention of the dictionary compilers, but many of the others did because they were refused seats in the legislature.

[39] These figures are based on a random sample (every third name) of the deputies excluded from the Councils on 19 Fructidor, Year V.

[40] Nearly half (47 percent) of the rightists simply excluded had held local revolutionary offices. According to Albert Meynier, only seventeen of the deputies scheduled for deportation were clearly royalists and active conspirators; sixteen were "réacteurs arrivés déjà plus qu'à moitié chemin entre la République et la royauté, mais hésitants encore et indécis"; and the rest were in some sense republican (vol. 1, *Le Dix-huit fructidor*, pp. 174–75).

TABLE 3
Office-holding and Legislative Experience of Directorial Legislators

Group	Old Regime (%)	Local Revolutionary (%)	Constituent Assembly (%)	Legislative Assembly (%)	National Convention (%)	Sat in Legislature of Year IV (%)	Year V (%)	Year VI (%)	Year VII (%)
Fructidor rightists (N = 54).....	17	54	4	22	18	72	98[a]	...	...
Floréal Jacobins (N = 84)......	8	40	6	18	32	13	11	100	5
Brumaire Jacobins (N = 59) ...	10	73	3	10	30	22	20	88	100
Directory sample (N = 200).....	13	69	7	8	32	46	53	52	51
Year IV sample (N = 91).......	13	67	12	16	67	100	...	...	...
Year V sample (N = 105)	18	64	10	10	42	70	100	...	...
Year VI sample (N = 103).....	14	73	6	5	23	40	60	100[b]	...
Year VII sample (N = 104)	11	71	4	4	12	16	28	66	100

Note.—Sources same as for tables 1 and 2.

[a] Carnot was not a deputy to the Year V legislature; he had been elected in the Year IV and then promoted ⋺ the Directory.

[b] These men were elected to the Year VI body but were never actually seated because of the coup of 22 Fl﹖⋎.

481

tion. Mersan was finally admitted to the Five Hundred in May 1797—after the rightist electoral victory—and he immediately joined the Clichy Club. Like most of the deputies scheduled for deportation in Fructidor, Mersan eluded arrest. He reemerged into public life under the Consulate, but once again he was forced out of his (now minor) office when he was identified as an active royalist agent. Yet under the Restoration, Mersan became known as a defender of Carnot's reputation. The political opinions of this secretive man are not easy to categorize, but it seems most likely that in 1797 he was one of many rightist deputies who favored a constitutional monarchical restoration.[41]

The careers of Léonard Gay-Vernon and Pierre-Joseph Briot illustrate some of the differences between the two Jacobin cohorts. Gay-Vernon, born in 1748 in a village in the Haute-Vienne, was a parish priest in a small town near Limoges before the Revolution. He was elected constitutional bishop of the Haute-Vienne and then was elected to the Legislative Assembly and the Convention, where he voted for the death of the king. From the first years of the Revolution, Gay-Vernon identified himself as a Jacobin, and one of his brothers, who was also a churchman, was a militant in the Limoges Club. In Brumaire, Year II, Gay-Vernon renounced his ecclesiastical functions. Although he withdrew cautiously from the public eye in the months after 9 Thermidor, Gay-Vernon was elected to the Council of Five Hundred in the Year IV and reelected in 1798 after an energetic legislative career. His fellow deputies voted to expel him in Floréal.[42]

Gay-Vernon's younger colleague Briot was born in the village of Orchamps (Doubs department) in the Franche-Comté in 1771; his father was a local tax official. After studies at the university in Besançon, Briot became an *avocat* in 1789, and the next year he was named professor of rhetoric at the Besançon *collège*. He quickly joined the new local Jacobin Club and became one of the editors of the

---

[41] For biographical information on Mersan, see Adolphe Robert, Edgar Bourloton, and Gaston Cougny, *Dictionnaire des parlementaires français*, 5 vols. (Paris, 1889–91), 4:353. Mersan was denounced to the police along with Lemerer as an agent of Louis XVIII (17 Ventôse, Year V). See *Mémoires de Barras, membre du Directoire* (Paris, 1895), vol. 2, *Le Directoire jusqu'au 18 fructidor*, pp. 339–43.

[42] Gay-Vernon was one of seven deputies named to a special commission of the Five Hundred to report on the royalist conspiracy which supposedly provoked the Fructidor coup. Considerable (but sometimes erroneous) information on Gay-Vernon's career can be found in A. Artaud, "Gay-Vernon, évêque constitutionnel et député de la Haute-Vienne," *La Révolution française* 27 (1894): 314–35, 447–67, 502–31. According to Suratteau, Gay-Vernon's expulsion was the "type même de 'floréalisation' pour vengeance personnelle"; La Revellière, Reubell, and Barras all disliked him (*Les Elections de l'an VI*, p. 374).

club's journal. Before May 31, 1793, Briot was known as a moderate, but after the purge of the Girondins, he moved closer to the Mountain. In the Year III Briot was jailed as a terrorist. The next year he was elected to the municipal government in Besançon, but the departmental administration annulled his election on the grounds that he was not old enough to hold office. Briot hastened to Paris to protest, and there he obtained a post in the Ministry of Police working for Merlin de Douai. After serving a third brief stint in the army, Briot returned to preside over the opening of a "Constitutional Circle" in Besançon and to take up his position in the *collège*. In the Year VI he was elected to the Council of Five Hundred, but he was not included in the purge of 22 Floréal. In the aftermath of 18th Brumaire, Briot was ejected.[43] Like most of the Jacobins, Briot and Gay-Vernon were small-town provincials to whom the Revolution offered an unexpected opportunity for social mobility—election to important local offices and then to national political prominence. The chief difference between them was one of age (Gay-Vernon was forty-one in 1789; Briot was only eighteen), though there may also be a difference here in convictions, for the Floréal purge included proportionately more regicides of the Year II (see table 4).

It is difficult to tie the clear political differences between the leaders of the right and the left to national social or political cleavages. An analysis of the constituencies of the proto-party politicians (see table 5) shows that the parliamentary parties under the Directory did not reproduce the ideological divisions of the Year II: the *parliamentary* right did not represent a "backward," underdeveloped, fanatically counterrevolutionary France, and for the most part, the parliamentary left did not represent an extremist, radical France.[44] The Directorial party leaders were not elected by depart-

---

[43] Apparently, the Minister of the Interior was not able to gather decisive information on the Doubs department in the Year VI. Suratteau, *Les Elections de l'an VI*, annex Y, p. 363. According to Woloch (see n. 17 above), Briot was an active Jacobin (pp. 144, 366, and 387). Briot was not listed as a member of the Paris Jacobin Club by Alphonse Aulard in "Les Derniers Jacobins," *La Révolution française* 26 (1894): 385–407. For Briot's career see Maurice Dayet, *Un Révolutionnaire franc-comtois: Pierre-Joseph Briot*, Annales littéraires de l'Université de Besançon, vol. 33 (Paris, 1960).

[44] Our conclusions here are compatible with Suratteau's maps of the election results for 1795–98 (Suratteau, *Les Elections de l'an VI*, pp. 298–300). We have also computed Pearson correlation coefficients for the forty-nine departments whose elections were annulled in the Fructidor coup: the results are almost identical to those given in table 5 for the Fructidor rightists (using the fifty-four deputies scheduled for deportation). The correlation with urban population, for example, is .25. The correlation with agricultural production is not significant, however, though the correlation with tax base is (.40). With both of these measures for implantation of the right, there is a slight correlation (.19) with the measure for Floréal Jacobinism. This most likely

TABLE 4

PREVIOUS LEGISLATIVE EXPERIENCE AND PERCENTAGE OF REGICIDES IN VARIOUS DIRECTORIAL PARLIAMENTARY GROUPS

Political Characteristic	Fructidor Rightists (%)	Floréal Jacobins (%)	Brumaire Jacobins (%)	Directory Sample (%)	Year IV Sample (%)	Year V Sample (%)	Year VI Sample (%)	Year VII Sample (%)
Regicides in group	7	22	15	14	27	18	10	5
Ex-Conventionnels............	18	32	30	32	67	42	23	12
Ex-Conventionnels who voted on king's death and voted for death sentence[a]........	40	86	64	51	50	50	45	45
Legislative experience before the Directory regime[b]	33	39	37	41	77	50	31	16

NOTE.—Categories and sources the same as for previous tables. The first measure, regicides in group, is misleading if taken out of context, e.g., the percentage of regicides in the Year IV sample is high because the Two-Thirds Decree mandated the election of two-thirds ex-Conventionnels, and since about half of the Convention voted for the death sentence, the Year IV sample was bound to contain a substantial number of regicides. This third measure gives the proportion of regicides as a ration based on the number of ex-Conventionnels who were present for the decisive vote. It shows that among the ex-Conventionnels in the various groups, those in both Jacobin cohorts were more likely to have been regicides than the ex-Conventionnels in any other group.

[a] This is the best measure of militant republicanism.

[b] Experience in any national assembly before the elections of the Year IV.

TABLE 5
CORRELATION COEFFICIENTS FOR DEPARTMENTAL SOCIAL,
ECONOMIC, AND POLITICAL VARIABLES

Departmental Variables	Fructidor Rightists[a]	Floréal Jacobins[b]	Brumaire Jacobins[c]
1. Population density (pop. 1798/area)[d]	.46*	.12	.25*
2. % urban population in 1806[d]	.23*	.15	.29*
3. Total literacy (1786–90)	.05	−.10	−.07
4. Distance of *chef-lieu* from Paris	−.32*	.01	.19*
5. Agricultural production in 1812	.20*	.09	.16
6. Tax base (fonçière 1791/ pop. 1798)	.19*	.01	−.13
7. Deaths in Terror (per 100,000 pop.)	.04	.03	.25*
8. No. of emigrés (per 100,000 pop.)	.07	−.08	.18
9. Death votes 1793[e]	.17	.15	.15

SOURCES.—(1) Marcel Reinhard, *Etude de la population pendant la Révolution et l'Empire* (Gap, 1961), pp. 48–49; (2) René Le Mée, "Population agglomérée, population éparse au début du dix-neuvième siècle," *Annales de démographie historique* (1971), pp. 455–510; (3) Michel Fleury and Pierre Valmary, "Le Progrès de l'instruction élémentaire de Louis XIV à Napoleon III, d'après l'enquête de Louis Maggiolo (1877–1879)," *Population* 12 (1957): 71–92; (4) Jacques Peuchet, *Statistique élémentaire de la France* (Paris, 1805); (5) Thomas D. Beck, *French Legislators, 1800–1834* (Berkeley, 1974), pp. 154–57; (6) P. E. Herbin de Halle, ed., *Statistique générale et particulière de la France et de ses colonies,* 7 vols. and Atlas (Paris, 1803), 3:390–97; (7) Donald Greer, *The Incidence of the Terror during the French Revolution* (Cambridge, 1935); (8) Donald Greer, *The Incidence of the Emigration during the French Revolution* (Gloucester, Mass., 1966).

[a] Percentage of Fructidor deportees per department.
[b] Percentage of Floréal Jacobins per department.
[c] Percentage of Brumaire Jacobins per department.
[d] The following departments were excluded from the analysis: Seine, Alpes-Maritime, Corse, Mont-Blanc, and Vaucluse.
[e] "Death votes" is a compound variable created from the appendix to Alison Patrick, *The Men of the First French Republic* (Baltimore, 1972) pp. 317–39. Death votes equals the proportion of "radical" votes cast to the number of deputies eligible to vote in the three decisive issues pertaining to the execution of Louis XVI.
* Correlation coefficient is significant at the 95 percent level. (This is the conventional level set by most social scientists to insure that the results are not due to chance. That the results are significant does not establish a causal relationship: the correlation coefficients are measures of association.)

ments strongly marked by the intense struggles of the period 1792–94. Only the Brumaire left correlates significantly with any of our three political variables (deaths in the Terror per 100,000 population), but this can be interpreted as a reaction to antirepublicanism in the Year II rather than as radicalism per se. Nor does there seem to be a dramatic difference here in socioeconomic base. Not much can be concluded about the constituency of the Floréal Jacobins, but

reflects a contest, with seesawing results, for political control in certain areas and should serve as a reminder that both the left and the right were important in some highly politicized areas (perhaps especially in the big cities).

the Fructidor rightists and young Brumaire leftists represented, in a sense, opposite ends of the same spectrum: the rightists were elected from densely populated, relatively urban, rich departments *near* Paris while the Brumaire Jacobins came from densely populated, relatively urban, not so rich departments *far from* Paris. This translates into a rather distinct political geography: the right flourished in the north, the northwest, and the Rhone valley; the left did best in the Massif Central, the south, and the periphery in general. There were significant political divisions in France at this time, but the weakness of our correlations should serve as a caution against drawing the conclusion that the political map of Directorial France was neatly or simply drawn. More local studies are needed before we can determine with greater certainty why the right and the left were more successful in some areas than in others.

No doubt the revival of the right in 1797 did threaten the moderate republic. There were four regicides (see table 4) among the rightist leaders scheduled for deportation in Fructidor, but in a sample of the deputies simply excluded from the Councils there were none (none of them sat in the Convention). Thus, though in some cases the rightist leaders were perhaps not demonstrably antirepublican, most of them were of dubious loyalty. More surprising, and of even greater significance, however, was the threat posed by the "majority" itself. If we look at random samples from the legislatures between 1795 and 1799 (the Year IV through VII), a clear trend emerges (see table 4): the number of parliamentary veterans and the number of regicides dropped dramatically from year to year. At first glance the party men appear to be relatively new to national politics (see also table 3), though the leftists seem to be somewhat more experienced than the rightists. But this difference between the party men and the center turns out to be illusory. At their installation the Councils had a very high proportion of veterans because the National Convention decreed that its successor in 1795 must have at least two-thirds of its members taken from the ranks of the Convention itself (the infamous Two-Thirds Decree). With each new election after that, however, the number of new men rose rapidly. Thus, though the rightists were newcomers in comparison with the other deputies in the early Directorial legislatures, the leftists seem quite veteran in contrast to the legislatures of 1798 and 1799. In the Year VII elections, over half (52 percent) of those elected had no previous national legislative experience—not even in the preceding Directorial Councils. Only fifteen regicides were elected, a tiny island of republican founders nearly lost in the flood of parliamentary neophytes.[45] Thus, ironically, the threat to republicanism came not from the harassed party leaders—at least not from those on the left—but from the "majority" itself. It was the influx of new men without firm republican convictions that made the 18th Brumaire coup possible.

III

The parliamentary right proved relatively easy to dismantle because of its own internal contradictions. After the coup of Fructidor, Year V, the right gave up its originally successful strategy of organizing the electorate on the local level; most rightists were in any case profoundly suspicious of "popular" sovereignty. Right-wing journalists and deputies recognized the need for party organization, but they had in mind a party by, of, and for the property owners. In 1796, the future Bonapartist Roederer made this view explicit: "Since the expression of the general sentiment and the initiative of opinion belong to the property-owners, since they are its guides and its organs, the government should give all its attention to their interests, to their discourses, to their readings, to the books and newspapers that circulate among them."[46] This was hardly the kind of view that would encourage popular mobilization. As a result, the Directory government was able to find ways to contain both the intrigues by foreign agents and the sporadic and usually ill-timed royalist uprisings on the country's periphery, and after 1797 the right faded as a threat to the moderate republic.

The left proved more persistent. From the start the claims of the left were more believable than those of the right; the Directory government could accuse the Jacobins of extremism, of terrorism, of anarchism, but it could not accuse them of antirepublicanism. More important, the left was difficult to muzzle, much less eliminate, and whenever persecution diminished, Jacobin clubs and newspapers reappeared. Jacobinism was not a mass movement, yet in its network of clubs it did bring together thousands of men of a "democratic persuasion," who championed the rights of the popular classes.[47] The Jacobin press assailed what it considered the two chief "factions" who threatened the principles of republican gov-

---

[45] These figures are based on a study of all the deputies elected in the Year VII listed in Auguste Kuscinski, *Les Députés au Corps legislatif, Conseils des Cinq Cents, Conseil des Anciens, de l'an IV. à l'an VIII* (Paris, 1905), pp. 289–322. We want to thank Bonnie Roe for her help in completing this part of the study.

[46] Quoted by Popkin, p. 216 (see n. 24 above).

[47] Woloch, chap. 6.

ernment: one that favored "oligarchic domination" and one that favored "monarchic domination." To these it contrasted the "natural patriotism" of the popular classes ("la classe la plus nombreuse").[48]

The elections of the Year VII (spring 1799) showed that the left had not lost its appeal despite the coup against it the previous year. No one was certain which side had won in the Year VII, but when the newly elected Councils convened in May, the Jacobins took the initiative.[49] Within a month, the Directory that had organized the 22 Floréal coup had fallen (in the *journée* of 30 Prairial, Year VII/June 18, 1799). In the summer, the Councils pushed through a new conscription law, a forced loan on the rich, and a harsh law of hostages—the so-called Jacobin laws. Prominent Jacobins were named to the government, left-wing newspapers reappeared, and the Jacobins reopened in Paris in the Manège as the Society of the Friends of Liberty and Equality.[50]

This resurgence of the left was short-lived. In August, the new Minister of Police Fouché closed the Jacobin Club, and Sieyès, a new Director, organized the legislative defeat of an indictment against those "Prairialized" two months before. In September, the Five Hundred decisively defeated General Jourdan's provocative proposal to declare *la patrie en danger* (the vote was 245 to 171); a new Terror seemed to have been averted, and it was now clear that the Jacobins did not command a majority in the Councils. Still, Sieyès and those of like mind were not satisfied. They wanted a thorough revision of the cumbersome constitution, a "new political edifice" that would resolve once and for all the nagging problem of popular participation. Boulay de la Meurthe expounded the "revisionist" position in the critical session of 19 Brumaire: "we want to nationalize the Republic. . . . They would introduce a new noble caste which would be much more intolerable than the one we have destroyed because it would only include that portion of the nation which is the most ignorant, the most immoral and the most vile."[51] Boulay urged support for the new leader of the "moral and constitutional movement."

---

[48] *L'Ennemi des oppresseurs de tous les tems (sic)*, no. 30 (11 vendémiaire, an VIII). This journal was a continuation of the *Journal des hommes libres*.

[49] See n. 32 for references.

[50] Aulard, "Les Derniers Jacobins."

[51] *Opinion de Boulay (de la Meurthe), sur la situation de la République, et sur le projet présenté par la commission chargée d'examiner la cause de ses maux, et d'indiquer les moyens de les faire cesser* (séance de la nuit du 19 brumaire an 8, à Saint Cloud).

Although the Jacobins had been defeated in the legislature by the end of the summer of 1799, the revisionists continued to use fear of the left as the justification of their program. And by now, the left and party organization as a political tool were indissolubly linked together, so much so that the Jacobins began to defend themselves explicitly as a party. The 1799 reincarnation of the *Journal des hommes libres* (*L'Ennemi des oppresseurs de tous les temps*) argued in a series of articles that "it can happen that the *patriots*, though they are united by the same love for the government, or rather, by consequence of this shared devotion to the maintenance of its *principles*, divide themselves into two *parties* because they do not agree about the person or the acts of those who *govern*. . . ." Faction and party should be distinguished: "The *factious* are those who attack the very principles of the *established government;* an immense majority renders the attack futile. If the *patriots*, men of *party*, attack by error these good *governers*, an immense majority will protect them."[52] Party, they claimed, is a natural occurrence when there is a divergence of views about particular governmental decisions or policy, but parties in a republic recognize the legitimacy of the principles of republican government. The Jacobins were arguing that they were a loyal opposition.

Bonaparte and his supporters rejected this possibility. In a proclamation issued late in the evening of 19 Brumaire, Napoleon declared, "J'ai refusé d'être l'homme d'un parti." And he vigorously denigrated the role of "factions" in the Councils: "Les idées conservatrices, tutélaires, libérales, sont rentrées dans leurs droits par la dispersion des factieux qui opprimaient les Conseils, et qui, pour être devenus les plus odieux des hommes, n'ont pas cessé d'etre les plus méprisables."[53] Napoleon's contempt for the politicians was general, but in fact the chief victims of the 18th Brumaire coup were the deputies, the clubs, and the newspapers on the left; the surest means of repressing them was the elimination of all political activity, whatever its inclination.

The liberal republic did not fail because its executive was too weak, or because its electorate was too apathetic, or even because its generals were too autonomous. The "weak" Directory itself compelled the alteration of the election results, called in the generals, and hounded the opposition's political clubs and newspapers. The moderates in the Councils and the executive paved the way for

---

[52] This was argued in a series of articles entitles "Quelques définitions à l'ordre du moment," 11–13 Vendémiaire, Year VIII (October 3–5, 1799).

[53] *Proclamation de général Bonaparte, le 19 brumaire, 11 heures du soir.*

military dictatorship with their own antiparty (chiefly antileft) policies. Their coups represented not so much an aimless "politique de bascule" as a determined resistance to the legitimation of any opposition. By 1799, a substantial group of them—enough to make a final coup—endorsed the technocratic, authoritarian, and antiparty vision of government that Napoleon put into practice, but which others before him had conceived. The "majority" had transformed itself and its government from within.

The Directory regime was thus caught in a trap of its own making. Because it was unwilling to participate in the introduction of a party system, the government found itself ordering the expulsion of many republican veterans; and as the hostility of the Directory to party activity became more and more apparent, fewer Frenchmen voted and even fewer were willing to stand for election. In the disaffected eastern department of the Meurthe, described by P. Clémendot as "a good example of those peaceful departments in which indifference to the regime contributed to its failure," voter turnout fluctuated from 10.6 percent in the Year V, to 18.9 percent in the Year VI, to 8 percent in the Year VII.[54] The meager evidence available seems to indicate that voting was higher in Jacobin regions and higher almost everywhere during the years of striking Jacobin resurgence (the elections of the Year VI). In the Jacobin stronghold of Toulouse, for example, voter turnout declined, but it did so from a relatively high level of participation: 71 percent in the year V (a victory for the Jacobins there), 46 percent in the Year VI, and 44 percent in the Year VII.[55] In the eastern town of Colmar, voter turnout for the national elections rose slightly from 28 percent in the Year V to 30 percent in the Year VI, and then it dropped to 13 percent in the Year VII.[56] Voter apathy was clearly a reaction to governmental manipulation; why vote if the government was going to juggle the results?

As a consequence of this process, new men with no clear political affiliation infiltrated the legislature. Most of them had made their marks in local Revolutionary offices: three-fourths of those elected in the year VII had local experience.[57] But they were definitely not republican venerables. The electorate turned away from the re-

---

[54] Pierre Clémendot, *Le Département de la Meurthe à l'époque du Directoire* (Raon-l'Etape, 1966), pp. 502 (for quote), 227, 267, and 311 (for electoral figures).

[55] Jean Beyssi, "Le Parti jacobin à Toulouse sous le Directoire," *Annales historiques de la Révolution française* 22 (1950): 28–54.

[56] Roland Marx, *Recherches sur la vie politique de l'Alsace préRévolutionnaire et Révolutionnaire* (Strasbourg, 1966), p. 61.

[57] See n. 45.

gicides, from parliamentary veterans in general, and looked instead to men who had not served in the national arena before. The political opinions of these men would be difficult to characterize without a more detailed study of individual legislators, but even one example can be instructive. Jacques-Thomas Lahary, a Bordeaux lawyer, was elected for the first time to the Councils in 1799 at the age of forty-seven. He had been a deputy to the town meeting in Bordeaux of 1789, which met to choose delegates for the regional meetings held as a preliminary to the Estates-General. In 1790 he was elected secretary-general of the district of Bordeaux, and in 1792 he was named to a high post in the ministry of Justice. After returning to the Southwest where he held other important local posts, Lahary was twice arrested, imprisoned as a suspect, and only released upon the fall of Robespierre. In the Year VI he was named the Directory's commissioner to the central administration of the Gironde department, but despite official support, he failed in his first campaign for a legislative seat. The following year he was elected to the Council of Ancients. As a reward for his cooperation, Lahary was later named to the Tribunate and the Legion of Honor by Napoleon.[58] Lahary was an early partisan of the Revolution and can probably be characterized as a moderate republican. Given his close brush with disaster under the Terror, it is not surprising that he actively opposed Constitutional Circles as a local agent of the Directory. What is most striking about him, however, is his absence from the political scene between 1793 and 1798. Lahary was not unknown to the electors of the Gironde, yet he certainly cannot be counted as an ardent republican.

The new men joined a legislature increasingly subject to the influence of men like Sieyès. Representative of this group in the Councils was the veteran deputy Antoine-François Hardy, a medical doctor who had represented the Seine-Inférieure since 1792. Out-lawed as a Girondin in 1793, Hardy returned to the Convention in the Year III and became an enthusiastic Thermidorian. In the Directorial Councils he helped prepare the coups against the parties and then, caught up in the growing technocratic orientation, he turned his energies to the reorganization of medical education. In the Year VIII Hardy quickly rallied to Bonaparte.[59] New men with

[58] For biographical information, see Robert et al., *Dictionnaire des parlementaires,* 3:537; and Woloch, p. 96.

[59] For biographical information, see Robert et al., *Dictionnaire des parlementaires,* 3:311–12. Hardy was a member of both the commission to report on the royalist conspiracy of the Year V and of the special commission that worked with the Directory to prepare the lists of deputies to be excluded in Floréal, Year VI. After the

half-hearted republican convictions and veterans obsessed with preventing a leftward drift of the republic—this was a lethal mixture for
parliamentary government.

Napoleon gathered the fruits of Directorial policy on that fateful
day in November 1799. The Parisian crowd had long since with-
drawn from the national or even the local political arena, and most
of the deputies seemed insensible. The remaining Jacobins in the
Five Hundred forced a military showdown, but when confronted
with bayonets, they dispersed. The Ancients proved docile and
obedient. In the days following the coup, many deputies fell over
themselves in the rush to curry favor with the new regime. When
news came in from the departments, it was equally reassuring: a few
individual administrators protested here and there, but most of the
political elite welcomed what promised to be the last in a parade of
coups.[60]

Bonaparte promised continuity with the principles of 1789–91, that
is, the consolidation of the Revolution in property and civil rights by
means of a well-ordered state. In fact, however, he delivered continuity with trends developing between 1795 and 1799; the Directorial regime's resistance to the establishment of a party system was
converted into a blanket suppression of all political activity. The
elections which had so troubled the delicate Thermidorian balance
were eliminated; appointment and cooptation were more straightforward and much more predictable than the encouragement of voter
apathy. The Directory had made a mockery of electoral politics, and
Napoleon took them at their word.

Soboul and Lefebvre may well be correct when they maintain that
Napoleon insured the dominance of the "propertied classes": quotations on the stock exchange did rise dramatically after the coup.[61]
What they gloss over—as do most historians of the period—is the
political process that made the Napoleonic coup possible and successful. Two trends stand out in the Directory period. The executive
took the initiative in throttling the opposition, and the legislature
came to be increasingly dominated by an antiparty, technocratic

---

Floréal coup the left press reported that on the eve of the coup Hardy had boasted to
dinner guests about his close work with the Directory (see, e.g., *Journal de Toulouse*
for 28 Floréal, Year VI). Hardy accepted the Directory's equation of royalists and
"anarchists"—in his words, they were "divisions of the same army." *Discours prononcé . . . 30 ventôse, an 6, jour consacré à célébrer la souveraineté du peuple.* His
*des commissions d'instruction publique . . . sur l'organisation des écoles de médecine,
1 frimaire, an VII.*

[60] Albert Vandal, *L'Avènement de Bonaparte,* 5th ed. (Paris, 1908), vol. 1, *La Genèse
du Consulat, Brumaire, la Constitution de l'an VIII,* pp. 403–44.

[61] See, for example, *Le Publiciste* for 19 Brumaire, Year VIII.

elite. Bonaparte brought together the different strands of this development; he became the ultimate Director—the legislature was reduced to impotence, parties lost their function with the abolition of elections, and the executive ruled without opposition. The supporters of Bonaparte became administrators of the new state, and politics per se was no longer a viable vocation. Tocqueville considered this a surrender of freedom. We have tried to demonstrate that the "majority" of the Directorial regime manacled itself by refusing to act on the imperatives inherent in representative government and a system of national elections. As a consequence, the Revolution's internal mechanism—the mobilization of the political classes, however widely or narrowly defined—was finally destroyed. Bonaparte and his supporters reaped that harvest in 1815.

Index

D

CONTRIBUTORS

KEITH MICHAEL BAKER is Anthony P. Meier Family Professor and Director of the Stanford Humanities Center and Professor of History at Stanford University.

T. C. W. BLANNING is Professor of Modern European History at Sidney Sussex College, Cambridge University.

SUZANNE DESAN is Associate Professor of History at the University of Wisconsin at Madison.

BILL EDMONDS is Senior Lecturer in History at MacQuarie University, Australia.

FRANÇOIS FURET is Professor at the Centre de Recherches Politiques Raymond Aron (E.H.E.S.S.) and the Raymond W. and Martha Hilpert Gruner Distinguished Service Professor of Social Thought at the University of Chicago.

VIVIAN R. GRUDER is Professor of History at Queens College, City University of New York.

PAUL R. HANSON is Professor of History and Chair of the History Department at Butler University.

JAMES N. HOOD is Associate Professor of History at Tulane University.

LYNN HUNT is Annenberg Professor of History at the University of Pennsylvania.

DAVID LANSKY, Ph. D., resides in Portland, Oregon.

COLIN LUCAS is Master of Balliol College, Oxford University.

JOHN MARKOFF is Professor of Sociology and History at the University of Pittsburgh.

MONA OZOUF is Director of Research at the Centre National de la Recherche Scientifique and Professor at the Centre de Recherches Politiques Raymond Aron (E.H.E.S.S.).

ALISON PATRICK is an Associate of the Department of History at the University of Melbourne.

JEREMY POPKIN is Professor of History at the University of Kentucky.

WILLIAM H. SEWELL, JR. is Professor of Political Science and History at the University of Chicago.

THEDA SKOCPOL is Professor of Government and Sociology at Harvard University.

TIMOTHY TACKETT is Professor of History at the University of California at Irvine.

DALE K. VAN KLEY is Professor of History at Calvin College.